REPRESENTATION and ELECTORAL SYSTEMS

Canadian Perspectives

REPRESENTATION and ELECTORAL SYSTEMS

Canadian Perspectives

J. Paul Johnston   Harvey E. Pasis

Prentice-Hall Canada Inc., Scarborough, Ontario

Canadian Cataloguing in Publication Data

Main entry under title:

Representation and electoral systems

Includes bibliographical references.
ISBN 0-13-773656-8

1. Representative government and representation -
Canada. 2. Elections - Canada. I. Johnston,
J. Paul (James Paul), 1940-   . II. Pasis,
Harvey E. (Harvey Edward), 1945-   .
JL167.R46 1990   324.6'3'0971   C89-094841-0

Prentice Hall, Inc., Englewood Cliffs, New Jersey
Prentice-Hall International, Inc., London
Prentice-Hall of Australia, Pty., Ltd., Sydney
Prentice-Hall of India Pvt., Ltd., New Delhi
Prentice-Hall of Japan, Inc., Tokyo
Prentice-Hall of Southeast Asia (Pte.) Ltd., Singapore
Editora Prentice-Hall do Brasil Ltda., Rio de Janeiro
Prentice-Hall Hispanoamericana, S.A., Mexico

ISBN 0-13-773656-8

Production Editors: Catherine Leatherdale, Amy Lui-Ma, Kelly Dickson
Cover Design: Bruce Farquhar
Coordinating Editor: Elizabeth Long
Production Coordinator: Sandra Paige, Anna Mascioli
Typesetting: CompuScreen Typesetting Ltd.

1 2 3 4 5 IG 94 93 92 91 90

Printed and bound in Canada by Gagné Printing Ltd.

Every reasonable effort has been made to find copyright
holders. The publishers would be pleased to have any
errors or omissions brought to their attention.

To my late mother
J.P.J.

and

To my parents
H.E.P.

CONTENTS

SECTION THREE Mechanisms For Distributing Elective Representation / 175

PREFACE

Representation and Electoral Systems: Canadian Perspectives examines the nature and function, implementation and consequences of political representation and electoral systems in Canada. The book is divided into the following five sections:

- Section One: Political Representation: Conceptual and Theoretical Issues
- Section Two: The Institutional Implementation of Political Representation
- Section Three: Mechanisms for Distributing Elective Representation
- Section Four: Electoral Systems: Types, Consequences, and Reform
- Section Five: Decision Rules and Collective Choice

Each section begins with an introduction and ends with discussion questions. Selected readings provide evidence for different viewpoints on the issues and controversies featured in the section.

Section One examines the meaning, nature, function, and system of political representation; who and what should be represented; and the criteria for fair, effective, and responsive representation. Section Two concentrates on the implementation of Canadian political representation in the legislature, bureaucracy, regions, judiciary, political parties, interest groups, and political systems with deep societal divisions. Section Three centres on the machinery, criteria, methods for and consequences of establishing seats and electoral boundaries in Canada. Section Four examines the different types of electoral systems, their political consequences, and reform of the system. Finally, Section Five analyses the conditions required for and the paradoxes of voting systems.

This volume contains some articles that have never been published elsewhere; it updates other previously published articles; moreover, this volume includes articles considered to be classics by academics in this field. The select bibliography complements the articles presented in this book, and should prove of invaluable assistance to students in their work on research papers.

This reader is appropriate for use in undergraduate courses on Canadian politics, parties and elections, political or electoral behaviour, empirical research, and selected problems in political science. The style of the reader permits instructors to use the entire reader or selected parts of it. In sections Four and Five, some instructors may consider that the mathematical and logical notations used in some articles are too difficult for their introductory students. The editors feel, however, that students can understand the major arguments presented in these excerpts even if they lack some mathematical and logical skills. Alternatively, instructors could teach their students the basic skills required to understand the notations.

The editors would like to thank the authors and publishers who granted permission for the printing or reprinting of their material. For practical reasons, however, we were unable to include some articles that we would have liked to include. We also want to thank Katherine Pacholok of Athabasca University for her secretarial assistance. Our thanks also to Catherine Leatherdale for her editorial assistance and to Patrick Ferrier, Maurice Esses, Elizabeth Long, Amy Lui-Ma, and Kelly Dickson of Prentice-Hall Canada Inc. for their help in publishing this book. We are grateful to Jon H. Pammett and Ian Greene for their helpful remarks as reviewers of the manuscript. The alphabetical order of the names of the editors could have been reversed for this volume, since we shared equally its development. Finally, we accept equal responsibility for any errors or omissions.

J. Paul Johnston
Edmonton, Alberta

Harvey E. Pasis
Athabasca, Alberta

June 1989

POLITICAL REPRESENTATION: CONCEPTUAL AND THEORETICAL ISSUES

INTRODUCTION

J. Paul Johnston

Ideas are not mere abstractions to be played with in semantic word games. Our ideas are directly tied to our experience of the world; we distinguish one thing from another, we interpret and categorize our experiences, we try to explain the nature of things and events, their causes, and the impact they have on us and other people. Ideas are the tools we use in perceiving, thinking about, and attempting to understand our experiences and those of other persons. Great ideas become the focus of thought and discussion throughout history, bridging not only the passing years but also the experiences of diverse cultures. The concept of political representation is an idea of that stature.

HISTORY OF REPRESENTATIVE PRACTICES

There is some dispute about the historical origin of the concept of political representation. Some scholars use the concept in describing the government and politics of ancient Greece and Rome; others question whether the idea of political representation was understood by the ancient Greeks and Romans.[1] Etymologically, the Latin word *representare* serves as the root for the family of terms we use in discussing such matters.[2] Roman political institutions appear to have served representative purposes, but the Romans did not use the word *representare* to refer to those institutions or to what the institutions accomplished. The practice of having one person formally represent another person came about as part of the judicial proceedings in the ecclesiastic (Church) and royal courts of medieval Europe. Its purpose was to ensure that all parties to a dispute acknowledged the jurisdiction of the court, and to do that they or their agent had to be present. The practice was later applied to the representation of corporate bodies, such as municipalities and guilds, in such proceedings. Still later, it was extended to the political realm, allowing representation of the interests of individuals and corporate bodies in deliberations of the affairs of state at the prince's court.[3] At first, only the two great "estates" of the medieval social structure, the landed nobility and the Church, were made regular participants in such deliberations. Usually, members of the feudal nobility spoke for themselves rather than as representatives of their estate, but the high-ranking clergy who represented the Church did so as agents of that corporate entity. In time, representatives of the towns and counties of the realm, the "Third Estate," joined the national assemblies and parliaments[4] which sprung up across Europe from the twelfth century forward. Many aspects of our modern conception of political representation find their origins in the medieval experience, but those origins also sometimes serve to confuse our contemporary understanding of the concept.

The form of government used in medieval Europe in no way could be described as "representative government." Medieval representatives did not generally come to the prince's Court at their own insistence; they were summoned to attend. And, while the feudal lords and the prelates of the Church were sometimes in a position to bargain with the prince about how the affairs of state and his policies would affect their Estates, those summoned to represent the common people of the towns and countries were there largely to serve as a source of information about local affairs, and as messengers, taking back news of the royal proclamations and rulings to the people they represented.[5] In a sense, they served as ambassadors of the Crown to their own localities. They did not "represent" those localities and their inhabitants in the modern sense of the word.

Today's concept of political representation was framed, in large part, by those who challenged the doctrines and practice of absolute monarchy in the sixteenth and seventeenth centuries, chiefly in England, and proposed the principles of modern constitutionalism and the concept of "limited government." Central to that concept is the claim that governments should be, as A.H. Birch puts it, "the servants of the public, not its masters."[6] Under limited government, rulers are not free to adopt whatever policies they see fit, but must wield their powers in ways that respect the interests of the people they govern, as the governed define their interests. Few people in the sixteenth and seventeenth centuries would have accepted that most members of the public were suited to the tasks of defining what those interests were and addressing them in governmental policies, or even that most people were interested in such matters. However, it was clear that some persons were capable of doing so on behalf of others, acting as spokespeople in promoting and defending the interests and concerns of the people, especially with regard to limiting the arbitrary exercise of royal prerogatives.

Such persons were the first modern political representatives, and the actions they took in that capacity formed the basis for our modern notion of political representation. However, many features of medieval government remained in play. Representatives were chosen not by common or lay members of the groups they represented, such as the Church, landed nobility, or municipality, but by those with property, wealth, or high social standing within the groups. They did not *make* governmental policy; rather, they served as spokespeople for those whose interests and lives would be affected by governmental policy—"standing in the place" of those persons in parliaments, congresses, and assemblies. And, they were still summoned to meet in the consultative bodies by the monarch.

Several other medieval representative practices and conventions were retained, but took on new significance as the doctrines of modern constitutionalism emerged. For example, the feudal notion of the Crown and its relation to the realm, as Walter Ullmann has described it, that "the Crown was to all intents and purposes the kingdom itself, symbolizing the incorporeal, legal bond which united king and kingdom,"[7] was still held to be true in an amended form, known as "the Crown in Parliament"; whenever the monarch met with the Houses of Parliament, the realm was thought to be represented there in its entirety. Thus, the representatives were considered persons who not only represented particular localities or segments of society but also the interests of the nation as a whole.

Similarly, the medieval convention that obliged a monarch to seek the counsel and support of the great "estates" of the realm before undertaking important policy initiatives on all matters said to "touch the Crown" was still observed. However, the convention was now considered to provide support for the newer claim that government was to be conducted "by the consent of those governed." The monarch's right to govern arbitrarily had been limited by the right claimed by his subjects, that they were bound to follow only those dictates to which their political representatives had given consent. Charles I literally lost his head through his insistence that he had the right to dissolve Parliament at his pleasure and to the right to ignore its counsel in policy matters. Modern political representatives had, by that point, established an effective role for themselves in making the laws and policies which governed the political community.

Impact of Modern Constitutionalism

The attempt to place constitutional limits on the powers of government, and, in particular, on the arbitrary exercise of those powers by a monarch, was largely a challenge of royal authority by members of the social and economic elites in seventeenth century England, though it took a decidedly more democratic turn with the Puritan Revolution at mid-century. However, political democracy as we know it today hardly flourished there, or elsewhere in Europe, at that time. Tory and Whig views of the constitution and the role of representatives in the practice of government were in conflict. The Tories defended the Crown and saw the role of representatives as closely derived from medieval practice. Representatives were to provide consent and counsel to the monarch on matters concerning the national interest, as well as matters of concern to particular groups; as ambassadors to the royal court, their job was to "express the grievances and represent the interests of their constituents."[8] The taking of policy initiatives and the administration of the affairs of state should, according to the Tories, remain under the control of the monarch. Whigs, on the other hand, called for limitation of the monarch's powers, the deliberation of policy matters by elected representatives, and the active participation of the representatives in governing the nation.

Two aspects of the Whig view of political representation are worthy of further comment. First, the Whigs held that representatives were not to serve as the instructed delegates of their constituents, but should act as independent "trustees," exercising their own judgment on behalf of the people they represented in dealing with matters of state. A century later, Edmund Burke would make this same notion famous in his speech to the electors of Bristol, renewing an earlier controversy about the relationship between representatives and their constituents that still exists. The second aspect of the Whig view warranting comment is their response to demands for the extension of political representation to those groups lacking direct representation. The basis for representation was still the local community as a corporate entity, and the interests of a given community, taken as a whole, were represented in the assembly, not those of individual citizens within the community. Some communities, particularly newer industrial cities, did not elect their own representatives. Moreover, the franchise was very narrowly defined, so that most persons living in communities with their own representatives were unable to participate in the elections held to choose them. The Whigs were not bothered by this situation, as their conception of political representation was an elitist one. To counter the movement for a more democratic basis of representation, they put forward the idea of "virtual representation": people lacking the franchise were still held to be represented by virtue of the fact that the community at large was directly represented, and they were members of that community. The Whigs also argued that those communities lacking direct representation were represented by virtue of the fact that it was the particular interests of a community that were represented in the assembly, and not its individual citizens; if any other community having the same interests as one lacking direct representation was directly represented, then so were the interests of the latter community.

While the idea of virtual representation seems quaint to us today, we use it implicitly in arguing that the interests of children are represented in the persons of their parents. More significantly, the idea of virtual representation points to the issue of when and under what circumstances political representation can be said to occur, that is, when is a person represented in the political process by another person, and under what circumstances? Similarly, the Whig notion of the representative as an independent trustee raises the question as to whether constituents are actually being represented if the person they elect is under no clear obligation to heed their wishes, acting instead on his own perception of what is in their best interests. The Whigs offered one set of answers to these questions; modern democratic thought offers another set. Whigs stressed the need for representatives and government to act *responsibly* in the interests of the whole community as seen by those best placed to discern those interests, rather than to *respond* to the immediate wishes and demands of particular interests or people. Only then could "peace, order, and good government" prevail, to borrow a familiar theme of the Canadian constitution. Modern democratic principles stress that political representatives be *responsive* to the expressed concerns of their constituents, that all citizens be directly and equally represented in the political process, and that citizens possess the means to render their representatives accountable for actions supposedly taken on their behalf.

Although arguments in favour of the modern democratic perspective were put forward by the Levellers and other radical thinkers in the English Puritan Revolution, the Whig views on these matters prevailed throughout the eighteenth century and up to the passage of the First Reform Act in 1832. However, radical views favouring a more democratic basis for representative government, gathered strength in England during that period. Similar views emerged in the American colonies and in France as the eighteenth century came to a close, inspiring the American and French Revolutions. Some thinkers, like Rousseau, argued that true political democracy was incompatible with representative forms of government, and that the only hope for instituting democracy resided in forming small, socially and culturally homogeneous communities, wherein the practice of simple, direct democracy could be re-established among citizens willing to forsake their own private interests to promote and defend the public interest shared by all. Others, like Joseph Priestly and Thomas Paine, were committed to representative government, but challenged the notion that Parliament was sovereign, arguing the doctrines of popular sovereignty: that the right to decide how a political community should be governed ultimately resides in its citizenry and cannot be irrevocably delegated to political representatives. Similarly, they maintained that each citizen had a natural right to be represented politically in the governmental process and to take an equal part in the selection of political representatives. These ideas exerted a powerful influence on the prevailing views of political representation and representative government. They continue to shape our thinking about these matters, providing a standard against which we now assess the meaning of the concept of political representation and the practical implementation of the principles that underlie it.

The Rise of Modern Liberalism

Over time, some of the ideas of the radical thinkers of the eighteenth century evolved into the doctrines of modern liberalism. Individualism was, and remains, the watchword of liberalism. Liberals are committed to the worth and the freedom of the individual. Liberalism continued to develop in the early and mid-nineteenth century, and liberals adopted a more extreme version of the notion that constitutional limits should be placed on the powers of government to control the activities of individuals: "that government is best which governs least." The primary job of government, from the liberal viewpoint, is to protect individual freedoms, provide circumstances in which such freedoms can be extended, and provide opportunities for individuals to improve upon their personal welfare. Similarly, the job of an elected representative is to ensure that the interests and individual freedoms of the persons he represents are defended and promoted, and, especially, to guard against governmental intrusions, purportedly made on behalf of others, upon the rights of individuals.

Such ideas were already widespread in the United States by the end of the eighteenth century, their attractiveness enhanced by the negative aspects of

British colonial rule that led to the American Revolution and a long history of local self-government. In England, liberal ideas became popular in the rising middle class in the early and middle part of the nineteenth century, providing as they did a compromise between older Whig notions and radical views: liberalism recognized the central role of individual enterprise in society and the diversity of interests it produces, and attempted to accommodate that wide range of interests in the formulation of public policy.

The Whigs had maintained there was one or two dominant interests in a constituency to be represented. Liberals maintained there was a diverse range of interests reflecting the private concerns of individual constituents that were or might be affected by governmental policies; interests were not considered to be tied closely to an area's social and economic organization, although one's opinions might be shaped in part by social and economic factors. The role of an elected representative being to represent the interests of his constituents as *they* saw them, a wide and diverse range of concerns had to be taken into account in formulating governmental policies. What serves the "public interest" would be determined through a process of rational deliberation, focusing on how policies would impinge on the interests of individuals, and taking care to prevent a dominant group or faction from infringing on the rights of individuals or imposing its view without due cause. For liberals, the role of representative institutions would be to provide the context in which these deliberations could take place on a full and open basis.

The industrially-based society emerging in Britain in the early and middle parts of the nineteenth century was becoming socially and economically pluralistic, though class differences were already pronounced. Among the working class, there arose a demand for reform of the system of representation that had prevailed through the long years of Whig dominance. Under the Whigs, the population sizes of constituencies varied sharply across the nation, allowing small "pocket" boroughs with few electors equal weight in terms of representation with a large city, like Liverpool. Members of Parliament were not paid for their services, so candidacy was largely limited to those of independent wealth or those on "retainer" to the wealthy. Property qualifications and other restrictions imposed severe limits on the franchise. Open voting meant that those who were able to vote were subject to duress or undue influence, and corrupt election practices flourished. The demand raised by the working class for reform was promoted by middle class radicals, and culminated in the passage of the Great Reform Act of 1832.

The Reform Act of 1832 established a uniform franchise for England and Wales (though it did not greatly extend the size of the electorate), and focused on what we would call the "redistribution" of representation. Rather than representing local communities arbitrarily, representation was distributed among constituencies in relation to their population size, although local community interests continued to influence the delimitation of constituency boundaries, as they do today. The new industrial towns were given representation, larger counties were given more than the traditional two members of Parliament, and many of the "pocket" boroughs were abolished. "Representation by population" added weight to the Leveller's earlier demand that representation be extended to all persons on an equal basis. "One person, one vote, one value" is a notion that continues to be a source of controversy.

Aside from the changes just noted, the Great Reform Act did not make further inroads on the existing system of representation; in many respects, the Act can be seen as a move by the dominant Whigs to accommodate some of the demands for reform without making wholesale changes. But, as Birch notes, "the old principles of representation were abandoned, and the gates were opened to further instalments of reform."[9] It was after 1832 that the Liberal view of representation took shape and became dominant in Britain and in the rest of western Europe, as it had in the United States. In both places, the representation of the interests of individuals became of primary concern, and the legislature, the main locus of representation within the governmental process, became a forum for contending views of what constituted the "public interest."

If the purpose of representative bodies is the presentation of contending views of the public interest, then any person having an opinion warrants having that opinion represented, and the franchise should be extended to all citizens in a fully democratic manner. As each person has an equal right to such representation, its provision should be on an equal basis. Such equality can only be accomplished within a system of representation if constituencies are equal in population size, so that each person's representative carries equal weight in deliberations and votes on matters before the assembly. Moreover, representation must be direct, for a person's interests and opinions cannot be truly represented by someone he or she did not choose. Taken together, these arguments led liberal reformers to call for full manhood suffrage, constituencies equal in population size, and electoral arrangements that would provide direct representation of the interests and opinions of as many members of the electorate as possible. Representation that is truly democratic in character would only come about, it was held, when such reforms were put in place.

Liberal reformers measured the representative character of a legislature by the extent to which its composition and procedures permitted the complete range of opinion within the citizenry to be taken into account in deliberations on a matter of policy. They believed that to be truly "representative" the legislature must mirror that range of opinions in debate. Consequently, nineteenth-century liberals, like John Stuart Mill, often advocated the adoption of proportional representation so that all shades of opinion would be represented in elected assemblies. Moreover, they encouraged procedural reforms that would enhance the opportunities for representatives to make the concerns of their constituents known.

How to arrive at policies which promote the general interest of all in representative government is problematic, a point that had been made forcefully by Rousseau. The Whig view of representation, incorporating Locke's views, had stressed majoritarianism, though under the Whig system of representation, majority sentiment was actually the sentiment of a relatively small segment of citizenry. While English liberals of the later period saw an underlying harmony of individual interests, American liberals of that time, such as James Madison, were not so optimistic, nor did they hold much faith in the "public regardingness" of ordinary citizens. In particular, they were anti-majoritarian, fearing that a dominant faction might forge a majority coalition of support that could rule tyranically, disregarding and oppressing minority interests. Their solution was to distribute representation widely in the form of a large number of relatively small, geographically-based constituencies. In this way, government could take advantage of the diversity of local interests found in a large nation, making it difficult to form majority coalitions that would persist from one issue to the next. Consequently, majority rule would involve shifting and cross-cutting majority coalitions of concurrent minority interests. Over time, what was truly in the "public interest" would be prudently indicated if the evils of factionalism and the threat of majority tyranny that were inherent in democratic practice were blunted in this fashion. The legacy of their views on this matter has been a continuing concern about the tension between majority rule and minority rights in the practice of representative government, and a continuing concern about how to identify what is truly in the common interest of all citizens if representative practices and institutions serve mainly to represent the concerns of individuals motivated largely by self-interest.

The tenets and practice of modern liberalism altered popular thought about the nature of political representation, the role it plays in democratic government, and the basis on which it is extended to the citizenry. By the end of the nineteenth century, however, the importance of liberalism was being downplayed, and two new features of social and political organization were taking shape: political parties were emerging as organizations designed to mobilize support in the mass electorate, and specific group interests were also being organized institutionally.

The Role of Parties

Modern political parties interposed a mediating agency between the elected representative and his constituents. Parties undertook the direction of election campaigns, selecting the issues that would be stressed in the campaign, nominating candidates, and recruiting support for them in the mass electorate. Although political parties in this modern form emerged in the American colonies in the latter half of the eighteenth century, they came into being in Britain only in the last quarter of the nineteenth century, and in the rest of western Europe at the end of that century. In large part, their creation was in response to the extension of the franchise under liberal reforms. Those persons seeking to gain office as elected representatives were now faced with the task of trying to canvass support in the mass electorate, rather than in a narrowly defined electorate; the task had become unmanageable, so candidates became dependent on party resources to carry out their campaigns, putting them rather at the mercy of party leaders, and limiting their independence of action in representing constituents should they be elected.

Candidates nominated were pledged to support and, if elected, to work to implement, the "party mandate", a program of policies developed by party leaders. The party mandate was taken to the electorate in appealing for the support of its members. According to the mandate argument, if a particular party won control of the government, it had been given a mandate by the electorate to implement its program of policies, and was bound to honour that commitment to those whose support it had solicited. Insofar as it had won control of the policy-making mechanisms available in a system of representative government, only those citizens who voted for the party would have effective representation in the making of governmental policy. Those who supported other parties whose candidates won office would be represented only in the fashion of having their concerns made known by the member representing their constituency. And those who voted for losing candidates in their own riding would ostensibly not be represented at all, for how could they be represented by someone whose views they had rejected? Such representation would be formalistic at most.

While the doctrine of a party mandate has seldom been invoked in its most stringent form, it still raises important issues about what constitutes representation and under what circumstances representation takes place. The policies put forward by a particular party reflect only the views of whatever segment of the electorate supports that party. If that segment is a relatively homogeneous dominant minority in the political community and use of a "winner-take-all" form of electoral system allows it to gain control of government through the electoral process, what is in the "public interest" may become rather narrowly defined. Moreover, the extent to which that policy program genuinely reflects the range of interests found within the support base of a given party will depend on the degree to which democratic practices are employed within the party in arriving at the program. And, finally, if the party recruits support broadly across different interest groups in a society and uses democratic processes to arrive at its policy program, there is the risk that the views of minority interests within its support base will not be incorporated in the specification of those policies due to the manoevrings required to form a majority coalition of support among party members. Clearly, the creation of political parties raises a host of issues concerning what constitutes representation and how it is accomplished in the political process.

The Impact of Interest Groups

In the early part of the twentieth century, the institutional organization of specific group interests also influenced thinking about the nature of political representation and how it can be effectively extended to citizens. Public opinion on matters of governmental policy is a rather vague thing (if it is a "thing" at all) under the individualistic view of society that was held by nineteenth-century liberals: a shifting amalgam of diverse individual opinions, rooted in current wants or dislikes. But when society is organized formally along lines of shared group interests, public opinion becomes something quite different: a set of competing points of view that reflect the functional basis of the group organization of that society. With the rise of business and employer organizations, trade unions, and farmers' cooperatives in the early part of this century, the basis for organizing public opinion regarding policy matters was created. A variety of theories of group representation and demands for reform of the system of political representation along such lines were also put forward. In Canada, that approach to reform was represented in Henry Wise Wood's ideas regarding group representation during his tenure as a leader of the United Farmers of Alberta, the agricultural producers' organization that evolved into a political party and governed Alberta from 1921 to 1935. Remaining true to Wood's philosophy, the UFA, with one exception, only ran candidates in rural ridings and provided cabinet representation for urban Albertans by offering pertinent ministerial posts to Labour Party MLAs from the city ridings.

If groups are seen to be the integral components of social and economic organization in society, they must have distinct interests which, it was held, should be represented in the political process. This perspective calls to mind the medieval notion that the Church, the landed nobility, and the townspeople should be represented in government; in that sense, the group perspective was a reaction against the individualistic conception of social life and its organization. Its advocates maintained that group interests could not be afforded the kind of representation they warranted in a system designed to accommodate the principles of liberal individualism, and that the dynamic interplay of contending interests arising from functional group relationships would not be represented in the political process. They advocated a variety of institutional reforms in order to create representative institutions wherein corporate interests could be brought forward and coordinated in a spirit of democratic cooperation. Representation in such institutions would be distributed to groups and functional organizations, not to individuals or local communities. A variety of special purpose agencies would need to be established to reflect the complex division of labour that had developed in modern mass industrial societies.

The use of geographically-defined constituencies is inappropriate to such purposes; hence, those who made such proposals advocated the use of what are known as "voluntary" constituencies. Each group would be allocated a specific number of representatives, elected by members of the group. Thus, for example, all farmers would be registered on a separate voters list, regardless of where they might reside in the country or province; they would be able to vote only in elections to choose representatives of the farming interest, for candidates seeking to represent that interest. Not only would this change the nature of the electoral process, but also the idea of who should be represented and on what basis. Arguments for the representation of persons only in their capacity as members of groups are no longer popular. But today, we see parallel demands for industry and consumer representation on regulatory bodies, and for proportionate representation of minorities in government bureaucracies.

CONTROVERSIES AND ISSUES

Our understanding of the nature of political representation and the ways and circumstances under which such representation is made available to citizens has been shaped by the history of representative practices. An analysis of political representation helps us to organize our understanding of the politics of a particular era. In medieval times and later, a representative was someone who was authorized to speak and act on behalf of another in his absence, and was empowered to enter into agreements and bind the other to them as if that person had entered into the agreements himself. In other words, a formal arrangement has been made by which one person is authorized to speak and act on behalf of another as though he or she were that person. In her authoritative analysis of the evolution of the meaning of the concept of representation in the Western political tradition, Hanna F. Pitkin labels this view of representation a "formalistic" one, since it rests on the formal arrangements through which one comes to act in the representative capacity. There is no concern for the substantive character of the representation, nor is the representation concerned with democratic politics. Instead, it is simply, as Pitkin calls it, an "authorization" account of the meaning of the concept of formalistic representation.[10]

The rise of modern constitutionalism in England presented another variant of the formalistic interpretation. The leading issue of the era was that of making the Crown responsible to the major interests in the society with regard to the exercise of governmental authority. Whig doctrines of constitutional government claimed a share in the formulation of governmental policy for parliamentary representatives; representatives were viewed as independent trustees acting on behalf of their constituents. To ensure that they exercised their discretionary judgment in the best interests of their constituents, the representatives were made accountable to the constituents by having to renew that authorization periodically through the electoral process. Between elections, however, constituents held no power to specify what their representative should do. Pitkin notes that this view of representation is also essentially formalistic in character, differing from the "medieval" view only in its focus on the formal arrangements by which the representative is made accountable to those persons he represents.[11]

While the Whigs held that an elected representative should act as he best saw fit, the Leveller's disagreed. Their answer to the question "To what extent is an elected member of a democratic assembly bound to present and conform to the wishes and views of his constituents as they express them?" would be "To the fullest extent!" To their way of thinking, an elected representative was no more than an agent who presented the views of his constituents and gave or withheld their consent to laws and policies, acting on their instructions. This same issue, rooted in the conflicts of seventeenth-century England, remains a lively source of controversy.

Another related issue is also a source of controversy today: whether and under what circumstances a representative's moral obligation to act "responsibly" should take precedence over responding to his/her constituents' demands? Proponents of populist democracy would argue that representation that does not respond to the expressed interests of the constituents is not representation at all. Whigs, both old and new, argue that a representative's first duty is to act in a responsible manner in discharging matters of state, and that doing so requires the freedom to exercise discretionary judgment. Accommodating the demands of one's constituents, they say, may not advance or protect their broader interests.

A third related issue reflects the different perspectives of seventeenth century Tory and Whig doctrines. Tories held that elected members of Parliament represented only the interests of their local constituencies, not those of the nation at large; only the monarch represented the nation as a whole. Whigs, on the other hand, saw members of Parliament as sharing in the making of policies that applied to the nation as a whole, and argued that in their decisions, elected representatives should set the interests of the nation above the localized interests of the communities that elected them. This position provided a rationale for freeing representatives from the control constituents might want to assert.

From the authorization viewpoint, anyone authorized to act politically for another is, by definition, a representative; similarly, any government that claims the authority to act for its citizens politically is, by that fact, a representative government. What a representative does after being authorized to act for another whose interests he represents, on what basis, and in what ways is completely left to his discretion. The accountability variant attempts to correct this situation by defining a representative as someone who acts for another *and* is subject to formal mechanisms of accountability. In a democratic context, the need to renew his authorization periodically through standing for reelection makes an elected representative formally accountable to his constituents. The Levellers and later radicals favoured short terms of office, thereby forcing the elected representative to renew his authorization and account for his actions frequently, parallelled today, for example, in the two-year term of office for members of the United States House of Representatives. However, although arrangements for accounting after-the-fact may be intended to encourage responsiveness and appropriate behaviour, they may not be effective. Formal controls do not force a representative to act responsibly if he or she chooses to act in an unethical manner and is willing to suffer the consequences after the fact! Similarly, if a representative chooses not to stand for reelection, the mechanism of accountability becomes ineffective.

Formalistic perspectives lack a clear vision of what substantive activities constitute "representing" someone. Anything that is done after being authorized to represent another is considered "representation," and the formal controls do not always provide for accountability, even after the fact. In essence, the nature of the relationship between the representative and those who are represented, mirrored in the ongoing activities of the former on behalf of the latter, is largely ignored except for the formal arrangements by which that relationship is initiated and renewed. Making government responsible to elected representatives, as the Whigs sought to do, is surely desirable, but does one gain its benefits if elected representatives need not be responsive to the wishes and needs of their constituents as constituents express them?

Another perspective of the nature of political representation focuses on the character of the relationship between the representative and his constituents. From this perspective, as Pitkin states, "Representation is a certain characteristic activity, defined by certain behavioral norms or certain things a representative is expected to do."[12] Expectations are also created as to how the constituents will behave. A constituent can use the established standards of behaviour to judge whether he or she is being represented well or badly.

Although many writers allude to the character of the relationship between the representative and his constituents, Pitkin reports that none have definitively presented political representation in these terms. Instead, they draw analogies to other roles. For example, a representative might be seen as an **agent** of the people he represents, reflecting the fact that he acts for them. Or, he may be portrayed as a **deputy**, calling attention to the fact that he acts in place of those he represents. Similarly, comparison may be made to **ambassadors** or **delegates**, deputies who act with specific instructions, limiting the commitments they can make on behalf of those in whose absence they are authorized to act. The Whig notion of the representative as a **trustee** or a **guardian** of the interests of the people he represents suggests that "representing" involves taking care of the constituents' interests. Comparisons have been drawn to the role of the physician, lawyer, or some other professional, suggesting that a political representative is someone with special skills enabling him to ensure that the needs and wishes of the people he represents are made known and taken into account in the making of governmental policies, more effectively, in fact, than his constituents could do on their own behalf. These analogies, separately and as a set, tell us something about the character of representation as a specific kind of substantive activity, about the role of the representative and his relationship to those he represents, and about the norms that should guide his conduct in carrying out that role. But we would be wrong to take the analogies too far.

We would also be wrong to take this perspective too far. It tends to portray representation as dyadic, between the representative and his constituents. While that may be true in certain respects, representation also exists in the body politic, linking the citizenry with its governors and the institutions of government. And this perspective, like the formalistic views, hinges on the notion of *agency*, or a person "*acting for*" others. But the concept of representation has also been used in the sense of "*standing for*" someone or something that is currently absent, symbolizing that which is absent.[13] This facet of its meaning is not reflected in agency views of representation, though it plays an important part in "political representation" as a concept.

The idea that representation involves "standing in place of" something that is otherwise absent is most straightforwardly indicated in that variant of this perspective which Pitkin calls "descriptive representation."[14] The rationale is that whatever "represents" replaces that which is represented, and can only do so if it reflects the character of that which is absent. John Adams held that a truly representative legislature "should be an exact portrait, in miniature, of the people at large, as it should think, feel, reason, and act like them."[15] Contemporary students of legislative representation mimic his view in their attempts to define the extent and quality of representation afforded to constituents by looking at congruence of policy views between a representative and his constituents. We also see this kind of thinking in the nineteenth-century liberal notion that a representative assembly should contain all variants of opinion on policy matters, and people from all walks of life, in like proportions to those found in the citizenry at large. And we see it again in the Levellers' notion that an elected representative should act as an instructed delegate, mirroring the views of his constituents.

This view surely captures the democratic notion that it is the will of the people, however diverse, that is to be expressed in the governmental process through the adoption of representative practices and institutions. But descriptive representation has obvious weaknesses. First, simply being like something or someone is not the same as representing it or him politically. Any sense of the activity of representing another in the governmental process is absent. Second, we might ask if constituents really want someone who is "like them" in as many ways possible as their representative? Would they not rather have someone who can effectively act on their behalf because he has the knowledge, skills, and experience they lack? If a certain portion of the citizenry is ignorant on some important matter of policy, should their ignorance be represented in the composition and views of the legislative assembly—and in like ratio? Does "congruence" really measure the existence and quality of representation? Third, is it possible for a representative to share, or even accurately reflect, the views of all of his constituents, given the diversity of opinion likely to exist there? Can he really present each of them with equal force, especially when on occasion they might conflict? Representing one's constituents seems to involve more than just "presenting" their opinions and concerns. Constituents could submit written documents instead, or give testimony to achieve *that* end. Fourth, what should be done if constituents have no views on some matter of policy? One can hardly represent something that does not exist, much less represent it accurately. This view of political representation leaves no room for representatives to take the initiative in defending and promoting the interests of those persons they represent, for them to show leadership.

A variant of descriptive representation focuses on how something or someone can represent something or someone else by symbolizing it in the minds of the people.[16] It was in this sense that the medieval monarch represented his realm in its entirety. It is also in this sense that the flag of a nation represents the nation. These two examples show that whatever represents something or someone else in this manner need not be a person and need not even resemble that which it represents. Pitkin notes that all that is really necessary is for people to accept it as symbolizing whatever it supposedly represents.

Say, then, that holding elections symbolizes the practice of representative democracy; if the elections are merely a sham, it does not matter because they symbolize democracy. Surely, we would not want to accept this position. People must *feel* that they are being represented, by whatever means that representation supposedly takes place, and the conditions under which they do or do not feel represented provide important information about what constitutes representation. But to feel represented is not necessarily to be represented in fact, and in any case, it does not indicate what is the substance of political representation, either as a principle or as a mechanism.

Each of the perspectives considered above offers a particular insight into and helps to identify important issues about the nature of representation. If we combine the insights gained from these different perspectives, we can come closer to understanding the concept. Let's regroup the issues discussed above in terms of three broad questions. First, there is the question of **who** should be represented? Should it be local communities as collectivities or the individual persons who compose them? What about corporate bodies, such as the Church or some other institution; or groups of like-minded persons, such as political parties and interest groups; or organizations that act for such groups, like trade unions, professional associations, and the like? For each alternative, questions arise about what is the intent of political representation and how it can best be accomplished. The answers differ because the focus differs. If we represent individuals, then we are likely faced with the need to accommodate diverse interests and opinions. If we represent local communities as collectivities or corporate bodies or groups or organizations, we may assume a homogeneity of viewpoint or interests that is not actually there. And, in any case, the institutional arrangements and the mechanics of extending representation will differ.

Second, there is the question of **what** should be represented. Should we represent broad, economically defined interests, as the Whigs and Edmund Burke maintained, or should it be the opinions and demands of individuals? Should we attempt to represent something called the "public interest," or can we do no more than represent the private interests of individuals as they touch upon public matters? Or should we represent "local interests," or what we take to be "national interests"? And who will define what is a "national interest"?

Might it simply be a "local" or "sectional" interest in masquerade? Similarly, if we are to represent the opinions of the constituents on policy matters, what do we do when they seem to have no opinions on such matters, or when the opinions they have conflict?

Third, there is the question of what the **nature of the relationship** between a representative and the people he represents should be. Should a representative act as an "independent trustee" or as an "instructed delegate"? If he acts as an instructed delegate, is there any real "representation" taking place, or is he simply a passive instrument through which his "masters' voices" are heard? If he acts as an independent trustee, how can it be ensured that the representative is responsive to his constituents' needs and wishes as *they* view them? Tension arises between a representative's being responsive to his constituents' demands and his obligation to act responsibly in representing their best interests, as well as those of others who are citizens of the wider national community. Those who are too ready to criticize the efforts of elected representatives should, perhaps, reflect on the issues reviewed here. Should we regard the role of a modern representative as that of a political specialist? Is the relationship between the representative and constituent a one-to-one relationship, or a one-to-many relationship? Indeed, an official like the president of the United States or the prime minister of Canada represents many different constituencies, each made up of many persons, some of whom may be members of more than one of those constituencies. How can their interests be determined? Or is the relationship a many-to-one relationship, as might occur in a multi-member district or in a case where several agencies represent the same person simultaneously? Or is it a many-to-many relationship, as in the case of a legislative body that collectively represents the citizenry of a given political community?

Who should be represented? What should be represented? And how? The theoretical issues arising from the rich complexity and subtlety of the concept of political representation must be addressed by those who study its implementation in modern politics.

* * *

The articles in Section One of this book were selected with an eye to achieving a blend of traditional and new issues, with perhaps slightly more emphasis on the latter, so as to indicate some of the directions recent thinking on political representation has taken.

Johnathan W. Still focuses on a long-standing question made more immediate by the 1970s "apportionment crisis" in the United States: how to determine when representation has been extended on an equal basis to citizens. He notes that political equality is an important principle of modern democracy, and that its fundamental status is reflected in the doctrine of "one person, one vote." Yet, he argues that existing definitions of the concept of "political equality" are generally too loosely drawn to be of much help in determining when representation has in fact been extended on an equal basis to citizens, and that such definitions are seldom linked to the features of the electoral systems through which representation is made available. He goes on to list six criteria closely tied to the electoral system that he feels give a clearer and more complete definition of the concept of political equality, and raises another issue that has gained much attention in recent years: what constitutes "effective" representation? The late Robert G. Dixon, Jr., a leading American authority on the law and politics of reapportionment, had argued that ensuring equal-sized constituencies in keeping with the "one person, one vote" doctrine did not ensure that the representation provided would be "fair" and "effective." In his attempt to redefine the concept of political equality as it applies to the provision of elected representation, Still sets as his goals fair and effective representation.

Duff Spafford's "Mill's Majority Principle" expounds on John Stuart Mill's notion that "true" representation means direct representation, and links this notion to the way in which Mill applies the "majority principle" within a representative democracy. Spafford shows that the arithmetic underlying Mill's majority principle requires that nearly all of the members of the electorate be directly represented in a legislature. His exposition also relates these matters to the role that political parties might play in mediating the representational linkage and to the argument for proportional representation that Mill espoused in his time.

Heinz Eulau and Paul Karps examine the traditional issue of representation as responsiveness. They criticise simplistic notions of descriptive congruence as a basis for evaluating the quality of the representation an elected representative provides his constituents, and go on to describe a multi-dimensional view of responsiveness. Its four components each reflect a different aspect of the role of the elected representative and the expectations connected with that aspect of the role.

Anthony H. Birch takes an approach that, to my knowledge, no one else has, and carries it off in a way that reflects his acknowledged expertise regarding the concept of political representation, the nature of representative institutions, and their historical evolution within the western political tradition. He looks at the nature and role of political representation in a modern democracy from the perspective of contemporary systems analysis. His effort focuses on identifying the functions that representative institutions serve in such political systems.

Birch's attempt to relate political representation to the workings of the system as a whole is complemented by the final selection in this section, taken from Hanna Fenichel Pitkin's authoritative text, *The Concept of Representation*. Pitkin argues that political representation may not be best viewed in terms of the dyadic relationship between the elected representative and his constituents. Rather, she suggests that it may be better seen as an emergent property of large-scale social and political arrangements in a complex mass society. In this respect, it is a collective enterprise and a collective phenomenon that depends as much on the culture and values of a society as it does on anything an individual representative does in his capacity as such. Pitkin proposes that all of the various institutions involved in the working of modern representative governments have a role to play in ensuring that political representation takes place. Her argument provides an excellent backdrop to the readings in Section Two, serving as a bridge between the two sections.

Notes

1. The use of representative practices and institutions in ancient Greece and Rome is discussed in J.A.O. Larsen, *Representative Government in Greek and Roman History* (Berkeley, Calif.: University of California Press, 1955), while the argument questioning their understanding of the concept is given in an essay by Heinz Eulau, "Changing Views of Representation," included in Heinz Eulau and John C. Wahlke, eds., *The Politics of Representation* (Beverly Hills, Calif.: Sage Publications, 1978), 36-9, 41.

2. Hanna Fenichel Pitkin, *The Concept of Representation* (Berkeley, Calif.: University of California Press, 1967), 2-3.

3. See Gaines Post, *Studies in Medieval Legal Thought* (Princeton, N.J.: Princeton University Press, 1964), Ch. 2-4.

4. S.E. Finer, "The Contemporary Context of Representation," in Vernon Bogdanor, ed., *Representatives of the People?" Parliamentarians and Constituents in Western Democracies* (Aldershot, Hants, England: Gower Publishing Company Ltd., 1985) 286.

5. See Helen M. Cam, "The Theory and Practice of Representation in Medieval England," *History* 38 (1953).

6. A.H. Birch, *Representative and Responsible Government* (Toronto: University of Toronto Press, 1964), 18.

7. Walter Ullmann, *Medieval Political Thought* (Harmondsworth, England: Penguin Books, Ltd., 1965), 153.

8. Birch, *Representative and Responsible Government*, 26. My account relies heavily on this source.

9. Ibid., 52.

10. Pitkin, *The Concept*, 39.

11. Ibid., 55-8.

12. Ibid., 112. My account relies heavily on that presented by Pitkin in Ch. 6 of *The Concept*.

13. Ibid., 11.

14. Ibid., Ch. 4. Again, my rendering closely follows Pitkin's.

15. Quoted in Pitkin, *The Concept*, 60.

16. Ibid., Ch. 5.

1. POLITICAL EQUALITY AND ELECTION SYSTEMS

Jonathan W. Still

Political equality is an important subject in contemporary political debate. Many political reform efforts (e.g., campaign finance reform, reform of presidential nominating procedures) are intended to increase the degree of political equality. Three of the last four amendments added to the United States Constitution have been similarly directed.[1] In 1978, Congress proposed an amendment to give full voting representation in Congress to the District of Columbia, and serious efforts are now being made to abolish the Electoral College and substitute direct election of the President. Thus, political equality is a topic of great contemporary concern.

But what is political equality? By what criteria is one to determine its presence or absence or whether a proposed change in political institutions will bring us closer to or further away from the condition of political equality? Let us begin by considering the definitions offered by some distinguished scholars.

In one of the best-known modern treatises on political economy, two very distinguished scholars, Robert A. Dahl and Charles E. Lindblom, define political equality in the following terms: "Control over governmental decisions is shared so that the preferences of no one citizen are weighted more heavily than the preferences of any other one citizen."[2] They later state as an operational criterion: "In elections the vote of each member has about the same weight."[3] The authors do acknowledge some ambiguity: "How equally weighted must votes be to have 'about the same weight'?"[4] But a more basic ambiguity is in the meaning of "equally weighted" votes. Does this mean that in any election each person casts one and only one vote? Does it mean that each person has the same chance of casting a vote which determines the outcome? Or does it mean that it does not matter who holds which preference, so that if preferences are interchanged among the voters the result of the election remains unchanged? These are all plausible interpretations of the above statements, yet as will be shown later, they do not all mean the same thing.

In a book containing many extensive discussions of the meanings of different concepts, Giovanni Sartori defines political equality in a single sentence: "The principle of political equality . . . is that every man counts for one vote, and that one man's vote is the equivalent of the next man's. . . ."[5] The first part of this definition seems clear enough, if it means simply that each person casts one and only one vote, but the second part is not clear. Does it mean the same thing as the first part, or is it intended to create an additional requirement? Does it mean that it makes no difference who casts which ballot? That every person has the same probability of casting a deciding vote? Or does it mean something else? It is certainly not possible to tell from the definition given.

Jonathan W. Still, "Political Equality and Election Systems," *Ethics* 91 (April 1981): 375-94. © 1981 by The University of Chicago. Reprinted by permission of the author and publisher.

Two distinguished political scientists, Austin Ranney and Willmoore Kendall, define political equality in these terms: "One characteristic that most persons regard as essential to democracy is political equality. A familiar way of describing this trait is 'one man, one vote,' which we take to mean that in a democracy political power must be equally shared by all its citizens, and no man should have any larger a share than any other man."[6] Do the authors mean to say that if each person casts one and only one vote (a literal reading of "one man, one vote"), "political power" is then "equally shared" by all citizens? Or must some other condition be satisfied? Later in their book, the authors modify their definition somewhat when they state; "Thus political equality means not only one man, one vote, but also an equal chance for each member of the community to participate in the total decision-making process of the community."[7] The authors note that "voting is just one part . . . of the total decision-making process,"[8] but even if attention is limited to the voting process, it is still not obvious what it means for each person to have an "equal chance" to participate. Does it mean an equal chance to cast a vote which decides the outcome, or simply that each person has one and only one vote, or that it does not matter who casts which vote? It is impossible to tell from the definition given. But as will be shown later, these possible meanings are not all equivalent.

All of the definitions of political equality examined above suffer from two major failings.[9] First, they are not formulated with sufficient analytical rigor. They do not state precise criteria for determining the presence or absence of political equality. This makes it difficult if not impossible to tell exactly what states of affairs would and would not qualify as achieving political equality. Second, these definitions are insufficiently (most of them not at all) related to the institutional mechanisms of elections and electoral systems. This makes it

difficult to determine the egalitarian (or inegalitarian) character of any particular election system, or whether a proposed change in electoral structures will move the situation closer to or further from the condition of political equality.

This article is intended to make a contribution to the rigorous analysis of the concept of political equality and its relationship to election systems. I will argue that political equality is not a single concept, but a group of distinct (though related) criteria which have not previously been adequately distinguished. Six criteria for political equality, and the relationships among them, will be examined. I will then discuss several applications which will show how these criteria may be used to illuminate the egalitarian character of electoral institutions and proposed changes in them.

One prefatory note is in order. Political equality is a concept with many aspects. There is, for example, an economic aspect (the influence of economic relationships on politics). There is also a sociological and psychological aspect (patterns of leadership and interpersonal influence, etc.) And there is an institutional aspect—equality among individuals in the formal structure of the decision-making process. I will be concerned here only with this structural aspect of political equality. While this is only one aspect of the problem, it is certainly an important part of a complete understanding of any political system.

I. CRITERIA FOR POLITICAL EQUALITY

What, then, is political equality? What criteria must be satisfied before it can be said that an election system treats everyone equally?

Perhaps I should first give a more precise definition of the term "election system." An election system is a procedure (a set of rules) by means of which the members of an organized society cast votes (conduct elections) to resolve issues concerning their governance. In general, election systems may be of three types: (1) direct decision-making processes (e.g., a referendum or a New England town meeting), in which the voters decide public policy questions directly; (2) elections of a single official (e.g., a mayor or governor) who will occupy a policy-making position; or (3) elections of a multimember body (e.g., a city council or state legislature) which has the power to decide questions of public policy. With one exception, the criteria to be discussed below will be applicable to all three types of election systems.

What is political equality? To begin the search, it might be useful to turn the question around and ask what political equality is not. The first thing which might come to mind is a situation in which some people are completely excluded from voting, or in which some people have five votes, others three or two, and still others only one vote each. Surely, political equality is absent under these conditions. This suggests the following criterion.

1. Universal Equal Suffrage: Everyone is allowed to vote, and everyone gets the same number of votes.

The number of votes allotted to each person is usually one (or one for each position to be filled). Thus, Universal Equal Suffrage calls for "one person, one vote" in a literal sense.

This criterion would appear to be an extremely simple one. But in practice even it can become complicated. For universal suffrage has never been truly universal, and no one has ever seriously suggested that it ought to be. Children are always excluded, though the age cutoff used has varied. Aliens are often excluded, as are insane people and convicted felons. Yet exclusions of this nature are generally not considered to negate the existence of universal suffrage. Hence, universal suffrage

will be interpreted here as meaning universal suffrage subject to the usual exclusions, without further discussion of what the usual exclusions are or ought to be.

If Universal Equal Suffrage is satisfied, does that mean that an election system is completely egalitarian? Or must some other criterion be satisfied? Suppose that a mayor is to be elected, or a referendum question decided, in a city containing 100 000 voters. Each person has one and only one vote, so Universal Equal Suffrage is satisfied. For the election, the voters are grouped into five districts. Four of the five districts contain 250 voters each; the fifth district contains 99 000 voters. Each district has one unit vote, which is awarded to the candidate, or position on the referendum issue, carrying the district. The winner is the candidate, or issue position, receiving a majority of the five unit votes.

It seems evident that not all votes "count the same" under this system, that in fact the votes of the 1000 people living in the four small districts "weigh more heavily" than the votes of the 99 000 people living in the one large district. Why? What is it about this system which causes this inequality? At first glance, the culprit might appear to be the very great disparity among the districts in the ratio of unit votes to number of voters. The voters in the small districts each have a one two-hundred-fiftieth "share" in a unit vote, while each voter in the large district has only a one ninety-nine-thousandth share in a unit vote. This difference suggests the following (awkwardly stated) criterion for political equality.

2. Equal Shares: Each voter has the same "share" in the election, defined as what that voter voted on divided by the number of voters who voted on it.

Equal Shares is difficult to define in general, but easy to define in practice. In the usual sort of general election at large for a single official (or referendum question), the result is determined directly by the votes cast. Each person's "share in the official" or "share in the decision" is then simply one divided by the total number of voters. If a unit voting system of the kind described above is employed, "share in a unit vote" becomes the relevant quantity. For a voter in any given district, the share in a unit vote is the number of unit votes assigned to that district divided by the number of voters in the district.

In elections for a multimember legislative body, the quantity is "share in a legislator." If all legislators are elected at large, each person's share is the number of legislators divided by the total number of voters. If legislators are chosen from districts, the share of a voter in a particular district is the number of legislators elected from that district divided by the number of voters in the district. If some legislators are elected at large and others from districts, one would compute each voter's share in the legislators at large and that voter's share in the district legislators from that voter's district. The voter's total share in a legislator is then the sum of these two quantities.

The definitions given above all assume that Universal Equal Suffrage is satisfied. If not, then one would presumably want to adjust the computation of shares to reflect this fact. For example, in a general election at large for a single official, each person's share in the official would not be one divided by the total number of voters, but the number of votes that person has divided by the total number of votes held by all voters. In particular, a person excluded from voting would have zero votes and therefore a zero share.

Universal Equal Suffrage and Equal Shares have one characteristic in common. Neither, in any way, relates the votes that are cast to the outcome of the election. This property seems peculiar in a criterion for determining the presence or absence of political equal-

ity. If all votes are to "count the same" or be "equally weighted" or "equally effective," one would think that would mean that, in some sense, all votes have the same impact on the outcome of the election. Yet neither of the two criteria examined so far is concerned with the relationship between the votes cast and the election result. This makes it likely that political equality could still be absent from an election system which satisfies Universal Equal Suffrage and Equal Shares.

As an extreme example, consider the following system for electing the mayor of a city with 100 000 voters (each of whom has one vote). The voters are divided into two districts, one containing 60 000 voters and having six unit votes, the other containing 40 000 voters and having four unit votes. All of the unit votes for each district are awarded to the candidate carrying the district, and the winner is the candidate who receives a majority of the ten unit votes. This system satisfies Universal Equal Suffrage and Equal Shares, but there is an obvious inequality among the voters. The election will be decided entirely within the larger district. Whoever wins that district wins the election, regardless of what happens in the smaller district. The votes cast in the smaller district are simply irrelevant to the outcome of the election; the voters in the smaller district have no chance at all to affect the election result by their votes.

What is the source of this inequality? One approach is to focus on the idea that the voters in the smaller district have no chance to affect the election result. Under this approach, votes would be equally weighted if all voters had the same chance to affect the election result by their votes. More precisely, the requirement would be that everyone have the same statistical probability of affecting the outcome of the election. To develop this approach, it is necessary to specify a statistical model, which will be discussed after the criterion is defined.

3. Equal Probabilities: Each voter has the same statistical probability of casting a vote which decides the election (under certain assumptions).

Several scholars have developed what are called "indices of voting power," all of which are based in one way or another on the idea that the "power" of a person's vote is measured by the statistical probability of that vote determining the election result.[10] The two most widely used are the Banzhaf index[11] and the Shapley-Shubik index.[12] While their conceptual bases differ somewhat, these indices will give the same or nearly the same index values in most situations.[13] The definition given above uses, in effect, the Banzhaf index; another way of stating the Equal Probabilities criterion is that each voter has the same Banzhaf index of voting power. The Banzhaf index has been chosen because it is the conceptually most appealing, and also (fortunately) the easiest to describe.

The "certain assumptions" referred to in the definition of Equal Probabilities are those constituting the statistical model on which the Banzhaf index is based. The Banzhaf index assumes, in essence, that the election is between two alternatives (for or against a policy proposal, or between two candidates for a single office, or two political parties seeking control of a legislative body), and that each voter favors one of these alternatives (there are no abstentions). Further, it is assumed that all possible voting combinations (specifications of which voters support which of the alternatives) are equally likely to occur; this is equivalent to assuming that each voter is equally likely to favor either alternative.

A person's vote is decisive if a change in that vote would have changed the election result (whether the policy is adopted or defeated, which candidate is elected to office, or which political party wins control of the legislature).

Since all voting combinations are assumed to be equally likely, the probability that a particular person's vote will be decisive is simply the number of voting combinations in which that vote is decisive divided by the total number of possible voting combinations. This probability is the Banzhaf index of voting power for that voter.[14] If these index values are the same for all voters, then the Equal Probabilities criterion is satisfied. In essence, the Equal Probabilities criterion requires that all voters have the same chance, or the same number of opportunities, of having their vote determine the election result, under the assumptions described earlier.

A general election at large satisfying Universal Equal Suffrage will also satisfy Equal Probabilities.[15] An election conducted by districts (either for unit voting or for the election of legislators), which satisfies Universal Equal Suffrage and Equal Shares, will not in general satisfy Equal Probabilities.[16] This will be true not only in extreme cases where one district controls the election, but also in any case where the district sizes differ.[17] However, in the special case where all districts are of the same size (i.e., contain the same number of voters and have the same number of unit votes or elect the same number of legislators), Equal Probabilities will be satisfied.[18]

If Equal Probabilities is satisfied, will all votes be equally weighted? Suppose that a five-member city council has the power to enact local ordinances; three of the five members must vote for an ordinance for it to pass. Each council member is elected from a separate district containing 20 000 voters. This system satisfies Universal Equal Suffrage, Equal Shares, and Equal Probabilities. In the city, there are two opposing groups of 36 000 voters, both of which would like to control the city council. The first group has 12 000 voters in each of three districts, while the second group has 7000 voters in each of four districts and 8000 voters in the remaining district. The first group is able to elect three members to the city council and secure the adoption of any ordinance it favors; the second group is unable to elect even one council member.

Although all voters may have had the same theoretical probability of casting a vote which decides the election, it would be difficult to argue that, in fact, the votes of the people in the second group had the same impact on the outcome of the election as the votes of the people in the first group. The inequality here would be particularly invidious if the districts had been deliberately designed to bring about this result; but even if it came about by accident, the inequality is real (and substantial) nonetheless.

What is the cause of this inequality? Note that if the voters in the two groups were to trade places (or stay put but cast each others' ballots), the second group would elect three council members and the first group none, exactly reversing the previous outcome. Thus, the different results for the two groups were due to their different positions in the electoral structure (specifically, their different distributions among the districts). The votes of the people in the second group "weighed less" because of where those people lived. This type of inequality would be eliminated if the outcome of the election would never change when different voters occupy different positions in the election system. This idea can be formalized into the following criterion for political equality.

4. Anonymity: The result of the election is the same under all possible distributions of the voters among the positions in the structure of the election system.

In essence, Anonymity[19] requires that the effect of people's votes be independent of the positions they occupy in the electoral struc-ture. Voters may trade places with each other in any possible manner, and the election result will not change. Another way of stating the Anonymity criterion is that the election result is the same under all possible permutations of preferences (concerning the election) among the voters. Voters may stay put and trade preferences (or ballots) in any possible manner, and the election result will not change. The name Anonymity derives from the idea that the election system treats the voters as anonymous in that the outcome does not depend on the identities of the voters holding particular preferences or particular positions in the electoral structure, but depends only on the set of preferences which are held.

Any permutation of the preferences among the voters (or of the voters among the positions in the electoral structure) can be broken down into a series of switches of preferences (or of positions) between two individuals. If any permutation changes the election result, then there must be some point in the series where a single switch of preferences (or positions) between two individuals changes the result. The Anonymity criterion provides that this can never happen. Thus, Anonymity guarantees that each individual's vote counts the same as everyone else's in the sense that it makes no difference whether that person casts the vote or someone else casts it, or whether it is cast from that person's position in the electoral structure or from someone else's position. What counts is the votes that are cast, not who casts them (or where they are cast from).

Is Anonymity sufficient for political equality? Consider a referendum on, say, a proposed bond issue. In the election, 60 percent of the voters vote for the bond issue, and 40 percent vote against. The bond issue is defeated, because a two-thirds vote in favor is necessary for passage. This system satisfies Anonymity; no matter how voters might trade places, the result will still be 60 percent in favor, which is short of two-thirds. Yet it could be argued that the votes of the bond issue opponents have weighed more heavily than the votes of the supporters, since the views of 40 percent have prevailed over the views of 60 percent. Similarly, it can be argued that any super-majority requirement will result in the same sort of inequality. This line of argument leads to the following criterion.

5. Majority Rule: An alternative favored by a majority of the voters will be chosen by the election system.

Note that this criterion does not attempt to deal with all situations. Specifically, it does not say what should happen if there are three or more alternatives, none of which commands a majority.[20] The Majority Rule criterion requires only that the election system be such that, if there is one alternative which has majority support, then that alternative will be chosen. Of course, if there are only two alternatives, then there will always be a majority choice.

One way to think of the difference between Anonymity and Majority Rule is in terms of what factors the "weight" of a vote is allowed to depend on. Anonymity requires that the weight of a vote not depend on who casts it or where it is cast from; but the weight is allowed to depend on the alternative for which it is cast. Majority Rule prohibits this latter form of "weighting" as well as the other types.

Does Majority Rule end the search for political equality? Not necessarily. Suppose that a ten-member city council is being elected at large; the ten candidates with the most votes are the winners. This system satisfies Universal Equal Suffrage, Equal Shares, Equal Probabilities, Anonymity, and Majority Rule. There are two slates of candidates seeking control of the council. In the election, 60 000 votes are cast for one slate, and 40 000 votes for the other slate. All ten candidates on the majority slate are elected. It could be argued that this result does not reflect "equally weighted votes." The majority group has been able to win one seat on the city council for every 6000 of its votes, while the minority group has received no seats at all for its 40 000 votes. If all votes are to count the same, then the number of votes producing one seat should be the same for both groups. In this case, that would mean that the majority slate would win six seats and the minority slate four. The majority group would still control the city council, but it would not have all the seats. This argument implies the following criterion for political equality.

6. Proportional Group Representation: Each group of voters receives the same proportion of the seats in the legislative body as the number of voters in the group is of the total electorate.

The groups referred to in this definition are groups of like-minded voters who support the same candidates. The intuitive idea which underlies Proportional Group Representation is that the legislative body ought to be a microcosm of the electorate, so each group ought to be represented in the same relative numbers as it would be if the entire electorate were to meet as a direct democracy.[21] In particular, a majority group should have a majority of the seats, but should not have all of the seats.

Although this criterion is defined in terms of groups, it has a natural interpretation in terms of the individual voter. If Proportional Group Representation is satisfied, then the ratio of seats to votes will be the same for all groups. Hence, each voter's share (legislators divided by number of voters supporting them) in the legislators which that voter supported will be the same for all voters in the electorate. In this way, Proportional Group Representation bears a certain resemblance to Equal Shares. The difference is that Proportional Group Representation treats voters as having a share only in legislators they supported, whereas Equal Shares will often treat voters as having a share in legislators they opposed and with whose policy views they may strongly disagree.

Unlike the previous criteria for political equality, Proportional Group Representation is applicable only to elections for a multimember body, and not to the other two types of elections (direct decision making and elections of a single official). When only one alternative is to be selected, Proportional Group Representation becomes impossible. Another way of looking at this is to say that in these cases Proportional Group Representation collapses into Majority Rule. With only one alternative to be selected, choosing the majority alternative is the closest one can come to proportionality.

* * *

Six distinct criteria for political equality have been examined above: Universal Equal Suffrage, Equal Shares, Equal Probabilities, Anonymity, Majority Rule, and Proportional Group Representation. Unfortunately, these criteria have not been sufficiently distinguished in previous work on the subject. When Dahl and Lindblom state that political equality requires that all votes have "about the same weight,"[22] do they mean that Anonymity must be satisfied, or Equal Probabilities, or Proportional Group Representation? When Sartori defines political equality as "every man counts for one vote, and . . . one man's vote is the equivalent of the next man's,"[23] does he mean that Universal Equal Suffrage must be satisfied, or Anonymity, or Majority Rule? When Ranney and Kendall state that "political power must be equally shared"[24] and that each person must have "an equal chance . . . to participate,"[25] do they mean Equal Probabilities, or Universal Equal Suffrage, or Anonymity, or one of the other criteria? Until these different criteria are adequately distinguished, the

and the distinctions among them are recognized and studied, the normative debate over which of them is (or are) required for "political equality," or which is (or are) essential to a democratic society, cannot even begin.

Failure to distinguish among these criteria can have other adverse consequences as well. One might be led into advocating, say, Universal Equal Suffrage when what one is really interested in is Anonymity, or one of the other criteria. Similarly, one might end up supporting an election system which satisfies, say, Equal Shares in the mistaken belief that it also satisfies Majority Rule, or some other criterion. These kinds of problems can be avoided only if the distinctions among the different criteria are clearly recognized and kept in mind. The six criteria elucidated above provide a framework for a more sophisticated analysis of the concept of political equality, in general, and of the egalitarian properties of specific political institutions in particular.

One obvious question about these criteria is the relationship (if any) among them. The manner in which they have been presented would suggest that they form a spectrum, or progression, of successively more stringent criteria; a nested sequence such that any election system satisfying one criterion will necessarily satisfy the preceding ones but not necessarily the subsequent ones. I will not elaborate on the point here, but this is almost in fact the case. There are a few exceptions, but they would not seem to be of much practical importance.[26] For election systems which are likely to be encountered in use, these six criteria can be thought of as a nested sequence.

That being the case, a natural question is how far along this spectrum one must go in order to reach "meaningful" political equality. Of course, answering this question inevitably involves a value judgment. My own tentative opinion is that one would have to reach at least Anonymity. It could be argued (along the lines indicated when the criteria were presented) that one would have to go further, that is, to Majority Rule or Proportional Group Representation. On the other hand, it could be argued that deviations from proportionality are necessary to get anything done,[27] and that the weighting of votes allowed by Anonymity (but not Majority Rule) is discrimination among the alternatives rather than among the voters.[28] But a violation of Anonymity means that there can be two groups of voters of exactly the same size, and one group can get what it wants while the other group cannot. In this situation, it is difficult to see how it can be said that each person's vote counts the same as everyone else's.

In addition to the six criteria presented here, other criteria for political equality could be developed which might conflict with some of these six. For example, in direct conflict with Proportional Group Representation would be "Equal Group Representation," which would require that each group have the same number of seats in the legislative body. This notion of equality defines the composition of the United States Senate and the United Nations General Assembly; it focuses more on the groups as entities in themselves rather than as aggregations of individuals. The six criteria presented earlier would appear to include all which have been commonly advocated in public debate or scholarly discussion as defining conditions under which it can be said that each individual's vote is the equal of every other's.

These six criteria can be used to evaluate (or, at least, illuminate) the egalitarian character of various electoral institutions. This can be done by analyzing the election system in question to determine how far along the spectrum it goes toward political equality. Similarly, the egalitarian character of proposed changes in electoral institutions can be evaluated (or illuminated) by comparing the point along the spectrum which will be reached if the change is made with the point

which the existing system is at. This will be done in the next section—with some surprising results.

II. APPLICATIONS

The six criteria for political equality developed in the preceding section would have little practical importance if it turned out that all existing election systems (and all reasonable alternatives to those systems) satisfied all of them, or none of them, or the same ones. But this is not the case. Existing (and alternative) political institutions differ substantially in how far along the spectrum they go toward political equality. This fact will be illustrated below by several applications of these criteria to actual political institutions and changes which have been proposed or made in them.

The first illustration is the US Supreme Court case of *Gray* v. *Sanders*,[29] decided in 1963. That case involved the Georgia county unit system for selecting the Democratic nominee for Governor (at that time, the Democratic nomination was tantamount to election). Each county was assigned a certain number of unit votes, all of which were awarded to the candidate carrying that county in the primary election. The winner was the candidate receiving a majority of the unit votes; a runoff between the top two was held if no candidate received a majority the first time around. Each voter had one vote in the election, and there were no significant exclusions,[30] so Universal Equal Suffrage was satisfied. The more populous counties had more unit votes than the smaller counties, but not nearly in proportion to population (or number of voters), so Equal Shares was not satisfied.[31] I will not go through the calculations here, but it can be shown that Equal Probabilities was likewise not satisfied.[32] Nor was Anonymity satisfied—even in a two-candidate race, a minority of the voters could elect their candidate if they were advantageously distributed with small majorities in counties having a majority of the unit votes (while the majority had large majorities in the remaining counties); if voters were to then trade places so that the distribution of opinion within each county was the same as statewide, the majority candidate would be elected instead (with all the unit votes). For the same reason, Majority Rule was not satisfied. (Proportional Group Representation is inapplicable, since this was an election of a single official.)

The Supreme Court declared the county unit system unconstitutional because it resulted in the unequal weighting of votes. This, the Court said, violated the principle of political equality. In what way? What criterion would have to be satisfied in order to have all votes equally weighted? Unfortunately, the Court did not say. The closest thing to a definition to be found in the Court's opinion is the statement, "The conception of political equality . . . can mean only one thing—one person, one vote."[33] Taken literally, this would mean that the Court considered political equality to be synonymous with Universal Equal Suffrage. But that could not be, for the county unit system satisfied Universal Equal Suffrage, a fact that the Court acknowledged.[34]

The Court was clear about one thing which would not be acceptable. Concerned that the Georgia legislature might attempt to retain the county unit system by assigning unit votes to counties in strict proportion to population,[35] the Court added a footnote at the end of its opinion to make it plain that this too would be unconstitutional: ". . . the weighting of votes would continue, even if unit votes were allocated strictly in proportion to population. Thus if a candidate won 6000 of 10 000 votes in a particular county, he would get the entire unit vote, the 4000 other votes for a different candidate being worth nothing and being counted only for the purpose of being discarded."[36] This makes it clear that the

Court did not consider Equal Shares to be sufficient for political equality, since the "reformed" county unit system it was discussing would have satisfied Equal Shares.

The Supreme Court did not explicitly state what election system would have to replace the county unit system. However, the Court's rejection of any form of county unit system left Georgia with little choice but to adopt the obvious alternative—a popular vote primary election with the winner being determined by the most votes received (as is traditional in the South, provision was made for a runoff between the top vote getters if no candidate received a majority in the initial election). It is easy to see that this system satisfies Universal Equal Suffrage, Equal Shares, and Equal Probabilities.[37] Anonymity is also satisfied, since the result depends entirely on the number of votes each candidate receives and not on their distribution. A candidate supported by a majority of the voters will always win (without a runoff), so Majority Rule is satisfied.

Thus, while the Court did not say how far along the spectrum one would have to go to reach political equality (beyond saying that Equal Shares was not sufficient), the Court was correct in its assumption that its decision would have a substantial impact on political equality. This can be seen quite clearly in Table 1. From a situation in which only the first criterion on the spectrum was satisfied, the Court's decision moved things all the way to the end of the spectrum with all criteria satisfied. By its decision in *Gray* v. *Sanders*, the Supreme Court accomplished a significant extension of political equality.

In 1964, one year after *Gray*, the Supreme Court decided the reapportionment cases.[38] These cases involved the legislative election systems used in six states, which were generally typical of the systems used in the remaining states as well. While the specific details of these systems varied from state to state, the general pattern was the same. State legislators were elected from districts (some single member, some multimember) by plurality vote. Universal Equal Suffrage was satisfied, as each voter had one vote for each legislator to be elected. Equal Shares was not satisfied, because the ratio of legislators to population varied among the districts.[39] Equal Probabilities was also not satisfied.[40] A group of voters constituting a majority in one district could elect a legislator, while an equal number of voters scattered among several districts could not, so Anonymity was not satisfied. A minority of the voters could win control of the legislature if they were distributed in a way giving them majorities in districts electing a majority of the legislators, so Majority Rule was not satisfied. And the fact that a minority of the voters could win a majority of the seats is also sufficient to show that Proportional Group Representation was not satisfied.

The Supreme Court held that this scheme was unconstitutional. Citing *Gray* v. *Sanders* as having "established the basic principle of equality among voters within a state,"[41] the Court ruled that this scheme resulted in the unequal weighting of votes in legislative elections. As in *Gray*, the Court did not say clearly exactly what criterion would have to be satisfied to attain political equality. But the Court did spell out what election system would have to replace the one it was invalidating.

Table 1   The Case of *Gray* v. *Sanders*
(Georgia County Unit System)

	UES	ES	EP	Ano	MR
Before	X	–	–	–	–
After	X	X	X	X	X

Note—For all tables: UES = Universal Equal Suffrage; ES = Equal Shares; EP = Equal Probabilities; Ano = Anonymity; MR = Majority Rule; PGR = Proportional Group Representation; X means the criterion is satisfied; – means the criterion is not satisfied.

The change ordered by the Court was that the districts be redrawn so that the population per legislator would be the same in all districts. Of course, this system satisfies Universal Equal Suffrage and Equal Shares. Since the district sizes could still differ, Equal Probabilities is not satisfied.[42] As before, a group of voters amounting to a majority in one district could elect a legislator, while an equal number scattered among the districts could not, so Anonymity is not satisfied. Similarly, a minority of the voters which is advantageously distributed among the districts could elect a majority of the legislators, so Majority Rule is not satisfied. This possibility suffices to show that Proportional Group Representation is also not satisfied.

The result of the Court's decision, in terms of political equality, can be seen in Table 2. It presents a sharp contrast with *Gray* v. *Sanders*. In both cases, the starting point was the same, with only the first criterion satisfied. But in *Gray* the result of the Court's decision was that all of the criteria were satisfied, whereas in the reapportionment cases, the Court moved the situation only one additional step along the spectrum. And the one criterion which the Court added, Equal Shares, was precisely the one criterion which the Court had explicitly said in *Gray* v. *Sanders* would not be sufficient for political equality! In the reapportionment cases, the Supreme Court used the same effusive rhetoric as in *Gray*, and it cited *Gray* for the principle of political equality. But what the Court apparently did not realize (or chose to ignore) was the fact that the consequences of its decision were far less than in *Gray* v. *Sanders*. In *Gray*, the Court accomplished a significant extension of political equality, but in the reapportionment cases, the Court accomplished virtually nothing.

Another illustration of the usefulness of distinguishing among the different criteria for political equality is provided by two constitutional amendments now being debated. The first is the amendment proposed by Congress to the states in 1978. That amendment would give the District of Columbia full voting representation in Congress, that is, two senators and a number of representatives dependent on population.[43] At present, the District has one nonvoting delegate in the House of Representatives and no representation in the Senate.

Table 2　Supreme Court Reapportionment Decisions

	UES	ES	EP	Ano	MR	PGR
Before	X	–	–	–	–	–
After	X	X	–	–	–	–

What would be the effect of this amendment on the state of political equality in congressional elections? As things stand now, citizens in the states can vote in congressional elections, but those living in the District of Columbia cannot. Hence, Universal Equal Suffrage is not satisfied. That being the case, it is not difficult to see that Equal Shares, Equal Probabilities, Anonymity, Majority Rule, and Proportional Group Representation are also not satisfied.

If the amendment is ratified, District citizens will be able to vote in congressional elections, and Universal Equal Suffrage will then be satisfied. However, since each state (and the District) will elect two Senators regardless of population, Equal Shares will not be satisfied, nor will Equal Probabilities.[44] Different voters will still be able to achieve different results with their votes, depending on their distribution among the states and congressional districts, so Anonymity will not be satisfied. Similarly, Majority Rule will not be satisfied, as a minority of the voters could still elect a majority of the members of Congress. For the same reason, Proportional Group Representation will also not be satisfied.

An alternative to the amendment which has been proposed is called "retrocession." Under this plan, the District of Columbia (or the residential portions thereof) would be ceded back to the state of Maryland (the District was originally part of Maryland). District residents would then be able to vote in congressional elections as citizens of Maryland.[45] Hence, Universal Equal Suffrage would be satisfied. However, for the same reasons as if the amendment is ratified, Equal Shares, Equal Probabilities, Anonymity, Majority Rule, and Proportional Group Representation would all not be satisfied.

These results are summarized in Table 3. It is evident that the proposed amendment would make little difference in terms of political equality. Compared to the present situation, the amendment would achieve only the first criterion on the spectrum. And compared to the alternative of retrocession, the amendment would accomplish nothing at all. It might be argued that Universal Equal Suffrage has a particular symbolic importance, but even so, it remains true that the amendment would achieve only a weak form of political equality. Thus, political equality is only a weak argument for the amendment compared to the present situation, and it is no argument at all for the amendment compared to retrocession.

Table 3　District of Columbia Constitutional Amendment

	UES	ES	EP	Ano	MR	PGR
Present	–	–	–	–	–	–
Retrocession	X	–	–	–	–	–
Amendment	X	–	–	–	–	–

Another constitutional amendment which has often been suggested is also intended as an extension of political equality. This amendment would abolish the Electoral College and substitute a system for the direct election of the President. Under the Electoral College system, each state is assigned a number of electoral votes equal to the number of Representatives it elects plus two, for its two Senators (the District of Columbia is given three electoral votes). All of the electoral votes for a state are awarded to the candidate winning the most votes in that state, and the candidate who receives a majority of the electoral votes is elected President. The proposed amendment would replace this system with a direct popular election in which the candidate winning the most votes nationwide would be elected, with a runoff between the top two if no candidate won at least 40 percent of the vote in the first election.

The Electoral College operates as a unit voting system for the election of the President. Universal Equal Suffrage is satisfied, as each voter has one vote in the election. Equal Shares is not satisfied, because the electoral vote of each state includes two votes for its two senators, regardless of population. It has been shown that Equal Probabilities is not satisfied.[46] The number of votes needed to win depends on how those votes are distributed among the states, so Anonymity is not satisfied. And the minority candidate could be elected in a two-way race, so Majority Rule is not satisfied.

If the direct election proposal is adopted, the Electoral College would be replaced by a popular election at large. This system would, of course, satisfy Universal Equal Suffrage and Equal Shares. Equal Probabilities would also be satisfied.[47] Since the result would depend entirely on the number of votes cast for each candidate and not on their distribution, Anonymity would be satisfied. Majority Rule would also be satisfied, as a candidate supported by a majority would always be elected.

The effect of the proposed constitutional amendment, in terms of political equality, can be seen in Table 4. Replacement of the Electoral College with direct election would result in a substantial extension of political equality. At present, only the first criterion on the spectrum is satisfied. Under a direct election system, all of the criteria would be satisfied. Thus, direct election of the President would be a major step forward in political equality.

Table 4 Electoral College

	UES	ES	EP	Ano	MR
Present	X	–	–	–	–
Direct election	X	X	X	X	X

As a comparison of Tables 3 and 4 shows, the effect of a direct election amendment on political equality would be much greater than the effect of the District of Columbia amendment. Direct election would assure each voter an equal chance to be decisive in the election. Direct election would guarantee that all citizens would cast equally weighted votes, regardless of where they lived. And direct election would also guarantee that a majority choice would always prevail in the election. The District of Columbia amendment would accomplish none of these things. For someone interested in political equality, a direct election constitutional amendment should have much higher priority than the District of Columbia amendment.

III. CONCLUSION

As the quotations presented at the beginning of this article illustrate, political equality is usually defined in very vague terms. Typical are phrases such as "one person, one vote," "equally weighted votes," "all votes count the same," "each vote is the equivalent of the next," "all votes have the same value," "each vote counts as a full vote," etc. This vagueness is both unnecessary and dangerous. It is unnecessary because it is possible to specify precise criteria for political equality. It is dangerous because one could be led into advocating one of several alternative political institutions in the mistaken belief that it will accomplish something which, in fact, it will not.

In this article, six distinct criteria for political equality have been defined and examined; Universal Equal Suffrage, Equal Shares, Equal Probabilities, Anonymity, Majority Rule, and Proportional Group Representation. These criteria form a spectrum of progressively more stringent conditions which an election system might satisfy. These criteria can have substantially different consequences, both conceptually and in practice, yet they have not been adequately distinguished in previous discussions of political equality.

The dangers inherent in confusing the different criteria are well illustrated by the Supreme Court decisions in *Gray* v. *Sanders* and the reapportionment cases. The Court thought that it was accomplishing the same thing in both cases. But in fact, the Court accomplished much less in the reapportionment cases than it had in *Gray*. Indeed, the only additional criterion achieved in the reapportionment cases was the very criterion which the court had said in *Gray* was not sufficient for political equality!

The differing consequences of alternative political institutions are also illustrated by the Electoral College and District of Columbia constitutional amendments. Abolishing the Electoral College in favor of direct election would result in a substantial increase in political equality in presidential elections. In contrast, the District of Columbia amendment would have only a minor impact on political equality in congressional elections, and no impact at all compared to the alternative of retrocession.

Political equality is an important concept. It deserves more careful analysis than it has received so far. Hopefully, this article has shown that precise thinking about political equality is possible. And the distinctions which careful thought reveals show, in turn, that the egalitarian characteristics of alternative election systems may be very different from what at first appears.

Notes

1. The Twenty-third Amendment (ratified in 1961) gave residents of Washington, D.C., a vote in presidential elections. The Twenty-fourth Amendment (1964) abolished the poll tax. The Twenty-sixth Amendment (1971) lowered the voting age to eighteen.
2. Robert A. Dahl and Charles E. Lindblom, *Politics, Economics, and Welfare* (New York: Harper & Bros., 1953), 41.
3. Ibid., 227.
4. Ibid., 278.
5. Giovanni Sartori, *Democratic Theory* (New York: Frederick A. Praeger, Inc., 1965), 335.
6. Austin Ranney and Willmoore Kendall, *Democracy and the American Party System* (New York: Harcourt Brace & Co., 1956), 16.
7. Ibid., 28.

8. Ibid., 27-8.

9. By presenting the quotations contained in the text, I do not intend to single out these particular scholars for special criticism. Many other examples could be given. See, e.g., Carole Pateman (*Participation and Democratic Theory* [London: Cambridge University Press, 1970], 43); Carl Cohen ("The Justification of Democracy," *Monist* 55 [1971]: 1-28, esp. 1); John Rees (*Equality* [New York: Praeger Publishers, 1971], 38-42); Gordon E. Baker (*The Reapportionment Revolution* [New York: Random House, 1966], 14-15); Robert A. Dahl (*A Preface to Democratic Theory* [Chicago: University of Chicago Press, 1956], 37, 67, 84).

10. For other indices different from (though related to) those mentioned in the text, see James S. Coleman ("Control of Collectivities and the Power of a Collectivity to Act," in Bernhardt Lieberman, ed., *Social Choice* [New York: Gordon & Breach Science Publishers, 1971], 269-300); and Peter C. Fishburn (*The Theory of Social Choice* [Princeton, N.J.: Princeton University Press, 1973], 53-5).

11. John F. Banzhaf III ("Weighted Voting Doesn't Work: A Mathematical Analysis," *Rutgers Law Review* 19 [1965]: 317-43; "Multi-Member Electoral Districts—Do They Violate the 'One Man, One Vote' Principle," *Yale Law Journal* 75 [1966]: 1309-38; "One Man, 3.312 Votes: A Mathematical Analysis of the Electoral College," *Villanova Law Review* 13 [1968]: 304-32).

12. Lloyd S. Shapley and Martin Shubik, "A Method for Evaluating the Distribution of Power in a Committee System," *American Political Science Review* 48 (1954): 787-92.

13. See William H. Riker and Lloyd S. Shapley ("Weighted Voting: A Mathematical Analysis for Instrumental Judgments," in J. Roland Pennock and John W. Chapman, eds., *Nomos X: Representation* [New York: Atherton Press, 1968], 199-216, esp. 204, n. 2); William F. Lucas ("Measuring Power in Weighted Voting Systems," Cornell University, Department of Operations Research, Technical Report no.

227 [Ithaca, N.Y., 1974] [available through the National Technical Information Service, U.S. Department of Commerce]); and Steven J. Brams (*Game Theory and Politics* [New York: Free Press, 1975], Ch. 5, 157-97).

14. This is the "unnormalized form" of the Banzhaf index. The "normalized form" is obtained by dividing each index value by the sum of the index values, so that the new index values will add up to one. The normalized form indicates the proportion of the total voting power which each voter possesses. If the number of voters is even moderately large, exact calculations would be impractical, and various approximation techniques must be used. This description of the Banzhaf index is intended only to give the reader a general idea of what the index is. Readers interested in calculating index values should refer to the sources in nn. 11-13 above.

15. The probability that one person's vote is decisive is simply the probability that the remaining voters are evenly divided between the two alternatives, assuming that each voter is equally likely to favor either alternative. Since this probability will necessarily be the same for all voters, the criterion Equal Probabilities is satisfied.

16. See Banzhaf, "Multi-Member Electoral Districts."

17. To return to the mayoral election example which preceded the definition of Equal Probabilities, suppose that there were three districts each containing 20 000 voters and having two unit votes, and a fourth district with 40 000 voters and four unit votes. Then Equal Probabilities would still not be satisfied, though there would no longer be any voters with a zero probability of casting a decisive vote.

18. In the mayoral election example, Equal Probabilities would be satisfied if there were five districts with 20 000 voters and two unit votes each.

19. The Anonymity criterion was developed by Kenneth May for application to direct decision-making processes, but it can be applied to the other two types of election systems as well.

Kenneth O. May ("A Set of Independent Necessary and Sufficient Conditions for Simple Majority Decision," *Econometrica* 20 [1952]: 680-4; "A Note on the Complete Independence of the Conditions for Simple Majority Decision," *Econometrica* 21 [1953]: 172-3). May preferred the term "equality" to "anonymity" as a name for his condition, but for obvious reasons the latter term will be used here.

20. The criterion has been limited in this manner because, if there are three or more alternatives with none supported by a majority, some complex problems arise involving the paradox of voting, the Condorcet choice (if any), strategic voting, etc. For an introductory discussion of some of these problems, with references to other sources, see Richard G. Niemi and William H. Riker ("The Choice of Voting Systems," *Scientific American* 234 [June 1976]: 21-7, 132). For a discussion of another problem which can arise when there is no single alternative supported by a majority, see Douglas W. Rae (*The Political Consequences of Electoral Laws*, rev. ed. [New Haven, Conn.: Yale University Press, 1971], 170-3).

21. See, e.g., Paul H. Douglas, "The Necessity for Proportional Representation," *International Journal of Ethics* 34 (1923): 6-26.

22. See, n. 3 above.

23. See n. 5 above.

24. See n. 6 above.

25. See n. 7 above.

26. One exception would be a three-member committee whose members have two, two, and one votes each, with three of the five votes necessary to a decision. This system satisfies Equal Probabilities, Anonymity, and Majority Rule, but not Universal Equal Suffrage or Equal Shares. However, since the two-vote members derive no advantage from their extra votes, it is unlikely that this system would ever actually be used. Another exception which might be of greater importance (but which involves only the last two criteria on the spectrum) would be proportional representation with a super-majority requirement in the legislature. In presenting the criteria, I have used some examples of election systems which are themselves quite artificial. However, these examples were used only for the purpose of clarifying the distinctions among the different criteria. For clarification purposes, it is often more helpful to use extreme artificial examples than real examples. For examples showing that real-world election systems do differ in terms of these criteria, see the next section.

27. This is the argument usually made by opponents of proportional representation (see e.g., Carl J. Friedrich, *Constitutional Government and Democracy* 4e [Waltham, Mass.: Blaisdell Publishing Co., 1968], 269-305).

28. This is, in effect, the approach taken by May. In addition to Anonymity, he defines a separate criterion called "neutrality" which prohibits discrimination among the alternatives (see May, n. 19).

29. 372 US 368 (1963).

30. Or, at least, so the Court assumed for purposes of its decision (372 US at 379).

31. The Court implicitly assumed throughout its opinion that the ratio of voters to population was the same in all counties, so that population could be used as a substitute for the number of voters.

32. Banzhaf has shown that in a unit voting system of the type which Georgia employed, the Banzhaf index for any voter will be approximately proportional to the number of unit votes assigned to that voter's county, divided by the square root of the county's population (see Banzhaf, "One Man, 3.312 Votes," 316). Applying this to the data given in the Court's opinion shows that Equal Probabilities was not satisfied.

33. 372 US at 381.

34. 372 US at 379.

35. While the litigation was in progress, Georgia had already amended the county unit system once to give the larger counties more unit votes, though still not in proportion to population (372 US at 372).

36. 372 US at 381, n. 12.

37. See n. 15 above.

38. *Reynolds* v. *Sims* (377 US 533 [1964] and five companion cases all decided on the same day. The more famous case of *Baker* v. *Carr* (369 US 186 [1962] had actually decided only that questions involving legislative election systems are justiciable questions, i.e., that federal courts have the power to decide such cases. The substantive decision did not come until two years later, in the reapportionment cases.

39. As in *Gray*, the Court implicitly assumed throughout that the ratio of voters to population was the same in all districts, so that population could be used as a measure of the number of voters.

40. See Banzhaf, "Multi-Member Electoral Districts," 1328.

41. 377 US at 560.

42. See Banzhaf, "Multi-Member Electoral Districts," 1330-2, 1334.

43. The amendment would also allow the District to participate, the same as a state, in the constitutional amendment ratification process.

44. See Banzhaf, "Multi-Member Electoral Districts," 1328.

45. District residents would also be able to participate in the constitutional amendment ratification process as citizens of Maryland.

46. See Banzhaf, "One Man, 3.312 Votes."

47. See n. 15 above.

2. MILL'S MAJORITY PRINCIPLE*

Duff Spafford

I wish—although this may surprise some hon. Members—that the majority should govern.
—J.S. Mill, from a speech in the House of Commons, July 5, 1867[1]

In his writings and speeches on the subject of electoral reform, John Stuart Mill calls upon an idea—a principle, as I make it out to be—whose meaning and place in Mill's thought have remained uncertain. This principle I call Mill's majority principle, and it is my purpose here to offer an account of it. In so doing, I hope to throw some light on an aspect of Mill's democracy which sorely needs it, namely his position on the matter of majority rule. In the received view of them, Mill's thoughts on majority rule amount to not much more than a series of alarms and reservations, things to be looked up in an index at "Majority, tyranny of." Mill feared majority rule, he sought ways to counteract it, he repudiated[2] it, even; he harboured a "distrust of the majority principle";[3] he called attention to the "'infirmities' of majority-rule systems";[4] he "was never able to assent without reservations to the straightforward democratic principle of majority rule"[5]—accounts vary, though more in degree than in kind. They vary especially from Mill's own, which is that he wished to "maintain the just ascendancy of majorities."[6]

Mill begins one of his discussions of majority rule and its implications for the conduct of elections in a democracy by remarking that

"the confusion of ideas here is great."[7] One source of confusion, he believed, was the mistaken notion that government by majority could be achieved without reform of the electoral system. Mill argued that the electoral arrangements in place in the Great Britain of his day made power rest, not in the hands of the majority of the electors by way of their representatives, but rather in the hands of a "majority of a majority" which might amount to a minority.[8] What was taken by many to be government by majority was possibly, even probably, government by minority.

Now those of Mill's commentators who have taken note of this "majority of a majority" argument have made quite different things out of it. John M. Robson has Mill holding by it that "government by majority is a delusion in itself,"[9] a reading which implies that Mill was disposed to cast aside the idea of majority rule as a will-o'-the-wisp. According to Dennis F. Thompson's interpretation of this argument, on the other hand, Mill meant not to dismiss but rather to affirm the principle of majority rule, or at any rate to affirm a version of that principle which holds that measures passed by parliament should be consonant with the wishes of a majority in the country.[10] Thompson does not go further into the matter, but he perceives that some construction of Mill's of the principle of majority rule has a part to play in Mill's case against the existing electoral system and in his case in favour of the electoral system of Thomas Hare. However, a note of ambiguity creeps into this interpretation with Thompson's suggestion that Mill, though he considered himself a democrat, did

Duff Spafford, "Mill's Majority Principle," *Canadian Journal of Political Science* 18 (September 1985): 599-608. Reprinted with permission of the author.

not consider himself a "majority-rule" democrat.[11]

The "confusion of ideas" of which Mill complained is, it may be suggested, a confusion of several ideas, each of which lays claim to the designation "majority rule"; Mill himself was to add one more to the roster. We have, to begin with, the idea of electing representatives by means of the plurality ("majority") decision-rule, and the idea of making decisions in representative assemblies by means of the majority decision-rule. If the former is held to be intrinsic to majority rule, then Mill, in rejecting the electoral system of his day, rejected majority rule. But it was Mill's contention that election by majority was not a necessary part of majority rule, that indeed it thwarted majority rule, correctly understood. What, precisely, we may now ask, did Mill take to be the correct understanding of the term "majority rule"—or, as he preferred, "government by majority"?

Mill's conception of government by majority, as I try to demonstrate below, is a conception which depends on a peculiar and complicated principle, the one of my title. I begin by setting out certain views on representation which underpin Mill's majority principle, then go on to define the principle itself and take note of one of its implications.

1

As Hanna Pitkin observes, Mill nowhere writes down an explicit definition of the term "representation."[12] But Mill does offer a very clear idea of what he means by a form of representation which he calls "direct" representation, and this, it turns out, is the very form of representation which figures in his majority principle.

Suppose an elector, Smith, casts his single vote at an election in favour of Brown, a candidate for a seat in a representative assembly. If Brown is elected, Smith becomes directly represented in the assembly, and directly represented by Brown. Thus an elector achieves direct representation in a representative assembly by the act of voting for a candidate who wins a seat in it. So much for electors who, like Smith, vote in winning causes at elections: they are directly represented. Now what of electors who vote in a losing cause in a constituency? They are, in the parlance of Mill's day, the "minority" in the constituency. Having failed to elect the candidate of their choice they are denied direct representation in the assembly, and Mill sees their position as follows:

> In every Parliament there is an enormous fraction of the whole body of electors who are without any direct representation, consisting of the aggregate of the minorities in all the contested elections, together with we know not what minorities in those which, from the hopelessness of success, have not even been contested. All these electors are as completely blotted out from the constituency, for the duration of that Parliament, as if they were legally disqualified. . . . Here, therefore, is a large portion of those whom the constitution intends to be represented, a portion which cannot average less than a third, and may approximate to a half, who are virtually in the position of non-electors. . . .
> . . . Not a man of them has any voice at all in determining the proceedings of Parliament.[13]

What Mill is urging in these passages, it will be seen, is the view that an elector who is without direct representation is without effective representation of any kind. Is it not a "great grievance," he asks in another place, that electors "willing and anxious to be represented, have no member in the House *for whom they have voted*?"[14]

An elector could be said to be represented only nominally by someone whose name he had passed over at the poll—by someone who, as Mill was wont to put it, the elector had voted "against"; and even this conceded too much if elector and member of the assembly were divided by their political opinions. Should they be of different political parties there could be no bond of representation between elector and elected. To assert that a Conservative member of parliament represented a Liberal elector was, Mill said, simply to assert a "falsehood."[15]

If we are to take the sense of what Mill meant by "representation" from the uses to which he puts the term in his argument for electoral reform, we must conclude that he meant by it direct representation and nothing else. For example, he writes: "Suppose . . . that in a country governed by equal and universal suffrage, there is a contested election in every constituency, and every election is carried by a small majority. The Parliament thus brought together represents little more than a bare majority of the people."[16] It is clear that Mill is assuming here that all those who vote in winning causes at elections are represented, and all those who vote in losing causes are unrepresented: the arithmetic allows of no other interpretation. For Mill, true representation is direct representation.

Let us return to our candidate Brown who, we will take it, has been elected, 60 votes having gone to him and 40 to his rival or rivals. The 60 electors who voted for Brown have a special status in that they and only they are directly represented by Brown. It is useful to have a way of designating them, and I will call them Brown's w-constituency. The entire 100 electors who took part in Brown's election I call his c-constituency. The 40 electors who are in Brown's c-constituency but not in his w-constituency are nominally represented by Brown, and there is little more to be said about them. Brown's real constituency is his w-constituency, the electors whose votes put him in office.

Now suppose a measure of some kind is brought before the assembly. There is a majority in its favour, and the measure is adopted by the assembly. Mill, for his part, has no quarrel at all with the use of the majority decision-rule in the proceedings of representative assemblies; indeed, he approves of it entirely. But he is after something more. He wants to inquire into whether a measure which has the approval of a majority within an assembly's walls also has the approval of a majority outside them—that is, whether there is a *popular* majority for the measure.

The difficulty here, of course, is that citizens do not declare themselves on specific measures as they come before the assembly, so how popular opinion stands with respect to those measures cannot be known at first hand. The door to popular opinion would appear to be firmly locked, but Mill proposes to force it with an assumption. "[Suppose] the representatives to express the mind of their constituents": so he states his assumption in one place, and the context leaves no room for doubt that, when he speaks of the representatives' "constituents," Mill means what I have called their w-constituencies.[17] He writes elsewhere: ". . . in an equal democracy (since the opinions of the constituents, when they insist on them, determine those of the representative body) the majority of the people, through their representatives, will outvote and prevail over the minority and their representatives."[18] In this last passage, Mill's assumption takes a more contingent form: the constituents' opinions will be acted upon by the representative "when they insist on them." Mill thought it unwise of constituents to make mere delegates of their representatives. On the other hand, he thought it prudent of those who framed democratic constitutions to suppose that constituents would do just that,[19] so it cannot be accounted out of character for Mill to assume, in his argument on electoral reform, that representatives faithfully transmit and act upon the views of those who elected them. Ideally, he believed, representatives would do this without urging, for a properly-designed electoral system would bring together electors and representatives of like opinion.

This assumption of Mill's has the effect of converting representative democracy into a kind of direct-democracy-by-proxy. Suppose a majority of the members of the assembly vote in favour of free trade in coal. If Brown is one of the majority, then we can chalk up 60 popular votes in favour of free trade in coal. From there we are to go on to canvass the other members making up the majority in support of free trade in coal, adding up their w-constituencies as we go. When we have the total, we are to compare it with the number of electors who voted in the election which constituted the assembly. If the former total is greater than one-half of the latter, Mill's majority principle obtains.

Mill leads us through these calculations (cast in a somewhat different way) in one of his speeches in the House of Commons:

> The majority in this House is got at by the elimination of two minorities. You first eliminate at the election the minority out of the House, then upon a division you eliminate the minority in the House. Now, it may very well happen that those combined minorities would greatly out-number the majority which prevails in this House, and consequently that the majority does not now govern.[20]

The majorities and minorities of this passage are numbers of electors. To assign a number to the "majority in this House" we first put aside all electors who voted in losing causes at the last election; let x denote their number. This leaves what I have called the w-constituencies; their sum I denote by w. We next put aside the w-constituencies of those representatives who, in a division in the House, are in the minority; the number of electors in this category is y. Having put to one side Mill's two grand minorities, we are left with the w-constituencies of the representatives who, in the division in the assembly, carry the day. Denote the number of electors in this last category by z.

The majority does not govern if the sum of x and y exceeds z. Since the sum of x, y and z is n, the number of electors who voted at the last election, this amounts to the proposition that the majority governs only if z is greater than one-half of n. For Mill's principle to hold generally, this last inequality must be satisfied with respect to every majority coalition which can be formed from the assembly's members.

We are now in a position to see what Mill meant to convey by the "majority of a majority" argument which he brought against the existing system of election. Upon an alternative rendering, his principle holds that the majority governs only if the following inequality is satisfied:

$$\frac{w}{n} \cdot \frac{z}{w} > \frac{1}{2}$$

Now w/n is the proportion of the electorate directly represented in the assembly. This proportion might be little more than one-half if there are two candidates and close contests in every (single-member) electoral district. The ratio z/w also might be little more than one-half in a close division in the assembly (indeed, might be smaller than one-half if the w-constituencies differ appreciably in size, but Mill does not raise this possibility).

Mill's point is that, even though each of w/n and z/w might exceed one-half, their *product*, a "majority of a majority" yielding z/n, might well fall short of one-half. He notes that under the existing system of election z/n might, in the extreme, amount to just over one-quarter.[21] He notes also that his majority principle would be satisfied even under the existing system of election if the assembly reached its decisions by the rule of unanimity,[22] which rule would make w and z the same number. However, as I have said, Mill had no second thoughts about the use of the majority decision-rule in assemblies. He looked not to z/w but rather to w/n for a solution to his "majority of a majority" problem. If w could be made sufficiently large in relation to *n*, his majority principle might obtain even though a division of the assembly threw up a *z*/*w* which barely exceeded one-half.

How large must *w*/*n* be? It can be shown that Mill's principle must be violated for some majority coalition of representatives unless *w*/*n* is large enough to satisfy the following inequality (framed for *s* an odd number, *s* being the number of seats):[23]

$$\frac{w}{n} > \frac{s}{s+1}$$

For example, if there are 99 seats in the assembly, then more than 99 percent of the electors must be directly represented if there is to be even the possibility that Mill's principle holds generally. That is, more than 99 percent of the electors must have voted in favour of candidates who won seats!

Mill asserted that *any* shortfall of *w* from *n* would place his majority principle in jeopardy.[24] The fact is that he had quite other reasons for holding, as indeed he did hold, that *w* should be made equal to *n*. Democracy was based on political equality, and there could be no such thing as political equality so long as some electors had representation—direct representation—while others went without it. True democracy required "representation of all."[25]

In the late 1850s a London barrister, Thomas Hare, devised an intricate method of election to whose objects and properties Mill gave his approval at once. Under Hare's method,[26] several (*s*) representatives are elected in an electoral district. Each elector submits a preference ordering of the candidates standing for election. Certain counting and sorting rules are then brought to bear on the set of preference orderings, and the method declares *s* winners and assigns each elector to the constituency of one of the *s*; every successful candidate ends up with a constituency *n*/*s* in number. An elector might, sometimes, find himself the constituent of one who ranked well down in his preference ordering. Still, his preferences had been consulted in the making of the assignment, and in that sense it could be said that the elector had chosen his representative. So much, in any case, Mill was prepared to say. With Hare's method of election in place, Mill wrote, "no elector would, as at present, be nominally represented by some one whom he had not chosen."[27]

Hare's method achieved "representation of all"; but it did more than that, for by way of its clever provisions came assurance that government would rest in the hands of the majority. In 1859 Mill wrote to Hare to apprise him of certain impressions which were abroad concerning his method of election, one of which impressions—a quite mistaken one, Mill thought—was that Hare's method would bring in rule by minority. Mill wrote in this connection: ". . . it is supposed that the plan would enable minorities to govern; whereas the fact is that *now* a minority very often governs (by being the majority of a majority) while under your plan a minority never could by possibility do so. It is the only plan which *ensures* government by the majority."[28] Only Hare's method could ensure government by majority, because only Hare's method held out the prospect of affording direct representation to every elector.

2

I have offered here an account of an idea which makes an appearance in a half-light in several of Mill's works. Mill sought to define a criterion of popular majority rule in a system of representative government, and the criterion he proposed is one which is of some interest still today. It is an implication of Mill's majority principle that a party which holds sway in a representative assembly must be a party which came to power with more than one-half of the popular vote cast in favour of its candidates. This notion of a popular mandate to govern is entertained today by proponents of proportional representation, one of whom, indeed, has asserted that the very "essence of a system of proportional representation is that no party can secure an absolute majority in the legislature unless it gains 50 percent of the vote."[29]

The source and foundation of Mill's majority principle are to be found in the tenets of direct representation which Mill opposed to the doctrine of indirect or "virtual" representation. "Am I represented by a member against whom I have voted, and am ready to vote again?" he asked;[30] and we know what he judged to be the appropriate response to the question. He went so far as to say that electors without representatives of their own choosing were "disfranchised."[31] Whatever is taken to recommend Mill's majority principle must also recommend its author's assessment of what is to count as representation, for the arithmetic of the majority principle will accommodate only direct representation.

Mill leaves his readers much room for speculation concerning the basis of his attachment to this rigid conception of representation. An understanding of why Mill insisted on direct representation would add something of value to our understanding of his unorthodox views on majority rule and his democracy in general.

Notes

*   A draft of this note was read at a meeting of the Western Canada chapter, Conference for the Study of Political Thought, University of Calgary, October 1984. I wish to thank Tom Flanagan and this Journal's referees for helpful comments.

1. *Hansard* n.s. vol. 188, July 5, 1867, 1103.

2. Robert Sugden, *The Political Economy of Public Choice* (New York: Halsted, 1981), 203: "... Mill repudiates the principle of majority rule ('the government of the whole people by a mere majority of the people') as undemocratic."

3. James Hogan, *Election and Representation* (Cork: Cork University Press, 1945), 127.

4. Elaine Spitz, *Majority Rule* (Chatham: Chatham House, 1984), 73.

5. J. H. Burns, "Utilitarianism and Democracy," *Philosophical Quarterly* 9 (1959): 168.

6. *Hansard* n.s. vol. 188, July 5, 1867, 1103.

7. J. S. Mill, *Considerations on Representative Government*, reprinted in John M. Robson, ed. *Collected Works of John Stuart Mill* 19 (Toronto: University of Toronto Press, 1977), 448. Hereafter, CRG, in *Collected Works* 19.

8. Ibid., 449. See also J. S. Mill, *Thoughts on Parliamentary Reform*, reprinted in *Collected Works* 19, 329.

9. John M. Robson, *The Improvement of Mankind: The Social and Political Thought of John Stuart Mill* (Toronto: University of Toronto Press, 1968), 229.

10. Dennis F. Thompson, *John Stuart Mill and Representative Government* (Princeton: Princeton University Press, 1976), 105-6.

11. Ibid., 8.

12. Hanna Fenichel Pitkin, *The Concept of Representation* (Berkeley: University of California Press, 1967), 4.

13. *Personal Representation: Speech of John Stuart Mill, Esq., M.P., Delivered in the House of Commons, May 29, 1867* (London, 1867), 7-8, 14.

14. *CRG*, in *Collected Works* 19, 450. Italics added.

15. *Hansard* n.s. vol. 188, July 5, 1867, 1104.

16. *CRG*, in *Collected Works* 19, 449.

17. *Personal Representation*, 14. The context is a numerical example which will not work out otherwise.

18. *CRG*, in *Collected Works* 19, 449.

19. Ibid., 505.

20. *Hansard* n.s. vol. 188, July 5, 1867, 1103.

21. *Thoughts on Parliamentary Reform*, in *Collected Works* 19, 329.

22. *Personal Representation*, 14. This, in spirit, was the solution to the "majority of a majority" problem proposed by John C. Calhoun. Calhoun depicts the problem in a quite different way. There is a majority party with a adherents and a minority party with b adherents, $b = n-a$. Further, the majority party contains a faction a' in number, $a'>a/2$, and the minority party contains a faction b' in number, $b'>b/2$. Suppose the majority decision-rule is in use. Then on any question of policy the a' can conclude the a and the a the whole (the n); and the a' govern, though they might make up little more than one-quarter of the whole (John C. Calhoun, *A Disquisition on Government and Selections from the Discourse* [Indianapolis: Bobbs-Merrill, 1953], esp. 32). We now suppose, to establish a parallel with Mill's treatment, that the a elect a representative A and the b a representative B, A taking up the position agreeable to the a' and B the position agreeable to the b'. Only when A and B take up the same position are the n bound by it. The required unanimity of A and B ensures that any policy adopted will accord with the wishes of a "true" (Calhoun's "concurrent") majority numbering $a' + b'$, a sum which must exceed $n/2$. It is a plausible conjecture that Calhoun's analysis of the "majority of a majority" problem prompted Mill's own. We find Mill, at a point in one of his speeches, adopting Calhoun's way of looking at the problem (but without, it should be added, adopting Calhoun's solution to it); see *Personal Representation*, 15, first full sentence.

23. If Mill's majority principle holds generally, then the $(s+1)/2$ w-constituencies which are smallest in size (number of electors) must together account for at least $(n+1)/2$ votes assuming odd n and s. The mean size of this subset of the w-constituencies must therefore be at least $(n+1)/(s+1)$, and the mean size, w/s, of all s w-constituencies can be no smaller. Therefore $w \geqslant s(n+1)/(s+1)$, and $w/n > s/(s+1)$.

24. *Personal Representation*, 15.

25. *CRG*, in *Collected Works* 19, 448 (chapter heading).

26. There were several versions of Hare's method. The version drawn upon here is—or so internal evidence would suggest, at any rate—the one Mill had before him when he wrote Chapter 7 of *CRG*. Its distinguishing feature is that every constituency is of size n/s. To avoid complication, I suppress Hare's (and Mill's) undertaking to make the nation the electoral district. The modern version of Hare's method is known as the single transferable vote. Its main principles are set out in W.J.M. Mackenzie, *Free Elections* (London: Allen and Unwin, 1958), Ch. 8.

27. *CRG*, in *Collected Works* 19, 455.

28. Mill to Thomas Hare, June 17, 1859, in *Collected Works* 15, 626. That representation under Hare's method (in the version here) satisfies Mill's principle can be deduced directly from the assumption that each representative has a w-constituency amounting to n/s electors.

29. Vernon Bogdanor, *What is Proportional Representation?* (Oxford: Martin Robertson, 1984), 59. Robert Sugden, in a recent article, cites an argument for proportional representation which holds that representation "should be designed . . . so that any majority of representatives are in a real rather than nominal sense the representatives of a majority of the citizens." This, it will be seen, is a rendering of Mill's majority principle. Sugden does not attribute the argument to Mill specifically, but he associates it with Mill's (and others') observations on the "majority of a majority" problem. See Robert Sugden, "Free Association and the Theory of Proportional Representation," *American Political Science Review* 78 (1984): 32.

30. *Personal Representation*, 14.

31. J.S. Mill, "Recent Writers on Reform," reprinted in *Collected Works* 19, 359.

3. THE PUZZLE OF REPRESENTATION: SPECIFYING COMPONENTS OF RESPONSIVENESS

Heinz Eulau and Paul D. Karps

The puzzle: "We have representative institutions, but like the Greeks we do not know what they are about."
—Eulau, 1967

With the publication in 1963 of "Constituency Influence in Congress" by Miller and Stokes, the direction was set for a novel approach to the study of political representation.[1] The virtue of this original study notwithstanding, the approach had some quite unexpected consequences for subsequent theoretical development and empirical research. Much of this development and research was due less to the impact of Miller and Stokes' innovative approach as such than to its vulgarization. The questions addressed in this paper are two: first, we propose to unravel the continuing puzzle of representation which was probably made even more puzzling by the thoughtless use of the concept of "congruence" which Miller and Stokes had introduced into discourse about representation; and second, we propose to explicate the concept of "responsiveness" by decomposing it into four components which seem to correspond to four targets of representation.

Heinz Eulau and Paul D. Karps, "The Puzzle of Representation: Specifying Components of Responsiveness," *Legislative Studies Quarterly* II: 3 (August 1977): 233-54. Reprinted by permission of the authors and the copyright holder, Comparative Legislative Research Center, University of Iowa.

THE MILLER-STOKES MODEL

Miller and Stokes (1963) themselves were well aware of the broader context of theory and research on representation,[2] but the focus of their particular analysis was a more limited one than "representation." They were interested in the degree to which "constituency control," rather than "party voting," determined congressional roll call behavior: "The fact that our House of Representatives . . . has irregular party voting does not of itself indicate that Congressmen deviate from party in response to local pressures" (45). The analysis addressed an old question: which factor, party or constituency, contributes more to variance in roll-call voting (all other things being equal)? The question had been previously asked in numerous studies relying, of necessity, on aggregate surrogate indicators of presumed district predispositions, most of them demographic or ecological.[3]

Miller and Stokes' research was a giant stride in the study of representation because it freed analysis from dependence on surrogate variables as indicators of constituency attitudes or predispositions. Miller and Stokes interviewed a sample of congressional constituents (voters and non-voters) and their respective congressmen (as well as non-incumbent candidates) whose attitudes in three broad issue domains they compared with each other, with congressmen's perceptions of constituency attitudes, and with corresponding roll call votes. Their tool of analysis was the product moment correlation coefficient and their mode of treatment was "causal analysis," which was then being introduced into political science. Miller and Stokes found the relationships among the variables of their model to vary a good deal from issue area to issue area, being strongest in the case of civil rights, weaker in the case of social welfare, and weakest in the case of foreign involvement. They concluded:

> The findings of this analysis heavily underscore the fact that no single tradition of representation fully accords with the realities of American legislative politics. The American system *is* a mixture, to which the Burkean, instructed-delegate, and responsible-party models all can be said to have contributed elements. Moreover, variations in the representative relation are most likely to occur as we move from one policy domain to another (56).

We have no quarrel with this general conclusion concerning the American system. We are bothered by the definition of what Miller and Stokes call "the representative relation" and its operational expression. This "relation" is the similarity or, as it is also called, the "congruence" between the four variables of the causal model that serves the purposes of analysis.[4] This specification of congruence as the expression of the representative relation has had great influence on later researchers, both those working in the tradition of, or with the data made available by, the Michigan group and those working independently with fresh data of their own.[5] The concern here is not this influence as such but rather the gradual erosion of alternative theoretical assumptions about representation of which Miller and Stokes themselves are fully cognizant. As a result of this erosion, what for Miller and Stokes (1963, 49) was only "a starting point for a wide range of analyses" became an exclusive

definition of representation: high congruence was interpreted as evidence of the presence of representation, and low congruence was taken as proof of its absence.

Whatever congruence may be symbolizing, it is not a self-evident measure of representation. Later researchers, poorly tutored in theories and practices of representation, tended to ignore this. Miller and Stokes, in order to use congruence as a measure, had stipulated three conditions for constituency influence or control. First, control in the representational relationship can be exercised through recruitment—constituents choose that representative who shares their views so that, by following his "own convictions," the representative "does his constituents' will." Second, control can be obtained through depriving the representative of his office—the representative follows "his (at least tolerably accurate) perceptions of district attitude in order to win re-election." And third, "the constituency must in some measure take the policy views of candidates into account in choosing a Representative" (50-51).

The electoral connection is of course only one of the links between representative and represented. And it should by no means be taken for granted that it is the most critical, the most important, or the most effective means to insure constituency influence on or control over public policies and the conduct of representatives. It is so only if one or all of the conditions for constituency control specified by Miller and Stokes are satisfied. This is also precisely the reason why attitudinal or perceptual congruence is not an exclusive measure of representation; it is simply the "starting point," as Miller and Stokes knew, in the puzzle of representation. Anyone who has the least sensitivity to the representative process recognizes that representatives are influenced in their conduct by many forces or pressures or linkages other than those arising out of the electoral connection and should realize that restricting the study of representation to the electoral connection produces a very limited vision of the representational process. Miller and Stokes themselves were eminently aware of this, as their "Conclusion" indicated. Yet, only three years after publication of their analysis, when two other analysts (Cnudde and McCrone, 1966), subjecting the Miller-Stokes data to an alternative causal analysis, found no support for recruitment as a condition of representation, constituency control was reduced to a purely psychological function in the representative's mind, and the danger of limiting the "representative relation" to attitudinal and perceptual congruence was demonstrated. Moreover, these analysts altogether ignored Miller and Stokes' important third condition for constituency influence through the electoral connection: constituents' taking account of the candidate's policy views in choosing the representative.

Indeed, Miller and Stokes themselves had the most trouble with this last condition. The overwhelming evidence of their research and that of others denies the condition: most citizens are not competent to perform the function which the model assumes—that elections are in fact effective sanctioning mechanisms in the representational relationship. Miller and Stokes gave a number of "reasons" for why representatives seem to be so sensitive about their voting records—for if voters do not know the record, this sensitivity is surely puzzling. They suggested that the voting record may be known to the few voters who, in close contests, make the difference between victory or defeat, and that the Congressman is "a dealer in increments and margins." They also speculated that the voting record may be known to opinion leaders in the district who serve as gatekeepers and conveyors of evaluation in a two-step flow of communication. But there is no evidence for this in their own research.[6]

THE CRISIS IN REPRESENTATIONAL THEORY

It would not yield further theoretical dividends to review in any detail the empirical studies of representation that, in one way or another, are predicated on the attitudinal-perceptual formulation of congruence that had served Miller and Stokes as a starting point but that, for most of their successors, became a terminal point. Most of these studies are distinguished by lack of historical-theoretical knowledge of representation and of independent theoretical creativity. In particular, they are cavalier in regard to a number of dilemmas that, by the middle sixties, had forced themselves on the attention of scholars interested in theoretical understanding of the problem of representation. That these dilemmas were articulated by different scholars at about the same time was probably coincidental, but the coincidence is important because it emphasized the possibility of alternative research directions.

First, representational theory made assumptions about citizen behavior that were negated by the empirical evidence. Wahlke, examining the role of the represented in the representational relationship, concluded that the evidence did not justify treating citizens as significant sources of policy demands, positions or even broad orientations that could be somehow "represented" in the policy-making process. Citizens simply lack the necessary information for effective policy choices to be communicated to their representatives, even if they were to make the effort to communicate. This being the case, Wahlke concluded that the "simple demand-input model" of representation was deficient. This is of course precisely the model that Miller-Stokes had in fact constructed in order to organize and explain their data. Wahlke suggested that a "support-input model" might be more appropriate.[7]

Second, given the limited capacity of the represented to formulate policy, a viable theory could no longer ignore the asymmetry of the representational relationship. Eulau suggested, therefore, that research should proceed from the structural assumption of a built-in status difference between representative and represented in which the former rather than the latter give direction to the relationship. Representational theory would have to deal with the tensions arising out of status differentiation rather than deny their existence (Eulau, 1967). Once status is introduced as a variable into the representational equation, the model of the representational relationship can be recursive, and the causal ordering of the relevant variables is likely to be reversed.

Finally, in a linguistic study of the concept of representation, Pitkin (1967) found the traditional theories of representation flawed. She advanced the proposition that representation, referring to a social relationship rather than to an attribute of the individual person, could be meaningfully conceptualized only as a systemic property. Representation might or might not emerge at the level of the collectivity, the criterion of emergence being the collectivity's potential for "responsiveness." Political representation "is primarily a public, institutionalized arrangement involving many people and groups, and operating in the complex ways of large-scale social arrangements. What makes it representation is not any single action by any one participant, but the over-all structure and functioning of the system, the patterns emerging from the multiple activities of many people" (221-22). Moreover, after considering every conceivable definition, Pitkin concluded that political representation means "acting in the interest of the represented, in a manner responsive to them" (209). However, there is also the stipulation that the representative "must not be found persistently at odds with the wishes of the represented without good reason in terms of their interest, without a good explanation of why their views are not in accord with their interests" (209-10).

Pitkin's formulation creates many measurement problems for empirical research. Concepts like "wishes," "good reason," "interest," or "views," are difficult to operationalize. She provides no clues as to how "responsiveness" as a systemic property of the political collectivity can be ascertained and how, indeed, it can be measured in ways enabling the scientific observer to conclude that representation has in fact emerged at the level of the political system. Pitkin's treatment seems to stress the condition in which the representative stands ready to be responsive when the constituents do have something to say. A legislature may, therefore, be responsive whether or not there are specific instances of response. In other words, Pitkin emphasized a potential for response rather than an act of response. There are considerable difficulties in empirically working with a concept stressing the possibility of an act rather than the act itself. Moreover, the formulation ignores Wahlke's injunction to jettison the demand-input model. Nevertheless, Pitkin's work had an almost immediate and profound effect on subsequent empirical research. (See Prewitt and Eulau, 1969; Muller, 1970; Peterson, 1970.)

Research on representation following the watershed year of 1967 has taken two major innovative routes. First, taking their cue from Wahlke's critique of the demand-input model, Patterson, Hedlund, and Boynton (1975) have used a support-input model that makes fewer requirements on the capacity of the represented to play a role in the representational process. However, their model continues to be based on congruence assumptions. Their analysis, conducted at the level of the individual, largely consists of comparison of the represented and representational elites in terms of relevant attitudes, perceptions and behavior patterns.

Second, taking a cue from Pitkin, Eulau and Prewitt (1973) transformed data collected at the level of individuals into grouped data, and conducted their analysis of representation at the macro level of small decision-making groups (city councils). In contrast to Patterson and his associates, Eulau and Prewitt stressed actual rather than potential response to constituent inputs, whether of the demand or support variety. In retrospect, it appears, they were harnessing "reactive" behavior rather than responsive behavior in Pitkin's sense, for they ignored the direction of the response— whether it was in fact "in the interest of" the constituents at the focus of representation. But these retrospective musings only suggest that the problem of conceptualizing representation in terms of responsiveness remains on the agenda of theory and research. As Loewenberg (1972, 12) has summed up the situation more recently:

> Representation ... is an ill-defined concept that has acquired conflicting meanings through long use. It may be employed to denote any relationship between rulers and ruled or it may connote responsiveness, authorization, legitimation, or accountability. It may be used so broadly that any political institution performs representative functions or so narrowly that only an elected legislature can do so. To a surprising extent, the Burkean conceptualization of the representative function is still in use, and Eulau's call for a concept adequate to modern concerns about the relationship between legislators and their constituencies has not been answered.

RESPONSIVENESS AS CONGRUENCE

Although the expectations or behavioral patterns to which the term "responsiveness" refers were implicit in the concept of "representative government,"[8] the term as such had not been used by Miller and Stokes or others as the defining characteristics of representation. By 1967, when Pitkin's work was published, the term struck an attractive chord as the ideals of "participatory democracy" were once more being reviewed in neopopulist movements that had intellectual spokesmen in the social sciences. Even though one should not expect a close affinity between the vocabulary of participation and the vocabulary of representation on logical-theoretical grounds, a term like responsiveness stemming from considerations of representative democracy could easily blend in with considerations of participatory democracy. When analysts of political participation like Verba and Nie (1972) came to pay attention to empirical work on representation, they had little trouble in linking, by way of an adaptation of the assumption of congruence, the concept of responsiveness to their work on participation. Interestingly, although they did not cite or refer to Pitkin's linguistic analysis, Verba and Nie found, on the one hand, that "responsiveness, as far as we can tell, rarely has been defined precisely, almost never has been measured, and never has been related to participation" (300). On the other hand, they acknowledged Miller and Stokes, who had not used the term: "Miller and Stokes in their analysis of the relationship between constituency attitudes and Congressmen, do deal with responsiveness in ways similar to ours" (300, n. 3).

Indeed, in examining and seeking to explain the effects of different degrees of citizen participation on the responsiveness of community leaders, Verba and Nie present a rechristened version of the congruence assumption of representation which they call "concurrence":

> Our measure of congruence depends on how well the priorities of the citizens and the leaders match. Several types of concurrence are possible ... our measure of the concurrence between citizens and community leaders measures the extent to which citizens and leaders in the community choose the same "agenda" of community priorities (302).

But they immediately raise the critical problem of causality: "whether we have the warrant to consider our measure of *concurrence* to be a measure of responsiveness. Just because leaders agree with citizens and that agreement increases as citizens become more active, can we be sure that it is citizen activity that is causing leaders to *respond* by adopting the priorities of the citizen?"(304).

In order to test for the causal relationship, Verba and Nie compared the correlation coefficients obtained for the relationship between "citizen activeness" and concurrence, on the one hand, and between "leader activeness" and concurrence, on the other hand. Finding that the correlations for citizens are "much stronger" than those for leaders, Verba and Nie concluded that their measure of concurrence "seems to be a valid measure of responsiveness to leaders" (331-32). But this mechanical comparison is not a test of causality at all in regard to the direction of responsiveness. In fact, it amounts to a false interpretation of the data. The correlations for citizens simply mean that more active citizens see things (priorities to be done in the community) more like leaders do than is the case with less active citizens; the correlations for leaders simply mean that the more active leaders see things more like citizens do than is the case with less active leaders. The strength of the coefficients, all of which are positive for both citizens and leaders, does not prove anything about the direction of causality—whether citizens influence leaders or leaders influence citizens, or whether citizens are responsive to leaders or leaders to citizens. It cannot be otherwise because Verba and Nie's measure of concurrence, like Miller and Stokes' measure of congruence, is neutral as to direction and requires that the direction of the relationships involved in the model be theoretically stipulated. There is no such stipulation in the Verba-Nie application of the concurrence measure to the question of linkage between leaders and led.

Causal analysis, then, does not free the analyst from defining his terms—be they power and influence, or be they responsiveness—in advance and stipulating the direction of expected relationships in advance.[9] The mechanical application of statistical tests of a possible causal structure does not necessarily model real-world relationships if the operational definitions of the model's components make no theoretical sense. Verba and Nie's two-edged use of the responsiveness, operationalized in terms of the directionless concept of concurrence, is intrinsically characterized by ambiguity. If concurrence is a measure of responsiveness of leaders to citizens, it cannot be a measure of responsiveness of citizens to leaders. If one were to take their comparison of the correlations between participation and concurrence for citizens and leaders as an indication of anything, it would have to be that leaders are responsive to citizens and citizens are responsive to leaders, varying in degree with degree of participation.

Pitkin, it was noted, had raised the importance of responsiveness as the critical characteristic of representation, but she had left the term undefined. Representatives, in order to represent, were to be responsive to their constituents, but Pitkin did not specify the content or target of responsiveness. Verba and Nie had taken a step forward by specifying public policy issues as the target of responsiveness. In focusing exclusively on congruence or concurrence in regard to policy attitudes or preferences, they ignored other possible targets in the relationship between representatives and represented which may also give content to the notion of responsiveness. By emphasizing only one component of responsiveness as a substantive concept, they reduced a complex phenomenon like representation to one of its components and substituted the component for the whole. But if responsiveness is limited to one component, it cannot capture the complexities of the real world of politics. It is necessary, therefore, to view responsiveness as a complex, compositional phenomenon that entails a variety of possible targets in the relationship between representatives and represented. How else could one explain that representatives manage to stay in office in spite of the fact that they are *not* necessarily or always responsive to the represented as the conception of representation as congruence or concurrence of policy preferences requires?

It deserves mention that Miller and Stokes (1963) had themselves realized that there are possible targets of responsiveness other than policy issues. They emphasized the "necessity of specifying the acts *with respect to which* one actor has power or influence or control over another." Their target, they conceded, was only the set of issues lying within the three policy areas of civil rights, social welfare and foreign involvement. But significantly they added, "We are not able to say how much control the local constituency may or may not have over *all* actions of its Representative, and there may well be pork-barrel issues or other public matters of peculiar relevance to the district on which the relation of Congressman to constituency is quite distinctive" (48). Miller and Stokes did not specify what they referred to as "other public matters." It is the task of the rest of this paper to suggest what some of these other targets of responsiveness might be.

seems to us, the complexity of the representational nexus requires. The first component is, of course, *policy responsiveness* where the target is the great public issues that agitate the political process. Second, there is *service responsiveness* which involves the efforts of the representative to secure particularized benefits for individuals or groups in his constituency. Third, there is *allocation responsiveness* which refers to the representative's efforts to obtain benefits for his constituency through pork-barrel exchanges in the appropriations process or through administrative interventions. Finally, there is what we shall call *symbolic responsiveness* which involves public gestures of a sort that create a sense of trust and support in the relationship between representative and represented. It is possible that there are other targets of responsive conduct which, in composition with the four here tapped, constitute the matrix of representational relationships. But the main point we are trying to make is this: responsiveness refers not just to "this" or "that" target of political activity on the part of the representative but to a number of targets. Only when responsiveness is viewed as a compositional phenomenon can the approach to representation-as-responsiveness recommended by Pitkin be useful. It is the configuration of the component aspects of responsiveness that might yield a viable theory of representative government under modern conditions of societal complexity.

COMPONENTS OF RESPONSIVENESS

There are four possible components of responsiveness which, as a whole, constitute representation. While each component can be treated as an independent target of responsiveness, all four must be considered together in the configurative type of analysis which, it

Policy Responsiveness

How the representative and the represented interact with respect to the making of public policy lies at the heart of most discussions of responsiveness. Responsiveness in this sense refers to the structure in which district positions on policy issues, specified as some measure of central tendency or dispersion, are related to the policy orientation of the representative—attitudinal or perceptual—and to his subsequent decision-making conduct in a given field of policy.

The premise underlying the specification of policy responsiveness is the presence of a meaningful connection between constituent policy preferences or demands and the representative's official behavior. This is what Miller and Stokes called "congruence" and what Verba and Nie called "concurrence." Whatever the term, the operational definition is the same: if the representative and his constituency agree on a particular policy, no matter how the agreement has come about, then the representative is responsive. There are, as has been noted, several problems with the model of representation built on the operationalization of responsiveness as congruence, notably the problem that congruence is neither a necessary nor a sufficient condition for responsiveness. The representative may react to constituency opinion, and hence evince congruent attitudes or behavior, yet not act in what is in the best interest of the constituency as he might wish to define that interest, thereby being in fact unresponsive. Further, the representative may make policy in response to groups and interests other than his constituents, including executive and bureaucratic agencies. Whether such conduct is also in the interest of his district as he sees it is an empirical question. But whatever the formulation and findings, it cannot be denied that policy responsiveness is an important component of representation.

The notion of policy responsiveness is implicit in some of the classic theories of representation. First of all, the controversy over mandate versus independence, whether the representative is a delegate or a trustee, though considered obsolete by Eulau (1967, 78-79) and in many respects resolved by Pitkin (1967, ch.7, 144-67), is still intriguing and relevant to the present discussion. For the debate is over whether the representative should act according to what *he* thinks is in the "best interest" of the constituency, regardless of constituency "wants," or whether he should follow the "expressed wishes" of the district, regardless of how he personally feels. The debate really turns on the competence of the citizenry in matters of public policy. For while the citizenry may know what it wants, it may not know what it needs. Secondly, therefore, an appropriate definition of policy responsiveness will be related to the classic issue of "district interest" as against "district will." There is no denying that the notion of policy responsiveness pervades empirical research on legislative decision-making, even when the issue of representation as a theoretical one is not raised. (For recent research, see Turner and Schneier, 1970; Kingdon, 1973; Clausen, 1973; Jackson, 1974; Matthews and Stimson, 1975.) However, precisely because this is the case, it is important not to ignore other components of responsiveness in the representational relationship. Exclusive emphasis on the policy aspects of responsiveness may give a one-sided view and may not help in solving the puzzle of representation.

Service Responsiveness

A second target for responsiveness to define the representational relationship concerns the non-legislative services that a representative actually performs for individuals or groups in his district. Service responsiveness, then, refers to the advantages and benefits which the representative is able to obtain for particular constituents. There are a number of services that constituents may expect and that the representative considers an intrinsic part of his role. Some of them involve only modest, if time consuming, requests, such as responding to written inquiries involving constituents' personal concerns, or facilitating meetings and tours for visitors from the home district. Newsletters or columns in local newspapers may be used to inform constituents of legislation that may be of interest and use to them. Much of this work is routine and carried out in regular fashion.

Another link in the chain of service responsiveness is often referred to as case work. (See Clapp, 1963.) Given his official position and presumed influence, the representative is in a position to solve particular problems for members of his constituency. The representative intervenes between constituents and bureaucrats in such matters as difficulties with a tax agency, delays in welfare payments, securing a job in government, and so on. Providing constituent services and doing case work constitute for many representatives more significant aspects of their representational role than does legislative work like bill-drafting or attending committee hearings. These "errand boy" functions deserve more theoretical attention than they have been given in contemporary research. In some important situations the representative may actually serve as an advocate and even lobbyist for special interests in his district vis-à-vis the legislature, departmental bureaucracies or regulatory agencies. This type of responsiveness is indeed crucial in trying to understand modern representative government.

This notion of service responsiveness seemed to underlie Eulau and Prewitt's (1973, 424-27, 649-50) operational definition of responsiveness. In their study of San Francisco Bay Area city councils, they initially divided these small representative bodies into those which seemed to be somehow responsive to constituent needs or wants and those which did not seem to be responsive. They then distinguished among the former councils those which were responsive to important standing interests in the community or attentive publics, and those which more often were responsive only to temporary alliances having a particular grievance or request. This conception of responsiveness, then, is based on the kind of group or individuals whom the representative perceives as being primarily served by his activities. Zeigler and Jennings (1974, 77-94), in a study of school boards, present a similar conception of responsiveness, conceptually distinguishing more sharply between "group responsiveness" and "individualized responsiveness." Both of these research teams, then, defined responsiveness in terms of the significant recipients of representational services.

That service responsiveness is an important element in representation should be apparent. Moreover, there is every reason to believe that it is increasing rather than declining. Until the middle sixties, it was generally assumed that case work and the advocacy of special interests bring advantages and benefits only to those who take the initiative in soliciting the representative's help. But as Fiorina (1977, 180) has recently pointed out, at least with reference to the federal level, increased bureaucratic activity in the wake of increased federal largesse to all kinds of population groups has also motivated congressmen to "undoubtedly stimulate the demand for their bureaucratic fixit services." The representative does not just respond to demands for his good offices and services; he has become a kind of hustler who advertises and offers them on his own initiative.[10]

This explication of service responsiveness has been entirely focused on the relationship between the representative and particular constituents. The representative can also be responsive in his unique role as a middleman in the allocation of more generalized benefits. We refer here to what has been traditionally called "pork-barrel politics" and to what we shall refer, for lack of a better term, as "allocation responsiveness." Both service responsiveness, whether initiated by the representative or not, and allocation responsiveness, which is always initiated by him, are important elements of representational behavior and important pillars in the representational relationship.

Allocation Responsiveness

It has long been recognized that pork-barrel politics in legislative allocations of public projects involves advantages and benefits presumably accruing to a representative's district as a whole. Although traditionally these allocations were seen as "public goods," with the expansion of the government's role in all sectors of society—industry, agriculture, commerce, health, education, welfare, internal security, and so on—the distinction between public and private benefits is difficult to maintain. Again, as Fiorina (1977, 180) has felicitously put it in connection with federal politics, "The porkbarreler need not limit himself to dams and post offices. There is LEAA money for the local police; urban renewal and housing money for local officials; and educational program grants for the local education bureaucracy. The congressman can stimulate applications for federal assistance, put in a good word during consideration, and announce favorable decisions amid great fanfare." Such allocations may benefit the district as a whole, or they may benefit some constituents more than others because they make more use of the benefits. The critical point to be made is that in being responsive as an "allocator," whether in the legislative or bureaucratic processes, the representative seeks to anticipate the needs of his clients and, in fact, can stimulate their wants.

Legislators' committee memberships sometimes serve as indicators of allocation responsiveness, as revealed in Fenno's (1973) studies of legislative conduct in committees of the US House of Representatives. A representative from a district that has a particular stake in a committee's jurisdiction will often seek a post on a parent committee but also on a particularly suitable sub-committee; such membership presumably enables him to act in a manner responsive to the best interests of his district and some or all of his constituents.

However, one cannot automatically assume that a legislator serving on a committee "not relevant" to his district is necessarily unresponsive and not interested in securing allocations. Legislators often seek preferment on important committees like Rules, Appropriations, or Ways and Means not because these committees are directly "relevant" to the interests of their constituents, but because they place members in positions of power and influence vis-à-vis administrative agencies which distribute benefits, such as the Army Corps of Engineers, the Park Service, or the Veterans Administration. These secondary bonds are probably as critical in securing benefits for the district as are the primary bonds resulting from "relevant" committee assignments. However, the secondary bonds have less symbolic value than do the primary bonds. And symbolic pay-offs, we shall see, are an important fourth component of representational responsiveness.

Symbolic Responsiveness

The fourth component of responsiveness is more psychologically based than the others. The first three components all somehow tap a behavioral aspect of representation: policy responsiveness is oriented toward the decision-making behavior of the representative in matters of public controversy; while service and allocation responsiveness are oriented toward particularized or collective benefits obtained through the acts of the representative. The representational relationship is not, however, just one of such concrete transactions, but also one that is built on trust and confidence expressed in the support that the represented give to the representative and to which he responds by symbolic, significant gestures, in order to, in turn, generate and maintain continuing support.

The notion of symbolic responsiveness has been alluded to by Wahlke (1971) in examining the role of the constituency in the representational relationship. He found little evidence for presuming that a district makes specific policy demands on its representative. Rather, he suggested the relevance of Easton's concept of diffuse support (1965, 247-340) as a key component in the relationship between the represented and their representative. He states that the "symbolic satisfaction with the process of government is probably more important than specific, instrumental satisfaction with the policy output of the process" (Wahlke, 1971, 288). The important question then becomes, ". . . how do representative bodies contribute to the generation and maintenance of support?" (290).

In an era of cynicism about the functioning of representative institutions, the ways in which representatives manipulate political symbols in order to generate and maintain trust or support become critical aspects of responsiveness. Edelman (1964, 1971), following the earlier work of Merriam, Lasswell, and Smith (1950), has emphasized the importance of symbolic action in politics. The need for giving symbolic reassurance is being demonstrated by the "reach out" efforts of the new President of the United States—walking down Pennsylvania Avenue after his inauguration, fire-side chats, telephonic call-a-thons, visits to economically stricken areas, being "Jimmy" Carter, and so on. The purpose of all of these symbolic acts is to project an image that the President is truly the people's representative and ready to be responsive to them. By mobilizing trust and confidence it is presumably

easier to go about the job of representation than would otherwise be the case.

Fenno (1975), in a paper on "Congressmen in their Constituencies," emphasizes the importance of political support in the representational relationship. The representative's "home style"—how he behaves *in* his constituency—is designed not just to secure constituent support and re-election but also to give the representative more freedom in his legislative activities when he is away from home. Symbolic politics has the purpose of building up credit to be drawn on in future contingencies. Although Fenno does not cite Wahlke at all, it is significant that his analysis approximates the "support-input model":

> . . . congressmen seek and voters may give support on a non-policy basis. They may support a "good man" on the basis of his presentation "as a person" and trust him to be a good representative. So, we might consider the possibility that constituent trust, together with electoral accountability, may also provide a measure of good representation. The point is not that policy preferences are not a crucial basis for the representational relationship. They are. The point is that we should not start our studies of representation by assuming that they are the only basis for a representational relationship. They are not (51).

Fenno's comments are all the more germane to the argument of this paper because it is interesting to note that this most eminent of legislative scholars deflates the prevailing obsession with policy responsiveness as the *sine qua non* of representation. In fact, much of what may appear to be policy responsiveness is largely symbolic responsiveness. From session to session, legislators on all levels of government—federal, state, and local—introduce thousands of bills which have not the slightest chance of ever being passed and, more often than not, are not intended to be passed. Yet representatives introduce these bills to please some constituents and to demonstrate their own responsiveness.[11]

RESPONSIVENESS AND FOCUS OF REPRESENTATION

Once the concept of representation-as-responsiveness is decomposed, policy responsiveness appears as only one component of representation and, perhaps, as by no means the dominant link between representative and represented. There is no intrinsic reason why responsiveness in one component of representation cannot go together with unresponsiveness in another. An individual or group may disagree with the representative's position and behavior on an issue of public policy and, as a result, may be unrepresented in this sense; yet, the same individual or group may be well represented by a person who is responsive by attending to their particular requests for some type of service. Similarly, it is possible for a representative to be responsive with regard to securing public goods for his constituency, while simultaneously being quite unresponsive with respect to issues of public policy. Finally, what matters in symbolic responsiveness is that the constituents feel represented, quite regardless of whether the representative is responsive in his policy stands or the services or public goods he provides for his constituency.

Moreover, even if attention is given only to policy responsiveness, research cannot simply neglect some of the classical questions of representational theory, such as the issue of representing the district's will as against its interest, or the issue of the focus of representation. It is easily conceivable that being responsive to a district's will—the wants of its people—may involve being unresponsive to a district's interest—the needs of its people. With regard to the focus of representation, being responsive to the electoral district may produce unresponsive behavior in the larger unit of which the district is a part and, of course, vice versa.[12]

In fact, a closer look at the question of representational focus will reveal further the potentially multidimensional character of the phenomenon of responsiveness. The representative can perceive his "constituency" in a multitude of ways,[13] thereby making the number of foci quite large. One might organize these possible foci into three categories. The first category entails a geographic focus; the representative may perceive his constituency in terms of nation, region, state, district, or any other territorial level of society. The second category would include particular solidary or functional groupings like ethnic, religious, economic, and ideological groups, whether organized or not. Finally, the representational relationship may have as foci individual persons ranging from distinguished notables to unknown clients in need of help and to personal friends.

Representational focus, then, can differ a great deal in each of these three ways. The crucial point, however, is that the focus of representation might vary with each of the four components of responsiveness. While one might find particular foci, according to the three categories, for policy responsiveness, one might find altogether different foci in regard to any of the other components of responsiveness. Any empirical combination is possible within relevant logical constraints. Empirical research has yet to address the relationship between modes of responsiveness and foci of representation, and untangle the web of complexity created by the relationship.

RESPONSIVENESS VERSUS RESPONSE

The generally confused and confusing use of "responsiveness," especially when linked to notions of "concurrence," is only symptomatic of a malaise that has come to characterize the "scientific" study of politics. The malaise is to substitute "theory construction" as a technique for substantive theory or theorizing. A younger scholar in the field, Fiorina (1974, 24), after reviewing the empirical research on representation of recent vintage, has come to a similar conclusion. We quote him precisely because he is not ignorant of or inimical to the new technological dispensations of our time:

> Too often it seems that the increasing availability of electronic computing facilities, data banks, and canned statistical packages has encouraged a concomitant decline in the use of our own capabilities. Rather than hypothesize we factor analyze, regress, or causal model. We speak of empirical theory as if it miraculously grows out of a cumulation of empirical findings, rather than as a logical structure one must carefully construct to explain those findings.

When Fiorina identifies "data banks" as one of the villains, he presumably implies that the user of these facilities has grown increasingly remote from his subjects of observation and lost touch with the humanity he is supposed to understand. Indeed, there are today users of survey research who have never interviewed a single person in their lives. Not surprisingly, therefore, causal models are being reified as if they described reality rather than being abstractions from reality. In the case of representational responsiveness, for instance, the causal direction has been assumed to point from the represented to the representative; the latter has been assumed to be the object of stimuli to which he responds (or does not respond) in the fashion of Pavlov's famous dog. But such a model, even if one provides for intervening attitudinal or perceptual processes, does not approximate representational relationships which are, above all, transactions

not necessarily structured in the ways of the S-O-R paradigm.

To appreciate the complexity of representational relationships as transactions, it is simply erroneous to assume that responsiveness—whatever component may be involved—is somehow the dependent variable in a causal structure. "Responsiveness" and "response" are not the same thing. On the contrary, a representative whose behavior is purely *reactive*—a condition that is hard to conceive on reflection but one that the "concurrence model" postulates—is the very opposite of a politically responsive person in Pitkin's sense. As that person has been chosen, elected, or selected from the multitude or mass to be a representative, that is, as he occupies a superior position in the relationship by virtue of his "elevation," one should expect him not merely to be reactive but to take the initiative. Whether he does or not is, of course, an empirical question; but the question cannot be answered by simply substituting an inappropriate model of causation for empirical observation and a viable theory of representation that would guide both observation and analysis.

As already suggested, the attractiveness of the notion of responsiveness in the most recent period has been due in part to the fusion of participatory and representational ideas about democracy. But in the participatory theory of democracy the leader—insofar as the model admits of leadership at all—is largely a reactive agent guided by the collective wisdom of the group. He is at best the executor of the group's will, indeed a human facsimile of Pavlov's dog. He reacts, presumably, but he is not responsive. One is in fact back to the "instructed-delegate" model in which there is no room for discretion in the conduct of the representative. A causal model of representation that draws its arrows only in recursive fashion from the represented to the representative cannot capture, therefore, the meaning of responsiveness in Pitkin's sense. It excludes ab initio what is yet to be concluded.

It is a grievous error, against which Fiorina wanted, to assume and to act as if the assumption were valid, that "causal analysis" will automatically yield "theory," or that by simple inversion of causal assumptions something meaningful will come out of a causal analysis. Theorizing involves something more than arbitrarily inverting the causal directions on the assumption that the resultant statistical structure will somehow reflect reality. It involves *giving reasons* and *justifying* the assumptions one brings into the causal analysis. It involves "going out on a limb," as it were, and saying something substantive about the phenomena being investigated, rather than

hiding behind the artifactual "findings" of a causal analysis that may be inappropriate in the first place.

A next step in the study of representation as responsiveness must take off from the compositional nature of the phenomenon. This step cannot be limited to simplistic measures like congruence or concurrence in connection with one component of a complex set of transactional relationships. Any inferences one may make about the functions of any one component of responsiveness in "representative government" must be related to inferences one may make about the functions of other components. Otherwise the puzzle of representation—having representative government but not knowing what it is about—will continue to bewilder the political imagination.

Notes

An earlier version of this paper was presented at the annual meeting of the Western Political Science Association, March 31-April 2, 1977.

1. Miller and Stokes (1963). A revised version is included in Campbell, Converse, Miller, and Stokes (1966, 351-72). We shall be citing the original article because we are only interested here in the theoretical aspects of the analysis which remained unaffected by the revision. The particular analysis was part of a much larger study of representation conducted in connection with the 1958 congressional elections.

2. In Footnote 2 of their original article Miller and Stokes refer to Eulau, Wahlke, Buchanan, and Ferguson (1959); Hanna F. Pitkin's then unpublished Ph.D. dissertation (1961), which presumably led to her later *The Concept of Representation* (1967); de Grazia (1951); and Fairlie (1940).

3. The two most significant studies of the fifties in this genre were: Turner (1951) and MacRae (1958).

4. The operational definition was expressed as follows: "In each policy domain, crossing the rankings of Congressmen and their constituencies gives an empirical measure of the extent of policy agreement between legislator and district." The measure itself was expressed as follows: "To summarize the degree of congruence between legislators and voters, a measure of correlation is introduced" (Miller and Stokes, 1963, 49 and n. 10).

5. See, e.g., Stone (1976, 8), where one finds the bland statement: "Representation is conceived as congruence or agreement between the behavior of the legislator and the opinion of the constituency on comparable policy dimensions." Compare this also with Clausen (1973, 128): "Given the principal orientation of this book, the policy orientation, representation is further defined as the congruence of the policy requirements of the constituency with the policy decisions of the representative."

6. Instead, to illustrate the constituency's sanctioning power through elections, Miller and

Stokes relied on data for a single Congressional district in a case which is both inappropriate and deviant, involving the defeat of Congressman Brook Hays in the Fifth Arkansas District where all *voters* in the sample (N=13) had read or heard "something" about Hays and his write-in opponent. But, as Miller and Stokes admit, the case was inappropriate: the voters probably knew little about Hays' legislative record in the previous Congress but punished him for his non-legislative role in the Little Rock school crisis. The Hays case indicated the power of an aroused electorate in an unusual situation; but even if they knew the legislative records of their representatives, electorates are rarely so aroused over any one of the many legislative issues with which representatives deal.

7. Wahlke (1971). The core ideas of this article were first presented by Wahlke in a 1967 paper before the Seventh World Congress of the International Political Science Association in Brussels, Belgium.

8. We could cite here, of course, an extensive "institutional" literature which has come to be neglected by "behavioral" students of representation. For a particularly useful recent introduction that paints a broad canvas, see Birch (1971).

9. The problem with causal analyses of phenomena like influence or responsiveness is that the direction of the relationships to which they presumably refer cannot be inferred from the causal structure of the statistical model that may be applied. The statistical model assumes the existence of a conceptual isomorphism between its ordering of the variables and their real-world ordering. The existence of a *possible* isomorphism between the direction of a political relationship and a causal relation between two variables in a statistical model was brought to the attention of political scientists in a series of papers by Herbert A. Simon. Attempting to define political power, Simon found that "the difficulty appeared to reside in a very specific technical point; influence, power, and authority are all intended as asymmetrical relations." It seemed to him that "the mathematical counterpart of this asymmetrical

relation appeared to be the distinction between independent and dependent variables—the independent variable determines the dependent, and not the converse." But, he pointed out in a significant passage that causal analysts seem at times to overlook, "in algebra, the distinction between independent and dependent variable is purely conventional—we can always rewrite our equations without altering their content in such a way as to reverse their roles." The problem, then, is one of giving operational meaning to the asymmetry that is implied in the definition of influence or power: "That is to say, for the assertion, 'A has power over B' we can substitute the assertion, 'A's behavior causes B's behavior.' If we can define the causal relation, we can define influence, power, or authority, and vice versa." See Simon (1957, 5). The most significant term in Simon's explication of the causal relation is "vice versa." It suggests that the definition of the "causal relation" and the definition of the phenomenon to be causally treated (here influence) are interdependent events. In other words: "If we can define influence, we can define the causal relation."

10. Unfortunately Fiorina then characterizes the new-style Congressman as an "ombudsman." This attribution is inappropriate because an ombudsman, though presumably available for the settlement of grievances, is not the kind of "hustler" whom Fiorina sees as coming on the stage of representation. Of course, both roles seem to be involved—that of ombudsman and that of hustler.

11. For example, Froman (1967, 36) found that in the 88th Congress (1963-1964) 15 299 bills and resolutions were introduced in the House of Representatives, whereas only 1742, or a little over 11 percent, were reported by committee.

12. For the distinction between "style" and "focus" of representation, see Eulau, Wahlke, Buchanan, and Ferguson (1959).

13. Fenno (1975) has also seen the need to decompose the concept of constituency. He suggests that congressmen perceive several distinct types of constituencies to which they respond in different ways.

References

BIRCH, A.H. 1971. *Representation*. London: St. Martin's Press.

CAMPBELL, ANGUS, PHILLIP E. CONVERSE, WARREN E. MILLER, and DONALD E. STOKES. 1966. *Elections and the Political Order*. New York: Wiley.

CLAPP, CHARLES. 1963. *The Congressman: His Job as He Sees It*. Washington: Brookings Institution.

CLAUSEN, AAGE R. 1973. *How Congressmen Decide*. New York: St. Martin's Press.

CNUDDE, CHARLES F., and DONALD J. MCCRONE. 1966. "The Linkage between Constituency Attitudes and Congressional Voting: A Causal Model." *American Political Science Review* 60 (March): 66-72.

DE GRAZIA, ALFRED. 1951. *Public and Republic*. New York: Knopf.

EASTON, DAVID. 1965. *A Systems Analysis of Political Life*. New York: Wiley.

EDELMAN, MURRAY. 1964. *The Symbolic Uses of Politics*. Urbana: University of Illinois Press.

———. 1971. *Politics as Symbolic Action*. Chicago: Markham.

EULAU, HEINZ. 1967. "Changing Views of Representation." In Ithiel de Sola Pool, ed., *Contemporary Political Science: Toward Empirical Theory*. New York: McGraw-Hill.

EULAU, HEINZ, JOHN C. WAHLKE, WILLIAM BUCHANAN, and LEROY C. FERGUSON. 1959. "The Role of the Representative: Some Empirical Observations on the Theory of Edmund Burke." *American Political Science Review* 53 (September): 742-56.

EULAU, HEINZ, and KENNETH PREWITT. 1973. *Labyrinths of Democracy: Adaptations, Linkages, Representation, and Policies in Urban Politics*. Indianapolis: Bobbs-Merrill.

FAIRLIE, JOHN S. 1940. "The Nature of Political Representation." *American Political Science Review* 40 (April-June): 236-48, 456-66.

FENNO, RICHARD F. 1973. *Congressmen in Committees*. Boston: Little, Brown.

———. 1975. "Congressmen in their Constituencies." Prepared for delivery at the annual meeting of the American Political Science Association.

FIORINA, MORRIS P. 1974. *Representatives, Roll Calls, and Constituencies*. Lexington. Mass.: D. C. Heath.

———. 1977. "The Case of the Vanishing Marginals: The Bureaucracy Did It." *American Political Science Review* 71 (March): 177-81.

JACKSON, JOHN E. 1974. *Constituencies and Leaders in Congress*. Cambridge, Mass.: Harvard University Press.

KINGDON, JOHN W. 1973. *Congressmen's Voting Decisions*. New York: Harper and Row.

LASSWELL, HAROLD D., CHARLES E. MERRIAM, and T.V. SMITH. 1950. *A Study of Power*. Glencoe, Ill.: Free Press.

LOEWENBERG, GERHARD. 1972. "Comparative Legislative Research." In Samuel C. Patterson and John C. Wahlke, eds. *Comparative Legislative Behavior: Frontiers of Research*. New York: Wiley.

MACRAE, DUNCAN JR. 1958. *Dimensions of Congressional Voting*. Berkeley: University of California Press.

MATTHEWS, DONALD R., and JAMES A. STIMSON. 1975. *Yeas and Nays: Normal Decision-Making in the U.S. House of Representatives*. New York: Wiley.

MILLER, WARREN E., and DONALD E. STOKES. 1963. "Constituency Influence in Congress." *American Political Science Review* 57 (March): 45-56.

MULLER, EDWARD N. 1970. "The Representation of Citizens by Political Authorities: Consequences for Regime Support." *American Political Science Review* 64 (December): 1149-66.

PATTERSON, SAMUEL C., RONALD D. HEDLUND, and G.R. BOYNTON. 1975. *Representatives and Represented: Bases of Public Support for the American Legislatures.* New York: Wiley.

PETERSON, PAUL E. 1970. "Forms of Representation: Participation of the Poor in the Community Action Program." *American Political Science Review* 64 (June): 491-507.

PITKIN, HANNA F. 1961. "The Theory of Representation." Ph.D. dissertation, University of California, Berkeley.

———. 1967. *The Concept of Representation.* Berkeley: University of California Press.

PREWITT, KENNETH, and HEINZ EULAU. 1969. "Political Matrix and Political Representation: Prolegomenon to a New Departure from an Old Problem." *American Political Science Review* 63 (June): 427-41.

SIMON, HERBERT A. 1957. *Models of Man.* New York: Wiley.

STONE, WALTER J. 1976. "Representation in the United States House of Representatives." Ph.D. dissertation, University of Michigan.

TURNER, JULIUS. 1951. *Party and Constituency: Pressures on Congress.* Baltimore: Johns Hopkins University Press.

TURNER, JULIUS, and EDWARD V. SCHNEIER, Jr. 1970. *Party and Constituency.* Baltimore: Johns Hopkins University Press.

VERBA, SIDNEY, and NORMAN H. NIE. 1972. *Participation in America: Political Democracy and Social Equality.* New York: Harper and Row.

WAHLKE, JOHN C. 1971. "Policy Demands and System Support: The Role of the Represented." *British Journal of Political Science* 1 (July): 271-90.

ZEIGLER, L. HARMON, and M. KENT JENNINGS, with G.W. PEAK. 1974. *Governing American Schools.* No. Scituate, Mass.: Duxbury Press.

4. THE FUNCTIONS OF REPRESENTATION

A.H. Birch

Normative theories of representation have nearly all been formulated to serve practical purposes, such as the justification of existing institutions or the promotion of political reforms. Most of the theories [so far discussed] emerged out of the debates on the American and French revolutions and the protracted discussions on the reform of Parliament and the extension of the franchise in Britain. The main political developments of the twentieth century —the growth of party discipline, the extension of government activities, the rise of one-party states and totalitarian systems, the emergence of the new states of the third world, the spread of violence—have given rise to a variety of theoretical writings but not to new theories of representation, with the one exception of the theory of responsible party government considered [in the previous chapter]. Because of this, the functions of political representation are normally discussed in a language which is slightly dated in character and tends to reflect the values of nineteenth-century liberalism. To overcome these limitations it is necessary for the student to disengage himself from the assumptions of liberal democracy and consider

A.H. Birch, *Representation* (London: Macmillan, 1971), 106-23, and 136. Reprinted by permission of the author and Phaidon Press Limited.

the issues in a broader perspective and a more analytical manner.

One scholar who has done this is David Apter, who has attempted to construct a theory of representation which is applicable equally to democratic and non-democratic systems, operating in societies at all stages of economic and political development. In Apter's formulation, the functions of political representation are defined as follows:

1. *Central control:* the ordered maintenance of discipline in a political system on a day-to-day basis.
2. *Goal specification:* the identification and priority ranking of policies; hence, a sharing in policy formulation on the basis of a longer term.
3. *Institutional coherence:* the continuous review, reformulation, and adaptation of the fit between boundaries of sub-systems, including the regulation of overlapping jurisdictions, and including as well, ideological adjustment.[1]

Unfortunately, these definitions are so wide in scope that they do not distinguish between the functions of representation and the functions of other elements in the political process. Central control, as defined here, is either a function of government as a whole or the function of a government's law-enforcement agencies: the business of public officials and policemen rather than of representatives. Goal specification is a function of all those concerned with policy making, whether or not they are representatives. Institutional coherence is one of the goals of policy makers, whoever they are. The definitions might apply to the role of the Communist Party in Russia or China, or a mobilizing party in a new state like Nkrumah's party in Ghana, but they cannot serve to distinguish the functions of representative processes from other processes in all kinds of political system.

Given that political representation fulfils a variety of functions, it is suggested that a two-stage classification may be helpful, in which three broadly-defined general functions are sub-divided into a larger number of specific functions, it being accepted that not all representative systems fulfil all the functions that they might fulfil. The general functions may be defined as follows:

1. *Popular control:* to provide for a degree of popular control over the government.
2. *Leadership:* to provide for leadership and responsibility in decision making.
3. *System maintenance:* to contribute towards the maintenance and smooth running of the political system by enlisting the support of citizens.

The specific functions may be defined as follows:

1. (*a*) *Responsiveness:* to ensure that decision makers are responsive to the interest and opinions of the public.
   (*b*) *Accountability:* to provide a way of holding political leaders publicly accountable for their actions.
   (*c*) *Peaceful change:* to provide a mechanism for replacing one set of leaders by another without violence.
2. (*a*) *Leadership:* to provide for the recruitment of political leaders and the mobilization of support for them.

(*b*) *Responsibility:* to encourage political leaders to pursue long-term national interests as well as reacting to immediate pressures.
3. (*a*) *Legitimation:* to endow the government with a particular kind of legitimacy.
   (*b*) *Consent:* to provide channels of communication through which the government can mobilize consent to particular policies.
   (*c*) *Relief of pressure:* to provide a safety valve through which aggrieved citizens can blow off steam and to disarm potential revolutionaries by engaging them in constitutional forms of activity.

It is suggested that a fully developed representative system will perform all of these functions, though the precise methods will vary from one system to another. Of course, most countries have representative systems which are only partially developed. For instance, the representative system of the USSR provides effectively for leadership, responsibility, legitimation and consent, but it is not very effective in the other four functions. Even systems which may be described as fully representative vary in their relative strengths. Thus, most observers would agree that the representative system of the Fourth Republic was more effective than that of the Fifth Republic in providing for responsiveness and peaceful change, but less effective in providing for leadership, responsibility and consent. It would in principle be possible to construct a profile for each representative system illustrating the way in which it fulfils these eight functions, though the extreme difficulty of measuring performance along these dimensions means that this would inevitably have to be based more on historical judgement than on quantitative research.

It will now be appropriate to consider the nature of these eight functions of political representation a little more fully.

POPULAR CONTROL

The main aim of liberal reformers in the past two centuries has been to use or to establish representative institutions in order to extend popular control over the actions of legislators and administrators. The achievement of a reasonable degree of control of this type is generally regarded as the essence of liberal democracy. As Mayo puts it: "a political system is democratic to the extent that the decision-makers are under effective popular control."[2] [As we have seen in earlier chapters,] much of the debate has turned on what Wahlke and Eulau have called the focus of representation:[3] to be specific, on the question of whether the need is to represent opinions or interests, individuals or groups, localities or the whole nation. But two other issues cut across the debate and must be taken account of in any theory of representation. One is the question of whether representatives are (or should be) concerned with the felt wants or the real needs of their constituents. The other is whether the control is (or should be) exercised before the event, by pressures and instructions, or after the event, by a system of public accountability.

The question of felt wants *versus* real needs has haunted political discussion ever since Rousseau distinguished between the particular will and the real will of citizens. Some democratic theorists of a Benthamite disposition have taken the view that actual, observable wishes and interests alone have reality, feeling that talk of a real will, like talk of a national interest, serves mainly to justify the tendency of political élites to impose their view of what is desirable on the whole country. But experience suggests that this view is too simple to be adequate.

In the first place, it has been shown time and time again that there is a wide range of political questions on which the majority of people have no settled views. To be sure, doorstep interviews can sometimes elicit a reaction from people who had no clear view before the interview was conducted, but such reactions do not survive the test of detailed probing by supplementary questions. Secondly, people's immediate wishes are often inconsistent. To take only the most obvious example, most people would vote for reduced taxes and increased government expenditures, which would add up to a budgetary deficit, but would vote against the inflation that this would cause. Representatives who felt themselves bound to promote only the immediate wishes of their constituents would find that on some issues they had guidance from only a minority, on others they had guidance that was clearly inconsistent, and on others again they had conflicting demands from different sections of the constituency. If political representation were solely of this kind the ineffectiveness of the representatives would probably mean that administrators and other non-representative persons would play a dominant role in the process of policy formation.

In fact most representatives do not feel themselves bound in this way. Thus, at the time of writing (1970) most British MPs are supporting the government's application to join the Common Market, in spite of the fact that opinion polls show a majority against the move, because the MPs believe that in the long run membership will benefit the nation. Equally, MPs supported the move to decimalize the currency not because this was wanted by the public but because it was thought that when people got used to it they would prefer it to the system of pounds, shillings and pence.

Even on those fairly rare occasions when MPs have a free vote on legislative proposals they do not necessarily feel bound to follow the expressed wishes of their constituents. Thus, capital punishment was abolished on a free vote when the polls showed a majority in favour of retention, the MPs acting partly on the belief that they had a duty to exercise moral and political leadership on this issue and partly on the belief that abolition would show that public fears about the loss of a deterrent to murder were unfounded. It was widely believed that if only the public had a better understanding of the psychology of murderers the public would be in favour of abolition, so that MPs who supported the reform could be said to be acting in accordance with the "real will" of the people; i.e. with what the people would want if only they were better informed and could free themselves of irrelevant prejudices.

In spite of the somewhat different political traditions of the United States, many American legislators also feel free to act on their own judgement of what is best for the people they represent. In their study of the role perceptions of representatives in four state legislatures, John Wahlke and his colleagues classified their respondents as delegates if they believed they should follow the expressed wishes of their constituents, as trustees if they believed they should act on their own judgement, and as "politicos" if their views contained a mixture of these beliefs. In seven of the eight legislative chambers a clear majority of those interviewed were classified as trustees.[4] In the justifications offered for this attitude, one common theme was the ignorance of the average voter. As one representative put it: "People are not capable to tell me what to do—not because they are stupid, but because they have limited access to the facts. If they had the facts, their decision would be the same."[5]

It is therefore arguable that the idea of responsiveness to public opinions and interests should be extended to include something wider than responsiveness to the day-by-day expressions of public attitudes. It is difficult to find a satisfactory term by which to describe this, as the concept of a "real will" has philosophical connotations to which many people object. Roland Pennock has attempted to deal with the problem by distinguishing between people's desires and people's interests.

> The distinction I am intending to make between "desire" and "interest" is the distinction between what is immediately demanded and what in the long run, with the benefit of hindsight, would have been preferred or would have contributed to the development of the individual into a person capable of making responsible decisions.[6]

The distinction is well drawn but it is doubtful whether the suggested terminology is helpful, because there are immediate and long-run interests just as there are immediate and long-run desires. Thus, a firm which applied for a bank loan to finance a new development would have an immediate interest in a favourable reply, but if the projected development were commercially unsound the long-term interests of the firm would be better protected by a refusal on the part of the bank.

However, the problem here is only a problem of terminology and does not reflect any basic confusion. The distinction can be expressed quite clearly in a paragraph, but there is no single word which can be used to denote it without ambiguity. If political science were a different kind of subject a new term or mathematical symbol could be coined for the purpose, but as things are the best course is simply to spell out the distinction in ordinary language. Almost everyone would agree that policy makers have a duty to take account of enlightened opinions and long-term interests as well as to respond to the immediate demands that are put to them. Some say that the concept of responsiveness should be stretched to include both kinds of response while others would say that the concept of responsiveness should relate only to expressed demands and opinions and the wider function should be considered under another heading, which is best called responsibility. From the point of view of empirical research the second alternative is certainly preferable, for expressed demands can be observed and perhaps measured while long-term interests can only be assessed and may always be a matter of controversy. For clarity in research design and analysis it is therefore desirable to keep a narrow definition of responsiveness, but without falling into the trap of assuming that this is necessarily more important than the other functions of representation.

The other question about popular control that must be mentioned is the question of when and how it is to be exercised. On this question people fall into three main groups. One group believes that the essence of popular control is control exercised in advance, by pressures or instructions or party programmes. Interest groups which appoint representatives to act as spokesmen clearly fall into this category. So do delegates to the Annual Conference of the Labour Party who regularly demand that conference decisions should be accepted as binding by the party's leaders in Parliament. Those American legislators who see themselves as delegates for their districts regard it as a necessary part of the democratic process that representatives should do their best to find out what their voters want and then do their best to achieve these aims. In the days when US senators were appointed by state legislatures it was quite common and considered quite proper for the senators to be given instructions on the line they should take. All politicians and writers who subscribe to the doctrine of the electoral mandate believe that the party programme, once endorsed by the electorate, should provide instructions and terms of reference for the incoming government.

Now, there can be no doubt that some kinds of representation lend themselves to control in advance. This is the case with all representatives who are appointed to act as agents, such as ambassadors and attorneys and spokesmen for pressure groups. The modern practice of consulting affected groups before drafting legislation means that there is ample opportunity for interested parties to instruct their representatives as to the line they should adopt.

However, elected representatives in a national legislature cannot normally be controlled in advance by their electors, for all the reasons given earlier. The only effective sanction on their behaviour, it is commonly argued, is that they face the risk of losing the next election if their decisions prove to be unpopular. On this argument the essence of popular control (and therefore the essence of democracy) is that legislators and ministers are accountable to the public for what they do while in office. The nature of this accountability clearly varies according to the nature of the party system. In a system characterized by loose discipline, such as the American system, elected persons may be held to account for their individual behaviour by published analyses of their voting records in Congress or a state assembly. In a disciplined party system with only two main parties, such as the British system, it is the government of the day which is held to account for its behaviour, with individual MPs having to accept the consequent loss or gain of popularity largely irrespective of their personal attitudes and behaviour. In a partially disciplined party system with several main parties, such as that of the Fourth Republic, the line of accountability is far from clear.

It has sometimes been argued that even this theory of popular control assumes too much. According to Joseph Schumpeter, defenders of liberal democracy should abandon the claim that the public is able to control or even to influence the actions of government and should fall back on the more modest and realistic claim that the system of competitive elections enables the public to choose between rival teams of political leaders. In Schumpeter's definition, the democratic method "is that institutional arrangement for arriving at political decisions in which individuals acquire the power to decide by means of a competitive struggle for the people's vote."[7]

One of Schumpeter's arguments is that democratic and representative systems of government can be distinguished more clearly from other systems in terms of processes than in terms of achievements. There are historical examples, he says, of dictatorial systems that served the will of the people better than some democratic systems have done. Certainly there have been dictators who claimed to be representatives: thus Adolf Hitler once declared, "My pride is that I know no statesman in the world who with greater right than I can say that he is the representative of his people."[8] Schumpeter put forward six other arguments, all of which are impressive, though as he was concerned with the definition of democracy rather than with the functions of representation there is no need to discuss them here. There can be no doubt that it is right to emphasize that the provision of institutional arrangements for competition between politicians, including the peaceful replacement of one set of leaders by another, is an important function that a system of political representation can serve. If we were concerned with the definition of liberal democracy it might be appropriate to say that no representative system could rightly be called democratic unless it fulfilled this function. But there have been and are many political systems which are in some degree representative although they do not provide for electoral competition, and [in a book on the concept of representation] it is sufficient to say that this is one of the eight functions that representation can serve.

LEADERSHIP AND RESPONSIBILITY

One of the many ways in which political activity differs from economic or social activity is that politics involves a sharp distinction between leaders and led. There are differences of power and status in economic and social activity, but almost everyone in society takes part and the personal influence that any one man or handful of men can have on the system is fairly small. Politics, on the other hand, is an activity which only a tiny minority of the population engages in on a full-time basis. All systems of government are in this sense oligarchic and a handful of political leaders can exercise immense power over their country. The selection of political leaders is a process of the utmost importance and it is a process which in many countries is performed by the representative system.

This is not the case in traditional systems of government where leaders are drawn from a ruling family or caste. Nor is it the case in military dictatorships where leaders are selected by the processes of military recruitment and promotion: which officer gets the top position in government depends on a mixture of political ambition, agility and good fortune, but there is normally a fairly small pool of senior officers from whom he emerges.

But in virtually all other types of government, democratic or dictatorial, in industrialized or developing societies, politicians are normally recruited and political leaders selected through the party system. Parties interest people in politics, persuade them to accept minor offices, choose between candidates for election, groom potential leaders for stardom, and mobilize support for them when they are successful. In parliamentary systems the representative assembly plays an important part in the process because an ability to perform well in debates is a necessary requisite for ministers. In Communist systems the assembly is relatively unimportant and top leaders are normally selected from the membership of the central committee of the party. The American system is exceptional in that cabinet posts sometimes go to presidential nominees who have never held elective office or been active in party affairs, but these are temporary posts and all career politicians have to make their way up through the party system.

If one of the functions of a representative system is the selection of political leaders, another is that of giving them sufficient support and scope for them to be able to balance conflicting pressures and formulate long-term plans for their government. With elections every four or five years the horizons of politicians are inevitably limited and "medium-term" might be a more realistic expression than "long-term," but at least it is generally thought desirable that political leaders should accept a broader responsibility than that of responding to day-to-day pressures.

One facet of this is that it is a function of political representation not only to articulate popular demands but also to provide for their integration. As V.O. Key said: "The problem of the politician or the statesman in a democracy is to maintain a working balance between the demands of competing interests and values. His task is not necessarily the expression of the 'general will' or the 'popular will'."[9]

Heinz Eulau struck a similar chord when he claimed that heterogeneous electoral districts were functional from the point of view of the political system as a whole: "The very circumstance of heterogeneity in the district tends to free the representative from being readily bound by a mandate, to make for discretion and political responsibility, and to enable him to integrate conflicting demands."[10]

Another facet of the matter is the need for political leaders sometimes to take decisions which are downright unpopular. Nobody wants conscription, higher taxes, credit restrictions or devaluation, but from time to time the national interest requires such measures. The Conservative leader Lord Hailsham put this very bluntly in his speech defending the rather severe budget of 1962: "When a government has to chose between a run on the pound and its own popularity, it has only one choice it can make. It makes it unwillingly. It must face unpopularity, loss of by-elections and even, if need be, defeat at a later general election. This is the price of responsible government."[11]

Walter Lippmann referred to the same need when he said: "Governments are unable to cope with reality when elected assemblies and mass opinions become decisive in the state, when there are no statesmen to resist the inclinations of voters and there are only politicians to excite and to exploit them."[12]

A third facet of the matter is that there occasionally arises the need for governments to undertake a major reversal of policy. The outstanding examples of recent years are President de Gaulle's decision to accept the demand of the Algerian Liberation Front for national independence and President Nixon's decision to engage in a gradual withdrawal of US troops from Vietnam. To carry through policy changes of this scale requires both powers of leadership and room for manoeuvre.

It follows that the function of responsibility has certain institutional implications. If responsiveness were the main function of a representative system it would be appropriate to have frequent elections and probably a rapid turnover of politicians. The function of public accountability implies that the turnover should not be too rapid, for unless representatives believe they have a fairly good chance of being re-elected the prospect of an election will not act as a check on their behaviour. The function of responsibility implies that elections should not be too frequent, for leaders need time both to carry through difficult policies and to persuade their followers that their less popular measures were justified.

This discussion of responsibility also emphasizes the value, in a modern state, of there being several levels of representation. One of the conditions of achieving both responsiveness and responsibility in government is that the raw demands made by local representatives and the spokesmen for particular interests should be transmuted by discussions within the representative system into more moderate demands which are more consonant with each other and with the interests of the nation as a whole. In this way the representative system acts not only as a set of information channels but also as a filter.

SYSTEM MAINTENANCE

Rousseau opened the third chapter of *The Social Contract* with the following observation: "The strongest is never strong enough to be always the master unless he transforms strength into right and obedience into duty." He added that force itself does not create right and that "we are obliged to obey only legitimate powers."[13] The wisdom of these remarks has been confirmed time and time again, and a study of history reveals only a limited number of ways in which rulers have been able to acquire an aura of legitimacy. For many centuries in many societies heredity was the chief source of legitimacy: kings were chosen from a ruling family and it was important to be able to show an unbroken line of descent from one generation to another. In some societies it has been believed that members of a particular caste or class had an exclusive right to govern: mandarins in China, brahmins in India, the nobility in feudal Europe, the landed gentry in eighteenth-century England. In other countries, and more recently, a particular kind of training has been regarded as a qualification to govern. In military dictatorships a military training is said to confer a sense of discipline, honesty and capacity to rise above sectional interests that is lacking among civilians. In Communist countries membership of the Communist Party, with the training and understanding that goes with it, is regarded as a necessary qualification to take a leading part in administration.

In the present era of history, however, election by popular vote is the source of legitimacy that appears to command the most widespread respect. The party that wins a majority of seats in a parliamentary election is thereby given authority to govern the country for a stated number of years. In Britain even the opponents of the policy mandate theory would agree that an election victory confers a "mandate to govern." This mandate, which implies no more and no less than a right to govern the country in whatever way the leaders of the majority party think proper, is however conditional upon the maintenance of the rules of the game regarding the electoral system. In the Second World War the parties formed a coalition government and agreed to put off the general election that was due in 1940 until Germany was defeated, and in 1945 the prime minister asked his parliamentary colleagues to extend his electoral truce until the war with Japan was also concluded. However, the Labour leaders proved unwilling to accept this proposal and without their agreement Churchill felt he had no option but to plunge at short notice into a general election.

In the United States not even a total war is allowed to interfere with the practice of holding national elections every other year, and the American insistence that political authority should be wielded by persons who can be seen to be the people's representatives leads to the practice of electing judges, district attorneys and other officials whose European equivalents are appointed by the executive. In the Soviet Union the Stalin Constitution of 1936 established direct popular election to a considerable hierarchy of legislative bodies, with the Supreme Soviet at the top. In practice the elections are non-competitive, but great importance is attached to a large turn-out and it is clearly believed that these representative institutions, even without competition, bolster the legitimacy of the government.

The other side of the coin is that a mass boycott of elections constitutes a public refusal to re-authorize the regime which is almost certain to endanger it. A good example is the partial boycott of the Nigerian federal elections in 1964: this was successful in only 70 constituencies out of 312, but it nevertheless caused a major constitutional crisis and spelled the beginning of the end of Nigeria's experiment with representative government.

The legitimizing function of representation can also be seen where representatives are appointed rather than elected. A commission of enquiry into industrial relations would lack legitimacy in the eyes of industrial workers unless it included at least one trade unionist among its members. The microcosmic representation of the various sections of the federation in the Canadian cabinet and Supreme Court helps to bolster the legitimacy of the federal government, while the customary inclusion of a Catholic and a Jew (and now a [Black]) among the nine members of the American Supreme Court does the same for that institution.

A related function of representation is the mobilization of consent. This was the original purpose of the older European parliaments, and though it would not now be said to be their main purpose it continues to be one of their more important functions. The liberal model of parliamentary government suggests that the electors control the representatives and the latter control the administrators, but on many issues the influence actually flows in the reverse direction. Problems are identified and policies framed within the administrative departments; ministers explain the proposals to their colleagues on the back benches; and the latter whip up support for the proposals by speeches in Parliament and in the country. The separation of powers prevents the process working so smoothly in the United States, which is one reason why the president has to use press conferences and public relations techniques to gain support for his policies, but there are many occasions on which speeches and campaigns by members of Congress help to persuade public opinion of the need for foreign aid, military intervention, increased taxes and other policies for which there is no spontaneous demand from the ordinary citizen.

The practice of official consultation with spokesmen for interest groups serves the same function. This is, of course, not really the intention of the interest groups, but if their negotiations with the administration are successful they are inevitably drawn into the position of agreeing (explicitly or implicitly) to persuade their members that the compromises they have arrived at are satisfactory. The general rule is that all channels of political communication tend to become two-way channels.

This rule can be seen very clearly in the operation of advisory and consultative committees. Thus, several of Britain's nationalized industries have consultative committees which were set up with the explicit purpose of representing consumers and bringing their complaints to the attention of the public corporations running the industries. In practice, close contact between the committees and the corporation officials has generally had the effect of persuading the committees that most public complaints are unjustified, and these numerous consumers' committees have on the whole been more successful in bringing the excuses and policies of the corporations to the attention of the public than in bringing public pressure to bear on the corporations. In 1970 public criticisms of the quality of British radio and television services led to the suggestion that a new Broadcasting Council should be established to oversee all the broadcasting media and deal with complaints from aggrieved members of the public. The *Daily Telegraph* made the following comment:

> Alas, this suggestion will not begin to solve the problem. It is our experience generally that boards which are set up to regulate and supervise some activity, whether on behalf of the government or the consumer, are soon captured by the industry in question and fashioned into its apologists.[14]

It is highly unlikely that this tendency is confined to Britain. The generalization that all channels of political communication become two-way channels can be supplemented by the generalization that, unless political passions are aroused, the party with most expert knowledge will tend to get the better of the argument. All representative institutions, if skilfully handled, can serve to mobilize consent to the policies of those actually running the industry, agency or government involved.

A closely related function of representation is that of relieving pressure on a regime from critics and dissenters. Representative institutions can do this partly by offering opportunities for grievances to be aired and partly by diverting the activities of potential revolutionaries into constitutional channels. Developments in British universities since 1968 provide a good example of this function. Faced with sit-ins and the prospect of other disruptive activities on the part of their students, university authorities have responded by creating new forms of representation. Student/staff committees have been established in each department and student representatives have been appointed to Senate committees and even to the Senate itself. The purpose of these moves, put bluntly, is to prevent the disruption of university life by student demonstrations and protests. The developments have other advantages, such as better communication and better understanding, but these are balanced (from the point of view of the university authorities) by the large increase in the amount of time spent on committee work. Very few people would maintain that universities run more smoothly or more effectively with student representation than they did without it in the past. The point is that they run more smoothly than they would now do without it, given the present mood among students. The object of the exercise is not to improve the decision-making process, but to moderate conflict and protect the essential features of the university system.

It is intrinsically difficult to find clear examples of disruption that did not occur, but there are ways in which the British parliamentary system serves the function of acting as a safety valve for grievances. The old slogan "redress of grievances before supply" sums up a long chapter of parliamentary history. Questions in Parliament are an outlet for grievances and the procedure whereby normal business may be suspended for an emergency debate constitutes another safety valve. Criticisms made in the 1960s of the ease with which ministers and officials could prevent an aggrieved citizen's case being re-opened led to the creation of the post of Parliamentary Commissioner, the British equivalent of the Scandinavian *Ombudsman.* If an MP fails to get satisfaction at Question Time he can now refer the grievance to the commissioner, who has power to call for confidential files and demand explanations from the civil servants concerned with the case. Another new development of the 1960s, this time arising from a new social problem rather than from a procedural problem, was the establishment of the Community Relations Commission and a set of Community Councils for race relations, which take up grievances and try to remove their cause by persuasion and pressure. The local Community Relations Councils are (to some extent) representative bodies in the microcosmic sense of the term.

Different examples can be found in situations of political conflict and potential revolt. After the Second World War the democratic regimes of France and Italy were threatened by the existence of large and well-organized Communist parties, each able to command about four million supporters. Though Communists were largely kept out of administrative positions no attempt was made to prevent them from competing in elections, and energies that might have been spent on the barricades were devoted to canvassing and other methods of soliciting votes. The socializing effect of membership of a legislative assembly was summed up earlier in France in the often-repeated comment: "There is more in common between two deputies only one of whom is a revolutionary than there is between two revolutionaries only one of whom is a deputy." It is hazardous to suggest causal relationships in history, but it is the case that the Communist threat to both these regimes has been contained and relieved over the past twenty years.

In the United States some recent troubles arise partly from the fact that extremist groups have taken to the streets instead of to the ballot box. The system would clearly be more secure if the Black Panthers and their allies would concentrate on election campaigns rather than on direct action. The alienation of some student radicals is another problem, as was evidenced by the sigh of relief that was heard in 1968 when large numbers of students went canvassing for Eugene McCarthy. It can be argued that one of the needs of the American political system is to engage its radical youth in some constitutional activities connected with the representative process.

Of course, representation by election does not always prevent grievances building up. For instance, the city of Londonderry has a sizeable majority of Roman Catholics among its citizens but careful drawing of ward boundaries has led to there being a safe and permanent majority of Protestants on the City Council. The resulting resentment among Catholics, combined with other exacerbating factors, had led to intermittent riots in the city over the past fifty years, and in 1969 a particularly serious outbreak of violence led the government to suspend the City Council and hand over its functions to a new body called the Londonderry Commission. The nominated members of the commission are thought likely to represent Catholic interests more effectively than before and the move has done something to relieve pressure on the regime. A similar function has been served by the decision to transfer some of the responsibilities of Northern Irish town councils in respect of housing to a new housing authority which contains a number of members nominated to represent the Catholic community.

If representative institutions are created with the object of relieving pressure on a regime, the timing of the exercise is crucial. After the Easter Rising of 1916, it was decided to create a new body called the Irish Convention to act as a forum for discussion between representatives of all groups, including the extremists. This move was too late, the Convention failing because it was boycotted by the extremist groups whose presence was most essential. On the other hand, the Conservative Party's promise before the 1970 election to create a Scottish National Convention was clearly too early, because the Scottish Nationalists do not pose a serious threat and the establishment of such a Convention would provide them with a new platform for their demands. It is possible to draw parallels from the academic scene, since some universities have suffered from the refusal of their authorities to meet student demands until it was too late to avoid trouble while, at the other extreme, it is noticeable that the two most liberal and progressive institutions of university education in Britain have suffered more from student violence than any of the others.

In conclusion it is suggested that this analysis of the functions of political representation could serve as a general framework for empirical research. It could be used as a starting point for the classification of representative roles and relationships, while representative systems could be assessed in terms of their performance along the eight dimensions indicated. It can also serve as a basis for classifying the considerable amount of research that has been done on political representation.

Notes

1. David E. Apter, *Some Conceptual Approaches to the Study of Modernisation* (Englewood Cliffs: N.J.: Prentice Hall Inc., 1968), 311.

2. Henry B. Mayo, *An Introduction to Democratic Theory* (New York: Oxford University Press, 1960), 60.

3. John C. Wahlke, Heinz Eulau, William Buchanan, and Leroy C. Ferguson, *The Legislative System* (New York: John Wiley and Sons, 1962), 270-2.

4. Ibid., 394.

5. Ibid., 274.

6. J. Roland Pennock, "Political Representation: an Overview," in J. Roland Pennock and John W. Chapman, eds., *Representation* (New York: Atherton Press, 1968), 13.

7. Joseph A. Schumpeter, *Capitalism, Socialism and Democracy* (New York: Harper Bros., 1942), 269.

8. Quoted in Mayo, *An Introduction to Democratic Theory*, 97.

9. V.O. Key, *Politics, Parties and Pressure Groups* (New York: Crowell, 1952), 10.

10. Heinz Eulau, *Micro-Macro Political Analysis* (Chicago: Aldine Publishing Co., 1969), 205.

11. *House of Lords Debates*, April 23, 1962.

12. Walter Lippmann, *The Public Philosophy* (Boston: Little, Brown, 1955), 46.

13. Rousseau, *The Social Contract* (London: Everyman's Library, 1913), 8-9.

14. *Daily Telegraph*, January 4, 1971.

5. POLITICAL REPRESENTATION

Hanna F. Pitkin

Representing as a substantive activity may often have seemed remote from the realities of political life. A political representative—at least the typical member of an elected legislature—has a constituency rather than a single principal; and that raises problems about whether such an unorganized group can even have an interest for him to pursue, let alone a will to which he could be responsive, or an opinion before which he could attempt to justify what he has done. These problems are further heightened when we consider what political science teaches about the members of such a constituency, at least in a modern mass democracy—their apathy, their ignorance, their malleability. Furthermore, the representative who is an elected legislator does not represent his constituents on just any business, and by himself in isolation. He works with other representatives in an institutionalized context at a specific task—the governing of a nation or a state. This reintroduces the familiar problem of local or partial interests versus the national interest, and the question of the political representative's role with respect to them.

Political representation need not raise any problems about the national interest; a symbolic head-of-state can stand for the nation without such a question even seeming relevant.

Or the institutional context may be such that one person or body may act for the nation, while another body is composed of local representatives who do not govern or act for the whole nation.[1] The problem of the national interest arises only in the context of a representative legislature, a body composed of persons representing (as we say) various constituencies, and, at the same time, supposed to govern the nation and pursue the national interest. That context has often led theorists to formulate the classical dilemma: If a man represents a particular constituency in the legislature, is his duty to pursue its interest or the interest of the nation as a whole?

As with the mandate-independence controversy, theorists seem far too ready to accept this as a true dilemma, with mutually exclusive alternatives. But, as with the mandate-independence controversy, there is something to be said for both sides. If a man represents a certain constituency, then, according to the argument [in the last four chapters], his obligation is to that constituency's interest. And in a practical sense, it is politically and socially important that local and partial interests should not be ruthlessly overriden and sacrificed in the name of the nation. On the other hand, someone has to govern and the national government must pursue the national interest. If the representatives as a group are given this task, they are thereby also given the national interest to look after. And, in a practical sense, it is politically and socially important that local and partial interests not be allowed to outweigh the needs and interests of the nation as a whole.

Hanna Pitkin, *The Concept of Representation* (Berkeley: University of California Press, 1967), 215-25, 227-35, 239-40 and notes 4-36 [1-33] and 43-50 [34-41]. © 1967 the Regents of the University of California. Reprinted by permission of the publisher.

It is possible to avoid one horn of this dilemma by shifting ground on who or what is represented. If the legislator represents his constituency, the substantive "acting for" view of representation suggests that he must pursue its interest. So, if we want to show that his obligation is to the national interest, we say that it is really the nation he represents. A number of European constitutions can be cited as illustrations:

> The members of the Reichstag are the representatives of the people as a whole, and shall not be bound by orders or instructions.
> The members of Congress are representatives of the nation and not of the colleges which elect them.
> The members of the two Houses shall represent the nation, and not the province alone, nor the subdivision of the province which elects them.
> Deputies shall represent the nation as a whole, and not the several provinces from which they are chosen.[2]

But such formulations are no solution to our theoretical dilemma; they simply reject one of the alternatives, opting for the national interest instead of constituency interest. Such representatives might as well be elected at large, nation-wide.[3] This position is the obverse of the diehard defense of constituency interest; both tend to obscure the relationship between constituency and nation, between part and whole. They take the choice to be genuinely either-or, as if constituency and nation were mutually exclusive and unrelated units. They suggest that for a representative elected in California to have the duty of "representing" the interest of the whole nation is the same as if he had a duty to "represent" the interest of New York. But of course this is not so; California is part of the nation. If we assume that a nation and its parts confront each other like two hostile nations, the prob-

lem is indeed insoluble. For then to admit that the national welfare is paramount would preclude representation of the locality. And, conversely, the locality could not be blamed for objecting to the emphasis on the national interest if that interest were necessarily hostile to its own.[4] But in fact, one of the most important features of representative government is its capacity for resolving the conflicting claims of the parts, on the basis of their common interest in the welfare of the whole.

A slightly more ambitious argument that frequently appears in the literature overcomes this weakness by postulating an automatic harmony between local and national interest. A sort of political "invisible hand" is supposed to prevent any real conflict. The nation is made up of its parts; so the national interest must be the sum of local or partial interests. The trouble with this argument is that it is false. We all know of cases in which the interest of some locality is in conflict with the national welfare. Moreover, this argument will not accomplish what its proponents expect from it, for it cuts both ways. A Congressman may say, "I'm here to represent my district. What is good for the majority of districts is good for the country,"[5] and take that to sanction his pursuit of his district's interest. But Burke can equally well maintain that every locality, being part of the whole, has a share in the national interest; and he can take that to sanction the representative's devotion to national welfare rather than constituency claims.

What is difficult here is the correct verbal formulation of the obvious facts: in a sense the nation is the sum of its parts, but in another sense the nation must sometimes ask some parts to sacrifice their welfare for its welfare. For a community to exist and persist, its members and subdivisions must benefit from its existence, have an interest in its perpetuation. In that sense each district is part of the whole, and the national interest is not a separate interest, hostile to its own. However, the national interest cannot just ignore or override the welfare of parts of the nation or even of individuals. In representative assemblies the national interest is often formulated out of the rival claims of interests and localities within the state. Yet sometimes a simple addition of these claims will not suffice; sometimes a direct, public-spirited attention to national welfare itself is required.

It would be useful to distinguish between what we might call initial-interest-claim, on the one hand, and final-objective-interest, on the other. The initial-interest-claim of a locality or group can be and often is opposed to the initial-interest-claim of the nation. But the nation also has an interest in the welfare of its parts and members, and they have an interest in its welfare. So, in theory, for each case there should exist an ideal final-objective-interest settlement (whether or not we can find it or agree on it), giving just the right weight to all considerations. A minor benefit to the whole nation purchased at the price of severe hardship to a part may not be justified. A minor benefit to a part purchased at the price of serious damage to the nation probably is not justified. About final-objective-interest one could say that the interest of the parts adds up to the interest of the whole, but such an optimistic formula must not be allowed to obscure the obvious conflicts in initial-interest-claim. Politics entails the reconciliation of conflicting claims, each usually with some justice on its side; the harmony of final-objective-interests must be *created*.[6]

The national unity that gives localities an interest in the welfare of the whole is not merely presupposed by representation; it is also continually re-created by the representatives' activities. As Charles E. Merriam has put it, "The generality of special interests must be woven into a picture" that is the national good.[7] There may be institutional systems in which this task is not performed by a representative body, where representatives plead their districts' cause before a monarch or other executive or national judge, who makes the final decisions. But this is not the typical situation in modern representative government.

The representative is, typically, both special pleader and judge, an agent of his locality as well as a governor of the nation. His duty is to pursue both local and national interest, the one because he is a representative, the other because his job as representative is governing the nation. The dual task is difficult, but it is neither practically nor theoretically impossible.

But there are other political realities to be considered, in addition to the problem of the national interest. The constituent, the voter who is to be represented, is not, of course, the rational, informed, interested, politically active citizen our formula seems to require.[8] Most people are apathetic about politics, and many do not bother to vote at all. Of those who do vote, the majority vote on the basis of a traditional party loyalty; sometimes personal characteristics of the candidate also play a role. But generally both personal characteristics and policy commitments are used to justify a pre-formed preference rather than as the basis for making a choice. The voters tend to ascribe to the candidate whatever policy they favor; few of them know anything about the Congressman's voting record. Decisions seem to be motivated mainly through contact with primary groups; people vote as their family, friends, and associates do. Thus voting decisions depend largely on habit, sentiment, and disposition rather than on rational, informed consideration of the candidate's or the party's stand on issues.

It would seem farfetched to imagine such voters in rational dialogue with their representative: "Why did you vote this way when we asked you to vote the opposite way?" "Ah, but

I know certain facts of which you are ignorant, had you considered that . . .?" "Well, yes, that does change matters. . . ." Surely nothing could be farther from what actually goes on in an election.

Similar problems exist when we turn to the representative and the realities of legislative behavior. Does the representative frequently consult his constituents' wishes, or, if not, does he apply his expert knowledge to a dispassionate, rational evaluation of what is best for them and the nation? Again, if these are one's assumptions, the facts would seem very disillusioning. For the legislator's position is far more complex than such a model would suggest. The modern representative acts within an elaborate network of pressures, demands, and obligations; and there is considerable disagreement among legislators about the proper way to perform their role.[9]

In the first place, the political representative has a constituency and constituents, not a principal. He is chosen by a great number of people; and, while it may be difficult to determine the interests or wishes of a single individual, it is infinitely more difficult to do so for a constituency of thousands. On many issues a constituency may not have any interest, or its members may have several conflicting interests.[10] And the representative knows of the voters' ignorance and apathy and irrationality, the diversity of their views and interests. Further, he seldom has access to accurate information about what views and interests they do have.[11]

In the second place, he is a professional politician in a framework of political institutions,[12] a member of a political party who wants to get reëlected, and a member of legislature along with other representatives. He must be sensitive to his political party (both local and national) and to various public and private groups and interests. As a member of the legislature, he occupies an office to which certain obligations and expectations are attached.[13] He must comply with its traditions and work within the framework of the rules and mores of the legislative body. He must get along with his colleagues, especially certain important ones among them.[14] To act effectively he must keep in mind not only the formal and informal rules of his legislative body but also its place in the whole structure of government.

In the third place, he will also have views and opinions, at least on some issues. He will feel that some measures are intrinsically unsound, immoral, or undesirable. At the same time, his opinions may, in turn, be shaped by those around him and his sources of information. His own opinion on a measure may be shaped by party leaders or other colleagues, by friends or effective lobbyists, or even by the mail. He himself may not be a reliable source of information as to just what shapes his opinion on some issue or even what determines his vote.[15] And issues do not come before him in isolation; issues are interrelated, and he may wish to compromise on some in order to gain on others.[16] A particular measure may have many parts, to which he responds in varying ways.[17] He also may see measures as having a significance beyond their immediate content, for example as part of an over-all party program.[18]

Thus in legislative behavior a great complexity and plurality of determinants are at work, any number of which may enter into a legislative decision. The legislator represents neither by a simple response to constituency desires nor by detached, Olympian judgment on the merits of a proposal. None of the analogies of acting for others on the individual level seems satisfactory for explaining the relationship between a political representative and his constituents. He is neither agent nor trustee nor deputy nor commissioner; he acts for a group of people without a single interest, most of whom seem incapable of forming an explicit will on political questions.

Must we then abandon the idea of political representation in its most common sense of "acting for"? This possibility has sometimes been suggested; perhaps representation in politics is only a fiction, a myth forming part of the folklore of our society. Or perhaps representation must be redefined to fit our politics; perhaps we must simply accept the fact that what we have been calling representative government is in reality just party competition for office. Yet, to "redefine" representation to equate it with the empirical reality of representative government, even if that reality displays no elements of what we would ordinarily call representation, seems pointless and misleading.

But perhaps it is a mistake to approach political representation too directly from the various individual-representation analogies— agent and trustee and deputy. Perhaps that approach, like descriptive or symbolic representation, leads us to expect or demand features in the representative relationship which are not there and need not be there. Perhaps when we conventionally speak of political representation, representative government, and the like, we do not mean or require that the representative stand in the kind of one-to-one, person-to-person relationship to his constituency or to each constituent in which a private representative stands to his principal.[19] Perhaps when we call a governmental body or system "representative," we are saying something broader and more general about the way in which it operates as an institutionalized arrangement. And perhaps even the representing done by an individual legislator must be seen in such a context, as embodied in a whole political system.

Political representation is primarily a public, institutionalized arrangement involving many people and groups, and operating in the complex ways of large-scale social arrangements. What makes it representation is not any single action by any one participant, but the over-all structure and functioning of the system, the patterns emerging from the multiple activities of many people. It is representation if the people (or a constituency) are present in governmental action, even though they do not literally act for themselves. Insofar as this is a matter of substantive acting for others, it requires independent action in the interest of the governed, in a manner at least potentially responsive to them, yet not normally in conflict with their wishes. And perhaps that can make sense and is possible even in politics, if we understand how and where to look for it.

Even if the representative does not examine his conscience as to the national interest on every issue, he may still be following a course of action designed to promote that interest. He may be playing his complicated role in the institutionalized political system in such a way that it strikes us as—that it *is*—representing. The mere fact that he is functioning within a representative system is, of course, no guarantee that he is truly representing; but it allows for more complex and long-range ways of representing than are possible for an isolated individual agent.

Similarly, although the political representative may ignore or even override constituency opinion, he may offer justifications, rationales, for doing so, in much the way that a substantive representative must be prepared to do. If we ask an American legislator whether he acts independently of constituents' wishes, and why, he is likely to answer in terms of his knowledge and their ignorance and true interest.

The majority of my constituents occasionally lack knowledge of relevant facts and circumstances. For me not to take this into account would be a violation of my oath of office as a legislator, not to mention my obligation to my own conscience, judgment and sense of duty.

I knew full well and without the slightest question that had the five thousand people who had written me been in the possession of the knowledge which was mine, at least a majority of them would have taken [my] position.

Much sentiment is manufactured and the result of gross misinformation.

. . . he replied that he knew but one way to ascertain the public opinion of Connecticut; that was to ascertain what was right. When he found that out, he was quite sure that it would meet the approval of Connecticut.

. . . they do not really understand the matter.

. . . they don't even know what a tariff is. . . . Of course they don't know what they're talking about.

I understand the problems of that area. I know what is best for the farm section. . . . I vote my convictions and hope that the constituents will follow these. They expect this—unless a real organized group is excited about something. They generally expect that you have more information than they do. . . . I try to follow my constituents—to ignore them would be a breach of trust—but I use my judgment often because they are misinformed. I know that they would vote as I do if they had the facts that I have. . . . I figure if they knew what I know . . . they would understand my vote.[20]

These statements are not evidence but illustration. Indeed, they could not serve as evidence, for legislators make any number of statements about why they vote as they do, and none of them need be accurate. But the statements suggest that the view of representing as substantive activity may not, after all, be too abstract and idealized for application to real political life.

It may even make sense to speak of the people—the ignorant, apathetic, nonpolitical citizens—as being capable of collective action

and judgment, as having, on occasion, a will or an opinion with which to confront their representative. But we must not succumb to an overly simplified picture of public opinion and popular will. Political scientists have long known that "voting is essentially a group experience."[21] We vote, indeed we perceive political reality, through the people with whom we are in contact. Most of us are reached by the mass media only in a two-step process, by way of other people's perceptions of and reactions to them. There can be a good deal of latent opinion in the behavior of individuals who may not be able to articulate their opinions at all. As one recent study has put it:

> The relation of Congressman to voter is not a simple bilateral one but is complicated by the presence of all manner of intermediaries: the local party, economic interests, the news media, racial and national organizations, and so forth. . . . Very often the Representative reaches the mass public through these mediating agencies, and the information about himself and his record may be considerably transformed as it diffuses out to the electorate in two or more stages. As a result, the public—or parts of it—may get simple positive or negative cues about the Congressman which were provoked by legislative action *but which no longer have a recognizable issue content.*[22]

The readiness of citizen A to vote for a certain candidate, derived from a causal conversation with B, who got it from overhearing C discuss an article in publication D—this readiness is, in a sense, a part of public opinion, even though A may not be able to muster a single reason for his vote, and may not care about the immediate issues. Perhaps it is to this kind of public opinion that the representative must be responsive, and can be responsible.

I am not suggesting an organic group mind. What the public does or thinks must (in theory) be translatable into the behavior or attitudes of individuals. I am only suggesting that his translation is not simple or obvious. The voting behavior of people in a representative democracy can respond to issues and policies, even if many individual voters do not respond directly to them. The process may be complex, involving an interaction among organizations, news media, and personal relationships. Even if most people vote in an irrational and uninformed response to primary group pressures, this does not preclude the system as a whole from displaying a degree of "rational" response.

All this is only meant to sketch a framework on which one could maintain what seems to me in fact the case: that political representation is, in fact, representation, particularly in the sense of "acting for," and that this must be understood at the public level. The representative system must look after the public interest and be responsive to public opinion, except insofar as non-responsiveness can be justified in terms of the public interest. At both ends, the process is public and institutional. The individual legislator does not act alone, but as a member of a representative body. Hence his pursuit of the public interest and response to public opinion need not always be conscious and deliberate, any more than the individual voter's role. Representation may emerge from a political system in which many individuals, both voters and legislators, are pursuing quite other goals. I am not suggesting that it must emerge from any particular system; there is no guarantee that it will. But it may emerge, and to the extent that it does we consider that system as being a representative government.

We must be cautious, also, about the absence of rational pursuit of the public interest by individuals. I do not wish to suggest that it is totally expendable, for I doubt whether any institutional framework could produce representation without conscious, rational, creative effort by some individuals. But there is latitude

in a political system for apathy, ignorance, and self-seeking. That the social institution can produce a "rationality" most individual members seem to lack is easier to believe at the level of the voter than at the level of the legislator. And this may well be because a higher degree of individual rationality, of conscious representing and pursuit of the public interest is required in the legislative system than in the public. Undoubtedly, creative leadership is needed in any political system, and such leadership does not just happen. But when we speak of political representation, we are almost always speaking of individuals acting in an institutionalized representative system, and it is against the background of that system as a whole that their actions constitute representation, if they do. . . .

But these many persons and institutions do not all represent in the same sense or in the same way. Political representation is as wide and varied in range as representation itself will allow. The most that we can hope to do when confronted by such multiplicity is to be clear on what view of representation a particular writer is using, and whether that view, its assumptions and implications, really fit the case to which he is trying to apply them. Consider one of the most significant expressions in the realm of political representation—"representative government." There are many ways in which a government may be said to represent, but not all of them correspond to the idea of a representative government. Any number of theorists have gone wrong in this respect, noticing only one sense in which a government may be said to represent, and immediately concluding that must be what "representative government" really means.

It is sometimes argued, particularly by authorization theorists, that every government represents its subjects in the sense that it has authority over them and makes laws for them.[23] Governments do have that authority;

the authority to make laws seems part of the very meaning of government. Yet authority is not coextensive with representation; one need not represent in order to have authority to issue orders. But a government also acts in the name of its subjects. Thus a slightly modified position would be that all governments represent in the formalistic sense that their actions not only bind their subjects but are attributed *to* these subjects.[24] The government acts, and we say that the nation has acted. Yet this kind of representing will not enable us to distinguish representative government from other forms; it would make "representative government" a redundancy.

Other theorists supplement the de jure authority of a government to act in the name of its subjects as a nation, with its de facto capacity to win support and obedience from them.[25] They may then argue that a government represents only to the extent that its decrees are obeyed and it is accepted by its subjects. This doctrine is close to the views of De Grazia and Gosnell, that representing is a matter of pleasing the represented. A representative government could be distinguished from other forms, under such a notion, by the high degree of obedience or consent or support it received from its subjects. And, as with De Grazia and Gosnell, the way in which that consent or support is engineered and achieved seems totally irrelevant: one may adjust the ruler to the ruled, but one may equally adjust the ruled to what he wants of them. Representative governments defined by the degree of their popularity need not have elections or other democratic institutions.

> The will on which a government rests may be democratic, even if oligarchic or plutocratic influences are powerful in creating it. It is quite possible that an interested minority may so control the avenues of information and suggestion that a majority will suffer persuasion contrary to their own interests. The decision of a leader may induce millions to support measures which they would have opposed if his prestige had been thrown to the other side.[26]

And all this seems perfectly compatible with representation and representative government.

Finally, some writers argue that a government is representative to the extent that it pursues the interest of its subjects and looks after their welfare, as distinct from merely being popular with them. "All government is somewhat representative," a writer tells us, "insofar as it identifies itself with the people's interests. . . ."[27] A representative government might, however, be distinguished, under such an approach, as one that pursues its subjects' interests to a very high degree.

But none of these senses in which one can say that (some) governments represent is what we mean when we speak of representative government. Whether governments have legitimate authority to bind their subjects, whether the subjects are obligated to obey, are largely philosopher's questions. For the ordinary layman or politician they simply are not problematical; laws are the kinds of things that ordinarily oblige and bind, just as promises are the kinds of things that one keeps. For anyone other than a speculative political philosopher, the right of government to bind its subjects is problematic only at times of resistance or revolution. Would-be revolutionaries might attempt to justify themselves by arguing that the government no longer represents them. And the international lawyer may have to decide which government is the legitimate spokesman for a nation, which in turn may depend on what government has effective control. Thus we may inquire whether the Peking government or that on Formosa properly represents China, or which government's delegation should represent the Congo in the United Nations.

There are occasions, also, when we become concerned with the "responsibility" of subjects for the actions of their government, meaning something different from the obligation to obey its laws. At the end of the Second World War and during the Nuremberg trials there was much speculation about the war guilt of the German people. Were they guilty of the atrocities committed in their name by the Hitler government? The kinds of arguments considered relevant here are undoubtedly familiar: How much popular support did Hitler have? How much resistance was there to him within Germany? How much did people know about what was being done? Did they approve of what they knew? But these questions are not coextensive with whether Nazi Germany was a representative government. We may agree that it was not. At most, the kind of information we want could be approximated by asking whether the German people would have supported a representative government that followed the same policies. Many people might argue the responsibility of the German people even though the Nazi government was not representative. We might agree, however, that in the case of a representative government the responsibility would be more clear-cut.[28]

But these are not at all the kinds of arguments we would normally consider relevant to deciding whether a particular government is or is not representative. By representative governments we mean to designate certain governments but not others. The United States, Great Britain, and Switzerland are usually regarded as representative governments. Dictatorships, true monarchies, and imposed colonial administrations are not usually so regarded. But is the Soviet Union a representative government? Is the Union of South Africa? Is Ghana? Is the United States, "really"? We know, at least in a general way, what the relevant arguments on such questions

are. They probably begin with whether or not the rulers are elected. But they soon range beyond this. We want to know how genuine the elections are, who has the right to vote, whether the elected officials have the real governmental power, and how much opposition is permitted.

Note, first, what subjects these questions do not cover. To decide whether a government is representative, we do not ask whether it has the authority to make binding laws in the name of its citizens. Every legitimate government has this authority. Nor do we ask how effective this authority is; a country does not necessarily have a representative government because its crime rate is low and disobedience is infrequent. Could we show that a government is representative by demonstrating that its policies are beneficient and promote the welfare of its subjects? This criterion, at least, seems more tempting. But the actions of a benevolent dictatorship might be directed toward the welfare of the populace, and make no concessions to anything resembling democratic participation. Surely this would not be a representative government. We do expect a representative government to promote the popular welfare, and perhaps think it unlikely that other governments will do so. But the fact that a government looks after the interests of its subjects is at most a piece of evidence, a necessary but not a sufficient criterion for calling it representative.

How about a government which keeps its subjects happy, whose policies are widely accepted by them? Could we show that a government is representative by demonstrating its popularity among its subjects? Here I think the temptation is very great to say yes, but we must be cautious. Could we not imagine cases to the contrary? Suppose that a drowsy tropical island (before the Second World War, we had better say) is delightfully administered by a benevolent despot from the colonial office.

The natives love him. But surely this is not a representative government. Or again, a dictator may perfect a new tranquilizing drug, and feed "happy-pills" to all his subjects so that they approve wholeheartedly of whatever he does. Surely not a representative government. Again, the contentment of the subjects is not sufficient to define representation.

Just as it is not enough to say that the individual representative who pleases his constituents represents them, so, at the level of government, it will not do to define representation by the acquiescence of the subjects. People may at time support a hereditary monarch; they may have nothing but good to say about a dictator (the critical members of the population having been removed). A dictatorship may have "active and preponderant" consent, but that does not make it a representative government.

> If support for the regime is manufactured by way of a monopoly of control over the media of mass communication, supplemented by severe coercion against oppositional elements. . . . If a political regime relies heavily on a highly organized propaganda monopoly, . . . and ruthlessly suppresses all political dissent, one must conclude that no amount of evidence of public support to the regime can prove that the people's genuine interests are not being exploited in the interest of the ruling few.[29]

By the same token, no amount of public support can then prove that the government is a representative one. When a ruler manipulates an inert mass of followers to accord with his will, we hesitate to say that he represents them. In the same way, if an interest group engages in a vast propaganda campaign to persuade the public in favor of some measure, we do not regard this activity as representation of the public.

It seems to me that we show a government to be representative not by demonstrating its control over its subjects but just the reverse, by demonstrating that its subjects have control over what it does. Every government's actions are attributed to its subjects formally, legally. But in a representative government this attribution has substantive content: the people really do act through their government, and are not merely passive recipients of its actions. A representative government must not merely be in control, not merely promote the public interest, but must also be responsive to the people. The notion is closely related to the view of representing as a substantive activity. For in a representative government the governed must be capable of action and judgment, capable of initiating government activity, so that the government may be conceived as responding to them. As in nonpolitical representation, the principal need not express his wishes, or even have formulated any, but he must be capable of doing so; when he does, his wishes should be fulfilled unless there is good reason (in terms of his interest) to the contrary. Correspondingly, a representative government requires that there be machinery for the expression of the wishes of the represented, and that the government respond to these wishes unless there are good reasons to the contrary. There need not be a constant activity of responding, but there must be a constant condition of responsiveness, of potential readiness to respond. It is not that a government represents only when it is acting in response to an express popular wish; a representative government is one which is responsive to popular wishes when there are some. Hence there must be institutional arrangements for responsiveness to these wishes. Again, it is incompatible with the idea of representation for the government to frustrate or resist the people's will without good reason, to frustrate or resist it systematically or over a long period of time. We can conceive of the people as "acting through" the government even if most of the time they are unaware of what it is doing, so long as we feel that they could initiate action if they so desired.[30]

Because this kind of political representation requires only potential responsiveness, access to power rather than its actual exercise, it is perfectly compatible with leadership and with action to meet new or emergency situations. It is incompatible, on the other hand, with manipulation or coercion of the public. To be sure, the line between leadership and manipulation is a tenuous one, and may be difficult to draw. But there undoubtedly *is* a difference, and this difference makes leadership compatible with representation while manipulation is not.[31] This is because leadership is, in a sense, at the mercy of the led. It succeeds only so long as they are willing to follow. Thus it is not incompatible with our requirement that the represented be able to get their way when they have an explicit will. Manipulation by a ruler, on the other hand, is imposed on the ruled, and threatens their capacity to reject a policy or initiate a new one. A person can be led and yet go of his own free will; something that is manipulated does not move itself. An inanimate object can be manipulated, but it cannot be led. Again, these are not just verbal games, but the right terms for naming a distinction in reality: the difference between democratic and dictatorial relationships between ruler and ruled. Only if it seems right to attribute governmental action to the people in the substantive sense do we speak of representative government.[32]

But all this makes the notion of representative government seem far more impressionistic, intuitive, and temporary than it really is when we use it. Judging a government to be representative is not merely a matter of a sort of over-all esthetic impression one has formed; though there may be difficult borderline cases, not all cases are borderline. Nor does this kind of representativeness fade in and out periodi-

cally. We do not say that a government is representative today, because it happens to be responding to popular wishes, and stops being representative the next day because it is frustrating them. Representative government is not defined by particular actions at a particular moment, but by long-term systematic arrangements—by institutions and the way in which they function. No particular act of compliance with popular demands is proof of a representative government, although a few serious cases of the frustration of legitimate popular demands will serve as counterevidence. John Plamenatz points out that a dictator might choose to do what his subjects want and nevertheless not be a representative. Only if he institutionalizes this decision, so that there is not merely occasional response when he pleases, but regular, systematic responsiveness, does he become a representative. And we tend to feel that this is impossible without elections. Our concern with election and electoral machinery, and particularly with whether elections are free and genuine, results from our conviction that such machinery is necessary to ensure systematic responsiveness. Our concern with the popularity of a regime is an attempt to find an operational measure for potential responsiveness. The fact that the people have no unfulfilled demands is an indication that they can get their demands fulfilled whenever they wish, but it is not conclusive proof. This is why a manipulated or coerced acquiescence does not satisfy us.

And here the formalistic accountability view, the descriptive view, and perhaps others as well become relevant to representative government. For only certain kinds of institutional arrangements will satisfy our requirements. An absolute monarch or dictator who chooses, for a reason of his own, to take public opinion polls and do whatever the people seem to want is not yet a representative government. We require functioning institutions that are designed to, and really do, secure a government responsive to public interest and opinion. Such a government may have a president, it may be headed by a prime minister, or it may be an assembly government. It may have geographic constituencies, proportional representation, or some other system of apportionment. It may have no political parties, weak ones, strong ones, many or few. All these forms may be representative governments; some are more successful than others.

For this purpose, our basic prerequisites seem very few. We would be reluctant to consider any system of representative government unless it held regular elections, which were "genuine" or "free."[33] We would be reluctant, further, to consider a government representative unless it included some sort of collegiate representative body in a more than advisory capacity.[34] We would not readily accept a system as representative in which the entire government was in the hands of a single ruler, even if he was subject to reëlection at regular intervals. Perhaps it is merely historical tradition that there should be a collegiate body composed of representatives of the various "parts" of the society. Perhaps it has to do with the persistent element of isomorphism or one-to-one correspondence in descriptive representation. Or perhaps it is simply that we cannot conceive that a political system could be truly responsive unless a number of minority or opposition viewpoints are officially active in its government. . . .

No institutional system can guarantee the essence, the substance of representation. Nor should we be too optimistic about the capacity of institutions to produce the desired conduct; even the best of representative institutions cannot be expected to produce representation magically, mechanically, without or even in spite of the beliefs, attitudes, and intentions of the people operating the system.[35] Madison's dictum that "the interest of the man must be connected with the constitutional rights of the place" has merit, but there is merit also in Tussman's, that in his capacity as citizen a man must "be concerned with the public interest, not with his private goods," that he "is asked public, not private questions: 'Do we need more public schools?' not 'Would I like to pay more taxes?'"[36] For this reason, too, we need to retain the ideal of the substance of representation in addition to our institutionalization of it. Without reference to such an ideal, how could we teach those intended to operate the institutions what we require of them? How else, indeed, could we remember it ourselves?[37]

Without institutionalization, as Martin Drath has pointed out, the ideal of representation would remain an empty dream, or at most would occasionally recur as a fitful, inexplicable blessing, which we have no power to produce or to prolong.[38] The historically developed institutional forms, the culturally ingrained standards of conduct are what flesh out the abstract ideal, give it practical import and effective meaning.[39] Thus the development and improvement of representative institutions, the cultivation of persons capable of looking after the interests of others in a responsive manner, are essential if the fine vision that constitutes the idea of representation is to have any effect on our actual lives. At the same time, we can never allow institutions, habits of conduct, the behavior of representatives, to become our standard and ideal. Whether the governments we conventionally call "representative" involve genuine representation always remains open to question. Whether what we designate as representation in the world really is (what we mean by) representation will always depend on the way in which its structure and functioning work out in practice.[40]

The requisite institutions have been different at different times in history.[41] But men have always striven for institutions that will really produce what the ideal requires; and institutions or individuals claiming to represent have always been vulnerable to the charge that they do not really represent. Application of the label "representative" seems to invite a critical appraisal: Is this a fiction, an empty formula, or is it really the substance of representation? Thus it has been argued "that representative government is the ideally best form of government for the very reason that it will not actually be representative in its character unless it is properly organized and conditioned. By its essential nature it is a system of trusteeship. . . . Institutions claiming to be representative can justify their character as such only to the extent that they establish and maintain such trusteeship."[42]

The concept of representation thus is a continuing tension between ideal and achievement. This tension should lead us neither to abandon the ideal, retreating to an operational definition that accepts whatever those usually designated as representatives do; nor to abandon its institutionalization and withdraw from political reality. Rather, it should present a continuing but not hopeless challenge: to construct institutions and train individuals in such a way that they engage in the pursuit of the public interest, the genuine representation of the public; and, at the same time, to remain critical of those institutions and that training, so that they are always open to further interpretation and reform.

Notes

1. Thus American Congressmen sometimes defend their attention to local needs by saying that the national interest is properly the concern of the Senate and the President. "What snarls up the system is these so-called statesmen—Congressmen who vote for what they think is the country's interest . . . let the Senators do that . . . they're paid to be statesmen; we aren't," says a Congressman cited in L.A. Dexter, "The Representative and His District," *Human Organization* XVI (Spring 1957)," 3. Cf. Gerhard Leibholz, *Das Vesen der Repräsentation* (Berlin: Walter de Gruyter, 1929), 188.

2. Constitutions of Germany, Portugal, Belgium, and Italy, cited in Robert Luce, *Legislative Principles* (Boston: Houghton Mifflin Co., 1930), 446-7; cf. Carl Schmitt, *The Necessity of Politics* (London: Sheed and Ward, 1931), 69. Martin Drath points out that such clauses did not originate as moralistic admonitions to the representative, but had a real and practical political significance. *Die Entwicklung der Volksrepräsentation* (Bad Homburg: Gehlen, 1954), 7-10.

3. Siéyès went so far as to argue that even the locally elected representative is really elected by the whole nation, and hence represents it. His speech in the National Assembly of 1789 is cited in Karl Loewenstein, *Volk und Parlament* (Munich: Dreimasken, 1922), 199. Samuel Bailey, *The Rationale of Political Representation* (London: R. Hunter, 1835), 137, argues that representatives should be elected nationally at large, if that were practical.

4. Misunderstanding of this distinction is common in the literature. Thus Luce cites the following passage from a speech by a delegate to the New Hampshire convention of 1902 *as an illustration of the way people prefer local to national interest:* "I had just as soon not be represented at all as to be represented by a man whose interests belong to another town, and who does not help our town." *Legislative Principles*, 506-7.

5. Cited in Dexter, "The Representative," 3.

6. Drath, *Volksrepräsentation*, 14; see also Sheldon S. Wolin, *Politics and Vision* (Boston: Little, Brown and Co., 1960), 63-6.

7. *Systematic Politics* (Chicago: University of Chicago Press, 1945), 140; also 145; Leibholz, *Das Wesen der Repräsentation*, 47-58; Rudolf Smend, *Verfassung und Verfassungsrecht* (Munich: Duncker and Humblot, 1928), 39-40.

8. On voting behavior see Joseph A. Schumpeter, *Capitalism, Socialism and Democracy* (New York: Harpers, 1947), 261, and these empirical studies: Paul F. Lazarsfeld, et al. *The People's Choice* (New York: Columbia University Press, 1948); Bernard R. Berelson, et al., *Voting* (Chicago: University of Chicago Press, 1954); Angus Campbell, et al., *The Voter Decides* (White Plains, NY: Row, Peterson and Co., 1954); Eugene Burdick and Arthur J. Brodbeck, eds., American Voting Behavior (Glencoe, Ill.: Free Press, 1959); Angus Campbell, et al., *The American Voter* (New York: John Wiley and Sons, 1960).

9. Dexter, "The Representative," 3; John C. Wahlke and Heinz Eulau, eds., *Legislative Behavior* (Glencoe, Ill.: Free Press, 1959), 298-304; John C. Wahlke, et al., "American State Legislators' Role Orientation," *Journal of Politics* XXII (May 1960): 203-27; H. Eulau, et al., "The Role of the Representative," *American Political Science Review* LIII (September 1959): 742-56; Charles O. Jones, "Representation in Congress," *American Political Science Review* LV (December 1961): 358-67.

10. Sabine, "What Is the Matter?" in A.N. Christensen and E.M. Kirkpatrick, eds., *The People, Politics and the Politician* (New York: Henry Holt and Co., 1941); G.D.H. Cole, *Social Theory* (London: Methuen, 1920), 103-16; Dexter, "The Representative," 4-5; Howard Lee McBain, *The Living Constitution* (New York: The Macmillan Co., 1948), 233; Eulau, et al. "The Role of the Representative," 747, 751; Schumpeter, *Capitalism, Socialism and Democracy*, 261; Jones, "Representation in Congress," 358-9, 365.

11. Dexter, "The Representative"; and "What Do Congressmen Hear: The Mail," *Public Opinion Quarterly* XX (Spring 1956): 16-27; H. Eulau et at., "The Role of the Representative," 749; Frank Bonilla, "When Is Petition 'Pressure'?" *Public Opinion Quarterly* XX (Spring 1956): 39-48; David B. Truman, *The Governmental Process* (New York; Alfred A. Knopf, Inc., 1959), Ch. 11; Jones, "Representation in Congress," 366-7.

12. Henry B. Mayo, *An Introduction to Democratic Theory* (New York: Oxford University Press, 1960), 102; Wahlke and Eulau, eds., *Legislative Behavior*, 117; Jones, "Representation in Congress," 359.

13. Robert M. MacIver, *The Modern State*. (Oxford: Clarendon, 1926), 196; Joseph Tussman, *Obligation and the Body Politic* (New York: Oxford University Press, 1960), 69, 75; Wahlke, et al., "American State Legislators' Role Orientation"; Wahlke and Eulau, eds., *Legislative Behavior*, 179-89, 284-93.

14. Dexter, "The Representative"; Wahlke and Eulau, *Legislative Behavior*, 204-17.

15. L.E. Gleeck, "96 Congressmen Make Up Their Minds," *Public Opinion Quarterly* IV (March 1940), 7; J. Turner, *Party and Constituency* (Baltimore: John Hopkins University Press, 1951), 12; Dexter, "The Representative"; Truman, *The Governmental Process*, Ch. 11.

16. Dexter, "The Representative," 5.

17. Jones, "Representation in Congress," 363-4.

18. Wahlke and Eulau, eds., *Legislative Behavior*, 298-304.

19. "Obviously important changes take place which make the substitute assembly far different from the direct meeting of the people." Alfred De Grazia, *Public and Republic* (New York: Alfred A. Knopf, Inc., 1951), 126.

"When one person represents a group, and still more when a number of persons represent different groups, the problem becomes much more complicated." John A. Fairlie, "The Nature of Political Representation," *American Political Science Review* XXXIV (June 1940): 466.

"My conclusion from this discussion is that the concepts connected with representation of individual persons by individual persons have no simple application to representative government." A. Phillips Griffiths and Richard

Wollheim, "How Can One Person Represent Another?" Aristotelian Society, Suppl. Vol. XXXIV (1960), 207.

See also Peter Laslett, "The Face to Face Society," *Philosophy, Politics, and Society,* ed. Peter Laslett (New York: The Macmillan Co., 1956).

20. The first three passages were elicited from New York State legislators by George W. Hartman, "Judgments of State Legislators Concerning Public Opinion," *Journal of Social Psychology* XXI (February 1945), 111; the fourth passage is from the autobiography of Senator George F. Hoar, 112-13, cited in Luce, *Legislative Principles,* 496; the fifth passage is a statement by a United States Congressman interviewed by Dexter, "The Representative," 3; the sixth is by a Congressman interviewed by Bonilla, "When Is Petition 'Pressure'?", 46-7; the last is a statement by a senior member of the House Agriculture Committee interviewed by Jones, "Representation in Congress," 365.

21. Lazarsfeld, et al., *The People's Choice,* 137. See also Elihu Katz and Paul F. Lazarsfeld, *Personal Influence.* (Glencoe, Ill.: Free Press, 1955); Edward C. Banfield, *Political Influence* (Glencoe, Ill.: Free Press, 1961).

22. Warren E. Miller and Donald E. Stokes, "Constituency Influence in Congress," 55; italics mine.

23. For instance, Karl Loewenstein, *Political Power and the Governmental Process* (Chicago: University of Chicago Press, 1957), 38-9; Eric Voegelin, *The New Science of Politics* (Chicago: University of Chicago Press, 1952) 37.

24. For instance, Georg Jellinek, *Allgemeine Staatslehre* (Berlin: O. Häring, 1905), Ch. 17.

25. For example, James Hogan, *Election and Representation* (n.p.: Cork University Press, 1945), 114; John P. Plamenatz, *Consent, Freedom and Political Obligation* (London: Oxford University Press, 1938), 12; Eulau et al., "The Role of the Representative," 743; Fairlie, "The Nature of Political Representation," 237; Avery Leiserson, *Administrative Regulation* (Chicago: University of Chicago Press, 1942),

3-9; Max Weber, *Wirtschaft und Gesellschaft* (Tübingen: J.C.B. Mohr, 1956), I, 25, 171-6. Gerhard Leibholz is particularly ambivalent between representation as authority and as effective authority: *Das Wesen der Repräsentation,* 140-1, 163-4; and *Strukturprobleme der modernen Demokratie* (Karlsruhe: C.F. Muller, 1958), 10-12.

26. MacIver, *The Modern State,* 197-98.

27. W.D. Handcock, "What Is Represented in Representative Government"? *Philosophy* XXII (July 1947): 107; cf. John Dewey, *The Public and Its Problems* (New York: Henry Holt and Co., 1927), 76.

28. For instance, Plamenatz, *Consent,* 16.

29. Christian Bay, *The Structure of Freedom* (Stanford; Stanford University Press, 1958), 322.

30. For representative government to exist, "the *possibility* for opposition must be considered sufficient." Charles William Cassinelli, Jr., "The Concept of Representative Government" (unpubl. thesis, University of California, Berkeley, 1950), 62.

31. Five criteria for distinguishing a "process of consent" from a "process of manipulation" in political elections are suggested by Morris Janowitz and Dwaine Marvick, "Competitive Pressure and Democratic Consent," *Public Opinion Quarterly* XIX (Winter 1955-56): 381-400. See also their book of the same title (Ann Arbor: University of Michigan Press, 1956) for an application. A useful discussion of the criteria of "free" elections is given in W.J.M. Mackenzie, *Free Elections* (New York: Reinhart, 1958), esp. the introduction and Part IV.

32. One must be cautious about the recent "economic" theories of democracy. Starting with Schumpeter, a number of writers have suggested that democracy may be regarded as a sort of economic marketplace in which votes constitute money, and would-be representatives are competitively trying to sell themselves to the buyers. Schumpeter defines democracy as "that institutional arrangement for arriving

at political decisions in which individuals acquire the power to decide by means of a competitive struggle for the people's vote," *Capitalism, Socialism and Democracy*, 269. Issues thus are not decided by the voters; the voters merely choose the "men who are to do the deciding." Marvick and Janowitz suggest that elections should not be considered as giving a mandate for certain action on issues, but as "a process of selecting and rejecting candidates . . . in competition for public office." "Competitive Pressure," 382.

A full theoretical development of this model has most recently been made by Anthony Downs, for whom, again, "the central purpose of elections in a democracy is to select a government." *An Economic Theory of Democracy* (New York: Harpers, 1957), 24. Policy decisions and ideologies are strictly secondary concepts in these theories. As Downs says, politicians in his model "never seek office as a means of carrying out particular policies; their only goal is to reap the rewards of holding office per se. They treat policies purely as a means to the attainment of their private ends, which they can reach only by being elected. . . . Parties formulate policies in order to win elections, rather than win elections in order to formulate policies." Ibid., 28.

This idea is derived from Schumpeter, who compares the competition of political parties to war; the decision of political issues is like the taking of a strategic position, not an end but a means. "Victory over the opponent" is "the essence of both games," *Capitalism, Socialism and Democracy*, 279. The voters are conceived as being at the mercy of what the parties offer them by way of programs and candidates; "If the alternative is a choice between demagogues, the electorate suffers; if the choice is between statesmen, the electorate gains. The quality of results is not guaranteed by the presence of competition." Janowitz and Marvick, "Competitive Pressure," 382.

A political system defined in this way is not necessarily a representative one, however; if our politics really corresponded to these models we would not call it representation. We

have merely to imagine a situation in which the electorate has a fairly explicit, articulate wish, but none of the political parties is willing to enact it. We can imagine such a situation, for example, in a society strongly divided on class lines, where a few parties, all from a single class, monopolize access to the legislature. Or we can imagine it in a colonial society in which nonwhites are permitted to vote, but only whites may sit in the legislature. In such situations a competitive selection of rulers might repeatedly fail to result in the enactment of a widely desired measure. We would be reluctant to call such a system representative government.

Now in all justice to Downs and Schumpeter one must add that they also wish to exclude such cases. They require that the candidate or parties seeking office engage in free competition, in the economic sense. Schumpeter, *Capitalism, Socialism and Democracy*, 272. (Janowitz and Marvick apparently do not understand Schumpeter's use of the term "free competition," for they argue that competition is no guarantee of good political results. They themselves require effective deliberation on the issues in the electoral campaign, but it is not clear whether they mean this to be a prerequisite for representation or merely for desirable, good representation. See also George Cornwall Lewis, *Remarks on the Use and Abuse of Some Political Terms* (Oxford: James Thornton, 1877), 98-9. Downs makes it clear that in his model new parties must arise whenever the old ones are not offering the people what they want. The concept is thus an analogue to economic free competition, in which the producer must supply what consumers want lest he be put out of business by a more responsive competitor. But such free competition on the political scene seems so farfetched as to raise doubts about the usefulness of the model. A second objection, more to the point of our concerns, is that, whether or not these models give an account of how democracy actually works, they are misleading if applied to the meaning of representation and representative government. The power to select one's rulers may result in representation, but it does not constitute representation (except possibly in the formal sense). What constitutes representation is the very responsiveness on issues which these models relegate to a secondary position. Mere selection of one man for a job by others need not make him their representative.

33. Cassinelli, "The Concept of Representative Government," and "Representative Government" (unpubl. diss., Harvard University, 1953). See also Bay, *The Structure of Freedom*; Mackenzie, *Free Elections*; Janowitz and Marvick, "Competitive Pressure."

34. "Now in this more conventional sense a monarch is not a representative. He is a ruler. The president is not a representative. . . . To catch our representative we have got to look where one group of people, formal or fundamental, has one member in some common body, and other groups have other members." Arthur F. Bentley, *The Process of Government* (Evanston, Ill.: Principia 1949), 450. See also Friedrich Glum, *Der deutsche und der französische Reichswirtschaftsrat* (Berlin: Walter de Gruyter, 1929), 33.

35. For a similar critique of liberalism and constitutionalism, see Wolin, Politics and Vision, esp. ch. 9.

36. *The Federalist*, No. 51, 265; Tussman, *Obligation*, 108.

37. Hans J. Wolff says that representation is neither a "zueinander" nor a "miteinander," but a "für einander," "und zwar nicht nur des Vertreters für die Vertretenen, sondern ebenso entsprechend der Vertretenen für den Vertreter. Darin liegt der tiefe ethische und soziale Gehalt der Vertretung, die grundsätzlich den Eigennutz überwindet und tiefer als im Versprechen und in der Gemeinsamkeit wurzelt in der gegenseitigen Treue." *Organschaft und juristische Person* (Berlin: Carl Heymanns, 1934), 5-6.

38. Drath, *Die Entwicklung der Volksrepäsentation*, 24. Drath reduces the force of his insight by confusing the substance of representation with a De Grazia-Gosnell sort of acceptance-of-the-government-by-the-people or the-people's-identifying-themselves-with-the-government. Ibid., 24-7.

39. This point is nowhere made better than in the writings of Michael Oakeshott, *Rationalism in Politics* (New York: Basic Books, 1962), esp. 118-26. But it is only half of the truth; Oakeshott robs us of the possibility of using an ideal abstracted from our institutions to criticize and change them.

40. Drath, *Die Entwicklung der Volksrepräsentation*, 13; Weber, *Wirtschaft*, II, 675; Merriam, op. cit., 139; Harold D. Lasswell and Abraham Kaplan, *Power and Society* (New Haven: Yale University Press, 1950), 165; Glum, *Der deutsche und der französische Reichswirtschaftsrat*, 25; Leibholz, *Das Wesen der Repräsentation*, 157-8.

41. Drath, *Die Entwicklung der Volksrepräsentation*, 7, 27-8. For a discussion of the American Revolution in this light, see Leibholz, *Das Wesen der Repräsentation*, 157-8; De Grazia, *Public and Republic*, 14, 22. The same kind of conflict is traced in medieval thought by Georges de Lagarde, "L'Idée de Représentation," International Committee of the Historical Sciences, *Bulletin* IX (December 1937): 426, 435. It is traced during the crucial Civil War period in England by Louise Fargo Brown, "Ideas of Representation from Elizabeth to Charles II," *Journal of Modern History* XI (March 1939): 23-40. [See also Appendix, below; for a more recent instance see Mackenzie, *Free Elections*, 175.]

42. Henry J. Ford, *Representative Government* (New York; Henry Holt and Co., 1924), 145-6. Ford attributes the view to John Stuart Mill.

DISCUSSION QUESTIONS

1. Discuss how the meaning of the concept of political representation has changed over the course of its history in response to political events.

2. Identify the basic quandary that underlies each of the following issues: (a) whether representatives should act as "independent trustees" or as "instructed delegates"; (b) whether their job is to represent primarily the local interests of their constituents or the interests of the nation; and (c) whether "responsible" representation compromises unduly the need to provide "responsive" representation that meets constituents' demands.

3. Can we piece together a full understanding of the meaning of the idea of "political representation" by combining the various partial views of its meaning described by Pitkin? If so, what would it entail?

4. Are Still's criteria of political equality logically compatible? If not, which ones are incompatible, and what causes that incompatibility?

5. What limitations does the adoption of Still's six criteria of political equality place on the kinds of electoral system that can be used if they are to be met?

6. How are the issues addressed in the selections by Still and by Spafford related? What central concerns are common to both accounts?

7. How do Mill's views on majority rule and the nature of representation reflect the spirit of Victorian liberalism and its agenda of electoral reforms?

8. What important implications do Mill's views on representation and the requisites of demo-cratic majority rule hold for those who advocate the doctrine of a "party mandate" or the need for "group representation"?

9. What "role expectations" do Eulau and Karps describe regarding the job of an elected representative, what means are available to ensure that they are met, and what problems of "focus" might arise in trying to meet them?

10. How are the aspects of "responsive representation" discussed by Eulau and Karps related to the various "functions" that Birch views representation as serving within a democratic political system?

11. Birch suggests that his analysis provides a general framework for doing empirical research on representation. Discuss what traditional and new issues regarding representation might be fruitfully studied by using Birch's framework.

12. To what extent does Birch's discussion of the functions representation has in a political system address the concerns Pitkin raises in suggesting that representation is an emergent property of the system of institutionalized arrangements for the collective practice of democratic government in a modern mass society?

13. How does Pitkin's claim that political representation is a collective enterprise involving many people and groups and operating through large-scale social arrangements alter the way we might regard the substance of traditional issues that focus on the relationship between an individual representative and those whom he/she represents?

THE INSTITUTIONAL IMPLEMENTATION OF POLITICAL REPRESENTATION

INTRODUCTION

Harvey E. Pasis

A democracy requires that public policies be "made, on a majority basis, by representatives subject to effective popular control at periodic elections which are conducted on the principle of political equality and under conditions of political freedom."[1] Section Two examines not only the elected representatives of legislatures but also other institutions that perform representative functions. These include the bureaucracy, the judiciary, the federal system, interest groups, and political parties. Criticism of representation in the Canadian regions and in the Northwest Territories is also presented, along with some reform proposals. Sections Three and Four will focus on whether political equality is achieved by designing mechanisms for distributing elective representation and by electoral systems, respectively. Finally, Section Five will centre on whether majority rule is followed in making collective choices. At the end of the book, you should be able to determine to what extent the definition of a democracy applies to Canada.

Representation is at the centre of any examination of liberal democracy, because, as John Courtney has argued, "its importance derives explicitly from the institutions it nurtures and serves and implicitly from the values its shapes and informs."[2] According to democratic theory, representation ought to lead to a representative government, which is "supposed to be an institutionalized arrangement whereby the elected are held accountable for their actions by periodic elections, and the governors are restrained by the collective vigilance of the elected assembly."[3] Electors are part of the legislative system, because legislators are supposed to be responsive to the views of the electorate and initiate policy on its behalf. However, because they must reconcile the views of their own consciences, their constituents, and organized interests, and at the same time vote with the view of their own political party, Canadian legislators find it difficult to be responsive to the views of the electorate.[4] In addition, backbenchers, who are not part of the cabinet, play a very limited role in policy-making in the Canadian federal and provincial parliamentary systems.[5]

Critics who want to increase the role and influence of private members in the formation of public policy have proposed that reforms should be made to the standing committee system, the review of delegated legislation, the procedures and administration of the House of Commons, and that the public should be made more aware of parliamentary institutions.[6] Groups like the Canada West Foundation advocate that changes need to be made not only to the House of Commons but also to the Senate, the cabinet, political parties, and the federal system, to satisfy the demands of Canadian regional representation.[7] However, C.E.S. Franks argues that calls for reforms of this nature are based on inaccurate comparisons of the Canadian parliamentary system with the American congressional one "in terms of representation of power, of decision-making and of balancing collective and special interests."[8] Furthermore, Franks argues that proposals making the Canadian Senate like the American one would reduce the ability of the federal government to stress the quality of programmes, justice, and economic development.

Proponents of descriptive representation argue that Canadian legislators ought to reflect the social characteristics of the population. At the federal level, this is certainly not the case, since Canadian legislators tend to constitute an elite that is not representative of the total population on the basis of age, education, and occupation.[9] Similar concerns have been expressed with regard to other institutions that perform representative functions, such as bureaucracies and the judiciary. Proposals for increasing the representation of French Canadians, aboriginal peoples, ethnic groups, women, the handicapped, and visible minorities, in the bureaucracies and the judiciary have been made, and in some cases implemented.[10]

A notable increase in the number of activities of interest groups, who bypass Parliament and parties to try to influence other political and bureaucratic policy-makers, has occurred recently. According to Khayyam Paltiel, this increase might lead to more participatory democracy, or advantages for established elite groups, or it might be an indication that modern industrial societies are ungovernable because of governmental overload.[11] In addition, if Paltiel and others[12] are correct about the decreased role of political parties in the policy process, the result is a different type of representation in which elective bodies (parties) are replaced or supplemented by non-elective bodies (interest groups).

Representation does not have to be based on a party system in which strict party discipline is followed. One alternative, as Gurston Dacks indicates in this book, is the proposal made by aboriginal peoples of the western Northwest Territories for a form of government based on consociationalism. This proposal requires that divergent social groupings and government institutions be represented sufficiently, so that politics is based on negotiation and consensus rather than conflict. Furthermore, representatives would consult the aboriginal peoples on all important issues, rather than follow party discipline.

According to Allan Kornberg, William Mishler, and Harold Clarke, a government's ability to achieve the ideals of representative democracy ought to be based not only on the evaluation of one representative institution or process but on the evaluation of those institutions and processes that generate and implement policies responsive to the public's needs and demands, including the consequences of federalism, political culture, and citizen political participation, and the role of political parties, interest groups, legislatures, bureaucracies, judiciaries, and the policy process. In their opinion, the provinces have moved toward representative democracy, but are inhibited by institutional factors from effectively representing the policy demands and needs of the public."[13]

In summary, then, a representative government can be implemented through various combinations of institutions and processes.

Notes

1. Henry B. Mayo, *An Introduction to Democratic Theory* (New York: Oxford University Press, 1960), 70. Similar definitions of democracy can be found in J. Roland Pennock, *Democratic Political Theory* (Princeton: Princeton University Press, 1979), 7, and T.C. Pocklington, ed., *Liberal Democracy in Canada and the United States: An Introduction to Politics and Government* (Toronto: Holt, Rinehart and Winston of Canada, Limited, 1985), 26.

2. John C. Courtney, "Parliament and Representation: The Unfinished Agenda of Electoral Redistributions," *Canadian Journal of Political Science* XXI (1988): 675-6.

3. Robert J. Jackson and Michael M. Atkinson, *The Canadian Legislative System: Politicians and Policymaking* 2e (Toronto: The Macmillan Company of Canada, 1980), 155.

4. Ibid.

5. Ibid., 170, and Allan Kornberg, William Mishler, Harold D. Clarke, *Representative Democracy in the Canadian Provinces* (Scarborough, Ontario; Prentice-Hall Canada Inc., 1982), 268.

6. James A. McGrath, *Report of the Special Committee on Reform of the House of Commons* (Ottawa: Queen's Printer for Canada, 1985), 61-9.

7. Peter McCormick, Ernest C. Manning, and Gordon Gibson, *Regional Representation: The Canadian Partnership* (Calgary: Canada West Foundation, 1981), 23-37.

8. C.E.S. Franks, *The Parliament of Canada* (Toronto: University of Toronto Press, 1987), 267-8.

9. Jackson and Atkinson, *The Canadian Legislative System*, 156-7.

10. For further discussion, see Kenneth Kernaghan and David Siegel, *Public Administration in Canada: A Test* (Toronto: Methuen, 1987), 445-51 and 482-90; and Peter H. Russell, *The Judiciary in Canada: The Third Branch of Government* (Toronto: McGraw-Hill Ryerson Limited, 1987), 164.

11. Khayyam Z. Paltiel, "The Changing Environment and Role of Special Interest Groups," *Canadian Public Administration* 25 (1982): 19 .

12. Ibid., 209.

13. Allan Kornberg, William Mishler, Harold D. Clarke, *Representative Democracy in the Canadian Provinces* (Scarborough, Ontario: Prentice-Hall Canada Inc., 1982), 268.

6. REGIONAL REPRESENTATION IN CANADA

*Peter McCormick, Ernest C. Manning
and Gordon Gibson*

It is obvious that regionalism has always been a factor in Canadian politics, and that in the past a variety of ways, both formal and informal, have evolved to accommodate it. Before we can justify the need for constitutional innovation in the pursuit of more effective regional representation, it will be necessary to consider each one of these devices in turn, and to suggest why they are no longer adequate.

1. THE HOUSE OF COMMONS

The fundamental principle of representation in the Canadian House of Commons, as in the national legislatures of all democratic countries, is "representation by population"—the representation that is given to any one part of the country is directly proportional to its share of the total population. The most immediate practical implication of liberal democracy, the political equality of "one person, one vote," is realized in the Commons.

The implication of this principle is that minorities, especially regional minorities, will tend to receive representation in the national legislature roughly proportionate to their share of the total population. Indeed, regional

minorities are assisted by a representational system in two ways, neither of which is insignificant. First, because the unit of representation is a geographically-delimited constituency, minorities that are concentrated in certain regions of the country fare much better than minorities of similar size that are dispersed over wider territories. Second, every federal country, and some non-federal countries, places some qualifiers on the principle of "representation by population" in order to enhance the representation of less populated areas.

In a very real sense, then, the House of Commons does represent the regions of Canada. It contains members of Parliament, directly elected within those regions, and directly accountable to the people of the region. It was suggested by Sir John A. Macdonald, and more recently (and surprisingly) echoed by Pierre Trudeau, that this representation in the Commons is sufficient to accord recognition to the regional differences and interests that are so pronounced in Canada.

That the regions are represented in the House of Commons is incontrovertible; that this representation is adequate to secure the necessary sensitivity to and recognition of regional particularities is more open to question. Several factors contribute to the inadequacy of such a suggestion:

i. The extent to which representation by population has been qualified by measures designed to over-represent regions of smaller

Peter McCormick, Ernest C. Manning, Gordon Gibson, *Regional Representation: The Canadian Partnership* (Calgary: Canada West Foundation, 1981), 23-37. Reprinted by permission of the publisher.

population has always been extremely moderate. These measures, so far as we are aware, are limited to the following:

a. At the time of their entry into Confederation, both Manitoba and British Columbia were given highly exaggerated estimates for their populations, with a corresponding increase in their representation in the House of Commons at least initially. It is generally thought that these inflated estimates were related more to the level of direct federal subsidies than to electoral representation.

b. The two northern territories have each been given representation in the House of Commons although their individual populations do not yet approach the normal "quota" for seats in the House; more recently, the Northwest Territories has been awarded a second seat based upon geographic rather than population considerations.

c. A variable floor has been set for the representation in the House of Commons for any specific province by the provision in the Representation Act (1974) that stipulates that no province may ever receive in the redistribution of seats following the decennial census fewer seats than it received under the previous redistribution. Newfoundland, New Brunswick, Nova Scotia and Prince Edward Island all seem to have been affected by this rule in the recent redistribution.

d. The complicated provisions for the allocation of seats in the current (1974) Representation Act require that the "electoral quotients" of "small" and "medium" provinces cannot be larger, and may be significantly smaller, than that of "large" provinces. Under the most recent redistribution, it took 81.1 thousand people to earn an additional constituency for Ontario, but only 77.5 thousand for Alberta, 70.6 thousand for Manitoba, and 66.2 thousand for Saskatchewan. The effect of these variable quotients was the addition of about seven seats to the four western provinces, over the number of seats that would

have been received under a distribution scheme using a single universal quota.

The net effect of these provisions is very modest, affecting less than twenty seats in a House of Commons that now has 282 members. In contrast, even a unitary system like that of the United Kingdom has established the practice of significantly over-representing regions such as Scotland and Wales in the national legislature by as much as 50% of that to which their population entitles them.

ii. The modest qualifiers to the principle of representation by population in the House of Commons are undermined by the automatic escalation clause that is built into the present Representation Act. This legislation guarantees a growing House of Commons into the indefinite future. Roughly speaking, that legislation generates for the 1971 census an electoral quotient reached by dividing the population of Quebec by 75; for the 1981 census, that quotient will be generated by dividing the Quebec population by 79, with similar four-seat increases for every subsequent decennial census. Unless the population of Quebec increases at a faster rate than that of Canada as a whole (and it has failed to do so since 1966), this ensures an increasing number of seats in the House after each redistribution. This dilutes the assurances of minimum representation to the smaller provinces. Until 1974, the four Atlantic provinces were guaranteed (under the "Senate Rule") a minimum representation in the House of Commons of at least 30 members out of a total of (about) 265, or 11.3%, no matter what happened to their population relative to the rest of Canada. Since 1974, they are guaranteed at least 32 members in a House of Commons that could pass 400 by the end of this century (depending upon what estimates we make of population trends in Quebec), and this is quite a different matter.

iii. The procrastination that is built into the decennial Canadian redistribution works against the representation of those regions that are enjoying a growing population, a factor that is obviously relevant to some of the current political discontent in Canada. Significant population shifts have taken place in this country in the last 20 years, yet the 1974 general election was still held on the basis of the redistribution that followed the 1961 census. Not until May, 1979 was an election held on the basis of the 1971 census; it seems probable that any redistribution derived from the 1981 census will not be used in a national election until 1988 (assuming quadriennial elections and normal time delays). Alberta's population is estimated to have passed the two million mark some time in 1979, but until the 1979 election its parliamentary representation was based on a 1961 population count of 1.3 million. This tardiness is inexcusable. The United States operates under the rule that any election taking place more than two years after the census must reflect the population shifts recorded at that census, even though the fixed total for the House of Representatives means that such redistribution must always involve the politically sensitive act of taking seats away from some states. The House of Commons would much better reflect the shifting regional balance of the country if:

—all elections held more than two years after census day must be based on a redistribution following from those census figures; and

—such a stipulation must apply, not just to the decennial census, but to the five-year census as well.

The combination of these two rules would ensure that the distribution of seats in the House of Commons would be based on population figures that were never more than seven years out of date; the present procedures allow a time lag of up to 18 years.

iv. The single member plurality vote system that is used for elections to the Canadian House of Commons has a distorting effect on representation for any region, in that it tends to exaggerate voting pluralities or majorities.

The problems and costs of such a system of representation have been known for some time,[1] and the recent regionalization of our formerly national parties is one of the consequences. Given regional discontent with national policies, the normal outcome for an election fought in such an electoral system is strong support for political parties other than the nationally dominant party, and when the discontent of a region of small population takes electoral form, it is normally relegated to the backbenches of the opposition side of the House. The self-perpetuating frustration of such a situation is one of the components of the present phenomenon of Western alienation, and one that is reinforced, rather than countered, by the House of Commons.

v. The basic principle of Canadian government is that of responsible government, the historical outcome of which has been the development in the Commons of disciplined political parties. Members may speak for their *regions*, but they must normally vote for their *party*, and in the *party* caucuses regional representatives suffer the same numerical disadvantage that they do in the House. The plight of regional representatives of this stripe is especially poignant when their party forms the government, and the frustration of Western Liberal MPs between 1968 and 1972 is not an accidental consequence, but one that is built into the Canadian political system.

vi. The fundamental and overwhelming weakness of the House of Commons as an adequate means for regional representation is built into the principle of representation on which it is founded. Precisely because representation in the Commons parallels the distribution of population, those regions of small population are necessarily put at a disadvantage relative to those regions of large population. This is the immediate corollary of representation by population. British Columbia is inevitably outvoted by either Ontario or Quebec. Calculations of electoral advantage on the part of governments will almost invariably lead to policies favoring areas of heavy population concentration over any smaller regional interests. To say this is not to vilify governments but to observe the imperatives of the system. Representation by population means large representation for regions with large populations, whatever disadvantage this might involve for underpopulated regions. What the P.C.I. expresses in abstract form, the House of Commons demonstrates concretely: the extent to which population, and therefore (under the present institutional arrangements) political power, is concentrated in one part of the country.

For these reasons, it is not correct to present the existing House of Commons as an adequate solution to the problem of regional representation, and democratically irresponsible to suggest that a lack of a regional voice is a legitimate punishment to be visited upon those parts of the country that failed to vote the "right" way. Such a suggestion assumes that Western Canadians can remember neither the frustration of the large contingent of Western Liberal MPs elected in 1968, nor the political dead-end into which the Progressive MPs of the 1920s were shunted by the operations of the parliamentary system of government. Such a suggestion assumes that Atlantic Canadians are unable to calculate the shrinking power base that representation legislation promises them within the only institution of the national government that is directly accountable, the House of Commons.

The House of Commons is capable of providing a forum for regional *input*, in which the concerns and fears of specific regions of the country may be articulated by the Members of Parliament who represent those regions. It is fundamentally unsuited to providing a mechanism of effective regional *power*, as the principles of majoritarianism and responsible government alike lead in quite a different direction.

2. THE SENATE

The existing Senate was originally created to serve the needs for regional representation, specifically the concerns of the Maritime provinces that their representatives might be overwhelmed in the lower house by the representatives from the central Canadian provinces. The composition of the Senate recognizes "Divisions" (three in 1867; increased to four in 1915), each of which is given equal representation of 24 Senators. Representation for Newfoundland and for the two territories is addition to this basic Divisional allocation.

It is not a controversial point to suggest that the Senate does not now, and probably never has, functioned effectively as a chamber for the special representation of regional interests and concerns. The reasons for this failure relate far more to the basic structure than to the personnel of the upper chamber. Some of the more obvious defects of the Senate as an instrument of regional representation include:

i. A major defect of the Senate is the fact that the status of an appointed body is increasingly suspect in an age that is dominated by a democratic ethos. An appointed legislative body carries with it the taint of anachronism; it is weakly grounded, and lacks the credibility to stand up to the lower house even were it so inclined. Unlike the United States, where the Senate is clearly the senior legislative body, in Canada Senators lack the status and credibility of members of the Commons. The Senate is, not a step forward in a political career, but the terminus. Without the challenge of future election campaigns, there is no incentive for the Senator to keep in touch with political opinion in the region he ostensibly represents, just as there is normally no incentive for concerned groups to regard him as a regular channel to the decision-making process. The relative freedom of the upper chamber, implied by the fact that the life of the government does not stand at issue in every major vote, is wasted in the curious political limbo into which the Canadian Senate is relegated. This aspect is further enhanced by the fact that one obvious source of Senate appointees is defeated candidates, federal and more rarely provincial, of the party that forms the national government. The Canadian Senate contains many individuals who cannot, or who can no longer, be elected; denied by the electorate the opportunity to represent their region through the front door of election to the provincial legislature or the House of Commons, they are given the chance to represent those same individuals through the back door of the Senate. In a democratic age, this further reduces the credibility of the chamber.

ii. If the fact of appointment is a handicap in itself, the mode whereby Senators are appointed further reduces its credibility as a device for regional representation. Senators are appointed by the Prime Minister of the day as an exercise of a power of patronage. There is no tradition of consultation with provincial premiers, although some such consultation may take place if the provincial government is of the same political stripe as the federal government. If the *fact* of appointment denies Senators the legitimacy of an electoral base, the *mode* of that appointment denies them the legitimacy of a provincial base. Accountable to no one, and beholden only to the Prime Minister (or possibly the party) that appointed him, the Senator represents his Division in a sense which is far removed from contemporary theories of democratic representation.

iii. A further defect of the Senate is the basis for representation. The units that are accorded equal representation in the chamber are not provinces, but "Divisions", a constitutional neologism created simply for this purpose, and one that remains suspect and arbitrary notwithstanding the fact that it is more or less reproduced in many proposed contemporary constitutional amending formulas. This manipulation of the concept of region has

resulted in an upper chamber whose representation is heavily skewed toward representation by population instead of reflecting the federal nature of the country. The two largest provinces, the central Canadian bogeyman that figures so largely in the politics of Canadian regional resentment, are given 46% of the upper house to go along with the 60% of the representation they currently enjoy in the lower house. The four western provinces, with 27% of the seats in the Commons, have only 23% of the Senate. The most penalized province is not Ontario (which receives about two-thirds the representation in the upper chamber that it enjoys in the lower), but British Columbia. Far from giving increased representation in the Senate to the smaller provinces, the Canadian system perpetuates the political dominance of the larger provinces in both chambers of the bicameral legislature. Canada is the only democratic federal system in the world in which the regions with the largest populations dominate both houses of the national legislature.

Table 1 Representation in Parliament by Province

Province/ Territory	% Representation in			
	Commons		Senate	
Newfoundland	2.5		5.8	
P.E.I.	1.4		3.8	
Nova Scotia	4.2		9.6	
New Brunswick	3.6		9.6	
		11.7		28.8
Quebec	26.6		23.1	
Ontario	33.3		23.1	
Manitoba	5.0		5.8	
Saskatchewan	5.0		5.8	
Alberta	7.4		5.8	
British Columbia	9.9		5.8	
		27.3		23.2
Yukon	0.4		1.0	
Northwest Terr.	0.7		1.0	

The atrophy of the Senate is disappointing in the light of its potential, and this is true in a double sense. FIRST, the Canadian Senate represents a waste of personnel, in that its membership contains a substantial wealth of experience and judgment. All indications are that a considerable proportion of the members take their legislative duties seriously, and it is commonly observed that the level of debate in the upper chamber is much superior to that of the Commons. Much of this is wasted, like a play well performed to an empty hall. SECOND, most other federal systems feature a strong upper chamber as an important device of federal conciliation, a major mechanism of regional accommodation. It is a chamber of real political power and practical political purpose. This wasted institutional space is one of the reasons why Senate reform is recurrently tempting to those who consider constitutional renewal.

Ironically, the formation of the first Canadian Senate was not without promising features. It was formed of prominent individuals nominated by provincial leaders. While hardly an ideal procedure (for the nineteenth century any more than the twentieth), this was certainly an improvement over the patronage-laden overtones of the present Senate.

None of this, of course, is to suggest that the Senate is useless or without power. Many analyses of the Senate have made the opposite point far too convincingly.[2] The point is that what power the Senate does deploy is for circumstances and controversies other than the protection or advancement of regional concerns. In terms of effective regional representation, the Senate is close to a dead loss.

3. THE CABINET

It has frequently been suggested that the Canadian political structure is inherently contradictory because it is an attempt to combine the decentralization of federalism with the central-

ization of the parliamentary system. However, one accommodation was sought from the beginning: Sir John A. Macdonald's first cabinet, and every Canadian cabinet since that time, has been formed with a careful eye to the representation of regions and interests. The intention is to generate a political decision-making body that is cognizant of the sensitivities and interests of all regions, and able to generate public policy that will respond optimally to these pressures. The most historically evocative example of such a cabinet was that formed by Laurier in 1896, which is considered to have brought together powerful political leaders from all parts of the country to form the national executive.

Since certain cabinet portfolios are especially sensitive to certain regions, the assignment to such a position of a regional representative further enhances the capacity of the cabinet to accommodate regional concerns and preoccupations. At one time, it was fashionable to list the set of political rules that governed the assignment of specific portfolios to specific regions; although this practice now appears to be followed less rigidly, the consideration remains. It would be, for example, a significant concession to western concerns to appoint a westerner as minister of transport or energy.

However, there are several problems to be considered when assessing the adequacy of careful cabinet formation as a device for the representation of regions. Again, we will stress those defects that directly relate to the structural features of the institution, as opposed to those that one might attribute to such historical accidents as individual personality.

i. The allocation of cabinet representation normally has a distinct tendency toward representation by population, the rough rule of thumb being one-third of the seats for Ontario, one-third for Quebec, two or three for B.C., and one each for the other provinces. The less populous regions are represented, but on a distinct minority footing. Saskatchewan can have one voice at the table, but Ontario has ten or eleven. Even if decisions are not made by strict majority rule (as they are not), the balance must tend to be in favor of the many, if only due to the increased opportunities to express a given region's point of view, and the allocation of a broader range of portfolios. No matter how carefully constructed, a cabinet can represent regional concerns only to a limited extent. It can serve as a means of *input* for less populous regions, but not as an effective means of political *power* for those regions.

ii. Although there is no direct logical connection between numbers and merit, there is a significant indirect connection which bears upon the capacity of the cabinet as an effective articulator of regional concerns. The Liberal Quebec caucus includes 74 members; the Liberal contingent from Manitoba includes only two individuals. All other things being equal, and with the best will in the world, it is far more likely that the Quebec caucus will be able to provide two individuals who are administratively competent, personally articulate, and politically influential. It is even more obvious that the Quebec caucus may be able, and the Manitoba caucus will be completely unable, to provide a third such individual. In all save the most unusual of circumstances, factors of merit and competence will amplify the straightforward numerical disadvantage suffered by regions of smaller population.

iii. The deliberations of the cabinet take place within the broader context of responsible government and the normal desire of a government to promote its own re-election in the next general election. Both within the House, and in the planning for electoral strategy, these calculations favor the interests of the larger regions over those of less populated regions whose support figures less prominently in the building of successful voting coalitions. It is Ontario, and not Manitoba or Nova Scotia, that will hold the balance in the next

election and determine the next government of Canada, and such a consideration can never be far absent from cabinet deliberations.

iv. The capacity of a region to achieve representation within the cabinet is dependent on its cooperation in electing members of the government party, there being no tradition of coalition government in this country. The recent political trend toward the regionalization of party support in this country is entirely inimical to a regionally representative cabinet. In 1979, it was Joe Clark who could not find enough Quebeckers to fill cabinet positions; in 1980, Pierre Trudeau generated western representation in his cabinet largely by appointing Senators. The same factors that undermine the appointed Senate as a regionally representative body undermine the credibility of an appointed Senator as a member of the cabinet.

v. The tradition of cabinet solidarity has reduced the effectiveness of regionally representative ministers by reducing their alternatives to two: defense of the cabinet position, or resignation in protest. In practical terms, the first represents surrender and the second defeat. Cabinet solidarity and strong parties make it impossible for regional cabinet ministers to muster cross-party support on regional matters. Instead, they must take their lumps in the give and take of a cabinet heavily skewed toward Central Canadian representation, and be satisfied with whatever crumbs fall their way. Sometimes the crumbs can be few, as western Liberals found between 1968 and 1972, even though there was strong Liberal representation in both Cabinet and Commons from the four western provinces.

vi. The tendency in recent years has been toward the strengthening of the office of Prime Minister and a corresponding decline in the power and significance of individual cabinet ministers. This has been exhibited in the rapid turnover of cabinet membership and the short terms most ministers serve in any one portfolio; the expanded activities of the Prime Minister's Office are part of the same process. This tendency toward a one-man show cannot be blamed upon a single person's character, since similar trends have been observed and deplored in other Western democracies. The problem is that while a cabinet may or may not be regionally representative in any meaningful sense, a single individual cannot be.

vii. Recent trends in the organization of political parties in Canada tend to reduce the extent to which cabinet members can effectively represent the regions from which they come. The age of regional chieftains like Jimmy Gardiner is over; as party systems diverge at the two levels, the "regional representative" is pushed into a curious limbo. Without the solid base that provincial organizational support provides, it becomes difficult to generate the independence and the indispensability that could provide leverage with a Prime Minister.

The federal nature of the cabinet stands as the major example of the way that the institutions of national government have evolved toward the accommodation of regional concerns and demands, and there can be no doubt that it has in the past served to reflect some concerns of some regions in national policy. However, the device suffers from the same basic limitation as regional accommodation through the House of Commons: cabinet and Commons both reflect majoritarian tendencies, with the unavoidable corollary of *less* representation and therefore *less* effective political leverage for those regions of less population. This inherent limitation has been aggravated by the recent polarization of party representation in the House of Commons.

4. POLITICAL PARTIES

Political parties themselves can function as informal, extra-constitutional, and highly effective devices for the reconciliation of re-

gional differences. This can best be accomplished by a political party that enjoys significant electoral strength in all parts of the country, and that has ties with provincial wings that are also competitive in their respective provinces. Under these conditions, the important sectional differences within the country are replicated within each party, and the compromises and trade-offs can be accomplished with less exacerbation of public feeling. The federal-provincial linkage can serve to reduce open confrontation between the two levels of government by providing intra-party communication channels between factions operating at the two levels. Such arrangements can permit a national party to survive a period during which it elects no MPs in a region without lasting alienation because the extensive organization of the provincial party provides effective if unofficial representation for that region. Saskatchewan during the Progressive revolt of the 1920s is a case in point.

Political parties in Canada are no longer capable of performing this function as well as they have in the past. Their capacity for integrating the diverse regions of the country has been significantly reduced by a number of factors, including the following:

i. The pattern of political support for the parties competing in national elections has become increasingly regionalized in recent elections. The Liberal party has, over the last decade, become weaker and weaker in the area west of the Lakehead, not just in terms of members elected (something that is always subject to fluctuations because of the single member plurality vote system), but in terms of percentage of popular support across the region and in all parts of it. The Conservatives, weak in Quebec since World War I, have gone from defeat to disaster, with even the bedrock 20%+ that seemed solid through the Diefenbaker years fading to less than 10%. Finally, the NDP has consistently failed to make a breakthrough in Quebec, and its support in

Ontario and the Atlantic provinces is sporadic and undependable. It could be suggested that in a very real sense, Canada no longer has any truly national parties. Correspondingly, the disputes which have regional overtones must take the form of a heated debate between parties, tending to reinforce the polarization that is already taking place.

ii. The provincial and federal party systems are being pulled apart, as voters support one party at the federal level and another at the provincial. The most extreme cases are the provinces of British Columbia (Socred/NDP at the provincial level and Conservative/NDP/Liberal in federal elections), and Quebec (PQ/Liberal in provincial elections, and so massively Liberal in federal elections one hesitates to dignify any other party by ranking it a contender). In both provinces, at least half the voting public must vote for a different party at the two levels to account for the persisting results. Since electoral volatility has increased, the national parties are increasingly making their appeals, not to large blocs of party faithful, but rather to floating pools of individuals with low degrees of partisan commitment. This reduces the extent to which a national party is dependent upon a provincial machine to deliver the voters, both because the provincial machine (when and where it exists) may no longer wish to cooperate, and because the voters on which the national party depends for its electoral success may not be the same voters that the provincial machine deploys for its own support. Correspondingly, the potential for a regional representative to possess his own support base (independent of the resources and appeal of the national leader) in the form of this provincial organization is similarly reduced. Political careerism replaces regional representation as a viable role for the region's elected representatives.

iii. The tendency over the last two decades has been increasingly toward the separation of the organization and leadership of provincial and federal parties sharing the same name. On several occasions, the most exciting political confrontations in the country have been those between a Prime Minister and a premier nominally from the same party. Certainly Joe Clark found that a "new style" of federalism did not emerge merely because he shared the same partisan label as most of the premiers. The pattern, so common in most countries, of political careers beginning at the provincial level and moving up to the national level is most unusual in Canada in recent decades, reducing the factors both of personal experience and shared cooperation.

iv. At one time, the need for corporate donations for financing the operations of political parties could be itself an integrating factor, in that both levels of the party were often obliged to go to the same donors for funds, enforcing a degree of coordination and cooperation. The recent trends in campaign financing, however, point a different direction altogether. The new requirements for the limitation of and reporting of corporate contributions, and for the subsidy of candidates or parties from public funds, contribute to the independence of the provincial and federal parties of the same name; indeed, in some provinces it has been the case that a party is obliged to create a separate provincial organization in order to receive such a subsidy from provincial funds.[3]

v. The parliamentary wings of the major national parties have completely escaped the control, and possibly even the influence, of their extra-parliamentary organization. It may, of course, be doubted that the extra-parliamentary wing ever dominated, and one observer[4] has suggested a cyclical pattern in the relation of parliamentary and extra-parliamentary wings. In the present context, the situation has become more critical. Although the major national parties are explicitly federal in their extra-parliamentary organization, with significant representation from every part of the country, their parliamentary wings have been becoming increasingly regionalized in their membership.

The decline of truly national parties with strong provincial wings is a fundamentally important development of Canadian politics in the twentieth century. Some scholars have identified the party system as the crucial factor in the maintaining and transforming of the "federal bargain." This contention certainly is plausible enough, although it is more realistic to depict the party system as the victim, rather than the creator, of the regional forces that have so fragmented Canadian politics. It is easier to decry the loss of the meliorating effects of informal accommodation through an integrative party system, than it is to devise solutions or repairs. Precisely because party systems register and reflect the social forces and pressures operating within the country, it is not possible to legislate their form or their internal dynamics. Sir John A. Macdonald's vision of the type of party system that would optimally operate the new Dominion—a Conservative party in power in Ottawa, with suitably subservient provincial wings in power in every province—has become, in both its major components, impossible to achieve. A more fitting commentary on the party system today is Premier Davis's comment before the 1980 election (possibly facetious, but with considerable substance) that if any of his supporters wanted to vote for Mr. Clark, he would not stop them. Precisely. So much for a party system that bridges and meliorates federal-provincial and national-regional strains and conflicts.

5. FEDERALISM

The most obvious means of achieving regional representation is federalism itself. One fundamental notion of federalism is the division of constitutional responsibilities between a na-

tional authority (to ensure uniformity in those matters where such universality is necessary or desirable), and regional authorities (to permit maximum opportunity for flexibility of the response to regional needs and preferences). Section 91 through 95 of the British North America Act attempt this difficult project for Canada. The other fundamental notion is that of concensus decision-making, rather than simple majoritarianism, at the national level.

To the extent that the division of powers is effective and appropriate, the problem of regional representation can be partly reduced. Those issues that are most regionally sensitive need never enter the national arena, while those issues that form the national agenda are, ideally, the least regionally divisive. The need would still remain to reflect regional sensitivity within national policy, but a careful division of powers could prevent the overload of the mechanisms that accomplished this.

There are several problems in attempting to resolve even part of the problem of representation through the division of powers, for a number of reasons including the following:

i. It is unlikely that it is possible to define lists of governmental powers clearly and unambiguously so as to make it possible to govern a country without clashes over jurisdiction. Human affairs do not neatly divide themselves into hermetically sealed compartments; human activities, and therefore political undertakings, are necessarily complex and messy. The first defect with the dream of removing the need for regional representation through exhaustive delineations of powers assigned to or shared by the two levels of government is that it is impossible; watertight compartments always leak, the efforts of judges notwithstanding.

ii. The project of drawing the line between provincial and federal jurisdictions becomes even more difficult in the modern era because modern society is more complex and interdependent than it has ever been in the past and because modern governments are called upon to attempt and accomplish far more things for far more people than has ever been the case before in human history. It is hard to think of any significant activity by either level of government that does not send very large ripples across the jurisdictional boundaries; conversely, it is hard to think of any problem of situation that could not be tackled at least in one aspect by either level of government invoking one of the general grants of power in the BNA Act.

iii. The division of powers tends to freeze the allocation of powers deemed appropriate for one sphere of government at a specific point in time. For example, it seems to be a commonplace to observe that "la survivance", the defense and survival of the French-Canadian culture, was one of the imperatives recognized by the Fathers of Confederation, and which resulted in education (inter alia) being assigned to provincial jurisdiction. However, it seems just as plausible, in the context of modern technology, to argue that the goal of "la survivance" is threatened if communication does not accompany education as part of the provincial arsenal. Even if the goal does not change in its essentials, changing circumstances may require different means to reach that goal.

iv. Even if the distinction between regionally sensitive issues on the one hand, and national agenda issues on the other, could ever have been made definitively, this no longer remains the case. The heaviest arguments now are over economic powers, with one side arguing that increased federal powers are necessary, and the other arguing that increased provincial jurisdiction is essential if regionally responsive economic policies are to overcome the current problems of the Canadian economy. The argument is not over details, but over the basics.

v. The rigidities and boundary problems of the division of powers are significantly off-set by the positive benefits and flexibility of *concurrency*, which cannot be achieved when regions confront the national government through their provincial governments, rather than being accommodated routinely within national decision-making processes.

6. SUMMARY

The rationale for considering regional representation, and for suggesting amplification of devices to this end as reasonable proposals to reduce the contemporary political malaise, is therefore quite straightforward. In such territorially diverse countries as Canada, there may exist regions distinctively different from other regions and from any composite national average, such that national policies responsive to a "mere" national majority may inadequately reflect the needs and preferences of the country considered as a whole. There is a need within the government of such a country for devices and instruments to provide special access to the demands of regional minorities. In the Canadian restaurant, blue-plate specials are not enough, and there must also be a large a la carte menu. The development of such instrumentalities, and both the appearance and the reality of special sensitivity to regional demands, becomes in itself a means of binding diverse territorial interests and generating both good will and common purpose, thereby reducing the pressures and resentment that lead to the articulation of hostile regional reactions.

This representation must be purchased at some cost to "one person, one vote" principles. The rationale for representing a region is not that it has some magic percentage of the national population, but that it constitutes a territorial diversity of significant proportions. Democratic anomalies comparable to the equal representation of Nevada and California in the U.S. Senate are unavoidable. Just as the "representation by population" agitation undermined the political stability of the pre-Confederation province of Canada, so the preoccupation with the majoritarian implications of "one person, one vote" principles must undermine the workability of any system that is truly federal in the sense of containing considerable diversities and cleavages that have organized themselves on a territorial basis.

A federal system is at best a qualified union, a bargain between people who trust each other only so far and always want to hedge their bets. The same air of tentative compromise must guide the ongoing administration of such a union. There is nothing wrong with this. Any democratic political system is committed to a sensitivity toward the interests and demands of minorities; in a federal system, it is especially important that this sensitivity be extended as well to *regional* minorities.

The devices, formal and informal, by which the Canadian political system has sought to accommodate regional differences are no longer adequate. Their sporadic and partial operation will no longer suffice in contemporary conditions. This is partly because structural defects in these devices have become more acute over time, and partly because the demands placed upon those devices by the increasing salience of regional concerns has increased in recent years. It is a fundamental prerequisite for any adequate program of Canadian constitutional change that it address this deficiency.

Notes

1. The classic statement is Alan C. Cairns, "The Electoral System and the Party System in Canada, 1921-1965," *Canadian Journal of Political Science* I: 1 (March 1968).

2. See e.g. Colin Campbell, *The Canadian Senate: A Lobby From Within* (Toronto: Macmillan, 1978).

3. Barry Wilson, *Politics of Defeat: The Decline of The Liberal Party in Saskatchewan* (Saskatoon: Western Producer Prairie, 1980).

4. Joseph Wearing, *The L-Shaped Party: The Liberal Party of Canada 1958-1980* (Toronto: McGraw-Hill Ryerson, 1981).

7. REPRESENTATIVENESS AND EQUAL OPPORTUNITY AND AFFIRMATIVE ACTION

Kenneth Kernaghan and David Siegel

Representativeness

The Meaning of Representative Bureaucracy

The values of responsiveness and representativeness are closely related in that the argument is frequently made that a more representative public service is a more responsive public service. This argument will be explored here in the context of a discussion of representative bureaucracy.

Representative bureaucracy is a tricky concept, and it has been interpreted in a variety of ways.[1] A strict interpretation of representative bureaucracy would require that the public service be a microcosm of the total society in terms of a wide range of variables, including race, religion, education, social class, and region of origin. However, there is disagreement in academic writings as to what purposes representative bureaucracy serves, what degree of representativeness is desirable, and what variables should be included. Proponents of representative bureaucracy recommend its adoption on the following grounds:

1. Public servants exercise significant power in the political system.

2. External controls over public servants by the political executive, the legislature, and the courts are inadequate to check administrative power and so to ensure administrative responsibility.

3. A public service which is representative of the total population will be responsive to the needs and interests of the general public and will therefore be more responsible. This central proposition of the theory of representative bureaucracy is based on several subpropositions:

   (a) If the values of the public service as a whole are similar to those of the total population, then the public service will tend to make the kind of decisions which the public would make if it were involved in the decision making.

   (b) The values of public servants are moulded by the pattern of socialization they experience before they enter the public service, that is, by such socializing forces as education, social class, occupational background, race, family and group associations.

   (c) The values arising from this socialization will not be modified by prolonged exposure to bureaucratic values.

   (d) The values arising from socialization will be reflected in the behaviour of public servants and therefore in their recommendations and decisions.

   (e) Thus, the various groups in the population should be represented in the

Kenneth Kernaghan and David Siegel, *Public Administration in Canada: A Text* (Toronto: Methuen Publications, 1987). 445-51 and 482-90. Reprinted by permission of Nelson Canada.

public service in approximate demographic proportion so that public servants will be responsive to their interests both in policy development and program delivery.

Critics of representative bureaucracy acknowledge the extensive power of public servants and the consequent need to provide controls to preserve and promote administrative responsibility. They contend, however, that the assertion that external controls are inadequate to ensure responsible administrative conduct requires more investigation. These critics also point to the logical and empirical failings of the theory of representative bureaucracy.

They contend first of all that in a representative public service the values of the public service *as a whole* will not be similar to those of the general population; rather, the values of *individual* public servants *may* be similar to the values of those groups in the population they are supposed to represent. Moreover, the public service as a whole does not make decisions; rather, decisions are made by individual public servants who, by acting on behalf of groups whom they represent, would serve the interests of particular segments of the public rather than the total population. Also, it is not sufficient for the public service as a whole to be broadly representative of the total population; for all interests to be represented in the decision-making process, each major administrative unit must be representative of the total population, especially at its senior levels where the most important recommendations and decisions are made.

Opponents of representative bureaucracy observe further that a public servant with certain social and educational origins will not necessarily share the values of persons outside the public service who have similar origins. The life-long process of socialization continues after entry to the public service, in the form of resocialization to the values of the service as a whole or of particular administrative units. Moreover, representatives of a specific group in the population, particularly if they achieve high office in the public service, are likely to be upwardly mobile and may well share the socio-economic and other values of those with whom they work, rather than of the group from which they came. In this regard, Peta Sheriff regrets the lack of research on the strength of preoccupational and post-occupational experience, and concludes that although "the very cornerstone of the representative bureaucracy thesis has no direct evidence to support it . . . the suspicion that pre-occupational socialization must have some influence is sufficient to maintain the thesis."[2] However, even if public servants continue to share the values of certain groups despite organizational socialization, these values may not be significantly reflected in the public servants' behaviour.

Thus, it is logically possible to have a representative public service which is not responsive, and a responsive public service which is not representative. Indeed, Meier and Nigro conclude that the most senior levels in the United States public service "are an unrepresentative demographic group holding quite representative attitudes."[3]

Canadian Writings

The major points of contention in a thought-provoking debate on representative bureaucracy in Canada[4] involve the extent to which the values of efficiency, effectiveness, neutrality, and responsiveness conflict with that of representativeness. In this debate, Donald Rowat objects to John Porter's sacrifice of representativeness for the sake of efficiency and suggests that both values can be achieved. He argues that representativeness "is essential to the efficiency of the bureaucracy, in the sense of the latter's effectiveness in a democratic, pluralistic society."[5] Porter asserts that persons of various social origins will be found in the bureaucracy in roughly the same proportion as in the population as a whole *if* government recruitment and promotion policies do not discriminate against particular groups, *if* educational facilities to qualify persons for public service appointments are equal as between these groups, and *if* these groups are equally motivated to join the public service. He contends that "in the theoretically ideal bureaucracy, the candidate for office neither gains nor loses as a result of ethnic, religious or regional origins."[6]

Rowat, who is more concerned with what can be realized in practice than with a search for a theoretically ideal bureaucracy, observes that Porter's conditions of equality do not exist and cannot be easily achieved. He contends that representativeness must be actively sought —even at the expense of technical efficiency and neutrality. Intelligent persons with the potential to rise to higher levels in the service could be recruited and provided with the required in-service education and training. Moreover, competent members of underrepresented groups could be brought into the public service from outside. Porter opposes the recruitment of outsiders on the grounds that this practice threatens the neutrality of the service and the concept of the bureaucratic career. He states that "since the basis of power associations are frequently ethnic, regional or religious, the idea that these groups should be represented in the bureaucracy contradicts the notion of the official as the servant of the state."[7] Rowat does not agree that the appointment of "bureaucratic outsiders" would endanger political neutrality, and he argues that a public service which complemented career public servants with outsiders would be more responsive, since a career bureaucracy tends to "lose contact with and lack understanding of the changing feelings, needs and desires of the great variety of people and groups found in our dynamic, pluralistic society."[8]

Rowat does not suggest that underrepresented groups should be represented in *precise* proportion to their presence in the total population, and he rejects the use of quotas for recruitment and promotion as unworkable. He does suggest, however, that recruitment to the public service should be guided by the principle of representation.

Porter objects on several grounds to Rowat's plea for representativeness. He first poses the basic question as to which of the many and varied groups in society should be represented in the public service. He then contends that Rowat's proposals for recruiting members of underrepresented groups and providing them with in-service training serve the principle of equal opportunity rather than representativeness. He states also that "in a society of classes, the upwardly mobile are seldom representative of the social interests from which they originated."[9] Finally, he notes the assumption in the theory of representative bureaucracy that political institutions are inadequate to cope with modern demands and questions the view that "ways can be found for governmental bureaucracy to make up for the deficiencies in our representative political institutions."[10]

Two decades after the Porter-Rowat debate, Wilson and Mullins expressed doubt "that members of a bureaucracy chosen from various relevant groups will be likely to act as agents or spokesmen for their groups and group interests."[11] Moreover, they concluded that support for representative bureaucracy "on the assumption that it would be politically representative in any meaningful sense is not only bogus, but also dangerous."[12] Like Rowat, Wilson and Mullins assert that technical efficiency should not be stressed at the expense of representativeness.

Another perspective on the issue of representative bureaucracy in Canada has been provided by Dennis Olsen,[13] who updated to 1973 the study of the bureaucratic elite conducted by John Porter in 1953. On the basis of an examination of data on the social background, career, and education of federal and provincial bureaucrats, Olsen concluded that, compared with the 1953 bureaucratic elite, the 1973 group is "more open, more heterogeneous, and probably more meritocratic." However, these changes have taken place very slowly, and he envisages for the future that the overall pattern will be characterized by a "marked persistence of both social class and ethnic preferences in recruitment."[14]

The Representativeness of the Canadian Bureaucracy

Data on the composition of the Canadian public service in relation to the total population show that the service is not a microcosm of Canadian society. A number of important groups are underrepresented in the service, and both the senior and middle echelons are unrepresentative of the general population. The middle ranks are more representative than the senior level, however, and are representative of the total population on the criterion of region of origin. Beattie, et al. concluded that compared to the senior bureaucracy the middle level was "quite open and heterogeneous." It drew "amply from a wide range of significant social categories in the Canadian mosaic —new and old-stock Canadians, the several regions of Canada, rural and urban areas, the various social class levels—all sectors, in fact, except the Francophone population of Canada."[15] By way of contrast, the senior level of the bureaucracy contained an overrepresentation of males, anglophones, the middle and upper classes, Ontarians, and the well educated. But Dennis Olsen, after comparing data from 1953 and 1973, concluded that the senior ranks have gradually become more representative of the general population. He asserts that "the new elite is drawn from a little lower in

the class system, ethnic representation is a little more balanced, the new elite is more highly educated than the old, and . . . a greater proportion of the new elite is made up of *career* civil servants."[16] Nevertheless, the senior level is not very representative of the total population. For example, 92 percent of the bureaucratic elite had university degrees compared to 8 percent of the male labour force; only 3 percent were women; and persons of British ethnic origin were substantially overrepresented, persons of French origin were slightly underrepresented, and all other ethnic groups were heavily underrepresented.[17] In terms of social class, the bureaucratic elite was primarily of middle-class origin and "only 15% of the bureaucratic elite . . . could be described as possibly of working class origin."[18]

It is not the policy of the federal government to establish in the public service a microcosm of the Canadian mosaic by pursuing exact demographic representation of all groups in society; rather, the government's aim is to achieve a more proportionate representation of a limited number of politically significant, but underrepresented, groups. In this regard, the Public Service Commission has stated that the underrepresentation of francophones, women, native peoples, and the handicapped "may have the effect of reducing the sensitivity of the Public Service to the needs of particular elements of the population."[19] Thus, a prime motivation underlying present efforts to represent these groups more adequately is to make the public service more responsive, both in the provision of policy advice and the delivery of services. As explained above, the assumption that representativeness will promote responsiveness is central to the theory of representative bureaucracy. The government also presumes that members of underrepresented groups who join the public service will remain sensitive to the needs and claims of these groups. In view of the deficiencies of the theory of representative bureaucracy outlined earlier, the benefits of representation in terms of increased responsiveness are likely to be less than anticipated. However, we know very little about the extent to which the expanded representation of francophones, women, and native peoples has had a policy impact by advancing the substantive interests of these groups.

Increased representation has effects which are not covered by the theory of representative bureaucracy. Representation has a symbolic impact, which explains in part its appeal to government officials and which helps to promote quiescence and stability in the Canadian political system. The statutes, regulations, and administrative units designed to increase the representation of francophones, women, and native peoples evoke symbols of equality of opportunity and upward mobility for members of these groups. In the name of equal opportunity, the government has instituted programs to recruit and train group members who have not enjoyed equal access to the public service. Also, recruitment to senior posts from outside the service and post-entry training geared to promotion to the higher ranks of the service demonstrate the opportunities for group members to attain senior policy-making posts.

These measures serve a partisan political purpose in that they help to sustain or increase electoral support for the governing party. Evidence of partisan motivation can be seen in the fact that, except for handicapped persons, the groups for whom increased representation has been sought have mobilized for political action and are highly visible and vocal in their demands for greater participation in the political and administrative systems. The government's efforts on behalf of francophones, women, and native peoples have brought about a more representative public service. It is not practicable, however, to attempt to represent proportionately all the myriad groups which make up the Canadian mosaic. Experience to date suggests that future government measures towards a more representative public service will be directed primarily to underrepresented groups which become politically influential.

The policies, practices and achievements of the federal government in respect of representative bureaucracy, equal opportunity, and affirmative action are explained further [in Chapter 21]. . . .

EQUAL OPPORTUNITY AND AFFIRMATIVE ACTION

The federal and provincial governments have adopted programs to promote equal opportunity for segments of the population that historically have been underrepresented in the public service. [As explained in Chapter 20,] the federal government is committed to improving the representation of certain "target groups," namely women, francophones, native people, the handicapped, and visible minorities. Among the provinces, there is some variation as to the particular groups considered to be inadequately represented. The underrepresentation of women is an important concern in all provinces, whereas concern about the participation of such groups as francophones and native peoples is limited to provinces where these groups make up a significant proportion of the population. The issues of representative bureaucracy and equal opportunity are closely linked in that the attainment of a representative public service depends largely on the extent to which equality of opportunity actually exists for various groups in society. Appropriate representation of these groups can be achieved most successfully when group members have equal access to the education and training required to equip them for government service, equal interest in working for government, equal knowledge of job vacancies in the public service, and protection from discrimination. Each of the target groups has been inequitably treated in more than one of these respects.

In the federal government, the Treasury Board Secretariat and the Public Service Commission have played the leading roles in developing, implementing and monitoring equal opportunity programs. The stated purpose of the programs is to ensure that all Canadians have equal access to employment in the public service and to redress historical imbalances in the representation of certain groups in the public service. To this end, the two agencies devised programs for francophones and women in the 1960s which were strengthened and supplemented by programs for indigenous people, visible minorities, and the disabled during the 1970s and 1980s.

These programs may be grouped into three categories, namely training and development, new or modified administrative units and practices, and vigorous recruitment. In the sphere of training and development, programs have included training opportunities to upgrade women in the Administrative Support Category for promotion to management posts; language training; and the Northern Careers Program for native people. Among new administrative structures in the Public Service Commission are the Office of Equal Opportunities for Women, the Office of Native Employment, and the Coordinators of Services to Handicapped People. Special efforts have been made through a variety of programs to recruit qualified persons from all the target groups. There has, for example, been a black persons employment program in Nova Scotia since 1973.

These programs to overcome artificial institutional barriers to public service employment are of limited use in overcoming attitudinal barriers, notably prejudice against the target groups, which exist not only in the public service, but in Canadian society as a whole. There is, however, an ongoing effort in government to "sensitize" public service managers to the importance of removing obstacles to equal access to public service employment. To ensure that managers are sensitive to this effort, success in enhancing the participation of these groups is now deemed to be one element of the managers' performance evaluation. The Public Service Commission has observed that "an important positive re-enforcement to managerial sensitization is the evaluation of managers vis-à-vis their utilization of human resources ... specifically with respect to the participation of under-represented groups."[20]

There have been complaints from public servants and from their unions that equal opportunity programs violate the merit principle and discriminate against candidates for appointment and promotion outside the target groups. The commission has responded by explaining that merit is a dynamic principle whose application requires the reconciliation of the values of efficiency and effectiveness, sensitivity and responsiveness, equality of access to public service employment, and equity. Moreover, according to the commission, the equal opportunity programs do not amount to reverse discrimination because individual abilities rather than group characteristics are emphasized in appointments and promotions.

The commission has opposed the setting of *quotas* for the employment of under-represented groups on the grounds that (1) it is very difficult to decide which groups or interests in society should be represented, and (2) quotas clash with the merit principle by creating two classes of public servants—those who received their jobs because they were meritorious and those who received them because they were members of an underrepresented group. The commission has, however, supported the Treasury Board requirements that departments set realistic *targets* for increasing the representation of the target groups. The commission asserts that these targets are not quotas; rather, they are described as yardsticks by which the government's success in attracting qualified candidates from underrepresented groups can be measured.

To assess the extent to which the federal government's equal opportunity programs have been successful, it is useful to examine briefly the experience of the three major target groups—francophones, women, and native people.

Francophone Representation

Barriers to equal opportunity for French-speaking persons have existed both in the government and in the francophone community itself for most of this century. During the post-Confederation period before the 1918 Civil Service Act, francophones were numerically well represented in the public service. They were not, however, as well represented as anglophones at the senior levels. Moreover, many of the francophone appointments rested on patronage, whereas the 1918 Act emphasized merit and efficiency. Especially after 1918, the public service was pervaded by an anglophone linguistic and cultural bias. Merit and efficiency were linked to formal education and technical qualifications. French-language or bilingual competence was not considered a component of merit or likely to enhance efficiency. Furthermore, written examinations and interviews for recruitment and promotion reflected anglophone values and the anglophone educational system to the disadvantage of francophones. Finally, the view was widely held that the Quebec educational system was a significant barrier to francophone representation because it emphasized education for such occupations as law, medicine, and the priesthood and did not therefore provide its graduates with the technical, scientific, and commercial skills required for appointment to the public service.

All these factors combined to reduce the motivation of francophones to seek or retain positions in the federal administration. The result was a decline in the proportion of francophones in the public service from 21.58 percent in 1918 to 12.25 percent in 1946 and a decline at the deputy minister level during the same period from 14.28 percent to zero.[21]

During the early 1960s, the so-called Quiet Revolution in Quebec focussed national attention on francophone grievances about their inadequate participation in the public service. And the Glassco Commission reported in 1963 that francophones were badly underrepresented in the service. The commissioners noted that public confidence in the public service will depend on "how representative it is of the public it serves," and to achieve representativeness "a career at the centre of government should be as attractive and congenial to French-speaking as to English-speaking Canadians."[22]

Then, in 1966, Prime Minister Pearson made his landmark statement on bilingualism in the public service in which he promised that the "linguistic and cultural values of the English-speaking and French-speaking Canadians will be reflected through civil service recruitment and training."[23] The Royal Commission on Bilingualism and Biculturalism, which reported in 1967, gave enormous impetus to this objective. Prime Minister Trudeau, in accepting in principle the broad objectives proposed for the public service in the commission's report, stated that "the atmosphere of the public service should represent the

linguistic and cultural duality of Canadian society, and that Canadians whose mother
tongue is French should be adequately represented in the public service—both in terms of
numbers and in levels of responsibility."[24]
Then, in keeping with the aim of the Official
Languages Act passed in 1969, the Treasury
Board established the Official Languages Program with three major objectives—providing
services to, and communicating with, the public in both official languages, enabling public
servants to work in the official language of
their choice, and achieving the full participation in the service of members of both the
anglophone and francophone communities.

In a concerted effort since the late 1960s to
increase francophone representation in the
public service, the major strategies adopted by
the government have included more active recruitment of francophones, the designation of
language requirements for public service positions, the establishment of French-language
units in the service, and the development of an
extensive language training system.[25] Individual public servants and public service unions
have severely attacked these measures on the
grounds that the measures violate the merit
principle and amount to reverse discrimination against anglophones. The government's
response to these charges is that bilingual competence is an element of merit, and that by
increasing the number of positions requiring
bilingual competence the government would
"increase the opportunities for qualified francophones and thus at one and the same time
preserve the merit principle and achieve the
goal of a more representative Public
Service."[26] These strategies have helped to reduce institutional barriers in the government
to francophone representation. Attitudinal
change is more difficult to measure, but there
appears to be less overt resistance to government programs in this area than there was

initially, and the public service milieu is now a
much more bilingual one. In addition, a significant perceived barrier in the francophone
community has been largely overcome in that,
since 1960, the Quebec educational system has
produced large numbers of university and college graduates with the requisite qualifications
for public service appointments.

A tangible indicator of progress is the fact
that francophones are now represented in the
public service in almost exact proportion to
their numbers in the total population—an increase from 12.25 percent of the service in 1946
to 27.8 percent in 1985. However, only 20.3
percent of the Management Category is composed of francophones. The Public Service
Commission concluded in 1977 that "the proportion of francophones in the federal Public
Service has not yet reached that 'critical mass'
that would allow the two language communities to survive, to be self-sustaining and to
come into their own, yet this is one of the
preconditions for efficient and high-quality
service to all Canadians."[27] The evidence provided in subsequent annual reports of the
commission—and of the Commissioner of Official Languages as well—reaffirms this conclusion. In 1985, the Office Languages Commissioner reported that "in spite of general
progress, the underlying problems are practically the same as those pointed out in every
Annual Report since 1980: Anglophones are
under-represented in Quebec and in the Administrative Support category; Francophones
are under-represented in management generally, . . . in the Scientific and Professional category and in bilingual regions outside Quebec."[28]

Female Representation

The underrepresentation of women in
Canada's public services has existed from
Confederation to the present day because of

obstacles to equal opportunity both in the government and in society generally.

By 1885, only 23 of 4280 public servants were women, and more than one-third of these were junior clerks in the Post Office Department. The proportion of women in the service rose gradually to 14 per cent in 1928 and to 18.7 percent in 1937. It accelerated during the war years and reached 35 per cent in 1943, but declined after the war and remained at about 27 percent during the 1960s.[29] Since, by 1970, women constituted about 30 percent of the total labour force, they were not badly underrepresented in the public service in relation to the private sector. However, they were—and remain—poorly represented at the senior levels of the service. In 1971, only 14.1 percent of officer positions in the service were held by women, whereas women made up 29.3 percent of the service as a whole.[30]

Before 1970, the government took little action to promote female representation in the public service. It was not until 1955 that the restriction against hiring married women for government employment was abolished. The Royal Commission on Government Organization (the Glassco Commission) noted in 1963 that the government had not fully implemented equality of treatment for women and called upon the government to show "creative leadership in providing equal opportunities for women."[39] In the 1967 Public Service Employment Act, sex was included along with race, national origin, colour, and religion as a basis on which it was forbidden to discriminate. Then, the Royal Commission on the Status of Women reported in 1970 that women do not enjoy equal opportunity to "enter and advance in Government Service, and that their skills and abilities are not being fully used there. Attitudes and practices seem to be at fault."[32] The commissioners made numerous recommendations to ensure equality of oppor-

tunity for women in the public service, and the government implemented most of these recommendations.

Barriers to equal opportunity for women have been similar in the public and private sectors of society. The under-utilization of women has generally been attributed to differences in formal education and work experience between men and women and to low career expectations, high absenteeism, and high turnover among female employees. Studies on the role of women in the public service conclude that these factors are not sufficient to explain fully the lower salaries and subordinate positions received by women. The attitude that women do not perform as well as men in managerial and supervisory positions helps to explain the underrepresentation of females at the senior levels of the service.

As with francophones, the government used a variety of strategies to remove barriers to female representation, including new administrative structures, active recruitment, and training. To date, the success of these government strategies to increase female representation has been modest, but progress is being made. Between 1975 and 1985, the percentage of women in the public service rose from 35.6 percent to 41.6 percent. At the end of 1985, women made up 82.7 percent of the Administrative Support Category and 7.8 percent of the Management Category.

The Representation of Native People

The underrepresentation of native people[33] in the public service is much more striking than that of francophones and women. The federal government estimates that native people constitute as much as 4 percent of the Canadian population, but as of December 1981, they made up less than 1.5 percent of the public service. Of these employees, 54 percent worked for the Department of Indian Affairs and

Northern Development, and the majority of the rest worked in five other departments. Less than 0.5 percent of positions in the Management Category were occupied by native people.

This underrepresentation of native people reflects the lack of effective native participation in the Canadian labour force as a whole, and results from a formidable array of institutional and attitudinal barriers to representation both in the government and in the native community. Native people have been isolated culturally and geographically from the mainstream of Canadian society. Inadequate educational facilities and opportunities have made it difficult for them to obtain the academic qualifications required for entry into the public service, especially at the senior levels. As a result of the small number of native people in the public service and of their concentration in the lower ranks, native people are not sufficiently aware of career opportunities in the more senior echelons. There is no visible cadre of native public servants whose achievements they are motivated to emulate. Furthermore, the government's recruitment practices tend to emphasize formal academic qualifications rather than practical experience, and to stress competence in the French or English languages rather than in a native language. Discriminatory attitudes towards native people, which are widespread in Canadian society, are found also in the public service.[34]

These various governmental and societal factors have combined to discourage native people from seeking positions in the service and to confine those who do enter primarily to lower-level positions. To overcome these obstacles, the federal government has adopted strategies similar to those used to increase the representation of francophones and women. New administrative units have engaged in active recruitment and training of native people.[35]

Affirmative Action

Despite its efforts to increase the representation of the target groups, the federal government is not satisfied that sufficient progress has been made. In June 1983, the government announced its continued commitment to a bureaucracy "that is representative of and responsive to the people it services,"[36] and introduced an affirmative action program to accelerate the participation in the public service of the target groups. *Affirmative action* was defined as "a comprehensive systems-based approach to the identification and elimination of discrimination in employment. It makes use of detailed analyses to identify and systematically remove employment policies, practices and procedures which may exclude or place at a disadvantage the three target groups"[37] (women, indigenous people, and handicapped people). The government stressed that the merit principle is to be preserved, and that the numerical goals being set were not quotas, but rather, "an estimate of what can be achieved when systemic barriers are eliminated and some temporary special measures are put in place to accelerate training and development experience."[38] The President of the Treasury Board announced that implementation of the affirmative action program would be viewed as a major consideration in the performance of deputy ministers. While this affirmative action program does not establish quotas, its use of temporary special measures, numerical goals, and pressure on senior bureaucrats to achieve these goals is likely to result in greater emphasis on the responsiveness/sensitivity components than on the efficiency/effectiveness components of public service merit.

The legal basis for affirmative action programs in the federal sphere of government was laid in 1977 by the Canadian Human Rights Act. This Act established the Canadian Human Rights Commission to investigate complaints about discrimination by federal departments, Crown corporations, and businesses under federal jurisdiction, to work out settlements in individual cases, and to promote the reduction of discriminatory practices through publicity and research. The wording of section 15(1) of the Act suggests that measures taken to redress historical imbalances in the participation of certain groups does not amount to "reverse discrimination."

More recently, the recommendations of the Royal Commission on Equality in Employment[39] and the coming into force of section 15—the equality rights section—of the Canadian Charter of Rights and Freedoms prompted the federal government to promote employment equity as part of its affirmative action program. It is especially important to note that affirmative action programs are protected under the Charter. Section 15 guarantees "equal protection and equal benefit of the law without discrimination" and then goes on to say that this guarantee "does not preclude any law, program or activity that has as its object the amelioration of conditions of disadvantaged individuals or groups including those that are disadvantaged because of race, national or ethnic origin, colour, religion, sex, age or mental or physical disability." In other words, preferential treatment for groups which have historically suffered from discrimination does not constitute reverse discrimination.

As explained earlier in this chapter, employment equity seeks to eliminate attitudinal and systemic barriers in public and private sector organizations to the equitable representation and remuneration of women and minority groups. The term *systemic barriers* (or systemic discrimination) refers to an employment policy, practice, procedure, or system that excludes or has a negative effect on women or minority groups, whether or not that effect was intended, and which cannot be justified as being job-related. For example, if 15 percent of the geologists in Canada are women, but only 6 percent of the geologists in the Department of Energy, Mines and Resources are women, the burden is on the department to show that this is not the result of discrimination. The explanation could be that the department requires that all the geologists it hires have ten years of working experience and that relatively few female geologists have that experience. Consideration would be given to removing this requirement because its impact is to penalize women more than men, even though no discrimination was intended by the requirement. The federal Employment Equity Act (Bill C-62), which was passed by the House of Commons in March 1986, requires employers who employ "one hundred or more employees on or in connection with a federal work, undertaking or business" to report annually to the government on the extent to which they have achieved results in promoting employment equity.

In September 1985, the federal government expanded its affirmative action program by announcing special measures to promote employment equity in the federal public service for members of *visible minority groups*.[40] These initiatives were in part a response to the recommendations of the House of Commons Special Committee on Participation of Visible Minorities in Canadian Society.[41] A government survey showed that members of visible minority groups are underrepresented in the public service in that they make up about 1.7 percent of the service compared to more than 4 percent of the labour force. The new measures to be introduced included revising employment application forms to allow members of visible minority groups to so identify themselves, providing estimates of the availability of qualified members of these groups in the labour market to help public service managers establish targets for hiring members of these groups, and incorporating a special section on visible minorities in training courses for public service managers.

CONCLUDING OBSERVATIONS

The management of human resources is a centrally important function of government which is closely related to several of the subjects examined [in] earlier [chapters]. Many of the issues discussed [in this chapter] are of an enduring nature; despite continuing efforts, they have not yet been resolved to the satisfaction of the government or its employees. Other issues have emerged more recently. One of these—equal opportunity—has such important political and administrative ramifications that it promises to have a continuing impact on public administration at all levels of Canadian government. [Another issue—collective bargaining—is of such pervasive and enduring significance in human resource management that it merits the separate treatment it receives in the next chapter.]

Notes

1. For an examination of the theory of representative bureaucracy and of its inadequacies, see V. Subramaniam, "Representative Bureaucracy: A Reassessment," *American Political Science Review* 61 (December, 1967): 1010-19; Arthur D. Larson, "Representative Bureaucracy and Administrative Responsibility: A Reassessment," *Midwest Review of Public Administration* 7 (April 1973): 78-89; Kenneth John Meier, "Representative Bureaucracy: An Empirical Analysis," *American Political Science Review* 69 (June 1965): 526-42; and V. Seymour Wilson and Willard A. Mullins, "Representative Bureaucracy: Linguistic/Ethnic Aspects in Canadian Public Policy," *Canadian Public Administration* 21 (Winter 1978): 513-38.

2. Peta E. Sheriff, "Unrepresentative Bureaucracy," *Sociology* 8 (1974): 449.

3. Kenneth John Meier and Lloyd C. Nigro, "Representative Bureaucracy and Policy Preferences: A Study in the Attitudes of Federal Executives," *Public Administration Review* 36 (July-August 1976): 467.

4. John Porter, "Higher Public Servants and the Bureaucratic Elite in Canada," *Canadian Journal of Economics and Political Science* 24 (November 1958): 483-501; Donald C. Rowat, "On John Porter's Bureaucratic Elite in Canada," ibid., 25 (May 1959): 204-7; and John Porter, "The Bureaucratic Elite: A Reply to Professor Rowat," ibid., 25 (May 1959): 207-9.

5. Rowat, 204.

6. Porter, "Higher Public Servants," 490-1.

7. Ibid., 490.

8. Rowat, 207.

9. Porter, "The Bureaucratic Elite," 208.

10. Ibid., 209.

11. Wilson and Mullins, Representative Bureaucracy," 533.

12. Ibid., 534.

13. *The State Elite* (Toronto: McClelland and Stewart, 1980).

14. Ibid., 82.

15. Christopher Beattie, Jacques Desy, and Stephen Longstaff, *Bureaucratic Careers: Anglophones and Francophones in the Canadian Public Service*, Research study no. 11 for the Royal Commission on Bilingualism and Biculturalism (Ottawa: Information Canada, 1972), 87.

16. Olsen, 82. (Emphasis in original.)

17. Ibid., 71-8.

18. Ibid., 79.

19. Public Service Commission, *Annual Report 1976* (Ottawa: Minister of Supply and Services, 1977), 15.

20. Public Service Commission, *Equality of Access: Equal Opportunity Programs and the Merit Principle* (Ottawa: Public Service Commission, 1982), 3.

21. V. Seymour Wilson and Willard A. Mullins, "Representative Bureaucracy: Linguistic/Ethnic Aspects in Canadian Public Policy," *Canadian Public Administration* 21 (Winter 1978): 520.

22. Royal Commission on Government Organization, *Report* (Queen's Printer, 1963) 1, 27-9.

23. House of Commons, *Debates*, April 6, 1966, 3915.

24. Ibid., June 23, 1970, 8487.

25. For information on the implementation and effectiveness of these strategies, see the annual reports of the Commissioner of Official Languages. On the history of language-training programs and the Office of the Commissioner of Official Languages, see the twelve-volume work by Gilles Bibeau, *Report of the Independent Study on the Language Training Programmes of the Public Service of Canada*, 1975. On the issue of language of work, see the special report of the Commissioner of Official Languages entitled *Language of Work in the Federal Public Service*, December 1982.

26. C.M. Drury, *Minutes of Proceedings and Evidence of the Standing Committee on Miscellaneous Estimates*, March 9, 1971, Issue no. 11:8.

27. Public Service Commission, *Annual Report 1977* (Ottawa: Minister of Supply and Services, 1978), 27.

28. Commissioner of Official Languages, *Annual Report* 1985 (Ottawa: Supply and Services, 1986), 41.

29. Stanislaw Judek, *Women in the Public Service* (Ottawa: Queen's Printer, 1968), 7-9, and Kathleen Archibald, *Sex and the Public Service* (Ottawa: Queen's Printer, 1970), 106.

30. Calculations based on Public Service Commission, *Annual Report 1971* (Ottawa: Information Canada, 1972), 44-5.

31. Vol. 1, 275.

32. Royal Commission on the Status of Women, *Report* (Ottawa: Information Canada, 1970), 138.

33. The term "native people" refers to status Indians, Inuit, Metis, and non-status Indians.

34. See *Native People and Employment in the Public Service of Canada.* A report prepared by Impact Research for the Public Service Commission, October 1976, 40-4.

35. See Public Service Commission, *Annual Report* 1985 (Ottawa: Supply and Services, 1986), 27-8.

36. Treasury Board, *Affirmative Action in the Public Service, News Release*, June 27, 1983.

37. Ibid.

38. Ibid.

39. *Report* (Ottawa: Supply and Services, 1984).

40. Treasury Board, *Special Employment Measures for Members of Visible Minority Groups, News Release*, September 9, 1985. These measures were expanded in mid-1986. See Treasury Board, *Enhanced Employment Opportunities to Help Visible Minority Persons and Other Affirmative Action Target Groups, News Release,* June 26, 1986.

41. Canada, House of Commons, *Equality Now! Report of the Special Committee on Visible Minorities in Canadian Society*, Issue no. 4, March, 8, 1984.

8. SHOULD THE JUDICIARY BE SOCIALLY REPRESENTATIVE?

Peter H. Russell

Is there also a need for a more representative mix of social backgrounds among members of the Canadian judiciary? In terms of social class, there can be no doubt about the unrepresentative character of the Canadian judiciary. Nearly all of Canada's judges are recruited from the ranks of moderately successful lawyers who have reached at least mid-career. A moderately successful, middle aged lawyer, while not necessarily rich is certainly not poor. There is a similar class bias in the parental background of the lawyers who become judges. This is true whether one looks at the top or the bottom of the judicial hierarchy. Adams and Cavaluzzo in their biographical study of the first fifty Supreme Court of Canada judges, found that only two of them were born into working-class families.[1] John Hogarth, in his study of Ontario magistrates, reports that "more than half the magistrates come from business or professional families, while not many more than one in ten of the general population are drawn from these occupational groups."[2] Bouthillier's research on the Quebec judiciary yields similar results. In particular he draws attention to occupation inheritance: the high number of judges raised in the families of judges and lawyers.

The unrepresentative character of the Canadian judiciary in a social class sense is a

fact. But is it also a problem, something that in a liberal democracy we should be seeking to change? I think not. It is important that social and economic barriers to legal education be removed, but to a large extent this has been done in Canada. Admission to law school now depends on academic marks and aptitude tests, not social connections. But, advantages of birth do remain: it helps a lot to grow up in an environment that nurtures an interest in the legal vocation or, more generally, an environment that makes the affluence and prestige of the lawyer the expected standard of success. Only the most fiendishly authoritarian regime would try to eliminate such advantages. Nor is there reason to believe that if more lawyers with working-class backgrounds were appointed to the bench, our courts would treat members of that class more fairly or leniently. Some very tough attitudes may be engendered in the person who has had to struggle and "make it the hard way." In his study of sentencing, Hogarth found that magistrates from working-class families were rather more punitive in their attitudes and beliefs.[3]

The uniformity in the class backgrounds of Canada's judges does not constitute, as Dennis Olsen has suggested, a "contradiction ... between liberal-democratic ideology and practice."[4] The ideal of liberal democracy is not a classless society without structure. The pluralism valued by liberals is not a wide-open, limitless pluralism in which truly all things are possible. [As we argued in the opening chapter,] the judiciary as part of the

Peter H. Russell, *The Judiciary in Canada: The Third Branch of Government* (Toronto: McGraw-Hill Ryerson Ltd., 1987), 164-9 and notes 60-83 [1-24]. Reprinted by permission of the publisher.

governing structure in any society will be supportive of its prevailing ideology. Through their legal education and professional experience, judges absorb the values and accommodate the interests that have shaped the law. That law—the law they must as judges interpret and apply—is no more neutral than it is fixed or certain. We should not expect judges in Canada to believe that private ownership of the means of production or exchange is evil or that poverty should be accepted as a defence for robbery. But within this common *Weltanschauung* there can be many grounds for differing with the outlook and sensitivities of the government of the day. It is here that political pluralism is needed in staffing the judiciary of a liberal state. We should be concerned about recruitment policies that favour partisan supporters of the government or crown attorneys over defence lawyers. As long as judges are recruited entirely from the ranks of successful lawyers (and that policy, as we have seen, is now well established in Canada) the bourgeois orientation of the Canadian judiciary is unavoidable. This may very well mean that when class issues are clearly at stake in adjudication, the Canadian judiciary is not impartial. R.M. Jackson, in his study of the English judiciary, notes how the class bias of English judges has been reflected in a series of questionable decisions concerning the rights of trade unions. But the remedy, Jackson suggests, is not to seek out working-class judges but to recognize that, given this limitation of the judiciary, industrial disputes should as far as possible be kept out of the courts and resolved by joint bodies, representing employers and workers.[5]

There are, however, some other ways in which the Canadian judiciary is unrepresentative, about which we should be more concerned. Aboriginal persons have not been appointed to the bench above the position of justice of the peace. Indeed, there are very few non-Caucasians among Canadian judges.

Also, less than 5 percent of Canadian judges are women. The under-representation of women is worse on the higher courts: in 1980 Pauline Jewett told the House of Commons that only twenty (3 percent) of the 657 federally appointed judges then serving were women and all but two of these had been appointed since 1971.[6] At that time there were no women on the Supreme Court of Canada or the superior courts of six provinces. Under-representation in these areas has more than a symbolic significance. It also means that insights and knowledge needed for intelligent adjudication are often lacking. Native Canadians who become judges are likely to be much better informed than Canadian judges have been up to now about the meaning and significance of aboriginal rights—rights which are now entrenched in the Canadian Constitution.[7] Black judges might call into question the harsher sentences given black youths in the Halifax Provincial Court.[8] Through their first-hand experience of "the deprivations of personhood," to use Pauline Jewett's phrase, women judges should be able to help Canadian courts respond more intelligently to claims of sex discrimination. It would surely be ridiculous to aim for a judiciary that precisely mirrored the diversity of the Canadian population. Without approaching that extreme, there is still much that could be done and much to be gained in moving the Canadian judiciary away from the vertical mosaic that John Porter described a generation ago.[9] Access to legal education has now been broadened to the point that it should be possible to appoint more members of under-represented groups without sacrificing quality. This is certainly true in the case of women, who by now constitute a significant proportion of the lawyers with ten years of practice.[10] Research on the result of President Carter's affirmative action approach to judicial appointments concludes that this policy, far from undermining merit selection, on balance improved the quality of appointments.[11]

LINGUISTIC AND REGIONAL REPRESENTATION

The need to reflect the constitutional ideal of official bilingualism in Canada's judicial process poses a distinctive representational challenge to the Canadian judiciary. The Constitution has always provided the right to use English or French in courts established by the federal Parliament and in the courts of Manitoba and Quebec.[12] In 1982 a similar requirement was added for the courts of New Brunswick.[13] The scope of this constitutional right has been broadly interpreted by the Supreme Court of Canada. In 1979, in the *Blaikie* case, the Court held that the right applies to administrative tribunals exercising judicial or quasi-judicial powers as well as to the regular courts, and is available to corporations as well as to individuals.[14] In provinces where the constitutional right does not apply, the need to resist Quebec separatism has created political pressure to provide bilingual court services. This is particularly true of Ontario which has the largest French minority. In 1984 that province inserted a clause in its Courts of Justice Act declaring English and French to be the "official languages" of its courts.[15] The act identifies areas of Ontario in which there is a significant francophone population and in these designated areas gives the litigant the right to require a hearing "before a judge who speaks both the English and French language."[16]

Bilingual judges (and juries), although not the only way, are certainly the most effective way of providing judicial services in English and French. In Quebec, because most francophone lawyers have been bilingual, it has not

been difficult to staff a bilingual judiciary. Thus, even though anglophones, in the modern period, have been under-represented on the Quebec bench,[17] members of Quebec's English-speaking community have always been able to have their cases heard by judges proficient in their language. The same has not been true for the French-speaking minority outside of Quebec, although in recent years Ontario has made an impressive effort in a practical, if not a symbolic, way to meet the Quebec standard. In other provinces a good many judges are taking advantage of the language training available under the auspices of the Canadian Judicial Council. However, in Manitoba and New Brunswick, where court service in French and English are constitutionally mandated, it would appear that not enough judges are proficient in French to give reality to the constitutional right to use French in court proceedings. While the Supreme Court of Canada in 1986 in the *Société des Acadiens Case* held that the language guarantee itself does not require that the judges hearing cases pleaded in French be able to understand French, it did refer to the common law requirement that parties in judicial proceedings be heard and understood.[18]

At the federal level, the Federal Court Act requires that at least eight of the Federal Court's twenty-five judges come from Quebec.[19] There is no such requirement in the act establishing the Tax Court of Canada, although that court too is constitutionally obliged to hear cases in both languages. The Supreme Court Act of 1875 required that two of the Court's judges come from Quebec. This requirement was not changed when the Supreme Court was expanded to seven judges in 1927 but was increased to three Quebec judges when the Court was increased to nine in 1949.[20] Of course, the rationale for this provision was not so much language as the need to provide judges with a background in Quebec's distinctive civil law. Indeed, the constitutional right to be heard in French in the Supreme Court of Canada was scarcely a reality until the 1960s. No translation services were provided and a majority of the judges could not understand spoken French.[21] As a result, Quebec lawyers appearing before the Court jeopardized their chances of winning if they chose to argue in French. Much has been done since then to remedy the situation. Instantaneous translation is available and newly appointed English-speaking justices take French immersion courses. Francophone lawyers may still feel that they will communicate more effectively if they argue in English. Nonetheless, it is interesting to observe how much more frequently in recent years bilingual Quebec lawyers will make a point of exercising their constitutional right to use French in the Supreme Court.

A representational pattern that has assumed the status of a constitutional convention is the representation of the major regions of Canada on the Supreme Court of Canada. This convention, like many others, cannot be stated with mathematical precision. Table [1] shows that while there has been some variation over the years in the number of judges from each region, for all but four years of this century the Supreme Court has included justices from Ontario, Quebec, the Atlantic provinces and the Western provinces. A prime minister who departed from this degree of regional representation would likely suffer serious political consequences. Thus geography is the most important representational factor in staffing the Canadian Supreme Court. Some attention has been paid to religion in that at least one-third of the Court has been Roman Catholic and it has usually included a Catholic from English-speaking Canada. However, until the appointment of Bora Laskin in 1970, no person of a non-Christian faith had served on the bench. The Court has been quite un-

representative in terms of ethnicity and gender.[22] Except for Laskin no person of a non-British or non-French heritage has been appointed. In 1982, Bertha Wilson became the first woman to serve on the Court.

Table 1 Regional Representation on the Supreme Court of Canada, 1875-1982

Year*	Quebec	Ontario	Atlantic Provinces	Western Provinces
1875	2	2	2	0
1888	2	3	1	0
1893	2	2	2	0
1903	2	1	2	1
1905	2	2	2	0
1906	2	2	1	1
1927	2	3	1	1
1949	3	3	1	2
1979	3	2	1	3
1982	3	3	1	2

* The years listed are years in which appointment to the Supreme Court altered the pattern of regional representation.

The fact that regional representation looms so large in appointments to the Supreme Court reflects the politics of the Canadian federation. Geography has been a consideration in appointments to the U.S. Supreme Court but no greater than religion and, in the modern era, not as crucial a factor as ideology.[23] The justification for this emphasis in the Canadian case is primarily symbolic. Justices do not function on the Court as representatives of their regions. The participation of the Quebec judges in Quebec appeals ensures that expertise in Quebec's civil law can be brought to bear on these cases. Regional expertise is much less salient for cases coming from common law Canada and there is much less of a regional pattern in panels of the Court dealing with these cases. Now that the Court's docket is concerned mostly with issues of federal law and constitutional law, the functional rationale for regional representation is weaker than ever. But at the same time the strains in the Canadian federation are such that it has become more essential than ever before to secure the allegiance of political elites in the various regions of Canada for national institutions such as the Supreme Court. Thus, for the foreseeable future the principle of regional representation will be observed and is likely to be recognized in any agreement reached by the current generation of political leaders on entrenching the Supreme Court in the Constitution.[24]

Notes

1. George Adams and Paul J. Cavaluzzo, "The Supreme Court of Canada: A Biographical Study," *Osgoode Hall Law Journal* (1969): 84.

2. Hogarth, *Sentencing as a Human Process* (Toronto: University of Toronto Press, 1971), 54.

3. Ibid., 212.

4. D. Olsen, *The State Elite* (Toronto: McClelland and Stewart, 1980), 52.

5. R.M. Jackson, *The Machinery of Justice in England* 7e (Cambridge: Cambridge University Press, 1977), 474-5.

6. House of Commons, *Debates*, 18 Dec. 1980, 5890.

7. For a critique of the Canadian judiciary's treatment of aboriginal rights issues, see Brian Slattery, "The Hidden Constitution: Aboriginal Rights in Canada," in Menno Boldt, Anthony J. Long, and Leroy Little Bear, *The Quest for Justice* (Toronto: University of Toronto Press, 1985).

8. See K.E. Renner and A.H. Warner, "The Standard of Social Justice Applied to an Evaluation of Criminal Cases Appearing Before the Halifax Courts," *The Windsor Yearbook of Access to Justice* (1981): 62.

9. John Porter, *The Vertical Mosaic* (Toronto: University of Toronto Press, 1965).

10. Pauline Jewett estimated in 1980 that women with ten years' professional experience constituted 15% of the total number of lawyers practising in Canada. House of Commons, *Debates*, 18 Dec. 1980, 5892.

11. Sheldon Goldman, "Carter's Judicial Appointments: A Lasting Legacy," *Judicature* (Mar. 1983): 343.

12. Constitution Act, 1867, s. 133; Manitoba Act, 1870, s. 23.

13. Constitution Act, 1982, s. 19(2).

14. *A.G. Quebec* v. *Blaikie* [1979] SCR 1066.

15. SO, 1984, c. 11, s. 135(1).

16. Ibid., s. 136(2). S. 136(3) establishes a right to bilingual juries when jury trials are held in districts designated in the statute. In Dec. 1986 this right was extended to the whole of Ontario, but in the superior court the demand for this service has been largely in Ottawa, Prescott, Cornwall, and Cochrane.

17. Bouthillier, "Profil du juge de la Cour Superieure," reports that in 1973, 15% of Quebec's Superior Court judges were English as compared with 19% of the population and 25% of the provincial bar, and overall only 5% of the provincially appointed Court of Sessions judges have been English.

18. *Société des Acadiens* v. *Minority Language School Board No. 30* [1986] 1 SCR 549.

19. SC 1985, c. 38, s. 11.

20. The Supreme Court Act, s. 6.

21. See Peter H. Russell, *The Supreme Court of Canada as a Bilingual and Bicultural Institution* (Ottawa: Queen's Printer, 1969).

22. For an analysis of these features of the first fifty appointments to the Supreme Court, see Adams and Cavaluzzo, "The Supreme Court."

23. For an analysis of the representational aspects of Supreme Court appointments in the United States, see John R. Schmidhauser, "The Justice of the Supreme Court: A Collective Portrait," *Midwest Journal of Political Science* (1959): 1-56. Abraham, *Judicial Process*, provides data on appointments since 1959.

24. This is more fully developed in Peter Russell, "Constitutional Reform of the Judicial Branch: Symbolic vs. Operational Consideration," *Canadian Journal of Political Science* (1984): 227.

9. THE CHANGING ENVIRONMENT AND ROLE OF SPECIAL INTEREST GROUPS

Khayyam Z. Paltiel

In the past two decades Canadians have witnessed a sharp increase in the number and activities of interest groups operating at all levels of government. Scarcely any decision or policy initiative—from the most minor zoning variance, to the location of hydro-electric transmission lines or airports, to conservation measures, to the launching of new welfare, educational or billion-dollar mega projects—fails to provoke the intervention of some organized body concerned about its impact on the interests of its members. The traditional forums of public debate and interest aggregation in Parliament and party appear to have been bypassed in the drive by group spokesmen to achieve direct access to political and bureaucratic decision-makers. The increasing number of interactions by way of information gathering and dissemination, advice and consultation, together with exchanges of personnel between the private, voluntary, para-public and governmental sectors in the process of priority setting, policy formulation, policy-making and implementation, suggests that the nature and role of the Canadian state has undergone a fundamental change.

To some observers this signifies a more participatory democracy; to some it appears to have compounded the advantages of those

Khayyam Z. Paltiel, "The Changing Environment and Role of Special Interest Groups," *Canadian Public Administration* 25: 2 (1982): 198-210. Reprinted by permission of The Institute of Public Administration of Canada.

elite groups already in possession of the skills and resources necessary to attract the support of those at the political command posts. But for others of a more conservative and pessimistic bent, this development is viewed as the source of the increasing ungovernability of modern industrial societies owing to the phenomenon of governmental overload. These observers have pointed to the multiplicity of conflicting demands on political and bureaucratic decision-makers which cannot be met because of inflationary pressures, industrial recession and the drain of capital resources to the oil-producing countries as a cause of the political instability evidenced by frequent changes of government. Furthermore, it has been alleged that among those most culpable for these pressures are the public interest groups.

The participatory democracy school directs attention to the search by senior bureaucrats and the political elite for a legitimizing consensus to justify policy and serve as a foundation for maintenance in office and governmental stability. The left-liberal or progressive school emphasizes the unequal bargaining power of groups, the advantages enjoyed by the economic elites in the policy process and the skewed character of the outputs. Preoccupied by the threat to the stability of liberal democratic regimes, the overload school fixes blame on excess demand for public services and the excessive growth of public sector institutions with their alleged rigidities, the solution for which is to be sought in the reduction of expectations and "smaller" governments. Its proponents underline the consequences of the studied evasion of the allocative and distributive problem in advanced capitalist societies; times of fiscal scarcity highlight the fragility of the pluralist attempt to convert politics into administration and emphasize its dependence on high levels of sustained economic growth. Each of these schools provides some useful insights into the nature, the actors, and the consequences of group activity. But both individually and together they fall short of providing an explanation for the burgeoning of the group universe and the part played by the pressure system in the Canadian political process. The latter must be sought in the political economy of the contemporary Canadian state and the structure of Canadian society.

Although their interpretations of the emergence of the contemporary interventionist, dirigiste, positive welfare state differ, followers of the neo-Marxian and the various liberal schools of political economy in Canada are all agreed on the relative decline of political parties, legislatures and Parliament in the policy-making process. All are also agreed on the shift of power and authority to the political executive in the form of the cabinet, and on the increasingly salient role of the bureaucracy, especially at its senior levels in ministerial departments, central agencies, regulatory commissions and public corporations.

The Canadian state in the view of neo-Marxists[1] such as Rianne Mahon shares the features common to advanced capitalist societies: "the organization of a significant portion of the working class; the plurality of capitalist interests; substantial direct state intervention in the economy; the 'transfer' of state power to the executive; and the concomitant development of a professional or 'bureaucratic' civil service."[2] In Canada these features are complicated by the federal nature of the state[3] and the significant economic role played by multinational, primarily American, corporations[4]; each of these features pose specific problems of harmonization in addition to multiplying the interests to be reconciled. Bourgeois hegemony, and the assurance of continued accumulation and its legitimation, are maintained through a system of unequal representation of interests mirrored in the very structure of the state. The administrative apparatus contains the threat from subordinate classes, integrates marginal groups and accommodates the divisions within the capitalist class and its fractions. This role is facilitated by the relative autonomy of the state and the organization of its agencies in a manner which reflects the hierarchy of values and the need for the perpetuation of capitalist society. Interests are represented relative to their status, authority, resources and power, but in a manner which permits them to be constrained for the greater good of the system as a whole. Each department or agency embodies and is surrounded by a cluster of groups seeking access and recognition. The key actors, however, are members of the senior bureaucracy whose common values and interchangeability assure harmonization in the interest of the maintenance of the capitalist politico-economic order.

In the neo-Marxist view, the image of the state as neutral arbiter is simply a convenient illusion masking the true nature of the Canadian political process. Interest groups are not simply the spokesmen of the private or voluntary sector but serve as instruments of social control for the benefit of the capitalist state. The neo-Marxists appear to deny the possibility that interest groups themselves may be gaining more autonomy over resources and capabilities, thus permitting them to acquire control over certain aspects of their environment. Furthermore, despite the specific disclaimer that they have adopted an instrumentalist view of the state—in common with the older classical or vulgar Marxism—it does appear that the process described by the neo-Marxists implies a self-awareness and self-consciousness on the part of politicians and administrators which mere verbal denials cannot belie. The apparent relegation of interest groups to passive reactors waiting to be managed flies in the face of current reality. Just as the state must enjoy a certain autonomy in order to perform its functions, so do interest groups seek to control certain aspects of their environment and maintain a degree of freedom of action.

Paul Pross and S.J.R. Noel also provide a political economic explanation of the contemporary environment and the role of special interest groups in Canada. Its economic basis is to be found in the shift from small-scale local business to large pan-Canadian enterprises serving national and world markets. The concomitant political transformation has been the rise of a powerful bureaucracy and the decline of the traditional party system. For Pross,[5] the key feature of current Canadian politics is the replacement of spatial by sectoral politics and the emergence of the administrative and special interest state. The principal event in this process in his view was the introduction within the public service of a merit system of appointment and a technocratic classification system. A functionalist administrative structure has produced a parallel structure of interest groups which has subverted the role of parties in the policy communication area. As representative government is reduced to the merely symbolic and as policy outputs are seen to be largely the result of the interface between public and private sector elites, the legitimacy of the regime, as well as its decisions, has begun to wither.

In contrast to Pross's thesis, Noel[6] pinpoints a change in the pattern of political clientelism as the principal element in the transformation of the Canadian state into its current bureaucratic form. Borrowing the concept from the political anthropologists, Noel distinguishes three forms of clientelism in Canada; personal patron-client bonds; the patron-broker-client relationship; the bureaucratic clientelism. One form appears to grow out of the other, moving from a simple dyadic system with weak horizontal links, to a triadic relationship marked by the broker-intermediary or broker-fixer, culminating in the blossoming of a multiplicity of highly sophisticated impersonal bureaucratized supervisory and intermediary public organizations with attenuated and weak local personal dyadic links. The key variable in the shift from one stage of clientelism to another lies not in the political arena but in the economic realm. The evolution of the Canadian economy—from a rural, extractive or fishing base personified by the individual entrepreneur to a large-scale enterprise such as canal and railway-building requiring large amounts of capital under the aegis of joint-stock companies backed by some form of government guarantees—accounts for the shift from Stage I to Stage II clientelism. The local notable gave way to the promoter and the fixer, politics moved from a non-competitive to a competitive basis. The cadre and brokerage parties were born and leadership passed to brokers able to organize and maintain grand coalitions of interests. Politics and business were inextricably intertwined as the organized political party replaced the personalistic politics of Stage I clientelism. Differences in political style and leadership within and among the provincial and the federal governments in Canada find their explanation in the overlap and lags of the development of areas, regions and provinces of Noel's three stages.

Stage III, or bureaucratic clientelism, results from the expansion and proliferation of government activities stemming from the transformation of the Canadian economy. Rapidly growing public bureaucracies have ceased to be the patronage resource and preserve of the traditional parties. The broadening role and scope of government public services at all levels has narrowed the sphere of party politics. The merit and the credentialist systems of recruitment have transformed the bureaucracies into independent, quasi-autonomous structures which have assumed many of the clientelist functions formerly carried out by the political parties and their leaders; this process is readily confirmed by studies of Canadian interest group behaviour.

Professor Noel rightly points out that the substitution of universalist for discretionary grants, distributions, and other government benefits has enhanced the role of the bureaucracy and imposed dependency on the ever-increasing circle of its clients. But it has weakened the support system formerly available to its nominal masters in the form of the political parties. Particular bureaucratic agencies may well exploit the dependency of their clients to bargain for expanded budgets, staff and scope; nevertheless, the erosion of the support available to the political parties has increased the fragility of the Canadian political system as a whole.

However, there is a gap in Noel's argument due to his failure to spell out the socioeconomic correlatives of Stage III. Bureaucratic clientelism is not simply marked by the expansion of government and the proliferation of the scope and power of the public bureaucracies. The private economic sector in Canada is itself highly concentrated and bureaucratized in the form of vast conglomerates and holding companies. The public bureaucracy has its counterparts in private corporate bureaucratic structures which possess large resources and have a considerable independence and autonomy; in their latest multinational form they are even able to dispose of a degree of coercion. To these must

be added trade unions and voluntary and professional groups which are not simply puppets of the public sector.

Certain bureaucratic clienteles are more dependent than the older political clienteles, but in the industrial sector it may safely be asserted that the clientele has resources which considerably reduce if not eliminate one-way dependency; in the corporately organized economic sector the dependence may be mutual. To confuse the powerful interest groups with the individual welfare recipient or isolated scholar or artist is to blur the degree of accommodation between private and public sector elites. The relationship between a local ballet company and the Canada Council cannot without distortion serve as a model for the interaction between Imperial Oil and the National Energy Board or the Canadian Petroleum Association and the Department of Energy, Mines and Resources; nor is it an appropriate model for the relations between such bodies as the Canadian Labour Congress and the federal Department of Labour.

The foregoing approaches stress the primacy of the bureaucratic phenomenon which precludes the treatment of interest groups as autonomous and independent actors in the political process. A general theory of the Canadian pressure system must begin by viewing interest groups as something more than mere passive clienteles, conveyors of information, or instruments of social control; but it must go on to explore the explosive consequences of escalating interest group demands and competition.

Much fruitful work has been done in recent years in the area of Canadian interest group behaviour.[7] Case studies have been carried out in the fields of competition policy, agricultural policy, energy, mining and other resource industries, as well as the organization and structure of numerous groups ranging from manufacturing to labour. Robert

Presthus[8] has examined the interaction of public and private sector elites. David Kwavnick has traced the struggle for recognition by way of the search by labour organizations for legitimacy and mandate;[9] along with others he has examined how federal-provincial relations and the distribution of legislative authority and administrative competence affect the structures, strategies and tactics of interest groups.[10] A few attempts have been made to construct a typology of interest groups in order to facilitate analysis. Thus Pross has tried a continuum framework in which to examine groups in terms of their degree of institutionalization, their characteristics, and their levels of communication with government.[11] Others have studied groups in terms of their functions, orientations, structure, origin and degree of mobilization. The most common categorizations, however, are those which attempt to classify interest groups in terms of their policy area or in terms of their purported constituencies.[12] Interesting as these studies are in systematizing information about interest groups, it has been pointed out that the conventional divisions are deceptive in that they imply a non-existent symmetry and pluralism which glosses over differences in size, resources and influence and camouflages the distinctions between the relatively poor public interest groups and the multitude of well-financed and staffed groups speaking for the myriad business interests. Another failing of the conventional policy classifications is their lack of grounding in a general theory of groups which would relate their organization goals, size and resources—both human and financial—to their policy areas. More important for our purpose is the fact that they cast little light on the factors encouraging the emergence and survival of pressure groups.

Few, if any, Canadian studies provide clues which would account for the growth in the number of groups and the impact of their resource base on their role and character. To fill the gaps I have drawn on a recent study by John L. Walker of the Institute of Public Policy Studies at the University of Michigan.[13] The findings are based on a 1980-81 survey of a comprehensive sample of all American voluntary associations open to membership "concerned with some aspects of public policy at the national level."

The bulk of the interest groups surveyed were organized around discrete occupational roles by a proportion of four to one; that is, almost 80 percent sought to protect some professional, industrial or bureaucratic interest while only about one-fifth were open to members without special occupational qualifications. Walker finds that most groups cluster on either side of the "central cleavage" in the American political system, namely, the business or profit-making sector on the one hand and the governmental, public or charitable sector on the other. However, in addition to the three mutually exclusive classes which embraced the majority of groups, there is a fourth category of occupationally based groups whose membership is drawn from both the public and private sectors. A fourfold typology of groups based on occupational roles thus results: three occupational sectors, private, public non-profit, and mixed; and non-occupational citizens's groups. The first includes trade associations representing private business and economic interests and professional bodies of those engaged in a "fee-for-service" or employed in private profit-making businesses. The second includes public sector trade associations and organizations of professionals working largely for non-profit agencies. The third, mixed class, draws members from both the private and public sectors by way of professional societies (e.g., planners) and some trade associations which include private and public agencies and corporations. The least homogeneous class is the category of citizen groups which are open to all regardless of their occupational affiliations but which do include professionals interested in the issue area.

The value of Walker's typology becomes clear in his study of the history and origins of interest groups. He found that more than half of all the groups still in existence were founded since 1945, with a sharp rise since 1960. Enhancing this trend has been the rapid relocation of group national headquarters from other cities to the nation's capital. But more significant from our point of view than the absolute growth of the interest group system has been the change in its composition. The biggest increase in numbers, and I daresay this holds true for Canada as well, has been the growth in the numbers and proportion of groups falling in the citizens' group category— those promoting an idea or cause in contrast to those with an occupational prerequisite. Whereas citizen groups were less than one-seventh of the total number founded before 1960, by 1980 this type constituted more than one-fifth of the total; and even more important, half the total number of citizen groups were established after 1960. Much of the sense of conflict and pressure felt by political leaders and senior bureaucrats may thus be attributed to this growth in citizen group numbers. This pressure was probably further enhanced by the confrontational public tactics used by the leaders of these groups to attract media attention and maintain the loyalties of their scattered and variegated membership.

The 1960s were characterized by an explosion of self-awareness among consumers, students, women and native groups and in Canada by Québécois nationalism and ethnic group self-consciousness. These social movements were accompanied by a bursting forth of clientelist groups, created in response to the elaboration of the welfare state during the same period. In turn, the emergence of these new formations galvanized established institutional groups into renewed action to protect themselves against the demands of the newly conscious and to restore a shattered equilibrium which had previously operated in their favour.

To some extent the growth of citizen groups can be attributed to demographic changes, including changes in the structure of the workforce, and the spread of higher education which coincided with a communications revolution, thus permitting the easy spread of the group's message and the recruitment of members. Important as these factors were, the most telling was the discovery by potential group leaders of new sources of support outside their immediate membership and followings. Lacking the advantages of an occupational community, the organizers of citizen groups had always faced the dilemma of the absence of start-up and maintenance funds and have had to depend on external funding. In the 1960s such resources were discovered in the shape of benevolent sympathizers, private foundations in search of an agenda, and most importantly, public agencies, bureaucrats and politicians in search of an expanded constituency, votes and political support. Whereas private-sector groups depend largely on their membership for support, external funding in the past twenty years has apparently played an ever-increasing role in the funding of citizen, non-profit and even the mixed-sector groups.

But governmental and bureaucratic patronage, as S.J.R. Noel has pointed out, like all patron-client relations, is an exchange relationship. Occasionally it is entered into in an effort to coordinate delivery systems or diffuse techniques. Recently patrons have disbursed funds in an effort to mollify social frustration and channel protest along peaceful lines through co-optation of the leadership. Most often, however, bureaucratic patrons make their disbursements to groups that share, support and will defend their view of social policy. Thus Walker finds, and I am reasonably certain that Canadian evidence would corroborate, that an overwhelming majority of groups receiving public funds would support and almost half would welcome increased governmental intervention in the economy and society. On the other hand, of those groups not receiving governmental assistance, almost two-thirds desire a decrease in government intervention.

Thus in place of a model which views citizens as the active proponents and legislators as the passive ratifiers of public demand, a pressure model of the policy process must take account, as Walker states and Noel implies, of the motives of the patrons of political action who seek support for an ever-expanding role and budgetary allocations through the sponsorship of clientelistic groups.

If this model is valid then the resolution of the problems of overload confronting modern governments and the alleged ungovernability of post-industrial societies must be sought elsewhere than in the simple reduction of competing and contradictory demands on government made by importunate pressure groups.

This search must of necessity review the principal explanations and views of the role of interest groups and their relation to the state in democratic societies. Contrary to the received wisdom in current popular writing and the participatory slogans of the 1960s, the traditional view of interest groups in liberal democratic thought was quite negative. Madison in the Federalist Papers warned of the dangers of faction. French writers in the tradition of Jean Jacques Rousseau spoke of "la républic une et indivisible," emphasizing the threat of particularist organizations to the general will thus providing the ideological underpinnings for the Le Chapelier law which inhibited the formation of private associations. Organizations such as trade unions were treated as criminal

conspiracies under the Combination Acts in the United Kingdom as they were under the Criminal Code in Canada until the 1870s.

The removal of these legal inhibitions to organizational activity followed a recognition of the growing complexity of industrial societies and the realization that individual claims were a reflection of one's position in the social and economic system. The revelations of the role of the lobbyists in the formulation of legislation and their influence on legislators and political parties by critics of the economic order on the socialist and Marxist left forced a revaluation of individualist doctrines and the Burkean view of parties. Beginning with scholar-journalists like Bentley who saw all of politics as group activity, the pluralist school emerged which sought to reconcile group activity with the traditional notions of majoritarian democracy. They envisioned the political system as a grand marketplace where competing groups articulated the demands of their members for legitimacy and access to the political decision-makers in the parties. Overlapping group memberships and a common commitment to democratic norms would together act as a brake on extremist demands. For their part the parties seeking office and confronted with the imperatives of democratic elections would be compelled to formulate consensual political programs by aggregating a set of group demands capable of appealing to a majority of voters of varied background. Through inter-group competition and the notion of polyarchy, the pluralists thought that they had produced a reasonable facsimile of the utilitarian ideal of the great good of the greatest number. Governments' role in the pluralist universe was to be little more than that which it had played in the era of laissez-faire liberalism. In addition to providing for internal security, external defence and the provision of a minimal number of major public works, it was to make up, compensate and where feasible correct the failures of the marketplace; but its prime function and that of the parties which controlled its levers was simply to act as a broker ratifying bargains struck amongst rival interests.

It did not take much research to demonstrate that the pluralist attempt to counter conservative and Marxian criticisms of liberal democratic practice foundered on its failure to take account of the unequal bargaining power of particular groups, notably in the business sector, the unequal distribution of resources and information, and restricted access. And it turned out that the much-vaunted notion of overlapping memberships was characteristic of the socio-economic elites and propertied groups, which thus constituted a multiple vote rather than a check on overweening demands. The pluralist reconstruction of democratic theory was also undermined by the growth of the interventionist state. Clearly the state is not a neutral arbiter. But if pluralism is not an accurate description of the political process in advanced capitalist democracies, it nevertheless survives as one if not the most accepted of establishment ideologies. But like all ideologies, it camouflages the true nature of the political process.

Two further attempts have been made to describe and prescribe for the role of interest groups in the Canadian political process. Robert Presthus, after one of the most exhaustive surveys of legislative, bureaucratic and private sector elites, has had recourse to the theories of elite accommodation such as consociationalism in order to describe the nature of the interaction among the three elites. He explains the closeness of their relationships on the basis of their common social and educational background and shared values. This is reinforced by features of Canada's political culture which he finds to be corporatist and favourable to state intervention in behalf of the private sector. Further, the deferential character of Canadian citizens and their passive role in Canadian politics—usually limited to voting—leaves the elites a great margin to manoeuvre and order affairs according to their common values. Although Presthus's work is full of tantalizing insights worthy of further investigation, they do not appear to grow out of his research findings. The burden of Presthus's research bears on the relationship between the three elites and not on the notions of corporatism, consociationalism and the nature of mass political participation in Canada, which thus appear as explanatory afterthoughts unwarranted by the research data presented.

Corporatism constitutes the fourth school of thought which has attempted to deal with group activity in Canada.[14] In some ways it is the oldest and most varied effort made by Canadian political theorists and analysts. Its oldest manifestation lies in the writings of Catholic thinkers in Quebec who sought to mitigate the social disharmony and class conflict of a rapidly industrializing society by recourse to Church doctrines on the role of intermediary bodies in the spiritual and political realm. The first quarter of this century also saw the agrarian revolt with its attack on the party system and the substitution of delegate democracy based on the representation of functional groups. Both movements were overtaken by events but they were echoed in part, probably unconsciously, by Mackenzie King. In his *Industry and Humanity* King first elaborated what has come to be known as the theory of liberal corporatism based on a tripartite system of functional representation. Designed at the outset to deal with the problems he had encountered in his work as industrial relations adviser to the Rockefellers, King's scheme spelled out the principles which were to be found embodied in the Roosevelt

New Deal of the 1930s and have been incorporated in many of the constitutions adopted in the postwar era in Sweden, Austria, Switzerland, West Germany and elsewhere. That these mechanisms were not adopted in Canada despite the repeated efforts of the Trudeau government may be attributed to the absence of disciplined interest group networks of employers and labour under powerful peak organizations and the fissiparous tendencies inherent in the nature of Canadian federalism.

Although the theorists of interest group liberalism, elite accommodation and liberal corporatism diverge in their descriptions, analyses and prescriptions regarding the role of interest groups in the political process, all appear to be agreed on the diminished role which political parties play in the policy process. The political parties in Parliament, which in the conventional presentation are the aggregators of the general interest, have been reduced to be the simple ratifiers of decisions taken elsewhere by bureaucrats and the party elites in consultation with the spokesmen of the interest groups. This fact is already embodied in the notion of elite accommodation and would be simply formally recognized in any proposed application of corporatist principles.

Realistic as this description may be, it nevertheless points to a fundamental source of instability in allegedly open democratic systems in which parties have ceased to play their traditional role. Easton has defined politics as the authoritative allocation of values. The decline of party implies that the allocative decisions which are the essence of politics have begun to escape control by the democratic electorate. Elections, as Meisel[15] has indicated, are reduced to simple plebiscites and the essential political struggle, as Lowi[16] has seen, becomes one for group legitimacy and access.

Any group which has these attributes is by definition entitled to an allocated share, the denial of which would threaten the mainstays of the regime. In the absence of coercion, social peace—given the propagation of competitive groups through bureaucratic patronage and private sector resources—can only be purchased by an ever-expanding economy and allocative system. Lacking a means to focus on the common interest, a purely private-regarding political culture may be rendered extremely fragile and unstable by economic stagnation and decline.

This suggests that only a public-regarding moralistic political culture which stresses a conception of the commonwealth as the basis for democratic government can cope with the otherwise intractable problems of governmental overload. Political activity in such societies would be a programmatic politics centred around some notion of the public good and devoted to the advancement of the public interest rather than the pursuit of patronage and private favour. Private-regarding conceptions of authority limit the capacity of parties to perform their aggregating function and mobilize broad majorities for the promotion of the general welfare.[17]

Although the transformation of political culture and the revival of parties lie beyond the scope of this paper, it appears that both are essential if the Canadian political system is to cope successfully with the problems posed by the evolution of special interest groups. Only a "creative politics" along the lines suggested by the late John Porter would galvanize the Canadian political process in a direction which would permit the disciplining of the interest groups which currently threaten the stability and legitimacy of liberal democracy in Canada.

Notes

1. A useful compendium of neo-Marxist views is to be had in Leo Panitch, ed., *The Canadian State: Political Economy and Political Power* (Toronto: University of Toronto Press, 1977).

2. See Rianne Mahon, "Canadian Public Policy: the Unequal Structure of Representation," ibid., 165-98.

3. See Larry Pratt, "The State and Province-Building: Alberta's Development Strategy," ibid., 133-62.

4. Mahon, "Canadian Public Policy," 168.

5. For a detailed statement see A. Paul Pross, "The Canadian Public Service and Special Interest State," prepared for O.P. Dwivedi, et. al., *The Administrative State: Canadian Perspectives—Essays in Honour of J.E. Hodgetts* (Toronto: University of Toronto Press, 1982).

6. S.J.R. Noel, "Patrons and Clients in Canadian Politics," paper presented to the annual meeting of the Canadian Political Science Association, Laval University, Quebec City, May 1976. A related version of this paper entitled "Leadership and Clientelism" appears in David J. Bellamy, Jon H. Pammett, and Donald C. Rowat, eds., *The Provincial Political Systems: Comparative Essays* (Toronto: Methuen, 1976), 197-213.

7. The best collection and bibliography on the subject is found in A. Paul Pross, ed., *Pressure Group Behaviour in Canadian Politics* (Toronto: McGraw-Hill Ryerson, 1975).

8. Robert Presthus, *Elite Accommodation in Canadian Politics* (London, Toronto and New York: Cambridge University Press, 1973).

9. David Kwavnick, *Organized Labour and Pressure Politics* (Montreal: McGill-Queen's University Press, 1972).

10. David Kwavnick, "Interest Group Demands and the Federal Political System: Two Canadian Case Studies," in Pross, *Pressure Group Behaviour*, 69-86.

11. Pross, "Pressure Groups: Adaptive Instruments of Political Communication," ibid., 1-26. Cf. A. Paul Pross, "Pressure Groups: Talking Chameleons" in Michael S. Whittington and Glen Williams, eds., *Canadian Politics in the 1980s* (Toronto: Methuen, 1981), 221-42.

12. For a summary of these typologies, see the chapter on "Interest Groups in Canada" in Richard J. Van Loon and Michael S. Whittington, *The Canadian Political System* 3e (Toronto: McGraw-Hill Ryerson, 1981), 406-43.

13. John L. Walker, "The Origins and Maintenance of Interest Groups in America," presented to the annual meeting of the American Political Science Association, New York City, September 1981.

14. For a review of corporatist ideology in Canada, see Khayyam Z. Paltiel and Clinton Archibald, "L'évolution de l'idée corporatiste au Canada," Actes du Colloque du Mons, 24-26 Avril 1978, in *Etudes Canadiennes*, numéro spécial, 1979: 61-80.

15. John Meisel, "The Decline of Party in Canada," in Hugh G. Thorburn, ed., *Party Politics in Canada* 4e (Scarborough, Ontario; Prentice-Hall Canada, Inc., 1979), 119-35. Cf. John Meisel, "Exorcising the Pluralist Heaven: Interest Groups in Canadian Society," prepared for the seminar on Canadian-United States Relations, Harvard University, October 30, 1979.

16. Theodore J. Lowi, *The End of Liberalism* (New York: Norton, 1979), passim.

17. These notions have been drawn from the detailed discussion in a paper by a Rutgers University academic, Michael T. Hayes, "Interest Groups and Political Culture: A Revision of Elazar's Typology," prepared for delivery to the 1981 annual meeting of the American Political Science Association in New York City, September 1981.

10. POLITICAL REPRESENTATION IN THE NORTHWEST TERRITORIES

Gurston Dacks

It is a rare week when the newspapers of the Northwest Territories do not carry a story that raises questions about representation. These questions reflect deep societal divisions and the fact that the government of the Northwest Territories has not yet achieved its mature form. The single-member constituency electoral system operates in the NWT as the basis for government which is becoming increasingly well-established. However, many northerners view this form of government with skepticism. They doubt its legitimacy and reject the system of representation on which it is based. This paper will examine the contending claims about representation which figure prominently in today's NWT, and the alternative responses which are being considered in view of these claims.

BASIC ISSUES OF REPRESENTATION

Representation is a relationship between those who govern and those who are governed. This relationship involves several elements. The first element may be termed "structural." Structural representation is the degree to which politically significant groupings have members in the structures of government in rough proportion to their numbers in society.

The second element may be termed "substantive." Substantively representing a constituency or other social grouping means "acting in the interest of the represented, in a manner responsive to them.... The representative ... must not be found persistently at odds with the wishes of the represented without good reason in terms of their interest."[1] Usually, a pattern of structural representation that closely reflects the differentiation in a society will produce a high degree of substantive representation. Substantive representation is particularly likely to follow from close structural representation if the structure of politics and government provides "institutional arrangements for responsiveness."[2] In other words, there must be a means by which the governed can express their wishes. Also, representatives must have the power to act in response to their constituents. Finally, there must exist mechanisms of accountability, of reward and punishment, which compel representatives to act in the best interests, if not always according to the wishes, of the governed.

For any particular system of government, such as that of the NWT, to be legitimate and effective, it must substantively represent the population in general, and, in particular, the major groupings which comprise it. This will be relatively easy to the extent that a society is homogeneous because the differences within it will tend not to be very contentious. It will not appear to be so important that the different interests in society are represented accurately in the structures of government because it can

An original essay written for this volume. The author is with the University of Alberta, Department of Political Science.

be assumed that the "public interest" will affect all of the groups in society in relatively uniform ways. None will be so disadvantaged by the way in which the public interest is defined as to question the system of representation that underlies the policy process. However, if a society is deeply divided concerning values, the concept of a single public interest becomes less meaningful, and representation becomes an important political issue. What government does will distribute benefits and costs unevenly among the groups. The divergent groups in society will seek to maximize their weight in government in order to promote policies that benefit their own group. Some will reject the existing system of representation and will want to alter it so that governmental decisions taken in the public interest respond to their needs.

The present colonial status of its government makes the Northwest Territories a laboratory for students of political representation. Because the form of the territorial government is neither entrenched constitutionally nor definitively accepted by a majority of the population, the possibility of fundamental change remains as it does nowhere else in Canada. Representation is such an important issue today because of the nature of major clusters of social groupings, hence political interests, in the NWT.

THE SOCIAL CONTEXT OF REPRESENTATION

The fundamental feature of the population of the Northwest Territories is its division along ethno-cultural lines. According to the 1981 census, aboriginal people comprise 58% of the territorial population. The Inuit, including the Inuvialuit—the Inuit of the western arctic—account for 35% of the population; the Dene —the Indians of the NWT—17%; and the Metis 6%.[3] The specific concerns of particular aboriginal groups differ, but the groups share important goals which set them apart politically from the non-aboriginal population. While the aboriginal people have come to accept, and some to take jobs, in the wage economy, they continue to cherish their relationship with the land, and in the case of the Inuit, with the coastal waters. They want to ensure that development that takes place on the land and water does not threaten their relationship with the natural environment. They want political power to decide whether and under what conditions exploration and extraction of oil, gas, and mineral deposits and transportation of the resources out of the North will occur. They also want power to decide wildlife management policy so they can continue to hunt, fish, and trap, activities fundamental to both their economic and spiritual well-being. They believe that the *Constitution Act, 1982* guarantees these powers to them as aboriginal rights. To clarify the nature of these rights and to benefit from them, the aboriginal peoples of the North have presented aboriginal claims to the government of Canada. A major concern of the aboriginal people is validation of their belief that the different native groups constitute peoples or nations, and that the collective identity of each group must survive for future generations. Only if their collective needs as peoples are recognized do they feel they will be able to improve the quality of their lives.

The goals and assumptions of the non-aboriginal people of the territories differ fundamentally from those of the aboriginal population. Whereas the aboriginal people feel a spiritual attachment to the land and a sense of responsibility as stewards of the land, the non-aboriginal population sees the land primarily as a source of economic opportunity, and mining and oil and gas development as more profitable than wildlife harvesting. Like most

North Americans, they base their political thinking on the assumptions of individualism and equality. Both their economic interests and their philosophic assumptions make most of them dubious about the aboriginal groups' pursuit of rights that are special, rather than universal, and collective, rather than individual.

While beliefs vary among the members of each of these groups, it is fair to generalize that the aboriginal people of the North want the northern society of the future to differ from that of southern Canada. They want new institutions of government in which they will be represented in ways that will help them remedy the social ills the conventional form of Canadian government has brought to Canada's aboriginal population.[4] In addition, the aboriginal people want a government in which they will feel comfortable. They want to make government decisions in ways that are familiar to them and that accommodate their customary approaches to questions of representation and political accountability, approaches which contrast with non-aboriginal political practice. For example, aboriginal political ideas emphasize individual self-determination rather than the representative principle. For this reason, aboriginal people would feel more comfortable with a delegate rather than a representative model of voter-legislator relations. They would prefer MLAs to consult them on all important issues. They would prefer that MLAs not be bound to strict party discipline which might prevent them from voting in accordance with constituent wishes. In contrast, the non-aboriginal population views responsible government based on disciplined parties contesting single-member constituencies as highly desirable. This system represents the majority of people and can be held accountable to them. Legislators can be viewed as representatives rather than delegates because they are seen as having been elected on the basis of party affiliation in a system which emphasizes party discipline—and the accountability it can provide—over the direct representation of the views of individual constituencies. In the minds of most members of the non-aboriginal population, the parliamentary system and the form of accountability it provides is the natural system of government for all parts of Canada.

Two examples illustrate how much aboriginal and non-aboriginal practices concerning representation and accountability differ. The first example is the process in the summer of 1988 by which the Dene and Metis agreed, with certain conditions, to confirm the Agreement in Principle negotiated by their leaders with the government of Canada for the settlement of their aboriginal claim. Once the agreement had been reached, meetings were held in all of the communities throughout the region covered by the claim, to explain the agreement to the Dene and Metis people. Then the Dene and the Metis each held their own week-long general assemblies, which were open to the public. At the Dene assembly, the chiefs and delegates from each aboriginal community were empowered to vote. At several points during the assembly, the main proceedings were suspended to allow the chiefs and delegates to consult at great length with the people from their regions who had travelled to participate in the assembly, and to receive instructions from their people. This example shows that the Dene practice is to disperse power widely among their people and to give the people close control over those they appoint to represent them. The other northern aboriginal groups display similar preferences about the political process. Contrast this with a second example, the process of creating and ratifying the Meech Lake Accord. This agreement was reached by eleven individuals who met in secret, did not consult during the process with the people they represented, and agreed that no amendments to the accord would be permitted, not even to accommodate the strongly-felt concerns of their constituents. Clearly, the locus of power and the extent of meaningful, mass participation differ greatly between these two cases. Northern aboriginal people want the future government of the NWT to enable them to accommodate these differences so that they can continue to manage the representative relationship in the fashion that makes sense to them.

THE CONSTITUTIONAL CONTEXT

This difference of political agendas has important and practical consequences in the NWT because it, alone of all the provincial and territorial governments, has not yet achieved its final form. The government of the Northwest Territories has travelled a great distance along the road to responsible government.[5] In 1975, the last appointed member of the territorial legislative assembly ceased to sit in it; since then all of the members of the assembly have been elected. An executive council or cabinet, composed completely of ministers who are MLAs, directs the policy process and administration of government under the government leader. While these features closely resemble those of provincial governments, significant differences mark the territorial government as immature. For example, party politics do not underlie the governmental process. Candidates seek office in territorial elections as independents. Because those who are successful sit as independent MLAs, the election itself does not determine who will lead the government and form its cabinet. Instead, the first item of business for the assembly after an election is to choose those of its members who will form the executive council. These individuals choose among themselves the individual, and he (to

date no woman has been selected) assigns ministerial responsibilities to his colleagues. Because the government leader does not actually select his ministers, his power over them is less than that enjoyed by the premiers and prime minister. This fact makes it difficult to hold the government leader, or the executive council collectively, responsible for any action undertaken by an individual minister. Indeed, the defeat of a significant motion or piece of legislation proposed by a minister does not bring down the government as it would elsewhere in Canada. The assembly could pass a motion dismissing the executive council, but this has never been attempted, let alone accomplished. Despite the rapid progress made since 1975, the absence of the basic test of confidence means that responsible government cannot be said to exist in the NWT.[6]

The government of the Northwest Territories is not fully mature in another sense; it is not constitutionally entrenched. The steps it has taken in the direction of responsible government represent only an informal agreement among the MLAs, and tacit permission from the federal government. The entire structure of the government of the NWT rests on an ordinary act of parliament which the government of Canada could change arbitrarily. Ottawa has indicated that it will not entrench a form of government for the Northwest Territories until aboriginal interests have been adequately protected, and until a consensus exists among the people of the Territories concerning the appropriate form of government.[7] This condition gives the aboriginal peoples of the NWT an opportunity enjoyed by no other aboriginal peoples in Canada's history. They are in a position to pursue a form of public government that will differ from the parliamentary model and thus represent them and guarantee their rights better than the parliamentary model has represented and protected the other aboriginal peoples of Canada.

STRUCTURAL REPRESENTATION

1. The Boundaries of the Polity

The first element in that consensus about the appropriate form of government involves answering a fundamental question of representation—what is the polity for which the system of representation is being designed? In a deeply divided society, it may not be possible to span the divergences of interest and culture and to allay the suspicions which separate the disparate groups. In such a society, it may prove impossible to create any system of representation which all of the groups will accept. Those groups that feel they have been disadvantaged by the status quo or that expect to suffer in the future will attempt radical change of the system of representation by altering the set of groups to be represented. In other words, they will attempt to alter the boundaries of the political system.

a. Division of the Northwest Territories

This is precisely the approach that has been taken by the Inuit, the aboriginal people who live above the treeline. For the last decade they have sought a division of the Northwest Territories roughly along the treeline.[8] The jurisdiction, Nunavut, to the north of the treeline, would benefit the Inuit in a variety of ways. It would provide them with an Inuit homeland, symbolic support for their view of themselves as a people, or cultural collectivity. More practically, it would give them a government with two crucial features. The first is that it would be a public government, like the federal, provincial, and municipal governments of Canada, hence would fall squarely within the bounds of Canadian convention rather than require some radical innovation the government of Canada might reject as untried. The second feature of a Nunavut public government is that the Inuit would be able to control it using the conventional Canadian approach to representation, election based on single-member constituencies. Because they comprise approximately 86% of the population of the region they want to become Nunavut,[9] it is very difficult to imagine a future in which they would not dominate the ballot box. With control of the public government and collective safeguards of their aboriginal rights after the settlement of their aboriginal claim, the Inuit, while respecting the Canadian *Charter of Rights and Freedoms*, would be excellently placed to determine their own future. They would, of course, face the limitations that governments of economic hinterlands usually face, but in dealing with severe problems of unemployment and social malaise, it would be they who make the decisions, rather than the government in Yellowknife that they find foreign in tone, unsympathetic, and inaccessible because of the very high cost of travelling the huge distances that separate it from most Inuit communities.[10]

b. Aboriginal Self-Government

It is not at all certain that Nunavut will come to pass. The ongoing inability of the group undertaking constitutional planning on behalf of the two proposed regions to agree on a boundary has stalled progress since 1982, when a territorial plebiscite narrowly approved the principle of division. It is not clear whether division would be approved if such a plebiscite were held today. However, if division were to occur, the aboriginal people of the western NWT would find themselves comprising only 43% of the population.[11] Even given a degree of over-representation of the smaller communities, which tend to be almost exclusively populated by aboriginal people, the existing system of representation would not guarantee them control of the government. Already a minority at the ballot box, the aboriginal people could be overwhelmed if large-scale oil or gas development brought great numbers of non-aboriginal people to the North, even if only for several years. In addition, despite efforts at affirmative action, the territorial public service grossly fails the test of structural representativeness at the middle and senior levels; the crucial contribution the public service makes to the policy process inevitably proceeds on the basis of non-aboriginal assumptions, no matter how sympathetic individual public servants may be.

These factors may prompt the aboriginal people of the western NWT to seek to redefine the boundaries of the polity. However, they will not be able to seek a geographic answer to their needs as the Inuit have. Because the majority of its aboriginal people live scattered throughout the western NWT, it is impossible to draw boundaries that would enclose them, while excluding the bulk of the non-aboriginal population. The aboriginal people of the western NWT may opt for a functional solution rather than a territorial one. They may press the government of Canada to establish aboriginal self-government with authority over those issues the aboriginal people feel are crucial to their cultural integrity and economic well-being. Throughout most of the 1980s, the aboriginal people of the western NWT did not actively pursue their own aboriginal self-government, although they supported the national campaign for the entrenchment of an aboriginal right to self-government in the Canadian Constitution. However, they have generally viewed the government of even a united, aboriginal-majority Northwest Territories with suspicion. In 1988, the government of Canada proposed an agreement-in-principle for the aboriginal claim of the Dene and the Metis, the aboriginal people who live below the treeline in the western NWT. The Dene and Metis endorsed this proposal only when Ottawa agreed to negotiate an acceptable form of aboriginal self-government. No official details regarding the form of government the aboriginal people of the western NWT seek are available. It is probable that they want to control for their people social programs such as education, social services, child welfare, and the administration of health care, as well as land use planning and wildlife management on the lands they will own as a result of the settlement of their claim. Ottawa can be expected to resist the Dene and Metis wish to control land and wildlife policy, even on their own lands, because this could interfere with the development of oil and gas Ottawa wants. With the stage set for conflict on this important issue, the future of aboriginal self-government in the West cannot be predicted. Indeed, it may merely be a negotiating position to lever concessions from both Ottawa and the government of the Northwest Territories. However, in view of the legitimacy three constitutional conferences have given it, the concept cannot be ruled out as a viable way for the aboriginal peoples of the western NWT to create a new polity, at least with regard to a great number of policy areas, and as a way to find an answer to the long-term problems the present system of structural representation in the NWT poses.

Aboriginal self-government would involve problems as well as promise. It is an untested and radical innovation. Moreover, it would leave in place a territorial government with significant powers, but over which the aboriginal people would have little influence. Aboriginal voters would probably continue to vote for MLAs for representation with regard to territorial matters. However, the MLAs who are aboriginal or who depend on aboriginal voters would undoubtedly be "second-class" legislators because of an inability to speak with authority when cultural issues such as education are being debated, since the territorial government would consider these issues only as they affect non-aboriginals. The territorial government, the public government, might come to be dominated by non-aboriginal legislators.

2. An Extended Residence Requirement

Recognition of potential problems like the ones described above may encourage the aboriginal people to seek to alter the system of representation in the territorial government rather than to form their own government. A fundamental change sought there is an extended residence requirement for voting. Presently, the length of the residence requirement is one year. In theory, a longer residence requirement would ensure that those who voted met what might be termed a "competence" requirement: they would be familiar with and sensitive to the unique features of northern politics. A longer residence requirement has also been justified by arguing a "community" requirement: that only those who have a significant commitment to a region and a significant likelihood of bearing the consequences of the decisions made by the people who are contesting an election—those who are really part of the community and not merely transients—ought to be allowed to vote. In practice, a longer residence requirement would benefit the aboriginal people because they have lived in the North all their lives, while many non-aboriginal people come North to work for a limited period of time, returning South at the end of their contracts. It is very difficult to gauge how much different residence requirements would shift the electoral balance between the aboriginal and non-aboriginal populations in the North.[12] Obviously, the longer the requirement, the larger the proportion of non-aboriginal people who would be denied the vote. In 1981, the Dene

Nation, representing the Indians of the NWT and the Metis Association of the NWT, proposed a residence requirement of ten years.[13] This requirement would certainly enable the aboriginal people to dominate the system of representation, but would certainly be judged unconstitutional for unjustifiably limiting the right to vote guaranteed in the *Charter of Rights and Freedoms*. It has been suggested that three years would be the longest residence requirement the courts would accept, with two years more likely to be the maximum acceptable.[14] Extending the residence requirement by an extra year would enhance the representation of the aboriginal population, but it would not guarantee it future domination over the system of representation.

3. Conventional Responses to the Special Representation Needs of Aboriginal Northerners

a. Regional Over-Representation

The aboriginal people of the NWT already benefit to a degree because the way in which the boundaries of territorial constituencies are drawn causes them to be over-represented. Most jurisdictions pay some attention to population densities when drawing electoral boundaries. They recognize that a dispersed population is hard for candidates to meet and for elected politicians to serve. The application of this principle in the vast and very thinly populated NWT creates some ridings with many fewer voters than live in urban ridings. For example, as a result of the most recent revision of constituency boundaries, in 1983, the electoral district of Hudson Bay was home to 383 residents, while Yellowknife South had 3822 residents.[15] Because the smaller constituencies tend to have a much higher proportion of aboriginal people than do the large, urban constituencies, aboriginal voters benefit from this deviation from the rule of individual equality in the electoral process. The over-representation factor is one reason why the majority of the members of the tenth and eleventh legislative assemblies of the NWT are aboriginal people.

Because of over-representation, the assembly meets the test of structural representation as far as the aboriginal people are concerned. However, it fails to meet their test of substantive representation. The organizations that speak for the aboriginal peoples of the territories seem unable to effectively use the aboriginal MLAs to advance their interests. In part, this difficulty is due to the absence of party organization in the assembly, making it very difficult for MLAs not in the cabinet to cooperate in pursuing a coherent strategy. In addition, the absence of party politics makes it impossible for aboriginal voters to vote for a cabinet and hold it accountable for its actions. Also, because the public service is largely non-aboriginal, it brings a non-aboriginal perspective to its contributions to policy. These and other factors often lead the territorial government to make decisions that conflict with the goals of the aboriginal peoples. Their pursuit of new forms of representation and government demonstrates that favourable structural representation in a legislature does not guarantee an adequate level of substantive representation in government.

b. Guaranteed Seats in the Legislative Assembly

This judgment has rendered obsolete arguments advanced in favour of guaranteeing a certain minimum percentage of seats in the assembly to aboriginal people, even if the proportion of the population they account for falls well below the guaranteed percentage of seats. The suggested guarantees would provide less than fifty percent of the seats, hence no certainty that the aboriginal people would be able to protect themselves from decisions of some future, culturally different majority. Recent proposals for guaranteed seats have tended to be part of more complex packages, such as the Denenedeh concept proposed by the Dene and Metis in 1981, which suggested as one of several options that the Dene and Metis together would elect a minimum of 30 percent of members of the assembly.[16] However, this option was backstopped with provisions for a senate composed entirely of aboriginal members with significant powers to review the legislation passed by the assembly. That the Dene and Metis felt a need to supplement the concept of guaranteed representation suggests that it will figure in the NWT's constitutional future, if at all, as part of a complex system of representation.

c. Regional and Local Government

Historically, the aboriginal people of the North did not rely on political representatives. Political decisions were made in small, local social groupings which took into account the views of all members of the group and built consensus. To this day, the aboriginal people prefer to place as little power as possible in the hands of distant representative institutions and as much as possible in local and regional governments. For example, a group of Dene elders included the following paragraph in its constitutional recommendations:

> The constitution of a new government in Denenedeh (the name prefered by the Dene for the western NWT) should reflect a decentralization of jurisdiction and powers to community and regional levels of government. People should have the right to make decisions about an issue which affects them alone or their region, without undue interference from other levels of government which do not have a specific interest in the issue.[17]

This wish has not been realized. The powers of local governments currently are limited to providing what are termed "hard services," such as water, sanitation, and fire protection, and to passing and administering by-laws. Regional councils also exist in the NWT, but their role is largely limited to advising the government of the NWT and to promoting cooperative activities among the communities in each region. Thus, neither the local nor the regional level of government has succeeded in meeting the need for a governmental structure dominated by the aboriginal people and exercising real power over the issues of land and wildlife management and cultural protection, which lie at the heart of aboriginal political concerns.

STRUCTURAL AND SUBSTANTIVE REPRESENTATION: PARTNERSHIP GOVERNMENT

Because conventional devices have failed to meet their needs, the aboriginal peoples of the NWT are looking for more fundamental innovations in the territorial system of representation. The quest that led them to consider aboriginal self-government and division has also led them to consider a new form of government for the western NWT, should division actually occur. Between 1982 and 1988, the leaders of the government and of the aboriginal groups of the western NWT worked through the Western Constitutional Forum (hereafter, the WCF) to devise a new form of public government for the western NWT. The WCF had two goals in devising the new system of representation and its underlying logic. The first was to develop a system of representation—both structural and substantive—that would embody the majoritarian principle to the extent that the government of Canada and the non-aboriginal population of the region

would be satisfied. Both are understandably anxious about any deviation from the liberal, individualist representational formula they view as natural and just. The second goal was to entrench constitutionally the collective rights of the aboriginal peoples and to ensure that the structures of representation and government would enable the aboriginal peoples to forcefully express their needs to government and reasonably expect responsive action from government.

Their approach borrowed from the European model of consociationalism. This concept evolved in political science from efforts to explain how certain European countries, such as Belgium, Austria, and Switzerland, have managed to contain the conflicts within their culturally divided societies, and to maintain political stability.[18] The essence of consociation is the sufficient representation of each of the divergent societal groupings and government institutions that ensure that politics involves negotiation and consensus rather than conflict ending in the imposition of the will of the majority. With this in mind, the WCF developed a model of government it called "partnership," clearly a less awkward and more familiar and inspiring label than "consociational." The model on which the thinking about partnership is evolving[19] rests on nine basic principles.

First, the society of the western NWT is to be conceived of as a partnership of cultural communities. Thus, it is more than a set of individuals whose only relationship to the state consists of the rights and responsibilities of the individual. Presumably, the cultural communities will be the non-aboriginal, the Inuvialuit, and the Dene/Metis, although the latter grouping could split into its two parts for constitutional purposes. It is essential to the partnership model that the rights of these cultural communities as participants in the new government of the western NWT be equal and symmetrical because the purpose of the new constitution is to protect all cultural communities equally. Put more bluntly, the constitution is more likely to be accepted by all cultural communities if its guiding principle is not the protection of only certain of the cultural communities—the aboriginal ones. As they relate to the public government, all cultural communities should be equal. Of course, the aboriginal communities will also enjoy aboriginal rights, but these flow from the Constitution of Canada, not from any preferred status under the territorial constitution. *Second*, the partnership constitution will contain a Charter of Collective Rights which will define the fundamental interests of each of the cultural communities. Each of the cultural communities will be able, as a matter of right, to protect and enhance these fundamental interests and thus to ensure its control over the direction and integrity of the evolution of its cultures. *Third*, each cultural community will enjoy a measure of segmental autonomy in the form of a council which will exercise complete legislative jurisdiction over those matters defined in the Charter as fundamental to its cultural interest.

Fourth, there will be a legislative assembly with jurisdiction throughout the new territory over all matters not assigned to the cultural community councils. The territorial electorate will be divided into separate cultural community voting lists, so that the members of the assembly will be elected by the respective cultural communities. To reduce the difficulty of individual members serving and relating to constituents over the whole of the new territory, multi-member constituencies, probably three in number, will be created. The number of seats allotted to each constituency will be roughly proportional to its total population, and the number of members elected by each cultural community will also reflect its proportion of the territorial population, except that the constitution will entrench some minimum

number of members below which a cultural community's representation will not be allowed to drop. The details of the electoral system have not been finalized. However, a general application of these principles would produce a thirteen-member assembly comprising four Dene/Metis, two Inuvialuit, and seven non-aboriginals. If a larger legislative body were deemed desirable, the 1981 population of the territory and the general rules suggested above would produce a twenty-five member body of nine Dene/Metis members, three Inuvialuit, and thirteen non-aboriginals.

Fifth, matters that do not touch on constitutionally-defined cultural concerns will be decided by a simple majority vote in the legislative assembly. *Sixth*, legislative enactments deemed by members of any of the cultural communities to significantly affect matters of cultural right must be approved by a majority of each of the cultural caucuses in the assembly. This principle provides a mutual veto structure that should reduce the anxiety any of the cultural communities would feel about being represented by a minority of members in the assembly; majority rule will not dominate cultural rights. *Seventh*, the executive will be composed of aboriginal and non-aboriginal members. It might be required that they be equal in number or, for flexibility in cabinet formation, some inequality might be permitted. Within limits, this would not jeopardize either of the groups because of the requirement that all executive decisions have the approval of a majority of the members of each of the cultural components of the executive. The exact procedure for structuring the executive and its relationship of responsibility to the assembly and to the cultural caucus that comprise it remain to be decided. Much will depend on whether political parties develop. However, it is clear that both forming and operating the executive will involve the politics of inter-cultural coalitions. *Eighth*, a priority of the new territorial government would be, while respecting the rights of ongoing employees, to increase the structural representativeness of the bureaucracy and the judiciary. Affirmative action programs already exist to make the cultural composition of both the bureaucracy and the judiciary more representative of the composition of the population. These programs would be strengthened and new ones implemented. For example, many job requirements could be rewritten to recognize skills aboriginal people have, which tend to be undervalued by job requirements based on southern Canadian models. *Ninth*, amendments to any of these arrangements would require the approval of either a majority of each of the cultural caucuses in the assembly, or a popular referendum showing majority support for the change in each cultural community.

All of these principles would be essential for the viability of a partnership government in the Northwest Territories, or the western portion of it should division occur. However, two of the principles raise fundamental questions about representation. The first is the system for electing MLAs to the assembly. The second is the structure and operation of the executive.

The essence of the proposed electoral system is that it provides for direct and guaranteed representation of the cultural communities. This approach requires separate voters lists for each cultural community with, for example, the Dene and Metis voters voting for Dene or Metis candidates to represent them, the non-aboriginal voters voting for non-aboriginal MLAs, and so on. One disadvantage of this system is that it undermines the principle of regional representation in two ways. The first is that it would require dividing the western NWT into three regions for electoral purposes, producing constituencies of enormous geographic scale. This result is inevitable, given that a partnership electoral system would be organized first to represent cultural communities, and only second to represent geographically-defined populations. The problem posed by constituency size would be met, not by subordinating the principle of group representation, but by ensuring adequate travel budgets for MLAs and adequate opportunities during legislative sessions for them to tour their constituencies to discuss legislative proposals with constituents. The second difficulty posed by a direct system of representing cultural communities is that it could bring cultural divisions in individual communities into sharper focus. For example, the town of Aklavik contains Dene, Metis, Inuvialuit and non-aboriginals. Under a partnership system, the Dene and Metis would vote for the Dene/Metis MLAs for the Mackenzie Delta and northern Mackenzie Valley region, while the Inuvialuit would vote for their MLAs, and the few non-aboriginals would vote for non-aboriginal MLAs. Besides drawing attention to the differences in such a community, the system would relieve individual candidates and MLAs of any need to build bridges among the cultural communities in order to fashion a coalition of electoral support. Politicians might seek to unify communities out of a sense of statesmanship, but they would not be compelled to do so electorally unless their own people favour this form of accommodation. One answer to this foreseeable problem is that political parties may well develop once some of the other fundamental issues—such as aboriginal claims—are resolved, and that intercultural accommodations could be managed within the context of these parties. It is also likely that the aboriginal MLAs will be encouraged to act as a caucus in the assembly if they appoint the aboriginal cabinet members together, rather than appointing them as representatives of the individual aboriginal groups. Such an approach, which may be necessary to keep the cabinet to a manageable size, could encourage other forms of collaboration among the aboriginal

MLAs, including working with one another to solve the problems of the towns they represent together.

Two simultaneous elections would be involved in an alternative system that balances the need for both cultural and geographic representation. Half of the assembly would be elected on the basis of direct representation and cultural communities, using separate electoral lists. The other half of the assembly would be elected at large, using a single unified voters list. The resulting twelve constituencies would be about the size of the present territorial ridings, permitting reasonably good contact between MLAs and constituents. The drawback to such a system is that it would create two classes of MLAs, the cultural community ones and the regional ones. It is unclear how or whether the regional MLAs could be involved in voting on matters of cultural importance. While their own cultural background should be easy enough to discern, it would be less easy in some cases to identify which cultural group voted them into office because they were elected by voters on unified voters lists. It would thus be difficult to identify the extent to which they considered themselves representative of and accountable to the respective cultural communities in their constituencies. It would certainly be impossible to argue that they would consider themselves to represent one cultural community to the exclusion of others such that they could take part in votes on matters of fundamental cultural importance. If they were excluded from these votes, they might come to feel that they had a special responsibility for the general matters coming before the assembly. Taken far enough, this opinion might lead them to try to confine the cultural MLAs to dealing with cultural matters. In view of all of these problems, a dual system of electing MLAs to achieve a balance between cultural and regional representation would build confusion and conflict into the assembly.

Representation based on culture will avoid this confusion, although it will not avoid conflict. To the contrary, it will bring into the assembly the fundamental dimension of conflict in northern society. This may make the legislative process difficult, but will at least give it a better chance of relating to social needs than if fundamental interests were not expressed. Possibly, the development of a party system could provide the motivation for mutual accommodation among these interests, and thus balance the tendency to conflict.

Representation based on culture has one final advantage: it can accommodate the different aboriginal and non-aboriginal preferences concerning representation and accountability. It would enable aboriginal MLAs to respond to the traditions of their people by regularly discussing policy matters with them, and particularly with elders and with the aboriginal organizations that have gained great importance in the North during the land claims process. They would not have to pursue similar consultations with non-aboriginal constituents, most of whom do not expect it, or risk accusations of favouritism from the non-aboriginal people who would want to be consulted just because the aboriginal people were receiving this consideration. For their part, non-aboriginal MLAs could operate as they and their constituents prefer—as representative rather than delegates—without offending aboriginal constituents by what would appear to be inadequate consultation with them. This would allow non-aboriginal MLAs more latitude to organize themselves in parties, giving their voters some degree of choice as to who will form the executive, and some ability to hold the executive accountable and to force it to represent them in the substantive sense.

This last possibility is a reminder that the structure and operation of the executive is the second aspect of partnership that raises fundamental questions about representation. While legislators may be responsible for acting in the best interests of society as a whole, there is no doubt that they are expected to represent their constituents and to be held accountable to them through the mechanism of the ballot box. Representation and accountability are more elusive concepts when applied to the executive, but they must apply at this level as well as at the legislative level because, in modern governments, the executive exercises great power. In a divided society like that of the Northwest Territories, the obvious question is "Whom is the executive supposed to represent?" A continuum of possible responses to this question can be described. At one end of the continuum would be a highly fragmented society, hence executive. As the forces of diversity appear more fundamental than the factors promoting unity, the task of the executive would be to represent the cleavages in society and to protect the distinct interests of the different groupings. Such a cabinet would function as a forum for negotiating; the concept of a "territorial interest" aside from a negotiated settlement would have little meaning. The other end of the continuum would be a relatively unified society, perhaps based on the need for people in a colonial setting to work together to overcome the external forces of economics and politics that otherwise would overwhelm them. An executive governing a relatively unified society would see itself as responsible primarily for the total area it governed, as a whole. It would, of course, have to aggregate different interests within its territory, but it would view this task primarily as one of defining a "territorial interest," that could be operationalized because of the underlying unity of society.

Each of the points on the continuum suggests a certain structure, hence pattern of accountability for the executive. To the extent that the differences among the cultural communities of the NWT dominate its future constitution, each cabinet minister might be selected by one of the cultural community legislative caucuses—all of the MLAs from that cultural community. If ministers could only be removed from office by their own cultural caucus, they would then be accountable to it. The leader would be selected by all of the members of the assembly. In assigning portfolios, the leader would have some control over ministers, but since he would be unable to dismiss them, he would have little ability to discipline them. Ministers would have substantial latitude to operate their departments as they wished; general policy and the activities of individual departments would become matters for negotiation among all of the members of the cabinet in what would essentially be a "weak leader" system. In this system, general decisions, that is, those without significant cultural implications, could be taken by a majority vote. However, decisions that might affect the cultural rights of the different peoples of the territory would require more unanimity to be approved. Perhaps each cultural community would have a veto over these decisions. Such a stringent requirement might make it too difficult for the executive to make decisions and operate effectively. It might be better to require only the approval of two groups on the executive—the aboriginal members and the non-aboriginal members—rather than of each of the cultural communities individually. The close accountability of ministers to their cultural caucuses would make cabinet secrecy and cabinet solidarity impossible. In such a situation, parties might develop, particularly if some fundamental and non-cultural issue arose in the territory. However, a party system would not be necessary to enable the voters to hold the government accountable because the lines of accountability would run between the ministers and their cultural caucus and not between the government and the electorate at large.

A more unified society would want to be able to hold its government more effectively accountable than this system does. It would want less delay in decision-making and better integration of government policy. An executive structure that would produce these results could be one in which the assembly chooses the leader. He or she in turn would select the members of the executive according to a formula that would guarantee each cultural group a certain proportion of the members. However, the cultural groups would exercise little control over their members of the executive because the leader's power to select and dismiss ministers would tend to make them dependent on him or her. The assembly could pass a motion dismissing the leader, but this measure would be so drastic and disruptive that they could be expected to resort to it infrequently. A strong leadership system could be expected to develop under rules like these. The leader would likely be able to organize cabinet secrecy and solidarity and, in view of the unity of the cabinet, parties could well develop to compete for the right to staff what would be a collective body under an identifiable leader, rather than a collection of cultural delegates.

Such a system might give too little control to the cultural communities. A compromise might see the leader appointing half of the executive members according to a formula which ensured representation from each of the cultural communities. The other half of the members would be appointed directly by the cultural community caucuses of MLAs. Such a system would tend to evolve two classes of ministers—the leader's team and the cultural delegates. However, it should ensure an adequate communication flow between the executive and the caucuses and that cabinet policy-making would take place in discussions in which the views of each of the cultural communities were forcefully represented.

There is no one partnership model. The variety of possibilities for structuring the legislative and executive units of a partnership government and the relationships between them make this clear. Rather there is a rich diversity of models. If any of these is chosen, it will be the model that both reflects the balance of political power in the territory and is deemed acceptable by the government of Canada, that has the last word on the constitutional structure of the territory. The aboriginal people will tend to prefer models that provide more guaranteed protection of their cultural interests because they have witnessed the costs borne by aboriginal peoples elsewhere in Canada when decisions are made by the majoritarian, strong-leader parliamentary system. The non-aboriginal people will tend to prefer the parliamentary system. However, each of the groups recognizes some merit in the other's position. The aboriginal peoples see the need for unified action to protect northern interests. A great many non-aboriginal people appreciate that aboriginal fears come from a valid reading of Canadian history, sympathize with the social stresses non-aboriginal life has brought to the aboriginal people, and recognize that constitutionally-entrenched aboriginal rights must be respected.

It is impossible to predict how all of these factors will work themselves out to produce a consociational government in the NWT, or the western part of it. It is not even possible to predict that any such government will come into existence. To date, the partnership concept remains just that—a concept. The delay in deciding whether division of the NWT will occur has distracted attention from the question of what form of government might follow division. In addition, the aboriginal groups, who must push for an innovative form of government if one is to be established, have been focusing their attention on the settlement of their aboriginal claims. As a result, the people of the western NWT have not been educated about the partnership model, nor have their opinions on it been sought. Whether it will actually come to pass and in what form will depend on several factors. One is whether the existing government of the NWT can show itself to be responsive to its aboriginal constituents. If they come to see it as more legitimate than they do now, they may decide that their time and energy would be better spent pursuing goals other than a new form of government. A second factor is the approach the aboriginal people will take if they are dissatisfied. If they opt for a form of self-government, they are less likely to push for a different form of territorial public government as they will be too busy setting up their own institutions. The non-aboriginal population could also be expected to resist changes to the government of NWT. They would feel that the aboriginal constitutional agenda will have been satisfied by aboriginal self-government, hence the territorial government should be based solely on the liberal-democratic values which have shaped the federal and provincial governments of the rest of Canada. A third factor is the fate of division. The population of aboriginal and non-aboriginal people is more balanced in the NWT all told than it would be in the western NWT after division. The non-aboriginal people of the western NWT would clearly be a majority of the population of the region, giving them no encouragement to support a constitutional innovation that would undermine the majoritarian principle. However, in a unified NWT, depending on residence requirements, and the impact of immigration on one hand and a high aboriginal birth rate on the other, they might feel at risk of being a minority at the ballot box. This could lead them to favour some form of the partnership model as a means of ethnic self-protection.

The partnership model stands as a possible alternative to the status quo in the NWT. Whether it will see the light of day depends on the energy with which aboriginal leaders pursue it. That in turn will depend on the unfolding of the three factors of governmental performance, the attractiveness of self-government, and the outcome of the division process.

SUBSTANTIVE REPRESENTATION: PARTY POLITICS

It has already been argued that "institutional arrangements for responsiveness" promote substantive representation. These arrangements involve the governed being able to express their wishes, representatives having the power to respond, and the governed having the means to hold their representatives accountable for the quality of their responses.

As both of the territories are gaining powers and financial responsibilities which resemble those of the provinces, politicians in the NWT meet the second of these three conditions. However, the lack of a party system at the territorial level means that the first and third features of "institutional arrangements of responsiveness" are absent in the NWT.

This situation has provoked considerable unhappiness. The lack of parties and cabinet solidarity make it easier for ministers to pursue their occasional inclinations to work at cross-purposes. When they change portfolios, no party policy or consideration of the party's accountability to the voters exists to ensure continuity in the administration of policy. While the government leader tries to maintain the coherence and continuity of his government, he cannot use several of the powerful arguments available to other first ministers in Canada to forge cabinet unity. Perhaps worst, if a minister makes an unpopular decision, for example, cancelling a high school promised to a region, the voters have no recourse. Unless the minister represents that region, the voters cannot vote against him personally, and they cannot vote against his party because he does not belong to one. Members run as independents, each in his or her own constituency. At the first session of the assembly following the election, all members are equally eligible to seek cabinet seats in a process whose outcome has proven unpredictable. Thus, it is impossible for voters to vote for a party or leader, or to pass judgment on the previous cabinet, when they cast their ballots. The result is that they vote on the basis of the perceived qualities of the candidates, including their sensitivity to local concerns. This tends to send to the assembly many members who see themselves as emissaries and supplicants for their region more than as representatives who gather to bring regional perceptions to bear on the task of defining the larger territorial interest.

Despite these problems, party politics have not come to the assembly (although federal elections in the NWT run on party lines). One explanation is that the absence of full responsible government makes it less crucial for the government to organize firm and predictable majority support in the assembly; unfavourable votes defeat legislation, but they do not defeat the cabinet. Another factor is that the aboriginal people view party politics at the territorial level with skepticism because they expect domination by the national parties. In that these parties assume a parliamentary model of government, their appearance would legitimize the present form of government in the NWT, and would stiffen the resistance of non-aboriginal residents to the kind of innovations in governmental structures the aboriginal people are seeking. In other words the premature introduction of party politics would help freeze the government of the NWT into a form that would not allow the aboriginal people to effectively pursue their interests or to apply their traditional concepts of representation and accountability to the public government process. Yet what is probably the most important reason for the non-partisan

nature of elections and the assembly is that the aboriginal people prefer to be represented by their own organizations, such as the Dene National or the Inuit Tapirisat, fearing that political parties might subordinate their concerns in the pursuit of some larger electoral strategy.

In view of these considerations, the aboriginals would be likely to vote against candidates who tried to run on the basis of parties, lest the development of parties undermine the ability of their own organizations to express their interests. The aboriginal people are likely to continue to rely on their own organizations to represent them until the basic legal and constitutional questions—land claims and the form of the future NWT government—are settled, because they want to be represented as aboriginal people, rather than through the mediating device of parties, in the discussions that will settle these questions.

The absence of party politics and fully responsible government allows for the effective representation of aboriginal interests through more powerful aboriginal organizations than might be possible if the government of the NWT were more mature. However, its immaturity limits the accountability and quality of representation the government of the NWT can offer northerners. Parties have a role to play in improving the representative process, but that role depends on the form of government the territory ultimately adopts and the system of representation that logic implies. If the southern, Westminster model becomes entrenched, the aboriginal people are likely to opt for aboriginal self-governments and to occupy themselves with the pursuit of opportunities presented by the settlement of their aboriginal claims. While they might play a modest role in the legislative assembly, they would not be able to argue very plausibly that its pattern of representation should accommodate their needs because they will be managing their social, cultural, and many of their economic affairs through their own governments and through the implementation of the settlement of their aboriginal claims. The legislative assembly could be expected to take its non-aboriginal assumptions to their logical conclusion, quickly setting up a system of responsible government. Disciplined parties could be expected to follow soon, and with them the southern Canadian system of representation and accountability. However, if the assembly develops along consociational lines or adopts some other way of representing the collective interests of the territory's cultural communities, MLAs will continue to behave more like delegates than like representatives. They would tend to remain accountable as individuals to their constituencies, a pattern in keeping with the aboriginal tradition of dispersing power as widely as possible. Political parties might appear, but would not likely exhibit much party discipline; nor would their members be likely to pursue responsible government, which would promote party discipline, because these developments would reduce their ability to represent the interests of their constituencies or cultural communities.

CONCLUSION

Twenty-seven years elapsed between the creation of Canada's original north-western territories in 1870 and their gaining responsible government in 1897. The evolution of the system of representation in the North is likely to take at least as long. In 1870, the government of Canada felt that the wishes of the western aboriginal peoples did not figure in its calculations about western government. Today, the government of Canada accepts that the aboriginal peoples of the NWT must be involved in any process leading to a new constitution for the territory. The constitution itself will be complex in order to balance the need for structural representation of both cultural and regional interests, for the mechanisms of accountability that will provide substantive accountability, and for a reasonable degree of efficiency. The complexity may express itself in a distinctively "northern" form of government or in a more "southern" form of government plus separate aboriginal self-governments. Because the compromises among these principles will involve fundamental values such as language and lifestyle, a new and distinctive form of government is only likely to appear if the aboriginal peoples of the territories apply a great deal of energy and strategic skill to dislodging the status quo. Most relevant to this discussion, questions of representation will lie at the heart of the debates that will shape the future government of most of Canada's northern frontier.

Notes

1. Hanna F. Pitkin, *The Concept of Representation* (Berkeley, California: The University of California Press, 1967), 209.

2. Ibid., 233.

3. M. Whittington, coordinator, *The North.* Research Study No. 72, The Royal Commission on the Economic Union and Development Prospects for Canada (Toronto: University of Toronto Press, 1985), 54.

4. See, for example, J.R. Ponting and R. Gibbins, *Out of Irrelevance* (Toronto: Butterworths, 1980), Ch. 1, and Canada, House of Commons, *Report of the Special Committee on Indian Self-Government* (Ottawa: Supply and Services Canada, 1983).

5. G. Dacks, *A Choice of Futures: Politics in the Canadian North* (Toronto: Methuen, 1981), 92-94; M. Dickerson and J. Cunningham,

"Administration, Government and Financial Arrangements in the NWT," in R. Aird, ed., *Running the North: The Getting and Spending of Public Finances by Canada's Territorial Governments* (Ottawa: Canadian Arctic Resources Committee, 1988), 43-65, and G.C. Eglington, "Matters of Confidence in the Legislative Assembly of the Northwest Territories, Special Committee on Rules, Procedures and Privileges," *Third Report* (Yellowknife: Legislative Assembly of the NWT, 1986).

6. Eglington, "Matters," 103. This situation also applies in the Yukon. However, the Yukon government is based on a party system, operates on the principle of responsible government, and, because the non-aboriginal population comprises about 70 percent of the territorial population, is viewed as legitimate by a majority of Yukoners. These factors almost guarantee that the structure and approach to representation of the future government of the Yukon will closely resemble those found in the provinces today.

7. David Crombie, Minister of Indian Affairs and Northern Development, Address to the Legislative Assembly of the Northwest Territories, *Hansard*, February 6, 1985, 11.

8. Details of their proposal are contained in *Building Nunavut* (Yellowknife: Nunavut Constitutional Forum, 1985). The document itself contains some interesting approaches to representation designed to ensure that Inuit culture is protected by over-representing the smaller communities in which Inuit culture is strongest, and by applying a three-year residence requirement for voting eligibility, which would prevent many non-aboriginals from taking part in elections (25).

9. Northwest Territories Legislative Assembly, Special Committee on the Impact of Division of the Northwest Territories, *Report* (Yellowknife: Government of the Northwest Territories, 1981), 5.

10. Nunavut Constitutional Forum, *Nunavut* (Yellowknife: Nunavut Constitutional Forum, 1983), 2.

11. M. Asch and G. Dacks, "The Relevance of Consociation to the Western Northwest Territories," in Western Constitutional Forum, *Partners for the Future* (Yellowknife: WCF, 1985), 60.

12. See, for example, N.M. Lalu, "A Statistical Analysis of Residency and Mobility Patterns in the Northwest Territories," in Northwest Territories Legislative Assembly Special Committee on Constitutional Development, *Residency Requirements* (Yellowknife: NWT Legislative Assembly, 1983).

13. The Dene Nation and the Metis Association of the Northwest Territories, *Public Government for the People of the North* (Yellowknife: Dene Nation and Metis Association, 1981), 17.

14. M. Posluns, "Residence Requirements Limiting Voting Rights to Permanent Residents," in *Residency Requirements*, 22.

15. The population data used were for 1982. Northwest Territories Electoral District Boundaries Commission, *Report to the Speaker of the Legislative Assembly* (Yellowknife: Legislative Assembly of the NWT, 1983), 10 and 11.

16. *Public Government*, 17.

17. L. Malloch, *Dene Government Past and Future* (Yellowknife: WCF, 1984), 37.

18. Consociation is discussed in the following works: B.M. Barry, "Review Article: Political Accommodation and Consociational Democracy," *British Journal of Political Science* 5: 477-505; K.D. McRae, *Consociational Democracy: Political Accommodation in Segmented Societies* (Toronto: McClelland and Stewart, 1974). Some political scientists have attempted to explain aspects of Canadian politics in terms of consociationalism. Examples are E.A. Aunger, *In Search of Political Stability: A Comparative Study of New Brunswick and Northern Ireland* (Montreal: McGill-Queen's University Press, 1981), and K.D. McRae, "Consociationalism and the Canadian Political System," in K.D. McRae, *Consociational Democracy*.

19. Asch and Dacks, *The Relevance*, 35-63.

11. REPRESENTATIVE DEMOCRACY RECONSIDERED

Allan Kornberg, William Mishler and Harold D. Clarke

We can still have a modern, viable theory of democracy which retains the notion of participation at its heart.
—Carole Pateman, *Participation and Democratic Theory*

REPRISE

It is doubtful if any real-world political system merits the designation "representative democracy." Indeed, only a small minority of the world's political systems even roughly approximate the model of representative democracy [set forth in this volume and] for very good reason. [As noted in Chapter 3,] such political systems rest upon particular configurations of economic social and cultural conditions and constellations of institutions and processes not present or present to only a very limited extent in most countries. [Throughout this book] it has been argued that the provincial political systems are among the minority that have travelled *some* distance along the road to being representative democracies. At least part of the reason they have been able to do so is because in varying degrees they have been endowed with or have achieved many of the prerequisites for the establishment and maintenance of such a political order.

With respect to the social and economic bases of democracy, data were presented [in Chapter 3] indicating that Canada, currently a country of some 24 million people, is one of the most industrialized, urbanized and affluent members of the international community. Canadians also are among the best-educated people in the world. Millions have graduated from secondary school and approximately one person in 10 has attended a college or university. Significant proportions of the population are members of the several professions or executives or proprietors of businesses. Millions of others pursue a variety of well-compensated blue- and white-collar occupations. Regarding political culture, large majorities of persons in all provinces have positive, if divided, political loyalties. Québécois excepted, most Canadians give very strong support to both the federal and their provincial political communities. Also, many citizens in all provinces combine reasonably high levels of social trust with positive views of the role of the state and what it can do to facilitate their general life satisfaction and, more specifically, their economic well-being. In terms of their political institutions, in every province citizens have the opportunity to vote for candidates for parliament, provincial legislatures and municipal councils. Millions regularly do so. At both the federal and provincial levels, large bureaucracies staffed by extremely well-educated public servants administer and independent judiciaries adjudicate the myriad rules and regulations of government. At both levels of the federal system there are political party organizations and interest groups in which people

Allan Kornberg, William Mishler, Harold D. Clarke, *Representative Democracy in the Canadian Provinces* (Scarborough, Ontario: Prentice-Hall Canada Inc., 1982), 260-84. Reprinted by permission of the publisher.

can participate to have their needs and interests brought to the attention of public decision-makers. Finally, occupants of and contenders for public elective offices long ago accepted the rules of the democratic political game. They abide by the results of elections, executive powers pass peacefully from one group of political actors to another and, with singularly rare exceptions, neither aspirants for various public offices nor current incumbents employ extra-constitutional means to achieve or maintain these positions.

In comparative perspective then, it is likely that Canada as a whole and each of the provinces more closely approximate the model of representative democracy than do a large majority of the other political systems in the world. Still, there are noteworthy differences in the degree to which the provinces exhibit some of the preconditions for representative democracy. Consider, for example, interprovincial differences in so fundamental a precondition of democracy as wealth. In the late 1970s Ontario alone contributed more than six times as large a proportion of the gross domestic product as the four Atlantic provinces combined. The per capita value of Alberta's gross provincial product was more than two and one-half times as great as Prince Edward Island's and per capita personal income rose sharply as one moved from Newfoundland westward to British Columbia. All in all, an examination of a variety of economic indicators reveals that there are three relatively distinct groups of provinces: the affluent (Alberta, Ontario and British Columbia); the moderately well-to-do (Quebec, Manitoba and, most recently, Saskatchewan); and the hard-pressed (New Brunswick, Nova Scotia, Prince Edward Island and Newfoundland).

The cultural environments in which provincial political systems operate also differ but the pattern of these differences is more complex and their extent should not be exaggerated. Consider, for example, the manner in which two of the most important psychological dimensions of political culture, trust in governmental elites and political efficacy, are distributed. In every province the level of the former seems higher than the latter, but the significance of the distribution of trust is more difficult to interpret. On the one hand, trust is reasonably high everywhere and some two-thirds of the populations of virtually every province believe that government officials are intelligent, honest and generally can be trusted to do what is right. On the other hand, similar proportions in every province feel that these same governmental officials waste a great deal of money, and people in every province frequently are not very complimentary in their evaluations of elected officials. In particular, they judge them to be poor managers of the economy. Consider, also, the findings that people in every province expect a great deal from governments, want them to do more of practically everything, but, at the same time, judge elected officials are unresponsive to their needs and demands and that they (the people) are incapable of doing much about this condition. Indeed, although provincial differences in political efficacy are discernible, the major determinant of efficacy clearly is not province of residence, but rather socioeconomic status.

The provinces also are characterized by limited variations in their underlying social cleavage structures. In his landmark study of social class and power, John Porter argued that Canadian society in the 1950s was marked by significant reinforcing cleavages.[1] This was especially the case in Quebec, where patterns of ethnicity, language, religion and socioeconomic status were such that Francophone Catholics tended disproportionately to be low-income, blue- and white-collar workers, whereas English-speaking Protestants of Anglo-Celtic origins predominated in the professional and business classes. Porter maintained that these reinforcing cleavages not only affected the distribution of power among various social groups, they also influenced the potential for social conflict and political instability. Although Quebec and other provinces are now considerably different from the societies of the '50s described by Porter, some cleavages still strongly reinforce one another. In Quebec, for example, religion, language and ethnicity reinforce one another, but religion and language now tend to crosscut socioeconomic status divisions. That is, most Francophones still are Roman Catholic whereas most Anglophones are Protestant. However, no longer are Francophones disproportionately confined to lower status, poorly-paid occupations while Anglophones dominate the upper status, high income positions. On average, ethnicity, language, religious affiliation and socioeconomic status reinforce one another most strongly in New Brunswick and Prince Edward Island and least strongly in Alberta. However, provincial differences in the extent to which societal cleavages reinforce one another are not great. Moreover, the inferences to be drawn from these cleavage patterns for representative democracy are not clear. One might be that in every province there is enough crosscutting to provide a firm social base for representative democracy. In contrast, however, it may be that although every province provides a social environment conducive to the establishment and maintenance of representative and democratic institutions, the prospects for these would be enhanced further if the social and economic cleavages of the several provincial societies crosscut to a greater degree than they do at present.[2]

Similar to societal cleavage patterns, only limited provincial differences were observed in attitudes and behaviour relevant to the achievement of representative democracy. Generally, people in the several provinces do not vary greatly in the extent to which they manifest an interest in politics, use issues as the primary basis for making electoral choices,

or participate politically in activities other than voting. Thus, for example, the proportions of citizens following politics at last "fairly closely" range from slightly over one-half in New Brunswick to slightly over two-thirds in British Columbia and the proportions who are moderately or very interested in politics and are sufficiently flexible in their attachments to political parties that they might exercise at least a rough and ready rationality when voting range from one-fifth in Nova Scotia to two-fifths in British Columbia. The number of such potentially rational voters in seven of the 10 provinces differs by 5% or less. There also is little variation in provincial standings in overall participation in electorally related activities. In every province most people confine their political participation to voting and one other activity, such as periodically discussing politics with friends and family—activities requiring little in the way of the commitment of time, energy or material resources.

To reiterate, it can be argued that every province is characterized by an economic, cultural and sociopolitical environment that provides some minimal basis for the achievement of representative democracy. However, it also can be argued that these environments are far from ideal and that the prospects for representative democracy would be enhanced if, in every province, material resources and educational opportunities were greater and distributed more evenly throughout the population, people felt more politically efficacious, were less ambivalent in their feelings about political officials, voted more often on the basis of informed and rational calculations, and made more and better use of the different types of political opportunities which are formally available to them.

When evaluating the tendency of people in all provinces to refrain from most kinds of political activity, it must be noted that some of the avenues for participation which are open in theory are less open in practice. With little difficulty people can try to convince family members, friends and associates that a particular party or candidate merits their electoral support. They can attend political rallies, listen to campaign speeches, put bumper stickers on their automobiles and signs on their lawns and, subject to the availability of funds, contribute to party coffers. But they may find it is more difficult to become involved in party organizational work on a sustained basis. Except when recruiting workers to perform mundane tasks such as stuffing envelopes, posting signs and canvassing, party officials are rather selective in their choice of people to whom they turn for assistance. Many of those who are asked and who do join parties often drop out, either temporarily, or permanently. In part, high levels of personnel turnover are a consequence of the routine and repetitive nature of most of the tasks associated with the principal goal of provincial parties, the election of candidates bearing their party labels. Turnover probably also is a function of the oligarchic nature of party organizations. Although parties perform critically important functions in provincial political systems, nowhere is the composition of parties' extralegislative organizations descriptively representative of cross-sections of the general public. Nor are these organizations' internal procedures fully democratic. Only a very small minority of rank-and-file party workers in any province participate in important activities such as the selection of candidates, the construction of the platforms on which candidates run, or the generation of the policies their legislative parties pursue when in office or opposition.

Regarding parties in the electorate, although data [in Chapter 5] indicate that provincial parties frequently have been successful in building coalitions that cut across major sociodemographic cleavages within provinces, the existence of such coalitions is not evidence of widespread citizen influence over party affairs. In truth, the vast majority of persons

identifying with a provincial party exercise no direct influence over either candidate and leader selection, or the formulation of positions on major policy issues. Further, [as argued in Chapter 4,] several provinces are characterized by tendencies toward one-party dominance. In these cases, it is doubtful whether electoral competition among parties gives voters generally, or party identifiers in particular, much in the way of indirect or post hoc influence over the governing party's candidate selection or policy formulation processes. Additionally, although it appears that many party identifiers may choose their parties on the basis of specific or more general policy concerns, many others evidently do not. From one quarter to slightly over one-half of party identifiers in every province have always identified with the same party and many of these persons have done so since childhood or adolescence. For many of these durable partisans, party attachments are largely affective, essentially irrational ties. It is highly unlikely that these persons are genuinely concerned about influencing the selection of party policies, candidates or leaders. Rather, party policies and candidates invariably are perceived as "good" simply because they bear the "right" party label. By fostering such positive perceptions, the unswerving allegiance of these durable partisans effectively negates their desire to influence the conduct of party affairs.

Limited participation and influence over the conduct of organizational affairs on the part of the rank-and-file is perhaps even more characteristic of major interest groups. Interest groups, like political parties, can perform important functions in a representative democracy. Inter alia, they can suggest policies and provide information to elected public officials. By so doing, they can help make those in positions of authority cognizant of the special needs and demands of particular segments of the public and provide them with data relevant to the design and implementation of responsive policies. By representing the interests of their members in this way, and by communicating the reactions of public officials to their members, interest groups help link individuals psychologically to government and the larger political system. They thereby can enhance the democratic nature of the polity and build support for the political community and regime as well as particular policies.

In practice, however, interest groups in every province function as highly biased channels of communication. Many elements of the public are not organized into interest groups at all or, if so organized, are enrolled in groups which lack effective access to political decision-makers. In fact, such access frequently is confined to business and professional groups. Membership in the most important of these is effectively restricted to persons who are affiliated with large corporations or are members of prestigious professions. Further restricting the representational utility of interest groups is their oligarchic nature. Even in (perhaps particularly in) "institutionalized" interest groups which are able to command the attention of party and bureaucratic elites, patterns of influence and control are such that only a minority of members has an effective voice—often only those who are full-time salaried officials at the very apex of the organization. "Issue" interest groups coalescing around a shared desire to communicate a specific, pressing need or demand to government provide more significant opportunities for rank-and-file participation. However, they also are generally less effective in influencing the conduct of public affairs than are the more institutionalized and resource-rich groups.

[In Chapter 5] it was argued that although both political parties and interest groups can play important roles in making representational processes operate effectively, the former are more appropriate instruments of representation because they can articulate a wider range of group interests and are more accountable to the public for their actions. At present, however, the ability of provincial political parties to perform representational functions is constrained by a number of factors. One of them is the method by which candidates are elected to provincial legislatures. Single- or multi-member plurality electoral systems introduce an element of distortion into the representational process because the proportion of a party's legislative seats rarely is perfectly congruent with the proportion of the popular vote it receives. In the post-World War Two period, the largest distortions have occurred in Alberta, Prince Edward Island and Ontario; the smallest in Manitoba, New Brunswick and Saskatchewan. In all provinces the effect has been substantial. More important, perhaps, than the distorting effect of a first-past-the-post electoral system, but related to it, is the tendency for a single party to control the government of a province for relatively long periods of time. At some point in their histories all the provinces have experienced this phenomenon. Since 1945 the governments of Quebec, Manitoba and New Brunswick have been subjected least often to relatively long periods of one-party control; those of Ontario, Alberta, Newfoundland and Saskatchewan most often.

Long periods of governmental control by a particular party can distort the representational process in two ways. First, one-party dominance may lead to the generation and implementation of public policies which disproportionately reflect the interests of one or more major institutionalized interest groups. The latter, because of their organizational structures and bountiful resources, are well-positioned to develop and maintain intimate relationships with the cabinet ministers and bureaucratic officials who formulate and administer policies that are especially important to the groups. Second, given the British-model parliamentary systems and disciplined legislative parties operative in each of the provinces,[3] the policy positions of substantial proportions of the provincial electorates who have voted for opposition party candidates may be under- or unrepresented for lengthy periods. The policies advocated by opposition members of a legislature receive very short shrift from a governing party which feels itself securely ensconced in power.

The argument that domination of government by a single party can distort the representational process rests in part on the assumption that parties promulgate different policies when in office. Although there is a long and continuing debate regarding the extent of policy differences among various parties in several of the provinces,[4] there is some empirical support for the notion that it makes a difference who governs. Two types of data are relevant in this regard. First, analyses of aggregate data on the health, education and welfare policies pursued by the provinces in the post-war period indicate that Liberal governments are more responsive to public welfare needs than are other parties. Conservative and Social Credit governments tend to be more responsive to educational needs, and NDP governments tend to respond (indeed to overrespond) to health needs. Further, survey data indicate that substantial percentages of the general public in all provinces believe that the party in power makes a great deal of difference. The electoral strength of the NDP in a province seems particularly important in conditioning public views of the extent of policy differences among parties; the percentage of persons in a province reporting it makes a difference which party is in power is almost perfectly correlated with the magnitude of electoral support for the NDP in that province.

This is not to say that the NDP is unaffected by the kinds of political forces that influence the behaviour of other parties in particular provinces. [As observed in the case study of health policy in Saskatchewan in Chapter 7,] even New Democrats, when in office, have their policy decisions affected by the leaders of major interest groups and senior members of provincial bureaucracies. Bureaucracies share legislative and executive functions with cabinets and legislative assemblies as well as perform traditional administrative tasks. Unlike members of governing and opposition parties in provincial legislatures, bureaucrats accountability to the public cannot be secured by the threat of electoral defeat. Rather, relationships between the executive, the bureaucracy and the legislature are designed, in theory at least, to preserve the political neutrality and anonymity of civil servants.[5] As a result, the public depends on the formal procedures of parliamentary government and the more amorphous informal subjective norms operative in the bureaucratic units themselves to secure accountability.

Formal accountability through the cabinet and legislature may break down under a variety of conditions. Ministers may refuse to accept responsibility for the actions of bureaucratic subordinates. Legislators may lack the resources (e.g., standing committees, expert staff, specialized information) or the incentives to oversee the activities of public servants. For their part, bureaucratic officials neither are invariably neutral in their policy positions nor always willing to toil in silent anonymity. In this respect, members of provincial bureaucracies may be in a dilemma in the sense that strict adherence to the canons of expertise, neutrality, equality and other "standard operating procedures" at times makes them appear to be representing their own rather than the public's interests. At other times, when bureaucratic officials establish too close and continuous relationships with interest group leaders, or treat groups who nominally are the objects of their regulations as cherished clients, appearance may give way to reality![6]

Arguably, representative democracy in the provinces might be enhanced if bureaucratic accountability to the legislature and the public could be increased. As indicated, however, the utility of formal mechanisms of accountability is constrained because even the largest and most professionalized province legislatures (i.e., those of Quebec and Ontario) do not perform the oversight function effectively. Individual legislators and the institutions of which they are members are much better conveyors of authority than they are exactors of accountability. British-model parliamentary systems such as those operative in the provinces with their often weak and ineffectual standing committees, their dependence for information on the bureaucracies they are overseeing and their lack of expert staff and the specialized information which such staffs can generate, are not equipped to perform oversight activities in a vigorous and systematic manner.[7] When one adds to these structural deficiencies the strongly felt need of individual MLAs in all provinces to devote much of their time to ombudsman and other constituency service tasks widely assumed to increase their chances of being reelected,[8] small wonder that provincial legislative bodies are not known for their ability to ensure that bureaucratic officials are responsive to the general public rather than to well-organized and powerful interest groups.

More generally, backbench and opposition members of provincial legislative bodies are not especially noted for their ability to influence the policy process. The several stages of the process—the identification of problems requiring governmental response, the establishment of a policy agenda by deciding among competing priorities and the formulation and implementation of specific programs intended to achieve broad policy goals—are dominated by provincial premiers, their cabinet colleagues, senior civil servants and the representatives of powerful interest groups. At best, individual MLAs can influence the initial and concluding stages of the process (i.e., the identification of public problems and the eval-

uation of the effectiveness and appropriateness of specific programs). Even then their influence depends more on the effective use of informal contacts with ministers and senior civil servants than participation in the formal deliberations of provincial assemblies. In all provinces, institutional factors currently inhibit the ability of legislators to represent effectively the policy demands and needs of their constituents.

If, in comparative perspective, the provinces basically are similar in the way their political institutions operate both to facilitate and to limit the achievement of representative democracy, the same cannot be said of the resources which they can bring to bear to meet public needs and demands. In this respect, given the importance many social theorists ascribe to societal wealth as a prerequisite for the establishment of a democratic political order, it is ironic that there is an inverse correlation between the wealth of a province and its overall level of responsiveness to public needs in education, health and social welfare during the post-1945 period. In fact, were it not that Saskatchewan, until recently one of the least affluent provinces, ranks so low in *overall* responsiveness, the correlation between wealth and low responsiveness would be almost perfect. It must be emphasized, however, that responsiveness, as we have measured it, is not simply a surrogate for the magnitudes of governmental spending in the several policy areas. For example, in the mid-1970s, per capita expenditures on health, education and welfare by Ontario and Alberta substantially exceeded those by Newfoundland and Nova Scotia. Yet, the latter two provinces ranked higher than Ontario and Alberta in overall responsiveness. It also will be recalled that the index of policy responsiveness does not measure the *quality* of public services a provincial government provides. Physicians in Newfoundland and Nova Scotia are no more skilled, nor are their hospitals better equipped than those of Alberta and

Ontario. Nor do Newfoundland and Nova Scotia enjoy superior schools or more effective social welfare programs. However, Newfoundland and Nova Scotia do perform better than Alberta and Ontario in providing a more equitable distribution of their scarce resources among competing public needs. In this sense the index of responsiveness is a measure of a provincial government's rational and effective behaviour in responding to public needs—its ability to do the best with what it has available.

We have seen that the ability of provincial governments to do the best with the resources available to them is influenced by a number of factors, not least of which are the actions of the federal government. Over the years the federal government consciously has pursued a policy of redistributing some of the country's wealth to less prosperous provinces to help standardize the quality of governmental services. For example, in the mid-1970s, the value of the per capita transfer payments from the federal government to the less affluent provinces of Prince Edward Island and Newfoundland were 265% and 170% greater than the grant to Alberta, now one of the country's richest provinces. The manner in which the provinces choose to spend these funds affects their level of responsiveness.

Levels of responsiveness are also affected by participation in federal-provincial cost-sharing programs. In this respect, in 1977, a number of changes were made in the arrangements under which the federal government assists the provinces to fund major programs in fields such as health and post-secondary education.[9] The federal government had a two-fold objective in initiating these changes. The first was to try to control the continuously escalating federal contribution to these programs; the second, to centralize authority and responsibility for the disposition of funds for the management of these programs in the hands of provincial governments. Preliminary indications are that although, for a variety of reasons, the proportion of the federal contribution to such programs actually has increased rather than diminished since 1977, the provinces have become more cost conscious and have tried to impose ceilings on expenditures, at least in the health field. Consequently, their overresponse to health needs, as measured here, has declined somewhat. Although any prediction respecting the continuation of this trend would be premature, it does appear that a major determinant of the ability of provinces to respond to public needs—in the sense of making the best use of their available resources—is the extent to which they are free to dispose of the federal contribution to these resources.

TOWARD REPRESENTATIVE DEMOCRACY

Thus far in this discussion three points deserve emphasis. First, none of the provinces conform to the model of representative democracy [set forth in Chapter 1]. All fall short of meeting the specified conditions in a number of ways. Second, and equally important, however, all of the provinces come closer to meeting the requirements of this model than do a large majority of the world's political systems. Third, although it is doubtless true that the provincial political systems and the economies, societies and cultures upon which they rest differ in a variety of significant ways, with reference to the model, they are much more alike than different. This being the case, it is possible to entertain ways of enhancing the extent to which the provinces approximate the ideals of representative democracy in terms of a series of reforms that are applicable in varying degrees to all.

Proposals for Reform

Over the years, scholars and interested laypersons alike have offered a great many proposals designed to foster representative democracy. Although these proposals are too numerous to make a systematic analysis of their relative merits possible, fortunately, many can be reduced to variants on a few major themes. At the most general level, they approach the problem of bolstering democracy in two ways. The first focuses on altering the environment of a political system, that is, on changing economic, societal and cultural factors that condition the conduct of political life. Scholars with this perspective frequently argue that changes in the structure of and relationships among social classes are crucial if Western political systems are to move any substantial distance along the road to representative democracy. Specifically, they contend, social and economic inequalities among classes must be dramatically reduced.[10] Such reductions would increase the levels of political interest, efficacy and knowledge among currently disadvantaged members of the public and contribute to an enhanced sense of community within and among groups. These changes, in turn, would lead to both quantitative and qualitative increases in citizen participation in political life. Widespread, informed political participation would make political leaders more responsive to citizen needs and demands. Moreover, questions of its instrumental value aside, political participation is a defining characteristic of representative democracy.

The second approach to fostering representative democracy focuses on one key idea: the efficacy of institutional change. In the voluminous literature on democratic government and politics, those who share this perspective frequently advocate the reform of legislative institutions.[11] Recognizing the shortcomings of contemporary Western democracies, and assuming that legislatures are *the* key representative bodies in these polities, they contend that changes in legislative structures will improve prospects for representative democracy. Thus, literally thousands of proposals have been made to provide legislators with greater opportunities to participate more effectively in policy formulation, oversee the activities of the executive and the bureaucracy, and enhance their ability to communicate with constituents, interest groups, the mass media and extraparliamentary party organizations.[12] Normally, these proposals involve limited institutional reforms such as strengthened committees (more, fewer, bigger, smaller, with more general or more specific mandates), more staff (for individual legislators, for parliamentary committees, for party caucuses), or changes in the conduct of legislative business (longer sessions, shorter sessions, more time for the opposition to speak against government legislation, more time for the government to implement its legislative program, etc.)

Some of the proposed changes in legislatures amount to little more than institutional tinkering and whether they would add anything of real substance to the quality of political life is questionable. Other recommendations for structural changes, however, appear to have greater potential. In this latter category are proposals to change the method by which legislative representatives are chosen. A perennially popular, albeit controversial, suggestion is to abandon the current electoral system in favour of some form of proportional representation.[13] In Canada, a long-time favourite is to alter the structure and functions of the Senate and change the method by which senators are selected to provide more equitable and effective representation of regional or provincial interests in Parliament.[14] More far-reaching are proposals which concern the division of legislative powers between levels of government in the federal system or the grafting onto the parliamentary form of government certain features of the congressional system such as powerful legislative committees.[15]

Analytically, the environmental and institutional approaches to political change are easily distinguished. Empirically, it is likely that any meaningful alterations in important political institutions would require commensurate changes in the economy, society and culture in which institutions are embedded. Such *reciprocal* relationships between the way in which a political system operates and its environment raise the possibility of "vicious" circles of causality which could inhibit substantial movement toward greater representative democracy. As C.B. Macpherson recently observed:

> The reduction of social and economic inequality is unlikely without strong democratic action. And it would seem . . . that only through actual involvement in joint political action can people transcend their consciousness of themselves as consumers and appropriators. Hence the vicious circle: we cannot achieve more democratic participation without a prior change in social inequality and in consciousness, but we cannot achieve the changes in social inequality and consciousness without a prior increase in democratic participation.[16]

The questions are, then, can one break out of these circles and, if so, how? Our response to the first of these questions is positive. In part, progress toward greater representative democracy is possible precisely because at least some of the requisites for such a political order already are in place. Because they are, incremental but nevertheless meaningful reforms in existing political institutions are possible. These, in turn, can lead to changes in the social, economic and cultural environments of the provinces, thereby initiating a spiral of effects, the cumulative results of which will be to enhance the quality of political life. Let us consider some specific possibilities.

Of the multiple loci for possible institutional change, the federal system is particularly important. The federal and other provincial governments and the mechanisms of the federal system (e.g., first ministers and interprovincial conferences) constitute key institutional elements in the environments of every provincial political system. In particular, the capacity of any province, large or small, to respond to the needs and demands of its citizens is affected by the amount and type of resources available to its government. Federal-provincial fiscal arrangements thus assume critical importance. Both the magnitude of the funds and the manner in which they are made available to the provinces have important consequences. It can be argued that federal cost-sharing programs, by offering money "with strings attached," constrain provincial policy-making because they channel spending toward programmatic areas for which funds are available and lead to the neglect of others. As a consequence, one recommendation for enhancing provincial responsiveness is to replace shared-cost programs with a system of block grants. The latter would provide the provinces with the latitude and flexibility required to spend money most effectively to meet various public needs and demands and, thereby, facilitate their ability to be responsive.

From the perspective of maintaining the integrity of the Canadian political system, a potential pitfall of such a strategy is its manifest provincial bias. Former Finance Minister John Turner reportedly described it as "combining the federal right to tax with the provincial duty to spend."[17] A possible consequence of augmenting the federal taxing/provincial spending pattern would be the serious erosion of support for the federal government and, perhaps, even for the very idea of an overarching Canadian political community. Thus, another proposal is that rather than simply making blocks grants to the provinces, the federal government should share more of its taxing authority—permitting the provinces to raise and spend additional tax revenues as they see fit. The objection to this recommendation, however, is that it would perpetuate, in fact, exacerbate, existing provincial economic disparities. The contention is that without federal intervention in the form of an equalization mechanism, the value of tax revenues of a province such as Alberta always will significantly exceed those of a New Brunswick. Other factors being equal, the "have" provinces always will have greater financial capacity to be responsive to citizen needs and demands than the "have nots."

Yet another and quite different recommendation is to enhance *federal* fiscal powers, particularly the ability of the federal government to redistribute wealth among the provinces. The argument is that current arrangements have proven inadequate. The poorer provinces are losing ground and, if the trend continues, the long-term viability of the national political community itself will become problematic. Essentially this is one of the principal justifications political leaders such as Prime Minister Trudeau have offered for strengthening the economic power and authority of Ottawa in any renewed federal system.[18]

Clearly, there is an inconsistency between these latter two proposals. Maintaining or enhancing federal fiscal powers constrains the ability of richer provinces to maximize responsiveness to *their* citizens. As noted, however, emasculating federal fiscal powers would deny poorer provinces the resources required to respond effectively to the needs and demands of their citizens. In our view, a compromise position that enables the federal government to maintain considerable redistributive authority is the proper solution. Although such a compromise might result in modest alterations in the existing fiscal powers of the federal government, the real reform required in this area is not structural but rather attitudinal. There is a profound need for political leaders and the

general public alike to recognize the implications of accepting the idea that people in *every* province are members of an overarching Canadian political community. All citizens of this community deserve the benefits of representative democratic government. As long as one is unwilling to abandon the concept of enhancing representative democracy in *all* parts of the country, the notion of ensuring that the less prosperous provinces have adequate resources to act responsively remains valid. That richer provinces inevitably will be unable to be as responsive as they might be is, in this perspective, a price that must be paid if advances in representative democracy are not to be restricted to the wealthy.

Irrespective of the possible impact these recommendations, if implemented, might have on the ability of provinces to move toward the achievement of representative democracy, the availability of adequate financial resources is a necessary but not sufficient condition for meeting this goal. In a full-blown representative democracy formal mechanisms of authorization and accountability encompassing legislators, bureaucrats and citizens are needed and would constitute an intricate and sensitive network of communication and control. In such a network provincial legislators would be more accurately apprised of the needs and demands of their constituents and would be able to hold their respective bureaucracies more accountable for the implementation of policy than is currently the case. Proposals such as freedom of information legislation which might open up government, and institutional reforms such as those recently proposed at the federal level by the Lambert Commission (the Royal Commission on Financial Management and Accountability)[19] provide a point of departure for constructing a more effective set of linkages between citizens' elected representatives and bureaucratic officials. The Lambert Report and various commentaries[20] on it are especially intriguing.

Although differing in detail, they call for re-vamping legislative committees, the provision of additional staff and other resources for such committees and for individual legislators and, perhaps most importantly, a rethinking of traditional procedures used to ensure public service neutrality and anonymity.

A political neutral and anonymous civil service is part and parcel of parliamentary government, as that process is currently under-stood. In fact, however, as Campbell and Sza-blowski,[21] Cairns,[22] and others have observed, senior civil servants currently are involved in making crucial *political* decisions. Moreover, they do so in an environment which effectively shields them and other important political ac-tors such as cabinet ministers and interest group representatives from public scrutiny. As a result, the public's elected representatives, no matter how intelligent and sensitive to public needs and demands they may be, have neither the requisite information to analyze and com-prehend the content of governmental pro-grams, nor the ability to assess their possible consequences. Accordingly, structural and procedural changes which would make gov-ernment operations more visible and amena-ble to public scrutiny, as well as changes which might improve the information-gathering and analysis capacities of legislators, could make a significant contribution toward the achieve-ment of representative democracy generally and the accountability of bureaucrats to elected public officials in particular.

The chain of communication and control required to make authorization and account-ability function more effectively has other weak links as well. Specifically, links between the general public and their MLAs need to be strengthened. The most obvious is the elec-toral connection, which enables an electorate to signal either pleasure or displeasure with an incumbent government by reelecting it or re-jecting its candidates in favour of those of a competing party. In a democracy, this is a powerful and authoritative message. Nonethe-less, as many political theorists have noted, electoral mechanisms, as they currently oper-ate in Canada and other Western countries, constitute very imperfect communications channels and very blunt instruments of popu-lar control.[23] Regarding the former, both in logic and in fact, elections frequently fail to convey clear signals about either the content of public policy preferences or the priorities voters assign to these preferences. Also, as noted previously, the plurality electoral sys-tems employed in all provinces tend to distort the actual distribution of party votes when these are translated into legislative seats.

The ability of elections to serve as in-struments of control in part is contingent upon the motives of political elites: more specifi-cally, their political career aspirations. Other than a normative desire to adhere to the canons of representative democracy, elected officials who entertain no, or only modest po-litical ambitions, have little incentive either to anticipate or to respond to public needs and demands.[24] For their part, there is very little voters can do other than render a post hoc negative judgment on the performance of such officials at the next election. Additionally, there are no guarantees that candidates of par-ties aspiring to power will be more responsive than the "rascals" whom the electorate may wish to "throw out," or that challenging par-ties will present policies which differ meaning-fully from those currently being pursued.

Is there anything which can be done to improve the operation of the electoral system? Clearly, political parties cannot be forced by legislative fiat to offer clearly distinguishable policy alternatives. Nor is it possible to legis-late officeholders' motives during their terms of office. However, it may be possible to mini-mize the distortion of election results that presently occurs when votes are translated into legislative seats. Some form of proportional representation, if adopted, might ensure that the composition of legislative assemblies would reflect more accurately the electoral strength of parties in a province.

Advocates of proportional representation long have argued that the major beneficiaries of such a system would be smaller, weaker parties which traditionally have had great difficulty either securing or maintaining a foothold in provincial legislatures.[25] Gaining greater legislative representation would provide them with continuing access to one of the most important platforms in a democracy for making their policy positions known. The adoption of proportional representation also would help to break the system of oligopolistic competition among dominant parties, thereby widening the range of policy choices available to the electorate and demonstrating that a vote for a small minority party is not necessarily wasted. Over time, the cumulative effects of proportional representation might well be the development of significantly more competitive and ideologically diverse provincial party systems. Increased competition among ideologically diverse parties, in turn, might have a salutary effect on responsiveness by encouraging electoral candidates to be more attentive to public opinion and facilitating the public's ability to make meaningful choices among clearly defined policy alternatives proffered by competing parties.

Opponents of proportional representation question both the validity of these claims and the appropriateness of the system for Canada. Regarding the former, they ask whether proportional representation would appreciably improve the competitive position of Liberals in Alberta and British Columbia, of Conservatives in Quebec and British Columbia, of the New Democratic Party in the Atlantic provinces, Quebec and Alberta, or of Social Credit in any province east of Alberta. The prospects of these provincial parties also would be impaired if, as seems probable, some version of a "five percent" regulation were adopted as part

of a proportional representation package. As it operates in some European countries, the regulation requires that a party receive a minimum of five percent (or some other stipulated figure) of the total vote cast before its candidates can be seated in the legislature. Although this rule makes it difficult for fringe groups espousing anti-democratic sentiments to gain a legislative platform for their views, if used in Canada, it also probably would impair the electoral prospects of some of the provincial parties referred to above.

As for the claim that proportional representation would encourage political parties to present more meaningful policy choices to voters, critics point out that most parliamentary systems employing proportional representation have coalition governments. These coalitions are formed *after*, rather than before an election and it is often very difficult to forecast which coalitions might occur. Moreover, because of the politics of coalition building, voters casting their ballots for party "A" on policy grounds may receive something quite different in the way of policy if the party becomes part of a governing coalition.[26]

There are other criticisms of proportional representation. For example, it is argued that proportional representation is inappropriate for parliamentary systems of the kind found in Canada. These function best when a single party is able to achieve the parliamentary majority required to govern. Proportional representation, however, increases the probability of coalition governments which may be fractious and unstable. The possible results include continuing policy stalemate, more frequent elections and general political instability.[27] Additionally, although they need not, polities employing proportional representation frequently have list voting and multimember legislative districts. Under these conditions, the likelihood of election is dependent upon a candidate's position on a party list; the higher the position, the greater the likelihood of election. These lists generally are prepared by small groups of upper-echelon, full-time, salaried, party organizational officials who, it may be assumed, are unlikely to slate candidates in favourable positions if their social and demographic characteristics or policy views differ markedly from their own (i.e., the list-makers'). In sum, list voting might make party organizations even more oligarchic and legislatures more unrepresentative than they are currently.[28]

These objections to proportional representation notwithstanding, it may be the case that in *some* provinces the claims of advocates of such systems might be realized without incurring problems such as those cited above. Given this possibility and the manifest need to eliminate, insofar as possible, the distorting effects of present provincial electoral systems, the pros and cons of proportional representation should receive more systematic and unbiased consideration than they appear to have to date.

In any event, neither proportional representation nor any other electoral mechanism will eliminate the need for political leadership. In this respect, representative democracies are no different than other political systems. In a representative democracy the division of political labour between governors and governed places an inescapably heavy burden on political leaders, irrespective of the process by which they are selected. Although generations of political theorists have spent a great deal of time and effort on the task, a permanent solution to the leadership recruitment problem remains elusive. Of course, a fundamental rationale for democracy is precisely that there are no foolproof means of ensuring that leaders will be responsive to the public. Leaders' internalization of democratic norms, their more general political ideologies, and their political ambitions all may make them adhere to public needs and demands, but ultimately citizens must assume responsibility for

protecting their own interests by active involvement in political life.

Unfortunately, as observed a number of times in this book, one of the most salient characteristics of political behaviour in all provinces is that few citizens do anything political but vote and occasionally discuss politics with friends and family. The pervasiveness of low levels of participation might tempt one to infer that little or nothing can be done to enhance popular political involvement. Such an inference would be unwarranted. After all, in every province a minority of persons *are* politically active. In terms of attitudes and beliefs, they are people with high levels of political interest who believe that they have the competence to influence the behaviour of those who govern, and assume that "who governs" can and does make a difference. Sociologically, political activists tend to be well-educated, middle-aged, upper and upper-middle class men with prestigious professional or managerial occupations. Indeed, these are literally the defining characteristics of the most politically active and influential persons— leaders of parties and interest groups and holders of elective and appointive public offices. Knowing who they are enables us to suggest ways in which more extensive and intensive citizen participation can be achieved.

Our first suggestion flows from the observation that there is a causal chain linking socioeconomic status and political participation. Upper and upper-middle class persons frequently have the material resources and leisure time that lead to the development of psychological orientations (e.g., political interest, efficacy and knowledge) conducive to political activity. Although in a free society it is impossible to redistribute societal goods and services to ensure that everyone has the material and temporal resources currently available to the upper and upper-middle classes, greater efforts in this direction are possible. Particularly important is improved access to educational opportunities for lower socioeconomic status persons, minorities and women. [As noted in Chapter 3,] since 1960 every province (with the assistance of the federal government) has significantly expanded its system of secondary and post-secondary education. These systems are in place and constitute the structural basis for providing more citizens with the educational resources conducive to more extensive political involvement. Greater access to educational opportunities is merely a beginning. Studies of the relevance of secondary and higher education for political socialization in Canada have concluded that during the course of their formal schooling most people receive little or no information about how their political institutions and processes function.[29] Consequently, a second recommendation is that, at a minimum, people receive basic factual information about the nature of their political system and how it operates. Although this proposal might seem modest it can have significant effects if, as we believe, the knowledge people acquire will enhance both their interest in participating politically and the feeling that they can do so effectively.

A third suggestion is to provide opportunities and encouragement for greater participation in the governing of ostensibly "non-political" institutions such as schools, factories and offices. Advocates of this approach contend that for too long a time overly narrow conceptions of what is and is not political have discouraged participation by defining the political process almost entirely in terms of the operation of institutions such as legislatures, parties and bureaucracies. These are institutions which most people have little personal knowledge of or experience with and, hence, they have been unwilling to try to participate, assuming they could not do so effectively. A broader conceptualization of the political process, one that encompasses institutions such as schools and the workplace, is, therefore, desirable—both for its own sake and because it

would encourage the development of attitudes conducive to participation in more manifestly political institutions. Regarding the desirability of a broader conceptualization of the political process, the argument is that societal institutions that organize work, education and leisure have a major impact on most people. It is within these structures that people spend substantial proportions of their daily lives. Consequently, widespread participation in their decision-making processes is desirable in and of itself.[30] Participation of this kind would enhance people's feelings of personal competence which, in turn, would stimulate even more intensive participation on their part. Equally important, what persons learn and experience within the confines of these institutions can be generalized and transferred to the political arena more narrowly defined.[31] The net result of greater participatory opportunities might well be an expanding spiral of political efficacy and participation. To reiterate, if people are given meaningful opportunities to participate in the decision-making processes of institutions such as workplaces and schools, they will acquire an enhanced sense of political competence. This will encourage them both to participate more intensively in such institutions and to extend their involvement to manifestly political institutions. The latter would produce strengthened feelings of competence, which would reinforce the desire to participate.

PROSPECTS FOR REFORM

Offering blueprints for political reform is not terribly difficult. Indeed, the construction of plans for utopian polities has been an intellectual pastime for political theorists since Plato. Unfortunately, attempts to put such reforms into practice generally have led to bitter disappointment. After suffering such disappointments, erstwhile reformers often have accepted the truth of the old adage that "the road to hell is paved with good intentions" and become political "realists." In recent times, among the most influential members of the realist school have been the elitist democrats who defend the status quo by arguing that only very limited reforms of the political systems of Western countries are either possible or desirable. From the vantage point of democratic theory, one can reject the normative thrust of these arguments.[32] However, their empirical aspects are more difficult to evaluate. A skeptic, reviewing the historical wreckage of so many of the schemes for political reform, is justified in asking just how likely it is that meaningful changes can be effected. The question is a valid one, but a precise response, unfortunately, is impossible.

[As has been indicated throughout this book,] a number of barriers exist to meaningful democratic reform. Most of these can be reduced to the observation offered earlier [in this chapter] of the strong circularities in relationships between societal change and political reform. Significant social changes require institutional reforms which are highly unlikely in the absence of thoroughgoing societal changes. Breaking out of these circles of causality through actions initiated by reform-minded political leaders is difficult since these leaders profit the most from existing political, social and economic arrangements. Accepting this reasoning, some critics would abandon Western liberal and democratic traditions entirely and place their hopes for achieving desired societal changes on violent revolution led by enlightened cadres of counter-elites.[33]

Evidence adduced in this and other studies of political attitudes and behaviour suggests, however, that we are not necessarily fated to be crushed between the "rock" of status quo and the "hard place" of violent revolution. For one thing, considerable research has shown that political elites tend to be the strongest proponents of democratic norms in contemporary Western countries.[34] To conclude, therefore, that "when push comes to shove" political elites invariably will abandon these norms in favour of some version of a narrow class interest is unduly pessimistic. For another, our analysis of voting behaviour [in Chapter 4] indicates that the burden of moving the polity in the direction of greater representative democracy need not rest entirely on the shoulders of political elites. Substantial numbers of persons in every province already demonstrate a capacity for effective participation in a representative democracy and presumably would be receptive to proposed reforms designed to improve the quality of political life. In short, there is no reason to accept the extreme pessimism of either radical critics of the motives and behaviour of political elites or elitist democrats who disparage the capacities and inclinations of average citizens.

Still to be answered, however, is the question of how we break out of the circles of causality which reinforce the status quo. Do we begin with the political elites and political institutions or with the general public and society at large when initiating processes of reform? One answer, we believe, is to attempt incremental but *non-trivial* modifications of existing economic, social and political institutions, using widespread perceptions of the need for change as a base on which to build a consensus regarding the desirability of specific reforms. Although such reforms probably will have to be initiated by political leaders, as noted, there are reasons to believe that both elites and the general public will be receptive to them. Moreover, there is reason to believe that this receptivity will increase concomitantly with a growing recognition that the social and economic foundations of the Canadian political system, like those of other Western polities, currently are being subjected to severe, perhaps unprecedented, stresses. These include pressures deriving from continuing high rates of unemployment and inflation, recurring shortages of various raw materials and foodstuffs, ever-shrinking supplies of fossil fuels with accompanying escalations of energy costs, massive environmental pollution and rapid technological changes that seriously disrupt traditional social patterns and threaten the survival of minority cultural groups. Within the Canadian context, some of these problems are felt acutely, others are more remote. On balance, however, these stressful conditions have profoundly shocked the Canadian political system and helped produce the continuing and widely recognized "Crisis of Confederation."

Paradoxically, this crisis may well provide an unprecedented opportunity to improve the quality of Canadian political life. The view that problems such as those cited above must be dealt with immediately and systematically already is widespread. This recognition has prompted numerous proposals for revamping different aspects of the political system. To date, with the exception of the federal government's attempts to entrench a charter of rights in a new constitution, virtually all of these proposals have focussed quite narrowly on the federal system. Altering the powers of the federal and provincial governments and changing the institutions of the former to increase the ability of the latter to voice their demands at the national level have been major topics of debate. By conceptualizing solutions to the problems facing Canadians in terms of relationships between the two levels of *government*, federal and provincial politicians and other participants (e.g., academics, journalists) in this debate have neglected the need to change institutions at *both* levels to enhance the responsiveness of the political system to popular needs and demands.

Although, as previous discussion has indicated, proposals to change the federal system are relevant to the task of building representative democracy, clearly, revamping federalism

is not enough. More extensive and profound institutional, societal and cultural changes are required. Prospects for such thoroughgoing changes are uncertain, but not necessarily bleak. Since the systemic stresses which produced the ongoing crisis are unlikely to be eliminated (although they may be ameliorated) by altering the structures of federalism, pressures for additional reforms are likely to continue. It is possible that these pressures will be in the direction of representative democracy. In this regard, it is trite, but nevertheless true that much will depend on how elites and members of the general public react when it becomes apparent that changes in federalism provide only partial answers to the serious problems confronting the country.

Scholarly opinion regarding how the complex of problems facing Canada and other Western countries will affect the long-term prospects for democracy is sharply divided. Michael Margolis, for example, is quite pessimistic. In his opinion, despite their apparent discontent, neither elites nor the general publics in Western democracies want real reform. Rather they support the status quo and will continue to do so because they believe existing governmental institutions can deliver an ever-increasing abundance of the goods and services that they have come to take for granted. As a result:

> Only when the resources that have sustained this growth [in the economies of Western countries] have nearly run out will any radical adjustments in policy occur. For the citizens' own good these adjustments will be imposed upon them by experts from the governing elite. The policies imposed may or may not be successful ... but the policy process will be neither liberal nor democratic.[35]

C.B. Macpherson, in another recent work on the future of democracy, is even more critical of elites, but his high regard for the potential of citizens to recognize the pressing need for change makes him guardedly optimistic about the future of Western polities:

> So we have three weak points in the vicious circle—the increasing awareness of the costs of economic growth, the increasing awareness of the costs of political apathy, the increasing doubts about the ability of corporate capitalism to meet consumer expectations while reproducing inequality.... [T]ogether, they conduce to a decline in consumer consciousness, a reduction of class inequalities, and an increase in present political participation.[36]

Both Margolis and Macpherson agree that the economic and social catalysts for change are present; they disagree about the likely directions of change. Margolis believes that citizens in Western countries are unlikely to abandon what Macpherson has called "consumer consciousness" to emphasize values such as a sense of community, a clean, healthy environment, a more equitable distribution of societal goods and political participation itself. Macpherson, in contrast, judges that the present crisis may have precisely this effect on people's values and the result will be breaks in the reinforcing relationships of elite domination and mass apathy which heretofore have inhibited movement toward greater democracy in all Western societies.

We do not know if either of these two rival hypotheses will be proven correct. Social and political systems are complex entities and forecasting the future is necessarily a risky business. Nevertheless, it is apparent that significant social and economic changes are occurring and that these probably will lead to equally substantial changes in Canadian political life. It also is evident that it requires, for political elites and citizens alike, a "leap of faith" to attempt to channel the processes of change in the direction of representative democracy by working to institute political, social and economic reforms such as those described in this chapter. But this is nothing new. Democratic theory always has been predicated on faith: faith in the capacity of people for self-government. To abandon this faith is tantamount to denying the possibility of representative democracy. To affirm it may be simply naive, but an alternative and more generous interpretation is that such an affirmation is at worst a secular analogue of "Pascal's wager." Granted, the stakes are not as high as those which concerned the 17th century French philosopher. Still, the possibility of achieving a genuinely representative democratic system in a more humane and participatory society makes the game well worth the candle.

Notes

1. John Porter, *The Vertical Mosaic* (Toronto: University of Toronto Press, 1965), passim.

2. See, for example, Arend Lijphart, "Typologies of Democratic Systems," *Comparative Political Studies* 1 (1968): 12; Douglas Rae and Michael Taylor, *The Analysis of Political Cleavages* (New Haven: Yale University Press, 1970), 86.

3. For a succinct description of the properties of such systems see Nelson Polsby, "Legislatures," in Fred I. Greenstein and Nelson Polsby, eds., *Handbook of Political Science* 5 (Reading, Mass.: Addison-Wesley, 1975), Ch.

4. On recent changes in the British parliament see John E. Schwarz, "Exploring a New Role in Policy Making: The British House of Commons in the 1970s," *American Political Science Review* 74 (1980): 23-47; and Philip Norton, "The Changing Face of the British House of Commons in the 1970s," *Legislative Studies Quarterly* 3 (1980): 333-58.

4. See Harold D. Clarke, "The Ideological Self-Perceptions of Provincial Legislators," *Canadian Journal of Political Science* 11 (1978): 617-34.

5. For a recent discussion of these relationships see Kenneth Kernaghan, "Power, Parliament and Public Servants in Canada: Ministerial Responsibility Re-examined," in Harold D. Clarke, et al., eds., *Parliament, Policy and Representation* (Toronto: Methuen, 1980), Ch. 7.

6. On the breakdown of bureaucratic neutrality and anonymity in Canada see Colin Campbell and George J. Szablowski, *The Superbureaucrats: Structure and Behaviour in Central Agencies* (Toronto: Macmillan, 1979).

7. A number of scholars have made this argument. See, for example, Audrey Doerr, "Parliamentary Accountability and Legislative Potential"; Paul G. Thomas, "Parliament and the Purse Strings"; and Colin Campbell and George Szablowski, "The Centre and the Periphery: Superbureaucrats' Relations with MPs and Senators," in Clarke, et al., *Parliament, Policy and Representation*, Chs. 8, 9 and 11.

8. Harold D. Clarke, Richard G. Price, Robert Krause, "Constituency Service Among Canadian Provincial Legislators: Basic Findings and a Test of Three Hypotheses," *Canadian Journal of Political Science* 8 (1975): 534.

9. See David Falcone and Richard J. Van Loon, "Public Attitudes and Intergovernmental Shift in Responsibility for Health Programs: Paying the Piper Without Calling the Tune," in Allan Kornberg and Harold C. Clarke, eds., *Political Support in Canada: The Crisis Years* (Durham, N.C.: Duke University Press, 1982), Ch. 8.

10. More radical exponents of the perspective have argued that this can *only* be accomplished if the present capitalist economic system is replaced by a socialist one.

11. This is not to say that concern for legislative reform is a recent phenomenon. Scholars long have been interested in the topic. See, for example, Gerhard Loewenberg, *Modern Parliaments: Change or Decline?* (Chicago Aldine Alherton, 1971).

12. For a selection of proposed reforms in the Canadian Parliament and provincial legislatures see the several papers collected in Clarke, et al., *Parliament, Policy and Representation*.

13. See, for example, Report of the Task Force on Canadian Unity, V. 1 *A Future Together: Observations and Recommendations* (Hull: Canadian Government Publishing Centre, 1979), Ch. 7.

14. Examples include E.D. Briggs, "The Senate: Reform or Reconstruction?" *Queen's Quarterly* 75 (1968): 91-104; Government of Canada, *The Constitutional Amendment Bill* (Ottawa: Ministry of Supply and Services, 1978); Task Force on Canadian Unity, *A Future Together*, 97-9; Colin Campbell, *The Canadian Senate: A Lobby From Within* (Toronto: Macmillan, 1978), Ch. 7.

15. For arguments regarding the need for strengthening legislative committees see Thomas, "Parliament and the Purse Strings," and Campbell and Szablowski, "The Centre and the Periphery," Chs. 9 and 11 in Clarke, et al., *Parliament, Policy and Representation*. Proposals for restructuring the federal system are legion. Recent examples include Task Force on Canadian Unity, V. 1 *A Future Together*, Ch. 7; and The Constitutional Committee of the Quebec Liberal Party, *A New Canadian Federation* (Montreal: January 9, 1980). A concise exposition of the Parti Québécois' proposal for sovereignty-association is contained in André Bernard, *What Does Quebec Want?* (Toronto: James Lorimer, 1978), Ch. 4.

16. C.B. Macpherson, *The Life and Times of Liberal Democracy* (Toronto: Oxford University Press, 1977), 100.

17. Falcone and Van Loon, "Public Attitudes and Intergovernmental Shift in Responsibility for Health Programs."

18. Pierre Elliott Trudeau, *The Constitution and the People of Canada* (Ottawa: Queen's Printer, 1969).

19. Royal Commission on Financial Management and Accountability, *Final Report* (Hull: Canadian Government Publishing Centre, 1979).

20. See, for example, Kernaghan, "Power, Parliament and Public Servants in Canada"; Doerr, "Parliamentary Accountability and Legislative Potential"; and Thomas, "Parliament and the

Purse Strings"; Chs. 7, 8, and 9 in Clarke, et al., *Parliament, Policy and Representation.*

21. Campbell and Szablowski, *The Superbureaucrats,* Chs. 7, 8.

22. Alan C. Cairns, "The Governments and Societies of Canadian Federalism," *Canadian Journal of Political Science* 10 (1977): 695-726.

23. A succinct summary of these arguments can be found in Macpherson, *The Life and Times of Liberal Democracy,* 82-92.

24. Joseph A. Schlesinger, *Ambition and Politics* (Chicago: Rand McNally, 1966), Ch. 1; Harold D. Clarke and Richard G. Price, "Parliamentary Experience and Representational Role Orientations in Canada," *Legislative Studies Quarterly* 6 (1981): 373-90.

25. For a recent argument to this effect see the Task Force on Canadian Unity, *A Future Together,* 105.

26. A.J. Milnor, *Elections and Political Stability* (Boston: Little, Brown, 1969), 91-8.

27. Ibid.

28. For an expanded version of this argument with reference to the proposals of the Task Force on Canadian Unity see Allan Kornberg, Harold D. Clarke, Arthur Goddard, "Parliament and the Representational Process in Contemporary Canada," in Clarke, et al., eds., *Parliament, Policy and Representation,* 20.

29. T.H.B. Symons, *To Know Ourselves: The Report of the Commission on Canadian Studies* (Ottawa: Association of Universities and Colleges of Canada, 1975), 65.

30. Macpherson, *The Life and Times of Liberal Democracy,* 103-5; Carole Pateman, *Participation and Democratic Theory* (Cambridge: Cambridge University Press, 1970), Chs. 3, 4; Peter Bachrach, *The Theory of Democratic Elitism* (Boston: Little Brown, 1967), Ch. 7.

31. Pateman, *Participation and Democratic Theory,* Chs. 3, 4; Gabriel Almond and Sidney Verba, *The Civic Culture* (Princeton: Princeton University Press, 1963), Ch. 12.

32. See, for example, Jack L. Walker, "A Critique of the Elitist Theory of Democracy," *American Political Science Review* 30 (1966): 285-95; Lane Davis, "The Cost of Realism: Contemporary Restatements of Democracy," *Western Political Quarterly* 17 (1964): 37-46; Graeme Duncan and Steven Lukes, "The New Democracy," *Political Studies* 2 (1963): 156-77.

33. The possible and desirable roles of elites in effecting political change has long been a topic of intense debate among radical critics of liberal democracies. See, for example, Henry B. Mayo, *Introduction to Marxist Theory* (New York: Oxford University Press, 1960), Ch. 5.

34. Two classic studies documenting this point are Herbert McClosky, "Consensus and Ideology in American Politics," *American Political Science Review* 58 (1964): 361-82; and James W. Prothro and Charles M. Grigg, "Fundamental Principles of Democracy: Bases of Agreement and Disagreement," *Journal of Politics* 22 (1960): 276-94.

35. Michael Margolis, *Viable Democracy* (Markham: Penguin Books Canada Limited, 1979), 186-7.

36. Macpherson, *The Life and Times of Liberal Democracy,* 106.

DISCUSSION QUESTIONS

1. How representative are legislatures, the bureaucracy, the judiciary, and interest groups, in Canada? Are the regions in Canada adequately represented at the centre?

2. How do you think political representation ought to be implemented in the Northwest Territories?

3. Explain with reasons the changes you would make in implementing political representation in Canada.

MECHANISMS FOR DISTRIBUTING ELECTIVE REPRESENTATION

INTRODUCTION

Harvey E. Pasis

Four characteristics distinguish a democratic political system from a non-democratic one. The first feature of a democracy is the requirement of the popular control of representatives.[1] Since voters do not decide each public policy at elections, they vote for representatives to stand for them at elections held at regular periods. The second characteristic is political equality or the equality of all adult citizens in voting. Political equality requires that each person should have only one vote that counts equally, that representation by population should be followed, and that the number of representatives elected should be proportional to the number of votes received. The third trait is the existence of political freedoms, such as freedoms of speech, assembly and organization, and freedom to seek political office. The fourth feature is that decisions among the representatives are based on majority rule.

Section One of this book examined the meanings and controversies concerning political representation. Section Two centred on how political representation in Canada is performed by several institutions and processes. Section Three concentrates on whether political equality in Canada is attained in designing mechanisms for distributing elective representation by examining constituencies or ridings, the different criteria used to establish them, the allocation of seats, gerrymandering, the use of computers, and the evaluation of the redistribution process in Canada. Section Four will focus on whether political equality is attained in Canadian electoral systems. Section Five will ascertain whether majority rule is followed in making collective choices.

CONSTITUENCY

Elected legislators in Western democracies normally represent a constituency or "a piece of territory, and their representative function is linked to the citizens who reside in that area."[2] Besides territorial constituencies, functional constituencies can be used to represent people in certain occupations, for instance, lawyers, and ridings based on population can be established for numbers of people.[3] The number of ridings is normally related to the voting system used, so that single-member constituencies tend to be found with plurality or majority voting and multi-member ones with proportional representation.[4] According to Michael Steed, multi-member ridings make for more balanced and localist representation[5] compared to single-member ones, since the former tend to favour the representation of legislators, especially of ethnic minorities and women, who live in the constituencies for which they seek election.

CRITERIA

Before discussing the criteria used for establishing constituencies, three terms need to be clarified. First, redistribution is the Canadian term that refers to the allocation of seats in a political system and the periodic drawing of constituency boundaries.[6] Secondly, apportionment is the American term for determining the number of seats, and thirdly, reapportionment or redistricting[7] is the American term for the description of electoral lines.

In Canada, representation by population has not been followed closely in drawing federal electoral boundaries from 1867 until 1966, because politicians constructed ridings based on municipal and county boundaries, classes, regions, community of interest, the campaign convenience of legislators and candidates, and the over-representation of rural areas compared to urban ones.[8] T.H. Qualter has criticised most of the reasons for not using population as a major criterion for establishing boundaries. For example, he has questioned the argument that a different type of representation was needed in rural ridings compared to urban ones since each type of riding had a different community of interest. This argument assumes that rural residents had a common interest very different from urban ones and that place of residence is the correct indicator for community of interest. Qualter has argued that non-geographic factors such as income, social status, occupation, education, age, sex, or religion may be more important variables in defining a common interest.[9] Without strict adherence to representation by population, extreme inequalities in the number of people existed between the largest and smallest Canadian constituencies[10] and rural residents had more seats than urban ones.

Similar criteria for the arguments about constituencies were made in the United States until 1962 when the Supreme Court ruled in Baker v. Carr[11] that state apportionments could not violate the equal protection of the laws clause of the Fourteenth Amendment of the American constitution. Later, the Court ruled in Reynolds v. Sims[12] that districts had to be based on equal population as nearly as was practicable, and that one man, one vote had to be followed. These decisions led to many more court cases to bring about more equitable and more representative federal and state apportionment and redistricting systems.[13]

Even after many court cases, disagreement still exists about the criteria of fair representation. Richard Morrill, for example, has argued that good quality districting has the following characteristics: districts of equal population; equal or proportional treatment of parties; respect for area of partisan loyalty; equal treatment of race/language groups with respect to changes for electing minorities; respect for maintaining political boundaries; respect for communities of interest; and contiguous and compact districts.[14] Similar arguments have been made by Bruce Cain[15] and Arend Lijphart, although the latter has been able to list sixteen criteria of fair representation.[16] However, the major dilemma is that many of the criteria are inconsistent with each other and may lead to contradictory proposals.[17] For example, if districts are designed to be equal in population size, compact, and contiguous, they may not be able to follow local boundaries.

These inconsistencies occur when geographically-defined electoral districts are used with plurality or first-past-the-post and majority electoral systems. One solution is to implement proportional representation in order to achieve fair representation.[18] In the next section of the book, the advantages and disadvantages of proportional representation and other electoral systems will be examined with respect to the attainment of fair representation.

ALLOCATION OF SEATS

In 1867, the British North America Act (now called the Constitution Act) specified the number of federal seats for each Canadian province; Section 51 required the recalculation of the number of seats every ten years starting with the census of 1871. Over time, exceptions were invented so that provinces did not lose seats. For example, the "senatorial clause" of 1915 prevented a province from having "fewer seats in the House of Commons than it had in the Senate."[19]

From 1867 until 1964, the federal government controlled the redistribution process either through a government bill or a committee of MPs[20] in order to try to draw the boundaries for its own benefit—a practice also found in the United States.[21] In 1964, non-parliamentary electoral boundary commissions, which were to follow statutory guidelines for the redistribution process, were established.[22] The Canadian commissions, borrowed from the Australian model,[23] are required to draw ridings based on each province's electoral quota within a +25% tolerance limit for each constituency. But starting with the 1987 redistribution, this limit could be ignored under extraordinary circumstances, and, in fact, several commissions did exceed the tolerance level for a few ridings in 1987. Each commission is required to conduct public hearings on its proposals, but final authority for the redistribution rests with the commission and not Parliament.[24] Thus, federal politicians have been removed from the machinery involved in the redistribution process in Canada, although they can still alter the rules for the allocation of seats[25] and the guidelines for the boundary commissions.

GERRYMANDERING

If governments are responsible for the redistribution process, then the criticism of gerrymandering or the drawing of ridings designed to give the government a maximum unfair advantage[26] is usually made by the opposition party. In 1872, 1882, and 1892, this criticism was made in the House of Commons by the Liberals. As R. MacGregor Dawson has shown, the establishment of ridings designed to produce a Conservative victory failed in 1882 because people did not vote the way the government predicted they would, and because the opposition made the gerrymander an issue in the campaign.[27]

   A gerrymander is difficult to create and to determine because it must assume that the electorate votes the same way in specific ridings from one election to the next. In addition, it omits the possibility that the voters may move from one riding to another between elections, thereby lowering and raising support for political parties in their old and new constituencies respectively. Voters who vote in one election and abstain in another and voters who are enumerated in one election and not in another are also not considered. Even if these unknowns were eliminated, gerrymandering cannot be isolated as the only factor responsible for significant voting patterns carrying over from one election to the next, since other issues and/or new candidates may also be important.

   Furthermore, politicians' intentions in drawing electoral boundaries must be determined in order to find out if they tried to obtain an advantage for their party and if they were successful in their endeavours. Although the gerrymander of 1882 is an exception, politicians do not readily volunteer information of this nature. Either they conveniently forget, will not discuss, or refuse to acknowledge their intention in drawing constituencies. Even if any boundary change in a riding from one election to the next is assumed to be intended to benefit the party in power, an examination of the election results in each poll does not indicate if the party obtained the desired advantage on account of the alteration. Since new issues, new candidates, and the other factors mentioned previously may produce the same effect as boundary changes, there is still the problem of determining which factor or factors caused the election outcome.

   Even if it is difficult to establish a gerrymander, politicians in the United States have managed to develop two types not well-known in Canada. The first is the affirmative action gerrymander that is designed "to maximize the political strength of minorities to the extent possible ... by giving minority groups a proportion of representation in the legislature as close as possible to their proportion in the population."[28] The second type is racial gerrymandering designed to reduce the chance of a racial minority, such as blacks or Hispanics, from being elected.[29] The latter type was held unconstitutional by the Supreme Court of the United States in 1960.[30]

   Twenty-six years later, the Supreme Court of the United States went even further to state that an intentional partisan gerrymander was unconstitutional if the electoral system consistently reduced "a voter's or group of voters' influence on the political process as a whole"[31] and if the effects of a plan were "sufficiently serious to require intervention by the federal court."[32] According to Guillermo Owen and Bernard Grofman, the definition and measurement of a gerrymander will likely be important in 1990s redistricting cases in the United States.[33] Although the courts have been significantly involved in the reapportionment process in the United States, exactly the opposite has occurred in Canada.

USE OF COMPUTERS

Computers were expected to play an important part in drawing constituency boundaries, especially when the courts in the United States stressed population as the main criterion to be used in reapportionments.[34] This has not occurred, although computers have been used to correct errors in census data and to assist in calculating population statistics based on hand-drawn plans.[35] At one time, the use of computers for drawing constituencies was thought to be scientific, non-partisan, or impartial. However, G.B. Norcliffe has shown that "the science of districting is not value-free"[36] since subjective decisions concerning the most important criteria in districting still have to be made by the programmer.[37]

A similar debate developed in England, where R.J. Johnston, et al., have argued and attempted to show that the use of computers would speed up the redistributions carried out by British Boundary Commissioners for England, the European Assembly, and local government wards.[38] Later, after several tests were conducted, G.P. Barnes, the Secretary of the Boundary Commission for England, published a contrary view. He argued that using a computer would probably extend the length of time needed to perform the redistribution, and that no advantage would be achieved by its use "because the selection of a distribution in each area"[39] required many subjective decisions by the Commission.

EVALUATION OF THE REDISTRIBUTION PROCESS

The consequences, results, or impact of changes in the redistribution process in Canada need to be examined. One type of study uses a statistical measure to determine the change in the population size of constituencies. For example, John Courtney used the Gini Index to measure the extent of constituency equality or inequality, and found "that a marked improvement in the equality of constituency populations"[40] occurred since the establishment of Canadian boundary commissions in 1964. Harvey E. Pasis found similar results for the 1986-87 federal redistribution proposed to Parliament.[41] However, the British Columbia Supreme Court has ruled that Section 15(1) of the Canadian Charter of Rights and Freedoms, which states that "Every individual ... has the right to the equal protection and equal benefit of the law ...," applies to a provincial redistribution in that province.[42] The Charter will likely also be relevant for the federal redistribution since Section 32(1)(a) indicates it applies to Parliament and the government of Canada. Therefore, some Canadian court will have to determine in the future if the United States' principle of equal representation for an equal number of people is to be followed in Canada federally and provincially.

A second type of study has examined the impact of reapportionment on public policy in the states and provinces with mixed results. Researchers like Yong Hyo Cho and H. George Frederickson found that apportionment variables were not more important than other political factors in influencing all policy areas, but that they were important in influencing civil rights and firearms control policies.[43] Similarly, Douglas Feig ascertained that reapportionment had an impact on state aid to local education in about one-half of the states and in state expenditures for public welfare in nearly all of the states.[44] According to Mathew McCubbins and Thomas Schwartz, reapportionment may have led to some policy changes because redistricting created in the U.S. House of Representatives a large metropolitan majority who developed policies for metropolitan voters rather than for rural ones.[45]

Other studies found that economic development variables like industrialization were more influential than political factors like malapportionment in shaping policies in the states.[46] Results of a Canadian study by Dale Poel were different, showing that both socioeconomic and political variables including malapportionment were important in influencing provincial legislation.[47] Another U.S. study found that no political party gained at the expense of the other and that incumbents did not benefit at the expense of challengers after redistricting occurred in the U.S. House of Representatives.[48]

In summary, then, the Canadian federal redistribution process, now conducted by federal boundary commissioners rather than by politicians, has moved towards equality of constituency populations, and has protected the number of seats held by the smaller provinces. Although it has not yet been interfered with by the judiciary, this is likely to change in the near future.

Notes

1. Henry B. Mayo, *An Introduction to Democratic Theory* (New York: Oxford University Press, 1960), 61. The remaining traits can be found on pages 62-69. Similar arguments can be found in J. Roland Pennock, *Democratic Political Theory* (Princeton: Princeton University Press, 1979), and T.C. Pocklington, ed., *Liberal Democracy in Canada and the United States: An Introduction to Politics and Government* (Toronto: Holt, Rinehart, and Winston of Canada Ltd., 1985).

2. Michael Steed, "The Constituency," in Vernon Bogdanor, ed., *Representatives of the People?: Parliamentarians and Constituents in Western Democracies* (Aldershot, Hants, England: Gower Publishing Company Ltd., 1985), 267.

3. Terence H. Qualter, *The Election Process in Canada* (Toronto: McGraw-Hill Company of Canada Ltd., 1970), 84.

4. Steed, "The Constituency," 268.

5. Ibid., 283-4.

6. Norman Ward, *Dawson's The Government of Canada* 6e (Toronto: The University of Toronto Press, 1987), 92.

7. Michel Balinski and H.P. Young, *Fair Representation* (New Haven: Yale University Press, 1982), 2.

8. T.H. Qualter, "Representation by Population: A Comparative Study," *Canadian Journal of Economics and Political Science* 33 (1967): 248-57.

9. Ibid., 254.

10. Qualter, *The Election*, 87.

11. 369 U.S. 186 (1962).

12. 377 U.S. 533 (1964).

13. Edward McWhinney, *Supreme Courts and Judicial Law-Making: Constitutional Tribunals and Constitutional Review* (Dordrecht: Martinus Nijhoff Publishers, 1986), 191.

14. Richard L. Morrill, "Redistricting, Region and Representation," *Political Geography Quarterly* 6 (1987): 243-4. Morrill has made similar comments in his *Political Redistricting and Geographic Theory* (Washington: Association of American Geographers, 1981), 21-27, and his "Redistricting Standards and Strategies After 20 Years," *Political Geography Quarterly* 1 (1982): 361-9.

15. Bruce E. Cain, *The Reapportionment Puzzle* (Berkeley: University of California Press, 1984), 53.

16. Arend Lijphart, "Comparative Perspectives on Fair Representation: The Plurality—Majority Rule, Geographical Districting, and Alternative Electoral Arrangements," in Bernard Grofman, et al., eds., *Representation and Redistricting Issues* (Lexington: Lexington Books, 1982), 145-7.

17. Ibid., 147. The incompatibility of criteria has also been recognized by Bernard Grofman in "Fair and Equal Representation," *Ethics* 91 (1981): 477-81; "Criteria for Districting: A Social Science Perspective," *UCLA Law Review* 33 (1985): 77-184; and in two articles with Howard Scarrow, "The Riddle of Apportionment: Equality of What?", *National Civic Review* 70 (1981): 242-54; and "Current Issues in Reapportionment," *Law and Policy Quarterly* 4 (1982): 435-74.

18. Arend Lijphart, "Comparative Perspectives," 155.

19. Representation in the Federal Parliament, Ottawa: Minister of Supply and Services, 1986, 5.

20. Norman Ward, "A Century of Constituencies," *Canadian Public Administration* 10 (1967), 110.

21. For a comparison of the drawing of boundaries in the United States and Britain, see David Butler and Bruce E. Cain, "Reapportionment: A Study in Comparative Government," *Electoral Studies* 4 (1985), 197-213.

22. Norman Ward, "A Century," 117.

23. For a comparison of the Canadian and Australian Commissions, see John C. Courtney, "Theories Masquerading as Principles: Canadian Electoral Boundary Commissions and the Australian Model," in John C. Courtney, ed., *The Canadian House of Commons: Essays in Honour of Norman Ward* (Calgary: The University of Calgary Press, 1985), 135-72.

24. For the development of provincial boundary commissions, see Qualter, *The Election*, 105-11; and R.K. Carty, "The Electoral Boundary Revolution in Canada," *American Review of Canadian Studies* 15 (1985): 273-87.

25. For two views on the allocation of seats, see Michael Coulson, "Reforming Electoral Distribution," *Policy Options* 4 (January/February 1983): 25-8; and M.L. Balinski and H.P. Young, "Fair Electoral Distribution," *Policy Options* 4 (July 1983): 30-2.

26. Qualter, *The Election*, 115.

27. R. MacGregor Dawson, "The Gerrymander of 1882," *Canadian Journal of Economics and Political Science* 1 (1935): 215.

28. Cain, *The Reapportionment Puzzle*, 166-7.

29. Morrill, *Political Redistricting*, 13.

30. Gomillion v. Lightfoot 364 U.S. 339 (1960).

31. Davis v. Bandemer 106 SCT 2798 (1986) at 2810.

32. Ibid., at 2811.

33. Guillermo Owen and Bernard Grofman, "Optimal Partisan Gerrymandering," *Political Geography Quarterly* 7 (1988): 6.

34. For a list of typical articles on using the computer for redistricting, see James B. Weaver, *Fair and Equal Districts: A How-To-Do-It Manual On Computer Use* (New York: National Municipal League, 1970), 95-6; Richard L. Morrill, "Ideal and Reality in Reapportionment," *Annals of the Association of American Geographers* 63 (1973): 463-77; and his bibliography in *Political Redistricting*, 66-76.

35. Charles H. Backstrom, "The Practice and Effect of Redistricting," *Political Geography Quarterly* 1 (1982): 356.

36. G.B. Norcliffe, "Discretionary Aspects of Scientific Districting," *Area* 9 (1977): 240.

37. Ibid., 245.

38. R.J. Johnston, "Political Geography of Contemporary Events II: A Reapportionment Revolution that Failed," *Political Geography Quarterly* 2 (1983): 317; and R.J. Johnson, S. Openshaw, D.W. Rhind, and D.J. Rossiter, "Spatial Scientists and Representational Democracy: The Role of Information-Processing Technology in the Design of Parliamentary and Other Constituencies," *Environment and Planning: C* 2 (1984): 57-66.

39. G.P. Barnes, "The Use of Computers in Redistributing Constituencies," *Electoral Studies* 6 (1987): 138.

40. Courtney, "Theories Masquerading," 162.

41. Harvey E. Pasis, "The Courts and Redistribution in Canada," *Canadian Parliamentary Review* 10 (1987): 8-9.

42. Re Dixon and Attorney-General of British Columbia (1987), 31 D.L.R. (4th) 546.

43. Yong Hyo Cho and H. George Frederickson, "Apportionment and Legislative Responsiveness to Policy Preferences in the American States," in L. Papayanopoulos, ed., *Democratic Representation and Reapportionment: Quantitative Methods, Measures and Criteria* (New York: Annals of the New York Academy of Sciences, 1973), 264.

44. Douglas Feig, "Expenditures in the American States: The Impact of Court-Ordered Legislative Reapportionment," *American Politics Quarterly* 6 (1978): 320.

45. Mathew D. McCubbins and Thomas Schwartz, "Congress, the Courts, and Public Policy: Consequences of the One Man, One Vote Rule," *American Journal of Political Science* 32 (1988): 409.

46. For a list of relevant articles and issues on this topic, see Thomas R. Dye, *Understanding Public Policy* 6e (Englewood Cliffs, N.J.: Prentice Hall Inc., 1987), 309-14.

47. Dale H. Poel, "The Diffusion of Legislation among the Canadian Provinces: A Statistical Analysis," *Canadian Journal of Political Science* 9 (1976): 626.

48. Amihai Glazer, Bernard Grofman, and Marc Robbins, "Partisan and Incumbency Effects of 1970s Congressional Redistricting," *American Journal of Political Science* 31 (1987): 701.

12. THE CONSTITUENCY

Michael Steed

Most members of representative assemblies represent constituencies. Even the formal exceptions, such as the members of the Israeli Knesset all elected on national lists, the 100 national members of the Japanese second chamber, the House of Councillors, or the 12 state deputies in Greece, in fact very often have clear links to particular localities or sections of the population and, since their election is in part due to support in that area or group, can be said to represent them. But for most parliamentarians, this link and representative function is formalised: a legally defined part of the process of nomination, of the presentation of candidatures to the electorate and of election. That almost always involves a distinct area of territory; even the rare exceptions to this rule are usually only partial, for example, the four Maori-elected members in the New Zealand Parliament sit for four territorial sub-divisions of that country and the Flemish and Francophone colleges used for the election of Belgium's 24 MEPs mix a voluntary linguistic division in Brussels with a territorial one in the rest of the country. The norm in Western democracies is very clear: elected representatives are each attached to a piece of territory, and their representative function is linked to the citizens who reside in that area.

Michael Steed, "The Constituency," in Vernon Bogdanor, ed., *Representatives of the People? Parliamentarians and Constituents in Western Democracies* (England: Gower Publishing Company Limited, 1985), 267-85. Reprinted by permission of the publisher.

But if the constituency is nearly universal, consciousness of its role in parliamentary and political life varies greatly. Certain assemblies, notably the British House of Commons, place great store on the distinct territorial link of each member, symbolised in the British case by the convention of referring to other members as "the Member for Somewhere" rather than by name. In other assemblies—especially in the view of politicians accustomed to the habits of those in the first category—constituencies play little or no role. This distinction has been carried into the European Parliament. By treaty, all MEPs are elected to represent the member states of the European Community. Yet in the official list of its members published by the Parliament of all the United Kingdom's 81 MEPs are designated, under the heading "Member State," "United Kingdom Member for Northumbria" (or whatever). The odd Irish MEP has chosen to follow suit, but otherwise all other MEPs are designated by their countries—even the single MEP elected for Greenland was designated "Denmark." In fact, though many MEPs are elected on national lists (French, Greek, Dutch, Luxembourgers, some Germans and the Danes apart from Greenland), the majority are elected in distinct territorial subdivisions of their states and from the formal point of view if MEPs from the United Kingdom represent sub-national constituencies, a majority of the European Parliament does so also. The difference between the UK's MEPs and the rest of this majority is in behaviour and consciousness, carried over from national politics.

The difference in attitude towards constituencies is thoroughly mixed up with a politically much more important difference—the voting systems used. It is not easy to distinguish the two dimensions, especially since those who approve of (or simply benefit from) the political consequences of the plurality voting system in Britain may well be finding it easier to defend their position by reference to (and exaggeration of) one of its subsidiary characteristics. While it is impossible to disentangle fully the question of various sorts of constituency from that of the various electoral systems used, if we focus carefully on the former we acquire a somewhat different perspective from that of most of the literature on electoral systems. Though plurality or majority voting is now normally associated with single-member constituencies, and proportional representation with multi-member ones, the full relationship is more complex.

THE DEVELOPMENT OF THE CONSTITUENCY IN WESTERN EUROPE

The complexity is well illustrated if we look at the history of the sub-division through which members of European representative assemblies have been chosen. The story of voting systems is relatively simple: plurality or majority (successive ballot) methods were almost universal in the nineteenth century, giving way between 1899 (Belgium) and 1921 (Norway) to proportional systems in almost all countries, with France and the United Kingdom the notable exceptions. In many states the switch to proportional representation involved a change from single-member to multi-member constituencies, but in several it did not. Furthermore, if we trace the development further back, we find a nineteenth century drift from multi-member to single-member constituen-

cies. This can only be understood against the background of a move away from earlier views of representation, which saw parliaments as representing distinct categories of society, most usually the notability, the clergy, the peasantry and the towns.

Parliaments deriving from this earlier view were often based on sub-divisions which were as much functional as territorial and whose size (in population or electorate) was unrelated to their scale of representation. Constituencies, if the modern word can be applied to them, were entities which existed independently of the electoral process and were represented as such—in the same way as today the United States Senate consists of two members from each state, regardless of size. When this formula was adopted for the US Senate, that had been the norm in the House of Commons with each English borough, county or university having two members, regardless of size. Progress in the nineteenth century involved moving away from the representation of corporate or territorial bodies to that of citizens, and so both a widening of the franchise and an equalisation of representation as between different categories.

In some countries this meant a sharp break as multi-cameral estates systems gave way to uni- or bi-cameral systems. In others, the transition came in stages, as various functional constituencies were assimilated into a single form of territorial sub-division. Most of these changes came early, though Finland only jumped from an archaic system of four separate estates to a modern parliament in 1906; distinct university representation within the House of Commons lingered until 1950; and segregated representation of urban and rural areas in a fixed ratio in Norway only went in 1953. Indeed, a vestigial element remains in the House of Commons today, with each of the 650 members designated as representing either a borough constituency or a county constituency.

The equalisation of representation was met in two ways—either by varying the number elected to represent one entity so as to reflect population, or by sub-dividing them into more equal-sized districts. Often both approaches were adopted. In Switzerland until 1848, each canton had a single delegate in the federal assembly. The 1848 Constitution provided for a federal assembly comprising a national council, in which representation reflects population, along with a states council. The federal law of 1850 defined 49 new territorial constituencies. Fifteen were intact cantons (or half-cantons), six with a single member and nine with two, three or four members. The remaining ten cantons, entitled by population to between four and twenty-three members, were sub-divided into 34 specially defined constituencies of which six elected a single member; eight elected two members; eleven elected three members; and the remaining nine four each.[1] But as population grew and shifted during the nineteenth century, additional members were assigned to the more populous constituencies, with no further sub-division, until the canton of Geneva elected *en bloc* eight members (it had been three in 1850) and the largest constituency elected nine. The divisions of 1850 became the fixed entities and the system only changed in 1919 when proportional representation for the national council was introduced operating at cantonal level, with four cantons (three of them in fact half-cantons) electing a single member and twenty-one between two and thirty-one. Proportional representation brought the restoration of the intact canton as the constituency and indeed the latter principle placed a certain limitation on the proportional principle; in the single-member cantons a proportional formula produces the same result as a plurality election.

Though the Swiss law of 1850 is a good example of the general drift of change in mid-nineteenth century Europe, mixing as it did sub-division and variable size to attain equal-ity of representation, Switzerland is unusual in then maintaining its multi-member constituencies for so long a period. Belgium retained mostly multi-member constituencies throughout the nineteenth century, using them for its change to proportional representation in 1899. Elsewhere the Chartist principle of equal-size constituencies was increasingly chosen as the means to ensure equal representation and that mostly meant single-member ones, though in 1850 the Netherlands adopted 34 two-member divisions to elect a 68-member chamber, with half the members coming up for re-election at a time.

The Netherlands moved to mostly single-member electoral divisions in 1887, with multi-member ones in the cities, and to a wholly single-member system in 1896. Denmark had adopted the single-member principle for the popular chamber, the Folketing, in 1849 (though in reverse to the Swiss mix, in 1855 an attempt was made to have a council of the realm covering the Danish provinces, Holstein and Schleswig, using multi-member election by the single transferable vote). In 1861 newly-united Italy took over the single-member constituency from the 1848 Piedmontese constitution. The North German Confederation in 1867 and imperial Germany in 1871 used single-member constituencies. Multi-member, indirect election in Norway gave way to direct election in single-member districts upon full independence in 1905. The Hapsburg empire only moved away from a complex, indirect system of estates and provincial representation in 1907, when it adopted single-member districts (except in Galicia, where double-member constituencies were used to facilitate German-Polish ethnic balance). France, as throughout its democratic history, experimented with the electoral system for political ends. The *départements* had been the (multi-member) constituencies at the outset of both the Second and Third Republics, but they were divided into single-member districts in 1875, restored for a multi-member election in 1885, and switched back to a single-member system in February 1889 (partly because, on the evidence of a by-election victory on 27 January 1889, the supporters of General Boulanger looked set to take every one of the thirty-eight seats in the Seine *département*).

Thus there was a clear general move among Continental democracies towards the principle of securing equal representation by equal-size districts. Most of the remaining states using administrative units with variable representation lay in the more backward corners of Europe, such as the Balkan states or Portugal (in fact a pioneer of a crude form of proportional representation, the limited vote), just as elements of the estates system survived into the twentieth century in the Austro-Hungarian empire or some Nordic states (then poorer rural countries, not the epitomes of welfare industrialisation they were to become). Among the European countries regarded as models or modern, only Belgium and Switzerland stuck to the multi-member principle.

Britain moved, though more gradually, with this tide of change. The big jump occurred in 1885; Gladstone, in presenting the case for the change which he acknowledged "as far as England is concerned is almost a novelty,"[2] claimed it as the "general system of Europe" and added "the whole of the representative systems of the civilised world which have this single-member system do not show the least desire at present to get rid of it."[3]

Two or three decades later, most single-member constituency countries in Europe were getting rid of these systems, as the wave of change to proportional representation rolled across the continent. Britain was to resist that tide and indeed stood quite alone in the consistency of its commitment to what had been a novelty in December 1884. This behaviour probably has more to do with how certain British parties viewed proportional representation than with how they viewed the uninominal principle. But, in view of the uniqueness of the British case in Europe, it is worth enquiring further into the British decision to adopt the novelty that has subsequently come to be seen as characteristically British.

THE BRITISH CASE

Table [1] sets out the changes in the character of constituencies in the House of Commons. Historically the House had consisted mainly of pairs of members sitting for entities which were also territorially defined—"Communal/ territorial" in the table. The main exception were the single members sitting for the less populous Scottish burghs and counties. In 1832 and again in 1868 progress towards equalisation of representation on a population basis involved both methods. The variation for intact counties from one to three members, and boroughs with one or two in 1832 and one to three in 1868, kept communities as constituencies, minimising special electoral boundaries. The expanding and newly represented boroughs did have boundaries drawn for them —but these were subsequent upon the decision about their representation and were intended to encompass the natural urban area and not to produce constituencies of a particular size. However, the largest counties (assigned four members each in 1832) were subdivided, creating essentially electoral entities. In Scotland, with its single-member counties and burghs, the single-member division also appeared— one alone, Clackmannan & Kinross (also containing parishes lying in Perthshire and one in Stirlingshire) in 1832, and then six more in 1868 when the three counties assigned two members, Aberdeenshire, Ayrshire and Lanarkshire, were sub-divided. These seven were the tiny trickle to precede the flood.

There were also three other types of constituency, neither a territorial entity, nor a subdivision of one. The City of London, with four

Table 1   Constituency Development in the United Kingdom

	1832*	1868*	1885	1918	1922*	1950*	1983
Communal/Territorial							
Single-member boroughs	86	123	81	37	36	26	-
Double-member boroughs	282	196	46	24	22	-	-
Treble-member boroughs	-	15	-	-	-	-	-
Single-member counties	39	35	31	31	23	20	3
Double-member counties	88	86	-	-	6	-	-
Treble-member counties	21	21	-	-	-	-	-
Communal							
Districts of boroughs	27	28	21	7	7	3	-
Territorial Divisions							
Single-member divisions	1	7	480	591	507	576	647
Double-member divisions	104	134	-	-	-	-	-
Treble-member divisions	-*	-	-	-	-	-	-
Quasi-functional							
City of London	4	4	2	2	2	-	-
Functional							
Universities*	6	9	9	15	12	-	-
Total	658	658	670	707	615	625	650
% Single member	23.3*	29.8*	91.9	94.8	93.7	100.0	100.0
% Divisions	16.0	21.4	71.6	83.6	82.4	92.2	99.5

This table shows the number (and percentage share) of members of the House of Commons elected for various types of constituency in the period following the redistributions effective in the years stated.

*Notes to table:-

i)   University constituencies were all double-member in 1832; three double-member and three single-member in 1868 and 1885; one treble-member, four double-member and four single-member in 1918; and one treble-member, three double-member and three single-member in 1922.

ii) Between 1844 and 1885 small changes were made consequent upon the removal of separate representation from a few small boroughs on grounds of corruption, including the creation of a treble-member territorial division (Southern Lancashire) in 1861.

iii) The proportion of MPs sitting for single-member constituencies outside Scotland was 17.2% in 1832 and 23.9% in 1868; in Scotland these proportions were 92.4% in 1832 and 88.3% in 1868.

iv) The changes made in 1922 were wholly consequent upon the secession of the Irish Free State and a reduction in representation of Northern Ireland; no changes were made in Great Britain.

v)   The total was raised to 640 in 1945, 630 in 1955 and 635 in 1974 without significantly affecting the distribution between different types of constituency.

members elected together until 1868, is the historic core of modern London, with few residents; increasingly as time went by, its members were elected to represent those who had businesses there but lived elsewhere. The concept of a constituency based on function is much clearer with the university Members, elected by the graduates of most (after 1918, all) universities, wherever resident. The districts of boroughs were collections of small towns, always in Scotland or Wales and sometimes quite a distance from each other; communities of interest based on residence but not continuous pieces of territory.

Until 1868, the voting system was simple plurality, with each elector able to exercise as many votes as there were seats to fill in his constituency. From 1868, the limited vote was used for the 40 Members from the City of London and the treble-member boroughs or counties; simple plurality for the remaining 618 members.

This was the complexity when the third major round of reform came to be debated in the 1880s. Reform involved the question of the franchise (the other major change in 1885 was to be the extension of the franchise to the bulk of the male rural working class), the voting system (advocates of proportional representation were beginning to organise) and redistribution (equal representation demanded a reallocation of seats away from declining rural areas to the growing cities and industrial regions). Both the major parties acknowledged the case for reform, but both were divided on the several distinct questions. The Liberal government decided to proceed separately on the franchise question, and introduced a franchise bill in February 1884 without committing itself on the voting system or on redistribution. This played into the hands of the Conservative opposition, who were able to offer vigorous opposition to the attempt to settle the franchise without a redistribution. Lord Salisbury, the Tory leader, could thus keep his party united, avoid opposing the principle of an extension of the franchise and avoid specifying his party's position on the other questions, whilst at the same time raising fears about Liberal intentions. In July 1884, the Tory majority in the House of Lords wrecked the franchise bill on the grounds that the issues needed to be dealt with together.

Up to that point, the Liberal government had resisted all attempts, whether by the opposition or by some of its own supporters, to get these other issues discussed. The related questions of redistribution, type of constituency and voting system thus mainly emerged in the debates in the first half of 1884 under procedural guise—or, in a monumental misunderstanding by the chairman of the nature of the question, through amendments to abolish the limited vote or to extend it to double-member constituencies (allowed to be debated because they were said to be about the exercise of the franchise and not the electoral system). On these Gladstone refused to commit himself or the government, arguing, for instance, that if the limited vote in treble-member constituencies were a good principle, it should be extended but, if bad, abolished, and this should be decided on principle and not as a by-product of the franchise debate. However, he did make his position clear on one matter: "I am not personally at all favourable to what is called the system of electoral districts . . . [which] would involve a great deal of unnecessary displacement and disturbance of traditions."[4]

The conflict, fanned in the summer by mass demonstrations in favour of franchise extension and against the House of Lords, was in process of being resumed in the autumn when the two party leaders agreed to meet in private. They agreed on a scheme for redistribution that, by applying the single-member principle, also determined the electoral system; in return, the Conservatives dropped their opposition to the Liberal proposals on the franchise. Matters were settled fast. Gladstone and Salisbury first met on 19 November 1884; on 27 November, Gladstone reported agreement to the Queen; he announced the agreement in detail in the House of Commons on 1 December; and the redistribution bill incorporating the proposals received its second reading on 4 December. Indeed, Jones's account narrows the crucial decision down to a shorter period: he quotes evidence that on 22 November the Liberal Ministers involved thought Salisbury was only concerned to get single-member seats in the suburban belt around London, and that they were faced with Salisbury's demand for comprehensive application of the uninominal principle (with the sole exception of the City of London) on 26 November.[5]

Only four days after that Gladstone spelt out the precise agreement. The City of London and the existing University constituencies were to continue (except that the former was to be reduced from four-member to double-member)—concessions to Conservative interests. Boroughs of between 50 000 and 165 000 inhabitants were to remain intact and double-member; the force with which Gladstone justified this treatment ("a unity of municipal life which, except for some great object, it is not desirable to violate or impair by severence"[6]) indicates sympathy on his part for the exception. Otherwise the uninominal principle was to be universally applied. All attempts during the passage of the redistribution bill to modify the compromise package failed, and what the party leaders decided on or about 26 November 1884 determined the British electoral system and the shape of the British constituency for the next hundred years.

Historians and biographers examining this episode have generally neglected the question of the electoral system. Interest has focused on the innovation of inter-party negotiation to resolve a constitutional conflict, and on the extension of the franchise in rural areas. The most detailed history of the episode, Andrew Jones's *The Politics of Reform, 1884*, concentrates explicitly on the "high politics" of what happened, registering its interest in "political in-fighting, the significance of duplicity as a means of conciliation, and the over-riding impact of ambition or frustrated ambition" (p. 237) rather than on the questions at issue. This may be understandable; the impact of the franchise-extension and the means of resolving constitutional crisis were probably of more importance to the development of the British political system in the late nineteenth century. But it is somewhat frustrating to the enquirer seeking to understand how Britain came to make a change which, arguably, has had a crucial impact on the subsequent hundred years of political development.

The historian's analysis which is most concerned with reform itself remains Charles Seymour's *Electoral Reform in England and Wales* published as long ago as 1915. However, it is not always clear, when he uses the terms "proportional representation" and "proportionate representation," where he is referring to representation of political opinion, where to that of population, and where to both. In a way, this uncertainty assists in understanding what happened in 1884, since this confusion was certainly present in many minds then. His account places the single-member district as one "device which would render the character of the legislature more representative," competing for consideration with other devices, namely (in modern terminology), the limited vote, the cumulative vote, the single transferable vote and the second ballot—in short, as one form of progress towards proportional representation.[7]

Gladstone's own defence of his conversion to the principle he had opposed in February 1884 put the case thus,[8]

> ... it is very economical, it is very simple, and it goes a long way towards that which many Gentlemen have much at heart—namely, what is roughly termed the representation of minorities; it may be termed the representation of separate interests and pursuits; but, give it what name you like, there is no doubt that by means of one-Member districts you will obtain a very large diversity of representation.

Salisbury's daughter's biography explains that he went for what she calls the "revolutionary feature of the new settlement,—i.e., the breaking up of the counties and big towns as units of multiple membership, and the practically universal introduction of single member constituencies of approximately equal size" in the cause of party unity. He saw it as one way to assure "the representation of social minorities ... [but] ... would have preferred, and in his speeches that summer had advocated, a more accurate and elaborate system of minority representation."[9] Other biographers do not dissent, though Lady Cecil's statement is the clearest evidence that Salisbury would actually have preferred some form of proportional representation within multi-member constituencies to the uninominal principal he eventually insisted upon.

The Commons debates on the redistribution bill show how widespread the belief was that single-member equal-size electoral divisions would produce fairer representation. Many members lamented the disappearance of the old community principle, none more so than Leonard Courtney who resigned from the government over what he saw as the introduction of a principle "contrary to the Constitutional idea of representation in Parliament,"[10] predicting (in a passage which appears to anticipate the safe seat) the "decay and atrophy of political energy and power,"[11] forewarning of the advent of adversarial politics "sharp lines of division, instead of making the people feel that they will belong to one community, will divide one section from another, and will set class against class"[12] and making as his most prescient claim "my great fear and anxiety is that it [the single-member seat] will be tenacious of life."[13] Courtney wanted the single transferable vote but would have accepted anything to keep multi-member, community constituencies, including the least proportional method of voting, the block vote by list. But a more common attitude was expressed by the Member for Mid-Lincs, who saw subdivision of cities as "calculated to destroy all *esprit de corps*, and what he might describe as the public and the corporate spirit of those great communities"[14] but felt nevertheless that if subdivision "did afford any kind of representation to minorities, it would be better than nothing at all."[15]

As Table [1] shows, traces of the older principle survived and momentarily (with the creation of one treble-member University constituency in 1918, and three double-member counties in Northern Ireland) resurfaced. A Speakers' Conference in 1917 unanimously recommended the restoration of the multimember principle for cities, but the government refused to accept the recommendation and the Commons followed suit. But by then the issue of the electoral system had become clearer and the 1917-18 debate revolved more around that. Constitutional conservatives, however, continued to lament the loss: thus Leopold Amery, the Member for a Birmingham division 1911-45, wrote two years after his final electoral defeat in 1945:[16]

> In so far as our system is historically one, not so much of individual votes as of communities and of important elements in national life, then there is certainly a case for considering the application of Proportional Representation to our larger cities. These are now chopped up into arbitrary constituencies with no characteristic corporate life.

However, the last handful of non-single-member divisions disappeared in 1950; three anachronistic Scottish districts of burghs lingered, Dumfermline burghs and Kirkcaldy burghs going in 1974 and the last, Stirling (unnoticed in its unique longevity) in 1983, while the 1972 Local Government Reorganisation Act removed the status of county boroughs and produced an almost universal system of counties big enough to require sub-division. At the 1983 election only three insular reminders of an older principle remained—Isle of Wight (94 226 electors), Orkney & Shetland (30 087) and Western Isles (22 822)—whilst the other 647 were all fairly equal-sized electoral districts with specially drawn boundaries.

THE MULTI-MEMBER MODEL

The norm in the rest of Europe is a variable size multi-member constituency which consists of an entity independent of the electoral process, combined with proportional representation. Switzerland epitomises this model. The cantons (and half-cantons) are the constituencies, which means that there has been only a single boundary change since 1919 due to the creation of the Jura canton. The number of deputies is adjusted automatically every ten years following the census; after the 1980 reallocation, there were five single-member constituencies and twenty-one electing between 2 and 35 members.

Countries with constitutionally defined states or provinces usually make those their constituencies. The 248 members of the German Bundestag elected on lists sit for the ten *Länder*. Representation varies greatly, as the largest *Land* (Nordrheinwestfalen) is more than twenty times more populous than the smallest (Bremen); however, numbers of seats are not fixed in advance but are determined after each election by the proportions of the

national vote cast in each *Land*. In Austria, the country was provisionally divided in 1919 into twenty-five constituencies, of a modest range of 4 to 13 members; in 1920 the first Austrian republic adopted a federal constitution but these twenty-five remained until 1971, when Austria switched to using its nine *Laender* as constituencies—the most populous (Vienna) having more than seven times as many electors as the smallest (Vorarlberg). In Belgium, the 1831 Constitution requires constituencies to be fitted within the boundaries of its nine historic provinces (which do not always fit with the controversial linguistic boundaries). In a complex system of two-tier constituencies set up in 1919, each province forms a constituency for certain purposes, but is also sub-divided into between two and five electoral *arrondissements*. The seats are assigned to the *arrondissements* following the decennial census, and range greatly, currently from 2 (Ypres and Neuchateau-Virton) to 34 (Brussels); in 1919 the range was from 3 to 26.

In Sweden the constituencies which came into use in 1921 largely but not wholly follow the boundaries of the 24 modern *län* (or counties), dating from 1862, rather than the ancient provinces (*landskap*). However, the two largest cities, Stockholm and Goteberg, are constituencies separate from their *län*; while a group of southern cities centering on Malmö form a "district of boroughs" constituency known simply as the "Four City Constituency." This sub-divides the three most populous *län* on an urban basis; the fourth most populous (Alvsborgslän), with a particularly awkward elongated shape, is sub-divided geographically into a North and South division. Thus, since 1921, there have been 28 constituencies. In 1970 a new constitution was enacted, making several changes including a substantial change in the type of proportional representation; a switch from population to the electorate as the basis for assigning members to constituencies;

and one chamber instead of the historic bicameral system. Yet the 28 constituencies remained unchanged with between 2 (the island of Gotland) and 31 (Stockholm city) members out of those seats in the new Parliament assigned to constituencies in advance.

The Swedish model of a set of constituencies based on, but not adhering absolutely to, administrative entities becoming fixtures (as with Switzerland 1850-1919) is followed in several other countries. In Greece, the *nomoi* (or prefectures) became the basis of a multi-member constituency system in 1886, and have so remained for most of the period since; but while 49 *nomoi* are intact constituencies, the largest, Attiki (containing Athens) is subdivided into five districts and the next (Thessaloniki) into two, making 56 constituencies. Italy's constituencies were set up by a governmental decree in 1946: this grouped the 92 provinces into 32 constituencies by combining the smaller ones. Nonetheless, the range of members was then from 7 to 36, even excluding the special (linguistic) single-member constituency of Aosta. With population shifts, the range has become 4 to 53, but no move has been made to revise the constituencies, either to conform to the twenty regions set up in 1948 or to adjust to the present distribution of population. The Netherlands has had eighteen constituencies since proportional representation was introduced in 1917, though the way the political parties operate the system makes them rather nominal so far as the voter or any theory of representation is concerned: three are the cities of Amsterdam, The Hague and Rotterdam; seven whole provinces; while the remaining four provinces are each divided into two constituencies.

Thus most European countries have found a way of meeting both the nineteenth century demand for equality of representation and the older principle of community representation by varying numbers rather than drawing boundaries. Constituencies have become fixtures in the political landscape, allowing a continuity of political life and normally a simple correspondence with administrative bodies, and with all the other public and social organisations that tend to arrange themselves around those areas of regional or local government. Changes are rare—but when local government boundaries are altered, consequential changes can be made instantly. Thus in 1970, Denmark reduced its multi-member constituencies outside Copenhagen from 22 to 14 so that they could continue to coincide with the *amtskrede*. In Finland there have been changes to the constituencies set up in 1906 on six occasions, three because of changes to the national boundary, two to county boundaries and only one (the separation of Helsinki city from the remainder of its country in 1952) a change not necessitated by other developments.

There remain three variations around this norm. In Spain the new Constitution of 1976 allows the principle of community representation significantly more weight than the objective of equality. The country's fifty provinces are the constituencies for the Congress of Deputies, with each province guaranteed two members plus an allocation on population. Consequently, although the largest province (Barcelona) had 45 times the number of inhabitants of the smallest (Soria) it had 33 deputies to Soria's 3, and six other sparsely populated provinces had the same effective minimum of three. This exaggeration of the representation of the less populated parts of Spain is accentuated by a Senate in which each province has equal representation. Norway, whose twenty constituencies are the counties, or *fylke*, also fails to allocate according to a numbers rule, significantly exaggerating the representation of the rural North and West.

A few countries create special multi-member divisions to avoid too great a range of numbers. The purest case is Malta, which uses specially drawn equal-size five-member constituencies. Ireland began in 1923 with a range of 3 to 9 members per constituency, but from 1947 has stuck to a narrow range of 3 to 5 and periodically draws special boundaries. France in the Fourth Republic used the *département* as its basic unit (with the less populous ones nevertheless guaranteed two seats) but subdivided all the most populous *départements* so that most constituencies lay in the range of 3 to 5 members. It is surely no coincidence that these three cases of combining the multi-member principle with sub-division are all influenced by the special boundary-drawing practice of the single-member constituency. France had returned at the end of Third Republic to the uninominal principle, and was to return to it once more in 1958. The proportional systems of Malta and Ireland are part of their British endowment, being the single transferable vote method, and with them came a presumption in favour of equal or similar-sized constituencies, even when multi-member.

The third variation is more substantial, being the attempt in some countries with proportional systems to keep a single-member seat element. The idea of doing this goes back to the early debates on electoral reform, when combining the uninominal principle with proportionality was sometimes advocated, especially in that part of the debate conducted in the German language. There the combination was sometimes termed the Geyerhahn method, after the Austrian scholar who put forward such a scheme in 1902.[17] Both Weimar Germany and the Austrian republic opted for a multi-member base to their proportional systems in 1919, but in 1920 Bavaria adopted a version of the Geyerhahn method. In this form (dubbed by the German historian of voting systems, Braunias "simulated uninominal voting"), voters in each constituency were presented with a simple contest between single candidates of each party. But the system of proportional allocation of seats, at the level of eight unions of constituencies each containing between 10 and 25 of them, and the practice of the parties in nominating candidates to stand in more than one constituency, meant that the uninominal principle applied more to the presentation of candidates than to the representation of constituencies. A single-member constituency could end up with more than one of its candidates elected; or with none; or even if with only one, that one elected by reason of the votes cast in other constituencies. The practice of multiple candidatures grew, and by 1928 scarcely a sixth of Bavarian deputies had stood and been elected only in one constituency.

Denmark had, in 1915, partially adopted the Geyerhahn method in another form. The capital city became a multi-member constituency with 24 members, and the rest of the country was divided into 93 single-member constituencies; in addition to those 117 constituency members, there were 23 supplementary seats. By an elaborate formula, operating at both national level and that of three regions (Copenhagen, Jutland and the islands), the supplementary seats were used to proportionalise the outcome in the constituencies. Used once, in 1918, this system came close to pure proportionality at national level, but the small departure (at most, one party had four too many, and another four too few seats) seems to have concerned the Danish parties.[18]

Consequently, Denmark moved to a purer system of proportional representation, and the vestigial element of mainly single-member nominating districts that remains deserves the term "simulated." After the Second World War, Italy considered the Geyerhahn method and another, also complex, version of it was adopted for the Senate. But that, too, is more a simulated than a real form of uninominal election.

At the same time, Germany moved towards a mixed system that is much closer to Geyerhahn's original proposal. Though often misunderstood (the system is a mixture of separate uninominal and plurinominal elements, but fully proportional), this system has come to be admired amongst some advocates of proportional representation in countries such as Britain, Canada and France. But though it is widely talked of in such circles as a distinct, and even only semiproportional, system, the West German electoral law is only one example of a combination which can be made in a variety of ways. At the technical level, the 1918 Danish system solves some of the problems which arise in the German law. More generally, the several varieties of the Geyerhahn method used in the German *Länder*, along with the contemporary Danish and Italian methods, exhibit a number of techniques, problems and effects that can be produced by combining proportionality with the single-member district.

EVALUATION

Most of the literature on electoral systems is essentially concerned with their effects on parties; very little has been written on the elements of electoral systems which are not mainly differentiated by their impact on the translation of party votes into seats, or their expected effect on party systems. That emphasis is appropriate—but it is a pity if it obscures the potential significance of other aspects of electoral systems. An attempt to evaluate the different types of constituency must be tentative, both because so little attention has been paid to it in any systematic manner and because there is such a heavy overlap with the two main types of voting system.

But even leaving aside the impact of electoral system on party, we are still dogged by the overriding proportional versus majority debate. Plurality and majority systems embody a "winner-takes-all" philosophy that may have much more profound effects than simply favouring some parties and disadvantaging others. Proportional systems reflect a high value placed on representativeness, and this may affect the behaviour of voters and politicians in more ways than the often-argued one of enabling them to vote without fear of wasting their ballot papers on unwinnable candidates. Some of the differences which will shortly be put forward as due to different sorts of constituencies could, at any rate in part, reflect these psychological effects of the ethos of voting systems.

Furthermore, our concern with type of constituency mixes two dimensions. There is the single-member versus multi-member choice; and the constituency based on distinct community as opposed to the constituency with specially drawn (equal-size) boundaries. The relationship between these two dimensions is confusing. The occasional single-member constituencies are mainly multi-member countries (for example, the few Swiss cantons, French-speaking Aosta, Swedish-speaking Åland islands in Finland) are usually highly distinctive small communities. Yet most single-member constituencies are thoroughly artificial, ephemeral pieces of territory which have no meaning outside the electoral context. The cases of more artificial multi-member constituencies (Ireland, Malta) are quite coincidentally the users of a special form of proportional representation. With care, some more general conclusions could be drawn from these cells of the matrix—but without care, these special cases may mislead.

Aware, therefore, of the complexity of the cases and the difficulty of singling out particular effects—as well as the more familiar problems in political science of attempting generalisations across varying national and cultural contexts, we will attempt conclusions in the form of three general propositions. The evidence for them varies. Some is clear, detailed and comprehensive, some is patchy and some more impressionistic. But even if some were disproved by subsequent research, there is surely enough to justify more attention to the constituency than has hitherto been accorded.

Variable-size constituencies make for more real community representation than single-member ones. There are constant complaints in uninominal countries, either that boundaries do not keep up with shifting population or that frequent changes disturb loyalties. The variable-size constituency allows a frequent adjustment to changing numbers but keeps outer boundaries constant. As a result, not only do public administrative organisations usually correspond to constituencies, but so do trades unions, farmers' associations and the plethora of social, cultural and other organisations that make up the public life of a modern democracy. Elected representatives and these communities of organisational networks relate easily to each other—with media circulation areas often coinciding. This makes for more real and relevant communication at the constituency level amongst those involved in public life.

Amongst political activists, this enables the networks of friendship and the stores of emotional capital invested in past political work to be maintained more easily, or at any rate for these elements in political life to fit more easily to the territories of elected representatives. Amongst the politically unconcerned, what matters more is whether the administrative units/constituencies have a historic or natural meaning. Long-standing cantonal or provincial boundaries, or big cities, engender a corporate identity, and when the constituency fits to such identity, the voter can relate more easily to the political structure. However, many of the administrative entities which form constituencies in modern Europe possess little of such identity.

Multi-member constituencies make for more balanced representation. When a party nominates for one place, it cannot consider balance. When it puts up two candidates, even a prime candidate and running mate as a replacement (for example, the French *suppléant* system or the US vice-president), it can make one partner complement the other and broaden its appeal. The more the places at stake, certainly up to double figures, the more it can balance. For the party will not only consider the balance of all its candidates but also the balance amongst those most likely to be elected. A party nominating, say, half a dozen people in winnable places on a list will be vulnerable if it includes no woman, or no one from a linguistic group forming a fifth of the electorate, or no one from a geographically distinctive quarter of the constituency. Consequently, nominating several candidates together becomes a highly sensitive and competitive affair in which careful balance of occupational, ethnic, geographical and other actual or potential sections of the electorate is the way to win votes. The same applies to noticeable political factions within the party.

The result is that multi-member systems tend to favour the representation of ethnic minorities and of women. The evidence for the ethnic effect is scattered but convincing, ranging from the German-Polish balance induced in Galicia quoted earlier, to the present in Britain of many more coloured councillors in London boroughs, which generally use multi-member wards, than in the rest of the country, which generally does not. The evidence on women is clear and systematic, and appears to mount to a fivefold multiplier, namely, culturally similar countries with multi-member systems of a substantial size have five times as many women in Parliament as those with single-member seats. The countries mixing uninominal with plurinominal election (for example, Germany since 1949, or the few British double-member constituencies before 1950) illustrate the effect well.

Multi-member constituencies make for more localist representation. The practice of political elites finding suitable constituencies wherever they can, graphically called parachuting in French, is a characteristic of uninominal countries. Generally in plurinominal states, elected representatives sit for the constituencies where they were living before they entered Parliament. The reason can be understood if we consider the prospects facing a would-be candidate, let us assume female. In a plurinominal system her party can probably win several seats in the constituency where she starts her political involvement. Amongst them will be, in all probability, one sitting member likely to retire before long or (if it is that sort of party) one who may be dislodged by political effort; it is worth her while, therefore, sticking around and working to win that seat. In a uninominal system, however, she may well happen to live in a constituency safely held by another party or, if in one of her own party's, a seat held by a healthy, young and ambitious man. To secure election she must go elsewhere.

Consequently, in plurinominal countries a candidate seeking nomination in a constituency where she has no local roots is looked at with suspicion: why cannot she make it in her own area? A few nationally known figures can escape the stricture, and with a small party likely to win only a few seats here and there it may not apply. But in general, the career structure of politics becomes one in which people come into Parliament from their home constituencies. Constituency representation means just that.

Such a restriction has been built into the single-member seat system of the United States by a combination of the residence rule and the primary system. But in Britain and France, the uninominal principle has encouraged candidates to move around the country seeking a point of entry into Parliament, and the career structure is one in which would-be candidates earn entitlement to consideration for the party's safe seats or good prospects by their willingness to fight a hopeless prospect elsewhere. Local ties are created after selection.

CONCLUSION

Thus for all the deeply-held belief amongst British MPs and MEPs that the British single-member constituency system involves a more real or worthwhile relationship between representative and electorate than do proportional systems, there is considerable reason to see the community-based and plurinominal constituencies used by most proportional systems as producing in several ways a more genuine constituency representation. The case is complex, and merits investigation more than firm conclusion. But it is clear from the history of the uninominal principle in Britain that it was not introduced to produce a closer relationship between MP and local community. It was brought in, perhaps for party advantage, perhaps because it was not understood, and certainly in the belief by some key figures that it was an advance towards more proportional representation, in the acknowledgement that it meant a sacrifice of an older tradition of more community-based representation. However, whilst Gladstone and Salisbury were monumentally wrong in their belief that it would make for fairer representation of minorities, perhaps Gladstone caught its appeal well when he urged its simple economy. Only that reflection on the strength of its simplicity, along with Courtney's warnings, stand the test of a hundred years of its practice in Britain.

Notes

1. Loi fédérale concernant les élections des membres du Conseil national (21 December 1850).

2. House of Commons Hansard, Vol. 294, 1 December 1884, col. 380.

3. Ibid., 4 December 1884, col. 685.

4. Ibid., Vol. 285, 28 February 1884, col. 129.

5. Andrew Jones, *The Politics of Reform 1884* (Cambridge: Cambridge University Press, 1972), 211.

6. House of Commons Hansard, 1 December 1884, col. 382.

7. Charles Seymour, *Electoral Reform in England and Wales* (New Haven: Yale University Press, 1915), 499-505.

8. House of Commons Hansard, Vol. 294, 1 December 1884, col. 380.

9. Lady Gwendoline Cecil, *Life of Robert, Marquis of Salisbury*, Vol. III, 1880-86 (London: Hodder & Stoughton, 1931), 122.

10. House of Commons Hansard, Vol. 294, 4 December 1884, col. 660.

11. Ibid., col. 673.

12. Ibid., col. 674.

13. Ibid., col. 674.

14. Ibid., col. 710.

15. Ibid., col. 709.

16. L.S. Amery, *Thoughts on the Constitution* (London: Oxford University Press, 1964e), 55.

17. Siegfried Geyerhahn, *Das Problem der verhältnismässigen Vertretung* (Tübingen and Leipzig 1902).

18. Karl Braunias, *Das Parlamentarische Wahlrecht*, Vol. II (Berlin and Leipzig, 1932), 235-42.

13. CRITERIA OF FAIR REPRESENTATION

Arend Lijphart

The following list of criteria of fair representation is not exhaustive, but it does include the criteria—some of which are widely accepted while others are more controversial—that are most frequently mentioned (see Grofman, 1981e; Grofman and Scarrow, 1981a; Niemi and Deegan, 1978):

1. Representation must be equal for each citizen. This is the basic one-person, one-vote, one-value principle. For single-member district systems, it means that the districts must contain equal numbers of citizens, in line with the *Westberry* v. Sanders[1] and *Reynolds* v. *Sims*[2] decisions of the U.S. Supreme Court (Tribe, 1978:739-741). For non-single-member districts, the criterion calls for representation that is equal per capita. The number of representatives in multimember districts must be proportional to the population being represented, or the number of votes cast by representatives elected from districts of unequal sizes must be weighted according to the population being represented (Grofman and Scarrow, 1981a:2-3).

Arend Lijphart, "Comparative Perspectives on Fair Representation: The Plurality-Majority Rule, Geographical Districting, and Alternative Electoral Arrangements," in Bernard Grofman, Arend Lijphart, Robert B. McKay, Howard A. Scarrow, eds., *Representation and Redistricting Issues* (Lexington: Lexington Books, D.C. Heath and Company, 1982), 145-52. Reprinted by permission of the publisher.

2. The boundaries dividing the electoral districts must coincide with local political boundaries as much as possible.

3. Electoral districts must be compact and contiguous in territory.

4. The boundaries of electoral districts should be drawn in such a way as to provide representation for political minorities (*sophisticated gerrymandering*).

5. The boundaries of electoral districts should be drawn in such a way as to provide representation for ethnic and racial minorities (*affirmative gerrymandering*).

6. The electoral system should not be biased in favour of any political party in awarding seats for a certain percentage of the total vote. This is the criterion of *neutrality*, the first of the four criteria of fair districting suggested by Richard G. Niemi and John Deegan, Jr. (1978:1304): "A districting plan which treats all parties alike in allocating seats per given vote totals is said to be neutral."

7. The electoral system should not be biased in favour of any racial or ethnic group in awarding seats for a certain percentage of the total vote. This is the Niemi-Deegan criterion of neutrality, extended to groups other than political parties.

8. The electoral system should have a wide range of responsiveness to changes in the electorate's party preferences. Niemi and

Deegan (1978: 1304-1305) define the range of responsiveness as "the percentage range of the total popular vote (for the entire political unit) over which seats change from one party to the other. Specifically, the low end of the [range] is the minimum percentage of the total vote required for a party to win at least one seat . . ., while the upper end is the minimum percentage of the total vote required to win all of the seats."

9. The electoral system should have a "constant swing ratio;" that is, the rate at which a party wins seats per unit gain in the percentage of its vote should be constant (Niemi and Deegan, 1978:1306). The principle that a party's share of the seats should be proportional to its vote share is a special case of this criterion.

10. There should be proportionality between the share of the seats won by any particular ethnic or racial group and its vote share. This criterion extends the above proportionality principle to groups other than political parties.

11. The system should be competitive in the sense that each party should have a chance of election in each district. Niemi and Deegan (1978:1309-1311) operationally define this criterion as requiring each party's vote to be in the 45- to 55-percent range in each district.

12. Each citizen should have equal power to affect the outcome of elections by casting the decisive vote (Grofman and Scarrow, 1981a:3-4). This voting power varies inversely with the square roots of the sizes of the district populations (Banzhaf, 1966).

13. Each citizen's vote should be "used" as much as possible toward the election of a candidate and the "wasted" vote should be minimized. The used vote is "the number of votes required by the winning party to attain a plurality and . . . represents the votes that are actually used to elect its candidate to office." It can therefore also be defined as "the size of the vote received by the party polling the second highest vote plus one." All other votes—the votes received by the winner that exceed the plurality and the votes of all losing parties—are wasted (Cohan, McKinlay, and Mughan, 1975:365). This criterion is similar to criterion 11 (competitiveness) in the case of a two-party system.

14. Each legislator's power in the legislature should be proportionate to the number of citizens he represents. Banzhaf (1966) argues that not only the citizen's power to affect election outcomes (criterion 12) but also his influence on legislation varies inversely with the square roots of the district populations.

15. There should be equal numbers of representatives working on behalf of equal numbers of citizens. As Bernard Grofman and Howard A. Scarrow (1981a:18-19) point out, representatives have many functions in addition to voting on proposed legislation, such as performing various services for their constituents: "Any system of representation, such as adoption of the square root principle or weighted voting in any form, which results in some citizens having a proportionately greater access to these personal services because it does not apportion equal numbers of representatives to equal numbers of citizens, would therefore be unfair."

16. A majority of citizens should be able to control legislative outcomes through their representatives (Grofman and Scarrow, 1981a:19-21). In other words, minorities of citizens should not be able to elect majorities of legislators. This is the basic majoritarian principle.

INCOMPATIBILITIES BETWEEN CRITERIA

Although each of the above sixteen criteria of fair representation can be satisfied individually (with one exception, to be discussed below), they cannot all be satisfied to their full extent simultaneously within the constraints of a plurality-majority system and geographically defined districts. Maximizing the value of one criterion will often require deviating from one or more other criteria. Moreover, the different criteria lead to different recommendations with regard to whether a plurality or majority rule should be adopted and with regard to the kind of electoral districts that should be instituted.

The one exception to the statement that each individual criterion can be fully satisfied is the criterion of minority group representation by means of affirmative gerrymandering. The problem is that drawing district boundaries in such a way as to achieve representation for one minority may affect adversely the chances that another minority living in the same general area will be represented. This was the dilemma facing the Supreme Court in *United Jewish Organizations of Williamsburg v. Carey*[3] when a choice had to be made between the right to minority representation of blacks and Puerto Ricans on the one hand and Hasidic Jews on the other (Wells, 1978a). As Pitkin (1967:87) points out, the problem of choosing which groups deserve representation is a general problem that is inherent in the norms of descriptive representation: "representation as *standing for* by resemblance, as being a copy of an original, is always a question of which characteristics are politically relevant for reproduction."

The conflicts between pairs of criteria are indicated in Table [1]. Four clusters of conflicts can be distinguished. The first is the well-known tension between the requirement of absolute per-capita population equality (criterion 1) and districts that follow local political subdivisions and that are compact and contiguous (criteria 2 and 3). The Supreme Court has recognized, and solved, this incompatibility by assigning a higher priority to the equal-population rule than to the secondary criteria of local boundaries, compactness, and contiguity (Tribe, 1978:746-747). Because the requirement that there should be equal numbers of representatives working on behalf of equal numbers of citizens (criterion 15) largely coincides with the criterion of per-capita equal representation, it is also in conflict with criteria 2 and 3. Finally, there may be a conflict between the latter two criteria if the local political subdivisions deviate significantly from compactness and contiguity. All of these conflicts may be alleviated by moving from single-member districts to multimember districts or weighted voting. At-large elections eliminate the problem by eliminating districts and district boundaries altogether.

The second cluster includes the conflicts between the local boundary, compactness, and contiguity criteria (criteria 2 and 3) on the one hand and the series of criteria that call for electoral districts that will serve political purposes such as minority representation, responsiveness, and competitiveness (criteria 4 through 11). To achieve these objectives, the criteria of congruence with local subdivisions, compactness, and contiguity will almost always have to be violated. The criterion of minimizing the wasted vote (criterion 13) is, in a two-party system, similar to the competitiveness criterion (criterion 11). Hence it, too, conflicts with criteria 2 and 3.

The third cluster includes the incompatibilities among the Niemi-Deegan criteria (criteria 6, 8, 9, and 11; see Niemi and Deegan, 1978:1311-1312). In particular, the competitiveness and responsiveness criteria call for very different districts. Here again, the criterion of

Table 1 Conflicts among Sixteen Criteria of Fair Representation under the Plurality-Majority Rule and Geographical Districts *(Criteria, by number—see text)*

	16	15	14	13	12	11	10	9	8	7	6	5	4	3	2	1
1	-	-	X	-	X	-	-	-	-	-	-	-	-	X	X	-
2	-	X	-	X	-	X	X	X	X	X	X	X	X	X	-	-
3	-	X	-	X	-	X	X	X	X	X	X	X	X	-	-	-
4	-	-	-	-	-	-	-	-	-	-	-	-	-	-	-	-
5	-	-	-	-	-	-	-	-	-	-	-	-	-	-	-	-
6	-	-	-	X	-	X	-	-	-	-	-	-	-	-	-	-
7	-	-	-	-	-	-	-	-	-	-	-	-	-	-	-	-
8	-	-	-	X	-	X	-	-	-	-	-	-	-	-	-	-
9	-	-	-	X	-	X	-	-	-	-	-	-	-	-	-	-
10	-	-	-	-	-	-	-	-	-	-	-	-	-	-	-	-
11	-	-	-	-	-	-	-	-	-	-	-	-	-	-	-	-
12	X	X	-	-	-	-	-	-	-	-	-	-	-	-	-	-
13	-	-	-	-	-	-	-	-	-	-	-	-	-	-	-	-
14	X	X	-	-	-	-	-	-	-	-	-	-	-	-	-	-
15	-	-	-	-	-	-	-	-	-	-	-	-	-	-	-	-
16	-	-	-	-	-	-	-	-	-	-	-	-	-	-	-	-

minimizing the wasted vote behaves like the competitiveness criterion.

The fourth cluster consists of conflicts between the four criteria of equality (criteria 1, 12, 14 and 15). These occur only when there is a system of mixed single-member and multi-member districts, a system of multi-member districts with different numbers of representatives per district, or a weighted voting system. In these situations, criteria 1 and 15 demand the numbers of representatives per district (or the numbers of legislative votes cast by the representatives) be proportional to the district populations, instead of proportional to the population square roots as demanded by criteria 12 and 14. The latter two criteria also violate the principle of majoritarianism because the square-root rule would lead to an over-representation of small districts, which together may contain only a minority of the population but may be able to elect a majority of legislators.

Of the sixteen criteria of fair representation, eleven are neutral with regard to the choice between the plurality and majority rules, but the remaining five lead to different recommendations. The basic majoritarian principle (criterion 16) obviously favours majority rule. Minimizing the wasted vote (criterion 13) is also more easily achieved when majorities rather than pluralities are necessary for election, and competitiveness (criterion 11) is similarly enhanced when the electoral contest is reduced to two candidates in a runoff election. On the other hand, it can be argued that the plurality rule favours cohesive minorities, which may be able to elect their candidates when the majorities are divided (criterion 4 and 5).

The divergent recommendations with regard to the type of districting that are implied by the sixteen criteria are of greater significance. These are outlined in Table [2]. Rather surprisingly, a majority of the criteria (1, 2, 3,

6, 7, 12, 14, 15 and 16) favour at-large elections and clearly do not favour single-member districts. The reason is that by eliminating districts, the equality, neutrality, and majoritarianism criteria are satisfied completely, and the problem of congruence with local boundaries, compactness, and contiguity disappears. The second most desirable type of districting according to these criteria are districts other than single-member districts because they offer more flexibility to achieve equality, compactness and so on, and because there is less risk of a deliberate bias against particular parties or groups.

A second cluster of criteria leads to the completely opposite advice of adopting single-member districts (criteria 8, 9 and 10). There is a well-known empirical relationship between the magnitude of electoral districts (that is, the number of representatives elected per district) and the degree of proportionality of the election results. In systems of proportional representation, proportionality increases as the district magnitude increases, but in plurality and majority systems, proportionality decreases with increasing district magnitude (Blondel, 1969:194-200). Hence the highest degree of proportionality—or the smallest deviation from proportional results—in a plurality-majority system is achieved when the districts are as small as possible. Criteria 9 and 10 are therefore satisfied optimally by single-member districts. Similarly, the range of responsiveness (criteria 8) is maximized by a high degree of proportionality and consequently also by single-member districting.

Two criteria (4 and 5) are maximized by weighted voting. The reason is that it is easier to gerrymander a district for the purpose of minority representation if the district can be small. One of the main advantages of weighted voting is to give representation to small districts without violating equal per-capita representation and without making the legislature too large and unwieldy. If weighted voting is not used, the second most desirable system from the point of view of minority representation is a system with single-member districts—either an exclusively single-member district system or a mixed single-member and multimember district arrangement.

The last two criteria, competitiveness and minimizing the wasted vote (criteria 11 and 13), similarly favour weighted voting. To devise districts in which the votes received by the two major parties are in the 45- to 55-percent range—assuming that the total vote of the parties falls outside this range—it is obviously an advantage to have as much flexibility as possible as far as district size is concerned. The second best situation, however, differs from that called for by criteria 4 and 5. Multimember districts or mixed multimember and single-member districts offer better opportunities for drawing the largest possible number of competitive districts than single-member districts. There is one important qualification to the above conclusion: if the over-all vote for each of the two parties is in the 45 to 55 percent range, at-large elections would be completely competitive and would therefore be the optimal method.

Three other patterns in Table [2] deserve special attention. First, although at-large elections are the ideal districting method according to nine of the sixteen criteria, they are not the second best method according to any of the other criteria. Secondly, mixed single-member and multimember districts are not optimal according to any of the criteria but they are among the second best methods according to all of the criteria. Thirdly, multimember districts are never optimal either, but they are also frequently, in eleven of the sixteen cases, among the second best solutions.

Table 2 Optimal and Second-Best Types of Districting According to Sixteen Criteria
of Fair Representation

Types	Single-Member Districting	Mixed Single-Member Multi-member Districting	Multi-member Districting	At-Large	Weighted Voting
1. Per-capita equality	-	X	X	XX	X
2. Local boundary fit	-	X	X	XX	X
3. Compact/contiguous districts	-	X	X	XX	X
4. Sophisticated gerrymander	X	X	-	-	XX
5. Affirmative gerrymander	X	X	-	-	XX
6. Unbiased toward parties	-	X	X	XX	X
7. Unbiased toward groups	-	X	X	XX	X
8. Responsiveness	XX	X	-	-	-
9. Constant swing ratio	XX	X	-	-	-
10. Proportional representation for groups	XX	X	-	-	-
11. Competitiveness	-	X	X	-	XX
12. Equal voting power	-	X	X	XX	X
13. Minimizing wasted vote	-	X	X	-	XX
14. Equal legislator power	-	X	X	XX	X
15. Equal representative power	-	X	X	XX	X
16. Majoritarianism	-	X	X	XX	X

Note: XX = optimal; X = second best.

Notes

1. Wesberry *v.* Sanders (1964) 376 U.S. 1.
2. Reynolds *v.* Sims (1964) 377 U.S. 533.

3. United Jewish Organizations of Williamsburg *v.* Carey (1977) 430 U.S. 144.

14. A CENTURY OF CONSTITUENCIES

Norman Ward

The drawing of constituency boundaries for the representation of a people in a House of Commons may strike one as an elementary though fundamental exercise. Canadian experience offers conclusive proof that an apparently simple task can become almost hopelessly complex, involving bitter partisan quarrels, tortuous rules for dividing the available seats among the provinces, mutually exclusive rules within any one province for the recognition of such varied phenomena as the sanctity of municipal boundaries and the rapid growth of suburbia, and all but endless arguments about the kind of body best suited for drawing constituencies at all. The burden of the Canadian record, indeed, is that there is no single permanent solution to any of these problems, except in the sense that a continuing series of ad hoc compromises can be considered permanent.

On the whole the division of seats among the provinces has occasioned less partisan controversy than any other major aspect of redistribution. Quebec had sixty-five seats in the legislature of the Province of Canada, and the least upsetting way of starting the new House of Commons in 1867 was to give Quebec the same sixty-five seats, and permit the other provinces representation in proportion: this produced constituencies whose populations averaged less than 20 000.

To protect any province from a sudden diminution in the number of seats allotted to it after any one census, it was provided that a province could not lose any seats unless its population, considered as a fraction of the Dominion total, declined by one-twentieth between censuses.[1] Except for the addition of a constitutional amendment in 1915 which guaranteed that no province could have fewer Members of Parliament than it had senators, these relatively simple rules remained in force unchanged until 1946.

From the beginning the rules were not held applicable to new provinces on their admission to Confederation, initial representation in Parliament being considered one of the negotiable terms of entry. Thus Manitoba in 1870 received four MPs instead of one, and British Columbia in 1871 six instead of one; Prince Edward Island, in a weaker bargaining position, in 1873 received six members instead of five. The Northwest Territories in 1886 received four members instead of two, and in 1903 territorial representation was raised to ten, instead of the six justified by the census of 1901, in anticipation of the western settlement boom. In a slower rhythm, the "one-twentieth clause" designed to protect the smaller provinces against sudden losses of seats, and then the constitutional amendment of 1915, served to modify the application of strict representation by population primarily among the older provinces.

A redistribution held on the existing rules and the census of 1941 would have seen only four of the nine provinces enjoying "rep by pop": Prince Edward Island and New Brunswick would have received extra seats because of the number of senators they had, and

Norman Ward, "A Century of Constituencies," *Canadian Public Administration* 10 (1967): 105-22. Reprinted by permission of The Institute of Public Administration of Canada.

Nova Scotia, Alberta and Ontario would have received extra representation because of the one-twentieth clause—in Ontario's case, eight extra seats.[2] Because of dissatisfaction with the operation of the rules, and the dislocation of population caused by the war, the government decided to postpone the redistribution that should have followed the census of 1941 until the cessation of hostilities. Its right to do so, and its right subsequently to alter the basis of provincial representation in the House of Commons without consulting the provinces, were severely challenged; but the government of Canada, supported by Parliament, has always held that the constitution of the House of Commons is purely a federal matter, and neither in the 1940s nor since has it made any concession in the face of repeated demands (emanating primarily from Progressive Conservative members and in later years from Quebec MPs) for the involvement of the provinces.[3]

The postponed redistribution was effected in 1947, after an amendment to the British North America Act in 1946 which created new rules for dividing seats among the provinces, which were amended in detail but not in principle in 1952. The rules currently in force, unlike their predecessors, fix a ceiling of 263 on the membership of the Commons. Two of these seats are reserved for Yukon and Mackenzie River, and each province's share of the rest is initially calculated on a strict "rep by pop" basis. However, the senatorial floor under each province's representation still applies, and if the foregoing calculation gives any province fewer MPs than senators, it is given the requisite number of additional members and the mathematical calculation is done over, omitting any province or provinces affected by the senatorial rule. In addition, since 1952 no province in a redistribution can be deprived of more than 15 percent of the representation to which it was entitled at the last redistribution, nor can a province lose seats if that loss would give it fewer MPs than a province with a smaller population. The latter proviso has not yet been called into play; the 15 percent rule (as intended) saved Saskatchewan two seats from 1952 to the redistribution based on the census of 1961, which has not yet been the basis for an election, and Nova Scotia one seat after the current redistribution. Extra seats given by the 15 percent rule are protected for only one redistribution i.e., after the census of 1961, Saskatchewan's loss of seats was calculated not from the seventeen seats it actually had, but from the fifteen to which the basic rules entitled it without the 15 percent rule.

The division of seats among the provinces (summarized statistically in Table [1]) bears no necessary relationship to the division of any one province into constituencies and, as suggested earlier, the manner in which this is done can be productive of profound differences of opinion. There are two fundamental questions: the rules, if any, to be followed in drawing boundaries; and the agency which does the actual drawing. The first of these questions in Canada always received a simple answer: until 1964 the House of Commons applied no rules whatever to the drawing of boundaries. Occasional attempts to adopt rules (most notably in 1903[4]) were made, but in the event each redistribution down to the latest was carried out as a freelance operation in which any rational boundary drawing was likely to be the result of coincidence or accident. Depending on the convenience of the influential, local or municipal lines were sometimes followed, sometimes not; new representation was sometimes given to those parts of a province which had grown most rapidly, sometimes not; seats were sometimes made as compact as possible, sometimes not; blocks of constituencies were sometimes given fairly equal populations, sometimes not. The one practice that was followed with reasonable consistency was that urban divisions were generally made more populous than rural, but even here urban divisions themselves varied enormously in size, and some rural divisions were larger than the smaller urban seats.

The results of all this can be shown by a few examples. The redistribution law currently in force was passed by a Parliament whose MPs were elected in 1963. The Chief Electoral Officer's report on the election of that year included, among other anomalies, the following statistics on constituencies. The smallest constituency in the country was Iles-de-la-Madeleine, Quebec, with a population in 1961 of 12 479, and the largest was the suburban Toronto seat of York Scarborough, at 267 252. The urban seats of Montreal ranged from 34 020 to 233 964, and those of Toronto (exclusive of the Yorks) from 53 155 to 88 988; the Yorks, surrounding Toronto, ranged from 89 709 to 267 252. The Winnipeg seats con-

tained 42.7 percent of Manitoba's total population of 921 686, but comprised only four of the province's allotment of thirteen constituencies. In Prince Edward Island, Kings had a population of 17 893, and Prince 40 894. New Brunswick's seats ranged from 23 285 to 101 736, and Nova Scotia's (exclusive of the two-member riding of Halifax, at 225 723) from 27 634 to 85 001. Saskatchewan, with no metropolitan areas, nonetheless had ridings whose populations varied from 37 937 to 95 575. Every province, in short, showed remarkable variations in the populations of its constituencies, and almost all the discrepancies had grown worse by the election of 1965, held on the same boundaries.

It would be easy to blame all this on the agencies that severally drew the constituencies' boundaries, but the agencies themselves were

Table 1   General and Partial Redistributions of Constituencies among the Provinces since 1867

Year	No. of seats	Ont.	Que.	N.S.	N.B.	Man.	B.C.	P.E.I.	N.W.T.		Yukon (and Mackenzie River)	Nfld.
1867	181	82	65	19	15							
1871*	185	82	65	19	15	4						
1872	200	88	65	21	16	4	6					
1873*	206	88	65	21	16	4	6	6				
1882	211	92	65	21	16	5	6	6				
1887*	215	92	65	21	16	5	6	6	4			
1892	213	92	65	20	14	7	6	5	4			
1903	214	86	65	18	13	10	7	4	10		1	
									Sask.	Alta.		
1907*	221	86	65	18	13	10	7	4	10	7	1	
1914	234	82	65	16	11	15	13	3	16	12	1	
1915*	235	82	65	16	11	15	13	4	16	12	1	
1924	245	82	65	14	11	17	14	4	21	16	1	
1933	245	82	65	12	10	17	16	4	21	17	1	
1947	255	83	73	13	10	16	18	4	20	17	1	
1949*	262	83	73	13	10	16	18	4	20	17	1	7
1952	265	85	75	12	10	14	22	4	17	17	2	7
1965-6	264	88	74	11	10	13	23	4	13	19	2	7

* Partial redistributions occasioned by special circumstances such as the addition of territory, etc.

only partly to blame. The failure of the House of Commons to establish any rules to govern the drawing of boundaries was one factor. Time and social changes provided another, for the constituencies established in 1952 (as is shown in Table [2]), while they varied markedly in population when created, had become far more varied by the elections of the early 1960s, after more than a decade of brisk urbanization around Canada's major cities, with parallel declines in population in some rural areas.

The agencies, nonetheless, were far from blameless, not only because they were too often dominated by partisan motives, but also because they permitted themselves to be forced to work hastily, and with inadequate information at their disposal. This was particularly true of the redistributions of 1872, 1882, and 1892, which were carried out through a government bill; in each case the government introduced a proposal which included a definition of the proposed ridings, based on the assumptions that the voting habits of electors were constant, and that Liberals and Conser-

vatives reached voting age and died off, and moved in and out of constituencies, in fixed ratios. The first three redistributions were plainly intended to benefit the party in power, the second two particularly so; none of the three was spectacularly successful in attaining its obvious purpose, and that of 1892, after which the governing party was all but annihilated in the areas it had most carefully gerrymandered, was a dismal failure.[5]

The next six redistributions (1903, 1914, 1924, 1933, 1947, and 1952) were effected by committees of the House of Commons; the standard procedure in each instance was for the government to introduce a general bill ordering a redistribution as provided for by the British North America Act and the latest census, but including no details on individual ridings. The bill was then (commonly after second reading) referred to a committee of the House, on which the governing party's majority was frequently conspicuous. Two distinct procedural patterns in redistribution by committee were discernible. The committee of 1903 consisted of seven members, four Liberals and

Table 2 Constituency populations in Canada after Selected Censuses

Population	1952 Seats* on 1951 Census	1952 Seats* on 1956 Census	1952 Seats* on 1961 Census	1966 Seats on 1961 Census
Under 20 000	4	4	3	1
20 000-29 999	6	4	5	4
30 000-39 999	32	24	19	1
40 000-49 999	73	60	52	-
50 000-59 999	74	59	48	49
60 000-69 999	36	41	36	74
70 000-79 999	27	27	34	99
80 000-89 999	8	16	22	36
90 000-99 999	2	16	8	-
100 000-199 999	1	12	33	-
200 000-299 999	-	-	3	-

* Includes two two-member seats.

three Conservatives, all of whom were leading members of their parties, and all of whom participated actively in drawing boundaries. The committee of 1952 consisted of thirty-seven members representing four political parties, many of whom were backbenchers; the bulk of the work of the 1952 committee was done by regional or provincial subcommittees, the main committee acting primarily as a clearing house for proposals from subcommittees. The governing party in 1952 held twenty-two of the committee's thirty-seven seats, and an effective working majority on all the subcommittees.[6] Between the simple pattern of 1903 and the complex one of 1952 lay fifty years of evolution in which the chief elements were the number of provinces in the Dominion, their changing populations, and the number of parties in the House.

The redistribution that followed the census of 1961 revealed two marked departures from previous practice: the use of committees of MPs was abandoned outright in favour of redistribution by non-parliamentary commissions; and the commissions were given statutory guidelines to follow in the drawing of boundaries. The second of these proposals, as noted above, had been made as early as 1903, when the Leader of the Opposition sought to provide rules for the first redistribution committee. The proposal to have boundaries drawn by a non-partisan body has a history going back before Confederation.

The first draft of the British North America Act noted of constituencies: "The readjustment to be made by an independent authority, as some of the Judges, to be specified in the Imperial Act."[7] The final draft of the Act evaded the issue by providing in Section 51 for redistribution "by such authority, in such manner, and from such time, as the Parliament of Canada from time to time provides"; subsequent cabinets, as we have seen, interpreted this to suit themselves. Since 1867 proposals for a non-parliamentary commission have

been made sporadically, not just during redistributions and not just by suffering Opposition MPs. In 1899 and 1900 the Liberal government proposed a board of high court judges to make what were considered corrections in the federal ridings in Ontario, and was thwarted each time by the Senate. In this century support for outside commissions has been variously expressed, and with increasing frequency, by spokesmen for the Cooperative Commonwealth Federation (later the New Democratic Party), the Liberal, and the Progressive Conservative parties, with leading members from each showing a particular interest in the topic. The interest culminated in a resolution offered to the House of Commons in 1962 by the Prime Minister, Mr. Diefenbaker.

Mr. Diefenbaker's resolution of course foreshadowed a government measure, and it followed chronologically several attempts by Mr. Douglas Fisher, a member of the C.C.F., to get the House to commit itself to the principle of redistribution by a non-partisan body. Mr. Fisher's proposals concentrated on the principle, and were fairly general, though on one occasion they included reading into the Hansard a detailed bibliography.[8] Mr. Diefenbaker's proposal, as he enlarged it in debate, was more specific, and an interesting indication of preferences which were to be important in subsequent debate. It provided for "an electoral boundaries commission" which could employ "such technical advisers and other staff . . . as it deems necessary."[9] "Parliamentary approval would be required" before the commission's electoral districts became effective.[10] The commission was "to recommend such change in the total membership of the house that would make a just and equitable reallocation of seats without serious dislocation or hardship arising from its recommendations on the number of seats in any one province."[11] The names of the commissioners were to be placed before the House, "and our present purpose is to see to it that four of them will be superior court judges and one the electoral commissioner. We hope that one of the judges will be a judge of the Supreme Court of Canada. Another will be a chief justice of a province, a man who in years past participated in public affairs ... and two others will be chief justices who have not participated in either parliament or legislature."[12] Mr. Diefenbaker's resolution passed, and the relevant bill was given first reading; the dissolution of 1962 prevented further progress in that Parliament, and no bill was introduced in the short Parliament of 1962-63.

The next major steps concerning redistribution fell to the Liberal government which took office in April of 1963. Like Mr. Diefenbaker's earlier resolution, the Liberals' plans included no changes in the rules for dividing constituencies among the provinces, so that no hope was held out that Saskatchewan would not suffer a major loss of representation. In other ways, the Liberal proposals departed markedly from Mr. Diefenbaker's. On November 26, 1963, Mr. Pickersgill, then Secretary of State, introduced a long resolution which prepared the way for two bills, one to establish the office of Representation Commissioner, the other to provide for the establishment of electoral boundaries commissions. Two bills, Mr. Pickersgill explained, were desirable for technical reasons, primarily because the Representation Commissioner and the expenses of his office were to become permanent parts of the electoral machinery, whereas many of the mechanical and financial provisions involved referred specifically to the redistribution under consideration. Mr. Pickersgill made it clear, and later repeated several times, that both bills were only technically government bills, and that in fact the government was ready to accept improvements suggested by any MP. Already, in anticipation of the measures, the Chief Electoral Officer had

visited other countries to study redistributions there, and informal all-party conferences to facilitate agreement had been held in Canada.[13]

Despite all this preparation, the second of Mr. Pickersgill's bills had a protracted and occasionally stormy passage through the House; the first, providing for a Representation Commissioner, passed readily, and members of the House expressed satisfaction with the appointment in the bill of the Chief Electoral Officer, Nelson Castonguay, as Commissioner. The bill providing for the boundaries commissions took a full year to get through Parliament, with prolonged delays because of disagreements over its major clauses.

In essence, the bill to provide for boundaries commissions was based on five propositions which, with the dispositions made of them, were as follows:[14]

1. Ten commissions, one for each province, were to be established. Mr. Pickersgill's argument for ten commissions was based primarily on the time which redistribution was expected to take, although mention was also made of the desirability of having local commissions familiar with local conditions. The minister had first considered four regional commissions, but plumped for ten after the Chief Electoral Officer's trip abroad took him to Australia, where one commission was employed for each state. Since the Conservatives had committed themselves to a single commission in 1962, they were sharply critical of the Liberal scheme but offered no amendment to it; a motion for four regional commissions was rejected by the House on April 16, 1964, and Mr. Pickersgill's proposal for ten was approved the same day.[15]

2. Each commission, in the original bill, was to consist of the Representation Commissioner, a chairman appointed by the chief justice of the province from among the members of his court, one member appointed by the

Prime Minister, and one by the Leader of the Opposition. (Provision was made for the appointment of a chairman if the prescribed formula could not be followed, and the chairman was to appoint members if the Prime Minister or Leader of the Opposition failed to act within a stated time.)

The proposed personnel of the commissions was so productive of controversy that the parties reached an impasse, and debate on the bill was suspended for weeks at a time. Concern over personnel took several forms. Despite the high regard in which the Chief Electoral Officer was held, for example, it was nonetheless feared that in his capacity as Representation Commissioner he might exercise a centralized control over all the maps, with the ten commissions acting merely as rubber stamps. Suspicion was also expressed over the preliminary exercises being drawn in his office before the commissions were even established (a duty imposed on him by the statute creating his office) particularly when the government refused to accept responsibility for making them public; the suspicion was partially but not entirely allayed when a delegation from each party was invited to view the exercises in the Commissioner's office. A Conservative motion to require production of the exercises was defeated 101-60 on May 14, 1964, in a division which belied the claim that the debate was entirely non-partisan.[16]

More serious difficulty arose over the other members of each of the ten commissions. No objection was made to the use of judges as chairmen; but the New Democratic Party took the lead in pointing to the potential dangers, in a supposedly non-partisan set of commissions, of having half the members in each instance appointed by the Prime Minister and the Leader of the Opposition, and on April 16, 1964, Stanley Knowles moved to have the chief justice of each province appoint the two additional members from among a stated list of qualified persons, including provincial public servants, university presidents, etc. Mr. Knowles was strongly influenced by the provincial redistribution commission in Manitoba, as was Mr. Pickersgill himself; but since the Conservatives had already accepted in preliminary discussions the proposal to have appointments made by the two major party leaders, they were chagrined and annoyed to find Mr. Pickersgill taking the Knowles amendment seriously. Debate on the relevant clauses was suspended from April to November, 1964, while a compromise solution was sought, and on November 10 the minister indicated that he now felt that the necessary appointments could be made by the Speaker. The Conservatives still favoured the original bill, and Mr. Knowles still favoured limiting the Speaker to appointments from specified classes of people; Mr. Pickersgill's motion for appointments by the Speaker, "from among such persons resident in that province as he deems suitable" passed on November 12.[17]

3. The bill declared that constituencies were to "correspond as nearly as may be to the electoral quota for the province"; i.e., the province's population divided by its number of seats. A commission could "depart from the strict application" of this rule to take into account special geographic considerations, such as sparsity or density of population, accessibility, size or shape; and to allow for community or diversity of interests. But in no case could a constituency's population vary more than 20 percent above or below the electoral quota.

The proposal to have constituencies conform as nearly as possible to the provincial electoral quota did not of itself produce much discussion; what did arouse the members' interest was the series of conditions considered significant enough to justify deviations from the quota, and particularly the statistical tolerance to be allowed above and below it. Mr.

J.J. Greene, a Liberal member, pointed out on March 12, 1964, that the commissions were not empowered to take "historical connotations" into account in departing from strict "rep by pop," but made no motion to require it. Another Liberal, Mr. M.J. Moreau, supported by spokesmen for all parties, late in the debate moved an amendment to permit commissions to consider not only the sparsity or density of population, but also the "relative rate of growth," and it passed on November 13.

Differences of opinion over the 20 percent tolerance to be allowed around the electoral quota not unnaturally divided the parties with strong rural support from those with strong urban bases, and the differences were marked. Of the one hundred constituencies with over 70 000 population, the Liberals in 1963 had won fifty-eight (including the dual seat of Halifax) and the Progressive Conservatives twenty-one; of the thirty-six seats over 100 000, the Liberals had won twenty-four and the Conservatives eight. Of the seventy-nine seats under 50 000, the Conservatives had won forty-one and the Liberals twenty-seven. The New Democratic Party had won only four seats below 50 000, but eleven of those over 70 000. In general, the Conservatives, Social Crediters, and members of the Ralliement des Créditistes, wanted the quota to be as large as possible, the bidding on their side ranging from $33\frac{1}{3}$ percent to 40 percent; the Liberal and New Democratic spokesmen favoured a low quota, the smallest figure mentioned on their side being 10 percent. Disagreement over the tolerance necessitated further delays in the bill's progress, and again it was not until November of 1964, after informal consultations, that the relevant clause was passed. An Alberta Conservative, Mr. Eldon Woolliams, moved on November 12 for a tolerance of 25 percent above and below the electoral quota, and his amendment passed the following day.[18]

4. Commissioners were permitted but not obliged by the original bill to hold hearings of representations by interested persons before making a report. Any such hearings were to be preceded by at least fifteen days' notice in the *Canada Gazette*, accompanied by a map showing the proposed boundaries. Any person intending to present a brief had to give the commission ten days' notice in writing.

No one objected in principle to having the commissions hold sittings to permit the general public to make representations about the proposed maps, and debate on the topic turned largely on the MPs' desires to make the public hearings as effective as possible. The clause finally agreed on without serious division obliged each Commission to hold at least one public sitting on its map, the sitting to be announced not only in the *Canada Gazette* but also in "at least one newspaper of general circulation in the province," the advertisement to include a copy of the map and a description of each constituency. Interested parties were given twenty-three days from the appearance of the advertisement to notify the commission of their intention to present a brief, and the commissions were expressly forbidden to hear representations which did not comply with this proviso.[19] Representations received by the commissions could be disposed of as the commissions saw fit.

5. The bill gave each commission one year in which to prepare its map, which was to be transmitted through the Representation Commissioner to the Speaker and thence to the House of Commons. Within thirty days (later amended to forty-five sitting days) of its presentation to the House of Commons, one-third of the MPs from any province could object in writing to their province's map, and the House by resolution could refer a map back to a commission for reconsideration. The commission then had thirty days to dispose of the objection as it saw fit, and report back through

the Representation Commissioner to the Speaker. After that, the House could take no further action under the proposed legislation.

The question of parliamentary review of the commissions' boundaries, in the light of the many objections to the maps subsequently registered by Members of Parliament, received surprisingly little attention during the bill's passage. Mr. Diefenbaker's proposal of 1962, as noted above, would have required parliamentary approval of the maps before they became effective. The Liberal bill of 1963-64 not only contained no such requirement, but made even reference of each map back to the relevant commission for reconsideration remarkably difficult.

It was the difficulty, rather than the principle, that caught the Commons' collective eye in 1964. Mr. Pickersgill said, on second reading of the bill, that the House appeared to be agreed on two general principles. One concerned the use of non-partisan commissions. "The second principle was that in doing this we should not abdicate the final responsibility which is imposed upon this parliament, and we would have to find some means of making sure that we did not just turn this matter over to a commission without any final power in parliament at least to object if any palpable and obvious errors seemed by the majority to have been made."[20]

Opposition members from the beginning objected that any significant group of members, not a majority of those present, should be sufficient to require the reconsideration of a map. They also argued that one-third of the members from a province was too high a proportion for the consideration by the House of any provincial map; such a proportion, they pointed out, would make it impossible for the Conservatives from Ontario to protest any Ontario map on their own, since they could not muster enough members, while it left the Liberal majority from Ontario free either to

accept or protest the map as they saw fit. The same problem in reverse applied to provinces where the Liberals held fewer than one-third of the seats, and to the smaller parties everywhere. The final clause, again after extensive discussion, provided that any ten members could object to any map and precipitate a debate in the House, after which the objection and a transcript of the relevant Hansard would be sent to the Commission involved without a resolution of the House.

Other aspects of parliamentary review of the commissions, it may be noted, were given little time, and subsequently the government, to the indignation of some leading Opposition members, was able to refrain from tabling papers relating to the internal affairs of commissions (because they were independent of the government), although information on costs was made available.[21]

The five major points outlined above do not exhaust the list of criticisms and amendments made to the bill (it was amended, for example, to permit the continuation of the two-member seats of Queens and Halifax if desired), but they cover the commissions' constitutions. In sum, Parliament created ten independent commissions, on each of which the Representation Commissioner was a full member (a fact which, coincidentally, neatly ensured that each commission initially had on it at least one French-speaking Catholic); the Chief Justice of each province appointed the chairman; and the Speaker appointed the two other commissioners from within each province. The commissions had one year in which to draw maps based on instructions which specified that they were for each constituency to adhere to the electoral quota, from which they could depart up to a maximum of 25 percent in either direction for reasons spelled out in the statute. Provision was made for public hearings on the maps, and parliamentary review, but in both cases the commissions' decisions were final. Any changes made in the boundaries after the one parliamentary debate on each were thus subject to no further public scrutiny, either in commission sittings or in Parliament.

The policy followed by the Speaker in making his appointments was not, as some MPs seemed to expect, to consult the party leaders in the Commons. Instead he consulted the Chief Justice in each province and, if he had been already selected, the chairman of each commission. In general, the Speaker attempted to find in each province a team consisting of a university head or professor, and a provincial civil servant whose position was likely to be some indication of his impartiality, such as the clerk of the assembly, or the chief electoral officer; where this failed, the Speaker sought other citizens of integrity. In some areas the Speaker paid particular attention to the religious and ethnic backgrounds of possible appointees. As a matter of courtesy, the Speaker sent each party leader in the House a list of his appointments.

The commissions began work early in 1965, and for several months thereafter little was heard from any of them. By late spring and early summer all the commissions had prepared their preliminary maps for publication in the *Canada Gazette* and "at least one newspaper of general circulation," and the requisite public hearings were held from early June through October. None of the commissions limited itself to the single sitting required by law; each scheduled several hearings in various parts of each province.

The nature and scope of the hearings, and the presentations made at them, varied widely from province to province. The Quebec commission heard 152 representations at eight centres, Ontario 75 at seven centres, British Columbia 44 at eight; on the other hand, the Nova Scotia commission heard only 11 briefs in five centres and the New Brunswick 3, though it had scheduled five sittings. The briefs ranged from requests to change a name to comprehensive attempts to redraft the commission's map. Since the law required the scheduling of hearings before it was known what representations, if any, were to be made at each, some commissions found themselves in the awkward position of having to travel considerable distances to open a sitting at which nobody was expected to appear, but without statutory power to cancel the advertised meeting. A few citizens, having failed to meet the deadline in giving notice of their intention to appear, found themselves willing and able to express opinion on a map, except that they could not legally be heard. Most briefs that were presented not unnaturally concentrated on one or a few constituencies within each province, and thus did not take into account each commission's responsibility to draw a whole map, not just a partial one aimed exclusively at satisfying only local interests. Few of the public hearings thus swayed the relevant commission to any great extent, and while a few changes of widely varying significance were made in a majority of the maps, most parts of most maps survived the sittings unscathed. The Ontario map sustained the greatest alteration as the result of public hearings.

When in due course maps reached the House of Commons they survived, in the main, again, although amendments were made to four. Since the Conservative whip, Mr. Eric Winkler, let it be known early that his party intended to challenge as many maps as possible as a matter of principle[22] (and the New Brunswick commission invited challenge by producing majority and minority reports), it was inevitable that many objections would be registered, and that Conservative members would play a leading role in speaking to them; nonetheless, it would be inaccurate to conclude that Conservatives alone protested the maps, for spokesmen for all parties had points to make, and it was indeed a Liberal who said:

"In my humble opinion no elected body of men sitting in this house or anywhere else could possibly have made a redistribution on this basis or could possibly have made a worse redistribution than has been done in this case."[23]

One hundred and fifty-eight MPs signed thirty-five objections involving all the provinces except Newfoundland, as shown in Table [3].[24] As an historical footnote, it should be added that Mr. Caouette took advantage of the foregoing announcement to draw the House's attention to a bill he had set down to repeal the *Electoral Boundaries Readjustment Act* altogether; but it was not proceeded with.

Table 3

Province	Objections concerning individual seats	all seats
Alberta	-	1
British Columbia	1	1
Manitoba	-	1
New Brunswick	-	1
Nova Scotia	3	-
Ontario	4	1
Prince Edward Island	-	1
Quebec	18	2
Saskatchewan	-	1

The debate on these objections, in the closing days of April, 1966, included criticisms not only of the maps but of the commissions themselves. A few members, pointing out that few of the commissioners had political experience, stressed the degree to which the maps failed to take into account the realities of maintaining political organizations. Some objected that the commissioners had given no reasons for their decisions (the law did not require reasons), some challenged the commissioners' knowledge of what they were doing, and Mr. Diefenbaker said of the Saskatchewan map that it "could not have been drawn anywhere else than in Ottawa, by somebody that does not know anything about Saskatchewan"[25] (the Saskatchewan map was drawn in its entirety in Saskatchewan, after the commission had rejected all the preliminary exercises drafted experimentally in Ottawa).

Almost all the substantive objections to the boundaries depended on the relative weight attached by the commissioners and the MPs to Clause 13 of the Act. The relevant portions read:

13. In preparing its report each commission for a province shall be governed by the following rules:

   (a) the division of the province into electoral districts and the description of the boundaries thereof shall proceed on the basis that the population of each electoral district in the province as a result thereof shall correspond as nearly as may to the electoral quota for the province . . .

   (c) the commission may depart from the strict application of rules (a) and (b) in any case where

   (i) special geographic considerations, including in particular the sparsity, density or relative rate of growth of population of various regions of the province, the accessibility of such regions or the size or shape thereof, appear to the commission to render such a departure necessary or desirable, or

   (ii) any special community or diversity of interest of the inhabitants of various regions of the province appears to the commission to render such a departure necessary or desirable,

   but in no case . . . shall the population of any electoral district in the province as a result thereof depart from the electoral quota for that province to a greater extent than twenty-five percent more or twenty-five percent less.[26]

A large proportion of the debate on the members' objection to the maps can be summarized in a single statement: the commissions took Section 13(a) as their main instruction, whereas the objecting members, virtually to a man, wanted greater use, and different use, of the flexibility allowed in Section 13(c). Member after member complained of the commissions' slavish addiction to numbers, and spoke well of "relative rate of growth," "accessibility," and "community of interests."[27] "Apparently," the main Quebec objection read, "the commission was much more concerned with numerical balance than with demographic, geographic and historical facts." To this general observation, echoed by many MPs, the maps' critics added a second objection: the commissioners had confined themselves strictly to the census of 1961, instead of using annual estimates of population changes published therafter by the Dominion Bureau of Statistics. (A reading of the act suggests that the law gave the commissions no alternative but to adhere to the census of 1961, on which the division of seats among the provinces was based.) A motion of Mr. Ian Watson's on May 4, 1966, to direct the commissions to "further consider all objections legally made to the respective commissions in the light of Section 13(c)(i) and (ii)" failed because he was unable to obtain the unanimous consent he needed for procedural reasons. A few members, it should be added, took advantage of the objections to the maps to say that they were completely satisfied with the new redistribution.

Virtually without exception all the members who spoke to the objections in the House referred only to part or all of the map for their own province, and not one appeared aware that as between the public hearings and the debates several commissions received contradictory and even mutually exclusive representations. The Saskatchewan commission, for example, received from the New Democratic Party at a public sitting a proposed map that was radically different from a map later sent to it by Progressive Conservative MPs after the debate in the Commons. The commission could not have accepted one map without rejecting the other in toto, and could hardly have accepted either without raising doubts about its character as an independent non-partisan body. The Saskatchewan commission also received at its public sittings a representation from a member which was considerably different from another submission signed by the same member as part of the objection registered to the map in the House of Commons. The same commission was told several times that "trading areas" should form the bases of constituencies; but the legislation did not mention "trading areas" (though presumably they could be considered a "community of interest"); and in any event those who favoured them offered contradictory proposals on boundaries. Such experiences were by no means confined to the Saskatchewan commission.

In the event, only the maps of British Columbia, Ontario, Quebec, and Manitoba were ultimately returned to the House with substantive amendments.[28] The alterations again varied from changes of name to changes of boundaries, and the Ontario commission, in quantitative terms at least, was most responsive to parliamentary criticism, effecting twenty-four amendments; the Quebec commission changed three names and four boundaries involving eight seats; the Manitoba commission one name and one boundary involving two seats; the British Columbia commission altered six seats. Most of the commissions' original boundaries thus stood throughout the public sittings and the formal objections in the House of Commons. (The Senate was given no role in the legislation, but the commissions' work was nonetheless criticized therein.)

The maps the commissions drew are not susceptible of ready generalization, but a few significant points may be made. The tolerance established by Parliament meant the end of the enormous disparities in constituency populations hitherto so common. At that, a total tolerance of 50 percent around a norm still permits substantial variation: the map for British Columbia, to take a random example, includes ridings whose populations on the 1961 census run from barely 55 000 to over 78 000. The tolerance has also reduced the massive rural-urban differentiation that was formerly considered acceptable: the riding named York-Scarborough has been reduced from 267 252 to 80 715, and Mercier from 233 964 to 74 204. It is still true that urban seats are larger than rural, a fact clearly acceptable to Parliament.

At the same time, the redistribution of the 1960s did not eliminate the anomalies that arise from guaranteeing each province at least as many MPs as it has senators: the largest of Prince Edward Island's four seats is barely 30 000 and the electoral quota for New Brunswick was 59 794, as compared with 67 001 for Nova Scotia, which has just one constituency more. Other results included the elimination of the two surviving two-member seats of Halifax and Queens, and a substantial increase in the number of seats allotted to the major metropolitan areas. The metropolitan area of Toronto (depending on how one defines "metropolitan") now includes at least twenty seats as compared with the eighteen it previously held, and Montreal twenty-five as against twenty-one.

The nature and extent of the shifts in constituencies occasioned by the redistribution of the 1960s has inevitably stimulated speculation about the effects on the fortunes of political parties, a consideration which was of course not within the purview of any of the commissions as they drew their boundaries. The most striking single aspect of the latest redistribution, indeed, was its impartiality, a characteristic which revealed itself in two unprecedented ways. The debates on the maps in the House of Commons, since they concentrated on objections, gave few opportunities to members who wished to speak in favour of the new system; even so, the debates were far less disputatious than those which had accompanied any previous redistribution. The official Opposition took the lead in criticizing the maps, but nonetheless a leading Conservative, Hon. Walter Dinsdale, said of the Manitoba map, "Under the circumstances I feel that the commission did the best job possible."[29] Furthermore no critic of the maps, whatever views he held of the ignorance, arrogance, or incompetence of the commission in his province, even raised the charge of partisanship. In the light of the debates which led up to the *Electoral Boundaries Readjustment Act* of 1964, the redistribution which followed must be regarded as a considerable success: Parliament succeeded in eliminating the vast disparities in constituency populations, and succeeded in taking the readjustment of boundaries out of partisan hands. Anyone who thinks these are not remarkable parliamentary achievements should examine closely some of the previous redistributions. It is perhaps fortunate that not all political problems in Canada take ninety-nine years to find a working solution; even so, the objections registered in the House of Commons to the results of the Act of 1964 suggest that the new system too may not be permanent.

Notes

1. See Norman Ward, *The Canadian House of Commons: Representation* 2e, Toronto, 1963, Ch. 2.

2. See Canada, House of Commons, *Official Report of Debates* (referred to hereafter as *Debates*), 1943, 192. Other distortions of "rep by pop" resulted from the holding of elections soon after the taking of a census, before a new redistribution based on the census had been effected. See Norman Ward, "The Redistribution of 1952," *Canadian Journal of Economics and Political Science* (Aug. 1953): 341-60.

3. See, for example, *Debates*, 1946, 2227 ff.; 1952, 1428-56; 1964, 10026.

4. *Debates*, 1903, 11441.

5. See R. Mac G. Dawson, "The Gerrymander of 1882," *Canadian Journal of Economics and Political Science* (May 1935): 197 ff.; Ward, *The Canadian House of Commons: Representation*, Ch. 2.

6. Ward, "The Redistribution of 1952," 351.

7. Joseph Pope, *Confederation Documents*, Toronto, 1895, First Draft of British North America Bill, s. 25.

8. *Debates*, 1958, 1088 ff.; 1960, 1040 ff.; 1960-61, 1160.

9. Ibid., 1962, 2645.

10. Ibid., 2646.

11. Ibid., 2649.

12. Ibid., 1962, 3044. The commission here described by Mr. Diefenbaker refers in the original text to a commission of six members, not five, apparently in error.

13. See ibid., 1953, 5109 ff.; and 3078-79.

14. The proposals are in Bill C-131, House of Commons, First Session, Twenty-sixth Parliament.

15. See especially *Debates*, Nov. 26 and 27, 1963; Mar. 10 and 12, April 16, 1964.

16. See ibid., Mar. 10, April 16, 22, 23 and 30, May 7 and 14, 1964.

17. See ibid., Nov. 27, 1963; Mar. 10, 11 and 12, April 16 and 17, Nov. 10 and 12, 1964.

18. See ibid., Nov. 27, Dec. 3, 1963; Mar. 10, 12, April 15, 16, 22, 23, Nov. 12, 13, 1964.

19. See ibid., Oct. 20, 1964.

20. Ibid., 1964, 739.

21. See ibid., Mar. 10, Oct. 20, 1964; Mar. 21, April 27, 28, May 26, 1966. The last attempt to obtain information about a commission's internal affairs was withdrawn on Oct. 20, 1966.

22. *Globe and Mail*, January 29, 1966.

23. *Debates*, April 29, 1966 (daily ed.), 4552.

24. Ibid., April 25, 1966 (daily ed.), 4215.

25. Ibid., April 29, 1966 (daily ed.), 4545.

26. *Statutes of Canada*, 13 Elizabeth II (1964), Ch. 31, s. 13.

27. E.g., see *Debates*, April 29, 1966 (daily ed.), 4504-5, 4522, and 4537.

28. Ibid., June 3, 1966 (daily ed.), 5915.

29. Ibid., May 4, 1966 (daily ed.), 4703.

15. REPRESENTATION IN THE FEDERAL PARLIAMENT

Elections Canada

REPRESENTATION

One of the crucial questions faced by the Fathers of Confederation in 1867 was how to make sure that every person in the four founding provinces was equally represented in the federal parliament, while at the same time guaranteeing that each region of the country would have a fair say in the daily workings of the new federation. So they adopted as a basic working principle, the idea of "representation by population," according to which each province would be allotted a number of seats which directly reflected its share of the total population in relation to Quebec's. Around it they designed a formula for calculating the number of seats in the House of Commons which would be allocated to each province.

From the start, however, they recognized the diversity of the new provinces in terms of their physical geography, cultural and political traditions, population size and rural and urban characteristics. As more provinces entered Confederation and as some regions grew and developed more than others, the diversity became more pronounced and a certain degree of compromise had to be built into the formula. As a result, the basic principle of representation by population inevitably began to evolve.

Representation in the Federal Parliament (Ottawa: Elections Canada, 1986), 4-17. Reprinted by permission of Elections Canada.

Many observers have commented before now that the history of Canada itself is one of compromise. Certainly, the question of the representation of the provinces in the House of Commons is a case in point. Yet in spite of this, it is fair to say that even today the principle of representation by population remains at the root of the electoral system. This will be illustrated in the following pages by a brief historical sketch of the evolution of the representation formula, followed by an explanation of the present formula, how it is applied to the population statistics in order to determine the number of seats in the House of Commons, and how these are then divided between the provinces and territories of Canada.

History of the Formula

Confederation to 1915

At Confederation in 1867, the *British North America Act* (BNA Act—now called the *Constitution Act*) established a parliament composed of two houses. The upper house, or *Senate*, was to consist of 72 non-elected members, or 24 representing each of the three *regions*—Quebec, Ontario and the Maritimes. The lower, popularly-elected house, or *House of Commons*, was to comprise 181 members representing the four founding provinces—82 for Ontario, 65 for Quebec, 19 for Nova Scotia and 15 for New Brunswick.

In order that each province's representation in the House of Commons would continue to reflect its population, Section 51 of the

Table 1 Representation since 1867

									Number of Seats			
Year	Canada	Ont.	Que.	N.S.	N.B.	Man.	B.C.	P.E.I.	N.W.T. / Sask.	Alta.	Yukon and N.W.T.	Nfld.
1867	181	82	65	19	15							
1871	185	82	65	19	15	4						
1872	200	88	65	21	16	4	6					
1873	206	88	65	21	16	4	6	6				
1882	211	92	65	21	16	5	6	6				
1887	215	92	65	21	16	5	6	6	4			
1892	213	92	65	20	14	7	6	5	4			
1903	214	86	65	18	13	10	7	4	10		1	
1907	221	86	65	18	13	10	7	4	10	7	1	
1914	234	82	65	16	11	15	13	3	16	12	1	
1915	235	82	65	16	11	15	13	4	16	12	1	
1924	245	82	65	14	11	17	14	4	21	16	1	
1933	245	82	65	12	10	17	16	4	21	17	1	
1947	255	83	73	13	10	16	18	4	20	17	1	
1949	262	83	73	13	10	16	18	4	20	17	1	7
1952	265	85	75	12	10	14	22	4	17	17	2	7
1966	264	88	74	11	10	13	23	4	13	19	2	7
1976	282	95	75	11	10	14	28	4	14	21	3	7
1987*	295	99	75	11	10	14	32	4	14	26	3	7

Note: The N.W.T. / Sask. column represents N.W.T. through 1903, and Sask. from 1907 onward.

* Date of proclamation of representation order.

BNA Act stated that the number of seats allocated to each province would be recalculated after each ten-year (decennial) census, starting with the census of 1871. The total number of seats was to be calculated by dividing the population of each province by a fixed number, referred to as the "electoral quota" or "quotient." This quota was to be obtained by dividing the population of the province of Quebec by 65, the number of seats granted for Quebec in the House of Commons.

This simple formula was to be applied with only one exception, "the one-twentieth rule," under which no province could lose seats unless its share of the national population had decreased by at least five percent (one-twentieth) between the last two censuses.

1915—The senatorial clause

In 1915, the first change was made to the original representation formula, when what is known as the "senatorial clause" was added. Still in effect today, the clause states that a province cannot have fewer seats in the House of Commons than it had in the Senate. In 1915 it had the immediate effect of guaranteeing four seats to the province of Prince Edward Island, a number which it has maintained ever since.

1946—Changing the formula

Dissatisfaction with the original formula, however, led to the development of a new set of rules, which were adopted in 1946 when the

BNA Act was amended. These new rules divided 255 seats amongst the provinces and territories based on their share of Canada's total population, rather than on the average population per electoral district in Quebec.

However, since the population of all provinces did not increase at the same rate, the representation of some provinces was found to be decreasing under the new formula. As Nova Scotia, Manitoba and Saskatchewan were all to lose seats after the 1951 census, the "15% clause" was adopted to prevent a too-rapid loss of seats in some provinces. Under the new rules, no province could lose more than 15 percent of the number of seats to which it had been entitled at the last readjustment. However, the same three provinces, plus Quebec, all lost seats after the 1961 census. The same four provinces, plus Newfoundland, would also have lost seats after the 1971 census, so in 1974 legislation was finally introduced to resolve this particular situation.

1974—The "amalgam" formula

In 1974, concern over the continuing loss of seats by some provinces prompted Parliament to adopt the *Representation Act, 1974,* which, amongst other things, guaranteed that no province could lose seats.

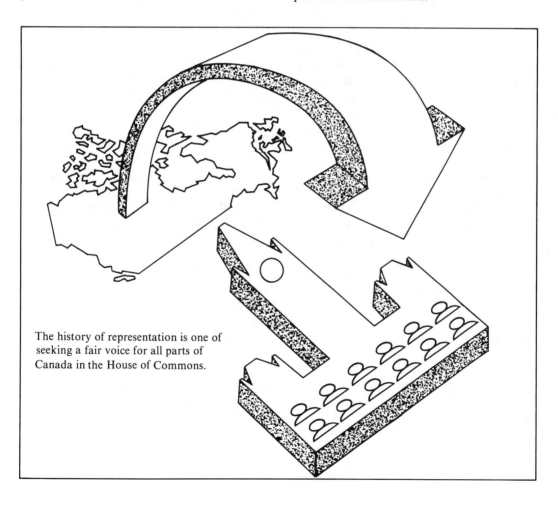

The history of representation is one of seeking a fair voice for all parts of Canada in the House of Commons.

During deliberations by the Standing Committee on Privileges and Elections in February 1974, it was stated:

> The objective must be adequate and realistic representation of all Canadians bearing in mind the historic undertakings arising out of the Confederation compact and its responsibilities. The allocation of seats (in the House of Commons) is at the very hard of the Confederation compromise.

A "compromise" was thus being proposed to deal with representation in the House of Commons. The new formula, the third in our history, was lengthy. As in the pre-1946 rules, Quebec was used as the basis for calculations, but there were three differences. First, Quebec was allocated 75 seats instead of 65. Secondly, the number of seats assigned to Quebec was to grow by four at each subsequent readjustment in such a manner as to slow down the growth in the average population of an electoral district. Thirdly, three categories of provinces were created: *large* provinces, those having a population of more than 2.5 million, *intermediate* provinces, namely, those with populations between 1.5 million and 2.5 million, and *small* provinces, with populations under 1.5 million. Only the large provinces were to be allocated seats in strict proportion to Quebec; separate rules were to apply to the small and intermediate provinces.

The amalgam formula was applied once, leading to the establishment of 282 seats in 1976.

THE PRESENT FORMULA

Following the 1981 census, calculations revealed that the amalgam formula would result in a substantial increase in the number of seats in the House of Commons both immediately and after subsequent censuses (369 seats were projected after 2001). Effectively putting a hold on the process which was already under way to reassign seats, Parliament passed the *Representation Act, 1985*. It came into effect in March 1986.

With the adoption of the *Representation Act, 1985*, the formula described in the amended Section 51 of the *Constitution Act* for calculating representation was greatly simplified.

The calculation is made in four steps in the following way:

1—Allocation to the territories

Starting with 282 seats, two seats are allocated to the Northwest Territories and one to the Yukon Territory, leaving 279 seats.

2—Calculating the electoral district average

The total population of the ten provinces is divided by 279 to obtain the *electoral quota or quotient*.

3—Dividing the seats

The theoretical number of seats to be allocated to each province in the House of Commons is calculated by simply dividing the total population of each by the quotient obtained in *2* above. If the result leaves a remainder higher than 0.50, the number of seats is rounded up to the next whole number.

4—Adjustments

Once the theoretical number of seats per province is obtained, adjustments are made in a process which is referred to as "applying the *senatorial* and *grandfather* clauses."

As we have seen, since 1915, the senatorial clause has guaranteed that no province will have fewer members in the House of Commons than it has in the Senate. Under the new grandfather clause, the most recent of the measures adopted to prevent loss of seats, no province will have fewer seats than it received

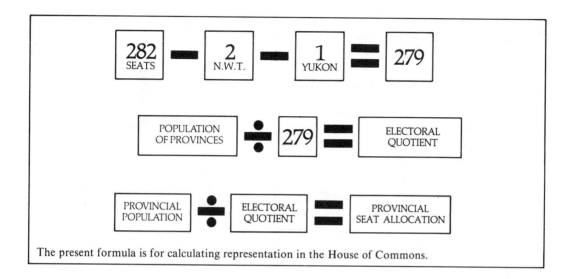

The present formula is for calculating representation in the House of Commons.

in 1976 (or had during the 33rd Parliament, when the *Representation Act, 1985* was passed).

Appended to this text is a table demonstrating how the latest formula has been applied to the census population figures obtained in 1981. Also at the beginning of this section is a table illustrating representation in the House of Commons from the date of Confederation to the present day.

READJUSTING THE BOUNDARIES

So far we have examined how the number of seats in the House of Commons is determined and what method is used to divide that number between the ten provinces and two territories of Canada. However, after the numbers are established according to the constitutional formula, the most difficult part of the exercise begins, namely, cutting up the country into *electoral districts*, sometimes referred to as *constituencies or ridings* in English and "comtés" in French.

The whole exercise is most properly known as "readjustment" of the electoral district boundaries, but is often referred to as "redistribution" and sometimes, particularly in other countries, as "redistricting." While the *Constitution Act* specifies that a readjustment must take place after each 10-year census, the rules for actually carrying out this enormous task are laid down in the *Electoral Boundaries Readjustment Act* (EBRA) of 1964. The main elements of the readjustment process will be outlined, following this brief historical note.

Historical Note

Up to and including the boundary adjustment following the 1951 census, the House of Commons itself was responsible for fixing the boundaries of electoral districts, through a committee appointed especially for that purpose.

Several authorities on the subject have documented the history of the process up to the 1960s. In effect there were no rules to guide the exercise at all. In the words of Professor Norman Ward[1], the process was a "freelance operation in which any rational boundary drawing was likely to be the result of coincidence or accident." Professor Terence Qualter[2] identified four informal "rules" which parliamentarians seemed to have followed in those days, namely: if the number of seats had to be reduced in a given area, 1) save the incumbents' districts; 2) cut out the districts of members who were not going to run again; 3) cut the seats of the minority party; and 4) if there is strong pressure to increase representation in heavily populated areas, increase the size of the House rather than reduce the representation in the rural areas.

The research done on this period reveals a considerable amount of "political" interference in the readjustment process prior to the 1960s. This was often referred to as "gerrymandering," a term used to describe the manipulation of riding boundaries so as to ensure, as far as possible, the re-election of the members of the governing party.

The Commissions Take Over

In the early 1960s, the decision was taken to assign the responsibility for readjusting electoral district boundaries to independent commissions, one for each province. Legislation to this effect was passed in November 1964. Each commission was to be chaired by a judge designated by the *chief justice of the province* and there were to be three other members. One of these was the *Representation Commission*, a public servant who was to sit on every commission. Although initially the other two members were to be political appointees, objections from opposition parties led to the legislation being amended so that finally the *Speaker of the House of Commons* was made responsible for making the two remaining appointments to each commission.

With the abolition of the post of Representation Commissioner in 1979 and the transfer of most of the duties to the Chief

A judge chairs each boundaries commission.

Electoral Officer of Canada, the current situation came into being, whereby a three-member boundaries commission is established for each province and the Northwest Territories, chaired as before and comprising two other members appointed by the Speaker.

The goal of a readjustment process that is completely free of any political association is reinforced by a provision in the *Electoral Boundaries Readjustment Act*, which specifies that no sitting member of the Senate or of a federal, provincial or territorial legislature can be appointed to a commission. In practice, many commission members, aside from the chairmen, are university professors or non-elected officials of legislative assemblies.

Public Input

When the rules for readjusting the federal electoral boundaries were laid down in 1964, members of Parliament realized that, in order for the process to be seen to be as completely fair as possible, it must not only be free from any political association but must also provide an opportunity for any voter to express his or her views on a commission's proposals. Conse-

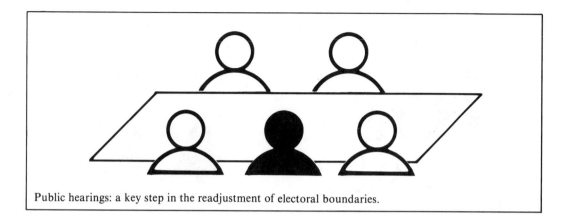

Public hearings: a key step in the readjustment of electoral boundaries.

quently, each commission actively seeks input by publishing maps in the newspapers and inviting the public to make known their opinions at *public hearings*, which are held at several different locations chosen to encourage the participation of as many interested people as possible.

Members of Parliament are not by any means excluded from this process of public involvement. Indeed, the process recognizes that they will invariably have strong views on both the names of the new electoral districts and where their boundaries will go. Therefore, members of Parliament are not only allowed to appear before a commission at the public hearings, but the legislation also provides the opportunity for them to object to the proposals of any of the boundaries commissions. The commissions must consider any objections but they are not obliged to make any changes as a result. In *all* cases, the final decisions as to where the boundary lines will be fixed rest with each commission.

Criteria—Where to Draw the Lines?

Once the commissions are given maps and documentation containing the relevant population data from the most recent decennial census by the Chief Electoral Officer of Canada, they have one year in which to make their proposals, hold public hearings and finalize their report. Their guidelines for this enormous task are found in the *Electoral Boundaries Readjustment Act* from which it is evident that the readjustment exercise is not simply a mathematical computation but, rather, a delicate balancing act which must take into account human interests as well as geographic characteristics. In the course of their work, they also receive technical and administrative assistance from the staff of the Chief Electoral Officer at Elections Canada.

The commissions are charged with dividing the territory assigned to them into a specified number of electoral districts, so that the population of each one will correspond "as closely as is reasonably possible" to the predetermined average (or "quotient"). But, in fixing the electoral district boundaries, they must take into consideration "the community of interest or community of identity in or the historical pattern of an electoral district ... and a manageable geographic size for districts in sparsely populated, rural or northern regions ...".

In order to accommodate these human and geographic factors, the commissions are allowed to deviate from the average population figure when setting their boundaries.

Boundary readjustment must take into account human interests and geographic characteristics.

While generally restricted to a maximum tolerance of 25 percent either way, a commission may, however, exceed this limit "in circumstances viewed by the commission as being extraordinary."

The Process of Readjustment

While the work of the commissions is indeed a crucial part of the readjustment exercise and may take up to one year or more to complete,

in fact, it is only one part of the exercise. The whole process may take two and one half years or more, from the time the Chief Electoral Officer of Canada receives the census data from the Chief Statistician through to the time at which the new boundaries can be used at a general election.

The following [tables] attempt to identify and to explain the main stages in the overall process of readjusting federal electoral boundaries. The relevant sections of the legislation are mentioned at each step.

Table 2   Preliminary Steps

1.
Allocation of Seats
*EBRA—Section 11(1) and Section 12

After the ten-year census, the Chief Statistician of Canada gives to the Chief Electoral Officer of Canada population data for each province and territory broken down by electoral districts and census areas.

Using these figures and the formula in Sections 51 and 51A of the *Constitution Act*, the Chief Electoral Officer calculates the number of seats to be allocated to each province and publishes the numbers so obtained in the Canada Gazette.

(continued)

Table 2 Preliminary Steps (*continued*)

2.

Establishment of Commissions

EBRA—Section 4

The members of the boundaries commissions are selected and appointed by the Speaker of the House of Commons and the appropriate chief justices.

Within 60 days from the time the Chief Statistician of Canada supplies the population data to the government and to the Chief Electoral Officer of Canada, the eleven electoral boundaries commissions must be established and charged with fixing the boundaries of new electoral districts.

The commissions are officially established by the Governor in Council (Cabinet).

Table 3   Commissions Prepare Proposals

3.

Public Hearings

EBRA—Section 17

Newspaper advertisements are published containing maps of the proposed electoral boundaries, as well as the time(s) and location(s) of public hearings, at least 60 days before the date of the first hearing is scheduled.

A commission must hold at least one public hearing before completing its report.

During the hearings, interested individuals, groups and MPs may appear to express their views on the commission's proposals, after notifying the commission in writing of their intention to do so.

4.

Completion of Reports

EBRA—Section 18

—No later than one year after receiving the population data, each commission must complete its report on the new electoral districts.

—The Chief Electoral Officer may grant an extension of up to 6 months when necessary.

Table 4   Reports Reviewed in Parliament

5.

Input by MPs

EBRA—Section 19 and Section 20(1)

Each commission's report is sent through the Chief Electoral Officer to the Speaker of the House of Commons, who must ensure that it is tabled and referred to a Committee designated to deal with electoral matters.

Written objections, each signed by at least ten MPs, may be filed with the Committee within 30 days of the tabling of a report.

The Committee has 30 days, longer if the House is not sitting, to discuss any objections to a report and return it to the Speaker.

Table 5   Finalizing the Boundaries

6.
Reports Go Back to Commissions
EBRA—Section 20(2) and Section 21

The Committee's minutes of proceedings are then sent back to the commission which decides whether or not it needs to adjust its report.

7.
Representation Order
EBRA—Section 22 and Section 25

The Chief Electoral Officer drafts a document called "representation order" describing and naming each electoral district established by the commissions and sends it to the Governor in Council (Cabinet).

The Governor in Council must publicly announce the new boundaries in a proclamation within five days of receiving the draft representation order, which must then be published in the Canada Gazette within another five days from that date.

The new boundaries cannot be used at an election until at least one year has passed between the date the representation order was proclaimed and the date that Parliament is dissolved for a general election.

---

*Electoral Boundaries Readjustment Act.

CONCLUSION

The preceding account shows the refinement that has taken place over the last 120 years in the formula for calculating the level of representation in the Canadian House of Commons, as well as the method for adjusting the electoral district boundaries.

The greatest change has undoubtedly taken place in recent decades. Since the 1940s, we have experienced three fundamental changes to the representation formula and one

major change in the boundary readjustment process. The readjustments which followed on the heels of the censuses of 1941, 1961, 1971 and 1981 were all delayed while such changes were made.

Canada is still a relatively young country, with the result that our electoral system is, of necessity, a dynamic one and subject to constant change. This being so, it will surely be worthy of continuing research and study as it adjusts in future years to meet the challenge of a growing and mobile population.

APPENDIX

Table 6   Calculations under the 1986 Redistribution Formula Using the 1981 Census Figures

Province or Territory	No. of Seats Established in 1976 and Comprising 33rd Parliament	Population 1981	*Quotient	Seats	Application of Senatorial and Grandfather Clauses	Total	Electoral Quotient
Ontario	95	8 625 107	87 005	99.133 (99)	-	99	87 122
Quebec	75	6 438 403	87 005	74.000 (74)	+1	75	85 845
Nova Scotia	11	847 442	87 005	9.740 (10)	+1	11	77 040
New Brunswick	10	696 403	87 005	8.004 (8)	+2	10	69 640
Manitoba	14	1 026 241	87 005	11.795 (12)	+2	14	73 303
British Columbia	28	2 744 467	87 005	31.543 (32)	-	32	85 765
Prince Edward Island	4	122 506	87 005	1.408 (1)	+3	4	30 627
Saskatchewan	14	968 313	87 005	11.129 (11)	+3	14	69 165
Alberta	21	2 237 724	87 005	25.719 (26)	-	26	86 066
Newfoundland	7	567 681	87 005	6.525 (7)	-	7	81 097
Northwest Territories	2	45 741	-	-	-	2	-
Yukon	1	23 153	-	-	-	1	-
TOTAL	282	24 343 181				295	

Detailed Calculation
1. Assign 2 seats to NWT and one to Yukon (3 seats).
*2. Use 279 seats and population (excluding NWT and Yukon) to establish quotient
   (24 274 287 ÷ 279 = 87 005).
3. Calculate number of seats per province using quotient; remainder rounded up if higher than 0.50.
4. Add seats to provinces pursuant to "senatorial clause" guarantee in the Constitution and new "grandfather clause" (based on 33rd Parliament).

Notes

1. Norman Ward, "A Century of Constituencies," *Canadian Public Administration* 10:1 (1967): 107.

2. Terence Qualter, *The Election Process in Canada*, (Toronto: McGraw-Hill, 1970), 99, 100.

16. REFORMING ELECTORAL DISTRIBUTION

Michael Coulson

Reform is needed of the redistribution process for federal constituencies (districts). The essential problems concern the distribution of districts among the provinces. Legislation for the second step, the drawing of boundaries within each province, is functioning well, although some politicians would like to see modest changes.

Proposals for reform of the part of the electoral process related to redistribution among provinces are not a new topic for debate. Some people may nevertheless consider the timing of this article inappropriate, perhaps even dangerous.

Canadian politicians have a propensity for changing the rules and delaying the decennial redistribution provided for in the British North America Act. In fact, not since 1933 has a redistribution been completed according to procedures determined prior to the publication of the census population totals by province.

At the present time a redistribution of federal electoral districts is under way. Commissions in each of the provinces and in the Northwest Territories have developed proposals and the first public hearings began in Manitoba in October 1982. My cry for reform is not intended to be disruptive of this ongoing redistribution. With all its deficiencies, the present formula applied to 1981 data will bring about a closer approximation between representation and population distribution than currently exists (which is based on 1971 data).

The contention of this article, however, is that a start in discussions towards reform must be made now, while interest is relatively high, in order for legislation to be in place prior to the results of the 1991 census of Canada. Repatriation of the Constitution in 1982 has added to the complexity of the reform process. The formula for distributing electoral districts among the provinces is written into the British North America Act. Revision would require participation by the provinces. Even proposals to remove the details of the formula from the Constitution, advocated by Professor Sancton of Western Ontario to the House Committee on Privileges and Election, would have to gain provincial support.

There are, of course, two levels of distribution to be discussed, that distributing electoral districts among the provinces and the process of delimiting the boundaries of electoral districts within each province. Both levels will be discussed in this article, but it is important to stress that alternatives to the present plurality voting system are beyond its scope.

Among Provinces

The present formula dates from 1974, is very complex in its structure and wording, and is commonly known as the Amalgam method. It

Michael Coulson, "Reforming Electoral Distribution," *Policy Options* 4 (January/February 1983): 25-8. Reprinted by permission of the publisher.

provides that no province shall lose electoral districts (seats in the House of Commons), that representation for Quebec shall increase by four seats with each redistribution, and that other large (over 2.5 million population) provinces shall increase their seats proportionately; small provinces (less than 1.5 million population) have their representation based on a quotient calculated on the basis of the *previous* census; intermediate provinces increase their number of districts at half the rate of small provinces.

Criticism has been directed at the rapid rate of increase in seats predicted for the House of Commons and at the arbitrariness of the method itself. A more general criticism is the great complexity of the formula. Indeed, minutes of the House Committee (Spring 1982) suggest that MPs do not understand the formula. Quebec was seen to be the key to controlling the size of the House, but in fact the Quebec quotient (average population per electoral district) controls only the representation from large provinces (Quebec, Ontario, British Columbia, in 1981).

The most comprehensive criticism of the Amalgam method has been provided by Balinski and Young, writing in *Canadian Public Policy* (1981). The criteria they cite as necessary for a fair distribution method are: ". . . the provinces' shares of representation should depend only on their relative rather than absolute sizes. . . . [A] larger province should never get fewer seats than a smaller province. . . . [A] growing province should never give up seats to a shrinking one. . . . [It] should not be possible to bring the provinces closer to their shares by a transfer of seats. . . . [A] method should be even-handed in its treatment of smaller and larger provinces. . . . [A] method should allow for the House of Commons to be fixed at any size that may be deemed desirable."

The Amalgam method is demonstrated to satisfy none of these criteria. Balinski and Young conclude that Canada should return to

"Webster's method with fixed floors and a predetermined house size." As with most solutions, this one has serious shortcomings.

The distribution of electoral districts has, since confederation, been guided by the principle of representation by population. This principle has persisted in the legislation even while its application has been diluted by a variety of special interest clauses. These latter might be summarized, euphemistically, as means of ensuring regional representation. Adequate regional representation has, in fact, become accepted as the second pillar necessary in any redistribution formula.

Two basic concerns seem to pervade the House of Commons regarding redistribution. First, a fear of returning to any formula which would allow a province to lose seats. Second, doubts as to the wisdom of allowing the number of seats in the House to increase at what is seen as an uncontrollable rate. Both positions can be sustained with reasoned arguments.

Such is the dynamic nature of the Canadian population that any strict application of representation by population would radically alter the composition of the House (see Table 1). All of the special interest clauses accumulated to 1971 were insufficient to prevent loss of seats to Newfoundland, Nova Scotia, Quebec, Manitoba and Saskatchewan, which provided the motivation towards the present formula.

The dynamism continues: in the decade 1971-1981 Alberta and British Columbia accounted for 42.15 percent of Canada's population growth. The principle of adequate regional representation is seen as essential by many members of Parliament; in practice, it is seen as no further loss of seats for any province.

Doubts over increasing the size of the House are often couched in terms of economics (operating costs per member) or logistics (space and time in the chamber). There are also real concerns about the dilution of the role of the individual member. On the other hand, Professor Courtney of the University of Saskatchewan suggested to the House Committee that a doubling of members would result in greater voter participation and better regional representation of political parties and ethnic and language minorities. He has few supporters among politicians at this time.

Attempts to resolve the conflicting positions often focus upon an ideal population per electoral district. Unfortunately, there is no agreement on what such a number should be. The practice in other countries (e.g., Sweden c. 24 000, United States c. 500 000) provides no guidance.

In Canada constituency populations over 80 000 occurred as early as the 1933 redistribution and not necessarily in densely populated urban areas (Nipissing 88 597, Welland 82 731, Spadina 82 127). A private member's

Table 1

	1981 Population	Distributions	
		Present[1]	Rep. by Pop[2]
Newfoundland	567 681	7	6
Prince Edward Island	122 506	4	1
Nova Scotia	847 442	11	10
New Brunswick	696 403	10	8
Quebec	6 438 403	75	74
Ontario	8 625 107	95	100
Manitoba	1 026 241	14	12
Saskatchewan	968 313	14	11
Alberta	2 237 724	21	26
British Columbia	2 744 467	28	31
Yukon	23 153	1	1
Northwest Territories	45 741	2	2
Canada	24 343 181	282	282

[1] Based on 1971 Census returns.
[2] Based on 1981 Census returns. Yukon and NWT are guaranteed seats.

bill has recently proposed a Canadian average of 200 000 population per electoral district before expansion of House membership should occur. More often than not debate on the question dissolves into arguments over limits in areal extent for a district. Gravitation of population towards metropolitan areas continues to aggrevate the problem of the size of northern districts. The implications of requiring such districts to approach a population of 200 000 are, I would suggest, beyond practical politics.

In summary, there is considerable support for retaining the House of Commons at its present size and for preventing any province from losing seats. Most would further admit that it is necessary to compensate rapid growth provinces for their increasing proportion of the Canadian population. This is a conundrum that calls for a pragmatic solution, if indeed there is a solution.

It is highly unlikely that any new formula adopted would allow a decrease in the representation of any province. This follows from the list of "players" in any process of reform, the provincial governments and members of the federal parliament. The general public is far less responsive to relative loss of representation in an expanding House than, understandably, to the very visible loss of an electoral district.

In practice this means that the provincial floors are those of the redistribution currently under way. The old Senatorial floors, with all their historical arbitrariness, are redundant, as they have been since 1974. If one accepts the reality of provinces never losing a district, then the range of options is more limited and one can address the problem of how fast the House of Commons should grow.

There seems to be more consensus, developed from disparate arguments, that if the number of seats in the House is to grow, then it should be as slowly as practicable. The solution of no further growth is not a practical one since it itself would require legislative approval and would penalize the "growth provinces". If slow growth is to be adopted as a criterion, then clearly the practice of using Quebec as the means of establishing a quotient for district population size must be abandoned. It is a slow growth province and its role has helped to inflate the size of the House. Similarly, the formula for small provinces must be abandoned since it results in allocation of extra seats to provinces whose quotients are already well below the national average.

Proportional Growth

The most effective and pragmatic solution would seem to be to award extra seats only to those provinces that have grown more rapidly than the provinces as a whole. For this we exclude seats guaranteed to the Yukon and Northwest Territories. In practice the procedures become: 1) no province may lose an electoral district through redistribution; 2) a national provincial quotient is established by dividing the total population of the provinces by the total number of existing members of Parliament from the provinces; 3) the number of seats for each province is determined by dividing a province's population by the national provincial quotient. Remainders of more than half the quotient are rounded up.

Finally, it would be well to continue a clause that provides that no province with a larger population can have less seats than a province with a smaller population, but more for contingency purposes than regular application.

The results of applying this procedure, which we shall term the Proportional Growth method, are compared with the current Amalgam method in Tables 2 and 3. The most recent factual population data is for 1981, which therefore provides the "best" comparison. A saving of twelve seats results. Quebec is

held to its floor of 75 seats. Strict application of the quota would yield only 74 seats for Quebec. When proportion of seats is compared to proportion of population, the new formula shows no improvement over the Amalgam method. Of great importance here is the limitation of additional seats to three provinces, effectively minimizing the redistributive effect of the method.

In practice any new formula will first be applied to 1991 population totals that exist only as projections today. Table 3 shows results for Statistics Canada projections, made in 1979. Provincial floors result from applying the Amalgam method to 1981 data, thus further distorting the representation by population principle. On projection I there is a saving of 27 seats in 1991 and 39 in 2001. For projection IV the savings are 19 in 1991 and 56 in 2001. What is more significant, this is achieved with no deterioration in the proportional distribution of seats compared to population.

These projections are illustrative only. New projections incorporating 1981 data will produce different provincial totals, but the overall Canadian results will almost certainly lie within the range given.

Two potential weaknesses of the Proportional Growth method should be mentioned. First, a province that experiences an absolute loss of population will retain its representation. Absolute losses have occurred in the past and are likely to occur in the future. Their magnitude, however, is small and relatively insignificant.

Second, an absolute loss in Canada's total population could be accompanied by growth in the size of the House of Commons due to one or more provinces experiencing "growth" greater than the national provincial average, and even though all provincial quotients were reduced. This is a highly unlikely scenario and special clauses to protect against significantly reduced provincial quotients seem unnecessary.

The Proportional Growth method favoured here conflicts with that of Balinski and Young, though the essential allocation method is that of Webster with the provincial quotient as the divisor and allocation of large remainders to extra seats, thus avoiding the present bias in favour of large provinces.

My proposal scores on its simplicity and its ability to favour representation by population without abandoning regional representation. The proposal accepts as an inevitable fact that provinces will not be allowed to lose seats in the House and thus, again inevitably, that some growth in the total number of electoral districts will occur. The thrust here is towards a practical solution rather than one with the mathematical finesse of Balinski and Young.

Boundary Commissions

The legislation controlling the distribution of electoral districts within provinces (and since 1974, the Northwest Territories) dates from 1964. Commissions are established in each province and they define each district, seeking for representation by population, but with population tolerances of plus or minus 25 percent to allow for a variety of specified conditions (Section 13, Electoral Boundaries Readjustment Act). The commissions have worked well and their performance has improved with experience even though there is no necessary continuity of commission membership from one redistribution to another.

At the same time, members of Parliament express a continuing unease with the work of commissions and the unpredictable nature of their decisions. In 1973, such unease translated into suspension of the legislation.

It is ironic that the politician's uncertainty over what boundary changes will be made to his district can be traced to the wide range of tolerance allowed by the Act and vigorously fought for by those same politicians. If a closer approximation to the provincial quota were required (say plus or minus 5 percent) then the options open to the commission would be greatly reduced.

Table 2

	1981 H. of C. Seats			Percentage Distribution (1981)		
	Prov. Quota	Propor. Growth	Amalgam Method	Pop.	Propor. Growth	Amalgam Method
Newfoundland	6.52	7	8	2.33	2.37	2.58
Prince Edward Island	1.41	4	4	0.50	1.36	1.29
Nova Scotia	9.74	11	12	3.48	3.73	3.87
New Brunswick	8.00	10	10	2.86	3.39	3.23
Quebec	74.00	75	79	26.45	25.42	25.48
Ontario	99.13	99	105	35.43	33.56	33.87
Manitoba	11.79	14	15	4.22	4.75	4.84
Saskatchewan	11.13	14	14	3.98	4.75	4.52
Alberta	25.72	26	27	9.19	8.81	8.71
British Columbia	31.54	32	33	11.27	10.85	10.65
Yukon	-	1	1	0.10	0.34	0.32
Northwest Territories	-	2	2	0.19	0.68	0.65
		295	310	100.00	100.01	100.01

Table 3

	Projection I				Projection IV			
	1991		2001		1991		2001	
	Propor.		Propor.		Propor.		Propor.	
	Growth	Amalgam	Growth	Amalgam	Growth	Amalgam	Growth	Amalgam
Newfoundland	8	9	8	9	8	9	8	9
Prince Edward Island	4	4	4	4	4	4	4	4
Nova Scotia	12	13	12	13	12	14	12	14
New Brunswick	10	11	10	11	10	12	10	12
Quebec	79	84	79	88	79	84	79	88
Ontario	110	123	121	137	105	122	112	137
Manitoba	15	16	15	17	15	16	15	16
Saskatchewan	14	14	14	14	14	16	14	16
Alberta	27	29	29	32	29	34	34	41
British Columbia	35	38	39	44	33	37	35	42
Yukon	1	1	1	1	1	1	1	1
Northwest Territories	2	2	2	2	2	2	2	2
	317	344	334	372	312	351	326	382

Based on alternative population projections by Statistics Canada, Cat #91-520, (Feb. 1979).

Mention should be made of some of the issues concerning use of the quotient. First, in 1974, the phrase "or relative rate of growth" was deleted from the Act. The result has been to greatly reduce the power of the commissions to apply the principle of representation by population. An electoral district has approximately a ten-year life expectancy. It was reasonably argued that commissions should attempt to keep a district within these tolerances throughout the ten-year period. Since 1974 the legislation has not supported this argument. In practice, however, the 1976 commissions were more successful than those of 1966 in keeping districts within tolerance limits.

Politicians seek to minimize changes to the boundaries of their districts during a redistribution. It is easy to be sympathetic to their position. Quite apart from organizational problems for parties and election administration, a sense of community in the district is strengthened by its stability and longevity. The Act, however, is silent on this matter and the commissioners are free to draw boundaries as and where they think fit. The issue is a delicate one since any wording would be subject to interpretation by both commissioners and politicians, and a probable point of continuing friction between them. It is noticeable that in 1976 the commissioners were more conservative in boundary revision than in 1966 or 1973.

Mr. Foster (Algoma) is trying to protect Northern Ontario against further loss of electoral districts (Bill C-211). At the root of the problem are the widely varying provincial boundaries within Canada. Because it has provincial status, Prince Edward Island is guaranteed four seats; Northern Ontario has to find its representation on the basis of province-wide quotients. Guaranteed representation for the territories can be cited in support of Northern Ontario's case, but one must remember the northern territories of Quebec, Manitoba, Saskatchewan, Alberta and British Columbia. They could all reasonably seek comparable protection through legislation.

Once again the discretion of a commission can be helpful. While a general pattern of lower populations for electoral districts of large areal extent has angered supporters of representation by population, it has done much to ameliorate the problems of northern electoral districts, problems of distance that can never be eliminated. For 1981 at least it is unlikely that Northern Ontario will lose another district, and Mr. Foster's bill loses its urgency for another decade. In 1976 the Ontario commission allowed an average 13.6 percent below the provincial quotient to Northern

Ontario districts. In 1981 these same districts average 14.8 percent below the provincial quotient, still well within the tolerance limits.

In summary, the present procedure for allocating electoral districts among the provinces is unsatisfactory. From the wide range of options available, the Proportional Growth method is preferable. It accepts as given the major concerns of politicians and yet provides a simple solution with only slow growth in the size of the House of Commons.

For the delimitation of electoral boundaries within provinces, the present legislation works well. Given the turbulent history of the electoral Boundaries Readjustment Act, it is important to recognize the arguments in favour of the status quo option in this matter.

17. FAIR ELECTORAL DISTRIBUTION

M.L. Balinski and H.P. Young

"In practice," charged Leon Trotsky, "a reformist party considers unshakable the foundations of that which it intends to reform."

Professor Coulson's call (in the January/February 1983 issue of *Policy Options*) for a reform in the method of apportioning the seats of the House of Commons is no exception. He considers "respecting political realities" the unshakable foundation. By it he means preventing any province from ever losing a seat, and incidentally any MP from ever being reapportioned out of his. This makes a mockery of Article 52 of the Constitution Act that says "The Number of Members of the House of Commons may be from Time to Time increased by the Parliament of Canada, provided proportionate Representation of the Provinces prescribed by this Act is not thereby disturbed."

Rep by Pop remains the constitutional aim and is the popularly accepted view of what is fair. It happens that there is one and only one method that can meet the ideal: it is the one that was first prescribed by the Act of 1867.

The intent of proportionate representation is simple enough. Take, for example, the year 2001 (with population projection 1) and suppose, as Coulson proposes that the House size is to be 334 seats (see Table 1). Then the perfect constituency size (X) is the total population 30 980 900 divided by 334, or X equals 92 757. The population of each province divided by X then gives the precise share of 334 that each deserves.

By this calculation Ontario deserves 128.476, but Prince Edward Island (PEI) only 1.432, the Northwest Territories (NWT) 0.955, and the Yukon 0.481. But usage—tradition or accepted practice—has it that provincial status guarantees at least 4 seats, while NWT and the Yukon are accorded 2 and 1, respectively. The fair share of the total 334 seats deserved by each province is, therefore, at least its minimum guarantee and otherwise its proportional share of what remains once the guarantees have been met. These may be calculated by adjusting X up to 93 929, the perfect constituency size for those provinces whose populations entitle them to more than the minimum guarantees, and dividing as before.

The intent is to give each province its fair share, so defined, of the total 334 seats. With PEI at 4, NWT 2 and the Yukon 1, Ontario's fair share becomes 126.873. But MPs are whole people and not remainders, so what should be done about .873? On this seemingly innocent question hangs not only a two-hundred-year-long history of constitutional and political conflict but a remarkably delicate mathematical problem and theory as well. (See our book, *Fair Representation: Meeting the Ideal of One Man, One Vote*, Yale University Press, 1982).

M.L. Balinski and H.P. Young, "Fair Electoral Distribution," *Policy Options* 4 (July 1983): 30-2. Reprinted by permission of the publisher.

Our intent here is to impart the essence of the theory and so to give a solid basis for the debate on parliamentary representation. Our approach has been to distill the common sense criteria that have been advanced over the years by political men into operational principles about what is fair, and to develop their logical implications.

History shows how tempting it has been to devise methods, in the prophetic words of Thomas Jefferson, "according to any crochet which ingenuity may invent, and the combinations of the day give strength to carry." The amalgam method and Coulson's scheme are testimony that the temptation still exists. The very meaning of amalgam—"a soft mass formed by chemical manipulation"—gives one an inkling of what the current method is like. We have explained in detail elsewhere (*Canadian Journal of Political Science*, December 1981) why it is so fundamentally bad. Here we concentrate on Coulson's method.

Coulson claims that his "proposal scores on its simplicity and its ability to favour representation by population without abandoning regional representation." What is the method? To obtain the solution for the year 2001 compute the perfect constituency size X of the provinces (excluding the territories) for a House size equal to the 1991 solution. A province receives either its population divided by X rounded in the usual way or its 1991 apportionment, whichever is larger. Coulson's method is indeed simple. And it meets its objective of "abandoning" no MP.

What is the method like in practice? Take the solutions that Coulson himself gives for two different published population projections to the year 2001 (Tables 1 and 2) and inspect them. The most evident drawback of the scheme, which it shares with the method it is supposed to reform, is the uncontrollable size of the House. The growth may not be as explosive as the amalgam's—334 instead of 370

for projection 1 and 326 instead of 381 for projection 4—but it still fails a fundamental principle: the method of apportionment should allow for the House of Commons to be fixed at any size that may be deemed desirable.

Consider Coulson's apportionment for the 2001 population projection 1 (Table 1). Should Ontario be satisfied with 121 seats when its fair share is 126.873? Should British Columbia with a fair share of 41.114 get 39 and Saskatchewan with a fair share of 10.236 get 14? The solution is riddled with situations that fail (as does the amalgam method) a second important principle: it should not be possible to bring the provinces' apportionments closer to their respective fair shares by a transfer of seats.

Consider also the Coulson apportionment for the 2001 population projection 4 (Table 2). Should Ontario, that deserves 116.306, accept 112 seats when Quebec, that deserves 74.705, gets 79? What concept of fairness justifies this transfer of four seats? And look a little further down the list: Saskatchewan's population is larger than Manitoba's, but it receives one fewer seat. Coulson's solutions fail to satisfy another obvious principle: a larger province should never get fewer seats than a smaller province.

The amalgam method avoids this pitfall by simply legislating against it. Indeed Coulson counsels a similar contingency clause, but he does not apply it. This principle should be met intrinsically, not by imposing an extra codicil.

Coulson's scheme is proposed as a reform of the amalgam method. Yet its solutions of the problems shown by Tables 1 and 2 seem to the naked eye worse than the amalgam's. In Table 1, 121 seats to Ontario deserving 126.873 is further from proportionality than 136 seats to Ontario deserving 140.841. As for Table 2, the amalgam solution is clearly closer to being proportional than Coulson's.

If "Proportionate Representation" means anything, it must mean that the provinces' allocations should depend only on their relative sizes and a growing province should never give up seats to a shrinking one. Yet both the amalgam method and Coulson's fail to satisfy this principle of proportionality.

In fact, the amalgam method and its supposed reform satisfy none of the principles of fair representation. However, of the infinity of all possible, conceivable methods there is exactly one that satisfies *all* of them: the 1867 method.

Known as Webster's in the United States (after the Senator who proposed it in 1832) it has also been called the method of "major fractions" and of "odd numbers." It rounds the fair shares in the usual way unless the rounding results in a House that is too large, in which case the "perfect constituency" X for the provinces is adjusted up until rounding gives the correct House size; if on the other hand the rounding results in a House that is too small, then the X is adjusted down until rounding works.

This is the method first used in Canada except that the X was taken to be the population of Quebec divided by 65 and the size of the House determined as a consequence.

The method of apportionment has been the target of many reformers. The 1867 method was amended in 1915 and then discarded in 1946. In turn, the 1946 method was altered in 1952 and then replaced by the amalgam method in 1974. Reforms are usually prompted by political considerations, not principles of fairness. 1974 was no exception. It seems that if the 1952 version had been used again, two very respected Members of Parliament would have found themselves in unfortunate situations. The Conservative ex-Prime Minister John Diefenbaker would have had to

run against the popular Otto Lang, and the Liberal, present Deputy Prime Minister, Allan MacEachen would have had to face the popular Robert Muir.

What should be done to reform the method of apportionment? If these principles of fairness are accepted, then it logically follows that the 1867 method is the one to use.

This leaves open two important choices: how large to make the House of Commons, and at what levels to fix minimum guarantees? Incumbents naturally push for an ever larger House. But the realities of a limited number of desks (around 150, with two members at each), not to mention the unwieldiness of a large body and its high cost, argue against it.

The fact is that in representation all that matters is the *share* of seats each province enjoys. Increasing the House indefinitely can be compared to inflating the currency as a device for making everyone richer. If no decrease in any province's seats is countenanced then the House size must be increased by leaps for otherwise all semblance of proportionality is lost.

It is inevitable that at some point Parliament will have to bite the bullet, fix the size of the House of Commons, and suffer provinces to gain or lose representation as they grow or shrink in population relative to one another. In our opinion, Canada should fix both the size of Parliament and the minimum guarantees once and for all and return to the 1867 method, with constituency size determined by the desired size of House.

By way of illustration Table 3 gives apportionments by this method for two different House sizes: 298 and 310 (the number projected by the amalgam method), assuming a minimum guarantee of 4 to each province, 2 to the Northwest Territories and 1 to the Yukon. In each case the loss of seats suffered by the

Table 1 Population Projection 1—Year 2001

	Population	Fair Share	1867 Method	Coulson	Fair Share	1867 Method	Amalgam
Ontario	11 917.1	126.873	127	121	140.841	141	136
Quebec	7 614.5	81.066	81	79	89.991	90	87
British Columbia	3 861.8	41.114	41	39	45.640	46	44
Alberta	2 835.0	30.182	30	29	33.505	34	32
Manitoba	1 185.3	12.619	13	15	14.008	14	17
Saskatchewan	968.0	10.306	10	14	11.440	11	14
Nova Scotia	931.8	9.920	10	12	11.012	11	13
New Brunswick	781.4	8.319	8	10	9.235	9	11
Newfoundland	620.0	6.601	7	8	7.327	7	9
Prince Edward Island	132.8	4	4	4	4	4	4
Northwest Territories	88.6	2	2	2	2	2	2
Yukon	44.6	1	1	1	1	1	1
Total	30 980.9	334	334	334	370	370	370

Populations taken from *Statistics Canada*, Cat. 91-520, February 1979, p. 38 and pp. 50-56. The Coulson and amalglam solutions depend upon apportionments of 1981 and 1991 (Coulson's solution is given in *Policy Options*, January/February 1983).

Table 2 Population Projection 4—Year 2001

	Population	Fair Share	1867 Method	Coulson	Fair Share	1867 Method	Amalgam
Ontario	10 133.5	116.306	116	112	136.359	136	135
Quebec	6 508.9	74.705	75	79	87.585	88	87
British Columbia	3 122.5	35.838	36	35	42.017	42	41
Alberta	3 080.3	35.354	35	34	41.449	41	41
Saskatchewan	1 211.3	13.903	14	14	16.300	16	17
Manitoba	1 169.0	13.417	13	15	15.730	16	17
Nova Scotia	1 008.5	11.575	12	12	13.571	14	14
New Brunswick	888.7	10.200	10	10	11.959	12	13
Newfoundland	671.1	7.702	8	8	9.030	9	9
Prince Edward Island	161.9	4	4	4	4	4	4
Northwest Territories	64.8	2	2	2	2	2	2
Yukon	32.9	1	1	1	1	1	1
Total	28 053.4	326	326	326	381	381	381

Populations taken from *Statistics Canada* (see Table 1), p. 38 and pp. 71-77. The same remarks as in Table 1 apply.

two prairie provinces, Manitoba and Saskatchewan, is about the same as the loss of seats also suffered by Nova Scotia and New Brunswick. The adjustment is proportional and balanced.

There is a moral to this tale. Instead of stooping to devious arithmetical devices, re-

formers should stand up and make a choice based on principles of fairness. In the words of the President of the Privy Council in 1974: "A just system of the representation of the people is the very life-blood of the democratic process."

Table 3 Apportionments by 1867 Method, 1981 Census

	Population	Present Appt.	Fair Share	1867 Method	Fair Share	1867 Method	Amalgam
Ontario	8 625 110	95	103.922	104	108.208	108	105
Quebec	6 438 400	75	77.575	78	80.774	81	79
British Columbia	2 744 470	28	33.068	33	34.431	34	33
Alberta	2 237 725	21	26.962	27	28.074	28	27
Manitoba	1 026 245	14	12.365	12	12.875	13	15
Saskatchewan	968 310	14	11.667	12	12.148	12	14
Nova Scotia	847 445	11	10.211	10	10.632	11	12
New Brunswick	696 405	10	8.391	8	8.737	9	10
Newfoundland	567 680	7	6.840	7	7.122	7	8
Prince Edward Island	122 510	4	4	4	4	4	4
Northwest Territories	45 740	2	2	2	2	2	2
Yukon	23 150	1	1	1	1	1	1
Total	24 343 190	282	298	298	310	310	310

The fair share and 1867 solutions assume each province is guaranteed 4 seats, the Northwest Territories 2, the Yukon 1.

18. WHAT IS GERRYMANDERING?

Robert G. Dixon, Jr.

Whenever "gerrymandering" is mentioned heads nod sagely for the conversation is then on familiar ground. Perhaps few persons recall the story of how an ancient Massachusetts "salamander" district was dubbed a "gerrymander" because of Governor Elbridge Gerry's hand in it, albeit a reluctant one.[1] But all are familiar with the practice of devising odd-shaped districts for political advantage— which is the historically derived and common popular usage of the term gerrymandering. Cartoonists, especially, have a field day in making "snakes," "turkey foots," "frying pans" and the like emerge from sets of revised districts. "Checker-board square" is the assumed ideal. Any significant deviations from such symmetry are deemed unclear and unjustifiable.

It may come as a surprise, therefore, to be told that this common understanding is highly unfortunate. It is unfortunate because it tends to preclude intelligent discussion of unfair partisan practices and results, in districting. It immediately casts attention in the wrong direction—toward superficialities of shape and size, rather than toward the political realities of district composition. These realities, as Robert Luce has so aptly observed, turn on the "accident of sleeping place."[2] It is the particular nature of this "accident of sleeping place" for a party's supporters which determines whether a set of symmetrical districts is fair, or is a cleansweep gerrymander for that party. Not to perceive this is to confuse form with function,

and even to prevent the asymmetrical designs dictated by considerations of political balance and minority representation, and dictated as well by normal preferences for giving some recognition to natural boundaries and political subdivisions.

Clearly misleading and wrong, therefore, are such definitions of gerrymandering as the following: (1) "the creation of legislative districts of grotesque form to produce a maximum number of districts with majorities for the party in charge of districting"; (2) "the application of contorted physical shapes for an intended partisan gain."[3] Little better is the following: "districting by political faith or race, not geography."[4] This last smacks of the "three monkeys" principle that gross results are acceptable if innocently caused.

More to the point are definitions of gerrymandering which speak of the "art of political cartography."[5] In simplest language, gerrymandering should be taken to encompass *all* apportionment and districting arrangements which transmute one party's actual voter strength into the maximum of legislative seats and transmute the other party's actual voter strength into the minimum of legislative seats. *Gerrymandering is discriminatory districting. It equally covers squiggles, multimember districting, or simple nonaction, when the result is racial or political malrepresentation.*

A. MYTH OF COMPACTNESS

A rule of compactness and contiguity, if used merely to force an explanation for odd-shaped districts, can have much merit.[6] Erected as a firm enforceable requirement, however, a rigid compactness-contiguity rule shifts attention

From *Democratic Representation: Reapportionment in Law and Politics* by Robert G. Dixon, Jr. Copyright © 1968 by Oxford University Press, Inc. Reprinted by permission.

from the realities of party voting to mere physical geography. Indeed, it would undercut the spirit of Chief Justice Earl Warren's oft-quoted statement about "people, not trees or acres," being the representational concern, if "people" denotes politically alert citizens.

For example, a recent article by a geographer sets forth a device for measuring gross perimeter of districts, and a geometric index of compactness.[7] These, combined with a 15 percent maximum deviation rule, are applied to create a set of suggested districts. The inference is that gerrymandering is thereby avoided and that fair districting is achieved, but there is not one line about the *political* effect of the proposed districts. Thus the crucial question about districting and gerrymandering—the impact on parties, policies, and programs, and on effective political competition—is not even considered.

The reality is that odd-shaped districts sometimes *may* facilitate unfair advantage of one party over another. The reality also is that odd-shaped districts may be one way, short of some proportional representation device, of avoiding "wasted votes," i.e., of ensuring some minority representation by recognizing a few relatively safe enclaves for the weaker party. In the latter instance questions of representation theory can be raised as to whether it is preferable for a minority to have its own voice in the legislature, or to be voiceless except through the dominant party. But in any event a rigid compactness rule will not provide satisfactory answers.

B. INSEPARABILITY OF GERRYMANDERING BY DISCRIMINATORY MULTIMEMBER OR SINGLE-MEMBER DISTRICTING

In a phrase, gerrymandering is *discriminatory districting*. For those states accustomed to using single-member districts for both houses of the legislature no further amplification is necessary. But what of those states which use some multimember districts, or that special variety of multimember districting known as floterial districts?

A "floterial district" has been defined as a "legislative district which includes within its boundaries several separate districts or political subdivisions which independently would not be entitled to additional representation but whose conglommerate population entitled the entire area to another seat in the particular legislative body being apportioned."[8] Although forbidden in Illinois in 1848 and Iowa in 1857, floterial districts have been common in the South.[9] In theory, they are a way of achieving greater arithmetic equality in situations where there are political subdivisions of varying sizes whose populations do not neatly accord with the representation ratio, while at the same time preserving the integrity of the boundaries of traditional political subdivisions.

The Supreme Court in *Reynolds* v. *Sims* suggested that use of floterial as well as multimember districts might be permissible to achieve some flexibility. However, Justice Douglas in his concurring opinion in *Kilgarlin*, the 1967 Texas reapportionment case, warned that multimember districting "allows the majority to defeat the minority on all fronts."[10]

Conceding that "all districting is gerrymandering," in the special sense to be noted below, there is still a major difference between the mild majority party biases which may unavoidably accompany use of single or multimember districting systems, and exaggerated biases. There is moral concern and there may well be constitutional concern when a majority can "defeat the minority on all fronts." It should be immaterial whether the defeat is accomplished by gross multimember districting which Justice Douglas had in mind (Texas districts ranged from single-member up to 14-

member) or by partisan creation of single-member districts. Functionally, there is no distinction. From the standpoint of minority representation (racial, political, or other) or party competition, the two forms of discrimination are simply alternative sides of a double-edged sword wielded by the controlling group. It follows then that there can be no logical distinction between these two forms of voter discrimination in regard to justiciability. If one is justiciable, so is the other.

C. ALL DISTRICTING IS "GERRYMANDERING"

To be brutally frank, whether or not there is a gerrymander in *design*, there normally will be some gerrymander in *result* as a concomitant of all district systems of legislative election. (A precondition of gerrymandering is use of a district system for election of legislators, or, of course, use of a winner-take-all at-large system. It cannot occur in a pure proportional representation system.) Marked disparities between a party's actual voting strength and its proportion of seats gained may be noted even under relatively equalized districts. For example, in 1966 in California a minority of the statewide congressional vote produced Democratic majorities in both houses of the reapportioned legislature, and a 21 to 17 edge in the unrevised congressional districts. By contrast, a Republican plurality of only 41 000 in a statewide total of nearly 900 000 produced a five to two Republican edge in congressional seats in Iowa. In New Jersey's revised congressional districts Democrats gained a nine to six edge in 1966 despite a Republican plurality in the popular vote.[11]

In a functional sense it may thus be said that *districting is gerrymandering*. The generalization applies both to single-member districting and to multimember districting. The former has been observed for years to create at least a mild bias in favour of the dominant party because it tends to win a higher percentage of districts than its statewide popular vote percentage. The latter creates a similar bias because of the winner-take-all feature. The normal majority party bias in single-member districts can be exaggerated by conscious partisan line skewing. This same bias in multimember districts can be exaggerated by increasing the number of legislators elected in each district, e.g., use of six-member districts, or higher, rather than two-member districts.

Perceiving these generic elements of districting makes the problem of achieving a just representation system no easier, but does permit the right questions to be asked. First, what range of "gerrymander in result" is tolerable? Some play in the joints of the political system is accepted. But hardly acceptable under democratic theory, or constitutional theory, are repeated inversions of popular minorities into governmental majorities, or distortions of two to one or greater in the ratio of votes cast to seats gained. Second, what kinds of reapportionment method will minimize *both* gerrymandering by design and in result? This question was explored [in Chapters XII to XIV] and the discussion culminated with a plea for consideration of bipartisan methods in apportionment-districting.

Third, failing use of bipartisan methods, and there often will be failure as states persist in using traditional partisan methods of districting, the next focus of inquiry emerges: Will courts curb gerrymandering excesses in the process of policing the equal population mandate for construction of American legislatures? In short, we are now brought back to *Baker* v. *Carr*. Rephrased, the key question is whether the old "political question" doctrine still lives to protect gerrymandering from judicial review, or whether gerrymandering, like unequal district population, poses a justiciable issue.

Notes

1. Although the particulars of the story vary, the term "gerrymander" probably arose from the following sequence of events: following a redistricting of Essex County, Massachusetts, Governor Elbridge Gerry signed the districting bill into law even though he was opposed to the soon-to-be-attacked provisions of the bill. A dialogue then occurred between portraitist Gilbert Stuart and another party, the identity of whom seems to be in conflict. Looking at a map of the redistricting printed in the *Boston Weekly Messenger* of March 6, 1812, Stuart noticed one fairly compact district encircled by another of distorted outline. He then sketched in a head, wings and claws and noted the likeness to a dragon. The other party considered it more like a salamander whereupon Stuart is alleged to have said, "Better call it a 'Gerrymander.'" It is ironic that a term bearing his name became such an epithet of opprobrium, since Gerry signed the bill only because he doubted the propriety of a governor's assertion of his veto power over a matter of such character. See Robert Luce, *Legislative Principles* (Boston: Houghton, Mifflin, 1930), 397-98.

2. Ibid., 393.

3. V.O. Key, *American State Politics: An Introduction* (New York: Knopf, 1956), 64-5; Charles P. Edwards, "Theoretical and Comparative Aspects of Reapportionment and Redistricting: With Reference to Baker v. Carr," *Vand. L. Rev.* 15 (1962): 1265, 1278.

4. Robert C. Brooks, *Political Parties and Electoral Problems* (New York: Harper Brothers, 1923), 437.

5. Andrew Hacker, *Congressional Districting* (Washington: Brookings Institution, 1964), 54.

6. In this spirit the Rhode Island Supreme Court has referred to constitutional requirement of "compactness" as being "peripheral in its thrust," forbidding a "complete departure" but leaving to legislative determination the degree of compactness which is "possible" in the total representation picture. Opinion to the Governor, 221 A.2d (R.I. 1966), 799.

7. Joseph E. Schwartzberg, "Reapportionment, Gerrymanders, and the Notion of Compactness," *Minn. L. Rev.* 50 (1966): 443.

8. Davis v. Mann, 377 U.S. 678, 686 n.2 (1964).

9. Luce, supra Note 2, at 377; A.Z. Reed, "The Territorial Basis of Government Under the State Constitutions," *Columbia University Studies* 40 (New York: Columbia University Press, 1911): 553.

10. 386 U.S. 120 (1967) 127.

11. See generally, Republican National Committee, *The 1966 Elections* (Washington, D.C., 1967).

19. THE COURTS AND REDISTRIBUTION

Harvey E. Pasis

For many years American courts have ruled that they lacked the jurisdiction to alter the reapportionment (called redistribution in Canada) of electoral districts or constituencies.[1] In 1962 the Supreme Court of the United States reversed its decision after a group of voters in Tennessee challenged the reapportionment that established wide disparities in population between urban and rural ridings for the state legislature. The court[2] ruled that the equal protection of the laws principle found in the fourteenth amendment to the Constitution gave the judiciary the authority to intervene so that democratic politics was effective. Two years later, the Supreme Court decided that the fundamental principle of representative government was equal representation for an equal number of people in congressional districts since legislators represented people, not farms, cities, or economic interests.[3] The same principle was also supported for state legislatures.[4]

In Canada, the voter had no legal basis to challenge the redistribution of federal and provincial electoral boundaries until Section 15(1) of the Canadian Charter of Rights and Freedoms, that states "Every individual ... has the right to the equal protection and equal benefit of the law ...", came into force recently. This Canadian clause about "the equal protection of the law" is similar to the "equal protection of the laws" clause found in the United States' Constitution. The Charter has been used in British Columbia to challenge the redistribution of provincial ridings that

had 15 or 16 times more electors in some ridings than others. The British Columbia Supreme Court ruled that Section 32(1)(b) of the Charter means the Charter applies to the legislature and government of each province for all matters within the authority of the legislature.[5] A ruling about the applicability of other sections of the Charter, including Section 15(1), to the redistribution of seats in British Columbia is expected in 1988. This case is important because a provincial court has decided that the judiciary has the authority to intervene in the redistribution process without indicating how it will do this until 1988. The Charter will probably apply also to the redistribution of federal electoral boundaries, because Section 32(1)(a) indicates that the Charter applies to the Parliament and government of Canada in respect of all matters within the authority of Parliament. Therefore, in the future some Canadian court will likely have to determine how equal or unequal the size of federal and provincial electoral ridings are and if the United States' principle of equal representation for an equal number of people is to be followed in Canada.

Fortunately, a measure called the Gini Index exists to aid any court. The Gini Index is a statistical measure used in the social sciences to show the level of inequality in the distribution of wealth, income, productivity, goods, social mobility and political equality. It has been applied to assessing redistributions and has been shown to be a better measure of inequality than the equal-share coefficient, the Schutz coefficient, the minimal-majority measure and the percent of goods held by the most favoured 1 percent of value holders.[6] The Gini scale ranges between 0, which is complete

Harvey E. Pasis, "The Courts and Redistribution," *Canadian Parliamentary Review* 10:3 (Autumn 1987): 8-9. Reprinted courtesy of Canadian Parliamentary Review.

equality, and 1, which is complete inequality. For example, complete equality (0) would occur when all the ridings in British Columbia had the same population and complete inequality would occur when one riding had all the population and other ridings had no people in them.

The following table indicates the Gini Index based upon recommendations of the federal electoral boundaries commissions for each province.

The lowest index indicates that the redistribution is approaching representation by population or an equal number of people in each riding. Since the federal electoral boundaries commission must follow specific rules in drawing boundaries, one should not expect the index to be 0.

The table demonstrates that Saskatchewan had the lowest index at .011 and Newfoundland had the highest at .167. By comparing the Gini indices, one could contend that the proposed federal redistribution for all provinces except Saskatchewan violate Section 15(1) of the Charter of Rights and Freedoms.[7]

The courts could accept a higher value of the Gini Index than the values shown for Saskatchewan but it seems likely that half of the federal redistributions could violate the Charter, if "the equal protection of the law" clause is to have any meaning in Canada. Thus

Table 1

Province	1986-87 Proposed to Parliament
Saskatchewan	.011
Manitoba	.035
Prince Edward Island	.042
Ontario	.051
British Columbia	.067
Quebec	.070
Nova Scotia	.073
Alberta	.077
New Brunswick	.098
Newfoundland	.167

a Canadian court could order the federal redistributions to be done again, even if they were eventually passed by Parliament.

In summary, then, Section 15(1) of the Charter of Rights and Freedoms has complicated federal and provincial redistributions in Canada, especially if a Canadian court agrees with the interpretation of the Supreme Court of the United States. Assuming that the Dixon case is not going to resolve all the issues, especially the applicability of the Gini Index, one solution is to have a reference case clarify this situation so that members of electoral boundaries commissions at the federal and provincial levels of government would know how to interpret the Canadian Charter of Rights and Freedoms.

Notes

1. *Colgrove v. Green* 328 U.S. 549 (1946).

2. *Baker v. Carr* 369 U.S. 186 (1962).

3. *Wesberry v. Sanders* 376 U.S. 1 (1964).

4. *Reynolds v. Sims* 377 U.S. 533 (1964).

5. *Re Dixon and Attorney General of British Columbia* (1987), 31 D.L.R. (4th) 546.

6. For a statistical explanation about the Gini Index, see H. Alker, Jr. and B. Russett, "On Measuring Inequality," *Behavioral Science* 9 (1964): 207-18; David C. Leege and W. Francis, *Political Research: Design, Measure-* *ment and Analysis* (New York: Basic Books Inc., 1974), 274-8; and Harvey Pasis, "The Inequality of Distribution in the Canadian Provincial Assemblies" *Canadian Journal of Political Science* V (1972): 433-6.

7. Although the data are not presented here, my preliminary findings indicate that all provincial redistributions have higher Gini indices than those at the federal level. Thus, courts may rule all provincial redistributions violate the Charter.

20. ELECTORAL DISTRIBUTION IN THE CANADIAN PROVINCIAL LEGISLATURES

Harvey E. Pasis

The Gini Index, a measure of inequality, is used to show how far the sizes of provincial constituencies deviate from equal population or equal number of voters. The index varies between 0, which is complete equality, and 1, which is complete inequality.[1]

When the Gini Index is applied to a set of data[2] for provincial elections in Canada, Table 1 shows that provincial constituencies are not drawn according to the criterion of equal size for each riding. For the most current provincial elections, Quebec, which has an independent boundaries commission, has the lowest index at .093 in 1985, and Prince Edward Island, which does not use an independent commission, has the highest index at .313 in 1986.

Table 1 also indicates that the index has always been reduced, compared to the previous index, whenever independent electoral boundaries commissions[3] have been established for the first time. For example, in Saskatchewan the index decreased from .196 in 1971 to .067 in 1975; in Alberta the index was reduced from .269 in 1967 to .191 in 1971; and in Manitoba the index was reduced from .275 in 1953 to .196 in 1958. Similar results were found for the first independent commissions used in Newfoundland in 1975; in British Columbia in 1986; and in Quebec in 1973.

Even when ad hoc commissions, criticised for possibly being partisan,[4] have been used for redistributions, the size of the index has gone down. For example, in Ontario the index went from .210 in 1963 to .170 in 1967; and in Nova Scotia the index dropped from .225 in 1974 to .156 in 1981.

These results indicate the electoral boundaries commissions, especially independent ones, employing specific rules, including a tolerance level[5] for the size of constituencies, have moved the provincial ridings closer to equality of representation in the legislatures. However, the British Columbia Supreme Court[6] ruled that the Canadian Charter of Rights and Freedoms applies to the legislature and government of each province, including the redistribution process, without indicating how it applied. Finally, in 1989, the British Columbia Supreme Court decided that provincial electoral ridings in British Columbia violated the right to vote guaranteed by Section 3 of the Charter, since representation by population was grossly violated under the electoral redistribution.[7] The Court also ruled that absolute equality or as near as practicable to absolute equality of the number of voters in each riding was not required. But the Court declared also that it would intervene on the constitutionality of electoral redistributions whenever a high degree of equality of voting power was undermined.

An original essay written for this volume.

Table 1   Gini Indices for Provincial Elections

	1911	26	28	30	33	34	35	36	37	38	39	40	41
Nfld													
NS													
BC			.287		.329				.367				.350
Que											.245		
Man								.297					.310
Sask						.182				.130			
NB													
Ont	.192												
PEI													
Alta		.225		.165			.178					.151	

	1944	45	48	49	51	52	53	55	56	58	59	60	62
Nfld				.179	.235				.220		.220		.248
NS												.261	
BC		.384		.371		.383	.386		.349		.359		
Que	.336								.355			.369	.384
Man		.348		.271			.275			.196	.200		.214
Sask	.136		.182			.159			.184		.169		
NB													
Ont					.244						.256		
PEI													
Alta	.187		.216			.216		.248			.278		

	1963	64	66	67	69	70	71	72	73	74	75	76	77
Nfld			.241					.262			.096		
NS	.270			.209		.212				.225			
BC	.349		.180		.190			.202			.226		
Que			.254			.267			.104			.120	
Man			.243		.096				.134				.177
Sask		.137	.176				.196				.067		
NB			.177			.183				.195			
Ont	.210		.170				.189				.131		.130
PEI			.277			.288				.308			
Alta	.263		.269				.191				.234		

	1978	79	81	82	83	84	85	86	87
Nfld		.128		.132			.116		
NS		.156				.164			
BC					.192		.157		
Que		.076				.093			
Man		.095					.108		
Sask	.100		.078				.114		
NB	.194		.199					.208	
Ont		.151					.171	.103	
PEI	.363	.304	.308				.313		
Alta		.190	.222				.170		

Sources: Harvey E. Pasis, "The Inequality of Distribution in the Canadian Provincial Assemblies," *Canadian Journal of Political Science* V (1972): Table I, 435 (corrected); and Reports of the Chief Electoral Officer for each province since 1972.

In the past, the relationship between the size of a territory or riding and its population size as the basis of representation has been discussed in provincial legislatures and then in commissions for those provinces that have them; similar discussions have occurred at the federal level.[8] The decision of the British Columbia court leads to the following questions: Will the courts now play a larger role in this discussion? What does equality of voting power mean? Will interest groups challenge provincial electoral boundaries and ask the courts to determine the meaning of "one man-one vote"?[9] Will the courts have to decide if provincial ridings are "reasonable" and "demonstrably justified in a free and democratic society," as required by the democratic and equality rights sections of the Canadian Charter of Rights and Freedoms? Because of the 1989 decision in British Columbia, the meaning of what constitutes fair and just representation is likely to be an important issue in the 1990s.

Notes

1. For an explanation of the Gini Index, see Hayward R. Alker, Jr., and Bruce M. Russett, "On Measuring Inequality," *Behavioral Science* IX (1964): 207-18; David C. Leege and Wayne L. Francis, *Political Research: Design, Measurement and Analysis* (New York: Basic Books, Inc., 1974), 274-8; and Harvey E. Pasis, "The Inequality of Distribution in the Canadian Provincial Assemblies," *Canadian Journal of Political Science* V (1972): 433-4.

2. The sources of the data from 1911 until 1971 are explained in Pasis, ibid., p. 434. The data from 1972 until 1987 are based on Reports of the Chief Electoral Officer for each province.

3. For a detailed discussion about the types of provincial commissions used, see Terence H. Qualter, *The Election Process in Canada* (Toronto: McGraw-Hill Company of Canada Limited, 1970), 105-11; and R.K. Carty, "The Electoral Boundary Revolution in Canada," *American Review of Canadian Studies* 15 (1985): 273-87.

4. Carty, ibid., 279.

5. The tolerance level beyond which the size of constituencies cannot be above or below is ±15% in Saskatchewan and ±25% in Newfoundland, Quebec, and Manitoba. For a further explanation, see Carty, ibid., 280.

6. Re Dixon and Attorney General of British Columbia (1987), 31 D.L.R. (4th), 546.

7. This is summarized from a copy of the unpublished decision of Dixon v. Attorney General of British Columbia dated April 18, 1989. The copy was obtained just prior to the publication of this book.

8. For the implications of the federal redistribution, see John C. Courtney, "Parliament and Representation: The Unfinished Agenda of Electoral Redistributions," *Canadian Journal of Political Science* XXI (1988): 684-5.

9. After the 1989 decision in British Columbia was made public, several civil liberties groups in Alberta considered challenging Alberta's provincial electoral boundaries. See *The Edmonton Journal*, Saturday, April 22, 1989, F8.

DISCUSSION QUESTIONS

1. Who should conduct redistributions in Canada?

2. What criteria should be used to draw electoral boundaries in Canada?

3. How should seats be allocated to each province for the House of Commons?

4. Should computers be used in the redistribution process? Why or why not?

5. What should the role of the Canadian courts be in the redistribution process?

6. Explain how theories of representation are and are not applied in the redistribution process in Canada.

7. What does fair representation mean?

8. Do gerrymanders exist in Canada?

9. What are the possible consequences of using different ways to carry out the redistribution process?

ELECTORAL SYSTEMS: TYPES, CONSEQUENCES, AND REFORM

DISCUSSION QUESTIONS

INTRODUCTION

Harvey E. Pasis

Specific mechanisms to distribute elective representation are associated with the different types of electoral systems referred to in Section Three. Section Four examines the advantages and disadvantages of electoral systems; their biases, such as the cube law; their impact or political consequences; and specific reforms proposed for the Canadian electoral system.

TYPES OF ELECTORAL SYSTEMS

Electoral systems—the ways in which votes are recorded and counted[1]—tend to be divided into majority and plurality types versus proportional representation, although other methods and classifications exist and will be examined later. The majority system requires the absolute majority of votes (half the number of valid votes plus one) and the plurality system requires the largest number of valid votes, which may not be the absolute majority, for a candidate to be elected. Canadian elections today use the single-member constituency plurality system or the first-past-the-post system. The simple plurality type tends to over-represent the party receiving a majority or plurality of votes in terms or the number of legislative seats it receives at the expense of the other parties. This bias is considered an advantage because one party can form a government with a majority of seats,[2] thus leading to stability. Canada is, however, an exception to this tendency, since minority governments, in which one party forms a government in the legislature with a minority of seats, have occurred federally and provincially. For example, a minority Conservative government was elected in the 1988 Manitoba provincial election. The plurality system is also considered easy for the voter to use and understand compared to other types.

   The share of seats won by a major party under the Canadian federal electoral system has been shown to be influenced by its "own share of vote, number of own candidates, number of minor-party candidates and (in one case) relative strength of the major party in size-classes of constituencies."[3] This system is also influenced by the geographic distribution of the popular vote, as Richard Johnston and Janet Ballantyne have ascertained: "The smaller the party, the more concentrated in one or a few provinces its vote should be, if it is to maximize its strength in Parliament. Conversely, the larger the party, the more dispersed across provinces its votes should be."[4] Thus, parties may examine several variables before planning their campaign strategy.

257

Proportional representation, the basic purpose of which is to represent majorities and minorities[5] by translating their votes into seats as closely as is proportionally possible, presents an alternative to majority and plurality systems. Although all electoral systems tend to favour the parties receiving a plurality of votes by giving them more legislative seats compared to the other parties, this bias is significantly greater in plurality and majority systems than in proportional representation systems.[6] Since the latter system tends to reward minorities with legislative seats, a minority or coalition government, in which two or more parties work together, will be formed. The formation of these types of government may be considered a disadvantage, if a majority government that does not represent minorities is the goal of an election. However, coalition governments have been successful in stable democracies like Switzerland and the Scandinavian and Benelux countries,[7] and minority governments have performed likewise in Canada federally and provincially.[8]

Supporters of the plurality system, like J.A. Chandler, have argued that this system leads to governments responsive to the voters, since the parties having a majority of votes will lose a large number of seats if they lose a small number of votes. In contrast, under proportional representation a party could afford to lose a large number of votes before losing a large number of seats.[9] On the other hand, Michael Laver has shown that "a rising third party can cause another party to win or retain seats despite its falling share of the vote ..."[10] under the plurality system without it being responsive to the electorate.

In the list system of proportional representation, parties nominate lists of candidates in multi-member ridings, the electorate vote for one party list or the other, and seats are given to the party lists in proportion to the number of votes received. In the single transferable vote system of proportional representation, the electorate votes for individual candidates rather than for party lists.[11] The single transferable vote is used in Ireland, where it has produced a high degree of proportionality between votes and seats, leading to stable governments.[12] However, critics have shown that this system does "not always respond positively to changes in individuals' preferences."[13]

Proportional representation is designed to reflect the voters' opinion in the legislature. However, if one assumes that it is the government and not the legislature that ought to reflect the opinion of the electorate as a whole, then the length of time a party is in government ought to be proportional to its vote during this time. Peter J. Taylor and Arend Lijphart call this ideal "proportional tenure." They have found that no "electoral system does particularly well in providing proportional tenure."[14] In addition, they determined that proportional representation "discriminates in favour of small centrist or special-interest parties and against large parties in general and ideologically extreme parties in particular."[15] Thus, biases exist in all types of electoral systems, although the extent to which they occur tends to vary from system to system.

Electoral systems can be classified by factors other than electoral method or formula. For example, Arend Lijphart uses five factors: electoral formulas; district magnitudes or the number of candidates elected in a riding; provisions for supplementary seats; electoral thresholds, or the minimum number of seats or votes required for any party to win a seat; and ballot structures, or whether the electorate votes only for candidates of one or more parties or among parties or candidates of different parties.[16] Andre Blais has proposed a scheme with six components: the nature of the constituency; constituency magnitude; the object of the vote; the number of votes allowed; the type of vote; and the formula. He also differentiates between systems based on the outcomes or the degree of disparity between the share of votes and seats.[17] The advantages of this classification are that it is systematic, and that the same variables can be applied to all systems.[18]

CUBE LAW

The cube law is another form of electoral bias; it warrants its own section because a diversified literature has been written on this topic. Originally applied in two-party contests using the plurality electoral system, it states "that the proportion of seats won by the victorious party varies as the cube of the proportion of votes cast for that party over the country as a whole."[19] The result is that the party with the largest number of votes usually wins a majority of seats with less than 50 percent of the vote. This law was justified mathematically and closely followed in the British general elections of 1935 and 1945. Other researchers ascertained that it was closely approximated for elections in the United States[20] and Australian[21] House of Representatives, and New Zealand[22] and Canadian[23] general elections. Later studies, after the reformulation of the cube law and the addition of other variables, such as district magnitude, number of districts, number of parties, and total size of the electorate and assembly, have applied it fairly successfully not only to plurality electoral systems but to proportional representation ones.[24]

The major criticism of the cube law is that no systematic[25] or theoretical explanation other than a mathematical one has been proposed to account for the relationship between seats and votes. Graham Gudgin and Peter Taylor challenge this criticism and argue that the cube law depends on "the size, spatial concentration, and political homogeneity of social-class clusters"[26] which seem to be similar among countries using the plurality system. Nevertheless, both the supporters and critics of the law agree that a bias does exist since the party with the largest number of votes usually wins a majority of seats with less than 50 percent of the vote.

POLITICAL CONSEQUENCES

Electoral systems and laws influence party competition, or the number of parties that can win seats. Maurice Duverger recognised this in what is often termed a sociological law: "the simple-majority single-ballot system favours the two-party system."[27] He also hypothesized that "the simple-majority system with second ballot and proportional representation favour multi-partism."[28] Later, William Riker revised the law as follows: "Plurality election rules bring about and maintain two-party competition except in countries where (1) third parties nationally are continually one of two parties locally, ..."[29] The revision is required to explain why third parties in Canada, such as the CCF-NDP and Social Credit, have elected MPs. Furthermore, Rein Taagepera and Bernard Grofman have shown that not only the election system but also the ideological cleavages or issue dimensions within a society interact to influence the number of parties, and that the number of parties can be quantified.[30]

The district magnitudes, or the average number of seats assigned to each district or riding, have been shown by Douglas Rae to interact with electoral formulae to influence party competition. He ascertained for twenty countries over a twenty-year period that proportional representation and high district magnitudes lead to nearly proportional results for the relationship between votes and seats, while plurality formulae and low district magnitudes lead to the greatest advantage for large parties over small ones in terms of the relationship between votes and seats.[31] Therefore, the number of parties is reduced, since small parties are often left out of the legislature. Building on the work of Duverger and Rae, Andre Blais and R.K. Carty found that electoral formulae and district magnitude also contribute to the establishment of one-party majority governments,[32] another political consequence.

Turning to Canada specifically, one finds in a study by Alan Cairns that the Canadian electoral system has important consequences for the party system, since it benefits the strongest major party and a weak sectional party (like the CCF-NDP) in terms of the relationship between their votes and seats. The electoral system also exaggerates the importance of cleavages found within sections or provincial boundaries, since contests between parties become contests between sections or provinces[33] such as East versus West or English Canada versus French Canada.

Critics, like J.A.A. Lovink, have argued that Cairns has exaggerated the importance of the electoral system for party policy, overstated its nationally divisive consequences, and underestimated its influence on the effective functioning of the parliamentary system.[34] Furthermore, Lovink has contended that other factors, such as the closeness of the next election, the distribution of safe and competitive seats among the parties, the party's being in or out of power, the size of the party in power in the Commons, and the regional base, policy preferences, and influence of the individual members of the party elite, may contribute to the success and failure of regional political parties and the regional policies that they adopt.[35] However, he has recognised the difficulty in measuring these political effects of the electoral system.[36]

William Irvine has contributed to this disagreement by showing in a recent comparative study that electoral systems do influence regionalism, since politicians do appeal to and spend resources in areas where they have the best chance

of success and ignore regions that are unfavourable to their party or are too
small to offer important political success.[37] This may help explain why the
Mulroney government had been announcing large federal projects and spending
in Quebec and not in Manitoba prior to the 1988 election.

This review has indicated that electoral systems, either alone or in combination with other variables, have important political consequences on the political system, not just in Canada but elsewhere.

REFORM

Changes have been proposed to reduce or eliminate the disadvantages and
biases in the Canadian single-member constituency plurality electoral system,
some of which have been examined previously. These proposed reforms[38] include implementing either proportional representation systems, or a combination of plurality and proportional representation systems, or simply adding
seats to the current plurality system. Although each proposal would solve some
of the weaknesses of the current system, two questions must be asked. First,
will the change to proportional representation or a combination of plurality and
proportional representation bring about perpetual minority government in
Canada?[39] This question leads us back to arguments for and against minority
governments, and about electoral systems producing stability or instability,
both of which were mentioned at the beginning of this essay. The second
question is whether other aspects of representation and their interrelationships
should be considered before changes are made to the electoral system. For
example, what are the appropriate forms of representation for the interrelated
electoral system, provincial governments, federal bureaucracy, interest groups,
and party system?[40] Some different viewpoints concerning various aspects of
representation have been presented in this book.

In summary, then, all electoral systems have strengths and weaknesses,
and all have political consequences, either alone or in combination with other
variables. Finally, proposals for electoral reform ought to consider how changes
to the electoral system might affect other aspects of representation.

Notes

1. Terence H. Qualter, *The Election Process in Canada* (Toronto: McGraw-Hill Company of
   Canada Limited, 1970), 129.
2. Arend Lijphart, *Democracies: Patterns of Majoritarian and Consensus Government in
   Twenty-One Countries* (New Haven: Yale University Press, 1984), 166.
3. Duff Spafford, "The Electoral System of Canada," *American Political Science Review* 64
   (1970): 175.

4. Richard Johnston and Janet Ballantyne, "Geography and the Electoral System," *Canadian Journal of Political Science* 10 (1977): 864.

5. Lijphart, *Democracies*, 150.

6. Ibid., 166.

7. Ibid., 111.

8. For a discussion on minority government, see Eugene Forsey, "The Problem of Minority Government in Canada," *Canadian Journal of Economics and Political Science* 30 (1964): 1-11.

9. J.A. Chandler, "The Plurality Vote: A Reappraisal," *Political Studies* 30 (1982): 92.

10. Michael Laver, "Coalition Bargaining, Interest Representation and Government Responsiveness," *Political Studies* 31 (1983): 655.

11. Lijphart, *Democracies*, 153.

12. Michael Gallagher, "The Political Consequences of the Electoral System in the Republic of Ireland," *Electoral Studies* 5 (1986): 263.

13. Gideon Doron and Richard Kronick, "Single Transferrable Vote: An Example of a Perverse Social Choice Function," *American Journal of Political Science* 21 (1977): 304.

14. Peter J. Taylor and Arend Lijphart, "Proportional Tenure vs Proportional Representation: Introducing a New Debate," *European Journal of Political Research* 13 (1985): 394.

15. Ibid., 394.

16. Lijphart, *Democracies*, 151-156.

17. Andre Blais, "The Classification of Electoral Systems," *European Journal of Political Research* 16 (1988): 108.

18. Ibid., 106.

19. M.G. Kendall and A. Stuart, "The Law of the Cubic Proportion in Election Results," *British Journal of Sociology* 1 (1950): 183.

20. James G. March, "Party Legislative Representation as Function of Election Results," *Public Opinion Quarterly* 21 (1957): 521-542.

21. Joan Rydon, "The Relation of Votes to Seats in Elections for the Australian House of Representatives, 1949-54," *Political Science* 9 (1957): 49-61.

22. R.H. Brookes, "Seats and Votes in New Zealand," *Political Science* 5 (1953): 37-44.

23. Qualter, *The Election*, 137-139. For a comparative study of the law, see Philip A. Schrodt, "A Statistical Study of the Cube Law in Five Electoral Systems," *Political Methodology* 7 (1981): 31-53.

24. Rein Taagepera, "Reformulating the Cube Law for Proportional Representation Elections," *American Political Science Review* 80 (1986): 489-504. For a new application to congressional districts in the United States, see Gary King and Robert X. Browning, "Democratic Representation and Partisan Bias in Congressional Elections," *American Political Science Review* 81 (1987): 1251-1273.

25. N.H. Chi, "Mathematical Modeling of Politics From Electoral Representation to Superpowers' Stockpiles," unpublished paper prepared for delivery at the annual meeting of the Canadian Political Science Association, Winnipeg, Manitoba, June 1986, 13.

26. Graham Gudgin and Peter Taylor, *Seats, Votes, and the Spatial Organization of Elections* (London: Pion Limited, 1979), 202.

27. Maurice Duverger, *Political Parties* (London: Methuen and Co. Ltd., 1964), 217.

28. Ibid., 239.

29. William Riker, "The Two-party System and Duverger's Law: An Essay on the History of Political Science," *American Political Science Review* 76 (1982): 761.

30. Rein Taagepera and Bernard Grofman, "Rethinking Duverger's Law: Predicting the Effective Number of Parties in Plurality and PR Systems—Parties Minus Issues Equals One," *European Journal of Political Research* 13 (1985): 341-352.

31. Douglas Rae, *The Political Consequences of Electoral Laws* (New Haven: Yale University Press, 1967), 138. For an update on some of Rae's findings, see J. O'Loughlin, "District Size and Party Electoral Strength: A Comparison of Sixteen Democracies," *Environment and Planning A* 12 (1980): 247-262.

32. Andre Blais and R.K. Carty, "The Impact of Electoral Formulae on the Creation of Majority Governments," *Electoral Studies* 6 (1987): 216.

33. Alan C. Cairns, "The Electoral System and the Party System in Canada, 1921-1965," *Canadian Journal of Political Science* 1 (1968): 62.

34. J.A.A. Lovink, "On Analysing the Impact of the Electoral System on the Party System in Canada," *Canadian Journal of Political Science* 3 (1970): 499.

35. Ibid., 505.

36. Ibid., 514.

37. William P. Irvine, "Measuring the Effects of Electoral Systems on Regionalism," *Electoral Studies* 7 (1988): 15.

38. For a detailed review of the many Canadian electoral system reforms, see William P. Irvine, "A Review and Evaluation of Electoral System Reform Proposals," in Peter Aucoin, ed., *Institutional Reforms for Representative Government* (Toronto: University of Toronto Press, 1985), 71-109; William P. Irvine, "Power Requires Representation," in George Cooper, ed., *Effective Representation* (Nova Scotia: The Institute for Research on Public Policy, n.d.), 43-49; and Andrew Treusch, "Electoral Reform in Canada: Proposals and Prospects," *Parliamentary Government* 1 (1980): 7-9.

39. Irvine, "A Review," 98-100.

40. For comments on both aspects of representation and on electoral reforms, see John C. Courtney, "Reflections on Reforming the Canadian Electoral System," *Canadian Public Administration* 23 (1980): 427-457.

21. THE CLASSIFICATION OF ELECTORAL SYSTEMS

Andre Blais

Electoral systems are back on the agenda of political science. In the 1980s a significant number of books have been published on the topic (Bogdanor 1981, 1984, Bogdanor and Butler 1983, Brams and Fishburn 1982, Cadart 1983, Dummett 1984, Grofman and Lijphart 1986, Katz 1980, Lijphart and Grofman 1984). This renewed interest has led to interesting new developments. For instance, Taylor and Lijphart (1985) have proposed a new criterion —proportional tenure instead of proportional representation—to evaluate electoral systems. Likewise, Taagepera and Grofman (1985) and Taagepera (1986) have suggested new laws to predict the number of parties, laws which implicitly or explicitly question traditional ways of conceptualizing electoral systems. Taagepera and Grofman (1985) argue that "pluralist elections can be thought of as a special case of list PR, with M = 1" (p.344). Such new findings highlight the necessity of rethinking the classification of electoral systems. The necessity of the task is indeed felt. Lijphart and Grofman (1984) note that they have "come to regard the dichotomy between PR and plurality as misleading" (p.5). Yet, they stick to the "misleading typology," as their own book starts with a discussion of plurality versus proportional representation and even concedes

later on that "PR and plurality may be the main alternatives in choosing an electoral system" (p.7).

The purpose of this paper is to look closely at how electoral systems are classified, to discuss the merits and limits of these classifications and, finally, to propose what I deem to be the most appropriate classification. The nature of the exercise is thus one of conceptual clarification and this sets out the limits of the paper. It does not attempt to describe actual systems, nor to explain their relative popularity or unpopularity, nor to assess their impact. It is assumed, however, that any work in this area has to rely on some sort of classification and that a "better" classification is likely to improve the quality of empirical analyses of the causes and consequences of electoral systems. Even though the approach is basically conceptual, the concerns underlying the analysis are concrete and practical. I am to design a typology which is not only aesthetically satisfactory but also useful and relevant. Finally, I do not wish to start from scratch and I will thus resort to present classifications to the greatest extent possible. Only if these classifications are shown to have serious weaknesses and if a better substitute can be identified will these classifications be replaced. In so doing, I am acknowledging that clarity is not the sole criterion of a sound classification but that simplicity is also crucial and thus that a typology should be as close as possible to the common usage of terms.

I will be concerned with direct electoral systems. Electoral systems are defined as *those*

Andre Blais, "The Classification of Electoral Systems," *European Journal of Political Research* 16 (1988): 99-110. Copyright © (1988) by D. Reidel Publishing Company. (Martinus Nijhoff Publishers.) Reprinted by permission of Kluwer Academic Publishers.

rules which govern the processes by which preferences are articulated as votes and by which these votes are translated into the election of decision-makers. The definition is similar to the one proposed by Rae (1969:14), except for the fact that it refers to decision-makers rather than to governments or parties. As in Rae (1969), electoral systems are equated with electoral laws and the latter are taken to be a subset of election laws, which correspond to the whole set of rules pertaining to the conduct of elections, including suffrage and registration requirements, districting procedures and campaign financing. For the sake of simplicity, I exclude indirect elections, which introduce complexities that are not crucial to the task.

1. EXISTING CLASSIFICATIONS

Surprisingly enough there has not been much thorough thinking about ways of classifying electoral systems. Seldom, in fact, is any comprehensive typology suggested. There have been, however, some classificatory schemes. Table 1 summarizes the one found in Lakeman (1974). The major distinction being made is the one between majority and proportional systems. She also distinguishes relative and absolute majority, and within each, single and multi-member constituencies. Amongst proportional systems the distinction has to do with the presence or absence of a party list and the degree of choice among candidates (in a party list).

Figure 1 presents the classification proposed by Bogdanor (1983). The basic distinction is still between majority (and plurality) and proportional systems and the whole classification is quite similar to Lakeman's. The sole addition concerns the geographical nature (national, regional, local) of the list and of the allocation procedure.

Table 1 Lakeman's Classification of Electoral Systems

1. *Majority systems*
   A. Relative majority
   1. single-member constituencies
   2. multi-member constituencies
   B. Absolute majority
   1. single-member constituencies
   a. second ballot
   b. alternative vote
   2. multi-member constituencies
   a. second ballot
   b. alternative vote
2. *Semi-proportional systems*
   A. Limited vote
   B. Single non-transferable vote
   C. Cumulative vote
3. *Proportional systems*
   A. Party list
   1. no choice between candidates
   2. choice of one candidate within a list
   3. choice of more than one candidate within a list
   4. choice of candidates not confined to one list
   B. Mixed systems
   C. Single transferable vote

Source: Lakeman (1974), Appendix 1.

Taylor and Johnston's (1979) approach is somewhat different (see Table 2). They first identify three major systems: those based on pluralities, those based on the expression of several preferences, and those based on a choice between party lists. In each of the first two, a further subdivision is made according to the number of members per constituency. The major distinction within list systems is between "impersonal" and "personal" votes, which reflects the degree of choice among candidates.

Finally, it is important to examine the classification used in Rae's influential book (1969). In fact, Rae chooses not to propose a

Figure 1   Bogdanor's Classification of Electoral Systems

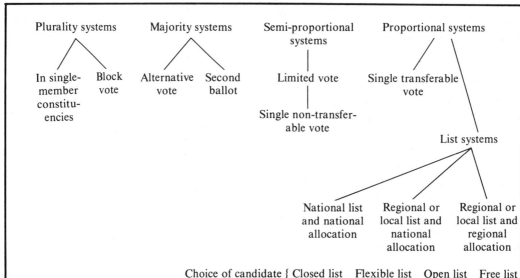

Source: Bogdanor (1983), 17.

full-fledged typology. He rather prefers to treat each of the three components of an electoral system—ballots, districts, and formulae—separately. He distinguishes categorical and ordinal ballots, majoritarian, plurality, and proportional representation formulae; as to districts, they are defined by their magnitude (Table 3).

Before discussing the actual content of these classifications, two comments would seem to be appropriate. First, there is a consensus about the criteria to be employed in the construction of a typology. These criteria, explicitly mentioned by Rae (1969) and by Taylor and Johnston (1979), are: (1) ballots, (2) districts, and (3) formulae. Secondly, the most basic distinction made in all cases is the one between majority (relative or absolute) and proportional systems, and refers to the formula, which is thus deemed to be the most crucial dimension of an electoral system. An exception could be Rae's approach which refrains from proposing a comprehensive typol-

ogy and who even notes that "too much attention is generally given to the effects of electoral formulae, while too little is given to effects of

Table 2   Taylor and Johnston's Classification of Electoral Systems

1. *Plurality systems*
   A. Single-member constituencies
   B. Multi-member constituencies
   C. Weighted plurality systems
2. *Preferential systems*
   A. Single-member constituencies
      1. alternative vote
      2. double ballot
   B. Multi-member constituencies: the single transferable vote
3. *List systems*
   A. Simultaneous lists
   B. Local lists
   C. Party lists
4. *Mixed systems*

Source: Taylor and Johnston (1979), Ch. 2.

Table 3   Rae's Components of Electoral
Systems

1. *Ballots:* categorical and ordinal
2. *Districts:* average magnitude
3. *Electoral formulae:* majority, plurality,
   proportionality

Source: Rae (1969), Ch. 2.

district magnitude" (p. 124), but as a matter of fact Rae himself first examines the effect of different electoral formulae and dedicates much more space to the impact of formulae than to the one of district magnitude or ballot structure. Moreover, nine of his thirteen differential propositions are concerned with electoral formulae. One of my tasks will be to assess the relevance of giving such a priority to formulae.

2. TOWARDS A NEW CLASSIFICATION

I shall proceed in the following fashion. I will first examine the very bases of the classification[1] and clarify the underlying rationale. I will then discuss the actual distinctions that are made with respect to each criterion, assess their merits and limits, and suggest ways to overcome these limits. I will finally look at the order in which the various distinctions are or ought to be considered.

A. The criteria

Rae (1969: 16) argues that the working of an electoral system can be divided into three phases: (1) balloting, (2) districting, and (3) formulae. Likewise, Taylor and Johnston (1979: 40) distinguished three basic characteristics: (1) the number of votes (i.e., ballots); (2) the number of representatives per constituency (i.e., districts); and (3) the way in which votes are allocated (i.e., formulae).

No explicit justification is provided by these authors for these criteria. In order to do so, it seems to me, one should start with the definition of an electoral system and sort out its implications. That definition indicates that the essential function of an electoral system is to translate votes into seats and that, as a consequence, one may distinguish three subsets of rules: (1) those that define how votes are cast, i.e., the ballot structure; (2) those that define how seats are structured, what I will call the constituency structure; and (3) those that define how votes are translated into seats, i.e., the formula. There thus seems to be a rationale for both Rae and Taylor and Johnston's claim that electoral systems have three basic dimensions and that rationale stems logically from the very definition of an electoral system.[2]

B. The distinctions

The major criteria underlying the classification of an electoral system having been clearly identified and justified, it is now possible to consider the actual distinctions that can be made with respect to each of these criteria. In each case, I will start with Rae's classification, which is the most systematic and explicit, point out weaknesses, and suggest ways to improve the classification.

1. The ballot structure

According to Rae (1969), there are two types of ballots: categorical and ordinal. The former "ask the voter to decide which one of the parties he prefers" and the latter "allow the voter to express a more complex, equivocal preference by rankordering the parties" (17). The categories are not exhaustive, as it does not take into account approval voting "which allows a voter to vote for or approve of as many candidates as he wishes" (Brams and

Fishburn 1983: 3), nor the limited or cumulative vote, under which the elector has a certain number of votes (Lakeman 1974: Ch. IV). Indeed, Rae is quite unclear about what exactly he means by ordinal ballots, since he considers panachage, which does not include any rankordering, to be ordinal.

The problem with this classification is that it deals with two dimensions at once. The first dimension is the number of votes allowed, which may be either one or equal to the number of candidates, of seats, or more than one but less than the number of seats (limited). The second dimension is the type of information the voter is asked to provide. As is well known, a piece of information can be nominal, ordinal, or numerical,[3] depending on the level of measurement which it entails (Blalock 1972). Nominal, ordinal, or numerical ballots can thus be distinguished on the basis of the quality of information they convey.

The ballot structure, however, cannot be reduced to these two dimensions. The fact is implicitly acknowledged by Rae (1969) himself, who, in his Table 2.1 which summarizes electoral laws, refers to party list and candidate ballots. Bogdanor (1983), Lakeman (1974), and Taylor and Johnston (1979) also refer to party list systems, though they do not mention the obvious opposite, that is, candidate ballots. Whereas the first two dimensions of the ballot structure—the number of votes and the type of vote—identify *how* voters are asked to reveal their preferences, the latter distinction indicates *whom*—individuals or groups of individuals—they can vote for.

2. The constituency structure

Rae's second distinction pertains to the magnitude of electoral districts. This leads to the well-known distinction between single-member and multi-member districts, which is used by Lakeman, and Taylor and Johnston. The latter distinction, however, hides the fact that there are substantial variations among multi-member districts (Rae 1969, Taagepera 1986) so that district magnitude should be construed as a numerical variable. This, of course, assumes that there are districts, which is obviously not always the case. It is thus essential to distinguish at-large and district elections (Engstrom and McDonald 1986). This shows that the second basic criterion cannot be defined as the district, as Rae (and others) suggest. It rather has to be constituency structure, with its two components: the nature of the constituency (the presence or absence of districts), and its magnitude.

3. The formula

Rae identifies three kinds of electoral formula: majority, plurality, and proportional representation. The distinction—a standard one—is, in our view, quite appropriate. The majority principle, of course, could be subdivided into absolute and qualified majority, as is the case, for instance, in the selection of the Pope (Favre 1977: 132, 177), but such a refinement does not seem to be necessary. Likewise, there are many variants of proportional representation (Taagepera and Shugart 1986) which need not be reviewed here.

Some authors also refer to semi-proportional systems (see Table 1 and Figure 1) to convey the image of a continuum from proportional to majority systems (Lijphart 1984:207). The limited vote and the single non-transferable vote are labelled as semi-proportional because they are "providing only rough accuracy of representation" (Bogdanor 1983: 8). Electoral systems can thus also be defined on the basis of the actual seat-vote relationship, i.e., the *disparity* between shares of votes and shares of seats, which is usually measured at the systems level by the deviation index (Loosemore and Hanby 1971). This type of classification is different from previous ones, in that it deals with the outputs of electoral laws rather than with the laws themselves.[4] No specific rule dictates the degree of disparity of an electoral system but a given *set* of rules defining the ballot structure, the constituency structure and the formula will typically produce a given degree of disparity. So while it is entirely appropriate to characterize electoral systems as being more or less proportional, it should also be clear that the distinction ought to be made on the basis of the actual outcome and not on the basis of the rules themselves. For instance, the single non-transferable vote is a plurality formula, multi-member district, one nominal vote system which produces moderately "proportional" outcomes (Lijphart et al. 1986).[5] The degree of disparity[6] can also be used as an overall characterization of electoral systems when precise information about the specific components is lacking (Blais and Carty 1987b).

The various distinctions that have been made are summarized in Table 4. I would claim that such a classification is superior to those usually proposed in many ways. It is an improvement over Rae's classification in that it clarifies and refines distinctions concerning the ballot structure and adds an important component of the constituency structure (its nature) omitted by Rae. It is even more an improvement over other classifications in that it is systematic. It enables one to identify the basic dimensions of electoral systems as well as the logical connections between these dimensions. It has the property of applying the same criteria to all systems rather than making different distinctions—the logic of which is not made clear—in various classes or sub-classes.

At the same time, the classification proposed here is simple. The number of dimensions (3) or even of total components (6) is small. The links between these dimensions and components are straightforward. Finally—and

this is an important consideration—it does not depart too much from existing classifications, so that it can be integrated into the literature rather easily. Indeed, our whole approach has been to start with what was deemed to be the most valuable classification proposed until now and to improve it whenever weaknesses were detected.

Finally, it should be specified that actual electoral systems may be a mixture of systems. This fact has led some authors to refer to "mixed" systems. But a mixture is a mixture, and the only way to identify a mix is to refer to its basic components, which I hope to have established here.

C. The order of distinctions

The last question to be addressed is whether the distinctions that have been made ought to be considered in any specific order. It was noted earlier that most classifications start with the distinction between majority, plurality, and PR systems and it has to [be] established whether that distinction (or any other) is more basic and should be given some priority. The approach here could be either empirical or conceptual. First, is there any evidence that any dimension or component has greater empirical import? The answer is clearly negative. On the one hand, it is very likely that importance varies according to the type of consequences being examined; dimension "A" may be more significant with respect to party fractionalization but dimension "B" with respect to party democracy. On the other hand, there are likely to be interaction effects: for instance, constituency magnitude may decrease disparity in PR systems but increase it in plurality systems (Taagepera 1984:101). Interaction effects imply that every variable is crucial and that none can be deemed to be the most important of all.

Table 4 The Dimensions in the Classification of Electoral Systems

A. *The Rules*
1. *The ballot structure*
   A. the object of the vote (lists/individuals)
   B. the procedure
   1. the number of votes
   2. the type of vote (nominal/ordinal/numerical)
2. *The constituency structure*
   A. its nature (whole constituency/districts)
   B. its magnitude
3. *The formula* (majority/plurality/proportionality)

B. *The Outcome:* The degree of disparity

On logical grounds, however, it could be argued that in order to make sense of the formula, one has to know the ballot and the constituency structures: ballots and seats have to be defined before votes are translated into seats. This is why, for instance, proportional representation is pointless in single-member districts, a fact implicitly acknowledged by Rae (1969: 140). As to the other two dimensions, it can be shown that constituency structure is prior to ballot structure. The reason is that in order to decide how voters will express their preferences, the desired outcome—how many candidates will be elected in what kind of constituency—has to be ascertained. For instance, there is no use resorting to a list system in a single-member constituency.

The actual implications of such logical considerations ought not to be overstated, however. The order in which the various distinctions are or ought to be examined depend more on theoretical and empirical considerations than on plain logic, such that the order should vary according to the particular topic or framework. In many cases, there may not

be any need for a specific order. The only strong conclusion that can be drawn is thus a negative one: there is no rationale to justify the logical priority given to formulae in most existing classifications.

3. CONCLUSION

When Rae (1969) assessed the state of research in electoral systems twenty years ago, the verdict was quite negative.

> The limitations of the existing literature reflect the three most persistent shortcomings of its component studies: (1) categories of analysis are seldom defined precisely, (2) data are almost never treated systematically, and (3) the standards of verification are usually left inexplicit. The properties of electoral laws—ballot form, districts, "formulae"—are not classified according to explicit, precise categories, and party systems are usually described in similarly vague terms. Data are often confined to the experience of a single country, and the population of facts is either small or, worse yet, undefined. Standards of evidence ... are typically left flexible or even unstated.... (p. 6).

Even though the field is still rather thin, in terms of quantitative output at least (Lijphart 1985), much progress has been made in the recent years, especially with respect to the systematic analysis of the consequences of electoral laws (see Taagepera 1986, Taagepera and Shugart 1986, Taagepera and Grofman 1985, Taylor and Lijphart 1985). However, the classification of electoral systems remains as vague and imprecise as it was twenty years ago, and this has prevented some interesting findings of empirical research to permeate the debate on electoral systems. Indeed, Sartori's (1970) assertion to the effect that "political scientists eminently lack ... a training in logic—indeed in elementary logic" (p. 1033) made also quite a time ago, still holds true (see also Sartori 1986).

In order to fill the gap, I have examined the major classifications that are used in the literature and pointed out their shortcomings. I have shown that the classification of electoral systems ought to take into account three basic dimensions which can be subdivided into six components: (1) the nature of the constituency (whole constituency/districts); (2) constituency magnitude; (3) the object of the vote (lists/individuals); (4) the number of votes allowed; (5) the type of vote (nominal/ordinal/numerical); and (6) the formula (majority/plurality/proportionality). I have also indicated that electoral systems can be distinguished on the basis of their outcomes, in terms of relative disparities between shares of votes and shares of seats.

Acknowledgements

I would like to thank Arend Lijphart, Rein Taagepera, Jean Laponce, Richard Johnston, Ken Carty, Duff Spafford, Vincent Lemieux, and Stephane Dion for their comments on a first draft of this paper.

Notes

1. Clearly identifying the basis of a distinction ensures that one of the fundamental logical criteria of a sound classification—that the distinction proceeds upon one, and only one, principle—is respected. See Cohen and Nagel (1934: 242).

2. Nohlen (1984) distinguished four "areas" of electoral systems: districts, candidacy, ballot structure, and translation of votes into seats. It will be shown later, however, that candidacy (individuals versus lists) can be conceived as a component of the ballot structure, a point implicitly acknowledged by Nohlen, who treats candidacy and ballot forms in the same section (4.2) of his book.

3. I leave aside the distinction between interval and ratio measurement, which is not of practical use here.

4. Taagepera and Shugart (1986) likewise note that electoral systems can be classified by legal inputs and by empirical outputs.

5. In fact, the average deviation index is 6.5% in single non-transferable vote elections, whereas it is 4.7% in PR systems and 11.5% in plurality systems (these figures are computed from the data base described in Blais and Carty 1987a, which includes 20 democracies).

6. I prefer disparity to proportionality or disproportionality in order to better distinguish the formula and the outcome.

References

BLALOCK, HUBERT M. 1972. *Social Statistics*. New York: McGraw-Hill.

BLAIS, ANDRE, and R.K. CARTY. 1987. "The Impact of Electoral Formulae on the Creation of Majority Governments," *Electoral Studies* 6.

BLAIS, ANDRE, and R.K. CARTY. 1987. "Electoral Formulae and Political Stability." University of British Columbia, mimeo.

BOGDANOR, VERNON. 1981. *The People and the Party System: The Referendum and Electoral Reform in British Politics*. Cambridge: Cambridge University Press.

BOGDANOR, VERNON. 1983. "Introduction." In Vernon Bogdanor, and David Butler, eds. *Democracy and Elections: Electoral Systems and Their Political Consequences*. Cambridge: Cambridge University Press.

BOGDANOR, VERNON. 1984. *What is Proportional Representation? A Guide to the Issues.* Oxford: Martin Robertson.

BRAMS, STEVEN J., and PETER C. FISHBURN. 1982. *Approval Voting.* Boston: Birkhauser.

BUTLER, DAVID E. 1984. "Reflections on the Electoral Debate in Great Britain." In Arend Lijphart and Bernard Grofman, eds. *Choosing an Electoral System: Issues and Alternatives.* New York: Praeger.

CADART, JACQUES. 1983. *Les modes de scrutin des dix-huit pays libres de l'Europe occidentale. Leurs resultats et leurs effets comparés.* Paris: Presses universitaires de France.

COHEN, MORRIS R., and ERNEST NAGEL. 1934. *An Introduction to Logic and Scientific Method.* New York: Harcourt.

DUMMETT, MICHAEL. 1984. *Voting Procedures.* Oxford: Clarendon Press.

ENGSTROM, RICHARD L., and MICHAEL D. McDONALD. 1986. "The Effect of At-Large Versus District Elections on Social Representation in U.S. Municipalities." In Bernard Grofman, and Arend Lijphart, eds. *Electoral Laws and Their Political Consequences.* New York: Agathon Press.

FAVRE, PIERRE. 1976. *La decision de majorité.* Paris: Fondation nationale des sciences politiques.

GROFMAN, BERNARD and AREND LIJPHART. 1986. "Introduction." In Bernard Grofman, and Arend Lijphart, eds. *Electoral Laws and Their Political Consequences.* New York: Agathon Press.

KATZ, RICHARD S. 1980. *A Theory of Parties and Electoral Systems.* Baltimore: Johns Hopkins University Press.

LAKEMAN, ENID. 1974. *How Democracies Vote: A Study of Electoral Systems.* London: Faber.

LIJPHART, AREND. 1984. "Trying to Have the Best of Both Worlds: Semi-Proportional and Mixed Systems." In Arend Lijphart, and Bernard Grofman, eds. *Choosing an Electoral System: Issues and Alternatives.* New York: Praeger.

LIJPHART, AREND. 1985. "The Field of Electoral Systems Research: A Critical Survey." *Electoral Studies* 4: 3-14.

LIJPHART, AREND, and BERNARD GROFMAN. 1984. "Choosing An Electoral System." In Arend Lijphart, and Bernard Grofman, eds. *Choosing an Electoral System: Issues and Alternatives.* New York: Praeger.

LIJPHART, AREND, R.L. PINTOR, and Y. SONE. 1986. "The Limited Vote and the Single Non-Transferable Vote: Lessons from the Japanese and Spanish Examples." In Bernard Grofman and Arend Lijphart, eds. *Electoral Laws and Their Political Consequences.* New York: Agathon Press.

LOOSEMORE, J., and V.J. HANBY. 1971. "The Theoretical Limits of Maximum Distortion." *British Journal of Political Science* 1: 467-477.

NOHLEN, DIETER, 1984. *Elections and Electoral Systems.* Trans. Derek Rutter. Bonn: Friedrich-Ebert-Stiftung.

RAE, DOUGLAS. 1969. *The Political Consequences of Electoral Laws.* New Haven: Yale University Press.

SARTORI, GIOVANNI. 1970. "Concept Misformation in Comparative Politics." *American Political Science Review* 64: 1033-1054.

SARTORI, GIOVANNI. 1986. "The Influence of Electoral Systems: Faulty Laws or Faulty Methods?" In Bernard Grofman, and Arend Lijphart, eds. *Electoral Laws and Their Political Consequences.* New York: Agathon Press.

TAAGEPERA, REIN. 1984. "The Effect of District Magnitude and Properties of Two-Seat Districts." In Arend Lijphart, and Bernard Grofman, eds. *Choosing an Electoral System: Issues and Alternatives.* New York: Praeger.

TAAGEPERA, REIN. 1986. "Reformulating the Cube Law for Proportional Representation Elections." *American Political Science Review* 80: 489-505.

TAAGEPERA, REIN, and BERNARD GROFMAN. 1985. "Rethinking Duverger's Law: Predicting the Effective Number of Parties in Plurality and PR Systems—Parties Minus Issues Equals One." *European Journal of Political Research* 13:341-353.

TAAGEPERA, REIN, and MATTHEW SOBERG SHUGART. 1986. *Seats and Votes: The Effects and Determinants of Electoral Systems.* University of California, Irvine, manuscript.

TAYLOR, PETER J., and AREND LIJPHART. 1985. "Proportional Tenure vs. Proportional Representation: Introducing a New Debate." *European Journal of Political Research* 13: 387-399.

TAYLOR, P.J., and R.J. JOHNSTON. 1979. *Geography of Elections.* New York: Holmes and Meier.

22. THE ELECTORAL SYSTEM OF CANADA

Duff Spafford

The working of the electoral system in Canada is investigated in this paper. The object is to identify the more important factors which go to determine the share of seats in the federal House of Commons won by a political party at a general election. Factors considered are share of vote, distribution of the vote and number of candidates in the field. The responsiveness of share of seats to variations in these factors is estimated by fitting linear equations by least squares to data for the fourteen federal general elections which took place in Canada between 1921 and 1965.

1. THE REPRESENTATION FUNCTION

The single-member-constituency system of election has cast up some rather puzzling results in Canada. Exhibited in Table 1 are shares of seats and shares of vote won by the parties contesting the general elections of 1930 and 1935. Two things stand out from the results. The first is that the electoral system apportions seats among the parties in a far from even-handed way: the party gaining the largest proportion of the vote is generously rewarded with seats at the expense of the other parties. This tendency, it should be said, is not

Duff Spafford, "The Electoral System of Canada," *American Political Science Review* 64 (1970): 168-176. Reprinted with permission of the author and The American Political Science Association.

peculiar to Canada but is observed wherever the single-member-constituency system is used.[1] Second, the system seems to suffer from a lack of consistency. Compare the fortunes of the Liberal party in the two elections: in 1935, with a slightly reduced vote, the party won close to double the share of seats it held in 1930. Again, compare the performance of the Progressive party in 1930 with that of the Reconstruction party in 1935. There is little evidence here of a simple relationship between a party's share of seats and its share of vote.

Now there is nothing in the rules of the single-member-constituency system of election to ensure that a party's share of seats will be related in a predictable way to its share of vote. In a two-party system, a party winning 40 percent of the vote might win anything from nil to close to 80 percent of the seats, depending on how the vote is distributed among the constituencies; with more than two parties, the range of possible outcomes is even greater. In fact, however, share of seats does tend to be closely dependent on share of vote in single-member-constituency systems—at least outside Canada. Dahl has fitted linear equations to time-series data for Congressional elections in the United States and found that more than nine tenths of the variance of share of seats was capable of explanation by the behaviour of share of vote.[2] In Great Britain, the so-called "cube law," which states that the proportion which party A's share of seats bears to party B's will vary as the cube of the proportion of A's share of vote to B's, has yielded quite accurate predictions of election outcomes. The implied relationship between share of seats and share of vote is non-linear. The rationale of the cube law has been investigated by the British statisticians Kendall and Stuart, who discovered that the construct rested on certain conditions governing the distribution of the proportions of vote won by a party in the constituencies.[3] The conditions were found to be approximately satisfied in Great Britain.

Table 1   Results of General Elections in Canada, 1930 and 1935

Party	Election of 1930		Election of 1935	
	Seats (%)	Vote (%)	Seats (%)	Vote (%)
Liberal	37.1	45.5	70.6	44.9
Conservative	55.9	48.7	16.3	29.6
Progressive	4.9	3.2	—	—
Co-operative Commonwealth Federation	-	-	2.9	8.9
Social Credit	-	-	6.9	4.1
Reconstruction	-	-	0.4	8.7
Other	2.0	2.7	2.9	3.7

Source: Howard A. Scarrow, *Canada Votes*, (New Orleans, 1962), Tables 24 and 28.

In Canada, neither the linear nor the cube-law hypothesis offers a convincing account of election outcomes. For the major (Liberal and Conservative) parties over the period from 1921 to 1965, no more than about three-quarters of the variance of share of seats can be explained by changes in share of vote, assuming linearity. The cube law, in its original (two-party) form, performs no better.[4] Considering that Canada is a multi-party system, the inapplicability of the cube law is not surprising. The mechanics of the cube law require, among other things, that the proportion of the vote needed to win a contest be one-half. In a three- or four-party system, a contest can be won with a good deal less than one-half of the vote, and the required proportion generally cannot be specified a priori.

There are, of course, many other forms of the relationship between a party's share of vote and its share of seats which might be canvassed. It seems unlikely, however, that the problem of explaining election outcomes in Canada is wholly or even largely one of discovering the correct functional form of a two-variable relationship. What does seem likely is that there are factors other than share of vote which play a part in the determination of election outcomes. To elicit the influence of these factors a multivariate analysis must be undertaken.

We begin by positing the dependence of the *i*th party's share of seats S_i on its share of vote V_i, K variables $X_1, \cdots, X_k$, and a variable *u*:

$$S_i = f(V_i; X_1, \cdots, X_k; u)$$

It is convenient to have a name for this relation, and "representation function" seems apt. The variables $X_1, \cdots, X_k$ are as yet unspecified factors which, along with V_i, exert systematic influences on S_i. The remaining variable, *u*, is an error term whose inclusion acknowledges the possibility of inexactness arising from incomplete specification, data errors and random disturbances. The expected value of *u* is assumed to be zero.

Two kinds of decisions must be made in the course of specifying the representation function. First, the form of the dependence of S_i on the independent variables has to be decided upon. We adopt the assumption of linear form, principally because of its simplicity. (Something more will be said about this assumption later on.) Second, the variables $X_1, \cdots X_k$ must be specified. Variables considered are numbers of candidates placed in the field by the several parties and an aspect of the distribution of the parties' vote among the constituencies. We discuss now the ways in which these variables may be supposed to figure in the representation function.

Number of candidates. The number of candidates presenting themselves for election has varied a great deal in recent Canadian experience. The major parties usually have contested all or almost all constituencies, though in several elections they named no candidates in many. The number of other ("minor-party") candidates has varied from fewer than one hundred to more than five hundred.

The proportion of vote necessary for victory in a constituency can be taken to be dependent in a loose way on the number of candidates in contention. For two candidates, something more than one-half of the vote is required; for three, it might be little more than one-third (though it might be a great deal more); for four, perhaps little more than one-quarter; and so on. A party winning 40 percent of the national vote might win relatively few seats in a two-party contest. In an election involving four parties, 40 percent of the national vote might be enough to win a majority of seats.

It is worthwhile to inquire more closely into the way in which variations in the number of candidates affect election outcomes. Suppose there are three parties, *A, B,* and *C*; and suppose further, for the sake of tidiness, that the voting population is fixed from election to election and everyone turns out. Each of the three parties enters a candidate in all *n* constituencies in election I. In a constituency *J*, *C*'s candidate finished a poor third in election I, and *C* does not name a candidate in *J* in election II. Imagine now that in the other *n*-1 constituencies the results of election II are identical in every respect with those of election I. The only changes in the system between elections I and II, then, are those following from *C*'s vacating *J*.

By abandoning a (by hypothesis) hopeless cause in *J*, party *C* will have augmented the "efficiency" of its vote in the following sense: the party wins the same number of seats as before, but with a smaller share of the total vote. We may be permitted to infer from this that, had it won as large a share of vote in II as in I, *C* could have won more seats in II.[5] That is, for a given share of vote, a party is predicted to win more seats when the number of constituencies it enters is reduced. There is a good deal of common sense in this prediction, which simply says that a given vote will yield more seats for a party when it is spread over fewer candidates.

Can it be taken for granted that the same reasoning applies when a party *increases* the number of constituencies it enters? There is a certain asymmetry here. It could be supposed that a party would abandon only palpably hopeless causes. One cannot suppose, however, that every new candidature is of the hopeless variety: the facts state otherwise. It remains, however, that the probability of a newcomer's winning a seat is quite small. Further, against the effects of a victory on a party's efficiency might have to be set the effects of perhaps a dozen defeats. The asymmetry must be allowed to stand, but it does not necessarily force a revision of the hypothesis that a party's efficiency will vary inversely with the number of its candidates.

We revert now to the simple model to examine the consequences for *A* and *B* of *C*'s decision not to contest *J*. Now it is clear that, because *C* wins the same number of seats with a smaller share of the vote in election II, *A* and *B taken together* must win the same number of seats with a larger share of the vote. At least one and possibly both of *A* and *B* will suffer a worsening in efficiency.

There is one case in which it can be predicted confidently that the efficiency of both *A* and *B* will be reduced. This case involves the following assumptions: (a) that, as a result of *C*'s vacating *J*, the number of votes going to each of *A* and *B* in *J* is larger; (b) that *C*'s stepping down does not cause the decision in *J* to be different. Assumption (a) seems fairly plausible even though arguable. It amounts to the supposition that, in election II, some of *C*'s adherents from election I days will go over to *A* and some will go over to *B*. Assumption (b) has somewhat less to recommend it. The former adherents of *C* might divide between *A* and *B* in such a way as to alter the decision. Suppose that *A* won *J* in election I but that in election II, with *C*'s candidate absent, *B* emerged the victor. The efficiency of *A*'s vote clearly will have deteriorated: the party wins a larger vote and fewer seats than before. But the effect on the efficiency of *B*, which wins a larger vote as well as more seats, is problematical. Since the assumptions represent sufficient but not necessary conditions, a worsening of *B*'s efficiency cannot be ruled out. Neither, however, can it be predicted with assurance.

In summary, our expectations take the following form. When a party reduces the number of its candidates, other things being equal, its efficiency will be improved; that is, for a given share of vote, the party will win more seats. The efficiency of at least one of its rivals must be reduced and that of all rivals might be. Effects of opposite kind can be anticipated throughout when a party increases the number of constituencies entered.

In the empirical work to follow, the number of candidates placed in the field by the *i*th party is denoted by N_i. For ease of interpretation of the coefficients N_i is expressed on the basis of an electoral system comprising 265 constituencies. (The actual number of seats varied over the 1921-65 period from 235 to 265.)

Distribution of the Vote. The share of seats won by a party will depend critically on the way in which its vote is distributed among the constituencies. The handling of distributional factors in an aggregative analysis is, it must be conceded, an awkward matter. Further, where more than two parties contend, as in Canada, such factors can be highly complex. There is, however, at least one aspect of the distribution of the vote which can be incorporated into the present analysis.

In Canada, at least until the most recent (1966) redistribution, substantial variation in the populations of constituencies has been permitted. Constituency populations have tended, moreover, to vary along a dimension which is relevant to the determination of voters' party preferences. Rural constituencies generally have contained fewer voters than urban constituencies. Because a rural seat contains fewer voters, it can be won with a smaller proportion of the *national* vote than is required to win an urban seat, other things being equal. Thus, the share of vote required to win a given share of seats might be relatively small if the vote is concentrated in small rural constituencies. It will be convenient to state the hypothesis in an alternative form: a party will win more (fewer) seats for a given share of vote, other things being equal, the greater its relative strength in small (large) constituencies.

To test this hypothesis it is necessary to devise an index representing the relative strength of a party in size-classes of constituencies. An index, denoted by B_i, was constructed in the following way. Constituencies larger than mean size (according to the number of votes cast) were identified, and the aggregate share of vote cast in favour of the *i*-th party in those constituencies calculated. This large-constituency share was then divided by V_i, the share of the vote received by the party over all constituencies, and the resulting quotient was multiplied by 100. An index of $B_i=110$, for instance, would connote that the i-th party's performance in large constituencies was 10 percent better, in relative terms, than its performance in all constituencies (e.g., the party might have won 55 percent of the aggregate vote in large constituencies and 50 percent of the aggregate vote nationally). A value of 100 would indicate that the party did equally well in large constituencies and all constituencies. The expectation is that the share of seats won by the ith party will vary inversely with B_i, other factors held constant.

II. EMPIRICAL ESTIMATES

We turn now to the task of estimating representation functions embodying the hypotheses set out. The representation functions are estimated by fitting linear regression equations to observed values of the relevant variables. The data pertain to the fourteen elections which took place in Canada from 1921 to 1965 and are displayed in an Appendix. Candidates are divided exhaustively into three groups: Conservative, Liberal and "minor-party," the latter group being a conglomerate of all candidates who are neither Conservative nor Liberal. Symbols used to present the variables and to identify political parties are listed below:

S_i: Share of seats (percent) won by the i-th party;

V_i: Share of vote (percent) won by the i-th party;

N_i: Number of candidates (basis 265 constituencies) placed in the field by the i-th party;

B_i: Index of relative performance of the i-th party in constituencies larger than mean size;

i = C: Subscript identifying Conservative party;

i = L: Subscript identifying Liberal party;

i = M: Subscript identifying minor parties.

Regression equations. For the Conservative party, S_C initially was regressed on the variables V_C, N_C, B_C, N_L, and N_M. It was found

that the coefficient of N_L was effectively zero; seemingly, conservative share of seats has not been sensitive to changes in the number of Liberal candidates., The variable was dropped and the equation fitted again, with the outcome:[6]

$$(1) \quad S_C = 2.897^{**}V_C - 0.241^{**}N_C - 0.819^*B_C$$
$$\quad\quad\quad (0.198) \quad\quad (0.099) \quad\quad (0.277)$$

$$+ 0.0550^{**}N_M + 53.49$$
$$(0.0098)$$

$$\overline{R}^2 = .964, \quad\quad S.E.E. = 3.39$$

The results are, on the whole, quite gratifying. Fit is good, all coefficients can be supposed with some confidence to differ from zero, and signs capable of prior prediction are as expected. The Conservative party's share of seats is shown to vary directly with its own share of vote and with the number of minor-party candidates, and inversely with the number of its own candidates and with its relative popularity in larger-than-average constituencies, other things held constant in each case. The standard error of estimate at 3.39 (percent of total seats) amounts to about nine seats in a 265-seat House of Commons.

A trial fitting of the representation function for the Liberal party turned up one variable (B_L) whose coefficient fell somewhat short of conventional significance levels and another (N_C) whose coefficient was patently insignificant. The latter only was discarded, and the equation became:

$$(2) \quad S_L = 3.217^{**}V_L - 0.356^{**}N_L - 0.821^*B_L$$
$$\quad\quad\quad (0.303) \quad\quad (0.146) \quad\quad (0.598)$$

$$+ 0.0656^{**}N_M + 62.85$$
$$(0.0129)$$

$$\overline{R}^2 = .902, \quad\quad S.E.E. = 4.97$$

Again, signs are as expected, although the coefficient of B_L is not significant. With $\overline{R}^2$ of .902 the fit of the equation is somewhat less close than that of the Conservative equation.

A rather different specification was adopted for the minor-party equation. It did not seem appropriate in the case of such a conglomerate to use an index of relative strength in constituencies of different sizes. Also, when V_M, N_M, N_C, and N_L were entered together as explanatory variables, a severe problem of collinearity arose. Minor-party share of vote is highly dependent on the number of candidates placed in the field by the several parties, and the consequent redundancy of information when the variables are entered in each other's presence makes it difficult to obtain reliable estimates of the coefficients.[7] If an estimate was to be made at all, it seemed necessary to jettison one or more of the variables. Unfortunately, all would appear to belong in the representation function, and dropping variables might be merely to exchange one source of unreliability for another. We might suppose, however, that, whatever other variables are relevant, V_M and N_M ought to figure in the equation.

(3) $\quad S_M = 1.237^{**} V_M - 0.0360^{**} N_M + 0.99$
$\qquad (0.233) \qquad (0.0117)$
$\qquad \overline{R}^2 = .718, \quad \text{S.E.E.} = 3.47$

Both coefficients are significant and the $\overline{R}^2$ is of a respectable order. However, the arbitrariness of this specification becomes evident when N_M is replaced by N_L. The fit of this equation (not shown) is as close as that of (3), and the coefficient of N_L turns out to be highly significant and *negative*. Replacing N_L in turn by N_C, the latter's coefficient also bears a negative sign though it is not significant. The negative signs persist through all configurations of variables. There are indications here that when a major party withdraws from contests the efficiency of the minor-party vote is *improved*, which in turn suggests that commonly such contests are won by minor-party candidates.[8] The tactics of multi-party politics no doubt figure in this phenomenon. A major party might withdraw from a contest with the hope

of delivering the constituency into minor-party hands and thwarting the ambitions of the other major party; or, recognizing that a minor-party candidate will win in any case, the major party might withdraw as a gesture of appeasement. The matter is, perhaps, of more historical than current interest, since in the last half-dozen elections the major parties have fielded complete slates of candidates with only a few exceptions.

The empirical estimates establish the importance of several factors in the working of the electoral system in Canada. In the case of the Conservative party, as many as four variables are shown to contribute significantly to the explanation of share of seats won; in the case of the Liberals, three. As noted, share of vote alone is able to account for only about three-quarters of the variance of share of seats won by a major party. The addition of numbers-of-candidates variables and an index representing one aspect of the distribution of the vote raises the proportion of variance explained to nine-tenths or higher. For the minor parties, the relevance of at least one variable besides share of vote is suggested, though because of collinearity the precise identity of the other variable or variables remains in doubt.

Some features of the system. From the coefficients estimated in equations (1)-(3) can be elicited a good deal of information concerning the working of the electoral system in Canada. We confine attention here to a few of the more important and interesting results.

The relationship which perhaps is of most interest is that between a party's share of seats and its share of vote when other factors are held constant. For the major parties, according to the coefficients of V_C and V_L in (1) and (2), a change in share of vote of one percentage point is transformed into a change in share of seats of about three percentage points in the same direction. Thus, in a House of Commons of 265 seats, an additional percentage point of vote won by a party would gain about eight seats. It is interesting that the estimated "incremental transformation rate" of 3.0 or thereabouts is quite close to the rate yielded by the cube law in Great Britain and to that estimated for Congressional elections in the United States.[9] That three systems should exhibit a regularity of this kind is indeed remarkable in view of the lack of formal restrictions on the transformation rate under the single-member-constituency method of election.

The transformation rate for the minor parties is substantially lower than the major-party rate. In fact, the coefficient of V_M in (3) is less than half those of V_C in (1) and V_L in (2). The minor parties are at a relative disadvantage, the most plausible explanation of which is the generally lower level of the minor-party vote.

This, however, raises a question concerning the form of the relationship between share of seats and share of vote. If, in general, the transformation rate varies with share of vote, the linearity assumption relied on thus far might not be suitable. Several rough-and-ready tests for non-linearity were carried out, and in none was its presence indicated. On the other hand, experimentation with disaggregated data, in which share of vote varied over a wide range, did turn up strong evidence of non-linearity. The following tentative explanation is offered: the underlying relationship between a party's share of seats and its share of vote is in fact non-linear; but over the limited range in which share of vote is observed in the present samples, the relationship can be closely approximated by a straight line.

When the number of minor-party candidates is increased, the share of seats won by a major party for a given own share of vote is augmented. According to equation (1), the increase in Conservative share of seats when an additional minor-party candidate enters the field is .055 percent (of the seats in the House); equation (2) offers an estimate of .066 percent in respect of the Liberals. There is no necessity

Figure 1

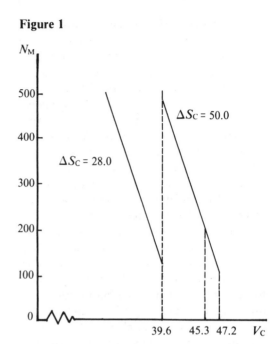

for the two coefficients to be equal: changes in minor-party activity could have quite different effects on the two major parties. However, the two sample coefficients here are within one standard error of each other, and the inference of no difference would seem to be called for.

The dependence of major-party share of seats on the number of minor-party candidates explains the ability of parties to win majorities in the House of Commons with much less than a majority of the vote cast in their favour. Figure 1 provides an illustration, using the coefficients for the Conservative party estimated in equation (1). Measured along the horizontal axis is V_C, and along the vertical axis N_M. The slanted lines ("equal-representation lines") trace out combinations of V_C and N_M which yield stated levels of S_C.[10] (It is assumed that the Conservatives contest all seats and perform equally well in large and small constituencies, i.e., $N_C = 265$ and $B_C = 100$). With 100 minor-party candidates in the field the Conservatives are estimated to require 47.2 percent of the vote to win 50 percent of the seats. Setting N_M at 200, some 45.3 percent of the vote is needed by the major party to win 50 percent of the seats; at 500, only 39.6 percent. In contrast, 39.6 percent of the vote is indicated to yield only about 28 percent of the seats when there are as few as 100 minor-party candidates in the field.

Since the independent variables in an equation are related to a common variable S_i, they can be brought into relation with each other to answer questions of this sort: By what amount must one independent variable be changed to compensate for the effect on S_i of a given change in another independent variable? Of special interest is the way in which variations in the "other" factors compensate for gains and losses in a party's voting support.

In this connection, the slope of the equal-representation lines in Figure 1 can be given a useful interpretation. The slope indicates the rate at which V_C must be substituted for N_M to maintain constant S_C. Holding N_C and B_C constant, we can write, from equation (1),

$$\Delta S_C = 2.897 \, \Delta V_C + 0.55 \Delta N_M$$

where Δ stands for "change in." Along a given equal-representation line, $\Delta S_C = 0$; hence,

$$O = 2.897 \, \Delta V_C + 0.055 \Delta N_M,$$

and the slope of the equal-representation line is

$$\frac{\Delta N_M}{\Delta V_C} = -\frac{2.897}{0.055}$$
$$= -52.7$$

Thus, an increase of about 53 in the number of minor-party candidates will have an effect on Conservative share of seats which just compensates for the effect of a decrease in its (the Conservative party's) share of vote of one percentage point. Put otherwise, the Conservatives can give up one percent of the vote for every 53 additional minor-party candidates in the field and maintain a given share of seats, other factors held constant.

Substitution rates can be calculated in a similar way to V_C in substitution with the other independent variables. Taking B_C,

$$\frac{\Delta B_C}{\Delta V_C} = 3.5$$

If there were a shift in the party's base of support towards small constituencies such that B_C fell by 3.5 (e.g., from 100 to 96.5) the party could win a given share of seats with a share of vote one percentage point smaller. Finally, for N_C,

$$\frac{\Delta N_C}{\Delta V_C} = 12.0$$

Withdrawing 12 Conservative candidates from the field has the same effect on S_C for given V_C as an increase in V_C of one percentage point. Substitution rates for the Liberal party, calculated from the coefficients in equation (2), are fairly similar throughout.

It would be useful, finally, to know something about the relative importance of the several independent variables in producing changes in election outcomes. As they stand, the regression coefficients do not offer a reli-

Table 2 Standard Regression Coefficients (Beta-weights)

Equation	V_C	V_L	V_M	N_C	N_L	N_M	B_C	B_L
(1)	1.37			-0.18		0.47	-0.22	
(2)		1.01			-0.31	0.64		-0.13
(3)			1.47			-0.85		

Source: Calculated from coefficients of Equations (1)-(3) and standard deviations of variables.

able basis for judging the relative importance of the variables: the size of a coefficient will reflect the (often arbitrarily-selected) units in which the independent variable is measured. For comparison to be meaningful, some standardization procedure is needed. Here we may make use of standard regression coefficients, often called Beta-weights, which show the change in the dependent variable, in own-standard deviation units, when an independent variable is changed by one own-standard deviation.[11] Beta-weights for the variables in equations (1)-(3) are shown in Table 2.

On the basis of the absolute values of the Beta-weights, own share of vote is the independent variable to which share of seats is most responsive in all three cases: a not unexpected result. Ranking next in importance throughout is number of minor-party candidates. We may conjecture that the seemingly eccentric changes in party standings which occur from time to time in Canadian elections are due largely to changes in the number of minor-party candidates. Reverting to the data of Table 1, it is doubtlessly significant that fewer than 100 minor-party candidates contested the election of 1930 while more than 400 contested that of 1935. The very substantial increase in minor-party participation in 1935 led to a correspondingly substantial increase in the efficiency of the Liberal vote.

Qualifications and a test. The empirical estimates are subject to several qualifications which ought to be recorded. First, certain specification problems which affect the interpretation of the coefficients are left unresolved. In the case of the minor parties, several formulations produced equally good fits; the major-party equations, fortunately, yielded less ambiguous results. The difficulties with the minor-party equation may be in part the result of lumping together all "other" candidates. Disaggregation would be desirable, but it would mean reducing the size of an already very small sample (no one third party's life spans the sample period). Second, it is possible that the estimated coefficients are biased because of the omission of relevant variables. The only way to guard against such biases is to bring all likely variables within the compass of he analysis. A few other variables were tried, but none appeared to add anything. It may be worth reporting that attempts to uncover possible effects of the periodic re-drawing of constituency boundaries (the effects assumed to be in favour of the party in power) turned up nothing. The results may reflect the method, which was distinctly unrefined. Third, a doubt concerning one of the variables must be confessed to. The index B_i is constructed from data which are subject to the influence of other explanatory variables, and its independence is open to question. The index is moderately correlated in the sample with several other variables (see correlation matrix, Appendix).

The general election which took place in Canada in 1968 offers a limited but valuable opportunity to test the capabilities of the equations. The relevant data (recorded in the Appendix) were inserted into equations (1)-(3) to produce the estimates shown in Table 3. For the Liberals and the minor parties, the equations perform very well; the estimate for the Conservatives is not so close to the mark. The results are as good as or better than one might have expected on the basis of the standard errors of estimate in the sample period.

Table 3   Estimated and Actual Shares of Seats, Election of 1968

Party	Estimated Share of Seats (%)	Actual Share of Seats (%)	Error (%)
Conservative	31.5	27.3	+4.2
Liberal	57.3	58.7	−1.4
Minor Parties	13.6	14.0	−0.4

Source: Estimated share of seats obtained by inserting values of independent variables (see Appendix) into equations (1), (2), and (3).

III. CONCLUSIONS

The most general conclusion to be drawn from the analysis is that the determination of election outcomes in Canada is a complex process in which the influences of several factors combine. By the use of regression analysis it has been possible to tentatively identify several—hopefully, the most important—variables which figure in the process. For the major parties, the variables shown to be relevant are own share of vote, number of own candidates, number of minor-party candidates and (in one case) relative strength of the major party in size-classes of constituencies. Certain problems stood in the way of a satisfactory account of minor-party share of seats, but the importance of at least one variable besides share of vote is indicated.

For the specifications adopted, the variable ranking next in importance to own share of vote is number of minor-party candidates. The greater the number of minor-party candidates in the field, the smaller the share of vote needed by a major party to attain a given share of seats, other things remaining constant. The regression coefficients provide a quantitative measure of the effect on the efficiency of the major-party vote of changes in the level of minor-party activity.

It is estimated that, for the major parties, an increase in share of vote of one percentage point will bring about an increase in share of seats of about three percentage points. This is similar to rates calculated for the two-party systems of Great Britain and the United States, but much larger than the rate estimated here for the minor parties in Canada.

In respect of method, the study offers some evidence of the potentialities of multiple regression analysis in the investigation of electoral systems. There can be few electoral systems so innocent of complexity that their working can be adequately described in a relationship between two variables, share of seats and share of vote. Other factors can—in Canada, at least, do—affect election outcomes.

Notes

* I wish to thank John C. Courtney and Peter C. Dooley for helpful criticism. Some preliminary results of this study were reported in a paper read at the annual meeting of the Canadian Political Science Association in 1967.

1. See Maurice Duverger, *Political Parties: Their Organiza tion and Activity in the Modern State* (London, 1954), esp. 373-374; and Douglas W. Rae, *The Political Consequences of Electoral Laws* (New Haven, 1967).

2. Robert A. Dahl, *A Preface to Democratic Theory* (Chicago, 1956), 148-149. Dahl regresses Democratic share of *major-party* seats on that party's share of *major-party* vote.

3. M.G. Kendall and A. Stuart, "The Law of the Cubic Proportion in Election Results," *British Journal of Sociology* 1 (1950): 183-196.

4. T.H. Qualter, in a recent study, puts forward a "modified cube law" for the multi-party case and applies it to Canada. Because of differences in intent and method it is difficult to compare Qualter's results with those presented here. See. T.H. Qualter, "Seats and Votes: An Application of the Cube Law to the Canadian Electoral System," *Canadian Journal of Political Science* 1 (1968): 336-344. It may be noted that both the two-party cube law and Qualter's "modified cube law" are special cases of the "weak proportionality" function proposed by Theil. See Henri Theil, "The Desired Political Entropy," *American Political Science Review* LXIII (June 1969): 521-525.

5. The inference would be fully justified if the representation function were continuous and

monotonic increasing. Obviously this requirement is not met in fact: the addition of a handful of votes to a party's total will not always result in additional seats won. It is sufficient for present purposes to assume that the probability of a party's winning an additional seat with a modest augmentation of its vote is not zero.

6. Shown in parentheses below the sample coefficients are the corresponding standard errors; $\bar{R}^2$ is the coefficient of determination corrected for degrees of freedom; S.E.E. is the standard error of estimate. Asterisks raised above the coefficients indicate significance level according to a two-tailed t-test, as follows: **significant at the .01 level; *significant at the .05 level. A useful and relatively non-technical introduction to regression analysis is Mordecai Ezekiel and Karl A. Fox, *Methods of Correlation and Regression Analysis* 3e (New York, 1959).

7. For a succinct discussion of this problem consult H.M. Blalock, Jr., "Correlated Independent Variables: The Problem of Multicollinearity," *Social Forces* 42 (1963): 233-237.

8. It seems clear that the minor parties have, on the whole, performed better when they were unopposed by one of the major parties, though the results are mixed. In the election of 1921, for example, the Liberal party did not name candidates in 33 constituencies, and in 28 of them minor-party candidates were successful; the Conservative party passed up 27 seats, of which only five were won by minor-party candidates.

9. The cube law implies a non-linear relationship between share of seats and share of vote, i.e., the incremental transformation rate is not a constant but rather varies with share of vote. However, James G. Marsh reports that for shares of vote ranging from 40 percent to 60 percent the cube law can be approximated closely by a linear equation which fixes the transformation rate at about 2.8. See James G. Marsh, "Party Legislative Representation as a Function of Election Results," *The Public Opinion Quarterly* XXI (1957/58): 521-542. Dahl (*A Preface to Democratic Theory* 148-149) elicited transformation rates for the Democratic party of 2.50 in House of Representatives elections and 3.02 in Senate elections.

10. The slanted (equal-representation) lines are truncated at $N_M = 100$ and $N_M = 500$ to remain well within the range of observed values of the variable in the sample.

11. See H.M. Blalock, Jr., *Social Statistics* (New York, 1960), 345.

APPENDIX
Data and Sources
Data:

Election	S_L	S_C	S_M	V_L	V_C	V_M	N_L	N_C	N_M	B_L	B_C
1921	49.4	21.3	29.4	40.7	30.3	29.0	228	235	254	96	97
1925	40.4	47.3	12.2	39.8	46.5	13.8	232	253	141	96	110
1926	52.2	37.1	10.6	46.1	45.3	8.7	238	252	83	98	106
1930	37.1	55.9	6.9	45.5	48.7	5.9	253	252	85	101	101
1935	70.6	16.3	13.1	44.9	29.6	25.4	263	251	450	97	100
1940	73.9	16.3	9.8	51.5	30.7	17.9	263	230	228	98	101
1945	51.0	27.3	21.6	41.1	27.4	31.5	262	221	545	100	101
1949	73.7	15.6	10.7	49.5	29.7	20.8	263	252	342	98	102
1953	64.5	19.2	16.3	48.9	31.0	20.1	265	248	384	95	102
1957	39.6	42.3	18.1	40.9	38.9	20.1	265	257	339	97	104
1958	18.5	78.5	3.0	33.6	53.6	12.8	265	265	301	97	101
1962	37.7	43.8	18.5	37.2	37.3	25.6	264	265	486	101	95
1963	48.7	35.8	15.5	41.7	32.8	25.4	265	265	492	104	93
1965	49.4	36.6	14.0	40.2	32.4	27.4	265	265	481	101	93
1968*	58.7	27.3	14.0	45.5	31.4	23.1	264	264	443	106	90

Sources: S_i, V_i, 1921-1958: H.A. Scarrow, *Canada Votes* (New Orleans, 1962); 1962-1968: *Report of the Chief Electoral Officer* (Ottawa) 25th-28th general elections; N_i, B_i computed from data in above sources, as follows:

$$N_i = \frac{265 n_i}{n}$$

where n_i is the number of candidates entered by the i-th party and n is the total number of seats in the (forthcoming) House of Commons;

$$B_i = 100 \left(\frac{\Sigma v_{ij}}{\Sigma v_j} \div V_i \right) \qquad v_j > \bar{v},$$

where v_{ij} is the number of votes won by the i-th party in the j-th constituency and $\bar{v}$ the mean number of votes cast in the n constituencies. Where not all constituencies were entered by the i-th party, data for uncontested constituencies were deleted in the computation of the index.

Data used differ slightly in some instances from those contained in the recent compilation by J.M. Beck in *Pendulum of Power* (Scarborough, 1968), which came to my attention too late to permit use here. The differences are small, and cannot be supposed to affect the argument.

*Not used in the calculation of regression coefficients.

Correlation Between Explanatory Variables

	V_L	V_C	V_M	N_L	N_C	N_M	B_L	B_C
V_L	1	−.43	−.17	.06	−.43	−.25	−.16	.22
V_C		1.00	−.81	−.27	.47	−.63	−.07	.42
V_M			1.00	.25	−.24	.85	.18	−.60
N_L				1.00	.24	.66	.35	−.42
N_C					1.00	.08	.29	−.24
N_M						1.00	.37	−.64
B_L							1.00	−.65
B_C								1.00

23. GEOGRAPHY AND THE ELECTORAL SYSTEM[*]

Richard Johnston and Janet Ballantyne

Does the single-member plurality electoral system encourage a party to make sectional appeals? As put, such a question would daunt the most energetic historian of party strategy.[1] But we can address a closely related question: does the single-member plurality system actually reward parties whose support is geographically concentrated and punish parties whose support is dispersed?

The answer depends upon the size of the party. In this paper, we shall test the proposition that Canada's electoral system gives seats in disproportionate numbers to parties whose votes are concentrated geographically. In this simple form, the proposition does not hold. We shall test a more complex proposition, involving the vote's very size as well as its geographic concentration, and extract from the test a general argument about party sectional strategy. The argument, applicable to virtually any level of geographic aggregation, has implications for the drawing of constituency boundaries, for decisions about the location of populations, and for the geographic impact of public policy and party campaign effort. We shall go on to argue that, in terms of electoral system incentives, the behaviour of the major parties and of the New Democratic party is paradoxical.

Richard Johnston and Janet Ballantyne, "Geography and the Electoral System," *Canadian Journal of Political Science* 10 (December 1977): 857-866. Reprinted with permission of the authors.

SOME BACKGROUND

Alan Cairns has taught us that Canada's single-member plurality electoral system manufactures regional differences more efficiently than it does parliamentary majorities. Its regional effect is twofold. First, differences between regions in a party's popular vote are exaggerated as they are translated into seats. This is the net national result of the fact that the party gaining the plurality in a specific region gains a disproportionate number of the region's seats.[2] The artificial exclusion of a party from seats in a region can set off a cumulative and self-reinforcing regional bias in the party's policy-making and campaign strategy.[3] Second, the number of seats a party gains in the country as a whole may depend on differences in its popular vote between regions:

> The case of the Reconstruction party provides dramatic illustration of the futility of party effort for a minor party which lacks a sectional stronghold. The treatment of the CCF/NDP by the electoral system is only slightly less revealing. This party with diffuse support which aspired to national and major party status never received as many seats as would have been "justified" by its voting support, and on six occasions out of ten received less than half the seats to which it was "entitled." The contrasting treatment of Social Credit and the Progressives, sectional minor parties, by the electoral system clearly reveals the bias of the electoral system in favour of concentrated support and against diffuse support.[4]

It is not clear whether Cairns means his argument to apply to all parties or only to small ones. Whatever his intentions, most readers have probably taken his argument to apply to parties of every size. Among practical politicians, Gordon Churchill seems to anticipate Cairns's reasoning and to extend it to major parties:

> The well-known decision of the Conservative party in 1957, acting on Gordon Churchill's maxim to "reinforce success not failure," to reduce its Quebec efforts and concentrate on the possibilities of success in the remainder of the country provides an important indication of the significance of calculations of sectional pay-offs in dictating campaign strategy.[5]

Could the success of Churchill's strategy indicate that the pattern Cairns observed for small parties holds for large parties as well?

A FIRST TEST

The proposition is relatively easy to formulate and test. We are predicting that a party will gain more seats per vote the more concentrated geographically is its vote. Accordingly, we need measures of "geographic concentration" and of "seats per vote."

The more concentrated geographically a party's vote, the greater should be the vote's geographic variance. As we shall deal with both large and small parties, the variance measure should not be sensitive to the party's size. The *coefficient of variation* of a party's popular vote across geographic units meets this condition admirably.[6] Over what units should the variation be measured? The general argument will apply to virtually any level of geographic aggregation. But, as Cairns's work embodies a concern with differences between provinces, we shall use as our measure of geographic concentration the coefficient of variation of a party's vote across provinces. The

larger the coefficient, the more concentrated in one or a few provinces is a party's popular vote.

The measure of seats per vote is straightforward. We shall calculate for each party in each election a *seat-to-vote ratio* in this way:

Party i's proportion of parliamentary seats
_____

Party i's proportion of
the national popular vote

This measure, like that we have chosen for geographic concentration, "corrects" for the size of the party.[7]

The relationship between two variables is best tested by the regression of one on the other. In our prediction, the geographic concentration stood as the independent variable and the seat-to-vote ratio as the dependent variable. Accordingly, we shall regress the seat-to-vote ratio on the coefficient of popular vote variation across provinces.[8] We shall do so for the five principal parties which contested national general elections in and since 1921. Altogether, this represents sixty-four data points.[9] Our prediction simply is that the regression coefficient attached to the geographic concentration measure will be significantly greater than zero. The prediction fails utterly:

$$Y_{ij} = 0.946 + 0.018 \ X_{ij} \quad F = 0.0156$$
$$(0.075) \quad R^2 = 0.0009$$

where:

Y_{ij} is the seat-to-vote ratio for party i in election j; and

X_{ij} is the coefficient of variation of party i's popular vote across provinces in election j.[10]

We cannot conclude that the regression coefficient on the geographic concentration measure is significantly different from zero. The efficiency of the vote would seem to depend not at all on the vote's geographic distribution.

FIRST MODIFICATION

Evidently, we cannot take the argument to apply to all parties. This leaves us with two questions. First, does the argument stand up to a comprehensive and systematic test for the parties Cairns considered most explicitly, small ones? Second, what happens in the case of large parties? To answer these questions, we shall perform regressions separately for small and large parties. The small parties in question are the Progressives, the CCF-NDP, and Social Credit in its various incarnations. The large parties are, of course, the Liberals and Conservatives. The small-party test will rest on thirty data points and the large-party test on thirty-four data points.

For small parties, the relationship is:

$$Y_{ij} = 0.146 + 0.526 \ X_{ij} \quad F \ = \ 17.232$$
$$(0.127) \quad R^2 \ = \ 0.381$$

where variables and statistics are defined as above. The small-party relationship is exactly as expected. The more concentrated across provinces the popular vote, the larger the number of seats the party wins per vote. For small parties, then, the electoral system poses incentives for sectional appeals.

For major parties, the relationship is:

$$Y_{ij} = 1.301 - 0.827 \ X_{ij} \quad F \ = \ 12.290$$
$$(0.236) \quad R^2 \ = \ 0.277$$

The relationship is exactly the opposite for large parties as for small ones. The more concentrated a large party's popular vote, the *fewer* seats it gains per vote. The electoral system could well move large parties to make appeals transcending regions.

If small parties benefit while large parties suffer from the geographic concentration of their vote, is there a magic threshold at which the direction of the relationship changes? In other words, where is the boundary between large and small parties? While the boundary may be obvious in Canada, it would not be so

in a system whose parties were more nearly equal in size than Canada's. In fact, regardless of the party system, there is simply no real point of discontinuity. While we have identified two oppositely signed regression coefficients, we have done so by imposing a linearity on each relationship. In reality, the function relating the party's seat-to-vote ratio to the geographic concentration of its popular vote must be curvilinear for all but the very smallest and the very largest parties and must be defined continuously across the range of party sizes. A moment's reflection will show why this is so.

THE GENERAL ARGUMENT AND FINAL TEST

The following examples will illustrate our contentions. First, consider extreme cases. A party with a total popular vote just sufficient, were the votes properly distributed, to yield a plurality in only one constituency reaches its maximum number of seats only if all of its votes lie in one constituency. Such a vote distribution is, of course, the most concentrated one possible. Any less concentrated distribution would yield the party no seats at all. Conversely, a party with a total popular vote just sufficient, were the votes properly distributed, to yield a plurality in every constituency reaches its maximum possible number of seats only if its votes are evenly distributed across constituencies. Such a vote distribution is the least concentrated one possible.[11]

Now consider a case between the extremes. A party with a total popular vote just sufficient to yield a plurality in, say, two of every five constituencies should have all of its votes in just that proportion of constituencies. If its votes were concentrated in fewer than two constituencies in five, the party would win commensurately fewer seats and would do so with unnecessarily large margins. The wasted votes were better located elsewhere. But the party could conceivably waste as many votes were they spread too thinly as it would were they concentrated too thickly. In our example, a party with votes in more than two constituencies in five would win fewer than two seats in five. Some votes would be dissipated in constituencies the party could not hope to win. The party's votes were better concentrated in fewer constituencies. A party between the extremes, then, can suffer if its votes are either too concentrated or too dispersed.

Our examples point to a general argument with two main elements. First, the more a party's actual vote distribution differs from the party's optimum one, the smaller will be the number of seats the party gains per vote. This should be true if the party's vote is either more concentrated or less concentrated than it should be. Second, the larger the party's popular vote, the less concentrated a distribution of votes the optimum one will be.

We shall express these contentions formally, by positing for a party a function relating its seats to the size and geographic distribution of its popular vote and by describing the function's implications. Having done so, we shall subject the function to the test of regression. One function which embodies both main elements of the general argument is:

$$Y_{ij} = b_0 + b_1 X_{ij} - b_2 Z_{ij} X_{ij}^2 + b_3 Z_{ij}$$

where, in addition to the variables defined above:

> Z_{ij} the party's proportion of the total popular vote in election j.

This function is by no means the only one compatible with the argument, but it is almost certainly the simplest. It describes a parabola concave downward over X_{ij}, but allows the axis of symmetry of the parabola to vary with Z_{ij}. If the party wishes to maximize the number of seats it gains per vote, the optimum geographic concentration of the vote will be:

$$X_{ij} = \frac{b_1}{2b_2 Z_{ij}} \qquad [12]$$

The larger the party's national popular vote proportion, Z_{ij}, the smaller must be the geographic concentration score, X_{ij}, at which the seat-to-vote ratio, Y_{ij}, is a maximum.

What are the implications of such a relationship? If the size of the vote increases, will the ratio of seats to votes increase as well? Whether or not it does depends on the size of the coefficients b_2 and b_3, and of the geographic concentration of the vote, X:

$$\frac{\partial Y}{\partial Z} = -b_2 X^2 + b_3$$

The more concentrated the vote, the more likely will a growth in its size (holding geographic concentration constant) yield a lower ratio of seats to the votes than before. Conversely, the more dispersed the vote, the more likely is its growth to improve its efficiency.

If the geographic concentration of the vote increases, will the ratio of seats to votes increase? Whether or not it does depends on the size of b1 and b2 and on both the popular vote's initial concentration, X, and the vote's size, Z:

$$\frac{\partial Y}{\partial X} = b_1 - 2b_2 ZX$$

In general, the larger the party's vote the more likely is an increase in its geographic concentration to reduce the ratio of seats to votes. Similarly, the more concentrated initially the vote, the more likely is an increment in that concentration to reduce the ratio of seats to votes. This, of course, has been only a restatement of our earlier contentions.

Does the function fit the facts? The test will employ the full sixty-four case party-election data set. This time, we regress the seat-to-vote ratio on the geographic concentration measure, the party's proportion of the national popular vote and an interaction term linking the two other independent variables. Defining the variables as before,

$$Y_{ij} = -0.375 + 0.853\,X_{ij} - 0.017\,Z_{ij}X_{ij}^2$$
$$\phantom{Y_{ij} = -0.375 + }(0.144) \quad (0.007)$$
$$+ 0.032\,Z_{ij} \quad F = 14.563$$
$$(0.005) \quad R^2 = 0.421$$

Each coefficient is significantly different from zero in the direction predicted by the general argument.[13]

SUMMARY AND IMPLICATIONS

There is no single, most efficient geographic distribution of the popular vote for all parties at all times. Rather, the optimum distribution varies with the size of the party. The smaller the party, the more concentrated in one or a few provinces its vote should be, if it is to maximize its strength in Parliament. Conversely, the larger the party, the more dispersed across provinces its votes should be. Similar arguments apply to the concentration or dispersion of the vote within provinces. Further, the effect of changes in the vote's geographic concentration varies with the magnitude of the initial concentration. The more concentrated the vote is initially, the less sense it makes to concentrate the vote still further. But a party with a relatively dispersed vote may well benefit from an increase in its concentration.

How does one increase or decrease the concentration of the vote? Three kinds of strategies seem pertinent. First, one can draw constituency boundaries with an eye to the efficiency of the popular vote. Second, one can actually move voters from place to place. Third, one can vary the geographic incidence of campaign effort or of the costs and benefits of public policy.

The gerrymander is the classic example of the first type of strategy. Even if the governing party assigns an equal number of voters to each constituency, it may still assign the voters in a way to maximize the efficiency of its own popular vote. It should spread its own pluralities as thinly as possible, so far as uncertainty permits. Thus it should win a large number of seats by a narrow margin. If necessary, it should confine its opponents to a few "hives," won by overwhelming opposition majorities:

> . . . Therefore let us re-distribute
> What constituencies are doubtful
> So as to enhance our prospects;
> Hive the Grits where they already
> Are too strong to be defeated;
> Strengthen up our weaker quarters
> With detachments from these strongholds;
> Surely this is true to nature
> In a mighty Tory chieftain![14]

In more prosaic terms, one relatively large party benefits from the dispersion of its vote while the other major party suffers from its vote's excessive concentration.

In a similar spirit, large blocs of voters can be transferred from constituency to constituency. The location of institutional populations, such as those in chronic or veterans' hospitals, universities, and the like, could affect a party's vote distribution. So could the location of low-income housing projects or, on a more grandiose scale, of new towns. Finally, there has been at least one occasion on which some of the armed services vote could be assigned virtually at will. In the 1917 general election, British soldiers serving with the Canadian Expeditionary Force and British subjects who had come to Canada from the United States in order to enlist were permitted to vote:

> Since military ballots would be counted in specific ridings, men without a Canadian domicile were to be left free to choose their own

district. . . . If there is one area in which MPs are not novices, it is election law. . . . [T]he law fulfilled a campaign organizer's dream—the right to deploy a clutch of reliable voters wherever the struggle was closest.[15]

The concentration of party effort and policy benefits on marginal areas, and the concomitant reduction of effort in both safe and hopeless areas, is an example of the third strategy.[16] Sometimes a major party will cut its losses and so increase the geographic concentration of its vote, as Churchill was alleged to have urged upon the Conservatives in 1957.[17] More often, however, major parties should try to spread their support relatively evenly across regions. They can do so by one of two means. One means is to couch appeals along a functional cleavage, such as social class.[18] The other means is to appeal simultaneously to the specific interests of each region, however much the appeal in one region may conflict with appeals in other regions. If Canada's major parties have chosen the latter,[19] such a choice could not be itself the result of the incentives embodied in the electoral system. Curiously, the party most likely to appeal along class lines, the NDP, is one which, were it making calculations of vote efficiency, would not make such an appeal. As a small party, it would as a rule gain more seats, the more concentrated its votes were in one or a few provinces. The incentives in the electoral system no more explain this strategic choice by the NDP[20] than they do the paradox that a major party may make regionally contradictory appeals in order to reduce regional differences in its popular vote.

Notes

*   The authors wish to thank Donald Forbes, David Rayside, Kathryn Fowler, and Charles Taylor for their comments and advice. Of course, none of these individuals share the blame for defects in the final product.

1. For a dispute on this question, see Alan Cairns, "The Electoral System and the Party System in Canada, 1921-1965," *Canadian Journal of Political Science* 1 (1968): 55-80; J.A.A. Lovink, "On Analyzing the Impact of the Electoral System on the Party System in Canada," *Canadian Journal of Political Science* 3 (1970): 497-516; and Cairns's reply to Lovink, ibid., 517-520. Cairns's original article is, of course, the point of departure for the arguments in this paper.

2. Cairns, "The Electoral System," 60-63. The logic of exaggerated regional differences is exactly the same as the logic of two other effects of single-member plurality systems: the disproportionate number of seats given parties with relatively large proportions of the popular vote and the exaggeration of swings from election to election. For the parameters of the first effect, see Douglas Rae, *The Political Consequences of Electoral Laws* (New Haven and London: Yale University Press, 1967), Chs. 4 and 5. For the second effect, see ibid., Table 5.2, and Edward R. Tufte, "The Relationship Between Seats and Votes in Two-Party Systems." *American Political Science Review* 67 (1973): 540-554.

3. Cairns, "The Electoral System," 64-72.

4. Ibid., 59-60.

5. Ibid., 65. See as well John Meisel, *The Canadian General Election of 1957* (Toronto: University of Toronto Press, 1962), 167-168.

6. The variance and its square root, the standard deviation, are both quite sensitive to the party's size. The smaller a party, the smaller will be its standard deviation, almost regardless of the degree to which its support is sectionally concentrated. The coefficient of variation corrects for this problem as it is calculated

as the ratio of the standard deviation (in this case, of the party's vote across geographic units) over the size of the party. The coefficient expresses the variation as a proportion of the party's size.

Some may feel uncomfortable with a variance measure taken as one of "concentration" rather than of "dispersion." Usually, one thinks of the variance as an indicator of the dispersion of a distribution *across the range of possible values.* The larger the variance, the more dispersed across the range the distribution is. The usage with geographic data is almost exactly opposed to the more common usage. The more dispersed over *space* (rather than over the range of possible values) is some attribute, such as a party's vote, the smaller are the differences between geographic units and, thus, the smaller is the geographic variance. Conversely, the more concentrated in one or a few geographic units the attribute is, the larger must be the difference between units and, thus, the larger must be the geographic variance. On the vagaries of areal measures and statistics, see Otis Dudley Duncan, Ray P. Cuzzort, and Beverly Duncan, *Statistical Geography* (Glencoe: Free Press, 1961).

7. This is the measure used in Cairns, "The Electoral System," Table II.

8. For elegant examples of the use of regression to explore aspects of the electoral system, see Rae. *The Political Consequences of Electoral Laws,* Ch. 4; Tufte, "The Relationship Between Seats and Votes"; and Duff Spafford, "The Electoral System of Canada," *American Political Science Review* 64 (1970): 168-176. Spafford did not consider, or at least did not report the consideration of, the distribution of the vote across provinces. He did, however, find a significant effect on the party's seat total of the distribution of its vote across constituencies of different sizes.

9. For the elections from 1921 to 1958 inclusive our data are taken from Howard A. Scarrow, *Canada Votes* (New Orleans: Hauser, 1962). The data for elections from 1962 to 1974 inclusive come from the Chief Electoral Officer's reports.

From 1921 to 1974 inclusive there have been seventeen general elections. Of course, the Liberal and Conservative parties have contested all seventeen. The Progressive party contested the four elections from 1921 to 1930 inclusive. The CCF-NDP and some version of Social Credit have contested all thirteen elections from 1935 to 1974 inclusive. We have treated Social Credit and the Ralliement des Créditistes as a single party.

Both Cairns and Spafford begin their studies with the 1921 election. That election produced a veritable quantum jump in the fractionalization of the Canadian party system. Estimates of the parameters of effects on the seat-to-vote ratio are probably not transferable from the post-1921 party system to the system in place before 1921.

10. The regression coefficient on X is unstandardized. The bracketed figure below the coefficient is the standard error of the coefficient. As a rule of thumb, a coefficient cannot be considered significantly different from zero unless it is at least twice its standard error.

11. The argument breaks down as the party's popular vote total exceeds that necessary to win a bare plurality in each and every constituency.

12. The point defined by $b_1/2b_2Z_{ij}$ is that at which Y is a maximum. The point is found by the partial differentiation of the seat-vote function with respect to X_{ij}, holding Z_{ij} constant:

$$\frac{\partial Y}{\partial X} = b_1 - 2b_2Z_{ij}X_{ij}$$

setting the differential equation equal to zero, and solving for X_{ij}. This yields:

$$X_{ij} = \frac{b_1}{2b_2Z_{ij}}$$

13. The coefficients are significant in spite of the considerable multicollinearity among the independent variables. The correlations between the independent variables are:

	XZ^2	Z
X	0.75	−0.87
XZ^2		−0.62

The national popular vote and the geographic concentration of the vote are related to each other more closely than each is to the interaction term. On the question of multicollinearity, see J. Johnston, *Econometric Methods* (New York: McGraw-Hill, 1972), 159ff.

14. Toronto *Globe*, June 3, 1882. This is taken from the epigraph to R. MacGregor Dawson, "The Gerrymander of 1882," *Canadian Journal of Economics and Political Science* 1 (1935): 197-221. For the pattern of redistribution in the 1882 case, see especially 210 and Appendix B.

15. Desmond Morton, "Polling the Soldier Vote: The Overseas Campaign in the Canadian General Election of 1917," *Journal of Canadian Studies* 10 (1975): 43-44. The number of soldiers actually eligible to assign their votes at will was not large. As it happened, many reassigned their votes illegally, but had their votes discarded as a result. See ibid., 48, 51.

16. See John M. Munro, "Highways in British Columbia: Economics and Politics," *Canadian Journal of Economics* 8 (1975): 192-204, and Donald E. Blake, "LIP and Partisanship: An Analysis of the Local Initiatives Program," *Canadian Public Policy* 2 (1976): 17-32. For an argument in the same spirit, but with respect to policy benefits distributed in response to the slightly more complex incentives embodied in the American Electoral College, see Gavin Wright, "The Political Economy of New Deal Spending: An Econometric Analysis," *The Review of Economics and Statistics* 56 (1974): 30-38.

The strategy described in the text and illustrated by Munro, Blake, and Wright corresponds to the "economic" approach described in Lovink, "On Analyzing the Impact," 502-504. Lovink suggests that the strategy of reinforcing strength be called the "patronage" strategy.

17. However much Churchill may have urged the party to cut its losses, the 1953-1957 shift in popular response to the party reflected no such strategy. As it grew from 1953 to 1957, the party's popular vote became *less* differentiated geographically. The party's vote declined in no region and displayed the greatest proportionate growth where the party had hitherto been weakest—on the prairies. In any case, according to Meisel, Churchill's advice to his party was more ambiguous than Cairns argued it to be (*General Election*, 167-168).

18. The distinction between functional and territorial cleavages is made in Seymour Martin Lipset and Stein Rokkan, "Cleavage Structures, Party Systems, and Voter Alignments: An Introduction," in Lipset and Rokkan, eds., *Party Systems and Voter Alignments* (New York: Free Press, 1967), 1-64.

19. For recent examples, see Walter Stewart, *Divide and Con: Canadian Politics at Work* (Toronto: New Press, 1973). The classic instance of mutually contradictory appeals must surely be those made by the Conservative party in 1911. The party's vote gained in English Canada on the basis of an Imperialist appeal. In French Canada, the party gained on the basis of an anti-Imperialist one. The irony is bitter even today.

20. Electoral system incentives may, however, explain some of the departure of the NDP from class-based appeals. See, for example, Stewart, *Divide and Con*, Ch. 4, especially 89-90, and Ch. 11.

24. ELECTORAL LAW AS A POLITICAL INSTRUMENT

Douglas Rae

What are the political consequences of electoral laws? How do these laws affect the interests of political parties and shape the development of party systems?

[In the foregoing chapters] I have presented a number of answers to these questions. [They are summarized at the end of each chapter and are catalogued together in Appendix A below.] The task that remains is to draw these tested propositions together as the basis for some general comments on the politics of electoral law. This chapter is meant to perform that task.

[Throughout the analysis] I have focused attention alternately on the short run (proximal) and the long run (distal) consequences of electoral laws for party competition. [In this concluding chapter] it will be useful to sort out these two strands of analysis, generalizing about each. The proximal effects operate at the conclusion of any single election when the legislative seats are allocated among the competing parties. The distal effects occur over the course of several elections, and follow from the proximal effects.

Proximal effects may be analyzed with great confidence since no intervening variable, save corruption, can disturb the relationship

Douglas Rae, *The Political Consequences of Electoral Laws* (New Haven: Yale University Press, 1967), Ch. 9, 133-147, "Electoral Law as a Political Instrument." Copyright © 1967 by Yale University Press. Second printing, April 1969. Reprinted by permission of the publisher.

between vote and seat distributions in a given election: the electoral system is the sole connection between the two.[1] When distal effects are considered, however, the redistributive bias of electoral systems becomes only one of an infinite array of competing factors—social, psychological, economic, even accidental— and it is not easy to decide how important the effects of the electoral law itself have been in producing the observed patterns of party competition. Let us consider the two kinds of effects separately, following the natural progression from proximal to distal, factual knowledge to speculative knowledge.

PROXIMAL CONSEQUENCES OF ELECTORAL LAW

For whosoever hath, to him shall be given, and he shall have more abundance: but whosoever hath not, from him shall be taken away even that he hath.

Matthew 13:12

Constants of Direction

The proximal effects of electoral laws upon political parties comport with the most literal understanding of Christ's prophecy. If a single pattern emerges from this study with status approaching a "law," it is the persistent bias of electoral laws in favour of strong parties as against their weaker competitors. The party which has many votes receives seats in "more abundance," but the party which does not have many votes is apt to receive fewer seats than its proportionate share or, worse yet, no seats at all. The prejudice of electoral laws—and here I include even the PR systems—in favour of strong elective parties and against weak ones is a very nearly universal fact of electoral life. This bias is reflected in three major findings:

1. Strong parties, typically those polling more than 20 per cent of the popular vote, usually receive more than proportionate shares of legislative seats; but weak parties —those polling less than 20 percent—generally receive less than proportionate shares of the legislative seats.[2]

2. The strongest single elective party almost always receives more than its proportionate share of the seats.[3]

3. The weakest elective parties, even after trivial candidates are discounted, are usually denied any representation whatever.[4]

As a result of these redistributions of competitive advantage, the structure of legislative politics is simplified. Parties are fewer in number; they are also, on the average, stronger. Small parties are often left out of the legislative arena, and the parties that are strong enough to obtain admittance are each likely to be stronger than they would be if electoral systems were neutral (i.e., perfectly proportional). In the categories of my analysis, these consequences can be summed up by saying that legislative party systems are less fractionalized than their elective counterparts, because electoral laws—*all* electoral laws—exert a defractionalizing effect.[5] The bias in favour of fewer, stronger parties is synonymous with the process of defractionalization.

Perhaps the most startling consequence of the defractionalizing process is the institutional creation of single-party legislative majorities.[6] When the voters fail to designate a governing majority, the electoral system may intercede to produce one by awarding a critical number of seats to the strongest of the minority parties. Indeed, almost two thirds of the legislative one-party majorities in the period studied were produced by this means.

These findings are not altogether inconsistent with the common-sense rule of social life: the rich get richer and the poor get poorer, most of the time. This tendency, which has been labeled "the multiplicative principle," is, according to Kaare Svalastoga, supported by a considerable evidential base.[7] It is also buttressed by common aphorisms like "money makes money," or "nothing succeeds like success." And if we remember that electoral laws are written by the leaders of parties strong enough to govern, the big party bias of actual electoral laws is not at odds with a certain disillusioned view of human nature.

There is strength in numbers. "Conformist" voters who support the leading parties are apt to be better represented (in a formal sense) than their countrymen who vote for the smaller parties. By proportionalist logic—John Stuart Mill's is the most lucid argument of the kind[8]—this is disturbing indeed. Legislatures are not clear mirrors of society; worse yet, they are always inclined to magnify the size of the "conformist" majority (or plurality) in the electorate, and to obscure many minorities. The question that is typically asked by the proportionalists is whether a given electoral law distorts representation in favour of the majority. My findings make it clear that the relevant question is not *whether* this distortion occurs, but *how great* is it?

Seen in a different light, the defractionalizing process is less disturbing. For the pragmatist, a more relevant question may be, "how can one make representative democracy work in a heterogeneous society?" How can one produce an effective flow of public policy without abandoning the elective principle in the face of many social cleavages which produce an equal number of political cleavages? How can one avoid legislative deadlocks of the kind which paralyzed the Fourth French Republic? How, within the institutional setting of liberal democracy, can one limit the divisive forces within the political system? If these are salient concerns, then the effect of electoral systems may be seen in a positive light. The defractionalizing process functions at once to: (a) improve the bargaining positions of governing parties, and (b) weaken the bargaining positions of non-governing parties. The extremes are the manufactured majority party and the weak party denied representation.

This speculation entails a number of assumptions which might be examined specifically in each country to which the argument is applied. First, it assumes that very strong "centrifugal" forces exist and threaten to obstruct the governing process. Second, it assumes that the leaders of strong parties wish to sustain the governmental process—an assumption that is inapplicable to, say, the large French and Italian Communist parties. Third, it implies that legislative institutions already enjoy a certain legitimacy. In short, this conjecture raises more questions than it answers.

Whatever becomes of these speculations, the actual pattern remains: electoral laws work to the advantage of strong parties and to the disadvantage of weak ones. Legislative party systems are therefore defractionalized, and in many cases legislative majorities are manufactured by electoral laws. As earlier analyses demonstrated, this pattern, in which strength is added to strong parties and taken away from weak ones, is a nearly universal consequence of existing electoral laws.

Since virtually all the disproportions are credited to strong parties instead of weak ones, the redistributive effects of electoral laws proceed in only one direction. No electoral laws systematically penalize strong parties to the benefit of weak ones. The main difference between electoral laws lies, therefore, on a single continuum between perfect proportionality (where no redistribution occurs), and extreme disproportionality (where strong parties benefit most and weak ones suffer most). While the extreme of perfect proportionality is never reached in actual practice, electoral laws differ in the degree to which they diverge from it toward the extremes of strong party advantage.

Variations of Degree

The degree to which seat allocations diverge from the condition of perfect proportionality is a function of two electoral law variables: (1) electoral formulae, and (2) district magnitudes. As a rule, PR formulae and high district magnitudes produce more nearly proportional results, while "first-past-the-post" formulae and low district magnitudes produce the greatest disproportionality (i.e., the greatest advantage for large parties over small ones). Let me consider the two electoral law variables individually, beginning with the electoral formulae.

Electoral formulae diverge from proportionality along two institutional dimensions. First, proportional representation formulae produce smaller deviations from proportionality than "first-past-the-post" formulae, whether the latter are based on pluralities or majorities.[9] Second, highest averages PR formulae diverge farther from proportionality than largest remainder PR formulae.[10] The first difference—between PR and "first-past-the-post" formulae—is by far the greater of the two.

It follows that PR formulae are likely to minimize (but not to eradicate) the general bias of electoral formulae in favour of strong parties. PR formulae give a smaller advantage to the strong elective parties and exact a smaller price from weak ones.[11] They give a smaller bonus to the strongest single elective party.[12] And, naturally enough, they are less apt to deny representation to elective parties.[13]

The proportionality of seat allocation also varies with the number of seats assigned to electoral districts—district magnitudes. Where many seats are allocated in each electoral district, the outcome is likely to approximate proportionality.[14] But where fewer seats are allocated in each district, outcomes are likely to diverge more sharply from proportionality.[15] This relationship is, however, curvilinear: as district magnitudes increase, disproportionality decreases at a decreasing rate.[16] Another way to put the same thing is: as district magnitude increases, the proportionality of outcome increases at a decreasing rate.[17] One need not be surprised that the bonus obtained by the strongest party declines as district magnitude rises.[18]

Since plurality formulae are always associated with a single-member district, it is hard to distinguish the disproportionality of these formulae from that of the single-member district's low magnitude. Indeed the distinction has no empirical meaning, except in the Australian case, where a majority formula is associated with a single-member district.

Given that the defractionalization pattern, which works in favour of fewer, stronger legislative parties, is a general fact of electoral life, it is also evident that specific institutions produce variations of degree within the pattern. Political ingenuity can render the defractionalizing pattern stronger or weaker through the manipulation of the institutional variables: electoral formulae and district magnitudes.

Suppose one wanted to design an electoral law that would maximize the defractionalizing pattern, producing strong advantages for strong parties, strong penalties for weak ones, and often "manufacturing" legislative majorities. The findings of this study suggest that the *single-member district* is the only necessary instrument. With these very low district magnitudes, the advantage of strong parties will be maximized, no matter what formula is used. Plurality and majority formulae will behave in the same way, defractionalizing legislative party systems by favouring fewer stronger parties. For that matter, even PR formulae would have the same effect in single-member districts. Because only one party can win in each district, the strong parties benefit at the expense of the weak ones, and legislative party systems are composed of fewer, stronger parties.[19]

Suppose, on the other hand, that one were worried about proportionality, and wished therefore to minimize defractionalization, giving each party its electoral due—no more and no less. Given these objectives, he should insist on a *PR formula*, preferably based on the *largest remainder procedure*, linked with *high district magnitudes* (i.e., many seats per district). It would probably not be worthwhile to expand the districts beyond ten or twenty seats, since the added proportionality seems to decline rapidly beyond that level. But with very low district magnitudes (i.e., less than six seats per district), even the largest remainder PR formula would produce a very substantial defractionalizing effect.

DISTAL CONSEQUENCES OF ELECTORAL LAWS

Do the short-run effects we have been discussing have long-run consequences for party systems? What are they? These questions can be answered only with considerable caution, since party systems are influenced by many variables—social, economic, legal, and political. Proximal effect of electoral law upon the legislative representation of parties is to be counted only one of many determining forces. And it is, secondly, impossible to sort out all the contributing factors, or to assign even approximate weights to them. Worse yet, electoral laws are themselves shaped by party systems.

In the face of these difficulties, one can only suggest limited connections. I have chosen to formulate my commentary in response to the question: "Where electoral laws do in fact make a long-run difference, which specific properties of electoral laws are apt to produce what differences?" By choosing to work within the assumption that electoral laws do exert long-run effects, yet without demonstrating this assumption's validity, I have settled for a very limited level of analysis. But to do more would require not one, but twenty or more, developmental studies, each devoted to a single country. The limited suggestions offered here may provide some guidelines for research of that kind, and may have at least tentative significance in their own right.

Party systems vary over a continuum, from non-fractionalization in one-party systems to extreme fractionalization in systems where a great many parties compete on about equal terms. Among the party systems analyzed in this study, the actual range of variation lies between two less distant points: US-style, two-party competition and Israeli-type multi-partism. Every party system, at any one point in time, may be assigned a place on this continuum, although (and this is important) individual systems may move along these scales, toward or away from the empirical extreme of two-party competition.

How do electoral systems influence the movement of systems on the fractionalization continuum? I wish to suggest that the pattern of proximal defractionalization described above is the source of whatever influence electoral laws have on the fractionalization of party systems. Where the pattern is strong—large parties are greatly advantaged—the electoral system exerts pressure on the system for two-party competition. But where the pattern is weak—large parties are only slightly advantaged—a weaker, often negligible, pressure is exerted in that direction. The defractionalizing pattern is a restraint on the fractionalization of party systems, and the effective pressure exerted by electoral laws varies with the intensity of the defractionalizing pattern itself. Multi-partism is most likely where electoral laws produce a weak defractionalizing pattern, and two-party competition most likely where the electoral laws produce a strong defractionalizing effect.

Now, according to my earlier comments, the defractionalizing pattern is complex. It entails at least five related subpatterns: (1) the advantage of large parties over small ones in the division of legislative seats; (2) the awarding of a "bonus" in seats to the strongest party; (3) the exclusion of small parties from the legislative arena; (4) the overall defractionalization of legislative party systems; and (5) the fairly frequent creation of "manufactured majorities" in legislative party systems. These are the subpatterns present in all electoral systems, but stronger in some than others, which constitute the defractionalizing process that seems so important. The question thus becomes, "What electoral law variables produce this syndrome?"

The answer to this question was foretold in the examination of proximal effects. Here let me recapitulate the effects of these institutions, with attention to the contribution they make to the shaping of party systems over time. Logically, the sequence of inferences is: (a) electoral law variables to intensity of the defractionalizing pattern, and, with less confidence, (b) the intensity of the defractionalizing pattern to the long-run fractionalization of the party system.[20]

What electoral law provisions intensify the defractionalizing pattern and therefore seem likely to exert pressure toward two-party competition? The answer is simple: the single-member district, or, failing that, small multi-member districts. In a single-member district, almost any formula[21]—the plurality is most common—is likely to advantage the strong parties and, in general, to establish the defractionalizing pattern. This much is confirmed by the analysis of proximal effects. But what about the long-range effects? The findings of the study show a fairly consistent association between single-member plurality formulae and two-party systems.[22]

A causal interpretation of this association falls upon several exceptions, the clearest of which are Canadian and Austrian. Nevertheless, the combination of the proximal defractionalizing pattern and the distal association with two-party competition suggests that the single-member district is likely to contribute to the development and sustenance of two-party systems. Other factors, such as regional minorities, may reverse this condition, as is the case in Canada. But, insofar as the electoral law exerts a controlling pressure, the single-member district is likely to press the system toward two-party competition.

And what arrangements are most likely to press party systems toward multi-partism, because they exert a very weak defractionalizing effect? These would be the institutions that optimize the proportionality of outcomes: largest remainder PR formulae, operating in high magnitude electoral districts. Because the outcomes are more nearly proportional under these provisions, the defractionalizing process is weakened. Is there an association between these arrangements and multi-partism? The study's findings show that there is:

1. In general, PR formulae are associated with more fractionalized elective and parliamentary party systems.[23]
2. Among PR formula electoral laws, those using the largest-remainder procedure are associated with greater fractionalization,

both elective and parliamentary, than are those using highest-average procedures.[24]
3. High district magnitudes are associated with greater fractionalization in both elective and parliamentary systems.[25]

The distal association between these institutions and high fractionalization, even when seen beside the weakness of the proximal defractionalizing pattern which they produce, does not suggest a simple *causal* relationship. It does, however, imply that insofar as the electoral law exerts a controlling pressure, these provisions are apt to press systems toward multi-partism and away from two-party competition.

These conclusions suggest that the statesman who must choose between electoral laws confronts a dilemma. On the one hand, he may opt for highly proportional election outcomes, in which case he is likely to encourage the fractionalization of party systems over time. Or, on the other hand, he may opt to encourage the development and maintenance of two parties, or less fractionalized multi-party competition, with the price being less proportional outcomes. These alternatives may not be inevitable, but the findings reported here make them seem probable: if proportionality, then multi-partism; but if two-party competition, then also a disproportional outcome.[26]

SUMMING UP AND LOOKING FORWARD

The general conclusions offered here are consistent with the specific findings of the study, yet a reasonable man might well have chosen to emphasize a different pattern. And I might well agree with *his* conclusions. Still another reader might well accept the study's findings, yet simultaneously find the general conclusions uninteresting or even, perhaps, misleading. Political discourse is marvelously subjective, especially when it touches upon issues with long polemical histories, and when it sweeps across national boundaries within which general agreement may have been reached.[27] Does this mean that the findings of this study—many of them known to the earlier literature—have added nothing useful to our knowledge about the politics of electoral law?

I hope, at least, that I have provided a number of touchstones with the facts of electoral politics. I am certainly prepared to suggest that the twenty propositions verified in this study are general and fairly accurate statements about the effects of electoral laws upon party competition. If so, it may be hoped that future arguments about the politics of electoral law will be more closely in touch with empirical reality and will, therefore, be more useful to political men who must choose between electoral laws.

But at least three series of related questions are implied, and left unanswered by the findings of the present study. First, what can a developmental analysis of elections in individual nations add to our understanding of the relationship between party system and electoral law? Despite its twenty-year span, the present study is concerned largely with correlational, not chronological problems. Is it not likely that a fairly general pattern of development—resting on a large set of variables, only one of which is electoral law—underlies the contemporary party systems we have been discussing? I am intrigued by the question.

Second, what are the consequences of electoral laws for the behaviour of individual politicians, operating within the confines of actual districts and party systems and moved by an infinite array of goals? How does the law shape their decision-making? And how, in turn, do these politicians act to shape the development of party systems? Further, how do the party systems so shaped come to influence the fate of electoral laws?

Third, how do party systems influence politics in general? What is the consequence of fractionalization for government stability and for the capacity of legislative politics to resolve the issues of the day?[28] How might defractionalization—the common bias of electoral systems in favour of a few strong parties—influence the fate of minorities as they compete with majorities? What are the consequences of electoral law and party system for the viability of the government-opposition tension which is so important to our cherished notion of liberal democracy?

These questions suggest three distinct directions for future research: (1) back in time toward the analysis of development; (2) inward toward the behavioral complexities of individual systems; and (3) outward toward the consequences of electoral politics for politics in general.

I have tried to isolate a series of general relationships between party system and electoral law for one period in the history of liberal democracy. These relationships have an interest of their own, and may add something to the century-old literature on the politics of electoral law. Hopefully, they will also facilitate the work of the scholar whose interests have carried him in one of the directions mentioned here or in yet another, unexplored direction.

Notes

1. Some complex proximal relationships, such as the one between district magnitude and proportionality cannot, however, be explained fully without district-by-district data.

2. Similarity Proposition One.

3. Similarity Proposition Two.

4. Similarity Proposition Four.

5. Similarity Proposition Five.

6. Similarity Proposition Three.

7. Kaare Svalastoga, *Social Differentiation* (New York: David McKay, 1965), 83-104.

8. Mill, *Representative Government*, 102-126.

9. Differential Proposition Four.

10. Differential Proposition Nine.

11. Differential Proposition One.

12. Differential Proposition Two.

13. Differential Proposition Five.

14. Differential Proposition Ten.

15. Differential Proposition Ten.

16. Differential Proposition Eleven.

17. Differential Proposition Eleven.

18. Differential Proposition Thirteen.

19. This assertion must be modified where parties which are weak on a national scale enjoy pockets of local support, enabling them to profit from the single-member district in those areas.

20. A third inference is from the degree to which an electoral system is presently fractionalized to the kind of electoral laws adopted for future elections.

21. The French double ballot may be an exception, although limited evidence suggests that it is not.

22. Differential Proposition Three and Similarity Proposition Seven.

23. Differential Proposition Six.

24. Differential Proposition Nine.

25. Differential Proposition Twelve.

26. The time-sequence data for the twenty-year period I have studied do not produce clinching evidence for these speculations: except for West Germany, there is no system which changes drastically in its degree of fractionalization. But that is not altogether surprising, since all of the systems, save Germany and Israel, had been in operation for many decades before the period covered by this study. Historical analyses of the individual systems would be of interest. I must conclude that association, but not sequential data, support my speculations.

27. For example, I would hazard the guess that informed Americans, and especially American political scientists, generally agree on the appropriateness of the single-member electoral law used in America.

28. Since our measure of fractionalization is based on the probability of partisan disagreement, the data reported in this study may have a direct relevance for this very interesting question.

25. RETHINKING DUVERGER'S LAW:
Predicting the Effective Number of Parties in Plurality and PR Systems—Parties Minus Issues Equals One*

Rein Taagepera and Bernard Grofman

1. THE HYPOTHESES

Two seemingly incompatible approaches have been tried to predict the number of political parties that will emerge in democracies. The first, associated with Duverger (1946a, b, 1951, 1954) and Sartori (1968), has focused on the nature of the electoral system. The second approach, associated with Downs (1957) and Lipset and Rokkan (1967), focuses on the nature and magnitude of the ideological cleavages within a society. In the first approach, institutional structures are the main driving forces. In the second approach, it is ideology which is paramount. Inspired in part by Lijphart (1984), we shall here attempt a synthesis of the two approaches.

Duverger's Law asserts that plurality elections favour two-party competition. Duverger has further proposed the hypothesis that majority runoffs and proportional representation (PR) systems favour multipartyism. Sartori (1968) has proposed that, within a multi-member district PR system, district magnitude (the number of seats in the district) is the best predictor of the number of parties that can be expected to contest the district—i.e., ceteris paribus, the larger the district magnitude, the greater the number of political parties.

Empirical support has been found to a greater or lesser extent for all these propositions. The UK, the USA, and New Zealand all have plurality elections and what is effectively two-party politics. Of the major countries using plurality elections, only India lacks a two-party system (Riker, 1982). Canada, which might appear another exception, with three major parties, has at the local level two-party politics—the two parties are simply not always the same two throughout the country. As for Duverger's hypothesis that majority runoffs and PR favour multipartyism, appreciable support is found for the latter proposition, especially if we amend it to substitute "list PR" for PR (see Duverger, 1985 forthcoming; cf. Sartori, 1985 forthcoming).

The arguments which lead us to believe list PR should facilitate multipartyism may or may not apply to the single transferable vote (STV), the other major form of PR. Furthermore, the arguments why list PR might foster multipartyism are considerably more compelling than the arguments for majority runoffs having that effect. Indeed, because of the use of single-seat districts, majority runoff may behave more like a plurality system than a PR system, and we will so treat it, although we

Rein Taagepera and Bernard Grofman, "Rethinking Duverger's Law: Predicting the Effective Number of Parties in Plurality and PR Systems—Parties Minus Issues Equals One," *European Journal of Political Research* 13 (1985): 341-352. Copyright © (1985) by D. Reidel Publishing Company. (Martinus Nijhoff Publishers.) Reprinted by permission of Kluwer Academic Publishers.

later point out special features of French electoral politics under the two-ballot system which foster something like four-party politics (cf. Duverger, 1980).

There are four cases cited by Riker (1982) as counter-examples to Duverger's hypothesis that PR fosters multipartyism: West Germany, Austria, Australia and Ireland. All but one of these cases can be distinguished away. West Germany has "too few" parties for PR, but this may be a consequence of a relatively high threshold (5% of votes) and the partial use of single-member districts which presents a psychological barrier to voters who do not wish to resort to ticket splitting. Moreover, Germany does have (as we shall show below) a 2½-party system rather than a pure two-party system. Ireland may have 'too few' parties, but Ireland uses districts of unusually low magnitude (three to five seats) which cannot allocate seats to many more than three parties. Moreover, as we shall later see, Ireland in fact has a nearly three-party system and is thus not really a good counter-example. Australia has the alternative vote, a form of runoff, which we regard as more akin to plurality than to PR, and it has 2½-party politics—albeit the third party is somewhat of an appendage to one of the two major parties. Austria, however, has been a true counter-example to Duverger's hypothesis because it has had effectively two-party politics despite list PR (the recent admission of the small, third party into the cabinet may change that).

This is another way in which Riker may have overstated the extent to which these four countries contradict Duverger's hypothesis. Asserting that the number of Australian parties has increased from two to three and then stabilized, Riker goes on to state: *"If the hypothesis* [about PR fostering multipartyism] *were true, however, the number should continue to increase. It has not."* (1982, emphasis ours.) Similarly, in discussing Ireland, Riker (1982) notes that the number of parties has

decreased (since 1927) despite use of STV. However, there is no need to interpret Duverger's hypothesis about PR and multipartyism as requiring that the number of parties must *increase over time.* All Duverger's hypothesis implies is that it is easier to have more than two parties under (list) PR than under plurality.

This is an important point, because, even if we accept Duverger's hypothesis, it tells us nothing about how many parties (more than two) we can expect. There is in fact great variation across PR systems as to the "effective number" of parties—with numbers ranging from just above two to over five (Lijphart, 1984). The effective number of parties, N, is calculated, following a procedure developed by Laakso and Taagepera (1979) and used by Lijphart (1984):

$$N = \frac{1}{\sum_{i=1}^{n} s_i^2} \qquad (1)$$

where s_i is the seat share of the i-th party. We shall focus on effective number of parties because we thus avoid the problem of whether to count the many minuscule splinter parties that may exist. The usual way to deal with them is introduce some cutoff point below which parties will not be regarded as significant in analysis, but this is fundamentally arbitrary.[1]

One of the most important extensions of Duverger's analysis from the institutionalist perspective is due to Sartori (1968), who focuses on the importance of district magnitude. Sartori's (1968) hypothesis that district magnitude will have a major impact on the number of parties in the system is well supported. Regardless of the seat allocation formula used, the "Break-even Percentage" of votes (at which a party starts obtaining its proportional share of seats, or more) shifts upwards as M increases (Taagepera and Laakso, 1980). This means that at smaller M fewer parties tend to obtain representation. Taagepera (1984) has found that the effective number of parties (N) in national assemblies tends to increase with increasing magnitude (M) approximately as

$$N = 1.15 (2 + \log M) \qquad (2)$$

when decimal logarithms are used. Note that list PR with M = 1 is identical to plurality in single-member districts; the formula yields N = 2.3 in this case. This formula represents a quantitative generalization of Duverger's Law. For a slightly different data base consisting of 39 electoral systems in 29 countries with a total of 350 elections, Taagepera (1985) obtained an r^2 value of 0.75 for a relationship slightly steeper than the one in equation (2): N = 2.03 + 1.45 log M.

Turning from the "institutionalists" to the "ideologues," it is much harder to find testable propositions. Lipset and Rokkan (1967) and Lijphart (1984, 149) may be interpreted as standing for the proposition that "the more axes of cleavage there are within a society, the greater will be the number of political parties." Note that this latter assertion is independent of the nature of electoral systems. It would appear to require that, if a society has few (many) axes of cleavage, it should have (many) parties regardless of the nature of the electoral system used.

Clearly, it ought to be possible to synthesize these two approaches. Consider, for example, the following fourfold table (Table 1).

Table 1

	"Plurality"	"PR"
A single issue dimension	two-party	?
Multiple issue dimensions	?	multi-party

The question marks in two of the cells indicate that it is not obvious how to predict outcomes in those cells. The institutional de-

terminism model would tell us that list PR systems should have multipartyism even if there was only a single axis of cleavage in the society, and that plurality systems should have only two parties even in the presence of many cleavages. The ideological approach would deny this. We have also put "plurality" and "PR" in quotation marks because the dichotomy puts the majority rule runoff or the alternative vote systems under the "plurality" label provided that those methods are used in conjunction with single-member districts, and the dichotomy puts nonlist multimember districts systems such as the Irish STV and the Japanese single nontransferable vote under the "PR" label. We propose the following tentative resolution, the predictive accuracy of which we shall examine later in the paper:

Hypothesis 1: The link between ideology, election type, and number of parties is as described in Table 2.

Table 2

	Plurality or majority in single-member districts	PR or semi-PR in multimember districts
A single issue dimension	two parties	two-three parties
Multiple issue dimensions	two-three parties	three or more parties

We shall now propose an even more specific hypothesis for the multiple-issue dimensions PR cell for list PR systems in that cell. Let I be the number of issue dimensions and N be the effective number of parties. Then it is proposed that for list PR systems, the effective number of parties (N) tends to be the number of issues plus one. Plurality elections can be thought of as a special case of list PR, with M = 1. Thus, if we apply this same proposed formula to plurality as well as list PR systems we find that, when I = 1, N = 2, and we can generalize:

Hypothesis 2: For the two cases on the main diagonal of Table 2 (i.e., one-issue dimension in single-member plurality or majority districts and multi-issue dimensions in PR multiseat districts)

$$N = I + 1 \qquad (3)$$

Thus, the hypothesis worded as "parties minus issues equals one" in the title of this article is now proposed to be applicable to plurality systems as well as to list PR systems (and to other systems). When I = 1 (a single left-right dimension, say) and plurality is used, we expect two-party politics, i.e., we have derived from Equation (3) *Duverger's Law as a special case.* If I = 2 and list PR is used, we expect three-party politics, etc. Thus, N = I + 1 can be thought of as a generalization of Duverger's Law.

In contrast to Equation (2), Equation (3) embodies an ideological, not an institutionalist, perspective.[2] Thus, to call 'N = I + 1' a generalization of Duverger's Law might seem to be misleading, since Duverger's Law, as originally stated, is commonly seen to stress the importance of electoral institutions, i.e., the plurality mechanism is seen as one which generates both "mechanical" and "psychological" pressure to hold the number of political parties down to two. This view, however, is in large part erroneous; while Duverger's Law is often thought of as a law about the functioning of plurality elections, we shall show that it is actually a law about the functioning of plurality elections in the *one*-dimensional context.

To make this argument precise we need to review the logic underlying the mechanism by which a plurality system facilitates two-party politics in the one-dimensional context.

Proposition 1. When voter ideal points are arrayed along a line (i.e., in single dimension) and voters choose the party/candidate which is closest to their ideal, the alternative corresponding to the ideal point of the median voter can receive a majority of the votes in pairwise competition against any other alternative.

Proof: See Black (1958).

Proposition 2. When voter ideal points are arrayed along a line and voters choose the party/candidate which is closest to their ideal, if there are only two political parties and each is driven by concern for vote-maximizing, then each will seek to locate at the position held by the median voter.

Proof: See Downs (1957).

Consider two parties L and R, with the voters and the parties arrayed along a line:

We have identified the position of the median voters as M. Clearly, if L moves towards M it will gain votes; the same is true for R. This position is in (Nash) equilibrium. As long as one party stays fixed, the other party cannot improve its vote share.

Proposition 3. If we now introduce an additional centrist party, C, the combination of a "mechanical effect" and a "psychological effect" under simple plurality will tend to eliminate one of the three parties.

Proof: Consider the following configuration:

Here, we would expect L to move towards M, and R to move towards M, since voters to the left of L or the right of R really have no choice (except abstention) that might be preferable to their voting for the party nearest their ideal point. If this happens, C is squeezed even if located exactly at M. Losing votes, it will lose even more in terms of seats. This is what Duverger (1951) refers to as the "mechanical" effect of plurality in making it impossible for one of the three parties to compete successfully:

$$\frac{M}{L \ \ C \ \ R}$$

Only in the central half of the segments from LC to CR does C get votes. If C's supporters are concerned about their ability to influence political outcomes, they will come to desert C and cast votes for L or R, the only two parties which have a real chance at victory. This is what Duverger (1951) refers to as the "psychological effect." In the social choice literature, it is known as the pressure towards strategic voting (Cain, 1978).

The diagrams and discussion above show that in one dimension, three-party competition is *unstable*, but two-party competition *is stable*.[3] The reason that Duverger's Law cannot be expected to apply when there is more than one issue dimension is that in such a case there will in general be no analogue to the median voter ideal point, i.e., no point which a majority prefers to each and every other point in the space and thus no single point in the space to which the mechanics of the pursuit of electoral advantage will inexorably draw each party. It is well known in the social choice literature that, in general, two-dimensional voting games (or voting games set in still higher issue dimensions) do not have a core, i.e., do not have a single point which is majority preferred to each and every other point in the space (McKelvy, 1978, 1979; Schofeld, 1978). When voting games lack a core the electoral dynamics posited by Duverger's Law simply cannot apply. Thus, Duverger's Law is really about one-dimensional political competition or, at least, political competition in which there are no cycles of majority preference—and in practice, that may amount to the same thing (Riker, 1982; cf. Feld and Grofman, 1985a, b).

For multi-dimensional plurality contests, even though two-party competition may be inherently unstable, certain configurations of three parties may be stable. For example, in the two-dimensional three-party case with three large, roughly equal-sized blocs of voters concentrated in the vicinity of X, Y and Z with other (smaller numbers of) voters scattered throughout the space, three parties located at these concentrations might be stable if the arrangement was like an equilateral triangle. But such stable configurations are empirically highly unlikely.

Having shown that Duverger's Law is fundamentally linked to the operations of plurality in one-dimensional issue space, we now turn to a test of our hypotheses linking the effective number of parties both with issues and electoral institutions.

2. EMPIRICAL TESTING

In order to test Hypotheses 1 and 2, we require specification of the number of issue cleavages in the society. Here we follow Lijphart (1984). Lijphart identifies the following seven dimensions, of which the first six closely follow the dimensions recognized by earlier analysis (Taylor and Laver, 1973; Sartori, 1976, 336-7; Dodd, 1976): Socioeconomic; Religious; Cultural-ethnic; Urban-rural; Regime support; Foreign policy; and Postmaterialism. Table 3 (taken from Lijphart, 1984: Table 8.1, p. 130 and Table 7.3, p. 122) shows the number of issue dimensions and the effective number of parties for 22 post-war democratic polities (France IV and France V are counted separately). The number of issue dimensions is not always an integer because Lijphart scored an issue dimension of medium salience as a half. The following hypotheses reflect the dichotomies in our earlier Table 2:

Hypothesis 1(a). Countries with unidimensional cleavages and elections in single-member districts have two-party systems.

There are two cases, the USA and New Zealand, both of which confirm the hypothesis.

Hypothesis 1(b). Countries with unidimensional cleavages and multimember districts will have between two and three parties.

There is only one case, that of Ireland, which with N = 2.8 confirms the hypothesis.

Hypothesis 1(c). Countries with multidimensional cleavages and single-seat districts will have between two and three parties.

There are five cases in this cell of Table 2 if we treat Australia's alternative vote as akin to a plurality system, as we believe it appropriate to do (cf. Katz, 1980), and also treat West Germany's mixed system as psychologically akin to plurality. Australia (with N = 2.5), West Germany (with N = 2.6), Canada (with N = 2.4), and the UK (with N = 2.1) confirm our hypothesis. France V (with N = 3.3) narrowly oversteps the limit (three parties), but France's unique second-round coalition alliances, in which certain parties by pre-concert drop out of the race in deference to a coalition partner with higher first-round voting support, encourage four-party politics nationally even while only two principal parties contest at the second round in each district (cf. Duverger, 1985 forthcoming and Duverger, 1980).

India is not among the countries considered by Lijphart (1984), but it, too, roughly fits our model with multidimensional cleavages and N = 3.2. We regard this account of India as more plausible than that in Riker (1982) which attempts to fit India into a one-dimensional situation which gives special status to the Congress party as a Condorcet (majority) winner and permits centrist parties which are Condorcet winners to have parties to both their right and left, thus allowing for multiparty

Table 3 Issue Dimensions and Effective Number of Parliamentary Parties in Twenty-two Democratic Systems, 1945-80

Country	Number of dimensions	Effective number of parties
Single-member districts		
United States	1.0	1.9
New Zealand	1.0	2.0
United Kingdom	1.5	2.1
Canada	1.5	2.4
Australia	2.5	2.5
France V	3.5	3.3
(West Germany)	2.0	2.6
Multimember districts		
Ireland	1.0	2.8
Austria	2.0	2.2
Luxembourg	2.0	3.3
Sweden	2.5	3.2
Denmark	2.5	4.3
Japan	3.0	3.1
Iceland	3.0	3.5
Italy	3.0	3.5
Belgium	3.0	3.7
Israel	3.0	4.7
Netherlands	3.0	4.9
Switzerland	3.0	5.0
Norway	3.5	3.2
Finland	3.5	5.0
France IV	4.5	4.9

Source: Lijphart, 1984 (Table 8.1, p. 130; Table 7.3, p. 122).

plurality politics. There are two difficulties with Riker's model. First, multi-ethnic politics in India makes it hard to fit into a one-dimensional framework. Second, even if the centrist party in a one-dimensional space were a Condorcet winner, it is not clear why its voting strength would not be nibbled away from both right and left (cf. Sartori, 1985 forthcoming), as was the case for the British Liberals around 1930.

Hypothesis 1(d). Countries with multidimensional cleavages and multimember districts will have three or more parties.

There are 14 cases in this cell of Table 2; for 13 of these our hypothesis is confirmed. The exception is Austria, with $I = 2.0$ and $N = 2.2$.

In sum, then, our first proposed reformulation of Duverger's Law and Duverger's hypotheses fits the data quite well. Now let us turn to Hypothesis 2, which states that for certain groups of countries we should have $N = I + 1$.

Before we look at the data, we must put the reader on notice as to one methodological point. Because of the nature of Lijphart's definition of issue dimension, there is a linkage between N and I. When estimating the number of issue dimensions (I) for a given country, Lijphart considers an issue dimension highly salient (1 point credit) or moderately salient (0.5 point) only if it is "dividing the significant or 'relevant' parties—the parties that have either coalition or 'blackmail' potential" (Lijphart, 1984, 128). Issues which divide parties internally (e.g., the language issue in pre-1970 Belgium) are not considered, nor are those which delineate minor parties.

Despite this linkage between issues and parties, Lijphart's (1984) definition in no way requires I to be any particular function of N. Assume for the moment that every issue dimension can contain only two opposite stands. Then one issue dimension can delineate only two separate parties. With two issue dimensions (e.g., ethnic and religious), the number of parties could be as low as two (perhaps Orthodox Greeks and Muslim Turks in Cyprus) or as high as $2 \times 2 = 4$ (German Protestants, French Protestants, German Catholics,

French Catholics in a hypothetical Switzerland). In general, for a given value of I, the number of parties generated could be as low as two and as high as 2^I. The highest values of I Lijphart finds (for Finland and France) are around 4, leading to a possible number of parties ranging from two to 16. This essentially covers the entire range of the number of parties ever observed in any democratic country. If we allow an issue dimension to contain more than two distinct positions (e.g., Protestant, Catholic, Muslim), the range shifts from somewhat more than two to considerably more than 2^I.

The point here is that Lijphart's estimates of the issue dimensions do not circularly emerge from the existing number of parties. For a given I, any practically conceivable number of parties remains possible. Conversely, for a given N, it takes very few issue dimensions to account for the number of parties, and countries tend to have more issue dimensions than they 'need' to generate the number of parties observed. What this means is that N and I are not rigidly interconnected by the very definition of these quantities. In principle, a wide range of combinations is possible for values of N and I.

We show in Figure 1 a plot of N versus I for all 22 of our cases. The regression line is

$$N = .8341 + 1.264 \qquad (4)$$

with a correlation coefficient of .75. This is very close to $N = I + 1$, and indeed this equation yields an almost equally high correlation.[4] Of course, we are looking at effective number of parties; counting minor parties would give us higher values of N.

Our second hypothesis is specifically about the 16 main diagonal countries in Table 3. Thus we should consider the best fit when omitting the UK, Canada, Australia, France V, West Germany, and Ireland. A glance at Fig. 1 shows that no appreciable improvement in fit is achieved. The plurality systems

Figure 1 The Relationship between N and I in Twenty-two Democracies

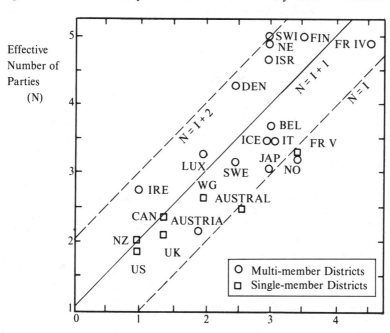

Number of Issue Dimensions (I)

(Canada, UK, West Germany) fit the general pattern. The single STV case (Ireland) has unexpectedly many parties, and the single-member districts with runoff or alternative vote (France V and Australia) have unexpectedly few parties, but the number of cases is much too small to draw any conclusions. The rule N = I + 1 seems to apply to all cells in Table 2 with an error range of ±1.

Thus we see that I alone can account well for differences in N across countries, even if we do not take electoral system into account. However, there is a link between type of election system and number of issue cleavages. Above 2.5 issue dimensions, multimember districts are the rule (the only exception being France V). Below 2.0 issue dimensions, single-member districts are the rule (the only exception being Ireland). It may well be that countries with many issue dimensions do purposely pick electoral systems which enable more than

two parties to survive (see Note 2). In particular, they may choose district magnitudes to satisfy this purpose. While the format of Equation (2) suggests that M affects N, the reverse is also possible. Combining Equations (2) and (3) could then express the tendency of issue dimensions to affect the choice of district magnitude.[5]

The connection between N and I was first established by Lijphart (1984: Table 8.4, p. 48), who provides a 3 × 3 cross-tabulation of countries grouped by low, medium, and high values of N and I. It is apparent from this table that N and I are interrelated and Lijphart (1984, 148) reports a .75 correlation between them.[6] However, Lijphart does not look at the slope of the regression line and thus does not derive the relationship N = I + 1. Given the remarkable strength of this relationship, it would seem that we have identified an important empirical rule. Nonetheless, although it is clearly important to have found a functional relationship such as N = I + 1 with such striking predictive power, it would still be desirable to hypothesize a mechanism which could account for that predictive power. This task, however, will require a separate paper.

Notes

* We wish to extend thanks for helpful comments to Arend Lijphart and Matthew Shugart, for typing of final copy to Cheryl Larsson of the Word Processing Center, School of Social Sciences, UCI, and to Dorothy Gormick for bibliographic assistance. The second author would also like to acknowledge the partial support of an NSF grant "Research into the Dynamics of Spatial Voting Games", Decision and Management Sciences Program.

1. For the parliamentary seat constellation .25–.25–.25–.25 one would expect and does obtain N = 4. For .35–.30–.15–.05–.05 one also obtains N = 4.00 so that this distribution is roughly equivalent to one with four equally large parties. The rather improbable constellation .49–.02–.02– ... .02–.01 (with 25 parties of 2% each) would also yield N = 4.00. The effective number of parties is connected to the well-known Rae "fractionalization" index F (Rae, 1971) through N = 1/(1–F). For a small number of effective parties, N is roughly equal to the actual number of parties with at least 10% of the vote, but N is more descriptive of the party strengths than the simple count in cases like the following two: .40–.40–.10–.10 and .40–.40–.09–.09–.02. If anything, the latter case has slightly more parties, as reflected in N increasing from 2.94 to 2.97, but the party count based on a 10% cutoff would suddenly drop from 4 to 2.

2. An alternative form of synthesis of the institutionalist and ideological approaches to predicting the number of parties would require longitudinal modelling of an interactive sort, i.e., the nature of issue cleavages in the society could affect the society's initial choice of election system, and the way in which political conflicts were resolved by existing electoral mechanisms could, over time, have an impact on the nature or the salience and intensity of societal cleavages.

3. Of course, we may have a multimodal distribution of voter preferences, or abstention from alienation/indifference effects, each of which will complicate the analysis, but still not really fundamentally affect the result except under very special circumstances. If, for example, there is also an 'alienation' effect. i.e., voters too far away from their most preferred choice abstain out of alienation from the political process, we'll have both L and R moving towards (but perhaps not quite reaching) the central location in M.

4. It often tends to be forgotten that the calculation of correlation coefficient r is symmetrical in x and y, but the same is not true of regression of y on x. In our case the regression of N on I yields N = 0.834I + 1.264, but the reverse regression of I on N yields the equivalent of N = 1.481I – 0.370. The simple equation N = I + 1 lies in between, although much closer to the first equation.

5. A formal combination of Equations (2) and (3) yields $M = 0.07(7.4)_I$. For I = 1, M = .5; for I V = 2, M = 3.8; and for I = 3, M = 28. It is, however, still too early to evaluate the merits of this cumbersome and non-intuitive formula.

6. Instead of using the effective number of parliamentary parties (i.e., N based on seat shares), one could also consider the effective number of electoral parties (i.e., based on votes shares) for which data are also available in Lijphart (1984, 160). Lijphart calculates the correlation of I with N (seats) only, and we agree that this is preferable on theoretical grounds. The correlation of I with N (votes) is slightly less good.

References

BLACK, D. 1958. *The Theory of Committees and Elections*. Cambridge: Cambridge University Press.

CAIN, B. 1978. "Strategic voting in Great Britain." *American Journal of Political Science* 22:639-655.

DODD, L.C. 1976. *Coalitions in Parliamentary Government*. Princeton, NJ: Princeton University Press.

DOWNS, A. 1957. "An economic theory of political action in a democracy." *Journal of Political Economics* 64:135-150.

DUVERGER, M. 1946a. "Les partis politiques." In Université de Bordeaux. *Conférences du Lundi (1945-1946)*. Bordeaux: Ed. Delmas, 21-32.

DUVERGER, M. 1946b. "Les partis politiques." *La Vie Intellectuelle* 20 (October): 62-73.

DUVERGER, M. 1951. "The influence of electoral systems on political life." *International Social Science Bulletin* 3: 314-352.

DUVERGER, M. 1954. *L'Influence des Systèmes Electoraux sur la Vie Politique*. Paris: Armand Colin.

DUVERGER, M. 1980. *Institutions Politiques et Droit Constitutionel: Tome I, Les Grands Systèmes Politiques* 16e. Paris: Presses Universitaires de France.

DUVERGER, M. 1985. "Duverger's Law: Forty years later." Forthcoming in B. Grofman, and A. Lijphart, eds. *Electoral Laws and Their Political Consequences*. New York: Agathon Press.

FELD, S.L., and B. GROFMAN, 1985a. "Who's afraid of the big bad cycle?" A little single-peakedness can go a long way." Unpublished manuscript.

FELD, S.L., and B. GROFMAN. 1985b. "Research note: Necessary and sufficient conditions for a majority winner in n-dimensional spatial voting games: An intuitive approach." Unpublished manuscript.

FELD, S.L., B. GROFMAN, and N. MILLER. 1985. "Cycle avoiding trajectories and the uncovered set." Prepared for presentation at the Weingart Conference on Formal Models of Voting, California Institute of Technology, March 22-23.

KATZ, R. 1980. *A Theory of Parties and Electoral Systems*. Baltimore: Johns Hopkins University Press.

LAAKSO, M., and R. TAAGEPERA. 1979. "Effective number of parties: A measure with application to West Europe." *Comparative Political Studies* 12:3-27.

LIJPHART, A. 1984. *Democracies: Patterns of Majoritarian and Consensus Government in Twenty-one Countries*. New Haven and London: Yale University Press.

LIPSET, S.M., and S. ROKKAN, eds. 1967. *Party Systems and Voter Alignments*. New York: Free Press.

LUCE, R.D. and H. RAIFFA. 1957. *Games and Decisions*. New York: Wiley.

MCKELVEY, R.D. 1978. "Intransitivities in multidimensional voting models and some implications for agenda control." *Journal of Economic Theory* 18:1-22.

MCKELVEY, R.D. 1979. "General conditions for global intransitivities in formal voting models." *Econometrica* 47: 1085-1112.

OWEN, G. 1983. *Game Theory*. 2e. New York: Academic Press.

RAE, D.W. 1971. *The Political Consequences of Electoral Laws*. New Haven and London: Yale University Press.

RIKER, W.H. 1982. "The two-party system and Duverger's Law: An essay on the history of political science. *"American Political Science Review* 76:753-766.

SARTORI, G. 1968. "Political development and political engineering." In J.D. Montgomery, and A.O. Hirschman, eds. *Public Policy* 17. Cambridge, Mass.: Harvard University Press, 261-298.

SARTORI, G. 1976. *Parties and Party Systems: A Framework for Analysis* 1. Cambridge: Cambridge University Press.

SARTORI, G. 1985. "The influence of electoral systems: Faulty laws or faulty methods?" Forthcoming in B. Grofman, and A. Lijphart, eds. *Electoral Laws and Their Political Consequences.* New York: Agathon Press.

SCHOFELD, N. 1978. "Instability of simple dynamic games." *Review of Economic Studies* 45:575-594.

STRAFFIN, P.D., and B. GROFMAN. 1984. "Parliamentary coalitions: A tour of models." *Mathematics Magazine* 57:259-274.

TAAGEPERA, R. 1984. "The effects of district magnitude and properties of two-seat districts." In A. Lijphart, and B. Grofman, eds. *Choosing an Electoral System: Issues and Alternatives.* New York: Praeger, 91-101.

TAAGEPERA, R. 1985. "Effect of district magnitude on party representation." Unpublished manuscript.

TAAGEPERA, R., and M. LAAKSO. 1980. "Proportionality profiles of West European electoral systems." *European Journal of Political Research* 8:423-446.

TAYLOR, M., and M. LAVER . 1973. "Government coalitions in Western Europe." *European Journal of Political Research* 1:237-248.

26. THE ELECTORAL SYSTEM AND THE PARTY SYSTEM IN CANADA, 1921-1965*

Alan C. Cairns

This paper investigates two common assumptions about the party system: (i) that the influence of the electoral system on the party system has been unimportant, or non-existent; and (ii) that the party system has been an important nationalizing agency with respect to the sectional cleavages widely held to constitute the most significant and enduring lines of division in the Canadian polity. Schattschneider, Lipset, Duverger, Key and others[1] have cogently asserted the relevance of electoral systems for the understanding of party systems. Students of Canadian parties, however, have all but ignored the electoral system as an explanatory factor of any importance. The analysis to follow will suggest that the electoral system has played a major role in the evolution of Canadian parties, and that the claim that the party system has been an important instrument for integrating Canadians across sectional lines is highly suspect.

Discussion of the respective merits of single member constituency electoral systems and various systems of proportional representation is frequently indecisive because of an inability to agree on the values which electoral systems should serve. Advocates of proportional representation base their arguments on democratic fundamentalism. They simply argue that each vote should have equal weight, and that the distortion of the voters' preferences by single member constituency systems is no more to be justified than the use of false scales by a butcher. This idealistic argument is countered by the opponents of proportional representation with the assertion that executive stability is a more basic consideration, and that it is well served by the propensity of Canadian type systems to create artificial legislative majorities. This controversy will not concern us further.

It may be noted, however, that critical analysis of the single member constituency system encounters a cultural bias in the Anglo-Saxon world because of the pervasive hostility shown to systems of proportional representation,[2] and the executive instability to which they allegedly contribute. Proportional representation has not been seriously considered as a possible alternative to the existing system. It exists in a limbo of inarticulate assumptions that it is responsible for the ills of the French political system, but it is given no credit for the sophistication and maturity of the Swedish political system.

Given this bias there is, no doubt, a tendency to transform a critique of the existing system into advocacy of proportional representation. The purpose of this paper, however, is not to advocate proportional representation, but simply to take a realistic look at some of the consequences of the prevailing system which have received insufficient attention. In any case, the habituation of Canadians to the existing system renders policy oriented research on the comparative merits of different electoral systems a fruitless exercise.

Alan C. Cairns, "The Electoral System and the Party System in Canada, 1921-1965," *Canadian Journal of Political Science* 1 (March 1968): 55-80. Reprinted with permission of the author.

THE BASIC DEFENCE OF THE SYSTEM AND ITS ACTUAL PERFORMANCE

If the electoral system is analysed in terms of the basic virtue attributed to it, the creation of artificial legislative majorities to produce cabinet stability, its performance since 1921 has been only mediocre. Table 1 reveals the consistent tendency of the electoral system in every election from 1921 to 1965 to give the government party a greater percentage of seats than of votes. However, its contribution to one party majorities was much less dramatic. Putting aside the two instances, 1940 and 1958, when a boost from the electoral system was unnecessary, it transformed a minority of votes into a majority of seats on only six of twelve occasions. It is possible that changes in the party system and/or in the distribution of party support will render this justification increasingly anachronistic in future years.

Table 1   Percentage of Votes and Seats for Government Party, 1921-1965

	% Votes	% Seats		% Votes	% Seats
1921	40.7	49.4(L)	1949	49.5	73.7(L)
1925*	39.8	40.4(L)	1953	48.9	64.5(L)
1926	46.1	52.2(L)	1957	38.9	42.3(C)
1930	48.7	55.9(C)	1958	53.6	78.5(C)
1935	44.9	70.6(L)	1962	37.3	43.8(C)
1940	51.5	73.9(L)	1963	41.7	48.7(L)
1945	41.1	51.0(L)	1965	40.2	49.4(L)

*In this election the Conservatives received both a higher percentage of votes, 46.5%, and of seats, 47.3%, than the Liberals. The Liberals, however, chose to meet Parliament, and with Progressive support they retained office for several months.

Note: The data for this and the following tables have been compiled from Howard A. Scarrow, *Canada Votes* (New Orleans, 1963), and from the *Report of the Chief Electoral Officer* for recent elections.

If the assessment of the electoral system is extended to include not only its contribution to one-party majorities, but its contribution to the maintenance of effective opposition, arbitrarily defined as at least one-third of House members, it appears in an even less satisfactory light. On four occasions, two of which occurred when the government party had slightly more than one-half of the votes, the opposition was reduced to numerical ineffectiveness. The coupling of these two criteria together creates a reasonable measure for the contribution of the electoral system to a working parliamentary system, which requires both a stable majority and an effective opposition. From this vantage point the electoral system has a failure rate of 71 percent, on ten of fourteen occasions.

This unimpressive record indicates that if other dysfunctional consequences of the electoral system exist they can be only marginally offset by its performance with respect to the values espoused by its advocates. In this paper discussion of these other consequences is restricted to the effect of the electoral system in furthering or hindering the development of a party system capable of acting as a unifying agency in a country where sectional cleavages are significant. Or, to put the matter differently, the stability which is of concern is not that of the cabinet in its relations to the legislature, but the stability of the political system as a whole. Has the electoral system fostered a party system which attenuates or exacerbates sectional cleavages, sectional identities, and sectionally oriented parties?

THE EFFECT ON MAJOR AND MINOR PARTIES

Table 2 indicates an important effect of the electoral system with its proof that discrimination for and against the parties does not become increasingly severe when the parties are ordered from most votes to least votes. Discrimination in favour of a party was most pronounced for the weakest party on seven occasions, and for the strongest party on seven occasions. In the four elections from 1921 to 1930 inclusive, with three party contestants, the second party was most hurt by the electoral system. In the five elections from 1935 to 1953 inclusive the electoral system again worked against the middle ranking parties and favoured the parties with the weakest and strongest voting support. In the five elections from 1957 to 1965 inclusive there has been a noticeable tendency to benefit the first two parties, with the exception of the fourth party,

Social Credit in 1957, at the expense of the smaller parties.

The explanation for the failure of the electoral system to act with Darwinian logic by consistently distributing its rewards to the large parties and its penalties to the small parties is relatively straightforward.[3] The bias in favour of the strongest party reflects the likelihood that the large number of votes it has at its disposal will produce enough victories in individual constituencies to give it, on a percentage basis, a surplus of seats over votes. The fact that this surplus has occurred with only one exception, 1957, indicates the extreme unlikelihood of the strongest party hav-

Table 2   Bias of Electoral System in Translating Votes into Seats

Year	| *Rank order of parties in terms of percentage of vote*									
	1		*2*		*3*		*4*		*5*	
1921	Libs.	1.21	Cons.	0.70	Progs.	1.20				
1925	Cons.	1.017	Libs.	1.015	Progs.	1.09				
1926	Libs.	1.13	Cons.	0.82	Progs.	1.55				
1930	Cons.	1.15	Libs.	0.82	Progs.	1.53				
1935	Libs.	1.57	Cons.	0.55	CCF	0.33	Rec.	0.05	Socred	1.68
1940	Libs.	1.43	Cons.	0.53	CCF	0.39	Socred	1.52		
1945	Libs.	1.24	Cons.	1.00	CCF	0.73	Socred	1.29		
1949	Libs.	1.49	Cons.	0.53	CCF	0.37	Socred	1.03		
1953	Libs.	1.32	Cons.	0.62	CCF	0.77	Socred	1.06		
1957	Libs.	0.97	Cons.	1.087	CCF	0.88	Socred	1.091		
1958	Cons.	1.46	Libs.	0.55	CCF	0.32	Socred	0		
1962	Cons.	1.17	Libs.	1.01	NDP	0.53	Socred	0.97		
1963	Libs.	1.17	Cons.	1.09	NDP	0.49	Socred	0.76		
1965	Libs.	1.23	Cons.	1.13	NDP	0.44	Cred.	0.72	Socred	0.51

Independents and very small parties have been excluded from the table.

The measurement of discrimination employed in this table defines the relationship between the percentage of votes and the percentage of seats. The figure is devised by dividing the former into the latter. Thus 1—(38% seats/38% votes), for example—represents a neutral effect for the electoral system. Any figure above 1—(40% seats/20% votes)=2.0, for example—indicates discrimination for the party. A figure below 1—(20% seats/40% votes)=0.5, for example—indicates discrimination against the party. For the purposes of the table the ranking of the parties as 1, 2, 3 . . . is based on their percentage of the vote, since to rank them in terms of seats would conceal the very bias it is sought to measure—namely, the bias introduced by the intervening variable of the electoral system which constitutes the mechanism by which votes are translated into seats.

ing a distribution of partisan support capable of transforming the electoral system from an ally into a foe. The explanation for the favourable impact of the electoral system on the Progressives and Social Credit from 1921 to 1957 when they were the weakest parties is simply that they were sectional parties which concentrated their efforts in their areas of strength where the electoral system worked in their favour. Once the electoral system has rewarded the strongest party and a weak party with concentrated sectional strength there are not many more seats to go around. In this kind of party system, which Canada had from 1921 to Mr. Diefenbaker's breakthrough, serious discrimination against the second party in a three-party system and the second and third parties in a four-parties system is highly likely.

Table 3 reveals that the electoral system positively favours minor parties with sectional strongholds and discourages minor parties with diffuse support. The classic example of the latter phenomenon is provided by the Reconstruction party in the 1935 election. For its 8.7 percent of the vote it was rewarded with one seat, and promptly disappeared from the scene. Yet its electoral support was more than twice that of Social Credit which gained seventeen seats, and only marginally less than that of the CCF which gained seven seats. The case of the Reconstruction party provides dramatic illustration of the futility of party effort for a minor party which lacks a sectional stronghold. The treatment of the CCF/NDP by the electoral system is only slightly less revealing. This party with diffuse support which aspired to national and major party status never received as many seats as would have been "justified" by its voting support, and on six occasions out of ten received less than half the seats to which it was "entitled." The contrasting treatment of Social Credit and the Progressives, sectional minor parties, by the electoral system clearly reveals the bias of the electoral system in favour of concentrated support and against diffuse support.[4]

Table 3   Minor Parties: Percentage of Seats and Votes

	Progressives		Reconstruction		CCF/NDP		Soc. Credit		Créditiste	
	votes	seats	votes	seats	votes	seats	votes	seats	votes	seats
1921	23.1	27.7								
1925	9.0	9.8								
1926	5.3	8.2								
1930	3.2	4.9								
1935			8.7	0.4	8.9	2.9	4.1	6.9		
1940					8.5	3.3	2.7	4.1		
1945					15.6	11.4	4.1	5.3		
1949					13.4	5.0	3.7	3.8		
1953					11.3	8.7	5.4	5.7		
1957					10.7	9.4	6.6	7.2		
1958					9.5	3.0	2.6	—		
1962					13.5	7.2	11.7	11.3		
1963					13.1	6.4	11.9	9.1		
1965					17.9	7.9	3.7	1.9	4.7	3.4

DISTORTION IN PARTY PARLIAMENTARY REPRESENTATION

No less important than the general differences in the way the electoral system rewards or punishes each individual party as such, is the manner in which it fashions particular patterns of sectional representation within the ranks of the parliamentary parties out of the varying distributions of electoral support they received. This sectional intra-party discrimination affects all parties. The electoral system consistently minimized the Ontario support of

the Progressives which provided the party with 43.5 percent, 39.7 percent, and 29.4 percent of its total votes in the first three elections of the twenties. The party received only 36.9 percent, 8.3 percent, and 10 percent of its total seats from that province. Further, by its varying treatment of the party's electoral support from Manitoba, Saskatchewan, and Alberta it finally helped to reduce the Progressives to an Alberta party.

An analysis of CCF/NDP votes and seats clearly illustrates the manner in which the electoral system has distorted the parliamentary wing of the party. Table 4 reveals the extreme discrimination visited on Ontario supporters

Table 4   Percentage of Total CCF/NDP Strength, in Seats and Votes Coming from Selected Provinces

	NS	Que.	Ont.	Man.	Sask.	Alta.	BC
1935 votes	—	1.9	32.7	13.9	18.8	7.9	24.8
seats	—	—	—	28.6	28.6	—	42.9
1940 votes	4.5	1.9	15.6	15.6	27.0	8.9	26.2
seats	12.5	—	—	12.5	62.5	—	12.5
1945 votes	6.4	4.1	31.9	12.5	20.5	7.0	15.4
seats	3.6	—	—	17.9	64.3	—	14.3
1949 votes	4.3	2.3	39.2	10.6	19.5	4.0	18.6
seats	7.7	—	7.7	23.1	38.5	—	23.1
1953 votes	3.5	3.7	33.4	10.1	24.6	3.7	19.7
seats	4.3	—	4.3	13.0	47.8	—	30.4
1957 votes	2.4	4.5	38.7	11.6	19.8	3.8	18.6
seats	—	—	12.0	20.0	40.0	—	28.0
1958 votes	2.7	6.6	37.9	10.8	16.3	2.8	22.2
seats	—	—	37.5	—	12.5	—	50.0
1962 votes	3.8	8.9	44.0	7.4	9.0	4.1	20.4
seats	5.3	—	31.6	10.5	—	—	52.6
1963 votes	2.6	14.6	42.6	6.4	7.3	3.4	21.5
seats	—	—	35.3	11.8	—	—	52.9
1965 votes	2.8	17.7	43.0	6.6	7.6	3.2	17.3
seats	—	—	42.9	14.3	—	—	42.9

Note: Percentages of votes do not total 100 horizontally because the table does not include Newfoundland, Prince Edward Island, New Brunswick, or the territories where the CCF/NDP gained a few votes but no seats.

of the CCF from 1935 to 1957. With the exception of 1940 CCF Ontario voting support consistently constituted between 30 and 40 percent of total CCF voting support. Yet, the contribution of Ontario to CCF parliamentary representation was derisory. During the same period there was a marked overrepresentation of Saskatchewan in the CCF caucus. The 1945 election is indicative. The 260 000 votes from Ontario, 31.9 percent of the total CCF vote, produced no seats at all, while 167 000 supporters from Saskatchewan, 20.5 percent of the total party vote, were rewarded with eighteen seats, 64.3 percent of total party seats. In these circumstances it was not surprising that observers were led to mislabel the CCF an agrarian party.

The major parties are not immune from the tendency of the electoral system to make the parliamentary parties grossly inaccurate reflections of the sectional distribution of party support. Table 5 makes it clear that the electoral system has been far from impartial in its treatment of Liberal and Conservative voting support from Ontario and Quebec. For fourteen consecutive elections covering nearly half a century there was a consistent and usually marked overrepresentation of Quebec in the parliamentary Liberal party and marked underrepresentation in the parliamentary Conservative party, with the exception of 1958. For ten consecutive elections from 1921 to 1957 Ontario was consistently and markedly overrepresented in the parliamentary Conservative party, and for eleven consecutive elections from 1921 to 1958, there was consistent, but less marked, underrepresentation of Ontario in the parliamentary Liberal party. Thus the electoral system, by pulling the parliamentary Liberal party toward Quebec and the parliamentary Conservative party toward Ontario, made the sectional cleavages between the parties much more pronounced in Parliament than they were at the level of the electorate.

The way in which the electoral system affected the relationship of Quebec to the parliamentary wings of the two major parties is evident in the truly startling discrepancies between votes and seats for the two parties from that province. From 1921 to 1965 inclusive the Liberals gained 752 members from Quebec, and the Conservatives only 135. The ratio of 5.6 Liberals to each Conservative in the House of Commons contrasts sharply with the 1.9 to 1 ratio of Liberals to Conservatives at the level of the voters.[5]

Given the recurrent problems concerning the status of Quebec in Canadian federalism and the consistent tension in French-English relations it is self-evident that the effects of the electoral system noted above can be appropriately described as divisive and detrimental to national unity. Brady and Siegfried, among others, have stressed the dangers which would arise should the lines of partisan division coincide with the "lines of nationality and religion,"[6] the very direction in which the electoral system has pushed the party system. This consequence has been partially veiled by the typically plural composition of the government party. In parliamentary systems, however, the composition of the chief opposition party, the almost inevitable successor to governmental responsibilities over time, is only moderately less significant. The electoral system has placed serious barriers in the way of the Conservative party's attempts to gain parliamentary representation from a province where its own interests and those of national unity coincided on the desirability of making a major contender for public office as representative as possible.[7] The frequent thesis that the association of the Conservatives with conscription in 1917 destroyed their prospects in Quebec only becomes meaningful when it is noted that a particular electoral system presided over that destruction.

The following basic effects of the electoral system have been noted. The electoral system

Table 5 Liberals and Conservatives: Percentage of Total Parliamentary Strength and Total Electoral Support from Quebec and Ontario

| | Conservatives | | | | Liberals | | | |
| | Ontario | | Quebec | | Ontario | | Quebec | |
	seats	votes	seats	votes	seats	votes	seats	votes
1921	74.0	47.1	—	15.5	18.1	26.6	56.0	43.8
1925	58.6	47.4	3.4	18.4	11.1	30.1	59.6	37.8
1926	58.2	44.9	4.4	18.7	20.3	31.7	46.9	33.4
1930	43.1	38.9	17.5	24.0	24.2	33.7	44.0	30.6
1935	62.5	43.1	12.5	24.7	32.4	34.4	31.8	31.5
1940	62.5	48.6	2.5	16.4	31.5	34.4	33.7	31.2
1945	71.6	52.7	3.0	8.3	27.2	34.6	42.4	33.3
1949	61.0	43.6	4.9	22.6	29.0	31.9	35.2	33.2
1953	64.7	44.2	7.8	26.0	29.8	32.6	38.6	34.2
1957	54.5	42.9	8.0	21.7	20.0	31.1	59.0	38.1
1958	32.2	36.2	24.0	25.7	30.6	33.3	51.0	37.8
1962	30.2	36.9	12.1	21.6	44.0	39.2	35.0	28.6
1963	28.4	37.8	8.4	16.0	40.3	39.1	36.4	29.3
1965	25.8	37.4	8.2	17.3	38.9	38.6	42.7	30.0

has not been impartial in its translation of votes into seats. Its benefits have been disproportionately given to the strongest major party and a weak sectional party. The electoral system has made a major contribution to the identification of particular sections/provinces with particular parties. It has undervalued the partisan diversity within each section/province. By so doing it has rendered the parliamentary composition of each party less representative of the sectional interests in the political system than is the party electorate from which that representation is derived. The electoral system favours minor parties with concentrated sectional support, and discourages those with diffuse national support. The electoral system has consistently exaggerated the significance of cleavages demarcated by sectional/provincial boundaries and has thus tended to transform contests between parties into contests between sections/provinces.

In view of the preceding it is impossible to accept any assertion which implies that the electoral system has had only trivial consequences for the party system. The Canadian party system in its present form would not exist had it not been for the highly selective impetus which the electoral system gave to its development. In more specific terms, it is evident that one of the most basic aspects of Canadian politics, its sectional nature, becomes incomprehensible if attention is not constantly focused on the sectional bias engendered by the single-member constituency system.

PARTY SYSTEM AS A NATIONALIZING AGENCY

The ramifications of sectional politics are highly complex. Given the paucity of literature on Canadian parties it is impossible to make categorical statements about these ramifications in all cases. Where evidence is sparse, the analysis will of necessity be reduced to hypotheses, some of which will be sustained by little more than deduction.

One of the most widespread interpretations of the party system claims that it, or at least the two major parties, functions as a great unifying or nationalizing agency. Canadian politics, it is emphasized, are politics of moderation, or brokerage politics, which minimize differences, restrain fissiparous tendencies, and thus over time help knit together the diverse interests of a polity weak in integration.[8] It is noteworthy that this brokerage theory is almost exclusively applied to the reconciliation of sectional, racial, and religious divisions, the latter two frequently being regarded as simply more specific versions of the first with respect to French-English relations. The theory of brokerage politics thus assumes that the historically significant cleavages in Canada are sectional, reflecting the federal nature of Canadian society, or racial/religious, reflecting a continuation of the struggle which attracted Durham's attention in the mid-nineteenth century. Brokerage politics between classes is mentioned, if at all, as an afterthought.

The interpretation of the party system in terms of its fulfilment of a nationalizing function is virtually universal. Close scrutiny, however, indicates that this is at best questionable, and possibly invalid. It is difficult to determine the precise meaning of the argument that the party system has been a nationalizing agency, stressing what Canadians have in common, bringing together representatives of diverse interests to deliberate on government policies. In an important sense the argument is misleading in that it attributes to the party system what is simply inherent in a representative democracy which inevitably brings together Nova Scotians, Albertans, and Quebeckers to a common assemblage point, and because of the majoritarian necessities of the parliamentary system requires agreement among contending interests to accomplish anything at all. Or, to put it differently, the necessity for inter-group collaboration in any on-going political system makes it possible to claim of any party system compatible with the survival of the polity that it acts as a nationalizing agency. The extent to which any particular party system does so act is inescapably therefore a comparative question or a question of degree. In strict logic an evaluation of alternative types of party systems is required before a particular one can be accorded unreserved plaudits for the success with which it fulfils a nationalizing function.

Assistance in grappling with this issue comes from an examination of a basic problem. In what ways does the party system stimulate the very cleavages it is alleged to bridge? The question can be rephrased to ask the extent to which an unvarying sectionalism has an autonomous existence independent of the particular electoral and party systems employed by Canadians. The basic approach of this paper is that the party system, importantly conditioned by the electoral system, exacerbates the very cleavages it is credited with healing. As a corollary it is suggested that the party system is not simply a reflection of sectionalism, but that sectionalism is also a reflection of the party system.

The electoral system has helped to foster a particular kind of political style by the special significance it accords to sectionalism. This is evident in party campaign strategy, in party policies, in intersectional differences in the nature and vigour of party activity, and in differences in the intra-party socialization experiences of parliamentary personnel of the various parties. As a consequence the electoral system has had an important effect on perceptions of the party system and, by extension, of the political system itself. Sectionalism has been rendered highly visible because the electoral system makes it a fruitful basis on which to organize electoral support. Divisions cutting through sections, particularly those based on the class system, have been much less salient because the possibility of payoffs in terms of representation has been minimal.

PARTIES AND CAMPAIGN STRATEGY

An initial perspective on the contribution of the parties to sectionalism is provided by some of the basic aspects of campaign strategy. Inadequate attention has been paid to the extent to which the campaign activities of the parties have exacerbated the hatreds, fears, and insecurities related to divisive sectional and ethnic cleavages.[9]

The basic cleavage throughout Canadian history concerns Quebec, or more precisely that part of French Canada resident in Quebec, and its relationships with the rest of the country. The evidence suggests that elections have fed on racial fears and insecurities, rather than reduced them.[10] The three post-war elections of 1921, 1925, and 1926 produced overwhelming Liberal majorities at the level of seats in Quebec, 65 out of 65 in 1921, 59 out of 65 in 1925, and 60 seats out of 65 in 1926. The Conservatives' weakness in Quebec derived from their identification with conscription, the hanging of Riel, and the punitive treatment they received from the electoral system. A contributory factor of considerable importance, however, especially in 1921 and 1925, was the vituperative tirade which the Liberals waged against Meighen and the Conservatives, stressing the 1917 crisis and exaggerating the dangers to Quebec should the Conservatives be successful. The 1925 campaign was described by Meighen as one in which "our candidates faced a campaign of hatred and racial appeal even more bitter than that of 1921. Paid organizers went from house to house advising the voters, particularly the women, that if

Meighen were elected Prime Minister a war with Turkey would be declared and that the entrails of their sons would be scattered on the streets of Constantinople."[11] In view of the ample evidence documented by Graham and Neatby of the extent to which the Liberal campaigns stirred up the animosities and insecurities of French Canada, it is difficult to assert that the party system performed a unifying role in a province where historic tensions were potentially divisive. The fact that the Liberals were able to "convince Quebec" that they were its only defenders and that their party contained members of both ethnic groups after the elections scarcely constitute refutation when attention is directed to the methods employed to achieve this end, and when it is noted that the election results led to the isolation of Canada's second great party from Quebec.[12]

More recent indications of sectional aspects of campaign strategy with respect to Quebec help to verify the divisive nature of election campaigning. The well-known decision of the Conservative party in 1957, acting on Gordon Churchill's maxim to "reinforce success not failure," to reduce its Quebec efforts and concentrate on the possibilities of success in the remainder of the country provides an important indication of the significance of calculations of sectional pay-offs in dictating campaign strategy.[13] The logic behind this policy was a direct consequence of the electoral system, for it was that system which dictated that increments of voting support from Quebec would produce less pay-off in representation than would equal increments elsewhere where the prospects of Conservative constituency victories were more promising. The electoral results were brilliantly successful from the viewpoint of the party, but less so from the perspective of Quebec which contributed only 8 per cent of the new government's seats, and received only three cabinet ministers.[14]

In these circumstances the election of 1958 was crucial in determining the nature and extent of French-Canadian participation in the new government which obviously would be formed by the Conservatives. Group appeals were exploited by the bribe that Quebec would get many more cabinet seats if that province returned a larger number of Tory MPs.[15] Party propaganda stimulated racial tensions and insecurities. A Conservative advertisement showed an outline map of Canada deeply cleft by a hatchet at the Quebec-Ontario border. Above it were the words: "The newspapers predict a shattering triumph for Diefenbaker." Below it the words: "Let us not isolate Quebec." Liberal propaganda retaliated with an advertisement which consisted of twelve outlined drawings of Diefenbaker comparing him to previous Conservatives who were stereotyped as anti-French.[16] Neither appeal was well designed to foster easy cordiality and an absence of suspicion and fear between French- and English-speaking Canada.[17]

The significance of Quebec representation in explaining the nature of the Canadian party system has often been noted. Meisel states that the federal politician is faced with the dilemma of ignoring the pleas of Quebec, in which case "he may lose the support of Canada's second largest province without the seats of which a Parliamentary majority is almost impossible. If he heeds the wishes of Quebec, he may be deprived of indispensable support elsewhere."[18] Lipson describes Quebec as the "solid South" of Canada whose support has contributed at different times to the hegemony of both parties, a fact which is basic in explaining the strategy of opposition of the two major parties.[19] An important point is made by Ward in his observation that Liberal dominance in Quebec contributes to "internal strains in other parties." He adds the fundamental point that it is the electoral system which "by throwing whole blocks of seats to one party" fosters

for that party a "special role as protector of the minority," while other parties are baffled by their inability to make significant breakthroughs in representation. Prophetically, as it turned out, he noted the developing theory that opposition parties should attempt to construct parliamentary majorities without Quebec, thus facing French Canadians with the option of becoming an opposition minority or casting themselves loose from the Liberals.[20]

Ward's analysis makes clear that the special electoral importance of Quebec and the resultant party strategies elicited by that fact are only meaningful in the context of an electoral system which operates on a "winner take all" basis, not only at the level of the constituency but, to a modified extent, at the level of the province as a whole. It is only at the level of seats, not votes, that Quebec became a Liberal stronghold, a Canadian "solid South," and a one-party monopoly. The Canadian "solid South," like its American counterpart, is a contrivance of the electoral system, not an autonomous social fact which exists independent of it.

The electoral system is to politicians as the price system is to businessmen. If the latter found marked differentials in the returns they received for their commodities in different sections of the country this would have, to say the least, important consequences for the staff in the salesroom. It seems clear that the staff in the salesroom of the political parties is importantly conditioned in its conduct by the imperfections of the political market in which the parties sell their goods.

Quebec constitutes the most striking example of the sectional nature of party strategy, electoral appeals, and electoral outcomes. It is, however, only a specific manifestation of the general principle that when the distribution of partisan support within a province or section is such that significant political pay-offs are likely to accrue to politicians who address themselves to the special needs of the area concerned, politicians will not fail to provide at least a partial response.[21] The tendency of parties "to aim appeals at the nerve centers of particular provinces or regions, hoping thus to capture a bloc geographical vote,"[22] and to emphasize sectional appeals, are logical party responses within the Canadian electoral framework.

ELECTORAL SYSTEM AND PARTY POLICY

The effect of the electoral system on party policies has already been suggested in part in the preceding indication of its impact on election campaigns. The inquiry can be extended by noting that the electoral system affects party policies both directly and indirectly. The direct effect flows from the elementary consideration that each party devises policy in the light of a different set of sectional considerations. In theory, if the party is viewed strictly as a maximizing body pursuing representation, party sensitivity should be most highly developed in marginal situations where an appropriate policy initiative, a special organizational effort, or a liberal use of campaign funds might tip the balance of sectional representation to the side of the party. Unfortunately, sufficient evidence is not available to assert that this is a valid description of the import of sectional considerations on party strategies. The indirect effect of the electoral system is that it plays an important role in the determination of who the party policy makers will be.

The indirect effect presupposes the preeminence of the parliamentary party and its leaders in policy-making. Acceptance of this presupposition requires a brief preliminary analysis of the nature of party organization, especially for the two major parties. The litera-

ture has been unanimous in referring to the organizational weakness of the Liberals and Conservatives. Some of the basic aspects and results of this will be summarily noted.

The extra-parliamentary structures of the two major parties have been extremely weak, lacking in continuity and without any disciplining power over the parliamentary party. The two major parties have been leader-dominated with membership playing a limited role in policy-making and party-financing. Although there are indications that the extra-parliamentary apparatus of the parties is growing in importance, it can be safely said that for the period under review both major parties have been essentially parliamentary parties.

Some suggestive explanations of this situation have been offered, particularly by Regenstreif. These include the absence in Canada of several important stimuli which have facilitated the development of party organization in the United States and Great Britain. The stimuli resulting from a powerful mass-membership left-wing party and by serious restrictions on campaign expenditures as in Great Britain, are absent in Canada. Unlike the American situation, Canadian parties are not responsible for voter registration. Compared to the United States, Canada also has a paucity of elections and elective offices, and party spoils have constituted a less attractive inducement to organizational work for the party.

In these circumstances of weak extra-parliamentary organization, it is evident that the parliamentary party, or more specifically, the leader and his trusted parliamentary colleagues, has had few institutional party restraints to contend with in the development of policy.[23] Thus, the contribution of the electoral system to the determination of the parliamentary personnel of the party becomes, by logical extension, a contribution to the formation of party policies.[24] Scarrow has asserted that "it is the makeup of the parliamentary party, including the proportional strength and bargaining position of the various parts, which is the most crucial factor in determining policy at any one time."[25] While this hypothesis may require modification in particular cases, it is likely that historical research will confirm its general validity. For example, the antithetical attitudes of Conservatives and Liberals to conscription in both World Wars were related not only to the electoral consequences of different choices, but also reflected the backgrounds and bias of the party personnel available to make such key decisions.[26] The generally much more solicitous treatment of Quebec and the French Canadians by the Liberals than by the Conservatives is similarly explicable. It is not accidental that bitter criticisms of family allowances as bribes to Quebec came from the Conservatives, while the recent emphasis on unhyphenated Canadianism has also been a Conservative contribution.[27]

The significance of the electoral system for party policy is due to its consistent failure to reflect with even rough accuracy the distribution of partisan support in the various sections/provinces of the country. By making the Conservatives far more of a British and Ontario-based party, the Liberals far more a French and Quebec party, the CCF far more a prairie and BC party, and even Social Credit far more of an Alberta party up until 1953, than the electoral support of these parties "required," they were deprived of intra-party spokesmen proportionate to their electoral support from the sections where they were relatively weak. The relative, or on occasion total, absence of such spokesmen for particular sectional communities seriously affects the image of the parties as national bodies, deprives the party concerned of articulate proponents of particular sectional interests in caucus and in the House, and, it can be deductively suggested, renders the members of the parliamentary party personally less sensitive to

the interests of the unrepresented sections than they otherwise would be. As a result the general perspectives and policy orientations of a party are likely to be skewed in favour of those interests which, by virtue of strong parliamentary representation, can vigorously assert their claims.

If a bias of this nature is consistently visited on a specific party over long periods of time it will importantly condition the general orientation of the party and the political information and values of party MPs. It is in such ways that it can be argued that the effect of the electoral system is cumulative, creating conditions which aggravate the bias which it initially introduced into the party.[28] To take the case of the Conservative party, the thesis is that not only does the electoral system make that party less French by depriving it of French representation as such, but also by the effect which that absence of French colleagues has on the possibility that its non-French members will shed their parochial perspectives through intra-party contacts with French co-workers in Parliament.[29]

The Conservatives have experienced great difficulty in recruiting capable French-Canadian representation into the hierarchy of the parliamentary party, a difficulty partly related to the discrimination of the electoral system which gave the party only a small pool of talent to work with. It has also been suggested that the parliamentary party has provided a most uncongenial habitat for those few French Canadians who did survive the rigours of electoral competition to take their seats as Conservative MPs. John R. Williams claims that the Ontario-dominated parliamentary group played an important role in the decline of the Conservative party in the King era.[30] The parliamentary party with its disparaging comments about Quebec and miserable treatment of French-Canadian colleagues seriously damaged the party in Quebec. French-Canadian Conservatives refused to run for re-election or crossed the floor to join the Liberals. On at least two occasions the departing French Canadians "publicly renounced the party because of the parliamentary group's hostility toward them and their race."[31] In marked contrast is the evidence of Ward that French-English relations within the Liberal party are "regarded by both as good," although they seem to be based on peaceful coexistence rather than on mutually intimate understandings.[32]

While a lengthy catalogue of explanations can be adduced to explain the divergent orientations of Liberals and Conservatives to Quebec and French Canada the electoral system must be given high priority as an influencing factor. A strong deductive case therefore can be made that the sectional bias in party representation engendered by the electoral system has had an important effect on the policies of specific parties and on policy differences between parties.[33] Additionally, the electoral system has helped to determine the real or perceived sectional consequences of alternative party policy decisions. Politicians engaged in party organizational and electoral work are, in Chubby Power's words, "inclined to gauge policies and administrations primarily in the light of their effect on the voting proclivities of the population, and to assess their value in terms of electoral success or failure, rather than on any other consideration."[34] This thesis, a practitioner's echo of Schumpeter's suggestion that politicians are individuals who deal in votes,[35] is far from constituting a total explanation of the factors which influence policy, but it is clear that no politician in a competitive party system can overlook the electoral consequences of his actions. In particular instances, the desire to win over a section in which the party is weak may lead to neglect of an area in which the party already has strong representation. King's courting of the prairie provinces and neglect of the Maritimes in the first half of the twenties constitutes a revealing instance of this phenomenon.[36] Whether a

party directs attention to the sections where it is strong, as a result of the assertiveness of intra-party spokesmen, or whether attention is lavished on a section where a major breakthrough is deemed possible, is a matter for investigation in each case. From our perspective the basic point is that both reflect the politics of sectionalism as stimulated by the single-member constituency system.

In some cases the sectional nature of party support requires politicians to make a cruel choice between sections, a choice recognized as involving the sacrifice of future representation from one section in order to retain it from another. This, it has been argued, was the Conservative dilemma in deciding whether or not Riel was to hang and in determining conscription policy in the First World War. Faced with a choice between Quebec and Ontario, in each case they chose Ontario. It should be noted that these either/or sectional choices occasionally thrown up in the political system are given exaggerated significance by an electoral system capable of transforming a moderate loss of votes in a section into almost total annihilation at the level of representation. If only votes were considered, the harshness of such decisions would be greatly mitigated, for decisions could be made on the basis of much less dramatic marginal assessments of the political consequences of alternative courses of action.

ELECTORAL SYSTEM AND PERCEPTIONS OF THE POLICY

A general point, easily overlooked because of its elementary nature, is that the electoral system has influenced perceptions of the political system. The sectional basis of party representation which the electoral system has stimulated has reduced the visibility of cleavages cutting through sections. The effect of this on the perceptions and conduct of political activists has already been noted. Academics have also been misled and frequently have imputed a monolithic partisan unity to the sectional particularisms of Canadian society.[37] The resultant misconception has identified particular sections with particular parties and particular parties with particular sections.[38]

It has been argued that the fragmentation of the electoral struggle into several hundred individual constituency contests, in contrast to the American system, prevents Canadians from identifying a "genuine regional influence" on election outcomes.[39] The fact is, however, that commentators have been far from reluctant to interpret election phenomena in sectional terms. A hasty survey of political literature finds Quebec portrayed as "the solid Quebec of 1921," western Canada described as "once the fortress of protest movements," since transformed "into a Conservative stronghold," eastern Canada depicted in the 1925 election as having "punished King for his preoccupation with the prairies," and the Conservative party described in 1955 as "almost reduced into being an Ontario party,"[40] when in the previous election 55.8 percent of its voting support came from outside that province.

The use of sectional terminology in description easily shades off into highly suspect assumptions about the voting behaviour of the electorate within sections. One of the most frequent election interpretations attributes a monolithic quality to Quebec voters and then argues that they "have instinctively given the bulk of their support" to the government[41] or it is claimed that "the voters of Quebec traditionally seem to want the bulk of their representation . . . on the government side of the House. . . ."[42] Several authors have specifically suggested that in 1958 Quebec, or the French Canadians, swung to Diefenbaker for this reason. To Regenstreif this was because otherwise he would have formed a government without French support, which would have meant

"that their entire way of life would be at stake. . . . Their solution was to help form the new government that was obviously going to be created anyway and thereby avoid the much-feared isolation that would otherwise be their lot."[43] A recent analysis of New Brunswick politics argues that the strong tendency for MPs from that province to be on the government side of the House "must be" because "it seeks to gain what concessions it can by supporting the government and relying on its sense of gratitude."[44]

The tendency of the electoral system to create sectional or provincial sweeps for one party at the level of representation is an important reason for these misinterpretations. Since similar explanations have become part of the folklore of Canadian politics it is useful to examine the extremely tenuous basis of logic on which they rest. Quebec will serve as a useful case study. The first point to note is the large percentage of the Quebec electorate which does not vote for the party which subsequently forms the government, a percentage varying from 29.8 percent in 1921 to 70.4 percent in 1962, and averaging 48 percent for the period 1921 to 1965 as a whole. In the second place any government party will tend to win most of the sections most of the time. That is what a government party is. While Quebec has shown an above average propensity to accord more than fifty percent of its representation to the government party (on eleven occasions out of fourteen, compared to an average for all sections of just under eight out of fourteen[45]) this is partly because of the size of the contingent from Quebec and its frequent one-sided representation patterns. This means that to a large extent Quebec determines which party will be the government, rather than exhibiting a preference for being on the government or opposition side of the House. This can be tested by switching the representation which Quebec gave to the two main parties in each of the eleven elections in which Quebec backed the winner. The method is simply to transfer the number of seats Quebec accorded the winning party to the second main party, and transfer the latter's Quebec seats to the former. This calculation shows that had Quebec distributed its seats between the two main parties in a manner precisely the opposite to its actual performance it would have been on the winning side on seven out of eleven occasions anyway.[46] It is thus more accurate to say that parties need Quebec in order to win than to say that Quebec displays a strong desire to be on the winning side.

One final indication of the logical deficiencies of the assumption that Quebec voters are motivated by a bandwagon psychology will suffice. The case of 1958 will serve as an example. In 1957 when there was no prediction of a Conservative victory, Quebec voters gave 31.1 percent of their voting support to the Conservative party. In 1958 that percentage jumped to 49.6 when predictions of a Conservative victory were nearly universal. On the reasonable assumption that most of the Conservative supporters in 1957 remained with the party in 1958, and on the further assumption, which is questionable, that all of the increment in Conservative support was due to a desire to be on the winning side, the explanation is potentially applicable to only one Quebec voter in five.

In concluding this critical analysis of a segment of Canadian political folklore it is only necessary to state that the attribution of questionable motivations to Quebec or French Canada could easily have been avoided if attention had been concentrated on voting data rather than on the bias in representation caused by the single-member constituency system. The analysis of Canadian politics has been harmfully affected by a kind of mental shorthand which manifests itself in the acceptance of a political map of the country which identifies provinces or sections in terms of the end results of the political process, partisan

representation. This perception is natural since elections occur only once every three or four years while the results are visible for the entire period between elections. Since sectional discrepancies between votes and seats are due to the electoral system it is evident that the latter has contributed to the formation of a set of seldom questioned perceptions which exaggerate the partisan significance of geographical boundaries.

ELECTORAL SYSTEM, SECTIONALISM, AND INSTABILITY

Individuals can relate to the party system in several ways, but the two most fundamental are class and sectionalism.[47] The two are antithetical, for one emphasizes the geography of residence, while the other stresses stratification distinctions for which residence is irrelevant. The frequently noted conservative tone which pervades Canadian politics is a consequence of the sectional nature of the party system.[48] The emphasis on sectional divisions engendered by the electoral system has submerged class conflicts, and to the extent that our politics has been ameliorative it has been more concerned with the distribution of burdens and benefits between sections than between classes. The poverty of the Maritimes has occupied an honourable place in the foreground of public discussion. The diffuse poverty of the generally underprivileged has scarcely been noticed.

Such observations lend force to John Porter's thesis that Canadian parties have failed to harness the "conservative-progressive dynamic" related to the Canadian class system, and to his assertion that "to obscure social divisions through brokerage politics is to remove from the political system that element of dialectic which is the source of creative politics."[49] The fact is, however, that given the historical (and existing) state of class polarization in Canada the electoral system has made sectionalism a more rewarding vehicle for amassing political support than class. The destructive impact of the electoral system on the CCF is highly indicative of this point. It is not that the single member constituency system discourages class-based politics in any absolute sense, as the example of Britain shows, but that it discourages such politics when class identities are weak or submerged behind sectional identities.

This illustrates the general point that the differences in the institutional contexts of politics have important effects in determining which kinds of conflict become salient in the political system. The particular institutional context with which this paper is concerned, the electoral system, has clearly fostered a sectional party system in which party strategists have concentrated on winning sections over to their side. It has encouraged a politics of opportunism based on sectional appeals and conditioned by one party bastions where the opposition is tempted to give up the battle and pursue success in more promising areas.

A politics of sectionalism is a politics of instability for two reasons. In the first place it induces parties to pay attention to the realities of representation which filter through the electoral system, at the expense of the realities of partisan support at the level of the electorate. The self-interest which may induce a party to write off a section because its weak support there is discriminated against by the electoral system may be exceedingly unfortunate for national unity. Imperfections in the political market render the likelihood of an invisible hand transforming the pursuit of party good into public good somewhat dubious.

Secondly, sectional politics is potentially far more disruptive to the polity than class politics.[50] This is essentially because sectional politics has an inherent tendency to call into question the very nature of the political system and its legitimacy. Classes, unlike sections, cannot secede from the political system, and

are consequently more prone to accept its legitimacy. The very nature of their spatial distribution not only inhibits their political organization but induces them to work through existing instrumentalities. With sections this is not the case.

Given the strong tendency to sectionalism found in the very nature of Canadian society the question can be raised as to the appropriateness of the existing electoral system. Duverger has pointed out that the single-member constituency system "accentuates the geographical localization of opinions: one might even say that it tends to transform a national opinion . . . into a local opinion by allowing it to be represented only in the sections of the country in which it is strongest." Proportional representation works in the opposite manner for "opinions strongly entrenched locally tend to be broadened on to the national plane by the possibility of being represented in districts where they are in a small minority." The political significance of these opposed tendencies "is clear: proportional representation tends to strengthen national unity (or, to be more precise, national uniformity); the simple majority system accentuates local differences. The consequences are fortunate or unfortunate according to the particular situation in each country."[51]

SECTIONALISM AND DISCONTINUITIES IN PARTY REPRESENTATION

It might be argued that the appropriate question is not whether sectional (or other) interests are represented proportionately to their voting support in each party, but simply whether they are represented in the party system as a whole proportionately to their general electoral strength. This assertion, however, is overly simple and unconvincing.

An electoral system which exaggerates the role of specific sections in specific parties accentuates the importance of sectionalism itself. If sectionalism in its "raw" condition is already strong, its exaggeration may cause strains beyond the capacity of the polity to handle. By its stimulus to sectional cleavages the electoral system transforms the party struggle into a struggle between sections, raising the danger that "parties . . . cut off from gaining support among a major stratum . . . lose a major reason for compromise."[52]

This instability is exacerbated by the fact that the electoral system facilitates sudden and drastic alterations in the basis of party parliamentary representation. Recent changes with respect to NDP representation from Saskatchewan, Social Credit representation from Quebec, and the startling change in the influence of the prairie contingent in the Conservative party, with its counterpart of virtually eliminating other parties from that section, constitute important illustrations. The experience of Social Credit since 1962 and more recent experience of the Conservative party reveal that such changes may be more than a party can successfully handle.

Sudden changes in sectional representation are most pronounced in the transition from being an opposition party to becoming the government party. As Underhill notes,[53] it is generally impossible to have more than one party with significant representation from both French and English Canada at the same time. That party is invariably the government party. This has an important consequence which has been insufficiently noted. Not only are opposition parties often numerically weak and devoid of access to the expertise that would prepare them for the possibility of governing, but they are also far less national in composition than the government party. On the two occasions since the First World War when the Conservatives ousted Liberal governments, 1930 and 1957, their opposition

experience cut them off from contact with Quebec at the parliamentary level. Even though the party was successful in making significant breakthroughs in the province in 1930 and especially in 1958, it can be suggested that it had serious problems in digesting the sudden input of Quebec MPs, particularly in the latter year.

The transition from opposition to government therefore is a transition from being sectional to being national, not only in the tasks of government, but typically in the very composition of the party itself. The hypothesis that this discontinuity may have serious effects on the capacity of the party to govern is deserving of additional research. It is likely that such research will suggest a certain incongruity between the honorific status symbolically accorded Her Majesty's Loyal Opposition, and an electoral system which is likely to hamper the development in that party of those perspectives functional to successful governing.

THE ELECTORAL SYSTEM AS A DETERMINANT OF THE PARTY SYSTEM

Students of Canadian politics have been singularly unwilling to attribute any explanatory power to the electoral system as a determinant of the party system.[54] Lipson has argued that it is not the electoral system which moulds the party system, but rather the reverse. Essentially his thesis is that parties select the type of electoral system most compatible with their own interest, which is self-perpetuation. He admits in passing that once selected the electoral system "produces a reciprocal effect upon the parties which brought it into being."[55]

Lipson's interpretation is surely misleading and fallacious in its implication that because parties preside over the selection, modification, and replacement of particular institutions, the subsequent feed-back of those institutions on the parties should not be regarded as causal. In the modern democratic party state, parties preside over the legal arrangements [of] governing campaign expenses, eligibility of candidates, the rules establishing the determination of party winners and losers, the kinds of penalties, such as loss of deposits, which shall be visited on candidates with a low level of support, the rules establishing who may vote, and so on. Analysis is stifled if it is assumed that because these rules are made by parties the effect of the rules on the parties is in some sense to be regarded as derivative or of secondary interest or importance. Fundamentally the argument concerns the priority to be accorded the chicken or the egg. As such it can be pursued to an infinite regression, for it can be asserted that the parties which make a particular set of rules are themselves products of the rules which prevailed in the previous period, which in turn. . . . It might also be noted that parties which preside over particular changes in electoral arrangements may be mistaken in their predictions about the effect of the changes. It is clear that the introduction of the alternative ballot in British Columbia in 1952 misfired from the viewpoint of its sponsors, with dramatic effects on the nature of the provincial party system which subsequently developed.

The only reasonable perspective for the analyst to adopt is to accept the interdependence of electoral systems and party systems and then to investigate whatever aspects of that interdependence seem to provide useful clues for the understanding of the political system.

In a recent article Meisel explicitly agrees with Lipson, asserting that parties are products of societies rather than of differences between parliamentary or presidential systems, or of electoral laws.[56] This argument is weakened by its assumption that society is something apart from the institutional arrangements of which it is composed. It is unclear in this dichotomy just what society is. While it may be possible at the moment when particular institutions are being established to regard them as separate from the society to which they are to be fitted, this is not so with long-established institutions which become part and parcel of the society itself. Livingston's argument that after a while it becomes impossible to make an analytic distinction between the instrumentalities of federalism and the federal nature of the society they were designed to preserve or express is correct and is of general validity.[57] To say therefore that parties are products of societies is not to deny that they are products of institutions. The only defensible view is once again to accept the interdependence of political and other institutions which comprise society and then to establish the nature of particular patterns of interdependence by research.

Confirmation of the view that electoral systems do have an effect on party systems is provided by logic. To assert that a particular electoral system does not have an effect on a particular party system is equivalent to saying that all conceivable electoral systems are perfectly compatible with that party system and that all conceivable party systems are compatible with that electoral system. This is surely impossible. Any one electoral system has the effect of inhibiting the development of the different party systems which some, but not necessarily all, different electoral systems would foster. To accept this is to accept that electoral systems and party systems are related.

APPROACHES TO A THEORY OF THE PARTY SYSTEM

This paper has suggested that the electoral system has been an important factor in the evolution of the Canadian party system. Its influence is intimately tied up with the politics of sectionalism which it has stimulated. Sectionalism in the party system is unavoidable as long as there are significant differences between the distribution of party voter support in any one section and the distribution in the country as a whole. The electoral system, however, by the distortions it introduces as it transforms votes into seats produces an exaggerated sectionalism at the level of representation. In view of this, the basic theme of the paper in its simplest form, and somewhat crudely stated, is that statements about sectionalism in the national party system are in many cases, and at a deeper level, statements about the politics of the single-member constituency system.

The suggested impact of the electoral system on the party system is relevant to a general theory of the party system but should not be confused with such a general theory. The construction of the latter would have required analysis of the import for the party system of such factors as the federal system, the relationship of provincial party organizations to the national party, the nature of the class system, the underlying economic and cultural bases for sectionalism, a parliamentary system of the British type, and many others. For this discussion all these have been accepted as given. They have been mentioned, if at all, only indirectly. Their importance for a general theory is taken for granted, as is the interdependencies they have with each other and with the electoral system. It is evident, for example, that the underlying strength of sectional tendencies and the weakness of class identification are interrelated with each other and with the electoral system as explanations of sectionalism in Canadian politics.[58] For any one of these to change will produce a change in the outcomes which their interactions generate. We are not therefore suggesting that sectional tendencies are exclusive products of the electoral system, but only that that system accords them an exaggerated significance.

Concentration on the electoral system represents an attempt to isolate one aspect of a complex series of interactions which is only imperfectly understood and in the present state of our knowledge cannot be handled simultaneously with precision. In such circumstances the development of more systematic comprehensive explanations will only result from a dialectic between research findings at levels varying from that of individual voters through middle-range studies, such as Alford's recent analysis of class and voting, to attempts, such as those by Scarrow and Meisel,[59] to handle a complex range of phenomena in one framework.

We can conclude that the capacity of the party system to act as an integrating agency for the sectional communities of Canada is detrimentally affected by the electoral system. The politicians' problem of reconciling sectional particularisms is exacerbated by the system they must work through in their pursuit of power. From one perspective it can be argued that if parties succeed in overcoming sectional divisions they do so in defiance of the electoral system. Conversely, it can be claimed that if parties do not succeed this is because the electoral system has so biased the party system that it is inappropriate to call it a nationalizing agency. It is evident that not only has the electoral system given impetus to sectionalism in terms of party campaigns and policy, but by making all parties more sectional at the level of seats than of votes it complicates the ability of the parties to transcend sectionalism. At various times the electoral system has placed barriers in the way of Conservatives becoming sensitively aware of the special place of Quebec and French Canada in the Canadian polity, aided the Liberals in that task, inhibited the third parties in the country from becoming aware of the special needs and dispositions of sections other than those represented in the parliamentary party, and frequently inhibited the parliamentary personnel of the major parties from becoming attuned to the sentiments of the citizens of the prairies. The electoral system's support for the political idiosyncracies of Alberta for over two decades ill served the integration of that provincial community into the national political system at a time when it was most needed. In fact, the Alberta case merely illustrates the general proposition that the disintegrating effects of the electoral system are likely to be most pronounced where alienation from the larger political system is most profound. A particular orientation, therefore, has been imparted to Canadian politics which is not inherent in the very nature of the patterns of cleavage and consensus in the society, but results from their interplay with the electoral system.

The stimulation offered to sectional cleavages by the single-member constituency system has led several authors to query its appropriateness for national integration in certain circumstances. Lipset and Duverger have suggested that countries possessed of strong underlying tendencies to sectionalism may be better served by proportional representation which breaks up the monolithic nature of sectional representation stimulated by single-member constituency systems.[60] Belgium is frequently cited as a country in which proportional representation has softened the conflict between the Flemish and the Walloons, and the United States as a country in which the single-member constituency system has heightened cleavages and tensions between north and south. Whatever its other merits, the single-member constituency system lacks the singular capacity of proportional representation to encourage all parties to search for votes in all sections of the country. Minorities within sections or provinces are not frozen out as they tend to be under the existing system. As a consequence sectional differences in party representation are minimized or, more accurately, given proportionate rather than exaggerated representation—a factor which encourages the parties to develop a national orientation.

Notes

* This is a revised version of a paper read at the thirty-ninth annual meeting of the Canadian Political Science Association at Ottawa, 1967.

1. E.E. Schattschneider, *Party Government* (New York, 1942), 62, 70; S.M. Lipset, "Party Systems and the Representation of Social Groups," *European Journal of Sociology* I (1960): 61-63, 80; M. Duverger, *Political Parties* (London, 1965), Book II; M. Duverger, "The Influence of the Electoral System on Political Life," *International Social Science Bulletin* 3 (Summer 1951); V.O. Key, *Public Opinion and American Democracy* (New York, 1961), Ch. 5. See also A. DeGrazia, "General Theory of Apportionment," *Law and Contemporary Problems* XVII (1952), and D.A. Rustow, "Some Observations on Proportional Representation," *Journal of Politics* XII (1950). F.A. Hermens, *Democracy or Anarchy?* (Notre Dame, 1941), and Enid Lakeman and J.D. Lambert, *Voting in Democracies* (London, 1955) discuss proportional representation from opposed viewpoints.

2. "We English-speaking peoples," stated Sir Richard Cartwright, "have made a sort of fetish of our present system, and appear to think that if you will only cut up a country or a province into equal divisions and give every man, wise or ignorant, rich or poor, the right to vote, you have devised a machine which will give you automatically a perfect representation. This is a huge mistake." *Reminiscences*

(Toronto, 1912), 314. See also F.H. Underhill, "Canadian Liberal Democracy in 1955," in G.V. Ferguson and F.H. Underhill, *Press and Party in Canada* (Toronto, 1955), 41-43.

3. D.V. Smiley, "The Two-Party System and One-Party Dominance in the Liberal Democratic State," *Canadian Journal of Economics and Political Science* XXIV (1958): 316-317, discusses the effects of the electoral system on major and minor parties. Schattschneider, *Party Government*, 74-75, and Pendleton Herring, *The Politics of Democracy* (New York, 1940), 182-183, note that the most important third parties in the United States have been sectional.

4. There is an unavoidable problem of circular reasoning here. There is an important difference between saying that the electoral system favours parties which *are* sectional and saying that the electoral system encourages parties to *be* sectional.

5. If 1958 is excluded as a deviant case the contrast is even more glaring, 727 Liberals from Quebec confronted 85 Conservatives, a ratio of 8.6 to 1, in contrast to the ratio of 2.1 to 1 which existed at the level of the voter.

6. A. Brady, *Canada* (London, 1932), 13-14; A. Siegfried, *The Race Question in Canada* (Toronto, 1966), 114.

7. McLeod is undoubtedly correct in his suggestion that national unity would be served if Canadians were "divided *across* ethnic barriers on lines of support for competing policies," but he fails to note the barrier which the electoral system has placed, at least historically, in the way of this objective. J.T. McLeod, "Party Structure and Party Reform," in A. Rotstein, ed., *The Prospect of Change* (Toronto, 1965), 18-19.

8. H. McD. Clokie, *Canadian Government and Politics* (Toronto, 1944), 81-83; McLeod, "Party Structure and Party Reform," 4-5, 9, 14; Brady, *Canada*, 102-103; A. Brady, *Democracy in the Dominions* 2e (Toronto, 1952), 110-112; R.M. Dawson, *The Government of Canada* 4e (Toronto, 1963), rev. by N. Ward, 469-70; J.A. Corry and J.E. Hodgetts, *Democratic Government and Politics* 3e (Toronto, 1963), Chs. 8-9; J.M. Beck and D.J. Dooley, "Party Images in Canada," Queen's Quarterly LXVII (1960): 433; F.H. Underhill, *Canadian Political Parties* (Ottawa, 1957), 4-5. For a critical discussion of brokerage politics see John Porter, *The Vertical Mosaic* (Toronto, 1965), 373-377.

9. The confusion over what the parties actually do is of long standing. Siegfried observed that Canadian statesmen "seem to fear great movements of opinion, and they devote themselves to weakening such movements. . . . Let a question of race or religion be raised, and . . . the elections will become struggles of political principle, sincere and passionate. Now this is exactly what is feared by the prudent and far-sighted men who have been given the responsibility of maintaining the national equilibrium." Less frequently quoted is the directly contrary statement that "The appeal to racial exclusiveness combined with religious bigotry is the first and last cartridge of the politicians of the Dominion. Before thinking of any other reason, or after all other reasons have been exhausted, they come to or return to this." Siegfried, *Race Question*, 113, 130. A similar contradiction is implicit in Robert Alford's statement: "Although the major parties are not distinctly Left and Right in their policies and appeals, they have, by that very token, been an *integrating* force in Canadian society, since they *emphasize* regional, religious, and ethnic representation and compromises rather than either universalistic or class representation." *Party and Society* (Chicago, 1963), 260; emphasis added.

10. Pierre Elliott Trudeau observes that French-Canadian Liberals have encouraged their potential supporters to use "their voting bloc as an instrument of racial defence, or of personal gain. Their only slogans have been racial slogans." "Some Obstacles to Democracy in Quebec," *Canadian Journal of Economics and Political Science* XXIV 3 (Aug. 1958), reprinted in Mason Wade, ed., *Canadian Dualism* (Toronto, 1960), 256.

11. Roger Graham, *Arthur Meighen: And Fortune Fled* (Toronto, 1963), 340. See also Graham, "Arthur Meighen and the Conservative Party in Quebec: The Election of 1925," *Canadian Historical Review* XXXVI (1955), for an analysis of this election in Quebec. For appeals to racial passions in 1921 and 1925 see Graham, *Meighen: And Fortune Fled*, 140-143, 340-343, and Blair Neatby, *Mackenzie King 1924-1932: The Lonely Heights* (Toronto, 1963), 73.

12. The impact of the conscription issue on party strategy and voter choice in Quebec is discussed in N. Ward, ed., *A Party Politician: The Memoirs of Chubby Power* (Toronto, 1966). Power suggests that with the exceptions of 1926, 1930, and 1935 it was an issue in every election from 1911 to 1940 inclusive.

13. John Meisel, *The Canadian General Election of 1957* (Toronto, 1962), 167-168.

14. This induced *Le Devoir* to observe "sombrely that the composition of the new Cabinet reduced Quebec 'to the status of a second-class, nearly a third-class province.' Neither the Conservative nor the Liberal parties, it argued, can rule without the support of at least twenty-five French Canadians in the House. 'And it is in the interest of the French-language group to be strongly represented in every government, whatever may be its party name; for every time that group has lacked an influential representation, French Canadians have been subjected to grave injustices.'" J.R. Mallory, "The Election and the Constitution," *Queen's Quarterly* LXIV (1957): 481.

15. D.H. Wrong, "Parties and Voting in Canada," *Political Science Quarterly* LXXIII (1958): 403.

16. J.M. Beck, "Quebec and the Canadian Elections of 1958," *Parliamentary Affairs* XII (1958-59): 95-96. Siegfried, *Race Question*, 163-164, 207-208 provides examples of the importance of French-English cleavages on election results and on party appeals at the turn of the century. As late as 1962, in some parts of Quebec, the Liberals tried to "link Diefenbaker with the historic 'Tory enemies' of French Canada. The names Borden, Meighen, Bennett, and Drew are still spat out as epithets by Liberal orators on the hustings." P. Regenstreif, "The Liberal Party of Canada: A Political Analysis," PhD thesis, Cornell University, 1963, 477.

17. By the 1963 election the politics of sectionalism once more reduced the Conservatives to a token effort in Quebec, "largely directed to holding the few seats they had. The Prime Minister himself did little more than show the flag. . . ." John Saywell, ed., *Canadian Annual Review for 1963* (Toronto, 1964), 23. In the 1965 campaign the major parties exchanged sectional insults, with the Liberals charging that the Conservatives did not have and would not gain meaningful representation in Quebec, to which the Conservatives retorted that the Liberals would lack representation elsewhere. John Saywell, ed., *Canadian Annual Review for 1965* (Toronto, 1966), 85.

18. John Meisel, "The Stalled Omnibus: Canadian Parties in the 1960s," *Social Research* 30 (1963): 383-384.

19. Leslie Lipson, "Party Systems in the United Kingdom and the Older Commonwealth: Causes, Resemblances, and Variations," *Political Studies* VII (1959): 27-28. See Ward, *A Party Politician*, 389, 392 for Power's recognition of the importance of Quebec to the Liberals.

20. N. Ward, "The National Political Scene," in Wade, ed., *Canadian Dualism*, 266, 272.

21. Sir Richard Cartwright argued in his *Reminiscences*, 352, that because the provinces differ in wealth and interests, "the temptation to the poorer provinces to sell themselves to the party in office is always very great and is certain to be traded on by practical politicians on both sides."

Graham, *Meighen: And Fortune Fled*, 299, 303, describes the pressures on Meighen to devise an attractive western policy as otherwise his party "has not the ghost of a chance on the prairies in an election." In contrast to King's assiduous courting of the prairie provinces, waffling on the tariff and promises of special western policies, Meighen decided to preach the tariff to the unconverted. He was rewarded with ten seats and King with twenty in 1925.

Liberal courting of British Columbia in 1925 by reducing rates on flour and grain going to Pacific ports for export is noted in Walter R. Sharp, "The Canadian Elections of 1925," *American Political Science Review* XX (1926): 111 n. 3. Lionel H. Laing, "The Pattern of Canadian Politics: The Elections of 1945," *American Political Science Review* XL (1946) provides a sectional interpretation of the 1945 election in terms of results and to a lesser extent of strategy.

22. H.A. Scarrow, "Distinguishing between Political Parties—The Case of Canada," *Midwest Journal of Political Science* IX (1965): 72. He also notes (75-6n) the tendency of a candidate to appeal for support "on the ground that only his party has a chance of winning office, and that consequently the voters of the district or region had better jump on the winning bandwagon if they want to be represented in the cabinet. Diefenbaker made wide use of this appeal in Quebec in 1958." Paul Hellyer appealed to prairie voters for Liberal support in the 1965 federal election to "elect more members to the Government side to make sure the views of this area are considered." (*Winnipeg Free Press*, 29 Oct. 1965).

23. The CCF seems to have been an exception. See Walter D. Young, "The National CCF: Political Party and Political Movement," PhD thesis, University of Toronto, 1965, for an analysis of the special role played by the central office, in effect by David Lewis, for long periods in the formation of policy and strategy.

24. The fact is that influence in caucus and party is conditioned by seniority. N. Ward, *The Canadian House of Commons: Representation* 2e (Toronto, 1963), 140-143, is relevant here with its implication that the spokesmen for the sectional strongholds of the party will enjoy a pre-eminent position compared to the more fluctuating representation where the party is weak.

25. "Distinguishing between Political Parties," 69. See also John R. Williams, *The Conservative*

Party of Canada: 1920-1949 (Durham, NC, 1956), 14-15, and Ward, "The National Political Scene," 268-270, for related comments.

26. See the interesting analysis of the 1935 election by Escott Reid which asserted that the difference in ethnic composition of the Liberal and Conservative parliamentary parties would incline the Liberals to isolationism and the Conservatives to a more imperialistic policy. "The Canadian Election of 1935 and After," *American Political Science Review* 30 (1936): 117-118.

27. See Regenstreif, "Liberal Party," 472-477, and Alford, *Party and Society*, 258, for party policy differences and party images related to French-English relations.

28. Other factors not considered here also influence party policy and attitudes. Meisel has cogently argued that the Liberals entered the 1957 federal election with a national approach remakably insensitive to regional needs, an approach born of long and intimate contact with a centralist-oriented civil service and a lack of feedback from backbenchers in the Commons. By contrast, the Conservatives, who entered the election as an Ontario party in terms of existing parliamentary representation, proved remarkably sensitive to the needs of regions and groups neglected by the Liberals. John Meisel, "The Formulation of Liberal and Conservative Programmes in the 1957 Canadian General Election," *Canadian Journal of Economics and Political Science* XXVI (1960).

29. In the mid-fifties Ward made the general point that all opposition parties had "little experience in dealing with French Canadians as trusted colleagues in caucus," with a resultant development of traditions reflecting that fact. "The National Political Scene," 267.

30. *Conservative Party*, 197-200.

31. Ibid., 197-198.

32. "The National Political Scene," 269-270.

33. The history of the CCF reveals that the sectional backgrounds of party MPs did not orient the party in the direction of its western supporters. In fact, the party rapidly moved away from its agrarian stronghold and be-

came, from the viewpoint of the national leaders, and especially David Lewis the most important person in the determination of party policy, a party with an urban, industrial, working class, and central Canada orientation. Young, "The National CCF," 127-128, 131, 132, 139-140, 148-149, 159-160, 166, 200-201, 204, 249-250, 310.

34. "Of course," he continued, "times and circumstances do arise where profound personal convictions conflict with party success or personal ambition, and where one must make decisions that one knows to be unpalatable to the voters." Ward, *A Party Politician*, 318.

35. J. Schumpeter, *Capitalism, Socialism and Democracy* 3e (New York, 1962), 285.

36. Neatby, *King: The Lonely Heights*, 66-67. See also 222-224.

37. E.P. Dean provides several striking examples in "How Canada Has Voted: 1867-1945," *Canadian Historical Review* XXX (1949). Duverger, who argued that "Parliamentary strength is always much more important than real strength in the country," provides a British illustration of the way in which this perceptual bias operates: "The fact that the Labour party had obtained only 48.7% of the poll in 1945 was completely obliterated by the fact that it controlled 390 votes in the Commons; public opinion itself considered Labour as having a strong majority." *Political Parties*, 400.

38. The provisions of Sections 51 and 51A of the BNA Act allocating parliamentary seats to provinces are important contributing factors in facilitating provincial or sectional interpretations of election results. As a byproduct the system precludes the possibility of electoral boundaries crossing provincial boundaries and makes the province a natural and easy unit for interpreting election results. In addition, of course, it transforms struggles over representation into struggles over provincial rights. I am indebted to professor Walter Young for drawing these factors to my attention.

39. J.E. Hodgetts, "Regional Interests and Policy in a Federal Structure," *Canadian Journal of Economics and Political Science* XXXII (1966), 10.

40. W.L. Morton, *The Kingdom of Canada* (Toronto, 1963), 450; R. Cook, et al., *Canada: A Modern Study* (Toronto, 1963), 254; Neatby, *King: The Lonely Heights*, 74, and Underhill, "Canadian Liberal Democracy in 1955," 40.

41. F.H. Underhill, *The Image of Confederation* (Toronto, 1964), 54.

42. McLeod, "Party Structure and Party Reform," 10. He adds that this is not "peculiar to Quebec."

43. P. Regenstreif, "The Canadian General Election of 1958," *Western Political Quarterly* XIII (1960): 362-363. See also Wrong, "Parties and Voting in Canada," 403-4.

44. H.G. Thorburn, *Politics in New Brunswick* (Toronto, 1961), 176. New Brunswick, Thorburn argues, "has been on the winning side whenever this could be divined with any accuracy before the election" (183); see also 49.

45. The sections have been defined as Maritimes/Atlantic, Quebec, Ontario, Prairies, and British Columbia.

46. In 1925 and 1957 the Liberals and Conservatives respectively have been identified as winners for the purpose of the above calculation.

47. Schattschneider, *Party Government*, 111. This point is made by Clokie, *Canadian Government and Politics*, 87-89, in a discussion implying that class cleavages are more real than sectional cleavages.

48. Porter, *Vertical Mosaic*, 373-377; F.H. Underhill, *In Search of Canadian Liberalism* (Toronto, 1960), 167.

49. *Vertical Mosaic*, 373-374.

50. Alford, *Party and Society*, 339; Porter, *Vertical Mosaic*, 368-369; V.O. Key, *Public Opinion and American Democracy*, 109; Key, *Politics, Parties, and Pressure Groups* 2e (New York, 1947), 152.

51. *Political Parties*, 383.

52. S.M. Lipset, *Political Man* (New York, 1963), 13. The extensive literature on crosspressures is relevant here with its emphasis that multiple group membership and identification have "the effect of reducing the emotion in political choices." Ibid.

53. *Image of Confederation*, 53-54.

54. For example, in recent articles Leon Epstein has specifically downgraded its importance, "A Comparative Study of Canadian Parties," *American Political Science Review* LVIII (1964): 48, 57-58, and McLeod, in an extensive catalogue of factors relevant to explaining the party system, does not discuss the electoral system, except for incidental mention of its contribution to single-party dominance. McLeod, "Party Structure and Party Reform," 9. The views of Lipson and Meisel are discussed in the following paragraphs.

　　Smiley is an exception in according some significance to the electoral system. He notes that the system favours sectionally based minor parties, and that it was "strategic" in destroying the Canadian two-party system between 1935 and 1953. "The Two-Party System and One-Party Dominance," 316-317.

55. "Party Systems in the United Kingdom and the Older Commonwealth," 20-21.

56. He supports his argument by noting that both the two-party system and its successor multi-party system existed within the same institutional framework. "The Stalled Omnibus," 370.

57. W.S. Livingston, *Federalism and Constitutional Change* (Oxford, 1956), 7-9.

58. Alford, *Party and Society*, 42-49, discusses various factors sustaining sectionalism.

59. Scarrow, "Distinguishing between Political Parties," and John Meisel, "Recent Changes in Canadian Parties," in Hugh G. Thorburn, ed., *Party Politics in Canada* 2e (Scarborough, 1967).

60. Lipset, "Party Systems and the Representation of Social Groups," 76-77; Duverger, *Political Parties*, 382-384.

27. ON ANALYSING THE IMPACT OF THE ELECTORAL SYSTEM ON THE PARTY SYSTEM*

J.A.A. Lovink

Analysis of the consequences of electoral laws has been rather narrowly focused. For most researchers, the sole aim has been to ascertain by historical and comparative study how a variety of electoral systems have affected (1) the number of parties winning legislative representation and (2) the distribution of seats among them. Few have shown earnest interest in exploring the effects of electoral laws upon party policies and campaign strategies; upon modes of political recruitment and nomination; upon the quality, independence, and role perception of legislators; or upon the extent to which individual citizens and minorities feel politically effacious and truly represented.

These gaps lend unusual interest to a recent effort by Professor Alan C. Cairns to identify the significance of the Canadian electoral system for the performance of the federal political parties as nationally unifying agencies.[1] His conclusion is that Canada's system of single-member constituencies with plurality vote[2] has so structured the political market and the regional composition of the various parliamentary parties that party policies and appeals have in practice been more sectional and sectionally divisive than unifying. In his own words:

J.A.A. Lovink, "On Analysing the Impact of the Electoral System on the Party System in Canada," *Canadian Journal of Political Science* 3 (December 1970): 497-516. Reprinted with permission of the author.

The basic approach of this paper is that the party system, importantly conditioned by the electoral system, exacerbates the very cleavages it is credited with healing. As a corollary it is suggested that the party system is not simply a reflection of sectionalism, but that sectionalism is also a reflection of the party system.

. . . Sectionalism has been rendered highly visible because the electoral system makes it a fruitful basis on which to organize electoral support. Divisions cutting through sections, particularly those based on the class system, have been much less salient because the possibility of payoffs in terms of representation has been minimal.[3]

He closes with a plea for study of the merits of proportional representation as an alternative to the existing electoral system. If accepted, these conclusions would clearly be of considerable theoretical, and perhaps even practical, importance. They therefore merit close scrutiny.

A SYNOPSIS OF CAIRNS' INDICTMENT OF THE ELECTORAL SYSTEM

Professor Cairns' argument is structured around six main propositions. These are:

1. Where party electoral support is not absolutely uniform throughout the country, the

electoral system creates regional or sub-regional differences in the "value"—in additional seats—of vote gains. These spatial differences in electoral payoff have encouraged parties to tailor their campaign appeals primarily to the assumed desires of those parts of the country where the rewards in seats are likely to be greatest. This strategy, induced by the electoral system, has served to perpetuate and reinforce the sectional divisions in Canada.[4] In Cairns' view, "one of the most basic aspects of Canadian politics, its sectional nature, becomes incomprehensible if attention is not constantly focused on the sectional bias engendered by the single-member constituency system."[5]

2. Indirectly, the electoral system has also had a regionally divisive effect on party policy between elections. This causal chain begins with the fact that the electoral system has historically produced parliamentary parties considerably more unbalanced in regional composition than the regional distribution of party electoral support. Coupled with the explicit proposition that as a rule the composition of the parliamentary party is probably 'the most crucial factor in determining party policy at any one time," and with the implicit proposition that MPs are primarily concerned with promoting the interests of their own section of the country, this fact leads to the claim that the electoral system has indirectly produced policies that are more severely biased in regional terms than would have occurred had the electoral system created less distortion in awarding seats for votes.[6]

3. As a result of the electoral system, each party's parliamentary representation has fluctuated far more, in total and in regional composition, than its electoral support. Because of this tendency to exaggerate vote losses or gains the electoral system has in-

troduced an element of crisis into many decisions that could otherwise have been faced with greater equanimity.[7]

4. Because of this same tendency to transform moderate changes in electoral support into major losses or gains in seats, the parties have had greater difficulty in establishing effective intra-party routines for regional accommodation and compromise than would otherwise have been the case.[8]

5. By fostering a regionally based politics, the electoral system has stood in the way of attempts to develop a more "creative," trans-sectional, class-based politics in Canada.[9]

6. These disadvantages are not offset by the commonly alleged virtues of the present electoral system as a device for securing effective parliamentary government. Measuring its performance from this standpoint by its success in producing majority government *and* an opposition having at least one-third of the seats in the House, Cairns shows that from 1921 to 1968 the electoral system failed one or both of these tests on ten of fifteen occasions, for a failure rate of 67 percent.[10]

All of these considerations lead Cairns to the conclusion stated earlier. They also form the grounds upon which he rejects the theory, advanced by some writers, that electoral systems do not have a major formative influence on party systems.[11]

MEASURING REGIONAL POLICY BIAS

Cairns' propositions are, without question, an imaginative and innovative contribution to the study of electoral systems. As this paper will argue, however, their empirical validity is impossible to assess on the basis of the evidence thus far adduced or otherwise readily available. Indeed, prima facie they appear to exaggerate the significance of the electoral system for party policy, to overstate its nationally divisive consequences, and to understate its contribution to the effective functioning of the parliamentary form of government. A crucial initial defect is their failure to come to grips with the meaning and systematic measurement of regional policy bias.

Regional policy discrimination is more difficult to identify and compare (for two or more parties) than Cairns' study would lead one to believe. Even the question of definition presents obstacles. What is meant by a "sectional policy"? What differentiates such a policy from one that is not sectional? Looking at some of Parliament's major concerns of recent years, should one consider unification of the armed forces, reform of the Criminal Code, changes in the Bank Act, medicare, proposals for reform of the tax structure, and foreign and defence policy generally as non-sectional policy decisions, on the grounds that they are all in some sense "national" in scope? Should the study of regional policy discrimination thus be restricted to decisions whose direct impact appears more regionally restricted, such as the continued extension of railway freight rate subsidies for western grain and for traffic between central Canada and the Maritimes, construction of the St. Lawrence Seaway, signing of the Columbia River treaty or of the United States-Canada automotive products agreement, and initiation of the regional economic expansion program?

Distinctions such as these are impaired by the likelihood that almost any apparently "national" policy will in practice affect the various regions differently, if only to the extent that their attitudes to the decision do not coincide. Typically, most of the "national" decisions mentioned above have not been regionally uniform in impact and/or in the responses evoked. It thus seems reasonable, at least for present purposes, to abandon any distinction between sectional and non-sectional policies, and to posit that most of Parliament's concerns possess some measure of "regional salience." To ascertain a party's regional policy bias (if any), one must examine all (or a representative sample) of its policies during a specified time, or a subset of all those policies somehow defined as "major" or "important."

To discover whether the policies pursued by each of Canada's federal parties over any given time span has on balance favoured some regions more than others and, if so, which party has favoured which regions most and least, one would need to know:

1. Each region's demands or policy preferences, often difficult to pinpoint because regional spokesmen disagree.

2. Each party's responses to these demands or preferences, commonly difficult to identify clearly either because the responses are ambiguous (intentionally or otherwise) or because they are partly hidden within the administrative apparatus (as in the instance of the government's professed endeavour to sell more wheat in 1969).

3. The environmental obstacles to a favourable response, such as a glut on an international commodity market, or lack or high cost of capital resources, or pressures from the international money market for fiscal retrenchment, all of which undoubtedly constrain the government more than the parties in opposition. Under such circumstances it may not be appropriate to characterize the government party as the less responsive.

4. The relative success of each party's responses in meeting a particular region's demands. In some cases responses will consist of a clear-cut affirmative or negative, or of specific financial commitments that can be easily compared. More often, however, the various party responses will comply partially with demands made, in which

case the more responsive party can only be identified by applying to the empirical findings the observer's own judgment (in the light of his understanding of the region's dominant values and priorities) and/or by resort to the judgment of others (within or outside the region) who are similarly informed.

Only after a time-consuming, complex, and inescapably subjective analysis of this kind will it be possible to make a defensible statement about the regional policy biases (during the period under study) of Canada's national parties. Such inquiries are badly needed.

ALTERNATIVE EXPLANATIONS OF REGIONAL POLICY BIAS

To push this critique a little further, let us now put aside the problem of policy analysis and consider the plausibility of the central hypothesis itself. Is it likely, as Cairns believes, that party differences in regional policy bias (if substantiated) will prove roughly congruent with differences in the regional makeup of the corresponding parliamentary parties (only partly a consequence of the electoral system) and that the first of these two variables is in large part a function of the second?

There are, as Professor Cairns notes, reasons why the composition of the parliamentary party should affect party policy. It is known that in all parties (except for the CCF/NDP)[12] the parliamentary party is substantially free from policy directives or restraints imposed by the party organization outside Parliament, and there is reason to think that in all parties the leaders cannot long retain their positions without steady public support from a large majority of their backbenchers. To retain this backing, the leadership cannot continually act in ways that are politically unpalatable to their parliamentary followers, whose policy

preferences will be influenced to varying degrees by the interests which they represent.

Yet it is not obvious that this need for a degree of leadership sensitivity to the wishes of backbenchers will produce a regional policy bias roughly matching the regional composition of the parliamentary party.[13] This outcome seems likely only under two alternative conditions: (*a*) if the parliamentary party effectively dominates the party élite in policy-making (be it directly, by majority-vote decisions on policy in caucus, or through customary deference by the party leaders to the parliamentary party's expressed and anticipated reactions) *and* insists on policy discrimination in favour of areas most strongly represented in its ranks; or (*b*) if each party's leadership, despite substantial autonomy in policy matters, typically chooses to pursue a policy strategy designed to please those areas where it has won most seats in the past, an approach which I shall call (for want of a better term) a "patronage" strategy.

With respect to the first part of the first of these conditions, much research still separates us from a general theory about the power relationship between leaders and led in Parliament, differentiating (as will probably be necessary) between types of policy decision, variations in relative party strength in Parliament, and such hard-to-measure factors as comparative leadership skill. For the present, however, it may be noted that the image of the parliamentary party dominating the élite in policy-making does not square with the existing literature on the subject, impressionistic and anecdotal though it is. The common view, as Professor Cairns puts it, is that within the parliamentary party the right to make policy lies "specifically with the leader and his trusted colleagues."[14]

As for insistence by the parliamentary party on policy discrimination in favour of areas most strongly represented in its ranks, it is a moot point how far backbenchers, if given control of party policy, would funnel benefits primarily to their own region. Some varying proportion (as yet unknown) of MPs would no doubt define their legislative roles as that of "trustee" or "politico," orientations that would lead them (sometimes, often?) to support policies not favoured by their constituents.[15] To the extent that this occurs, another of the footings of Cairns' hypothesis will have weakened.

What about the second condition that seemed necessary to finding a close relationship between a party's regional policy bias and the regional makeup of its parliamentary party? Does the available evidence (fragmentary once again) suggest that party élites typically opt for the "patronage" type of policy strategy identified earlier or do they appear to be following a variety of approaches to the distribution of political benefits and costs?[16]

The latter picture seems the more true. Before and during election campaigns, for instance, parties generally seek to appeal primarily to those areas where their chances of seat gains and losses are greatest, at the expense of those where they are either very strong and very weak.[17] At these times, as Cairns points out, they probably come closest to behaving like business entrepreneurs in trying to maximize the marginal return (in seats) on investment (of policy benefits).[18] It remains unknown, however, how long in advance of an impending election this strategy is typically adopted, and whether it may not have been the permanent or normal strategy for some party élites and for some political conditions, such as periods of minority government. That this may be a question of some significance for party policy is suggested by the differences between Columns 2 and 3 in Table 1. It is to be noted, moreover, that for one of the two parties shown in that table Column 3 resembles Column 1 more closely than does Column 2; to the extent that there is a likeness between Column 1 and any of the other columns, the potential significance for policy of the electoral

system as such is clearly reduced.[19] It remains to be seen, of course, whether the relationships between these three distributions were similar in earlier years.[20]

This "economic" approach appears to be only one of several competitors to the so-called "patronage" strategy. Cairns himself identifies another when he notes that:

> In particular instances, the desire to win over a section in which the party is weak may lead to neglect of an area in which the party already has strong representation. King's courting of the prairie provinces and neglect of the Maritimes in the first half of the twenties constitutes a revealing instance of this phenomenon. *Whether a party directs attention to the sections where it is strong, as a result of the assertiveness of intra-party spokesmen, or whether attention is lavished on a section where a major breakthrough is deemed possible, is a matter for investigation in each case.*[21]

Similar hopes of an electoral breakthrough may or may not explain why in 1969 the federal Liberal party appeared to assign a higher priority to solving the needs of Canada's economically depressed areas than to meeting those of the major population centres or why the Progressive Conservative party seemed to match or exceed the government party in solicitude towards Quebec's desires and to outdo it in professed sympathy with the demands of the urban areas.[22] In each case, their policies were quite contrary to what the regional composition of the parliamentary parties would have suggested.

Finally, of course, there is the likelihood that many decisions arise from no electoral strategy of any kind, stemming instead from conceptions of the national interest, from tradition and inertia, from leadership preferences or whims, or from oversight, ignorance, and other sources of irrationality.

It seems reasonable to believe, therefore, that any close correlation between party differences in regional policy bias and differences in

Table 1   Four Hypothetical Correlates of Regional Policy Bias, Calculated from the Results of the 1968 Canadian General Election (percentage of total)

Province or region	National vote (1)	Seats won (2)	Marginal seats won and lost* (3)	Seats won plus marginal seats lost* (4)
Liberal party				
Maritimes	9.0	4.5	8.9	7.1
Quebec	31.7	36.1	22.3	32.4
Ontario	37.1	41.3	41.1	40.0
Prairies†	13.2	7.7	18.8	12.4
BC	9.0	10.3	8.9	8.1
Total	100.0	99.9	100.0	100.0
N	3 696 945	155	112	210
Progressive Conservative party				
Maritimes	16.5	34.7	12.3	23.5
Quebec	18.3	5.6	11.1	7.8
Ontario	36.9	23.6	42.0	32.2
Prairies†	22.2	36.1	30.9	33.9
BC	6.1	0	3.7	2.6
Total	100.0	100.0	100.0	100.0
N	2 554 880	72	81	115

*"Marginal" seats have arbitrarily been defined as those which the party in question won or lost by a margin equal to or less than 10 percent of the total valid vote. This definition has some drawbacks, but seems adequate for the present (largely illustrative) purpose.

†Includes the Yukon and Northwest Territories.

Source: Canada, *Report of the Chief Electoral Officer, 1968*; all calculations by the writer.

the regional makeup of the respective parliamentary parties will be partly spurious. The second of these two variables is probably only one of many factors influencing policy, competing (in an as yet undetermined and no doubt variable way) with such other factors as proximity of the next election; the distribution among the parties of safe and competitive seats; whether the party is in or out of power; if in power, the size of its contingent in the House; and, not least, the regional base, policy

preferences, and relative influence of individual members of the party élite.

Of all these supposed sources of party differences in regional policy bias, all but the third to last should lend themselves to some kind of assessment, however crude. The influence of the party's position (in or out of office), on the other hand, is likely to remain uncertain. To gauge it, one would need to estimate how far differences between the government party and (say) the official opposition in such respects as information resources and environmental constraints themselves accounted for differences in policy. To assert that such differences in each party's "life situation" are likely to account for a certain measure of policy disagreement is not to argue that opposition parties behave irresponsibly (that is, advocate policies that they *know* they would not themselves pursue if in power), or that their policies can never be taken as true expressions of alternative conceptions of the national interest. It is to suggest, rather, that the often covert pressures on a government party are (in relation to those on other parties) so numerous and compelling that it is reasonable to doubt that the official opposition, if suddenly transplanted into office, would then in fact carry out all the policies it had theretofore advocated. It is to argue that *some* of these policies would not have been advanced had the party known then what it learned in office, and were thus the product of a different life situation and not of a true difference in attitude to regional demands.

To test this proposition, one would need to contrast the policies of successive governments sustained by different political parties, under conditions of ceteris paribus, a requirement rarely if ever met in the "real world." It can be no more than plausible, therefore, that as a rule the policy disagreement between government and opposition parties will be less than it seems and the "true" differences between them unknowable.

For clarity, the foregoing discussion may be summed up as follows. First, it has *not* been argued that the federal political parties in Canada have displayed no regional policy biases, or that they have lived up fully to their reputation as agents of national integration. The contention has been, rather, that no reliable judgment on this matter is possible until the necessary research has been done. Secondly, it has *not* been argued that the electoral system has had no effect on party poli-

cies. To the contrary, it has been acknowledged that the regional composition of the various parliamentary parties (only in part an effect of the electoral system) has probably created pressures for an equivalent bias in party policy. What has been argued is that this factor is only one (and not necessarily the most important) of many factors influencing party policies, and that it is, therefore, implausible to burden the electoral system with major responsibility for such regional policy bias as further inquiry may document.[23]

THE ELECTORAL SYSTEM AS PROMOTER OF SECTIONALISM

Let us now turn to the view that the nationally divisive consequences of the electoral system go considerably beyond any responsibility it may have for regional policy discrimination in Parliament. "Centrifugal" pressures also arise, it has been asserted, because the importance which the electoral system places on the geographic location of support gives the parties a strong incentive to frame their election appeals in local and sectional terms. The very formulation of such policies has acknowledged and reinforced regional identities to the extent where, at least in Professor Cairns' opinion, Canadian sectionalism must be regarded as to a major degree an outgrowth of the electoral system.[24] Moreover, without this incentive to cater to local and regional interests (that is, without the need to worry about the spatial distribution of voting support), the parties would have had a greater interest in building class-based rather than sectional political coalitions. The resulting difference of approach would not only have introduced the "creative" thrust of class conflict into Canadian politics, but would also have countered the dangers of national disintegration, classes being in a poor position to secede when disgruntled.[25]

To evaluate these propositions, we need to know much more than we do. Data are needed, in particular, on the *extent* to which the electoral system influences the policy choices presented to the electorate, and on the relative strength of regional and cross-cutting class or group identities in Canada.[26] Regarding the first of these questions, there is now no way of telling how much of the present policy posture of the two largest political parties is a response to the manner in which the electoral system has structured the political market, as opposed to the character of that market as such. By extension, it is difficult to foresee how much their behaviour would change (how class-oriented they would become) if the spatial aspects of that electoral system were to be abandoned (that is, if proportional representation were adopted).[27] And one of the main reasons for this uncertainty is that we do not really know very much about the Canadian political market. Although a certain amount of published empirical research has delved into the political salience of social class in Canada,[28] we are still far from being able to position Canada with confidence on a societal (ideal-typical) continuum marked at one pole by purely regional and no cross-cutting class or group cleavages, and at the other by purely class or group and no regional cleavages.[29] *Presumably the market pressures on party policy become increasingly unidirectional and compelling as one approaches either end of this spectrum, thereby commensurately reducing whatever influence the prevailing electoral system might otherwise exert.*

The relevance of these observations to the proposition that the content of party policies and appeals would be significantly altered by adopting proportional representation can be best illustrated by means of Figure 1. If the relationships there depicted are valid, then the accuracy of the proposition can be seen to depend entirely on the degree of influence the electoral system exerts on party policies (reflected hypothetically by the distance between the curves and the abstract "no influence" line) and on Canada's location on the societal cleavage continuum.[30] Thus, if position A on the horizontal axis should turn out to be most appropriate, then the proposition would have to be regarded as false because no major changes in policy would result no matter which of the three influence curves proved most valid. In this event, there would be little sense in generating the conflict which would surely attend attempts to change the electoral system. It would then be better (because conflict is in principle undesirable and to be avoided until major gains are expected) to delay such initiatives until greater homogeneity of regional conditions and interests and an associated "nationalization" of political issues had substantially strengthened cross-cutting class or group cleavages.

On the other hand, should position C best reflect reality, then it would matter very much which of the influence curves is right. The proposition would then be false only if the electoral system emerged as a very minor influence on party policy. Barring this contingency, a switch to proportional representation might indeed have important consequences for the nature of Canadian politics.

To sum up thus far: (1) it is not clear to what extent the federal political parties have pursued regionally discriminatory policies; (2) it is doubtful that major responsibility for whatever discrimination there may have been can reasonably be placed on the electoral system; (3) much more research is needed before we can know how far the sectional nature of Canadian politics can be blamed on the impact of the electoral system on party policy. In short, it must be concluded that Professor Cairns' confident indictment of the electoral system is premature and, perhaps, unduly severe.

Figure 1 Hypothesized Relationship between Societal Cleavage, Two Types of Electoral Systems, and the Nature of Party Policies and Appeals

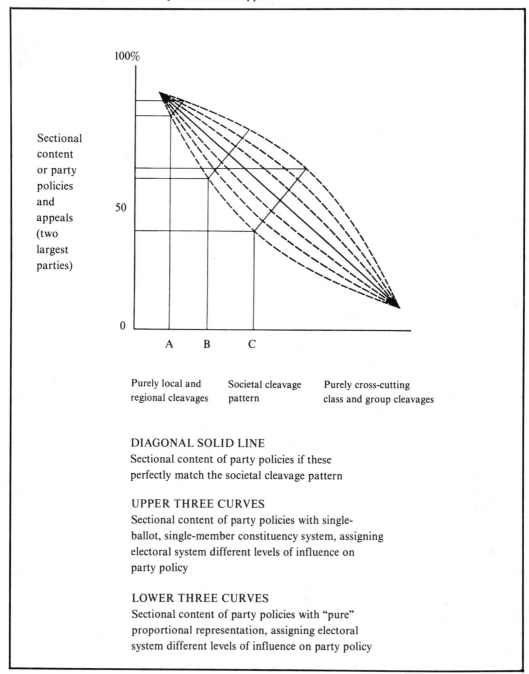

100%

Sectional content or party policies and appeals (two largest parties)

50

0

A   B   C

Purely local and   Societal cleavage   Purely cross-cutting
regional cleavages   pattern   class and group cleavages

DIAGONAL SOLID LINE
Sectional content of party policies if these
perfectly match the societal cleavage pattern

UPPER THREE CURVES
Sectional content of party policies with single-
ballot, single-member constituency system, assigning
electoral system different levels of influence on
party policy

LOWER THREE CURVES
Sectional content of party policies with "pure"
proportional representation, assigning electoral
system different levels of influence on party policy

OTHER ASPECTS OF THE ELECTORAL SYSTEM

Thus far we have looked only at the electoral system's effects on party policy and have ignored its meaning for the conduct and control of government. The greater visibility of these aspects will permit a briefer discussion.

The supreme virtue usually ascribed to the plurality-vote, single-member constituency system is that it promotes the effective working of parliamentary government by improving the chances that one party will win a majority of the legislative seats. In Professor Cairns' view, the Canadian electoral system has since 1921 failed to deliver this payoff of majority government on six of a possible thirteen occasions (see Table 2). On four other occasions it has reduced the combined strength of the opposition parties to less than one-third of the House—arbitrarily selected as the minimum required for effective opposi-

Table 2 Percentage of Votes and Seats for Federal Government Party, 1921-68

	Votes	Seats		Votes	Seats
1921	40.7	49.4(L)	1949	49.5	73.7(L)
1925*	39.8	40.4(L)	1953	48.9	64.5(L)
1926	46.1	52.2(L)	1957	38.9	42.3(C)
1930	48.7	55.9(C)	1958	53.6	78.5(C)
1935	44.9	70.6(L)	1962	37.3	43.8(C)
1940	51.5	73.9(L)	1963	41.7	48.7(L)
1945	41.1	51.0(L)	1965	40.2	49.4(L)
			1968	45.5	58.7(L)

*In this election the Conservatives received both a higher percentage of votes, 46.5%, and of seats, 47.3%, than the Liberals. The Liberals, however, chose to meet Parliament, and with Progressive support they retained office for several months.
Source: Cairns, "The Electoral System," 56. Data for 1968 have been calculated by the present writer from the *Report of the Chief Electoral Officer.*

tion. Cairns thus concludes that the electoral system has failed to perform as promised on ten out of fifteen occasions, a "failure rate" of 67 percent.[31]

This conclusion is questionable. Its criterion of success—that the electoral system invariably awards the party winning the largest share of the popular vote between one-half and two-thirds of the seats in the House of Commons, no more or less—is unreasonably stringent. No electoral system could meet this standard, since to meet it requires the power to determine not only seat shares but vote shares as well. Appropriately, therefore, no more appears to have been claimed for the present electoral system than that it tends to give the party with the most votes nationally a disproportionately large share of the seats, thereby enhancing its prospects of forming and sustaining a government.[32] By this more modest and reasonable standard, the electoral system has failed only once in fifteen instances (see Tables 2 and 3).[33] Although the help supplied on six of these occasions was not enough to yield a majority government, the pressure to form coalition governments in the true sense has been less than it would have been had vote and seat shares been more nearly identical.

Most benefits involve costs.[34] In this case the costs may be counted partly in terms of the frequency with which the electoral system has deprived the "losing" parties of enough seats to mount an "effective opposition," and partly in terms of the way in which it has distributed this penalty in seats among them.

The first of these two costs has been imposed, in Cairns' calculation, on four out of fifteen occasions, all instances when the opposition parties together failed to secure one-third of the seats in the House. A slight lowering of the minimum number of seats required for effective opposition, from an arbitrary one-third to an arbitrary one-quarter of the House (or from 88 to 66 seats in a 264-member

Table 3 Bias of Electoral System in Translating Votes into Seats: Rank Order of Parties in Terms of Percentage of Vote

Year	1		2		3		4		5	
1921	Libs.	1.21	Cons.	0.70	Progs.	1.20				
1925	Cons.	1.017	Libs.	1.015	Progs.	1.09				
1926	Libs.	1.13	Cons.	0.82	Progs.	1.55*				
1930	Cons.	1.15	Libs.	0.82	Progs.	1.53*				
1935	Libs.	1.57	Cons.	0.55	CCF	0.33	Rec.	0.05	Socred	1.68*
1940	Libs.	1.43	Cons.	0.53	CCF	0.39	Socred	1.52*		
1945	Libs.	1.24	Cons.	1.00	CCF	0.73	Socred	1.29*		
1949	Libs.	1.49	Cons.	0.53	CCF	0.37	Socred	1.03*		
1953	Libs.	1.32	Cons.	0.62	CCF	0.77	Socred	1.06*		
1957	Libs.	0.97	Cons.	1.087	CCF	0.88	Socred	1.09*		
1958	Cons.	1.46	Libs.	0.55	CCF	0.32*	Socred	0*†		
1962	Cons.	1.17	Libs.	1.01	NDP	0.53	Socred	0.97*		
1963	Libs.	1.17	Cons.	1.09	NDP	0.49	Socred	0.76		
1965	Libs.	1.23	Cons.	1.13	NDP	0.44	Créd.	0.72*	Socred	0.51*
1968	Libs.	1.29	Cons.	0.87	NDP	0.49	Créd.	1.20*		

Independents and very small parties have been excluded from the table.

The measurement of discrimination employed in this table defines the relationship between the percentage of votes and the percentage of seats. The figure is devised by dividing the former into the latter. Thus 1—(38% seats/38% votes), for example—represents a neutral effect for the electoral system. Any figure above 1—(40% seats/20% votes) = 2.0, for example—indicates discrimination for the party. A figure below 1—(20% seats/40% votes) = 0.5, for example—indicates discrimination against the party. For the purposes of the table the ranking of the parties as 1, 2, 3 . . . is based on their percentage of the vote, since to rank them in terms of seats would conceal the very bias it is sought to measure—namely, the bias introduced by the intervening variable of the electoral system which constitutes the mechanism by which votes are translated into seats.

*Parties that did not poll at least 5 percent of the valid vote in at least five provinces; such parties are described in the text as "regional third parties."

†The Social Credit party secured 2.6 percent of the popular votes in 1958, but won no seats.

Source: "The Electoral System," 58. Data for 1968 have been calculated by the present writer from the *Report of the Chief Electoral Officer.*

House—not an impossible concession) reduces the frequency with which this cost has been incurred to once in fifteen occasions (see Table 2).

The second set of costs, relating to the apportionment of seat penalties among the opposition parties, can be measured in various ways. One way of stating it is to note that since 1921 the electoral system has discriminated against the second largest electoral party on nine out of fifteen instances (60 percent), against regional third parties on five out of fourteen instances (36 percent), and against third parties with diffused national support on

twelve out of fourteen instances (86 percent) (see Table 3).[35] Another approach is to compare the relative impact of the electoral system on the opposition parties considered in pairs. By this measure, the largest opposition party has had an advantage over regional third parties on three out of twelve occasions (25 percent), and over national third parties on nine out of twelve occasions (75 percent). The same comparison for regional and national third parties gives the former the advantage on every occasion (100 percent). Finally, the bias ratios in Table 3 may be averaged, giving the largest opposition party, regional third parties, and national third parties scores of 0.87, 1.03 and 0.61 respectively.

Whatever measure is used, the differential impact of the electoral system is as generally described by Professor Cairns. That is, to the extent that the size of the parliamentary party is a factor (and it is clearly only one factor), (1) the credibility and challenge of the official opposition as an alternative government has been diminished somewhat more often (and more severely) than it has been enhanced; (2) the pressure from the left has always been attenuated, often acutely; and (3) the formation of regional protest parties has usually been encouraged. Whether all of these consequences are "costs" of the electoral system depends on the values of the observer; in any event, they will be important entries in any full "cost-benefit" analysis.

Inseparable from the electoral system's distortion of the votes-seats relationship is its well-known tendency to exaggerate moderate oscillations in vote shares into often spectacular fluctuations in seat shares.[36] Cairns acknowledges this trait several times, always as a morbific phenomenon. He objects to it on two grounds: (1) because it has occasionally (as in the Riel and conscription controversies) transformed into political crises decisions whose electoral consequences could otherwise have been weighed more calmly; and (2) because the conditions of "feast or famine" in regional parliamentary representation that can result (viz. the Conservative experience with Quebec)[37] hinder the parties in working out an internal routine for regional communication and compromise.[38] Considering these points in reverse order, it seems evident that the latter turns on a conception of the parliamentary party's role in policy-making that was suspected earlier in this paper of undue generosity. Briefly restated, the view taken earlier was that the makeup of the parliamentary party (present and past) undoubtedly affects party policy, but (at least in the two largest parties) only as one

of many factors and not the most important of these. It seems more plausible to regard the integration of new members as primarily a function of the outlook and values of the party leadership, a variable whose linkage to the electoral system is so loose (that is, admits of so many intervening variables) that it seems a bit Draconian to consider the electoral system more than a minor accomplice to possible failures in party integration.

The crux of the other objection seems to be that by turning moderate gains or losses in electoral support into gross changes in legislative representation the electoral system sometimes subjects policy-makers to pressures that have no legitimate basis in the preferences of the electorate at large. At such times, the continued support of a large number of voters may be obliterated by the defection of a much smaller dissenting minority. The electoral system is faulty, in other words, because it violates the principle of majority rule. It gives undue weight to the preferences of minorities, and allows them to hold policy-makers to ransom in a way that no system of proportional representation would permit.

From this majoritarian charge there is no escaping: a plurality system of election, by allowing minorities to carry the day, is undeniably anti-majoritarian. From many points of view, this is undoubtedly a vice. Yet by giving self-conscious, sectionally concentrated minorities more than proportionate influence on those few issues about which they are most "intense," such an electoral system may well be a long-run condition of their remaining within the political system.[39] Whether these costs are worth paying can obviously not be answered in the abstract, but will depend on the nature of the demanded concessions as they occur and on the contemporary and expected payoffs (tangible and intangible) from continued union.

On a different plane the artificial volatility in party seat shares obviously has the effect of promoting a more frequent and extensive turnover in public office, and in party office as well (party leaders being easier to displace when not in power). What consequences this relative ease of dislodging powerholders may have, however, is not entirely clear. It may (as is often assumed in assertions of the value of close inter-party competition) heighten the sensitivity and responsiveness of powerholders to political demands. A lively debate on the validity of this traditional assumption is currently in progress.[40] It may also stimulate greater political participation and a deeper sense of political efficacy than would obtain under a more proportional electoral system, where political changes are (all other things being equal) less dramatic.

Whether this last set of benefits is realized no doubt hinges in large part on the effect of adopting some form of proportional representation upon (1) the number of parties and (2) the clarity and variety of electoral alternatives.

1. On the nexus between electoral system and number of parties, the writings are voluminous but the findings contradictory.[41] As might be expected, numerous other factors interact with the electoral system as influences on the number of parties seeking and winning legislative representation, but the relative impact of these forces (or indeed their total number) remains unknown. Unanimous agreement would probably be confined to the rather primitive proposition, as stated by Professor Robert A. Dahl, that proportional representation is a sufficient but not a necessary condition for finding more than two parties.[42] The literature thus offers little help in estimating the effect on the number of parties of adopting a "moderate" form of proportional representation in Canada; an ad hoc analysis and weighting of relevant variables is necessary. Only a radical expansion in the number of parties is clearly improbable.[43]

2. As regards the clarity of electoral alternatives (as distinct from their content, discussed earlier),[44] no conclusions independent of a solution to the previous question seem possible. If the number of parties increases after proportional representation is adopted, then the specificity of their appeals will probably rise; if not, not.

One last factor that no adequate "cost-benefit" analysis could ignore is the electoral system's effect on the character and working of the House of Commons. How would abandoning the single-member constituency affect the process of candidate recruitment; the backgrounds, local ties, attitudes, and other characteristics of candidates nominated and elected; the ability of some MPs to build up a personal following and a measure of independence from their parties; and the way in which MPs generally define their task and goals? Adoption of some of the "milder" forms of proportional representation would probably alter these relationships very little; a switch to some of the "pure" forms might, depending on the state of the "political market," reorient them radically.

THE PROSPECTS OF PROPORTIONAL REPRESENTATION IN CANADA

As this paper has sought to make clear, measuring the political effects of the electoral system calls for far more knowledge of Canadian politics than we now have. Thus, to speak confidently about the relative influence of the electoral system on party policies and campaign appeals we must first know: (1) how the parties have responded to political demands; (2) how influence over the decisions made in Ottawa is distributed and how much weight is attached to electoral considerations; and (3) how strong cross-class, regional cleavages are in relation to cross-regional, class cleavages.

At this stage, then, only the direct consequences of the electoral system stand out plainly. Stating these summarily, it has furthered majority and one-party government, quickened the turnover in political leadership, helped regionally based third parties, and hurt the political left. As such, it is clearly to the present partisan advantage of three of the four legislative parties. Moreover, its first two consequences are easily portrayed (and are widely seen) as in the public interest.

While the electoral system thus stands secure against imminent reform, its buttresses may in future be undercut either by a decline in the electoral strength of the two largest parties to rough equality with a burgeoning NDP, or by a change in the political culture hostile to continued distortion in the representation of party preferences, or (most likely) by concurrent changes in both of these directions. Faced with a persistent diminution in their strength, the two older parties may either merge or they may coalesce in self-protection in support of some form of proportional representation, whose attractions will by then already have been heightened by the recurring failure of the present system to deliver either majority or one-party government. Until such a political realignment has begun, further research into the effects of the present electoral system will be mainly of theoretical interest.

THE ELECTORAL SYSTEM AS DETERMINANT OF THE PARTY SYSTEM

As the reader may have noticed, several parts of the preceding discussion have intruded upon the perennial dispute over the role of the electoral system as a determinant of the party system. One side of this debate is upheld by writers like Grumm, Epstein, and Lipson,[45] all of whom see electoral systems as (in Epstein's words) "more the results than the cause of

party systems."[46] Once in place, electoral systems do have reciprocal effects, but their impact is seen as marginal in relation to the other forces working on the party system.

A most explicit dissent from this view comes from Cairns, who indicts these writers for failing to perceive that electoral systems, even though initially shaped (and perhaps subsequently reshaped) by party systems, nonetheless exercise a powerful reciprocal influence. Freed of this error, they might have investigated the relationship more closely, whereupon they would surely have come to regard the electoral system with greater respect. In a systemic world, Cairns argues, understanding is furthered by assuming interdependence and exploring it, not by prematurely classifying phenomena as either cause or effect.[47]

This debate has something of a dialogue of the deaf, in that the participants are evidently addressing themselves to different questions. The first set of writers are mainly seeking to explain why certain countries have one type of electoral system and not another, or why one electoral system has on occasion been exchanged for a different one. Their perspective is explicitly comparative and historical. Analysis of the effects of electoral systems once adopted is of secondary concern. Cairns' orientation, on the other hand, is the exact reverse. He expresses little interest in the reasons why Canada has one electoral system and not another, or in positing the prerequisites for change in our electoral system.[48] His perspective is totally non-comparative and oriented to the past only as a source of data on the effects of the present system, his single concern.

It is evident that this disagreement turns more on differing emphases and priorities than on points of substance. It is also plain that both of these lines of inquiry are indispensable, and that conclusions about the role of electoral systems as a determinant of party systems relying exclusively on one or the other are almost bound to under- or over-state the case. Both of these approaches can be improved by consistent use of a multivariate focus. It is not especially helpful, in other words, to show (as do many comparative studies) that electoral systems have failed *by themselves* to preserve party systems from change, and have typically been adapted in response to such changes. What is needed, rather, is comparative study of the interaction between electoral systems and other probable determinants. By the same token, case studies and future comparative studies of the indirect consequences of electoral systems for (say) party policies and campaign appeals, the tone and success of political bargaining, and the background and role perception of legislators will need to concentrate on measuring the electoral systems' *relative* influence on these phenomena. What some of the other relevant factors may be has been suggested in several places earlier in this article.

Notes

* I should like to thank Professors E.R. Black, J.C. Courtney, P.M. Leslie, and R.E.B. Simeon for their criticisms of an earlier draft of this paper.

1. "The Electoral System and the Party System in Canada, 1921-1965," *Canadian Journal of Political Science* 1: (March 1968): 55-80.

2. From 1921 to 1965, the period of Cairns' study, there were two double-member constituencies in Canada, Queen's and Halifax. For the elections of 1921 to 1930, there was a third, Ottawa. At present all constituencies are single-member.

3. Ibid., 64.

4. Ibid., 64-68.

5. Ibid., 63.

6. Ibid., 68-71.

7. Ibid., 71-72.

8. Ibid., 76.

9. Ibid., 74-75.

10. Ibid., 56-57. The data have been reworked to include the results of the 1968 federal general election.

11. Ibid., 77-78.

12. The relationship between the parliamentary and extra-parliamentary parties while the CCF was in power in Saskatchewan suggests that the difference in this respect between the NDP and the other parties may well diminish de facto if that party should win office federally. See Evelyn Eager, "The Paradox of Power in the Saskatchewan CCF, 1944-1961," in J.H. Aitchison, ed., *The Political Process in Canada* (Toronto, 1963), 118-135.

13. Since the electoral system is only partly responsible for the regional composition of the parliamentary party, a relationship between the latter variable and regional policy bias short of rough congruence would make it difficult to maintain Cairn's contention that the electoral system exercises an "important" influence on party policy.

   This point is reinforced when one considers that part of the distortion in the votes-seats relationship may not be attributable to the electoral system at all, but to deviations from the one-man-one-vote principle of apportionment that are remediable without changing the electoral system. How much of the distortion is traceable to this last factor does not seem measurable.

14. Cairns, "The Electoral System," 69.

15. For an attempt at measuring the role perceptions of Canadian MPs in 1962, see Allan Kornberg, *Canadian Legislative Behavior* (New York, 1967), Ch. 6.

16. These references to alternative strategies should not be taken as suggesting that party policy is invariably the result of careful calculation. They are intended only as a convenient means of distinguishing between different types of policy-sets, however arrived at.

17. Cairns, "The Electoral System," 64-68. John Meisel's data for the 1957 general election did not indicate a close relationship between the party leaders' campaign itineraries and the size of the margin separating the parties in previous elections. *The Canadian General Election of 1957* (Toronto, 1962), 153-155. The fit might be closer, however, if one were to compare leaders' itineraries with *contemporary* evaluations of the margins separating the parties from seat to seat.

18. Cairns, "The Electoral System," 67. A model of party behaviour along these lines is presented in Anthony Downs' well-known *An Economic Theory of Democracy* (New York, 1957).

19. The reader's attention may have been caught by the small differences in Table 1 between Column 1 and Column 2 for the Liberal party, again suggesting that in this instance the potential significance for policy of the electoral system *as such*, even assuming pursuit of a "patronage" strategy, cannot be rated very high. Comparable data prepared by Cairns for Ontario and Quebec for 1921 to 1965 show, however, that such small differences have not been typical. "The Electoral System," Table v, 61.

Column 4, which combines Columns 2 and 3, has been included in Table 1 because intuition suggests that this last distribution may be a more likely correlate for party policy than either of the other two. All other things being equal, and to the extent that electoral considerations influence policy at all, it seems as unlikely that the policy claims of "safe" and "marginal" areas should carry equal weight as that the policy claims of "safe" areas should be ignored altogether. On the one hand, threats of loss of electoral support if policy demands are rejected are bound to be taken more seriously if they come from "marginal" areas.

On the other hand, intra-party pressures and the need to maintain party unity make it inconceivable that the demands of "safe" areas should be continually rejected.

20. The writer has in progress a historical study of inter-party electoral competition in Canada. An increase in inter-party competition over time (that is, a rise in the proportion of seats classifiable as "marginal") would probably mean that the differences between Columns 2 and 3 were greater in the past than now. A decline in inter-party competition would probably mean the opposite.

21. "The Electoral System," 71 (italics added). The next sentence, after the section quoted above, reads: "From our perspective the basic point is that both [of these strategies] reflect the politics of sectionalism as stimulated by the single-member constituency system." This may be true (although it must be conceded that only one or neither of these strategies may have been adopted for the reasons stated). Nonetheless, it may be observed that to the extent that these strategies are combined over time their associated regional policy biases will tend to cancel out. As was argued earlier (n. 19 above), it is highly unlikely that either strategy would be pursued to the total exclusion of the other.

22. These descriptions of party policy are highly impressionistic, being subject to all the earlier-mentioned difficulties of measuring regional policy bias, but are based on the following considerations. As far as the needs of the economically depressed areas of the country are concerned, these were acknowledged very soon after the 1968 general election by creation of a Department of Regional Economic Expansion, by assigning responsibility for its affairs to one of the (reputedly) most influential members of the cabinet, and by passage of the Regional Development Incentives Act. By comparison, the government's attitude towards demands for help from the large urban areas seemed (at least up to the end of 1969) less sympathetic, as was also alleged publicly by the Honourable Paul Hellyer upon his resignation from the cabinet. *Globe and Mail*, Toronto, April 25, 1969, especially 8. For the

reactions of the Prime Minister and the leader of the opposition to Mr. Hellyer's views, see *Can. H. of C. Debates*, April 24, 1969, 7893-7895, and April 25, 1969, 7976-7984. Some of Mr. Hellyer's complaints have been echoed by Liberal backbenchers from urban constituencies like Barnett Danson (York North) and Philip Givens (York West). Ibid., October 27, 1969, 108-109; December 8, 1969, 1715-1718; *Globe and Mail*, November 22, 1969, and February 12, 1970. Conservative policy, meanwhile, was to demand more active federal involvement in the cities and the creation of a Commons Committee on Urban Affairs. *Debates*, December 8, 1969, 1700-1736. The Conservative party's contemporary desire to please and accommodate Quebec seemed manifest in the leader's apparent support for the "two founding peoples" concept in his 1968 campaign and, for instance, in the support which he and most of his followers subsequently gave to the Official Languages Act. Ibid., May 16, 1969, 8790-8794; May 27, 1969, 9123-9124.

23. Qualifiers like "major," "primary," and "important" are notorious obstacles to clarity of description. To reduce this hazard, the word "major" as used above should be interpreted to mean "from one-third to one-half" (of the responsibility for regional policy bias), and thus as weaker than words like "primary" and "principal." In Cairns' analysis, the word most often used to classify the effects of the electoral system is "important." Given the thrust of the context in which it appears, I consider it justified to interpret his term as equivalent to "major."

24. That, at any rate, appears to be the meaning of the assertion already quoted above.

25. Cairns, "The Electoral System," 74-75.

26. This very question is begged by Maurice Duverger's statement that "Divisions of Public opinion arise not only from natural differences between citizens but also from external factors, of which the most potent is the electoral system. *To that extent* political divisions represent a pattern imposed on public opinion from without rather than a reflection of differences existing within public opinion." *Political Parties*, trans. Barbara and Robert North (London and New York 1954), 386 (emphasis added).

27. There are, of course, many kinds of proportional representation, *all* of which distort the votes-seats relationship to some extent, although less than do plurality-vote, single-member constituency systems. Douglas Rae, *The Political Consequences of Electoral Laws* (New Haven and London, 1967), especially Chs. 2, 4, and 5. In Canada, it is unlikely that spatial considerations would ever be totally abandoned (as in "pure" or nation-wide proportional representation). But even a moderate form of proportional representation (which might, for insistance, divide the country into ten-member constituencies not crossing regional boundaries) would bring votes and seats into quite close correspondence.

28. S. Peter Regenstreif, "Some Aspects of National Party Support in Canada," *Canadian Journal of Economics and Political Science* XXIX: 1 (February 1963): 59-74; Robert R. Alford, *Party and Society* (Chicago, 1963), especially Ch. 9; John Meisel, ed., *Papers on the 1962 Election* (Toronto, 1964); John C. Courtney and David E. Smith, "Voting in a Provincial General Election and a Federal By-election: A Constituency Study of Saskatoon City," *Canadian Journal of Economics and Political Science* XXXII: 3 (August 1966): 338-353; James W. Simmons, "Voting Behaviour and Socio-economic Characteristics: The Middlesex East Federal Election, 1965," ibid., XXXIII: 3 (August 1967): 389-400; John Wilson, "Politics and Social Class in Canada: The Case of Waterloo South," *Canadian Journal of Political Science* I: 3 (September 1968): 288-309.

Professor Cairns' view of this question is ambiguous. In one instance he asserts that "the emphasis on sectional divisions engendered by the electoral system has submerged class conflicts. . . ." In another he says that "given the historical (and existing) state of class polarization in Canada the electoral system has made sectionalism a more rewarding vehicle for amassing political support than class." In a third instance he maintains that the single-member constituency system discourages class-based politics "when class identities are weak or submerged behind sectional identities." Further on there is a reference to "the strong tendency to sectionalism found in the very nature of Canadian society. . . ." "The Electoral System," 74-75.

29. For an interesting discussion of the development process from predominantly cross-class, territorial conflict patterns to predominantly cross-constituency, class conflict patterns, see Stein Rokkan, "Electoral Mobilization, Party Competition and National Integration," in Joseph LaPalombara and Myron Weiner, eds., *Political Parties and Political Development* (Princeton, 1966), 241-265. He points out that the pattern of change has varied from country to country, and has been slow where there has been a strong local consensus, a tradition of rural territorial representation, and no deep urban-rural cleavage. Ibid., 256-265.

30. The implicit assumption that the influence of the electoral system on party policy is equally strong in the two cases considered may be wrong, and the curves may in fact differ in shape. This contingency will not affect the argument, however, so long as the curves continue to converge sharply towards each end of the cleavage spectrum.

31. See n. 10 above.

32. See, for instance, E.E. Schattschneider, *Party Government* (New York, 1942), 74-75; Donald V. Smiley, "The Two-Party System and One-Party Dominance in the Liberal Democratic State," *Canadian Journal of Economics and Political Science* XXIV: 3 (August 1958): 316.

33. In 1957 the Liberal party received a greater share of the total vote than the Progressive Conservative party but won a smaller number of seats. As Table 3 shows, the Conservative party owed its capture of the government in part to discrimination in its favour by the electoral system.

34. I realize that not everyone considers majority and one-party government as a "benefit," but to defend my use of this term within the limited scope of this article is impossible.

35. I have defined "regional third parties" as those that failed to poll at least 5 percent of the valid vote in at least five provinces. Other third parties have been classified as "national." An alternative criterion for differentiating between these two types of party might be the number of seats contested. If the cutting point in this case is set at 100 seats contested, the results are virtually identical to those reported in the text.

36. In Great Britain and the United States the relationship between vote and seat shares has been found to be roughly cubic in nature. In other words, if A and B are parties in a two-party situation, seat share A: seat share B = vote share A^3: vote share B^3. A similar relationship has been found to exist in Canada, provided two-party, three-party, four-party, and five-party contests are considered separately. See Terence H. Qualter, "Seats and Votes: An Application of the Cube Law to the Canadian Electoral System," *Canadian Journal of Political Science* I:3 (September 1968): 336-344, and sources there cited on the British and American experience. Compare, however, a recent study by Duff Spafford, who shows that a major source of the fluctuation in major-party seat shares in Canada has been the variation in the number of third-party candidates. "The Electoral System of Canada," *American Political Science Review* LXIV (March 1970): 168-175.

37. The number of Conservative MPs from Quebec has varied since 1921 as follows: 1921, 0; 1925, 4; 1926, 4; 1930, 24; 1935, 5; 1940, 1; 1945, 2; 1949, 2; 1953, 4; 1957, 9; 1958, 50; 1962, 14; 1963, 8; 1965, 8; 1968, 4.

38. Cairns, "The Electoral System," 71-72, 76-77.

39. For discussion of the "intensity" problem in democratic theory, see Robert A. Dahl, *A Preface to Democratic Theory* (Chicago and London, 1956), especially Ch. 4; W. Kendall and G.W. Carey, "The 'Intensity' Problem and

Democratic Theory,": *American Political Science Review* LXII (March 1968): 5-24.

40. See, for instance, T.R. Dye, *Politics, Economics and the Public* (Chicago, 1966): R.E. Dawson, "Social Development, Party Competition, and Policy," in W.N. Chambers and W.D. Burnham, eds., *The American Party Systems* (London and Toronto, 1967), 203-237; A.G. Pulsipher and J.L. Weatherby, Jr., "Malapportionment, Party Competition and the Functional Distribution of Governmental Expenditures," *American Political Science Review* LXII (December 1968): 1207-1219, and LXIII (June 1969): 528-531; C.F. Cnudde and D.J. McCrone, "Party Competition and Welfare Policies in the American States," ibid., LXIII (September 1969): 858-866; I. Sharkansky and R.I. Hofferbert, "Dimensions of State Politics, Economics, and Public Policy," ibid., 867-879; J.L. Walker, "The Diffusion of Innovations among the American States," ibid., 880-899; B.R. Fry and R.F. Winters, "The Politics of Redistribution," ibid., LXIV (June 1970): 508-522.

41. For some of the most useful studies, see Schattschneider, *Party Government*, Ch. 4; Duverger, *Political Parties*, 203-255; critiques of Duverger's work by Colin Leys and Aaron B. Wildavsky, reprinted in Harry Eckstein and David F. Apter, eds., *Comparative Politics* (New York, 1963), 305-315 and 368-375 respectively; Enid Lakeman and James D. Lambert, *Voting in Democracies* (London, 1955); John G. Grumm, "Theories of Electoral Systems," *Midwest Journal of Political Science* II (1958), 357-376; S.M. Lipset, *The First New Nation* (Garden City, NY, 1967), Ch. 9; Giovanni Sartori, "European Political Parties: The Case of Polarized Pluralism," in LaPalombara and Weiner, *Political Parties and Political Development* 137-176; Rae, *The Political Consequences of Electoral Laws*.

42. *Political Oppositions in Western Democracies* (New Haven, 1966), 351. Rae has subsequently found a "strong association" between plurality formulae and two-party systems, but his definition of a two-party system ("those in which the first party holds less than 70% of the legislative seats, and the first two parties together hold at least 90% of the seats") weakens this finding by including countries like the United Kingdom among the two-party systems. *The Political Consequences of Electoral Laws*, 93-95.

43. As is argued by Sartori, the adoption of proportional representation is unlikely to open the way to "extreme" party pluralism where it is met "by an already structured and stabilized party system." "European Political Parties," 167-176.

44. See 344-345 above.

45. Grumm, "Theories of Electoral Systems"; Leon D. Epstein, *Political Parties in Western Democracies* (New York, 1967), 37-45; Leslie Lipson, "Party Systems in the United Kingdom and the Older Commonwealth: Causes, Resemblances and Variations," *Political Studies* VII (1959): 12-31.

46. *Political Parties*, 37. For a similar view, see Frank J. Sorauf, *Political Parties in the American System* (Toronto, 1967), 27-32.

47. "The Electoral System," 77-78.

48. Cairns thinks he knows already why Canada has one electoral system and not another: Canadians share a "cultural bias" against systems of proportional representation. Moreover, habit has so ingrained the present system that any hope of change would be illusory. Ibid., 55-56. It may be noted that evidence supporting these propositions is virtually nonexistent, and that Cairns himself calls them into question by advocating study of the merits of adopting proportional representation in Canada.

28. POWER REQUIRES REPRESENTATION

William P. Irvine

THE CASE FOR REFORMING THE ELECTORAL SYSTEM TO PRODUCE MORE REGIONALLY BALANCED PARTY CAUCUSES

The Quebec referendum on May 20th produced *déblocage*. The impetus for constitutional rearrangement is greater than it has been for some years.

While Prime Minister Trudeau announced that everything was negotiable, he set two basic conditions: the enshrinement of certain rights from attack by any government, and the preservation of real power for the federal government. Getting agreement on these constitutional changes may require some important changes in the institutions that preside over those rights and powers.

Changes are necessary to make federal institutions more representative. Most Canadians would agree that we need a policeman to ensure our rights and to preside over policies for redistribution, for the free flow of people and capital, and so on. Many Canadians, however, are not entirely convinced that they can trust the present federal government or courts to be that policeman. There is always the fear that they might end up in league with the attackers.

I leave aside the question of reform of the judicial system, and focus on reform of the electoral system. Our Parliament does, of course, represent all parts of Canada, but neither our government, nor our opposition, does. This poses problems, primarily for the legitimacy of the federal government but also for the capacity of the opposition to take over the government.

At the level of conflicts of interest, this means that the caucus of the governing party is unable to fulfil its primary function. It cannot report to ministers how their plans will affect and be perceived in all parts of the country. It cannot offer a voice to important interests in different sections of the country. It cannot speak authoritatively, either for or to, all sections of the country.

This has never been clearer than in the results of the last two federal elections. In May of 1979, it seemed that Canada would have to deal with a Quebec referendum with a federal government having only two elected members from Quebec. The situation was different, but no happier, after the February 1980 election. Western alienation has been mounting for years, and our federal government will have to deal with that. And again, the federal government has been virtually shut out of a crucial region.

William P. Irvine, "Power Requires Representation," in George Cooper, ed., *Effective Representation*, Options Reprints Series (Halifax: The Institute for Research on Public Policy), n.d., 43-49. Reprinted by permission of the publisher.

There are optimists who feel that this situation is episodic. Indeed, some feel that both problems—the weakness of the Liberals in the west and the weakness of the Conservatives in Quebec—will be solved at one stroke, by the retirement of Prime Minister Trudeau. This is simply not so.

It is true that the Progressive Conservative party has in the past been able to win seats in Quebec. In 1958, Mr. Diefenbaker won 50 seats there. It is also true that the Liberals have been able to win seats in all the western provinces. In 1968, Prime Minister Trudeau did just that—winning 27 seats, four of them in Alberta.

These are very attractive trees and worthy of note, but the forest remains dark and foreboding for both parties. Surely, what is most striking is the inability of the parties to consolidate their victories. It is striking, but it is not inexplicable.

Our present electoral system produces a very weak relationship between the votes cast for a party and the seats won by that party. In translating votes into seats, it over-represents the leading party in any area and under-represents the parties that are placed second and third.

The under-representation is increasingly sharp as a party gets weaker. The Liberals get well over one-fifth of the votes cast west of Ontario but win only two of the 80 seats—less than three percent. The Progressive Conservatives have retained the support of thirteen percent of the Quebec electorate but get only slightly more than one percent of Quebec's seats.

Liberals *are* weak in the west. No monkeying with the electoral system will change that. But a person now has to be close to a masochist to campaign as a Liberal in the west. Trying to build a local organization, to encourage good candidates to come forward, and to attract people to participate in policy discussion within the party may be equally fruitless, and even more thankless. The same situation holds for the Progressive Conservative party in Quebec. Both parties do find good people to run under their banners—but only once.

This is the explanation for the parties' inability to consolidate their breakthroughs. There is no incentive for particularly able people to devote themselves to political careers within the party and nurture local roots for it.

The effect of the electoral system is aggravated by the images of the parties. They are seen by many potential candidates as hostile environments. They feel that even if they do get elected, in some 1958 or 1968-type sweep, it will take them a while to be able to influence their parties. The "while" just isn't there. They will probably lose at the next election. It is vital that someone represent the west in the Liberal caucus and Quebec in the Conservative caucus. Acquiring influence to represent effectively takes time. It requires commitment from the potential representative. Such a commitment is presently irrational.

Figure 1 Seats and Votes of Major Parties, by Region, 1980

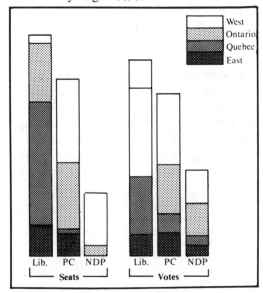

Its absence is equally unfortunate. There is a feedback mechanism at work. Inability to elect a significant number of members regularly means few people to tend the party organization. It means, for those who are elected, near isolation within the caucus. The lack of influence means that regionally attractive policies are less likely to be forthcoming, and that regionally-sensitive ministerial talent is rare. The lack of organization means that even the good policies may not earn their reward.

Lack of influence and organization make it difficult for a party to attract votes in its region of weakness. Without votes, and votes which must be bunched in particular constituencies, caucus influence will decline further. So will commitment to organizational development. The cycle begins again. Weakness breeds weakness. There is the danger that parties could eventually lose further electoral support and not just parliamentary support.

From analysts of the American Civil War to the Task Force on Canadian Unity, writers have commented on the danger of having political parties confined to a single region of a large country. Canada has been, and continues to be, fortunate in having nationally oriented parties at the federal level. They find it increasingly difficult, however, to maintain this orientation given the contrary incentives of the electoral system.

Moreover, they find it difficult to persuade Canadians that they are national parties. Most observers see only the party caucuses. It is easy for them to conclude that the Liberal party is the spokesman for Quebec and has no western support. It is easy to draw the opposite conclusion about the Progressive Conservatives. These are the parties as they appear on the left side of Figure 1.

The right side is generally unseen. Canadians might be surprised to discover that more than one vote out of every ten cast for the Progressive Conservative party was cast by a Quebecker, and that there are more Progressive Conservatives in Quebec than in Manitoba and Saskatchewan combined. Similarly, one Liberal voter in every seven lives west of Ontario, and there are more Liberals, almost 700 000, in the west than in Montreal. There are more in Alberta and British Columbia than there are in Toronto.

The problem is to increase their visibility. This means changing the electoral system—the set of rules that determines how votes cast get translated into parliamentary seats.

Many people and groups have suggested possible reforms. The Task Force on Canadian Unity briefly outlined one approach in its report, *A Future Together*, before the 1979 election. I published a book (*Does Canada Need a New Electoral System?*) shortly after that election. The 1980 results stimulated the NDP to renew a proposal made a couple of years before. The Canada West Foundation also recently produced another design for electoral system reform.

Other proposals abound. Designing electoral systems has become a cottage industry which could burgeon with the appointment of the parliamentary committee promised in the April, 1980 Throne Speech. The four I have mentioned are diverse enough to illustrate the major considerations.

Avenues for Change

The four proposals all preserve the single-member constituency that we now have. The authors seem to agree with the general view that having a single member of Parliament responsible to a defined body of electors offers certain advantages. My own proposal would have reduced our present number of constituencies by one-third. The Canada West Foundation proposal includes a 10 percent reduction in the number of constituencies, while the NDP and Pepin-Robarts approaches both leave the present constituencies untouched.

In order to correct the over- and under-representation of the present system, all four proposals must add a number of non-constituency seats—that is, seats whose occupant is decided on a different basis than are occupants of constituency seats. The proposals differ somewhat in allocating the non-constituency seats. The NDP proposal gives ten to each of five regions: British Columbia, the Prairies, Ontario, Quebec, and the Atlantic Provinces. The Task Force on Canadian Unity proposed that its additional seats should first be divided among the political parties according to the proportion each received of the national vote. In 1980, for example, the Liberals would receive 27 of the 60 additional seats for their 44.3 percent of the national vote. The Progressive Conservatives would receive 19, having won slightly less than one-third the national vote and the NDP would obtain 12 for about one-fifth the national vote.

My own proposal, and that of the Canada West Foundation, divided the additional seats on a territorial basis, assuring that each province's total parliamentary delegation remains proportionate to its overall share of the Canadian population.

These differences in initial allocation have potential constitutional implications which I shall address later.

The four proposals differ in their secondary allocations as well. The NDP proposal is to allocate the regional seats according to proportions garnered of the regional vote. The Canada West proposal is very similar. Since it operates at a provincial level, it allocates additional seats according to proportions of the provincial vote.

Quebec, which is both a region and a province, may serve as an example. Of the 10 seats it would get under the NDP proposal, 7 would go to the Liberals, and 1 each to the Progressive Conservatives, the NDP and the Socreds. The 15 seats for Quebec under the Canada West system would also be allocated

proportionately to the vote; 10 for the Liberals, 2 for the Progressive Conservatives, 2 for the NDP and 1 for the Social Credit party. The general philosophy behind each proposal is that in each region, a vote is a vote for purposes of the additional seats.

The Pepin-Robarts philosophy is different. It allocates seats to parties in the first step. For that allocation, a vote is a vote wherever it is cast. At the second stage, it allocates the parties' additional seats to provinces. At this stage, its philosophy is "a vote for party X is a vote for party X, whether it is cast in Alberta or in Quebec or anywhere else." That manifestly is not true in our present constituencies: 176 000 Liberals in Alberta get no representation; 1 675 000 Liberals in Ontario, about 10 times as many, get 52 representatives.

Treating each party successively, the Pepin-Robarts system distributes the additional seats to correct these distortions. After dealing with the malrepresentation of Liberals exemplified above, it would correct the similar distortions in representing Progressive Conservative or NDP voters. (We have already seen that 373 000 Conservatives in Quebec get one MP; 357 000 in Manitoba and Saskatchewan combined 12 MPs. Similar distortions for the NDP could also be reported.)

My own proposal was based on the most radical of the philosophies of representation: A vote is a vote, no matter where it is cast and no matter for whom it is cast. It would work to correct the distortions at the constituency level by over-representing at the provincial level those parties who have the hardest time translating votes into seats. It thus shares elements of all the above systems.

In Quebec, for example, the Liberals got almost 99 percent of the seats with 68 percent of the votes and the Conservatives got just over 1 percent of the seats for 13 percent of the votes. I proposed a large number of additional seats for Quebec, 44 against 50 constituencies. I would then allocate the provincial seats disproportionately to the Progressive Conservatives to assure them 13 percent of Quebec's overall parliamentary representation, and also over-represent other parties at the provincial level to bring them to the parliamentary strength warranted by their [votes].

A Cost-effective Appraisal

The consequences of these proposals for the present House of Commons (assuming that the votes continued to be cast in the same proportions) are shown in Tables 2 to 5, and may be compared with the current patterns in Table 1. Table 3 is taken from the draft paper for the Canada West Foundation. The others are my calculations; since the NDP proposal is on a regional basis, I have had to guess at the allocation of seats among the Atlantic and Prairie provinces.

A number of things are immediately apparent. First, the Liberals would still form a majority government under all proposals but the completely proportional one I have suggested. In all cases, however, that majority is reduced and becomes quite precarious (one seat) under the NDP proposal. Secondly, all proposals do change the regional complexion of the party caucuses, but in quite varying amounts.

One can do a rough "cost effectiveness" analysis of the four proposals. Any listener to open-line shows will know what the primary cost is. A common reaction to electoral system change is "We already have too many MPs who don't do anything." Whether such low esteem of our parliamentarians is general or justified will not be discussed here, but it is a fact that most schemes of electoral system reform would increase numbers in the House, implying increases in salary, overhead for space, support staff and office expenses, and so on.

The additional number of MPs, then, could be taken as a rough index of the cost of electoral system change. The proposals range from a net increase of 48 for Canada West to a net increase of 72 for my proposal.

To measure the effectiveness we have to specify exactly what is wrong with the present electoral system. The defects are numerous. There is the pure insensitivity to voter preferences, since many candidates get to Parliament with the support of less than half their constituents. There is the exaggeration of voter shift. From 1979 to 1980, Progressive Conservative support fell from 36 to 33 percent of the electorate, but that party's seats in Parliament fell from 136 to 103, a decline of 12 percent of the House.

British students have claimed that this tendency of our electoral system encourages short-run coping rather than long-run problem solving. In this regard, we may note research suggesting that few governments manage to resist the temptation to inflate their economies before elections and deflate them afterwards; Edward Tufte (*Political Control of the Economy:* Princeton University Press) could find only eight democracies where such a cycle was not in evidence. All have highly proportional electoral systems.

However, the present debate in Canada focuses on one particular defect of the electoral system: its tendency to produce party caucuses unrepresentative of the party vote. Let us then take this as the measure of benefit from any reform proposal. The following may be defined as the representation gaps: Liberal seats from Manitoba westward, Progressive Conservative seats in Quebec, New Democratic seats from Quebec eastwards. Additional seats in these categories may be rated as benefits.

The tables show that the proposals have quite different representational payoffs. The NDP proposal produces only 2 Conservative seats in Quebec (a gain of 1), 3 NDP seats in the east, and 7 Liberal seats in the west (a gain of 5). Overall then, the NDP proposal increases the size of the Commons by 50, but improves representation by 9, a benefit to cost ratio of .18. Similar calculation shows the Canada West proposal to have a ratio of .27, the Pepin-Robarts proposal to have a ratio of .58, and my own proposal to have a ratio of .69.

It must be said that, in this calculation, the measure of benefit is unsophisticated, and many will protest that my suggested measure of cost is inadequate. They see the biggest cost of electoral system reform as government instability or indecisiveness.

Would We Invite Instability?

Let us agree in the first place on the limits of institutional tinkering. Electoral system reform will no more turn Canada into Weimar Germany or Fourth Republic France or present-day Italy than it will turn us into present-day Germany or France. How an institution works depends very much on the history of conflicts in the host society. The cases of system instability are marked by much more profound class and/or religious cleavages than any that have marked Canadian history. Moreover, in the 1920s German and present Italian cases, important sectors of society had a very short history of participating in the political process, and the party systems did not have histories as long as those of the major Canadian parties.

Secondly, we must note that only a fully proportional electoral system is likely to make minority government more probable than it already has been in Canada. Whether this should be counted as a cost or not would require a long discussion and analysis.

Thirdly, while our present electoral system works against the representation of political forces that are small and evenly spread, it is quite vulnerable to a regionally concentrated protest movement. In 1962, Social Credit sup-

port was primarily concentrated in Quebec. In that province, the party took 35 percent of the seats with 26 percent of the votes. Politicians in Saskatchewan are now taking seriously the threat of Richard Collver. Any new party or leader that could put together 35 to 40 percent of the vote in some province like Quebec or Saskatchewan or Alberta could win a very large share of the seats in that province.

This, not the Rhinocerous or a Marxist Party, is the most probable threat to the present federal party system. Against such a threat the present electoral system offers *less* protection than would a more proportional one. Therefore, I do not think that I have understated the cost of the proposed reforms.

Could Reform be Soon?

Given the immediacy of the need for action, particularly action to rebuild the legitimacy of central institutions, electoral system reform has the advantage of being the most quickly accomplishable. Speed here is to be assessed in terms of the number of governments that must agree. Since the Supreme Court judgement on the Senate reference, changing that institution now requires a formal amendment. Change in the Supreme Court itself might be within the sole competence of the federal government, but this is not entirely clear.

Electoral system reform, by contrast, is likely to be within the sole competence of the federal Parliament. This does not mean that decision will be quick. Any new system should have broad legitimacy and support from all parties. But it does mean that electoral reform could be brought about more quickly than changes in other institutions.

A possible stumbling block to electoral system change is Section 52 of the British North America Act, which provides that provinces are to be represented in the House of Commons in proportion to their populations.

This poses no obstacle to my proposal, nor to the one of the Canada West Foundation. Both are explicitly designed so that total provincial parliamentary delegations are proportionate to population. There may be more of an issue with respect to the NDP or the Pepin-Robarts proposals. The former creates five regions, each entitled to an equal number of additional seats. The latter gives representation to parties first, and uses the seats to correct the most severe instances of *party* under-representation. As a consequence, the number of representatives from any province may vary by one or two from election to election.

Even so, there should not be a serious constitutional impediment, at least for the Pepin-Robarts proposal. The Parliament of Canada has, by itself, readjusted the numbers of MPs for each province in the House of Commons, most recently in 1974. So far, it has done so in close conformity to the principle of representation by population. Could it do so while departing from this principle?

Another way of asking the question is: do the provinces have such an interest in the principle of representation that the electoral system in that respect is not solely part of the federal constitution? In the Senate reference case, the Supreme Court did find that provinces had an interest in the maintenance of the Senate. Moreover, it found this to be so despite the fact that provinces do not appoint Senators and cannot hold them responsible in any way. It might, therefore, come to a similar conclusion about representation by population in the Commons.

One cannot predict what the Court would do. It may be however that the Court's reasoning with respect to the Senate depended on the history of pre-Confederation discussion about the Senate. The Court quoted Macdonald and Brown to the effect that smaller provinces had an interest in the Senate as a source of protection for their interests. They are unlikely to find such claims for the principle of representation by population. In the absence of such claims, would the Court conclude that the principle of representation by population was of interest only to the federal government, and hence part of the constitution of that government?

It is possible that the question could be avoided completely for the Pepin-Robarts proposal. While it does lead to some departure from representation by population, the magnitude of that departure is so small as to be of no practical significance. The number of Commons seats to which provinces are now entitled is determined after each decennial census, with quite long delays in many cases. The

Table 1   The Actual Distribution of Seats in the House of Commons after the 1980 Election

	Lib.	*P.C.*	*NDP*	*Other*	*Total*
Newfoundland	5	2	0	0	7
Prince Edward Island	2	2	0	0	4
Nova Scotia	5	6	0	0	11
New Brunswick	7	3	0	0	10
Quebec	74	1	0	0	75
Ontario	52	38	5	0	95
Manitoba	2	5	7	0	14
Saskatchewan	0	7	7	0	14
Alberta	0	21	0	0	21
British Columbia	0	16	12	0	28
Yukon Territory	0	1	0	0	1
Northwest Territories	0	1	1	0	2
Total	147	103	32	0	282
Percent Liberal	52				

Table 2 The 1980 Distribution of Seats in
the House of Commons under NDP
Proposal

	Lib.	P.C.	NDP	Other	Total
Newfoundland	6	3	1	0	10
Prince Edward Island	2	2	0	0	4
Nova Scotia	7	7	1	0	15
New Brunswick	8	5	0	0	13
Quebec	81	2	1	1	85
Ontario	56	42	7	0	105
Manitoba	3	7	7	0	17
Saskatchewan	1	9	7	0	17
Alberta	1	22	2	0	25
British Columbia	2	20	16	0	38
Yukon, N.W.T.	0	2	1	0	3
Total	167	121	43	1	332
Percent Liberal	50				

present distribution of seats slightly under-
represents Quebec and Ontario. In 1971, Quebec had 27.95 percent of the population and
obtained 26.60 percent of the seats. Ontario
had 35.71 percent of the population and obtained 33.69 percent of the seats.

Had the Pepin-Robarts system been in
place for the 1979 and 1980 elections, the
under-representation of Ontario would have
been diminished (but not eliminated) by the
allocation of extra seats. The under-representation of Quebec would have been corrected
slightly in 1979 and would have remained unchanged after the 1980 election. With respect
to these provinces, then, the Pepin-Robarts
system brings a justifiable improvement in
parliamentary position.

For some other provinces, the Pepin-
Robarts system would have produced short-
falls from strict representation by provincial

population at one election or the other, and
occasionally at both. In no case is the shortfall
as great as four-tenths of one percent.
Discrepancies of such magnitude are about the
same size as the discrepancies introduced by
the decision to ignore fractional remainders
(which cost Ontario one seat in the 1974 redistribution) or by the decision to increase the
number of seats for the Northwest Territories
from one to two. In the Senate reference case,
this last is explicitly held acceptable because it
(and Senate representation for the North) "did
not *in any substantial way* (my emphasis) affect federal-provincial relationships." Enacting
the Pepin-Robarts electoral system proposal
seems within the competence of the federal
government on the same ground even if it were
held that provinces do have an interest in representation in the Commons.

Choosing Provincial Members

The proposed provincial members would not
represent particular constituencies, but are
meant to represent whole provinces. They
would, of course, be elected by provincial
voters. The more votes cast for the Progressive
Conservative party in Quebec, for example,
the more members it would be assured from
that province. Reform simply tries to ensure
that Conservative voters in Quebec can get
representation even if they are not bunched in
one or two constituencies.

Reform would mean, however, that we
have to pay close attention to the process of
selecting these provincial members. In many of
the proposals, their nomination will be crucial.
The nomination process may decide, in part at
least who is successful.

This is not, however, very different from
the present situation. Present nomination processes may account for the under-representation of women in the House of Commons.

In any case, how provincial representatives are nominated will affect their status and legitimacy. It will determine whether a member is seen as a representative from the west to the Liberal caucus or as a representative of the Liberal caucus to the west.

There are two general ways to make the choice of candidate: let the voters do it, or let the party do it. Some have suggested that the additional seats be filled by the highest runners-up in constituency contests. Others propose province-wide primaries with seats to be filled in order of preference with the primaries. One could adopt a multi-member constituency with the single-transferable-vote method of election as another way of letting voters choose which of several party representatives might be returned to Parliament.

There is a general difficulty with all of these. Each leads members of the same party to compete against each other. Indeed, this intra-party competition will be much stronger than inter-party competition. With a highest-runner-up or single-transferable-vote system, candidates will feel it unlikely that they could replace a partisan opponent but will try to get an advantage on co-partisans. They might try to do so by assiduously courting a single-issue group, (a pro-capital punishment group, for example, or an anti-immigrant group). They might try to do so by espousing the policy line of the locally popular party. It is as if the NHL scoring championship were decided solely on the basis of goals scored. Members of a forward line would start stealing the puck from each other as they got into the opponents' end.

The purpose of the reform exercise is to strengthen parties as organizations that can embrace Canadians from 11 provinces. It should not be coupled with a method that would serve to destroy the organization. Both coordination and leadership require a party to be able to do some things on its own responsibility. Deciding on who might be provincial representatives, to my mind, is one of those things.

The alternative, therefore, is to have provincial members elected from lists chosen by the political parties. But who is the party? The answer to this question goes a long way to deciding who is being represented. Leaving list-making solely to the national leader might look too much like an avenue for cronyism. It would, in any case, be a system most likely to be seen as representing the party to the region, rather than the other way.

Still, the leader cannot be left out. When Mr. Stanfield excluded Leonard Jones in 1974 he was exercising his prerogative to protect what he believed the Progressive Conservative party stood for. We need to balance the interests of the national party and of its provincial organization.

My preference is for the selection of provincial lists to be predominantly up to provincial party organizations. How they would proceed could be left to the parties, but there is no reason that lists could not be drawn up well in advance of elections and perhaps, even ratified by party conventions in each province.

Some principles would have to be established spelling out a role for the national leader. A number of avenues might be followed. The national leader might be allowed to veto names from the list but not to insert names. He could be allowed to pick the first name but have no voice on the rest. He could be allowed to rearrange order on the list by one or two ranks but not to delete names.

Whatever one's own preference, list-formation is a most important matter. The parliamentary committee, proposed in the 1980 Throne Speech, is the logical body to decide the question. It may be sufficient to say simply that the national leader of the party must sign the lists submitted to the chief electoral officer. This would allow the parties to choose their own internal procedures. Parliament might want to go farther, however, and state explicitly a role for provincial associations of the federal parties. To do this would be further encouragement for parties to maintain vital associations in all provinces.

Any new electoral system has to be accepted by Canadians, and particularly by the areas now most under-represented in major party caucuses. A reform not seen as helping to resolve the representation problem is probably worthless. The parliamentary committee, through public hearings and consultation with national organizations and their provincial affiliates, is the best forum to work out a broad consensus on such a reform.

Legitimacy

Political science is a "soft" science, and "legitimacy" may be one of its softest concepts. We are not quite sure how to measure legitimacy, but there would be little dissent from the following proposition about its source: a government or decision-making body is accepted as legitimate if a group is confident that its interests are heard within it. If public opinion polls show greater feeling of closeness to provincial governments than to the federal, it is because such governments are seen as closer to the people. For the federal government, the problem of sheer distance has recently been complicated by the problem of under-representation and mis-representation.

Electoral system reform would make a marginal but still important contribution to rectifying this. Even the most effectively redistributive electoral system would not dramatically change the picture shown in our Figure 1. It would not alter the fact that the Liberal caucus draws its largest contingent from Quebec. Under the present electoral system, Quebec supplies half the Liberal caucus.

Even under the Pepin-Robarts proposal Quebec would make up more than 42 percent of the caucus; but the west would make up

almost 13 percent, ten times the weight it has now. This is good for the west; it would have its share of Ministers, parliamentary assistants and parliamentary committee chairmen, all of whom would add to the sensitivity of the executive. It would also be good for the Liberal party; no longer would it be seen in the west as "them."

Exactly the same could be written for the Progressive Conservative party. It would still be a strongly western caucus under the Pepin-Robarts formula: 42 percent as opposed to the 50 percent drawn from there now; but 10 percent of its caucus would represent Quebec—again, ten times the weight that Quebec has now.

Provinces have, and will continue to have for the foreseeable future, important roles in defining the national interest of the country. Electoral system reform would allow a national government, of whatever party, to have

Table 3 The 1980 Distribution of Seats in the House of Commons under the Canada West Foundation Proposal

	Lib.	P.C.	NDP	Other	Total
Newfoundland	5	3	1	0	9
Prince Edward Island	3	2	0	0	5
Nova Scotia	6	6	1	0	13
New Brunswick	7	4	1	0	12
Quebec	80	3	2	1	86
Ontario	58	44	8	0	110
Manitoba	3	6	8	0	17
Saskatchewan	1	8	8	0	17
Alberta	2	22	1	0	25
British Columbia	2	17	14	0	33
Yukon, N.W.T.	0	2	1	0	3
Total	167	117	45	1	330
Percent Liberal 51					

Table 4 The 1980 Distribution of Seats in the House of Commons under the Pepin-Robarts Proposal

	Lib.	P.C.	NDP	Other	Total
Newfoundland	5	2	0	0	7
Prince Edward Island	2	2	0	0	4
Nova Scotia	5	6	1	0	12
New Brunswick	7	3	0	0	10
Quebec	74	12	3	2	91
Ontario	59	46	12	0	117
Manitoba	4	5	7	0	16
Saskatchewan	3	7	7	0	17
Alberta	6	21	1	0	28
British Columbia	9	16	12	0	37
Yukon, N.W.T.	0	2	1	0	3
Total	174	122	44	2	342
Percent Liberal 51					

Table 5 The 1980 Distribution of Seats in the House of Commons under the Irvine Proposal

	Lib.	P.C.	NDP	Other	Total
Newfoundland	4	3	2	0	9
Prince Edward Island	3	2	0	0	5
Nova Scotia	6	5	3	0	14
New Brunswick	6	4	2	0	12
Quebec	64	12	9	9	94
Ontario	50	43	26	0	119
Manitoba	5	7	6	0	18
Saskatchewan	4	7	7	0	18
Alberta	6	17	3	0	26
British Columbia	8	15	12	0	35
Yukon, N.W.T.	2	1	1	0	4
Total	158	116	71	9	354
Percent Liberal 45					

an independent conduit to opinion in all segments of the country. Nationally based parties could seek to amalgamate these opinions into their own versions of national interest. These versions would attach less weight to the institutional interests of provincial governments, but still might be sold to residents in all parts of the country. A national party caucus might compete more effectively with the federal-provincial conference or the inter-provincial conference as a forum for working out national policies. Competition among representative bodies could only be in the interests of the represented.

29. REFLECTIONS ON REFORMING THE CANADIAN ELECTORAL SYSTEM

John C. Courtney

ELECTION RESULTS AND A PARLIAMENTARY CONSTITUTION

Criticism is sometimes levelled at the present electoral system because it makes it possible, following an election, for a government to be formed by a party which has won fewer votes but more parliamentary seats, or even fewer votes and fewer parliamentary seats, than its leading opponent. The implication of this criticism seems to be that the percentage of electoral votes rather than the number of parliamentary seats should be the determinant of which party forms the government. History seems to be on the side of the critics to the extent that in all but four of the thirty-one elections since Confederation the party forming the government after the election had received more electoral support than its closest opponent.[1] It should be noted however, that this particular attack on the electoral system is different in one important respect from the one noted previously about the very simple act of equating votes with seats. The level of the argument has moved away from the black-and-white logic of electoral calculus (is the share of seats more or less than the share of votes and what do we care to make of it?) into the grey conventions of a parliamentary constitution. The magic of numbers, when ex-

John C. Courtney, "Reflections on Reforming the Canadian Electoral System," *Canadian Public Administration* 23 (1980): 430-441, 448-457. Reprinted by permission of The Institute of Public Administration of Canada.

pressed simply as "votes versus seats," may have blinded the critics to a truth that is more readily apparent to our political leaders. That truth has to do not so much with the electoral system as with the constitution and with the nature of political change when expressed through more than two competing parties.

Surely the point should be that neither the number of seats nor the percentage of votes (or, for that matter, the two together) in isolation from a whole host of other variables should be expected to resolve the question of which party, or which coalition of parties, should form the government. Normally the question never arises. But when it does, no matter which electoral system is used, the outcome and the fairness of an election would have to be judged in relation to a number of practical political variables. What were the parliamentary and electoral strengths of the parties at the time of the preceding election? What was the composition of the Parliament at dissolution? What issues and policies tended to distinguish the parties from one another during the campaign and capture the interest of the voters? What will be the probable voting alliances between and among the parties once Parliament gets under way? These questions, and others, suggest that post-election decisions call for informed political judgment.

One need not necessarily subscribe to the view that politicians are overly well-endowed with judgment, but it is hard to deny that they have a keen sense of survival which has a direct bearing on their judgment. If, as happened in the two recent examples cited by the critics, 1957 and 1979, the political winds were found to be blowing against a governing party even though it was returned with more votes but fewer seats than its major opponent, and if no party had an overall majority of seats in the new Parliament but one party had clearly seized the political momentum from the other, prudent political leaders would be almost certain to see to it that the government changed hands. No other course of action would be in their interests.

The essential point is that in neither 1957 nor 1979 was the Liberal government of the day *forced* to step down, for in neither of those elections was the government in fact "defeated." In both instances had the Liberals chosen to stay on they could have sought the support of the new House of Commons when it first met, for the elections had failed to give any one party a clear majority of seats. That the Liberals chose to resign reflected their judgment that they could not survive long, if at all. Politicians know only too well a constitutional principle occasionally overlooked by analysts and commentators. That principle, interpreted by our political leaders in relation to the mood of public opinion as well as in relation to the number of seats controlled by their political competitors, was explained in the simplest terms by Walter Bagehot: "The Cabinet which was chosen by one House of Commons has an appeal to the next House of Commons."[2] Following the 1925 election Mackenzie King was obviously familiar enough with the principle (and with the Progressives) to know that the government he headed might just as well try to carry on, even though his party had received only 40 percent of the vote compared with the Tories' 46 percent. That the Prime Minister may have misjudged the situation, given the relatively short life of his government, was a comment on his political acumen and on the subsequent difficulties his government brought on itself, not on the method of electing MPs.

But let us assume, for the sake of argument, that the electoral system had been different at the time of the 1957 and 1979 elections.[3] Would the Liberal prime minister of the day have made the same decision to hand in his resignation and to turn over the reigns of power to his principal opponents? One can, of course, only speculate about the course of action that the respective governments would have taken. But it must be admitted that had some proportional electoral scheme been in use, the option of staying in office and of testing the mood of the newly elected Parliament would have been relatively more attractive to the Liberals as they discussed their future moves. The point is that if, having weighed the alternative courses of action before him, either Mr. St. Laurent in 1957 or Mr. Trudeau in 1979 had chosen to stay in office, his claim to have done so would have been a good deal easier to have justified because his party had received the largest share of the total popular vote in the election. Admittedly all sorts of other considerations would have had to have been taken into account (principally in the form of answers to the questions posed above about interpreting an election's outcome), and the decision to resign may well have been reached in both cases. But the need to have resigned would have been less apparent than it actually was in both instances, and the arguments that could have been mounted against resignation would certainly have carried more weight.

It stands to reason that the interpretation accorded election results will depend not only on what these results are but on how they were produced. Some might think, for example, that had the Pepin-Robarts formula for determining the number of parliamentary seats been in effect in 1979 the government would have changed hands, as in fact it did, from Liberal to Conservative (see Table 1). But this is not in itself self-evidently true. It ignores four critical factors. With the Pepin-Robarts formula: (1) the Progressive Conservative share of the total seats available would have been less than it was in the election itself; (2) the combined Liberal-NDP vote in the House would have been more than enough to have sustained the Trudeau government had it chosen not to resign following the election; (3) the number of Social Credit MP's would not, in itself, have been sufficient for the Conservatives to govern, as it was in the actual election; and (4) Mr. Trudeau would have had as part of his arsenal in support of holding on to power a perfectly legitimate reference to the Liberal share of the popular vote *and* to the number of additional Liberal MP's entering the House because of the workings of the redistributive mechanism of the reformed electoral system. The Liberals would have led all other parties in both the vote and the number of extra members of Parliament. Clearly under the Irvine proposal (Table 1) the chances of a change in government following the 1979 election would have been even more remote than they would have been with the Pepin-Robarts plan.

The whole matter may be speculative, but it is not frivolous. Given the Liberals' long-run dominant position in Canadian politics (the party has been in office nationally for all but

Table 1 1979 election results

	Actual results May 22	Pepin-Robarts Plan	Irvine Plan
Progressive Conservative	136	158	131
Liberal	114	138	139
New Democratic Party	26	37	66
Social Credit	6	9	15
Other	-	-	3
Total	282	342	354

twelve of the last sixty years) and their proven skill at surviving as the governing party in minority parliaments, the issue has to be addressed seriously. It raises a fundamental question about the likelihood of *ever* changing the party in office in Canada if a reformed electoral system were introduced. Recent Canadian political history is not at all encouraging about the prospects of political change in Canada. Only twice since 1935 have the Liberals resigned, and on both occasions the resignations have followed election "defeats." Yet even in both those "defeats" the party managed to win more votes than any of its opponents: two percentage points more than the Tories in 1957 and four percentage points more in 1979. The Liberals have, with the exception of the big Diefenbaker win in 1958 and the slight Conservative win in 1962, gained the largest number of votes in every one of the last fifteen elections. These references to the Conservative victories of 1958 and 1962 would appear to challenge the line of argument about the Liberals' firm grip on power. Yet the point about both of those elections is that they were timed, shaped and fought only because events had taken the turn that they did in 1957. The groundwork for the massive Diefenbaker win of March 1958 was laid in June 1957. Had the St. Laurent government not resigned following the election in 1957; had it argued that the number of votes more than the number of seats should determine which party ought to form the government; had it presented a Speech from the Throne, a budget, and several pieces of legislation to Parliament which it knew that the CCF and the Social Credit could easily support or, alternatively, defeat only at their own peril; and had Mr. St. Laurent, then 75, stepped down in favour of a younger man who would have been free to fashion the government in his own image— what then? The set of conditions may be more complex than the old one about Napoleon (had he been six feet tall would the history of Europe have been different?), but the answer may well have been the same to both questions. One cannot honestly tell, but as the above argument suggests, one can make an educated guess.

Certainly new voting alliances among the three or four parties in the House of Commons, possibly leading to formal governing coalitions, should not be ruled out under a different electoral system. Parliamentary parties can reasonably be expected to adjust their behaviour to different conditions. But no one at this point can confidently predict the direction and magnitude of the adjustments that lie ahead. Based on the evidence of the last few elections, the NDP would probably benefit the most from a changed electoral system, the Conservatives the least. As Professor Irvine notes, the NDP would occupy a strategic parliamentary position under a reformed system, for neither of its opponents would likely again be in a position to win a clear majority of the seats.[4] The NDPs increased parliamentary strength would enhance its bargaining powers and its impact on public policies as it went about making the most of a truly competitive bidding situation. But would its competitors' political and parliamentary skills and abilities be equal? The record of the past two decades speaks for itself. The Liberals are far and away the more successful party at garnering the NDPs support in minority parliaments. Given the skills and experience of their parliamentary leadership as well as their propensity to be totally flexible on policy, the Liberals stand an excellent chance of out-performing the Conservatives when it comes to attracting NDP support. Compare the minority governments of the past two decades—those of Mr. Diefenbaker and Mr. Clark with those of Mr. Pearson and Mr. Trudeau—and the point seems all too obvious. The NDP might be the big winner in terms of the proportion of seats gained

under a reformed system, but it would almost certainly be the Liberals who would be the big winner in solidifying their grasp on power.

ELECTIONS AND POLITICAL CHANGE

Critics of the electoral system are likely to tell us, as one did following the 1979 election, that a particular change in government "owed more to the accidents of the electoral system than it [did] to any expression of national will."[5] In one sense, of course, that sort of assertion is right. Transfer a few thousand Liberal and Conservative votes in 1979 and the government would not have changed hands. But in itself that kind of claim proves nothing, for every electoral system will have its "accidents" of one sort or another. Whether they are greater or fewer in number under different electoral systems is a matter for empirical investigation and argument. The fact remains that they do happen and that the fate of governments will sometimes be so determined.

In another sense such a claim is wrong. It is a mistake to describe a change of government as if it were the product of some sort of balancing act or political equation: more an accident of the electoral system must mean less an expression of national will, or vice versa. The error results from a misunderstanding of what constitutes an 'expression of national will' and from confusion over the extent to which the electoral system can be isolated from other variables as the cause of the difficulties.

If the politicians, party strategists and journalists were agreed on anything with respect to the 1979 election it was that a larger than usual number of voters wanted a "change of government." To some analysts the extent to which the results reflected that desire for change became the test by which the national will would be expressed in the election. Yet once the election was over it was obvious that those who had subscribed to the national will school of thought had been caught in a trap of their own making, for Quebec had tended to vote one way and the rest of the country had tended to vote another. Compared to 1974 the Liberal share of the vote had actually gone up in Quebec; elsewhere it had gone down. The 1979 results portrayed graphically a linguistic/ regional split, which left the commentators with little alternative but to conclude that there had been no clear-cut expression of national will and that regional tensions had been exacerbated. As the extent of the split had been magnified by the workings of the plurality vote system, Canadians were told a reformed electoral system was needed.

An "expression of national will" is an unfortunate figure of speech to use in relation to Canadian elections. Survey research has contributed substantially to our knowledge of the reasons people have for voting as they do, but only rarely has it produced evidence of a sufficient cluster of reasons on a truly national scale to enable us to conclude that the will of the electorate was like-minded enough to constitute a *national will.* The extent to which the 1979 election was actually about a change of government is a good case in point.

As in any election, the desire for a change of government is bound to vary in its intensity from person to person and in its shape from region to region. Given that the strengths of the parties running against the Liberals in 1979 varied according to constituency and province, those voters who felt strongly enough about the need to effect a change of government had no realistic chance of bringing about that change unless they maximized the effect of their vote. To do so they had to cast it for the candidate most likely to defeat the Liberal candidate. In some parts of the country this meant voting Conservative, in others it meant

voting NDP or, perhaps, Social Credit. By reminding ourselves of this we can better appreciate the lack of uniformity of the anti-government vote—or, more precisely, the lack of uniformity in the total vote of which part was cast in the hope of changing the government. The winds of political change are not unidirectional in a country as diversified as Canada. They twist and swirl according to local barometric pressures, one of which is the shape and condition of parties realistically competing with one another in various parts of the country.

Another is the relative popularity of the provincial government at the time of a federal election. That local or provincial matters are sometimes more important than federal ones in determining how an individual votes in a federal election should never be ignored in accounting for election results. The "time for a change" strategy the Conservatives designed for their national campaign was doomed to failure in Quebec from the outset. Had all things been equal at the time, Quebecers may have been more receptive to a call for a change of government. But things tend not to be equal in politics, and 1979 was no exception. The future of Quebec, more specifically the Parti Québécois' determination to redefine the relationship between Quebec and the rest of Canada, was an issue of considerable importance in that province in 1979. For a substantial part of the electorate the federal election provided an opportunity to score points against the provincial government. The Conservatives, who were at a loss to counter the widely held view that only the Liberals could argue the federal case against the PQ, found through their own polls that between 55 and 60 percent of the Quebec electorate were of the opinion that the best way to register a protest against the provincial government was to vote for the federal Liberals. Given that sort of widespread sentiment the magnitude of the

Liberal victory in Quebec was the safest prediction to be made about the election.[6]

It was widely recognized in both 1979 and 1980 that the Conservatives were no match for the Liberals in Quebec. While it is true that the faults and weaknesses of the Tories in Quebec stemmed to some extent from the cumulative and circular hardships imposed on the party through the workings of the electoral system in the 1960s and 1970s (policy, candidates and leader were weak because the party never won, and the party never won because policy, candidates and leader were weak), the extent to which the electoral system should be singled out for blame is by no means clear. Other possible explanations of Tory weaknesses in the province would have to include the historical ghosts with which Quebec Tories have had to live for decades. Their haunting presence underscores how difficult it is to be a Tory in Quebec and, conversely, how easy it is to be a federal Liberal there. This would not necessarily change if the electoral system were altered. If blood is indeed thicker than water, and if political memories in Quebec do happen to last longer than they do elsewhere, then the Conservatives may never overcome the impact of the triple legacy of Riel, the Manitoba Schools question and First World War conscription, even though these events themselves belong to the distant past and have been overtaken by ones infinitely more important to the well-being of modern Quebec. No matter what electoral system is employed, the fact remains that it is in the Liberals' interests to remind Quebec voters that historically Conservatives have been on the "wrong side" on too many occasions to be trusted. Robert Stanfield and Joe Clark paid a heavy price for leading an historically unpopular party in Quebec. The problems they faced were not caused exclusively, or even largely, as John Diefenbaker proved in 1958, by the electoral system. Modern Conservative leaders have been the

unwitting heirs to a handful of critical decisions from Macdonald to Meighen—decisions which have now entered the mythology of Quebec politics as "proof" of the anti-Quebec bias of the Conservative party. By definition, electoral reform aims at correcting faults of the electoral system. But too much should not be held out on its account when nothing short of a major historical rewrite would enable a party to overcome its past.

SWELLING THE PARLIAMENTARY RANKS

Electoral reformers plead the case for some type of electoral system that would award seats to parties otherwise unable to gain a share of seats roughly equal to their share of votes. (The particulars of the various proposals are not directly relevant to the general argument; it is sufficient to note that the principal electoral reforms proposed to date in Canada contemplate some redistributive or topping-up device to bring seats more in line with votes.)[7] It does no injustice to the case of the reformers to suggest that their reasoning is simple. If, to carry on with the Quebec example, the Conservatives only had had some additional members sent to Ottawa in 1974 as a result of a "fairer" electoral system, the party's task in that province during the next five years and in the elections of 1979 and 1980 would have been so much easier.

There appear to be two basic principles behind the reasoning. It is thought that a reformed electoral system would undermine the charge that a party is hopelessly without support in a region, and that a different electoral system would promote greater sensitivity within a party to the aspirations of the people in the region from which it traditionally gets few MPs. Although different in kind, both principles are largely perceptual in nature. One relates to the perception *of* a party by its opponents and by the electorate; the other concerns the perception *by* the party, specifically the party leadership, of regional problems. The claims are both strong ones, built on a seemingly irrefutable logic which gives them a natural appeal: increasing a party's parliamentary support in a region enhances its credibility in that region and increases its sensitivity to the region and its problems.

CREDIBILITY

According to Professor Fox a reformed electoral system would have the following advantage:

> There would be less foundation to the charge that the Liberals do not represent the West, that the Tories are a washout in Quebec, that the NDP is not a national party, and that Social Credit is a dying force limited to Quebec.[8]

Does it necessarily follow that a more equitable distribution of seats will accomplish all that is suggested on its behalf? The truthful answer, of course, is that no one in fact will know with certainty until the alternatives have been tried. But in the absence of actual electoral experimentation what does Canadian political experience suggest? Would there, for example, be any less likelihood of the Tories being considered a washout in Quebec simply because a few more members from that province were added to their caucus through some "topping-up" device? Perhaps not. If the electoral system were changed, the nature of the attacks on the Conservatives by their Quebec opponents and the misgivings about the Tories on the part of most Quebec voters would almost certainly be different than under the plurality system. But their consequences could very well be the same.

Any political party will use as part of its electoral arsenal whatever ammunition happens to be available. Under Mr. Trudeau's leadership in four federal elections the Liberal party in Quebec found it politically advantageous to exploit the weakness and inconsistencies of Conservative policies on national unity: *deux nations*, or not? special status, or not? negotiate sovereignty association, or not? (It need scarcely be added that the Liberals were not always honest in their portrayal of the Conservative positions, but for the sake of scoring electoral points that hardly mattered.) In 1979 and 1980 the Trudeau Liberals effectively squeezed what remained of the Conservative party out of Quebec. But had the electoral system been altered previously in some way to make it possible for a few Tories to be sent to Ottawa because the party had received a certain share of the popular vote, what then would have happened to the kind of argument that the Liberals would have employed in Quebec in the federal elections from 1968 to 1980?

Almost assuredly, the Liberals would have supplemented their attack on what they alleged to be the Conservative party's fudginess and inconsistencies on the national unity question with an attack on the very principle of voting Tory *at all*. Whereas under a plurality system the Liberals could rest assured that a vote cast for the Conservatives would have had virtually no effect on the outcome of the election because of the Tories' generally hopeless position in Quebec, an electoral scheme which distributes seats according to share of votes makes it imperative for a party to keep its opponent's share as small (and its own share as large) as possible.

Naturally the Conservatives in Quebec could be expected to base part of their electoral strategy on the claim that "as a vote for the Tories will now actually count for something, by all means don't hesitate to give it to us—Vote Conservative." Given that sort of assertion, one could presumably make a case for predicting an increase in the level of voter efficacy which, in turn, could lead to an increase in the Conservatives' share of the total vote. But the incentive to maximize support would work for all parties under a reformed electoral system, not simply the underdogs. Is it any less reasonable to assume that the Liberals, who since at least 1917 have not shied away from using any sort of argument in Quebec against the Conservatives, would have failed in 1979 and 1980 to have campaigned on something like the following: "As only the Liberals can stand up to Lévesque, it is in Quebec's interests to make certain that *as few votes as possible* are cast for the Conservatives—Vote Liberal locally and make certain that your vote does not contribute to the election of Conservatives from the province-wide lists." Or let us assume that, in 1968, the Tories had chosen Marcel Faribault to run at the top of their provincial list, a spot that would have guaranteed his election. What might the Liberals than have said? "If you seriously believe, as we do, that this man is a threat to the future of our country because of his support for a policy that even his own leader rejects, *deux nations*, then you have no choice but to help minimize the amount of support that he might be able to claim that his party enjoys in Quebec—Vote Liberal." As the opportunity to vote *against* something or someone has a powerful attraction to the electorate, these are not purely speculative matters. Accordingly the Conservative vote could well have gone down in Quebec in recent elections rather than remaining the same, or going up, because of a reformed electoral system.[9]

Nor is it necessarily idle speculation to imagine the Liberals describing with scorn those Quebec members who were elected simply because their party happened to have received a particular share of the popular vote. "Tories in Ottawa from Quebec? Only because

of the electoral system! The great majority of Quebecers did not want PCs 'representing' them, yet we are stuck with this crowd because of the workings of the electoral system." The possibility of creating, as it were, two classes of MPs may not be entirely remote given the penchant of Canadian politicians to argue their case by grabbing at the nearest straw, whatever it may be. One could easily imagine the attacks by parliamentarians on one another; to the purely partisan ones could be added those which distinguished between the types of members sitting in the House of Commons.[10]

What is striking about the Liberal victories in Quebec from 1968 to 1980 is their magnitude. At the constituency level the party employed its considerable organizational strength to a point far beyond that of bringing in enough support to be certain of winning the seat. The massive wins in the Montreal area constituencies are a good case in point. In 1979, for example, all twenty-four seats were won easily by the Liberals, the total Liberal party vote having been 70 percent to 11 percent for their nearest rivals, the Conservatives. What was remarkable about those seats was the combined turnout figure of 78 percent. It was marginally better than that of the province as a whole and it was at a level one does not normally associate with an urban system so overwhelmingly dominated by one party. (In the twenty-three Toronto area seats the turnout was 81 percent in 1979, but here the spread between the PCs and the Liberals was less than one-half of a percentage point.) The Quebec figures suggest an extraordinary capacity on the part of that province's Liberals to get out the vote even when the party does not need it to win handily. What emerges is the picture of a party which, in spite of the obvious advantage bestowed on it by the plurality system, nonetheless successfully mobilizes the electorate on the party's behalf. It has accomplished this through its leadership, its organization, its attacks on the provincial government, and its ability to project itself as the only true defender of Quebec interests in Ottawa. None of these would necessarily change if the electoral system were altered. Indeed, if the Liberals had had the added incentive of *having* to maximize their own support in order to keep the Tories' share of the total vote as small as possible, how much better would they have done? It is an intriguing question to which there may well be no satisfactory answer. But it would be a mistake to think that the Liberals in Quebec, had the electoral system been different, would not have tried to have turned the situation to their advantage. Perhaps somewhere along the line they might even have singled out the small band of Quebec Tory MPs chosen under a non-plurality system as proof of the extent to which the party was in fact a washout in that province, by noting that all but two or three of them had had to rely, as it were, on the back door in order to enter the House....

REPRESENTING THE PEOPLE

One would be hard-pressed to find a country more preoccupied with the representativeness of its political institutions than Canada. Its government and political institutions, from cabinet through to party conventions, are invariably constructed as tiny replicas of the larger mosaic. The more they are geographically and linguistically "balanced" (anglophones/francophones, Maritimes/Westerners/Central Canadians, and Quebecers/non-Quebecers) the greater the likelihood they will be held to be "representative." Little wonder that Canadians quickly find fault with parliamentary caucuses that are dominated by or, alternatively, almost totally without membership from, some of the country's regions and its principal demographic groups.[11]

One's natural response to the existence of unbalanced parliamentary caucuses is to "correct" their balance. Is the Tory caucus short of Quebecers, or the Liberal caucus short of Westerners? Then bring some in. If this means reforming the electoral system, so be it. The difficulty with that kind of response is that it can create new problems, the answers to which either are unknown or are of the sort which would not necessarily make matters better. The present electoral system lends encouragement to a party's leadership seriously intent on increasing its support in those areas in which it has few, if any, elected members. In fact it is an irony of the current system that a party's weakness in one region one day might account for its success there the next. Whether this would also be true of a reformed electoral system is not certain.

National political parties in Canada are loose amalgams of disparate regional, linguistic and economic interests scrambling for a spot more or less around the centre of the political spectrum. Their leaders share at least one trait in common—a recognition of the need to forge acceptable intraparty coalitions. Whether the parties would remain as broadly based, as relatively free of doctrine and ideology, and as accommodative of regional and linguistic differences under a reformed electoral system no one can predict with certainty. But one possibility should not be overlooked. It could be that a modified electoral system would encourage a dramatic rethinking on the part of many party activists and strategists about the need to continue directing an appeal to that area of the country in which the party is weak. Given some kind of proportionate scheme, each of the three existing parties would reasonably expect to have at least a few MPs elected in its weaker regions.[12]

Yet a party may discover that its optimal electoral strategy would be to concentrate on winning additional support in areas of its electoral strength rather than in areas of its electoral weakness. That discovery could lead party activists and influential strategists to question the appropriateness of continuing accommodative campaigns. They might argue that the party's principal electoral trouble spot had been "looked after" by virtue of the electoral system and that it would be pointless to continue deploying scarce resources in pursuit of extra support there when those resources could be used to greater effect elsewhere. The strategy, optimal or not, might have such a simple and plausible ring to it that a party's leadership would find it difficult to be as accommodating and as conciliatory as it might otherwise be. A reformed system might, in other words, diminish the capacity of political leaders to persuade colleagues, supporters and voters of the need to display the political equivalent of the military victor's greatest attribute—continued goodwill to the vanquished. The implications for national unity could be profound.

Without question there is an enormous challenge facing the Tories in Quebec and the Liberals in the West. But in that challenge lies a great incentive for developing organizational skills, for recruiting credible candidates and for devising acceptable policies. Lacking the fullest reason for attending to these, an accommodating political system such as Canada's could well lose some of its will for mediating the country's diverse regional and linguistic demands. If because of the redistributive workings of a reformed electoral system the Conservatives had been awarded some twelve to fifteen Quebec MPs in 1979, or the Liberals a similar number from the West in 1980, what would then have happened? Certainly the caucuses would have been more truly "representative" and the cabinets would have been much closer approximations of the classic Canadian example. But the more "balanced" parliamentary parties and cabinets might have come at the expense of a more genuine attempt to understand a region's grievances as well as the

leadership's recognition of the need to do something about them. The primary danger of designing a scheme to meet a particular problem comes when, having implemented the scheme, its results are mistakenly thought to have met the grievances which originally gave rise to the problem.

The reformers will argue, of course, that the Conservatives and Liberals have organized, recruited and devised as best they can in their respective weak spots in the past and all to no avail, and that almost any alternative is preferable to the present system. While there is some truth in this diagnosis, the cure they propose may be based on too restricted an understanding of what constitutes political representation in Canada. Perhaps nothing is needed so much as a fuller appreciation of the variety of ways in which representation is carried out under the present electoral and party system. A brief reference to one or two of those ways illustrates the point.

The results of the 1980 election presented the Liberal weakness in the West in stark terms. When it is recalled that three out of four voters in Western Canada supported a party other than the Liberals, that party's poor showing is not surprising given the workings of the plurality system. But the extent to which the Liberals fared badly may in itself have a salutary effect on the behaviour of the new government exceeding that which any proportionate scheme could have ensured. In this respect a post-election comment by one influential Western Liberal is revealing. Asked by Mr. Trudeau to recommend ways of giving the West some sort of presence in the new government, Lloyd Axworthy concluded after consultations with party officials in the West that:

> One paradoxical, but encouraging, result of the election outcome ... was the sharpening effect it [had had] on Liberal attitudes.
>
> Unlike past election results, in which the party has been able to elect a few members from provinces such as Saskatchewan and

British Columbia, the shutout in three provinces ... had a chastening effect.

The party can no longer avoid facing the lack of support it gets in the West and now realizes that only its performance on problems of importance to the area will determine whether it can rebuild the support it once had.[13]

Time will tell how chastening the effect of the election will prove to be. In the meantime the question remains: had some topping-up scheme awarded a handful of seats to the Liberals in each of the Western provinces would Mr. Axworthy's assessment of his party's mood have been the same? More to the point, would he have been asked by his leader to have given an assessment at all? It is doubtful. In that sort of situation it would have been easy to have argued that the problem of representing the West had been taken care of. Western Canadians might be quick to point out that it had also been taken care of in 1968, 1972, and 1974 when twenty-seven, seven and thirteen Western Liberal MPs were elected respectively.

Of course, prime ministerial responses to electoral weakness can take a variety of forms. One or two of Mr. Clark's moves following the 1979 election deserve mention because they suggest a different and potentially valuable way for Canadians to look at the concept of representation. Apart from naming both Quebec Tory MPs and two Quebec senators to the cabinet, Mr. Clark could do little more on that front. Yet as he was determined that his government should be neither embarrassingly insensitive to, nor totally unaware of, Quebec issues and problems, and as he was convinced that his party had a special obligation to lend credibility to its claim of being truly national, he sought ways of ensuring at least some francophone presence at the ministerial and prime ministerial levels. Several key political positions in the Prime Minister's Office, including Assistant Chief of Staff and Senior Communications Adviser, were filled with Quebecers. Every minister was directed by the Prime Minister to include at least one francophone in his exempt salary (political) staff, and Marcel Massé, with a good deal of attendant publicity, was brought in as Clerk of the Privy Council. These moves suggested a political-bureaucratic response to the problem at hand. Although this may be far from ideal in the public's eye as a replacement for the short supply of Quebecers and francophones in the Tory caucus and the cabinet, the move nonetheless may warrant closer scrutiny for its contribution to the whole policy-making process and to the notion of representation. Did the 'representative' character of the PMO and the ministers' personal staffs, for example, ease relations with those francophone civil servants who might otherwise have feared domination by an "English-speaking" government? Did it promote respect and trust between ministers and their staff? Was this the sort of news that gradually filtered through the system as a sign confirming Mr. Clark's declared intention of making certain that Quebecers in general, and francophones in particular, could not accuse his government of having abused them? Did Mr. Clark's actions, in other words, ensure that some form of representation was forthcoming whereby Quebecers would justifiably conclude that even though they lacked actual representation on the government side of the House, they had been accorded virtual representation in the government itself?[14]

These are the sorts of questions to which answers need to be found before the present electoral system is condemned on the grounds that it fails to represent Canadians. Professor Pitkin sheds light on a difficulty Canadians experience with the concept of representation. If one tends to think, as Canadians do, of a body such as a legislature, or a party caucus, or a cabinet, only as a "pictorial representation or a representative sample of the nation, [then one] will almost inevitably concentrate on its composition rather than on its activities."[15] Commentators might reflect on the wisdom of continuing to single out the regional and linguistic composition of cabinets and caucuses as the yardstick by which they are claimed to be representative, when that comes at the expense of judgments that ought to be formed about the capacity of these bodies and of the larger political system to act for Canadians in the fuller sense of the term "representation."[16]

Broadly based and middle-of-the-road as they are, Canadian parties place few structural or ideological barriers in the way of their leaders. A leader convinced that a changed electoral strategy or party policy would benefit his party can alter course with generally little internal opposition, as critics as well as friends of Canada's party system sometimes note. Accordingly, a national leader serious about trying to overcome his party's weakness in a region is not totally without options. He might promote policies favourable to the region, or he might strike an electoral bargain with a powerful provincial or regional party. In either instance a leader would have properly assumed his obligation to have sought honourable ways of overcoming his party's electoral deficiency. In so doing he would have performed a representational role in the sense of having acted for a region's interests by promoting his party's interests.

It is when the great majority of voters in a region view a party leader with suspicion (seeing him perhaps as non-conciliatory, or as indifferent to that region's concerns), and when such a view coincides with that leader's ability or unwillingness to form political alliances with important groups or parties in that region, that the party he leads is certain to pay a heavy electoral price in the province or region directly affected. Mr. Meighen's Conservatives in Quebec and Mr. Trudeau's Liberals in the West illustrate the point. By the same token, when one party benefits enormously from its leader's personal popularity in a region, other parties do not have much to show for their electoral efforts in the area. Mr. Diefenbaker's Conservatives on the prairies and Mr. Trudeau's Liberals in Quebec left little for their opponents to win. But such electoral strengths and weaknesses are not written in stone. As leaders, issues and policies change in Canada, so do voting preferences. In the late 1930s political obituaries were being written about the Conservative party. It was widely seen as a spent force in federal politics and in most provincial systems. Yet forty years later the Progressive Conservatives not only formed the government in Ottawa (for the second time in the four decades), they were also in power in seven provinces. In mid-1979 some commentators speculated that the Liberal party was on the verge of extinction as a genuinely national party. They reached the conclusion that unless the electoral system were reformed to award seats more in relation to a party's vote, the Liberal party might soon be reduced to little more than its Quebec power base. The 1980 election gave the lie to that prediction. Finality, Disraeli noted, is not the language of politics.

DESIGNING ALTERNATIVES

To pretend that all is well with the present electoral system in Canada would be a mistake. But to think that all would necessarily be better with a reformed system could prove to be an even bigger mistake. Too many questions remain to be answered before the current electoral system is altered. Not enough is yet known about recent political events to be able to judge the accuracy of the dramatic and immediate post-election claims about the representational crisis that Canada is said to be facing. Not enough is yet known of the likely impact on Canadian politics of a modified electoral system, and as it is reasonable to assume that different electoral conditions will prompt different behaviour on the part of at least some voters, candidates, leaders and parties, the implications of such changes for Canadian government and politics are uncertain. Not enough is yet known of the particulars of the various reform proposals to enable an informed judgment to be made about the relative merits of one scheme over another or, indeed, about the appropriateness of any of them as ways of ensuring that improvements in the political system will result from changes in the electoral system.

To single out the electoral system for exclusive attention at the expense of other topics potentially more relevant to representation in Canada would be a mistake. Further debates over the electoral system will be incomplete if they fail to take into account the wider context within which representation occurs. It would be helpful to know, for example, what Canadians see as the appropriate representational mix among their electoral system, provincial governments, federal bureaucracy, lobbies and party system. As the power and authority of government bureaucracies, provinces, and professional and economic pressure groups have grown in recent years, have these institutions come to play such a large representational role in the life of Canadians that the typical voter is less concerned with the complexion of federal party caucuses and cabinets as representational institutions than the reformers have implied? If so, this would have an obvious bearing on some of the claims put forward by the reformers.

A statement in the Pepin-Robarts Report illustrates the point. In pressing its case for a reformed electoral system the Task Force on Canadian Unity states:

> Our research of experience in other federations indicates that when party membership in the central parliament becomes concentrated in regional blocks it is an advance signal of eventual disintegration. The regional polarization of federal political parties corrodes federal unity. Because we see developing signs of such a situation in Canada we have come to the conclusion that electoral reform is urgent and of very high priority.[17]

It would have been helpful had the Task Force included a reference to the countries or to the types of parties or party system on which their research was conducted. This sort of information is essential to establishing the comparative value of the claim of "eventual disintegration" and in knowing whether the countries studied had, like Canada, highly developed regional/ linguistic differences and, at the same time, a set of parties each with its own regional support base but an unquestioned commitment to a united country.

But the important point is that so far as Canada itself is concerned such a claim may not be an entirely accurate one. It implies that regionally based but nationally weak federal parties damage federal unity, whereas more nationally based ones do not. Given what they displaced at the time, the Progressives, Social Credit and CCF might have had something to say on that matter had it been raised in the 1920s and 1930s. That regional protests are now all but certain to be voiced through the *established* national parties rather than, as was the case fifty to sixty years ago, through parties created expressly for the purpose, is bound to have an effect on the character of the parties themselves and, ultimately, on Canada's highly institutionalized three-party system. But that is not in itself proof of a corroding federal unit. It may well be that federal unity is as well protected through regionally strong federal parties as not, although that would clearly depend, among other things, upon the accommodative processes at work at the time in the political system.[18]

The Pepin-Robarts claim also ignores the possibility that other groups and institutions, notably pressure groups and bureaucracies at the federal level, may have more than offset whatever corrosive effect the "regional polarization" of federal parties has had on federal unity. It could be that supporting regionally strong, *but nonetheless federal*, parties is more than ever an option that Canadians find they can pursue with impunity because at least part of their political interests have come to be represented in ways that were previously nonexistent, unimportant or ineffective. If, in time, it is shown that the criticisms of the regional and linguistic imbalances of caucuses and cabinet are based on too limited an understanding of what constitutes truly effective representation, then the need to alter the electoral system may well be a good deal less pressing than the reformers have suggested.

If future research on the Canadian electoral system is sufficiently wide-ranging, as it should be, it will lead to a variety of alternatives being considered. One possibility worth exploring would be to leave the electoral system as it is but to adjust other institutions in such a way as to correct to some extent the abuses to which the present electoral system contributes. The problems inherent in a modified electoral system would thereby be avoided even though many of the reformers' objections would be met.

For example, a simple, yet novel, alternative would be to increase substantially the size of the House of Commons. This might not, as it would first seem, compound the current difficulties. Instead it may help to alleviate them. The suggestion is based on the premise that we should investigate ways of making more of Canadian political demography than we do. We have tended in the past to all but ignore the sociological fact that party support is geographically concentrated within areas varying in size from blocks and small neighbourhoods in cities to enormous sections of townships, municipalities and counties. Yet perhaps that is the very sort of characteristic of Canadian politics that can be turned to our advantage. Let us

say, for the sake of argument, that the size of the House of Commons was doubled to 575 members with no change in the current electoral system. What would be the impact on the distribution of sets by party and by region? To what extent would that distribution change over time and to what extent would it benefit or hurt parties in their areas of traditional strength and weakness? Would the existence of constituencies half their current size in population make it easier for political minorities such as Conservatives in Quebec, Liberals in the West, and the NDP in southern Ontario to elect MPs? By using our rich and readily available election data from the Chief Electoral Officer, and the simulating electoral boundaries according to the kinds of practical standards which the various electoral boundary commissions have applied in the redistributions of the 1960s and 1970s, it would be possible to speculate on the kinds of election results such a change would have produced in the last few elections.[19]

Indeed, a House of Commons twice its current size, but elected on the basis of the present electoral system, might bear looking into on other grounds as well. Such a change would avoid at least a few of the problems associated with electoral reform to which some parliamentarians and other politicians take exception. These relate specifically to the fear that classes of MPs would be created under different electoral conditions and that more power would be concentrated in the hands of a party's leadership to determine which candidates would be elected according to the methods available. There may be other quite unintended benefits, although at this stage that is impossible to tell. Certain questions come to mind to which answers would be helpful in judging the appropriateness of such a scheme. Would a House of Commons twice its present size reduce the power of the whips? Would it lead to greater independence on the part of backbenchers? Would it narrow the gap between a party's share of the votes and seats? Would it enhance Parliament, at the expense of extra-parliamentary sources, as the pool from which cabinet material and party leaders would be drawn? If it seemed that an affirmative answer could be given to such questions, a possibility not totally beyond reason, then the case for a House of Commons with a substantially increased membership would be strengthened.[20]

This illustration has been chosen simply because it underscores the need to consider as wide a variety of alternatives as possible and to ask as many different questions of the alternatives possible. What should be abundantly clear is that there are good reasons to warrant continued work on the subject of electoral reform in Canada. What is a good deal less clear is the direction that future research should take. If the problem were simply one of correcting regionally lopsided parliamentary caucuses and cabinets, then almost by definition the line of reasoning would lead one to tackle the electoral system and to advocate some proportionality in the way votes are translated into seats. Yet the simple route may

prove to be the most damaging, for it ignores some of the possible implications of electoral change. It is not self-evidently true that matters would be improved by designing caucuses or cabinets as truer replicas of regional and linguistic electoral support, for it is what happens after that takes place that is significant. This essay has argued that some of the benefits claimed on behalf of electoral reform are open to dispute. Party sensitivity and credibility may not be enhanced, and the incentives which now exist for a party's leadership to pursue accommodating practices could well be diminished. It is possible that following a change in the electoral system particular gains, such as more balanced political institutions, might be more than offset by larger losses to the political system. But these are debating matters to which nothing could make a greater contribution than survey research before they are weighed in the balance for the final time. The need for sound empirical studies explaining the likely impact of a reformed electoral system on Canadian government and politics is all too obvious.

Notes

1. The exceptions were the general elections of 1896, 1925, 1957, and 1979.

2. *The English Constitution*, 4th impression (London: Cox and Wyman Ltd., 1965), 69. In practical terms the only conditions under which such a maxim would apply are those of minority governments. On this important point, see Sir Ivor Jennings, *Cabinet Government* 3e (London: Cambridge University Press, 1965), 491-492.

3. As will be noted later, a different electoral system may give rise to different voting behaviour. For the purposes of this analysis the assumption has been made that voting behaviour remains the same. Irvine notes that

while such an assumption is necessary, it does lack plausibility. Unfortunately there is no choice. (William P. Irvine, *Does Canada Need a New Electoral System?* [Kingston: Institute of Intergovernmental Relations, Queen's University, 1979], 54.)

4. Ibid.

5. Anthony Westell, "Election System Undemocratic," *Star-Phoenix* (Saskatoon, 9 June 1979), 45.

6. This point is developed further in John C. Courtney, "Campaign Strategy and Electoral Victory: The Progressive Conservatives and the 1979 Election," in Howard R. Penniman, ed., *Canada at the Polls, 1979* (Washington:

American Enterprise Institute for Public Policy Research, forthcoming).

7. Details of the two most widely discussed proposals, the Pepin-Robarts and the Irvine formulae, are to be found in the Pepin-Robarts Report Canada, Task Force on Canadian Unity, *A Future Together: Observations and Recommendations* (Ottawa, 1979), 104-106, 131, and Irvine, *New Electoral System* 52-58, 90-94.

8. Fox, *Politics: Canada* 4e (Toronto: McGraw-Hill Ryerson, 1977), 312.

9. By the same token Jack Horner would have properly expected to have headed the list of prominent "at large" Liberals nominated in the province of Alberta as a whole at the time of the 1979 election. How much good would that have done the Liberals in that province at that time? Mr. Horner's province-wide candidacy could well have been as counter-productive to the Liberal campaign in the entire province, possibly leading to *fewer* votes being cast for the Liberals in Alberta in 1979, as it turned out to be in the Crowfoot constituency in the election. One is missing a feature of Canadian party competition if one assumes that had some proportionate vote scheme been in effect at the time of, let us say, the 1974 election, the Liberals would not subsequently have gone out of their way to attract one of the stars of the Conservative frontbenches (Jack Horner) to their side of the House. No party, whatever the electoral system may be, would pass up an opportunity to entice whomever it could from the other party. Did the Liberals need yet another Quebec MP in 1977 when they attracted Jacques Lavoie from the Tory benches to their side?

10. See the comments of Mark MacGuigan and Walter Baker in Simpson, "Rep by Pop." 7, critical of a "topping-up" scheme on the ground that it creates "classes" of MPs. See Irvine, *New Electoral System*, 56-57.

11. There are many ways in which the term "representation" is used—some proper, some not. Perhaps the description widest of the mark appeared in Quebec's Green Paper, which suggests that the voter is represented only when the candidate for whom he has voted has in fact won the election. Conversely the elected member is seen as representing only those who have voted for him (Quebec, Green Paper on the Reform of Electoral System, *One Citizen: One Vote* [Ministre d'etat à la Reforme électorale et parlementaire, 1979], 15-33). A similar interpretation is implied by Professor Irvine in his letter to the editor, *Globe and Mail*, 6 March 1980, 6. For the clearest exposition and critical analysis of representation, see Hanna Fenichel Pitkin's outstanding work, *The Concept of Representation* (Berkeley: University of California Press, 1967).

12. At some point a redistributive electoral scheme compensates not only for electoral inadequacies but also for party disorganization and internal weaknesses. How far should a reformed system go in awarding seats to parties unable to organize their own internal affairs? The NDP is so lacking in membership and organization in Quebec that at the time of the party's national leadership convention in 1975 Quebec NDPers were entitled to send only 65 delegates of the national total of 1256—the sixth lowest entitlement by province. Significantly, the Quebec party fell far short of filling its entitlement. Only 35 of its 65 positions were occupied. Had Professor Irvine's plan been in effect the year earlier for the 1974 election, the party that was able to find only 35 Quebec delegates for its national convention in 1975 would have had 7 MPs from Quebec.

13. *Globe and Mail*, 28 February 1980, 8. Mr. Robert Bochstael (Lib.—St. Boniface) had joined Mr. Axworthy in assessing the post-election situation in Western Canada.

14. The distinction between *actual* and *virtual representation* was first drawn by Edmund Burke. See Pitkin, *Concept of Representation*, Ch. 8. On the topic of representative bureaucracy in Canada, see John J. Carson, "Bilingualism Revisited," Kenneth Kernaghan, "Representative Bureaucracy: the Canadian Perspective," and V.S. Wilson and W.A. Mullins, "Representative Bureaucracy: Linguistic/Ethnic Aspects in Canadian Public Policy," *Canadian Public Administration* 21 (Winter 1978): 489-547.

15. Pitkin, *Concept of Representation*, 226.

16. For Professor Pitkin's argument that representation should be viewed as a "substantive acting for others" see *The Concept of Representation*, Ch. 10, and Pitkin, ed., *Representation* (New York: Atherton Press, 1969), 1-23.

17. Pepin-Robarts Report, 105. Of course it is important to learn from the experience of other countries. But as each political system is unique, cross-national comparative references are sometimes of limited value. Accordingly, caution should be exercised in basing an argument for change on electoral experiences abroad. The German system has recently attracted considerable interest in Canada. Although it has a good deal to commend it, the system was designed to deal with a particular postwar situation and a set of problems quite removed from the kind Canada is now facing. Two of its specifics (two votes per voter and no by-elections to fill vacant seats) suggest a philosophically different attitude in Germany from that in Canada with respect to what an election is expected to accomplish.

18. For an account of the political, statutory and legal moves that work to the advantage of the three national parties already competing in the system, see John C. Courtney, "Recognition of Canadian Political Parties in Parliament and in Law," *Canadian Journal of Political Science* 11 (March 1978): 33-60.

19. The Chief Electoral Officer's reports provide constituency results in an ideal form for social scientists—by polls (each designated urban or rural) averaging 150-200 voters. For information on electoral boundaries one could consult the reports of the Representation Commissioner, the preliminary and final reports of the various Electoral Boundaries Commissions, and the relevant minutes of the Commons Committee on Privileges and Elections. For more on redistribution in Canada, see Norman Ward, "A Century of Constituencies," *Canadian Public Administration* 10 (March 1979): 105-122, and Norman Ward. "The Representative System and the Calling of Elections." *Canadian Journal of Political Science* 6 (December 1973): 655-660.

20. A substantially enlarged House of Commons would help to reduce two prominent and worsening features of Canadian parliamentary representation: (1) the discrepancy between the number of seats to which the less populated provinces are entitled compared to the number of seats awarded to the more populated provinces; and (2) the geographic size of many of the less populated constituencies. If British experience with a large House of Commons (635 MPs) is any guide, backbenchers in Canada would be more independent of their party whip, and parliamentary career routes would be relatively better established and more clearly defined than they are at present. The size of the gap between a party's share of the seats and its share of the votes is a matter of logic. The larger the House of Commons, the closer its number of seats approximates the number of voters. Reductio ad absurdum, one seat per voter would be optimal.

DISCUSSION QUESTIONS

1. Explain the advantages, disadvantages, and biases of different types of electoral systems.

2. Explain the political consequences of electoral systems in general and the Canadian electoral system in specific.

3. What variables besides electoral formulae influence party competition?

4. Explain with reasons the appropriate combination of forms of representation that ought to exist among the redistribution process, the electoral system, the party system, the bureaucracy, the parliamentary system, the judiciary, provincial governments, and interest groups in Canada.

DECISION RULES AND COLLECTIVE CHOICE

DISCUSSION QUESTIONS

INTRODUCTION

J. Paul Johnston

The selections in Section Five are notably different in approach from those in previous sections. Each of the authors has adopted the rationale and analytic framework associated with the "theory of social choice" in his evaluation of representative democracy's ability/inability to make "collective" decisions.

Perhaps the easiest way to understand the notion of a social choice is to contrast social choices with choices we make for ourselves as individuals. Consider a person planning to buy a new car. Presumably, that person will survey the different makes and models available, noting the features of each. Armed with that information, the person will then evaluate each car against some criterion or set of such criteria, such as price, fuel economy, maintenance costs, appearance, capacity, and the like. On the basis of these considerations, the person will choose the particular kind of car best suited to his or her needs, desires, and resources. While this scenario presumes that the choice is made after rational consideration of the alternatives' merits, that need not have been the case. Nonetheless, the final selection is made solely by the individual in question. He or she will bear the consequences of the decision, whether it was a wise choice or not.

By contrast, a "social choice" is made by or for a society as a whole. Democratic principles generally require that the individual members of a society participate jointly and on an equal basis in the decision-making process by which a choice is made among alternatives, say, candidates for some public office or different courses of action that could be taken regarding some matter of public concern. However, social choices need not be made according to democratic principles, but could be made by a monarch or an oligarchy. The alternative would still be chosen for the society as a whole, and, in that sense, would still be a "social" choice. A social choice, then, is one that is made for, and is binding upon, the members of some social collectivity.

Under democratic principles, the outcome of the decision-making process, the selection of a particular alternative or set of alternatives from those under consideration, is jointly determined by all those persons eligible to take part in the process. The outcome is a "collective decision:" one collectively determined by the preferences of all those persons eligible to participate in making the decision. Some procedure serves to combine the preferences of all the participants into one decisive result. Voting is such a procedure. It is, however, only one of several such procedures. For example, Quaker societies arrive at collective decisions through discussion and deliberation of alternatives until some "sense of the meeting" has been identified to which all (or most) would adhere, no vote being taken. Similarly, collective decisions can be reached through negotiation among persons eligible to take part in the decision-making process. In both of these examples, the procedure used in "social" in another sense, as well: the participants are able to interact with one another and influence one another's preferences regarding the alternatives being considered. Voting can also be social in this sense if the participants are able to "campaign" for or against the choice of certain of the alternatives, interacting with one another and influencing one another's preferences during the process of reaching a decision. But voting need not be social in this sense. Individuals could be kept separate from one another and given a ballot listing the alternatives available, then asked to indicate the alternative (or alternatives) they prefer. A final collective choice would be made on the basis of some decision rule from the aggregated individual choices. These several ideas about the ways in which a social collectivity can make social choices are integral to the theory of social choice.

Social choice theorists are concerned with the quality of the social choices arrived at using a particular procedure and with how the properties of a procedure affect the quality of the social choice and the opportunities individual participants have to determine what social choice is made. They ask if the social choices are reached in some fashion that is defensible as a process of rational judgment, carried out collectively, and if the choices are consistent with the set of the participants' individual preferences. Then, they attempt to identify the properties of particular kinds of collective choice procedures, ascertain the effects those properties have on the making of collective decisions, and determine the kinds of social choices that result.

Suppose we were to determine what the collective preferences of the electorate were regarding the relative merits of the candidates in a recent election. The results from a Canadian election would only tell us how many voters ranked a given candidate first according to whatever criteria they used in evaluating the merits of the several candidates; or, *presumably* how many ranked that candidate first, for there is no evidence that each of them *actually* voted for the candidate he or she judged best. If we presume that the voters actually did rank-order the candidates (or at least some subset of them), the aggregate results tell us nothing about such rankings except that, for a given voter, the choice indicated on his ballot was preferred to some other alternative or alternatives.

One way to get around this problem might be to ask voters directly how they ranked the alternatives, or to require them to provide such a ranking via the ballot they cast. Some electoral procedures do just that: they ask the voter to rank the alternatives from first to last on the ballot paper used. "Ordinal" ballots like these provide information about the full ordering of candidates, reflecting the voter's relative preferences. Or do they? What is to stop a voter from misrepresenting his or her true preference ordering when marking the ballot? Similarly, what is to prevent a voter from misrepresenting that ordering when asked about it directly, either before or after expressing it (or some part of it) by casting a ballot in the election? These difficulties have prompted social choice theorists to adopt a different approach to determining collective preferences. They *posit* a particular set of individual preference orders, then derive what collective choice would be made, if any, under a given choice procedure.

A question of interest to a social choice theorist is what properties a given collective choice rule (or procedure) has. Two approaches can be taken here. One can try to identify the properties of a known procedure for aggregating individual preferences or choices and analyse how they affect the social choice(s) made under use of that procedure. This amounts to identifying the "axioms" upon which social choices under that procedure are made. Alternatively, one can specify certain desirable properties that a particular collective choice procedure (rule) should have, expressing them as "axioms" or as "conditions" that the procedure should meet in aggregating individual preferences or choices to arrive at a collectively-based result. Then, one attempts to identify a collective choice procedure (rule) that can accommodate that set of axioms and conditions. In both instances, a formal model of the collective choice situation is produced, and deductive reasoning is used to draw conclusions about the performance of the model and predict what empirical outcomes its use would produce.

Social choice theorists consider a wide range of desirable properties in such endeavours. An obvious one is that the collective choice procedure should be "decisive": that is, it should enable a social choice to be made based upon the aggregated individual preferences or choices. If it selects only one alternative, that is, makes a unique social choice, it is said to be "strongly decisive" or "resolute." Another property might specify the kinds of "social preferences" to be generated by the aggregation rule: are they to be "orderings" or simply pairwise collective preference relations or a set of pairwise relations. A third property might be the requisite that the procedure be "nondictatorial." A "dictatorial" procedure is one that would always choose the alternative favoured by a particular individual, regardless of the preferences of other individuals; "nondictatorial" procedure prevents this kind of result. A related property is that of "anonymity," sometimes called "symmetry." A procedure is "anonymous" when each person's preference or choice has equal weight in the aggregation procedure used, so that no one's preference counts more than another's, and hence they are interchangeable in that regard. Any "anonymous" procedure is also "nondictatorial" so its desirability is obvious; it has been taken to express the basic value of political equality underlying the "one person, one vote" doctrine. Another property is "manipulability," when the collective outcome can be manipulated to a person's advantage through strategic voting, or the agenda can be controlled in procedures with a sequence of intermediate steps, or the criteria used in evaluating the alternatives can be manipulated. Gibbard, and later, Satterthwaite, have shown that a procedure must either be "manipulable" or "dictatorial." And, if all procedures that are "nondictatorial" are necessarily "manipulable," then it can be shown that an unconditionally "best" voting strategy does not exist under those procedures.

Several of the properties mentioned above are concerned with the "fairness" of the procedure used. Another is the property of "neutrality." A decision rule is said to be "neutral" ("dual") if it is not in any way biased in favour of a particular alternative. For example, in order for the members of the United States Congress to override the President's veto of some piece of legislation, each chamber must pass the legislation again, but with a two-thirds majority favouring it. Hence, the decision rule applied in that instance is based in favour of the status quo, that is, in favour of maintaining the veto. Fairness is also essential to a property that can be called "responsiveness." Suppose that a vote is taken to choose one of a pair of alternatives, **x** or **y**, and **x** wins. Then suppose that one voter, who either voted for **y** or abstained, has a chance of heart and changes to support of **x**. If a new vote is then taken with all other voters voting as they did before and **x** still wins, then the voting procedure is said to be "positively responsive" (or "monotonic"). It would surely be perverse if **x** were not to be chosen in those circumstances, so this condition is sometimes called "nonperversity." Another set of conditions that relate to the "responsiveness" of a procedure are associated with an argument by the economist, Vilfredo Pareto: if all persons eligible to take part in the collective decision-making process except one are indifferent between the choice of **x** or **y**, and that one voter prefers **x** to **y**, then under the Pareto principle the society should choose **x** over **y**. Similarly, if everyone in the society is individually indifferent as to the choice between **x** and **y**, then the society should be indifferent between them in terms of the social choice to be made. In the first instance, **x** is said to be "Pareto-wise better" than **y**, whereas in the latter one, the society is said to be "Pareto-wise indifferent" between **x** and **y**. These notions lead to the idea of a "Pareto optimal" choice. In the examples given here, **x** would be the "Pareto optimal" choice if there were no other alternative in the set "Pareto-wise better" than it.[1] A final, related property is "unanimity": if every individual in the society prefers **x** to **y**, then **y** should not be made the social choice of that society.

Another set of properties focuses on the rationality of the decision procedure and its outcomes. One of the properties deals with the irrelevance of other alternatives in choosing between a given pair of alternatives; that is, the choice between a pair of alternatives should be based only on the merits of that particular pair of alternatives and not on the availability or merits of some other alternative. Other properties deal with the logical consistency of the choices made. For example, a choice procedure should not permit contradictory outcomes. Similarly, if we divide the set of participants in the process into two subsets and **x** is the choice made by a given procedure in each subset, then **x** should also be the choice that will be made if the procedure is used when the two subsets are combined. Another consistency property deals with cases wherein a social choice is made through a sequence of intermediate stages, each of which involves choosing among those alternatives or some subset of them. This is the kind of procedure used in legislative bodies when amendments are proposed to a main motion. First, a vote is taken on the amendment, and then on the main motion, either as it was or in amended form, depending on the outcome of the first vote. If the agenda, or sequence in which the voting proceeds, does not bias the result in favour of a particular alternative, the procedure is said to yield a result that is "path independent."

A final property is concerned with the domain of preference orderings that can occur within the set of individuals composing the society. If all possible preference orderings can occur, then the domain is said to be unrestricted. In a sense, this condition reflects the liberal ethic that all possible opinions should be taken into account in making a collective choice.

It has been shown that certain combinations of these properties are incompatible, since no decision procedure can satisfy all of them at the same time. Kenneth Arrow's famous "impossibility theorem" is an example of one such proof. Arrow showed that, if we require that "social preferences" should be orderings of the alternatives at the collective level, then the conditions of "unrestricted domain" and "independence of irrelevant alternatives," the Pareto principle, and the condition of "nondictatorship" cannot be met simultaneously by any social choice procedure capable of generating orderings as "social preferences" at the collective level. Why? Because the first four conditions jointly produce a dictatorial result. Arrow's results cast a large grey cloud over the prospects of setting out a collective choice rule that would accommodate the conditions specified, seeing that each has merit.

Numerous attempts have been made to get around Arrow's sweeping conclusion, usually by weakening or dropping one of the conditions that he included in the model. One of the more notable attempts was made by A.K. Sen. Sen reasoned that in many social choice situations it is not necessary for the social preferences generated by a collective choice rule to be orderings, as Arrow had specified. This amounts to dropping the transitivity axioms on the social preference relations or, to put it another way, to adopting a social decision function rather than a social welfare function as the collective rule of choice. Sen was thus able to escape the dictatorial outcomes produced by Arrow. But there was little to celebrate, since the dictator of Arrow's proof was simply replaced by an equally autocratic oligarchy. Thus, if one wanted to maintain all the remaining conditions in force while discarding the transitivity axioms, one would have to accept that the social choices made by the decision function would always be the outcomes preferred by a small oligarchy of the participants.[2] Others have altered the oligarchies to the status of a "collegium" of members, any one of whom would have a "veto" over what social choice is made, but nothing like the free and equal collective decision-making process assumed under liberal democracy has been achieved.

Another question raised by social choice theorists is what kinds of outcome a given collective decision procedure produces. In particular, they have been interested in how the outcomes produced by different procedures differ when they are each applied to the same set of individual preference orders, and how the outcomes a given procedure yields differ when the composition of the set of individual preference orders is varied. The former can be illustrated with the help of Example 1. When four different collective choice procedures are applied to the set of preference orderings displayed there, a different outcome is chosen as the social choice by each procedure. The majority rule, based on the voters' first choices, yields no decision whatsoever, since no alternative receives a majority of the first choices. Under the electoral procedure we use in Canada, the plurality rule (also based on first choices), "A" wins with a total of 23 first choices, more than any other alternative. But note that a *majority* of the individuals also make "A" their least desired alternative! However, these two procedures only make use of part of the information available in the preference orderings. What would happen if we used a procedure that made use of more, if not all, of that information? The "alternative vote" procedure does that. If it is used, then "B" is the social choice of this electorate. However, that procedure does not use all the information for all of the voters in the electorate. The "Borda Count" procedure does do that. When it is used, the overall winner chosen is "C." Which choice is best here?

EXAMPLE 1

Given:
(a) Three candidates, parties, or policies: A, B, and C.
(b) An electorate of sixty persons, all of whom vote.
(c) The assumption that each person is capable of forming a complete, transitive preference ordering of the alternatives, and does so.
(d) The following distribution of persons, according to their respective preferences orderings:

> I.   A>C>B: 23 persons hold this ordering.
> II.   B>C>A: 20 persons hold this ordering.
> III. C>B>A: 15 persons hold this ordering.
> IV.   C>A>B: 2 persons hold this ordering.

When there are more than two alternatives, majority rule fails to select an outcome that can be taken as the social choice. Recognition of this fact by the Marquis de Condorcet more than two hundred years ago led him to propose a means of using majority rule effectively in such circumstances. He suggested that we use the full information in the preference orderings to make pairwise comparisons of the alternatives, pitting each against the others in two-way contests. For example, with the set of alternatives here, "B" would defeat "A" by a majority of 35 votes to 25 votes. The overall "Condorcet winner" would be the alternative that defeated all the remaining alternatives in such two-way contests. For the data given in Example 1, the Condorcet winner is "C," which was also the choice made by the Borda Count procedure. Moreover, we have a "majority rule" rationale to undergird the claim that "C" is the best choice in this situation.

Another feature of the Condorcet procedure is appealing as a basis for making collective choices. If we carry out all three of the paired comparisons possible in Example 1, we see that not only is "C" the majority winner over "A" and "B" in terms of aggregated preferences, but "B" wins over "A," as well. Using these results, we can form a social preference ordering for the electorate as a whole, namely: C>B>A. We could do the same thing by ordering the vote counts produced for the alternatives by the Borda Count procedure. In this instance, the two results would match. Of course, we know from Arrow's theorem that this means that one or more of the conditions he specified as desirable must have been violated here.

Unfortunately, this seemingly attractive feature of the Condorcet procedure depends upon the range of the individual preference orderings in a given situation. In particular, it only occurs when that range is restricted so that certain orderings do not occur. For example, in the case considered above (Example 1), there are no preference orderings at the individual-level in which "C" is ranked last. Consider the following situation in which there are only three individuals whose preference orderings of the three alternatives are to be aggregated by the Condorcet procedure:

(1)   A>B>C
(2)   B>C>A
(3)   C>A>B

When we apply the procedure here, "A" defeats "B" by a 2 to 1 majority, "B" defeats "C" by the same majority, and finally, "C" defeats "A" by that same margin. Thus, in terms of the social preferences, "A" is preferred to "B," "B" is preferred to "C," but "C" is preferred to "A," thereby forming a "cycle" of collective preference relations, rather than yielding a transitive ordering of them. Moreover, there is now no "Condorcet winner" here. This result is known variously as the "paradox of voting" and the "majority paradox." It is one of a number of paradoxes of voting that have been identified for different kinds of collective choice procedures.[3]

The various principles of social choice that have been discussed in this essay, along with the arguments framed in terms of them, and the proven theorems about social choice that follow from those arguments apply to most or all situations in which collective decision-making is used to arrive at a social choice. In particular, they apply to the making of such choices in both simple, direct democracies and representative democracies. Most of the applications, as they relate to single direct democracies, are relatively clear and straightforward. Under representative democracy, however, a hierarchy of collective decision-making situations is created. For example, elections are carried out to select representatives who then take part in collective decision-making on our

behalf in committees and legislatures. Although the election of a specific representative may provide those who voted for that person with the "best choice" in
terms of their policy preferences, there is no guarantee that those policies will
be the ones chosen in the legislative voting that occurs at the next stage in the
hierarchy. Moreover, institutions such as legislatures employ a complex set of
collective decision-making procedures that may be, and often are, nested under
one another in a hierarchical or partly hierarchical fashion. Simply tracing and
evaluating the consistency of the collective decisions made at each level and
stage in that process is itself a complicated task. And that is only one aspect of
evaluating the quality of the collective decisions made, the performance of the
kinds of procedures used to make such decisions, and the degree to which both
can be seen to incorporate and reflect the basic values and principles that are
the normative basis for the practice of representative democracy.

Social choice theory provides an approach in which the features of collective decisions, the procedures used to make them, and the context in which they
are made can be described in reasonably precise terms. The tools of formal
modelling and logical reasoning are applied to the task of identifying problems
that arise in making decisions and in finding the limits of those problems, if not
actual solutions to them. Recently, social choice theorists have attempted to
derive empirical predictions about these matters that can be tested against
actual data. At the same time, they have reformulated a number of the traditional problems and questions regarding the practice of representative democracy in terms they can address through formal modelling and logical reasoning.
In that respect, they have been as attentive to the normative problems as they
have to those which, to some, seem "merely procedural." And, in the latter
regard, they have taught us that, in politics and government, it is often what is
"merely procedural" in making collective decisions that turns out to be most
important.

*   *   *

The selections in Section Five provide an overview of the social choice
theory approach to the making of collective decisions under representative
democracy.

Peter C. Fishburn's selection provides a broad-ranging review of the work
that has been done by social choice theorists on the various aspects of the
electoral process, from the nomination process to the determination of the final
outcome in an election. He identifies the central questions addressed in each
instance and the important findings resulting from social choice theoretic research. His piece is heavily annotated, treating as it does matters which lie at
the heart of a representative democracy. It also serves as an overview of the
components of the collective decision process, presenting them in a readable
and non-technical manner.

Hannu Nurmi's piece, "On the Properties of Voting Systems," reflects what
traditionally has been a central concern of social choice theorists: evaluating the

properties of voting procedures through the use of axiomatic models that identify those properties and describe both their relationship to one another and their consequences in precise, logical fashion.

In the next selection, Fishburn and Steven J. Brams present a clear and entertaining discussion of some of the paradoxes of voting that can occur when preferential voting procedures are used. This piece should be of special interest to Canadian students of politics, since the procedures that Fishburn and Brams describe as producing these paradoxes were actually used in provincial elections in Alberta and Manitoba for almost three decades. Moreover, they have been favoured by those who want to adopt some form of proportional representation system that still retains the Anglo-American emphasis on choosing among candidates rather than among parties.

The next two selections should be read as a pair. In the first, Terrence J. Levesque analyses the social choice that delegates to the 1983 Progressive Conservative leadership convention made in choosing their new leader. Levesque argues that the procedures used in making that choice were not "neutral"; rather, they were "biased against the candidate who represented a compromise between the two front runners." Levesque identifies John Crosbie as the "Condorcet winner" who would have been the best choice there, but was overlooked because of the non-neutrality of the procedures. In that regard, Levesque argues that the Tories may well have "shot themselves in the other foot." In his selection, Peter Woolstencroft rebuts Levesque's claims, arguing that they take insufficient note of the "linkages between institutional contexts and behavior." Woolstencroft maintains that features of the institutional context of a leadership convention mean that delegates' individual preferences are actually shaped on location by the nature of the procedures employed. In that regard, he disputes the notion that the adopted procedures working to frustrate the expression of fixed preferences brought to the convention setting. Finally, he claims that choosing appropriate choice rules to govern collective decision-making processes is a task that is more complex than simply adopting certain principles of social choice theory.

William H. Riker has been for some time one of the most eminent and forceful proponents of the social choice theory approach. In his selection, he argues the case for liberal democracy against that put forward by the proponents of populist democracy, whose arguments trace back to the Levellers in seventeenth-century England. This selection highlights Riker's continuing efforts to relate the principles of the social choice theory perspective to the grand issues of democratic theory as they apply to representative government.

Finally, in a relatively recent effort, Bernard Grofman and Scott C. Feld grapple with one of the most challenging issues of modern political thought: Rousseau's "general will." They offer a resolution of the seeming contradiction in attempting to arrive at collective decisions that are based on the "general will" of the society through procedures that seem to do little more than aggregate the conflicting private wills of individual citizens into what Rousseau called "will of all." Drawing on arguments rooted in Condorcet's thinking about collective choice in society, they put forward an exciting new way of dealing with this age-old issue. Since it was in part due to this problem that Rousseau rejected the principles of representative democracy, the relevance of Grofman and Feld's contribution is heightened for students of representative government.

Notes

1. Amartya K. Sen, *Collective Choice and Social Welfare* (San Francisco: Holden-Day, Inc., 1970), 21.
2. Ibid., 76-77.
3. See, for example, the selection by Peter C. Fishburn and Steven J. Brams included in this section; Charles R., Plott, "Axiomatic Social Choice Theory: An Overview and Interpretation," *American Journal of Political Science* XX (1976): 513-517; and Peter C. Fishburn, "Paradoxes of Voting," *American Political Science Review* LXVIII (1974): 537-546.

30. DIMENSIONS OF ELECTION PROCEDURES: Analyses and Comparisons

Peter C. Fishburn

1. INTRODUCTION

During the past two centuries, students of democratic institutions have debated the merits of a vast array of election procedures. Significant new research on the analysis and comparison of voting procedures has been done in the past two decades. Most of this work has focused on specific segments of the general problem of election system design, leaving a somewhat fragmented picture of the whole.

My aim here is to outline an integrative perspective for the evaluation of election procedures that could provide direction for further research. I shall begin with remarks on the historical search for better procedures, followed by a schematic of the electoral process which identifies key aspects of the process. I then comment on the general purpose and particular objectives of elections, and list twelve major dimensions of the electoral process that deserve consideration in any comprehensive evaluation of alternative election procedures. A selective overview of research on the dimensions and their interconnections concludes the paper.

2. HISTORICAL PERSPECTIVE

Recent interest in election procedures dates from the advent of modern democracies by way of the French and American Revolutions.

Peter C. Fishburn, "Dimensions of Election Procedures: Analyses and Comparisons," *Theory and Decision* 15 (1983): 371-397. Copyright © (1983) by D. Reidel Publishing Company. (Martinus Nijhoff Publishers). Reprinted by permission of Kluwer Academic Publishers.

Two eighteenth-century Frenchmen, Jean-Charles de Borda and the Marquis de Condorcet, have had a lasting influence on the theory of elections.

In a paper first printed in 1781, Borda [9] (translated in de Grazia [28]) advocated an election method based on *ranked voting* for selecting one candidate from three or more nominees. Given three nominees, Borda proposed that each voter indicate his first, second, and third choices. These choices would be awarded 3, 2 and 1 points respectively for that voter. The candidate with the greatest point total would be declared the winner. This procedure generalizes in a straightforward way when there are four or more nominees, or when several candidates are to be elected from the slate.

Borda argued that the *plurality* method (vote for one candidate), which in his context would elect the candidate ranked first by the most voters, is flawed. In particular, it might elect an *anti-majority candidate*, i.e., a candidate that would lose to each of the others in pairwise majority voting. According to Borda, the plurality method is defective because "electors cannot make known in a sufficiently complete manner their opinion on the various candidates before them" (de Grazia [28, p. 44]), whereas his method will elect the candidate who has the greatest merit to the voters.

Three criticisms of Borda's method will be noted here. First, the equal spacing of points awarded for first choice, second choice, and so forth, is rather arbitrary [28, p. 49], despite Borda's appeal to the principle of insufficient reason [28, p. 44] and Laplace's probabilistic argument [85] in its defense.

Second, as Laplace and others pointed out, it is vulnerable to strategic voting whereby some electors will rank their favourite's strongest opponents last even though these opponents may not be their least-preferred candidates. When confronted with this, Borda replied that his method was only intended for honest men. Of course, the plurality method is also liable to strategic voting, as when electors vote for their second choices because their favourites have no chance of winning. A related type of strategy applies to Borda's method.

Third, Borda's method may fail to elect a *majority candidate*, i.e., a candidate who would defeat each of the others in pairwise majority voting. In fact, Condorcet [24] gave a three-candidate example with a majority candidate who would lose under every Borda-type point assignment that awards more points to a first choice than a second choice and more points to a second choice than a third choice.

Although Condorcet sympathized with Borda's proposal, he felt strongly that a majority candidate ought to be elected when one exists. Methods that adhere to his dictum are sometimes referred to as *Condorcet procedures*. Condorcet procedures implement one notion of majority rule and provide winners who are robust against challengers.

Condorcet's name is also associated with the famous *paradox of voting*, or phenomenon [of] cyclical majorities, which occurs when every candidate would be defeated by some other candidate in pairwise majority voting. Condorcet's position for determining a winner in the absence of a majority candidate was so cryptic as to be unclear (Black [7, pp. 174-177]).

The trend begun by Borda was especially evident during the latter half of the nineteenth century in England. Thomas Hare published a book [64] in 1861 on proportional representation which advocated a system that tends to elect representatives of sizable minorities when several candidates were to be chosen for seats in a legislature. Hare systems—also known as *preferential voting* or methods of single transferable vote—are still used for major elections in Australia, Ireland and South Africa.

As in Borda's method, preferential voting asks voters to rank the candidates. When only one candidate is to be elected, a candidate with more than 50 percent of the first-place votes wins. If no candidate exceeds this figure, the candidate with the fewest first-place votes is scratched and the ballots are revised as if that candidate were never present. Scratching continues until some candidate surpasses the 50 percent quota of firsts on the revised ballots. With only three candidates, this is operationally similar to *plurality voting with a runoff* between the two candidates who get the most votes on the first ballot. It is not a Condorcet procedure.

When several candidates are to be elected, the 50 percent quota is lowered accordingly (33^+ for two seats, 25^+ for three seats, . . .), and the election/scratching process continues until all seats are filled. All candidates whose first-place votes pass quota are elected; elected candidates are removed from the ballots before the next round; voters whose first-place candidates are elected have less weight assigned to their ballots in later rounds; and if no candidate passes quota in a round, the one with the least weighted first-place votes is scratched.

Although this description is incomplete, it illustrates the system-building propensity of the Victorian period. Later evidence from America of this propensity is provided by Hoag and Hallett [70].

Other contributions to the theory of elections in the Victorian period were made by C.L. Dodgson (Lewis Carroll) and E.J. Nanson. Dodgson's work is described in the excellent historical part of Duncan Black's book [7]. Nanson's paper [98], first read in 1882, criticizes a number of voting methods and includes several passages on voting strategy. He advocated a Condorcet procedure based on ranked voting and Borda point counts. At each stage in the tally process, all candidates with below-average Borda count are scratched, ballots are revised accordingly, and the process continues until a single candidate remains.

In the present century, the most notable contribution to the theory of elections was made by Kenneth Arrow [3]. Arrow showed that a few apparently reasonable criteria for socially ranking three or more candidates on the basis of ranked ballots were mutually incompatible. In one version, his criteria allow all possible combinations of individual rankings, require one candidate to be ranked ahead of another in the social ranking if all voters prefer the former to the latter, force the social ranking between any pair of candidates to depend only on the voter's preferences between those two candidates, and prohibit a dictatorial voter—one whose preferences become the social preferences.

Arrow's insights sparked a veritable flood of research and writing, a portion of which appears in Sen [115], Fishburn [40], and Kelly [78]. The upshot of much of this work is a widespread belief that, even in an idealistic sense, there is no such thing as a flawless election system for choosing one of three or more candidates. As soon as we modify or replace one procedure to avoid its more obvious shortcomings, others appear, and the quest for better procedures continues.

Modern attitudes toward elections have been shaped by Enlightenment thought and Scottish common-sense philosophy that led to the doctrine of the freedom and moral responsibility of men to control their destiny, coupled with the doctrine of egalitarianism—belief in human equality in social, political and economic spheres. These principles ushered in modern forms of participatory democracies in place of theocracies and the divine right of kings.

These attitudes were already at work in the thought of Borda and Condorcet. According to Black [7, pp. 159-171], Condorcet wished to define and defend a system that would elect the right candidate; he ultimately equated 'right' with the will of the majority. That is, the judgment of the majority of well-informed electors in a society reveals what is right for that society. Needless to say, minorities continue to challenge this principle, at least until they attain power to become majorities.

The right to be an elector was of course initially reserved for elite minorities, such as the landed aristocracy. Although some countries still have elite electorates, enfranchisement movements have won the vote for most citizens of age in the 'free democracies.'

Although many of my later remarks are motivated by large public elections, most apply to elections on any scale. Indeed, the work of some of our historical figures was guided by problems in small electorates such as academic departments and clubs. But the theory of elections does not constrain the size of the electorate despite the fact that the viability of a specific procedure may depend crucially on the nature of the electorate.

3. THE ELECTORAL PROCESS

Figure 1 presents a schematic of an electoral process. The main inputs to the voting part of the process—candidates, electorate, and ballot or response mechanism—are shown near the top of the figure. Each of these is determined

Figure 1   Electoral Process

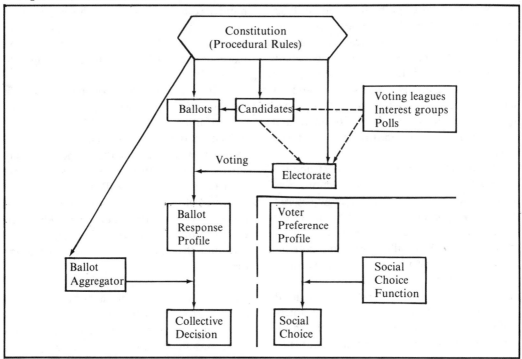

in part by a set of procedural rules, called a constitution, as indicated by the arrows from the top box. In many cases, an election commission or board is responsible for enforcing the constitution.

The constitution specifies the nomination process by which candidates become eligible for election; it identifies the electorate by a set of qualifications; and it describes the type of ballot to be used and how the ballot must be marked to be counted. The other primary function of the constitution is to specify how ballots are to be aggregated to determine a winner or collective decision. This is shown on the left part of the figure.

Figure 1 illustrates a single-ballot election. Elections with runoffs or multiple ballots would require more elaborate diagrams. Note

also that most constitutions have self-amendment provisions, so that candidates could be constitutional amendments.

Once candidates and the electorate have been determined, and information has been exchanged, the voters cast their ballots. We usually view balloting as an act of conscious choice. The cast ballots comprise a ballot response profile, which is processed by the ballot aggregator to compute the collective decision.

The two dashed lines into the electorate box on the figure identify informational inputs to voters prior to balloting. These inputs come from candidates, voting leagues, interest groups, polls, and other sources of information and persuasion. The horizontal dashed line suggests inputs that can influence candidates' positions.

The upper and lower left parts of Figure 1 depict the actual election process. The lower right part identifies constructs of theorists that have guided much of their thinking. Given the candidates and electorate, a voter preference profile describes each voter's feelings about the candidates. It is often assumed that voters' preferences can be described by rankings of candidates, but other assumptions are sometimes made.

The social choice function transforms the voter preference profile into a social choice, which usually has the same form as the collective decision for the actual process. If the collective decision is a single candidate, so is the social choice—but not necessarily the same one. If the collective decision is a ranking of two or more candidates, the social choice is also a ranking.

I have drawn the lower right part of the figure to suggest a mirror image of the lower left part. In fact, the two are often quite different. In the first instance, the type of ballot may preclude a direct correspondence between ballot response profile and voter preference profile, as when plurality voting is used and preferences are rankings. Even if ballots are intended to elicit the information in the voter preference profile, strategic voting and abstentions can confound comparison between the two.

If the social choice function is a Condorcet procedure that operates on rankings, but plurality voting is used, then the ballot aggregator must differ from the social choice function. On the other hand, if ballots follow the format of the voter preference profile, then the aggregator and the choice function can operate similarly, i.e., follow the same algorithm for computing a winner. However, even when ballots mimic preferences, there may be good reasons for the ballot aggregator to differ from the social choice function. In particular, if the social choice function has attractive theoretical properties but is computationally complex, one may prefer a simpler aggregator that retains most of the desirable features of the social choice function but is easier for the electorate and interest groups to comprehend and accept.

The preceding remarks indicate why the actual outcome or collective decision and the social choice—a "best" outcome under perfect information about voters' preferences—may differ. Recently, more attention has focused on the design of election procedures that have high propensities to produce collective decisions that are the same as the corresponding hypothetically-best social choices under the assumption of known preferences and the presumption that the social choice function specifies the right way to compute winners on the basis of voters' preferences. I shall return to this later.

4. DIMENSIONS OF ELECTION PROCEDURES

I take for granted that the overarching purpose of a democratic election procedure is to provide a means by which decisions can be made by an electorate on matters that affect the well-being of its members, or of the individuals in a more inclusive group, in such a way that the decisions thus made faithfully reflect the judgments of the electors on what best promotes well-being. As a corollary, I assume that the main purpose of analysing and comparing election procedures is to identify those best able to accomplish their intended purpose.

An indication of the immensity of the task of analysing and comparing election procedures, and the progress made thus far, can be gotten by considering various dimensions of elections. I shall note here twelve major dimensions, which are discussed in a bit more detail later.

An initial factor that bears on the dimensions listed below is the *particular objective* of an election. This specifies the type of collective decision desired, say, to elect a mayor, or choose a budget, or rank the contestants in a competition. Clearly, the ballot and ballot aggregator must be consonant with the particular objective.

It may also be important for evaluative purposes to distinguish between policy elections and representative elections. In the policy case, electors are to decide a policy issue such as the school tax for next year or whether to adopt a proposed constitutional amendment. Representative elections involve the choice of a person (president, legislator) or persons (school board) who will make a number of policy decisions on behalf of the electorate.

I shall not deal directly with how particular objectives ought to be determined, or with the larger question of which aspects of community life ought to be decided by elections. I assume in effect that particular objectives are specified, and proceed from this point.

Table 1 lists the twelve major dimensions. Although the list is surely nonexhaustive, I believe that it includes most salient factors in a reasonable arrangement.

The first dimension, *nomination process/agenda formation*, includes the procedural rules for determining specific candidates (age, residency, petition requirements, etc.). The nomination phase often has balloting implications involving ballot positions, order of voting, and so forth.

The latter factors may also appear as part of *candidate strategy*. Stands taken or avoided on policy issues, allocation of campaign funds, and schedules of personal appearances are included in this dimension.

The *nature of the electorate* involves the procedural rules that specify who can vote and, as a consequence of those rules, the demographics of the electorate. Physical dis-

Table 1   Some Dimensions of Election Procedures

1. Nomination Process/Agenda Formation
2. Candidate Strategy
3. Nature of Electorate
4. Voter Psychology
5. Voter Strategy
6. Ballots
7. Ballot Response Profile
8. Ballot Aggregator
9. Evaluative Aspects of Aggregation
10. Collective Decisions and Social Choices
11. Costs and Financing
12. Effects on Institutions

persion of the electorate can bear on comparisons among procedures, as may its general intelligence. A complicated scheme for choosing the head of a mathematics department may be impractical for the election of a U.S. senator.

Consideration of *voter psychology* can be very important in designing good election procedures. Complex systems may discourage voting, and some voters will shun procedures they perceive as unfair or rigged against their interests. Formation of voters' opinions about candidates, the ability of candidates or their backers to shape voters' preferences, and the type of ballot used to record preferences are relevant to this dimension.

Information about other voters' preferences as revealed by committee discussions, polls, and so forth, forms an important input to *voter strategy*. Different information may lead a voter to vote differently. Another factor in voter strategy, especially in small, cohesive electorates, is what a voter reveals to other voters. Advantage might accrue from disguising one's true feelings. Vote trading across elections is also germane.

Types of *ballots* or, more generally, the mechanism by which voters' expressed preferences are revealed or recorded, can affect elections. Some people will vote differently on a secret ballot than they would on an open ballot. A complicated mail ballot may be more likely to end up in the wastebasket. Some people are intimidated or confused by voting machines. Orders in which candidates are listed on a ballot may be important, and in sequential-elimination voting the point at which a candidate enters the voting may affect his chances.

The *ballot response profile* is dictated by the type of ballot. Its connection to the voter preference profile has received more attention in recent years.

The *ballot aggregator* has been a focal point for election theorists since the days of Borda and Condorcet. Aggregators must not allow ties unless a further tie-breaking step—such as decision by a nonvoting chairman, or a further vote in another voting body—is specified.

Discussions of ballot aggregators often focus on *evaluative aspects of aggregation*, including criteria of fairness to voters and candidates. Serious defects in aggregation methods are sometimes discovered by checking them against evaluative aspects.

Insofar as social choice functions are believed to yield good social choices, comparisons between *collective decisions and social choices* can provide valuable information for the comparison of election procedures. Since voters' true preferences are seldom known precisely, such comparisons entail interesting methodological issues.

Costs and financing of elections range from costs to voters of registering and going to the polls, to costs incurred by candidates and their backers, to costs borne by the public for campaign financing, balloting, and ballot counting. In some cases, public costs of multiple ballots or runoff elections could outweigh perceived advantages of multistage elections.

The final dimension, *effects on institutions*, is a primary concern of people and interest groups who are either threatened by change or else believe that they are disadvantaged by existing procedures. A political party that thinks its power will be dissipated by a new procedure will naturally try to block its adoption. An interest group with little power that believes it will benefit from a change is likely to push for that change. Consequently, a crucial factor in the comparison of election procedures is the probable effects they would have on the democratic process, its institutions, and associated interest groups over a period of time.

5. NOMINATION AND AGENDA FORMATION

The rest of the paper provides a very brief and selective review of dimensions introduced in the preceding section. We begin with the topic of nomination and agenda formation, followed in order by candidate strategy, the nature of the electorate and voter psychology, and voter strategy. The final sections discuss aggregation, costs, and institutional aspects.

When the number of candidates is not fixed by the constitution, nomination rules and a host of other factors can either limit or encourage entry. Riker [109] shows how strategic voting with the plurality procedure could explain the rise and fall of third parties in a putative two-party system. Brams and Straffin [14] model the changes of third parties under plurality voting and approval voting as a function of parties' positions on a left-right ideological axis and the distribution of voters' preferred positions along this axis. Unlike plurality voting, *approval voting* (Weber [133]; Brams and Fishburn [12]; Morin [95]) allows each voter to vote for any number of candidates. Each candidate checked by a voter gets a full vote from that voter, and the candidate with the most votes is elected. Although Brams and Straffin suggest that approval voting may be a greater barrier to entry than plurality voting, this is a moot point.

The strategic entrance of phantom candidates or stalking-horses by other candidates' backers is an old topic, but it has not been widely researched. Campbell [18] notes that sequential elimination by sincere majority voting is robust against manipulation by stalking-horses, but strategic voting could cloud the picture. However, McKelvey and Niemi [92] prove that sophisticated voting (a form of strategic voting defined later) for procedures that take successive majority votes between subsets of candidates, will elect majority candidates when they exist. The ability of a procedure to avoid manipulation by phantoms or fringe candidates seems important to its acceptability.

Given a fixed slate of three or more candidates and sequential-elimination majority voting, Black [7] observes that if voting is sincere —on each vote every voter votes for his preferred candidate—and there is no majority candidate, then candidates who are voted on last have an advantage. However, Farquharson [35] argues that under sophisticated voting, the earlier a candidate is voted on, the better his chances.

Plott and Levine [105] comment on the absence of models that capture subtle features of parliamentary procedures, and show how an agenda builder can fashion an agenda for successive majority votes between disjoint subsets of candidates to maximize the likelihood that a preselected candidate will win.

Fixed-slate agenda manipulation is of course precluded by many election procedures, such as plurality voting, Borda's method, and approval voting. Successive elimination procedures that depend only on a single-ballot response profile and not on a predetermined order of voting can be "manipulated" only by the actual votes.

6. CANDIDATE STRATEGY

Several topics that impinge on candidate strategy were mentioned in the preceding section. I assume here that the candidates and extra-vote agenda aspects are specified.

I find it convenient to think of candidate strategy as either active or reactive. An active strategy tries to persuade voters of the virtues of a candidate's positions or qualifications. A reactive strategy responds to pressures from interest groups, and seeks a position that appeals to a winning coalition of voters (Riker [108]). The two modes often intertwine during a campaign.

In an area that overlaps with voter psychology, Granberg and Brent [57] discuss how major contenders in large elections use polling data to determine where the public stands on issues, and how they try to manage voters' impressions. They comment on the strategy of inattention to and deliberate ambiguity on issues, and present evidence which shows that most voters will give estimates of where candidates stand. They argue further that such estimates tend to be systematic and interpretable by theoretical models.

Models of the effects of the allocation of campaign funds to different districts or states have been developed by several investigators, including Brams and Davis [11], Shane [120], Young [139], and Aldrich [1].

A large number of papers discuss the effects of candidates' positions in single-dimensional and multidimension issue spaces on their chances of being elected. Downs's book [31] initiated this theme. Within a two-party context with a single-issue dimension, his model shows that platform positions will converge to the position of the median voter if both parties try to maximize their changes. Further work has generalized Downs's model by allowing abstentions, multiple issue dimensions, and uncertainty, and by considering intra-party leadership (Coleman [23]), the sequence of nomination and election (Aranson and Ordeshook [2]), and the candidate's own preferences (Wittman [135]). A few key references to the literature of "spatial analysis" are Hinich and Ordeshook [69], Davis, Hinich and Ordeshook [26], McKelvey [91], and Kramer [83].

The work cited in the preceding paragraph focuses on plurality voting with two candidates. Very little has been done with many candidates and other types of voting.

7. THE ELECTORATE AND VOTER PSYCHOLOGY

Many people, including Lipset [87], Campbell, et al. [17], and Key [80], have analysed electorates in detail. Part of this literature seeks to explain voting patterns on the basis of demographic and economic (Kramer [81]; Fair [34]) factors. A related issue is whether voters act rationally (Harsanyi [66]; Riker and Zavoina [112]; Shapiro [121]) and, if so, what version of rationality characterizes their behaviour.

Downs [31] and Tullock [128] argue that the costs of voting exceed its benefits—including the probability of casting a decisive vote (Good and Mayer [56]; Chamberlain and Rothschild [19]), hence that voting is irrational. Related models of the rationality of voting are discussed by Riker and Ordeshook [111] for two-candidate elections, and McKelvey and Ordeshook [93] for multicandidate elections, given plurality voting and maximization of expected utility (von Neumann and Morgenstern [132]; Fishburn [37]). Ferejohn and Fiorina [36] examine minimax regret behaviour (Savage [114]) in place of utility maximization, and Hinich [68] offers empiri-

cal evidence for abstention arising from voter alienation and indifference in the spatial analysis context.

As far as I am aware, almost no work has been done on voter turnout as a function of the type of election procedure. In one instance, Kau and Rubin [77] suggest that turnout would increase in US presidential elections if the electoral college were abolished.

Another facet of voter psychology, which affects social choice analyses as well as ballot design and aggregation, is the form of voters' preferences. A common assumption is that voters can rank the candidates, but some people go beyond rankings to preference intensities (Kendall and Carey [79]; DeMeyer and Plott [29]; Straffin [126]) or von Neumann-Morgenstern utilities (Hildreth [67]; Harsanyi [65]), while others presume only partial rankings (Deacon and Shapiro [27]) or probabilistic preferences (Intriligator [74]; Fishburn and Gehrlein [48]).

8. VOTER STRATEGY

Since abstention was considered above, I shall focus here on voting as such. Examples of voter strategy for plurality and Borda's method were noted in Section 2. In fact, Gibbard [54] and Satterthwaite [113] prove that all reasonable election procedures for electing one of three or more candidates are subject to strategic voting, or are not "strategyproof." That is, there are situations in which some voter by voting contrary to his sincere preferences can secure a collective decision that he prefers to the one that obtains when he votes sincerely.

This result and related facts about strategic voting are included in Kelly [78] and Pattanaik [102]. Recent theoretical extensions are given by Ishikawa and Nakamura [75], Hylland [73], and Chichilnisky [21]. Restrictions on individual preference orders that render some procedures strategyproof are discussed by Kalai and Muller [76], Brams and Fishburn [12], and Border and Jordan [10].

As with agenda manipulation, strategic voting often requires detailed knowledge of other voters' preferences if it is to be effective. Even in large, dispersed electorates, polls often provide sufficient information to encourage such voting. There are, however, certain types of election procedures for which a voter need not know anything about other voters' preferences to determine his best voting strategy if he assumes that other voters will also use "optimal" strategies. To elaborate, let us say that one strategy *dominated* another if, regardless of how everyone else votes, the first strategy yields an outcome as preferable as (and in some instance better than) the outcome for the second strategy. Suppose all voters use undominated strategies. Then, within this restricted context, some of a voter's originally undominated strategies may be dominated by others. If these secondary-dominated strategies are eliminated for all voters, and this process is continued, we may arrive at a unique "eventually undominated" strategy for each voter. Such a strategy is called *sophisticated*. If more than one strategy remains undominated for a voter at the end of the elimination process, they might all be referred to as sophisticated.

The first systematic treatment of sophisticated strategies is due to Farquharson [35], who discussed their use in sequential binary elections where successive votes are taken between subsets of candidates until a winner emerges at [the] end of some branch in the voting tree. This has been pursued by Kramer [82], McKelvey and Niemi [92], and Moulin [96], who note that sophisticated voting often leads to the same outcome as would sincere voting. For example, Condorcet candidates will be elected by sophisticated voting for some binary election processes.

Within the past few years, a great deal of effort has been devoted to finding ballot mechanisms and aggregation procedures that will encourage people to vote sincerely, or to vote strategically in such a way that the likely outcome will be similar to the sincere-voting outcome or will have certain desirable characteristics. I shall return to this later in discussing collective decisions and social choices, but note one further development here. Peleg [103] shows that there are election procedures based on ranked ballots that always have equilibrium strategies for voters—at equilibrium, no voter can gain by voting differently—which yield the same outcome as the sincere strategies. Although the type of procedure discussed by Peleg (an elimination method that gets rid of "worst" candidates first) is not immune to criticism, it has several nice properties (Dutta and Pattanaik [33]; Oren [101]).

Another topic germane to voter strategy is logrolling or vote-trading (Buchanan and Tullock [15]), which often arises when each of several proposals is to be voted on separately. In such a case, a "candidate" is a subset of proposals; the collective decision is the set of winning proposals. By making voting deals among themselves, some voters may obtain a candidate that they prefer to the collective decision that would arise without such deals. Discussions of logrolling include its tie to spatial analysis (Tullock [129], an axiomatic investigation with independent preferences (Wilson [134]), and its beneficial and harmful effects (Riker and Brams [110]). A valuable summary of this and related topics in public choice is provided by Mueller [97, pp. 406-407].

9. BALLOTS AND AGGREGATION

The Australian ballot, printed by the government with the names of all authorized candidates, and to be cast in secrecy, was an important election reform of the nineteenth century.

The widespread use of voting machines in the present century is believed by some to be another improvement since it would appear to reduce opportunities for fraud and yield more reliable tallies. Although considerations of voter psychology suggest that participation and other aspects of voter behaviour can be materially affected by the type of ballot—secret versus open, ranked versus nonranked, and so forth—little research seems to have been done on this question.

Of far greater concern to election theorists have been the nature of the aggregator and its implications for fair elections and voter strategy. As suggested earlier, much of the research on aggregation has been based on voter preference profiles and social choice functions. I shall focus on social choice functions in the present section although, with sincere voting and full participation, my remarks could apply also to the ballot response profile and ballot aggregator. The link of voter behaviour and strategy between the two modes will be pursued further in the next section.

Given a voter preference profile—a list of all voters' sincere preferences in some form—what is the best possible social choice, and how will this change as the profile changes? Borda gave one answer, Condorcet another. As mentioned previously, the question may lack an answer, but comparisons of old and new proposals will continue to be made so long as we perceive room for improvement.

Following much of the literature, I shall allow the social choice for a given profile as determined by the social choice function to consist of more than one candidate, and refer to the social choice under this possibility of tied candidates as the *choice set*. Actual aggregation procedures must of course have tie-breaking provisions.

Analyses of social choice functions centre on conditions, or axioms, that one might want such functions to satisfy. These conditions embody notions of fairness, equity and consistency. Dozens are noted in the books by Sen [115], Fishburn [40], Kelly [78] and Pattanaik [102], and in review articles by Plott [104], Fishburn [43] and Sen [117, 118]. Six examples are:

anonymity: the choice set doesn't change when two voters' preferences are interchanged;

neutrality: if two candidates exchange places in all voters' preferences and one is in the choice set before the exchange, the other will be in the choice set afterwards;

Pareto efficiency: if all voters prefer one candidate to another, the latter will not be in the choice set;

monotonicity: if a candidate in the choice set moves up in a voter's preferences, all else unchanged, it will remain in the choice set;

Condorcet's principle: a majority candidate is the only candidate in the choice set;

partition consistency: if the voters in a profile are divided into two groups and a candidate would be in both groups' choice sets, then it will be in the choice set for the original profile.

We note three uses of such axioms. First, they are used to characterize specific types of social choice functions. For example, May [90] shows that anonymity, duality, and a stronger form of monotonicity are necessary and sufficient for simple majority with two candidates. Other axiomatizations have been given for Borda's method (Young [137]), ranked-voting generalizations of Borda's method (Young [138]; Smith [124]), approval voting (Fishburn [45]), and a form of Condorcet procedure (Young and Levenglick [140]), among others.

Second, combinations of some axioms have been shown to be mutually incompatible, indicating that no social choice function can satisfy all the "desirable" conditions that one might want it to satisfy. Arrow's theorem and related results were mentioned in Section 2 (Arrow [3]; Kelly [78]); Young and Levenglick [140] prove that anonymity, neutrality, Pareto efficiency and partition consistency are incompatible with Condorcet's principle; and Sen [116] and Blau [8], among others, show that certain notions of liberalism clash with other basic conditions.

Third, varieties of social choice functions have been compared across a spectrum of axioms to see which axioms each function satisfies and which it violates. Two informal but very useful studies in this vein are Nanson [98] and Niemi and Riker [99]. More formal studies include Fishburn [44], which compares nine Condorcet functions on eleven axioms; Richelson [107], which analyses six basic functions over twenty conditions; and Weber [133] and Brams and Fishburn [12], which compare approval voting to related procedures.

Some violations of specific axioms by certain social choice functions are subtle enough to be labeled as paradoxes. These include violations of monotonicity in Borda-type elimination procedures (Smith [124]), preferential voting (Doron and Kronick [30]), and other social choice functions (Fishburn [47]), and violations of Pareto efficiency by sequential majority elimination (Harary, Norman, and Cartwright [63, pp. 313-314]). More general discussions of paradoxes appear in Fishburn [42] and Niemi and Riker [99], and Gehrlein [51] gives a thorough review of Condorcet's paradox of voting.

Other comparisons of social choice functions include the relative likelihoods that different non-Condorcet procedures will choose a majority candidate (Fishburn [41]; Chamberlain and Cohen [20]; Gillett [55]; Fishburn and Gehrlein [49]), the probability that different functions yield the same choice set (Fishburn [38]; Gehrlein and Fishburn [52]), and the robustness of different Borda-type scoring systems to preserve the winner when a loser is removed (Gehrlein and Fishburn [53]).

Several additional topics in social choice theory that relate to aggregation are the distribution of power in voting bodies (Shapley and Shubik [122]; Banzhaf [4, 5]; Dubey and Shapley [32]), restrictions on voter preference profiles that guarantee a weak (ties allowed) majority candidate (Black [7]; Sen and Pattanaik [119]; Fishburn [40]; McKelvey and Wendell [94]; Maskin [89]), and the use of lotteries in making social choices (Zeckhauser [141]; Shepsle [123]; Fishburn [39, 46]; Barbera [6]).

10. COLLECTIVE DECISIONS AND SOCIAL CHOICES

Suppose that, whatever collective decision is made, we want the process that produces it to be anonymous, Pareto efficient and monotonic with respect to voter preference profiles that might arise. That is, the actual process is to emulate some social choice function in a designated class.

This would be theoretically trivial if the voter preference profile were known, but that is seldom the case. Therefore we would like to devise a process, including a ballot and aggregator, that will encourage people to vote in such a way that the collective decision will be in the choice set based on the unknown voter preference profile. A process that does this is said to *implement* the social choice function (class); the task of determining when such processes exist and of describing them when they do is the problem of *incentive compatibility* (Hurwicz [72]).

To illustrate, suppose a nine-member committee is to decide how much of next year's budget to devote to a major activity. We assume that each member will arrive at an ideal amount, with preference decreasing as one moves away from the ideal in either direction. Then the median of the nine ideal points is a majority candidate (Black [7]). Suppose the committee decides as follows: each member writes down one amount on a slip of paper, and the median of the ballot amounts becomes the collective decision. It is easily seen that each member has a unique dominant strategy, or *straightforward* strategy (Farquharson [35]), namely, to ballot his ideal. Thus, every voter has an incentive to vote sincerely. Since dominant strategies elect the majority candidate, the process implements every Condorcet social choice function in this specialized context. Moreover, since dominant strategies are sincere, the ballot-aggregation process is said to be *straightforward*. A complete characterization of straightforward processes in a general context is given in Dasgupta, Hammond, and Maskin [25].

Earlier, I mentioned the work of Farquharson [35] and others, including Moulin [96], who identify processes that encourage sophisticated voting (not necessarily sincere) which leads to desirable outcomes, and to the work of Peleg [103] and others on equilibrium strategies that yield collective decisions based on ranked voting that have some nice characteristics.

In fact, the literature of incentive compatibility is already quite large despite the fact that the earliest works (Hurwicz [71, 72]; Vickrey [131]; Farquharson [35]; Clarke [22]; Groves [59]) are comparatively recent. The majority of chapters in Laffont [84] as well as two journal issues (Tideman [127]; Hammond, Groves, and Maskin [62]) are devoted to the subject. Excellent technical introductions and surveys from the latter issue are Dasgupta, Hammond, and Maskin [25] and Groves [60].

The incentive-compatibility literature extends well beyond traditional election theory since much of it is economically focused. It is often addressed to the planning process and the provision of public goods. One problem not mentioned above that has motivated some of this work is the free-rider problem (Olson [100]; Groves and Ledyard [61]), and several proposed implementation schemes involve taxes or monetary transfers among individuals (Clarke [22]; Green and Laffont [58]; Groves [60]; Mas-Colell [88]). Despite its orientation, most of this work is relevant to election procedures in a broad sense, and the incentive compatibility problem is of central importance to the design of good procedures.

A further concern for collective decisions versus social choices is whether voting procedures, incentive compatible or otherwise, do in fact elicit the types of voting (sophisticated, sincere, and so forth) that they are designed for. This loops us back into the general topic of voter behaviour, including abstention and turnout, and responses to different types of procedures (Sections 7 and 8). It also raises the issue of how to estimate the congruence between voters' true preferences and their cast ballots or "revealed preferences" (Frey and Kohn [50]; Smith [125]; Brams and Fishburn [13]).

11. COSTS AND FINANCING

I have already mentioned the effects of personal costs on voting behaviour (Section 7) and the allocation of campaign funds (Section 6) as important aspects of elections. A related economic factor is government expenditures in electoral districts. Following Kramer [81] and Lepper [86], who note correlations between economic conditions and aggregate voting patterns, Wright [136] argues that differences across states in per capita federal spending can be largely explained as a consequence of attempting to maximize electoral votes by the party in power. Other aspects of economic policy may have a similar purpose.

Cost differentials of election procedures, such as between a primary election conducted by a single ballot versus one that uses a runoff election, can of course be a decisive factor in the choice of a procedure.

12. INSTITUTIONAL EFFECTS

Political philosophies of the past two centuries have helped shape the institutions of modern democracies, including the ways they elect their leaders and representatives. In the relatively stable era of the last few decades, research on institutional effects has tended to focus on political parties and their changes over time (Downs [31]; Riker [108]; Rae [106]; Butler and Stokes [16]; Upton and Särlvik [130]).

Whether in the context of a local club or a nation, any proposal for substantial changes in election procedures is likely to meet opposi-

tion, often because of perceived harm to institutional interests. It therefore falls to proponents of change not only to consider effects along our earlier dimensions but also to evaluate how structures of the concerned society may be affected if proposed changes are adopted.

13. CONCLUSION

This paper has identified dimensions of the electoral process that bear on the evaluation and comparison of election procedures, and sketched research work in these dimensions. It has sought to provide an integrative sense of the task of the design of good procedures that could be used to guide further efforts in this area.

References

[1] ALDRICH, J.H. 1980. *Before the Convention: Strategies and Choices in Presidential Nominating Campaigns.* Chicago: University of Chicago Press.

[2] ARANSON, P.H., and P.C. ORDESHOOK. 1972. "Spatial strategies for sequential elections." In R.G. Niemi and H.F. Weisberg, eds. *Probability Models of Collective Decision Making.* Columbus, Ohio: Charles E. Merrill, 298-331.

[3] ARROW, K.J. 1951. *Social Choice and Individual Values.* 2e, 1963. New York: Wiley.

[4] BANZHAF, J.F. 1965. "Weighted voting doesn't work: a mathematical analysis." *Rutgers Law Review* 19: 317-343.

[5] BANZHAF, J.F. 1968, "One man, 3312 votes: a mathematical analysis of the electoral college." *Villanova Law Review* 13: 304-332.

[6] BARBERA, S. 1977. "The manipulation of social choice mechanisms that do not leave 'too much' to chance." *Econometrica* 77: 1573-1588.

[7] BLACK, D. 1958. *The Theory of Committees and Elections.* Cambridge: Cambridge University Press.

[8] BLAU, J.H. 1975. "Liberal values and independence." *Review of Economic Studies* 42: 395-401.

[9] BORDA, JEAN-CHARLES DE. 1781. Mémoire sur les élections au scrutin, *Histoire de l'Académie Royale des Sciences.*

[10] BORDER, K.C., and J.S. JORDAN. 1981. "Straightforward elections, unanimity, and phantom voters." Social Science Working Paper 376, California Institute of Technology.

[11] BRAMS, S.J., and M.D. DAVIS. "The 3/2's rule in presidential campaigning." *American Political Science Review* 68: 113-134.

[12] BRAMS, S.J., and P.C. FISHBURN. "Approval voting." *American Political Science Review* 72: 831-847.

[13] BRAMS, S.J., and P.C. FISHBURN. 1981. "Deducing preferences and choices in the 1980 presidential election." *Electoral Studies* 1: 333-346.

[14] BRAMS, S.J., and P.D. STRAFFIN. 1979. "The entry problem in a political race." Mimeographed.

[15] BUCHANAN, J.M., and G. TULLOCK. 1962. *The Calculus of Consent.* Ann Arbor: University of Michigan Press.

[16] BUTLER, D., and D. STOKES. 1974. *Political Change in Britain* 2e. London: Macmillan.

[17] CAMPBELL, A., P.E. CONVERSE, W.E. MILLER, and D.E. STOKES. 1960. *The American Voter.* New York: Wiley.

[18] CAMPBELL, D.E. 1979. "Manipulation of social choice rules by strategic nomination of candidates." *Theory and Decision* 10: 247-263.

[19] CHAMBERLAIN, G. and M. ROTHSCHILD. 1981. "A note on the probability of casting a decisive note." *Journal of Economic Theory* 25: 152-162.

[20] CHAMBERLAIN, J.R., and M.D. COHEN. 1978. "Toward applicable social choice theory: a comparison of social choice functions under spatial model assumptions." *American Political Science Review* 72: 1341-1356.

[21] CHICHILNISKY, G. 1980. "A general result on strong manipulability." Economic Discussion Paper No. 51, Columbia University.

[22] CLARKE, E.H. 1971. "Multipart pricing of public goods." *Public Choice* 11: 17-33.

[23] COLEMAN, J.S. 1972. "The positions of political parties in elections." In R.G. Niemi, and H.F. Weisberg, eds. *Probability Models of Collective Decision Making.* Columbus, Ohio: Charles E. Merrill, 332-357.

[24] CONDORCET, MARQUIS DE. 1785. *Essai sur l'application de l'analyse à la probabilité des décisions rendues à la pluralité des voix.* Paris.

[25] DASGUPTA, P., P. HAMMOND, and E. MASKIN, 1979. "The implementation of social choice rules: some general results on incentive compatibility." *Review of Economic Studies* 46: 185-216.

[26] DAVIS, O., M. HINICH, and P.C. ORDESHOOK. 1970. "An expository development of a mathematical model of the electoral process." *American Political Science Review* 64: 426-448.

[27] DEACON, R., and P. SHAPIRO. 1979. "Private preference for collective goods revealed through voting on referenda." *American Economic Review* 65: 943-955.

[28] DE GRAZIA, A. 1953. "Mathematical derivation of an election system." *Isis* 44: 42-51.

[29] DEMEYER, F., and C.R. PLOTT. 1971. "A welfare function using 'relative intensity' of preference." *Quarterly Journal of Economics* 85: 179-186.

[30] DORON, G., and R. KRONICK. 1977. "Single transferable vote: an example of a perverse social choice function." *American Journal of Political Science* 21: 303-311.

[31] DOWNS, A. 1957. *An Economic Theory of Democracy.* New York: Harper and Row.

[32] DUBEY, P., and L.S. SHAPLEY. 1979. "Mathematical properties of the Banzhaf power index." *Mathematics of Operations Research* 4: 99-13.

[33] DUTTA, B., and P.K. PATTANAIK. 1978. "On nicely consistent voting systems." *Econometrica* 46: 163-170.

[34] FAIR, R.C. 1978. "The effect of economic events on votes for president." *Review of Economics and Statistics* 60: 159-173.

[35] FARQUHARSON, R. 1969. *Theory of Voting.* New Haven: Yale University Press.

[36] FEREJOHN, J.A., and M.P. FIORINA. 1974. "The paradox of not voting: a decision theoretic analysis." *American Political Science Review* 68: 525-536.

[37] FISHBURN, P.C. 1970. *Utility Theory for Decision Making.* New York: Wiley. Reprinted by Krieger (New York: Huntington 1979).

[38] FISHBURN, P.C. 1971. "A comparative analysis of group decision methods." *Behavioral Science* 16: 538-544.

[39] FISHBURN, P.C. 1972. "Lotteries and social choice." *Journal of Economic Theory* 5: 189-207.

[40] FISHBURN, P.C. 1973. *The Theory of Social Choice.* Princeton: Princeton University Press.

[41] FISHBURN, P.C. 1974. "Simple voting systems and majority rule." *Behavioral Science* 19: 166-176.

[42] FISHBURN, P.C. 1974. "Paradoxes of voting." *American Political Science Review* 68: 537-546.

[43] FISHBURN, P.C. 1974. "Social choice functions." *SIAM Review* 16: 63-90.

[44] FISHBURN, P.C. 1977. "Condorcet social choice functions." *SIAM Journal of Applied Mathematics* 33: 469-489.

[45] FISHBURN, P.C. 1978. "Axioms for approval voting: direct proof." *Journal of Economic Theory* 19: 180-185.

[46] FISHBURN, P.C. 1978. "Acceptable social choice lotteries." In H.W. Gottinger and W. Leinfellner, eds. *Decision Theory and Social Ethics, Issues in Social Choice.* Dordrecht, Holland: Reidel, 133-152.

[47] FISHBURN, P.C. "Monotonicity paradoxes in the theory of elections." Forthcoming in *Discrete Applied Mathematics.*

[48] FISHBURN, P.C., and W.V. GEHRLEIN. 1977. "Towards a theory of elections with probabilistic preferences." *Econometrica* 45: 1907-1924.

[49] FISHBURN, P.C., and W.V. GEHRLEIN. 1982. "Majority efficiencies for simple voting procedures: summary and interpretation." *Theory and Decision* 14: 141-153.

[50] FREY, R.L., and L. KOHN. 1970. "An economic interpretation of voting behaviour on public finance issues." *Kyklos* 23: 792-805.

[51] GEHRLEIN, W.V. 1981. "Condorcet's paradox." Mimeographed, University of Delaware.

[52] GEHRLEIN, W.V., and P.C. FISHBURN. 1978. "Probabilities of election outcomes for large electorates." *Journal of Economic Theory* 19: 38-49.

[53] GEHRLEIN, W.V., and P.C. FISHBURN. 1980. "Robustness of positional scoring over subsets of alternatives." *Applied Mathematics and Optimization* 6: 241-255.

[54] GIBBARD, A. 1973. "Manipulation of voting schemes: a general result." *Econometrica* 41: 587-601.

[55] GILLERTT, R. 1980. "The asymptotic likelihood of agreement between plurality and Condorcet outcomes." *Behavioral Science* 25: 23-32.

[56] GOOD, I.J., and L.S. MAYER. 1975. "Estimating the efficacy of a vote." *Behavioral Science* 20: 25-33.

[57] GRANBERG, D., and E. BRENT. 1980. "Perceptions of issue positions of presidential candidates." *American Scientist* 68: 617-625.

[58] GREEN, J., and J.-J. LAFFONT. 1977. "Characterization of satisfactory mechanisms for the revelation of preferences for public goods." *Econometricà* 45: 427-438.

[59] GROVES, T. 1970. *The Allocation of Resources under Uncertainty.* Ph.D. dissertation, University of California, Berkeley.

[60] GROVES, T. 1979. "Efficient collective choice when compensation is possible." *Review of Economic Studies* 46: 227-241.

[61] GROVES, T., and J. LEDYARD. 1977. "Optimal allocation of public goods: a solution to the 'free rider' problem." *Econometrica* 45: 783-809.

[62] HAMMOND, P.J., T. GROVES, and E. MASKIN, eds. 1979. *Review of Economic Studies* 46-2.

[63] HARARY, F., R.Z. NORMAN, and D. CARTWRIGHT. 1965. *Structural Models: An Introduction to the Theory of Directed Graphs.* New York: Wiley.

[64] HARE, T. 1861. *The Election of Representatives, Parliamentary and Municipal: A Treatise.* London: Longman, Green.

[65] HARSANYI, J.C. 1955. "Cardinal welfare, individualistic ethics, and interpersonal comparisons of utility." *Journal of Political Economy* 63: 309-321.

[66] HARSANYI, J.C. 1969. "Rational-choice models of political behavior vs. functionalist and conformist theories." *World Politics* 21: 513-538.

[67] HILDRETH, C. 1953. "Alternative conditions for social orderings." *Econometrica* 21: 81-94.

[68] HINICH, M.J. 1978. "Some evidence on non-voting models in the spatial theory of electoral competition," *Public Choice* 33: 2, 83-102.

[69] HINICH, M.J., and P.C. ORDESHOOK. 1969. "Abstentions and equilibrium in the electoral process." *Public Choice* 8: 81-106.

[70] HOAG, C.G., and G.H. HALLETT. 1926. *Proportional Representation*. New York: Macmillan.

[71] HURWICZ, L. 1960. "Optimality and informational efficiency in resource allocation processes." In K.J. Arrow, S. Karlin, and P. Suppes, eds. *Mathematical Methods in the Social Sciences*. 1959. Stanford: Stanford University Press, 27-46.

[72] HURWICZ, L. 1972. "On informationally decentralized systems." In C.B. McGuire and R. Radner, eds. *Decision and Organization*. Amsterdam, North-Holland: 297-336.

[73] HYLLAND, A. 1980. "Strategy proofness of voting procedures with lotteries as outcomes and infinite sets of strategies." Mimeographed, Harvard Uniersity.

[74] INTRILIGATOR, M. 1973. "A probabilistic model of social choice." *Review of Economic Studies* 40: 553-560.

[75] ISHIKAWA, S., and K. NAKAMURA. 1979. "The strategy-proof social choice functions." *Journal of Mathematical Economics* 6: 283-295.

[76] KALAI, E., and E. MULLER. 1977. "Characterization of domains admitting non-dictatorial social welfare functions and non-manipulable voting procedures." *Journal of Economic Theory* 16: 457-469.

[77] KAU, J.B., and P.H. RUBIN. 1976. "The electoral college and the rational vote." *Public Choice* 27: 101-107.

[78] KELLY, J.S. 1978. *Arrow Impossibility Theorems*. New York: Academic Press.

[79] KENDALL, W., and G.W. CAREY. 1968. "The 'intensity' problem and democratic theory." *American Political Science Review* 62: 5-24.

[80] KEY, V.O. 1966. *The Responsible Electorate*. Cambridge, Massachusetts: Harvard University Press.

[81] KRAMER, G.H. 1971. "Short-term fluctuations in U.S. voting behavior 1896-1964." *American Political Science Review* 65: 131-143.

[82] KRAMER, G.H. 1972. "Sophisticated voting over multidimensional choice spaces." *Journal of Mathematical Sociology* 2: 165-180.

[83] KRAMER, G.H. 1977. "A dynamical model of political equilibrium." *Journal of Economic Theory* 16: 310-334.

[84] LAFFONT, J.-J., ed. 1979. *Aggregation and Revelation of Preference*. Amsterdam: North-Holland.

[85] LAPLACE, MARQUIS DE. 1812. "Leçons de mathématiques, données à l'École Normale en 1795." *Journal de l'École Polytechnique* 2.

[86] LEPPER, S.J. 1972. "Voting behavior and aggregate policy targets." Cowles Foundation Discussion Paper No. 341, Yale University.

[87] LIPSET, S.M. 1960. *Political Man*. New York: Doubleday.

[88] MAS-COLELL, A. 1980. "Efficiency and decentralization in the pure theory of public goods." *Quarterly Journal of Economics* 94: 625-641.

[89] MASKIN, E. 1978. "Social welfare functions on restricted domains." Mimeographed, Massachusetts Institute of Technology.

[90] MAY, K.O. 1952. "A set of independent necessary and sufficient conditions for simple majority decisions." *Econometrica* 20: 680-684.

[91] MCKELVEY, R.D. 1975. "Policy related voting and electoral equilibrium." *Econometrica* 43: 815-843.

[92] MCKELVEY, R.D., and R.G. NIEMI. 1978. "A multistage game representation of sophisticated voting for binary procedures." *Journal of Economic Theory* 18: 1-22.

[93] MCKELVEY, R.D., and P. ORDESHOOK. 1972. "A general theory of the calculus of voting." In J. Herndon, ed. *Mathematical Applications in Political Science VI*. Charlottesville: University Press of Virginia, 32-78.

[94] MCKELVEY, R.D., and R.E. WENDELL, 1976. "Voting equilibria in multidimensional choice spaces." *Mathematics of Operations Research* 1: 144-158.

[95] MORIN, R.A. 1980. *Structural Reform: Ballots*. New York: Vantage Press.

[96] MOULIN, H. 1979. "Dominance solvable voting schemes." *Econometrica* 47: 1337-1351.

[97] MUELLER, D.C. 1976. "Public choice: a survey." *Journal of Economic Literature* 14: 395-433.

[98] NANSON, E.J. 1883. "Methods of elections." *Transactions and Proceedings of Royal Society of Victoria* 19: 197-240.

[99] NIEMI, R.G., and W.H. RIKER. 1976. "The choice of voting systems." *Scientific American* 234: 21-27.

[100] OLSON, M. 1965. *The Logic of Collective Action*. Cambridge, Massachusetts: Harvard University Press.

[101] OREN, I. 1981. "The structure of exactly strongly consistent social choice functions." *Journal of Mathematical Economics* 8: 207-220.

[102] PATTANAIK, P.K. 1978. *Strategy and Group Choice*. Amsterdam: North-Holland.

[103] PELEG, B. 1978. "Consistent voting systems." *Econometrica* 46: 153-161.

[104] PLOTT, C.R. 1971. "Recent results in the theory of voting." In M.D. Intriligator, ed. *Frontiers of Quantitative Economics*. Amsterdam: North-Holland, 109-129.

[105] PLOTT, C.R., and M.E. LEVINE. 1978. "a model of agenda influence on committee decisions." *American Economic Review* 68: 146-160.

[106] RAE, D.W. 1967. *The Political Consequences of Electoral Laws*. New Haven, Connecticut: Yale University Press.

[107] RICHELSON, J.T. 1979. "A comparative analysis of social choice functions, I, II, III: A summary." *Behavioral Science* 24:355.

[108] RIKER, W. 1962. *The Theory of Political Coalitions*. New Haven, Connecticut: Yale University Press.

[109] RIKER, W.H. 1976. "The number of political parties: a reexamination of Duverger's Law." *Comparative Politics* 9: 93-106.

[110] RIKER, W.H., and S.J. BRAMS. 1973. "The paradox of vote-trading." *American Political Science Review* 67: 1239-1247.

[111] RIKER, W.H., and P. ORDESHOOK. 1968. "A theory of the calculus of voting." *American Political Science Review* 62: 25-42.

[112] RIKER, W.H., and W.J. ZAVOINA. 1970. "Rational behavior in politics: evidence from a three person game." *American Political Science Review* 64: 48-60.

[113] SATTERTHWAITE, M.A. 1975. "Strategy-proofness and Arrow's conditions: existence and correspondence theorems for voting procedures and social welfare functions." *Journal of Economic Theory* 10: 187-217.

[114] SAVAGE, L.J. 1951. "The theory of statistical decision." *Journal of the American Statistical Association* 46: 55-67.

[115] SEN, A.K. 1970. *Collective Choice and Social Welfare*. San Francisco: Holden-Day.

[116] SEN, A. 1970. "The impossibility of a Paretian liberal." *Journal of Political Economy* 78: 152-157.

[117] SEN, A.K. 1977. "Social choice theory: a reexamination." *Econometrica* 45: 53-89.

[118] SEN, A.K. "Social choice theory." Forthcoming in K.J. Arrow and M.D. Intriligator, eds. *Handbook of Mathematical Economics*, Vol. III. Amsterdam: North-Holland Publishing Co.

[119] SEN, A.K., and P.K. PATTANAIK. 1969. "Necessary and sufficient conditions for rational choice under majority decision." *Journal of Economic Theory* 1: 178-202.

[120] SHANE, H.D. 1977. "Mathematical models for economic and political advertising campaigns." *Operations Research* 25: 1-14.

[121] SHAPIRO, M.J. 1969. "Rational political man: a synthesis of economic and sociopsychological perspectives." *American Political Science Review* 63: 1106-1119.

[122] SHAPLEY, L.S., and M. SHUBIK. 1954. "A method for evaluating the distribution of power in a committee system." *American Political Science Review* 48: 787-792.

[123] SHEPSLE, K.A. 1970. "A note on Zeckhauser's 'Majority rule with lotteries on alternatives.'" *Quarterly Journal of Economics* 84: 705-709.

[124] SMITH, J.H. 1973. "Aggregation of preferences with variable electorate." *Econometrica* 41: 1027-1041.

[125] SMITH, J.W. 1975. "A clear test of rational voting." *Public Choice* 23: 55-67.

[126] STRAFFIN, P.D. 1980. *Topics in the Theory of Voting.* Boston: Birkhäuser.

[127] TIDEMAN, T.D., ed. 1977. *Public Choice* 29-2.

[128] TULLOCK, G. 1968, *Toward a Mathematics of Politics.* Ann Arbor: University of Michigan Press.

[129] TULLOCK, G. 1970. "A simple algebraic log-rolling model." *American Economic Review* 60: 419-426.

[130] UPTON, G.J.G., and B. SÄLVIK. 1981. "A loyalty-distance model for voting change." *Journal of the Royal Statistical Society* A144: 247-259.

[131] VICKREY, W. 1961. "Counterspeculation, auctions, and competitive sealed tender." *Journal of Finance* 16: 8-37.

[132] VON NEUMANN, J., and O. MORGENSTERN. 1947. *Theory of Games and Economic Behavior* 2e. Princeton: Princeton University Press.

[133] WEBER, R.J. 1977. "Comparison of voting systems." Mimeographed.

[134] WILSON, R. 1969. "An axiomatic model of logrolling." *American Economic Review* 59: 331-341.

[135] WITTMAN, D. 1977. "Candidates with policy preferences: a dynamic model." *Journal of Economic Theory* 14: 180-189.

[136] WRIGHT, G. 1974. "The political economy of new deal spending: an econometric analysis." *Review of Economics and Statistics* 56: 30-38.

[137] YOUNG, H.P. 1974. "An axiomatization of Borda's rule." *Journal of Economic Theory* 9: 43-52.

[138] YOUNG, H.P. 1975. "Social choice scoring functions." *SIAM Journal of Applied Mathematics* 28: 824-838.

[139] YOUNG, H.P. 1978. "The allocation of funds in lobbying and campaigning." *Behavioral Science* 23: 21-31.

[140] YOUNG, H.P., and A. LEVENGLICK. 1978. "A consistent extension of Condorcet's election principle." *SIAM Journal of Applied Mathematics* 35: 285-300.

[141] ZECKHAUSER, R. 1969. "Majority rule with lotteries on alternatives." *Quarterly Journal of Economics* 83: 696-703.

31. ON THE PROPERTIES OF VOTING SYSTEMS

Hannu Nurmi

WHAT PROPERTIES ARE DESIRABLE?

Non-dictatorship

Quite obviously if one is interested in *voting* procedures one does not deem dictatorial procedures desirable. And yet to determine whether a procedure is dictatorial or not may not be quite straightforward. A combination of quite innocent-looking properties may imply a dictatorship. A case in point is the combination of the independence of infeasible alternatives and what is called the weak axiom of revealed preference (WARP) (see Plott 1976, 550). The former property requires that only the change of the voter preferences concerning the feasible alternatives can change the social choice. The latter, in turn, is a kind of consistency property to be discussed shortly. Any procedure having these two properties is dictatorial, i.e., the procedure chooses as if there were an individual whose preference always determines the social choice. Thus, if the independence of infeasible alternatives and WARP are viewed as consistency properties, non-dictatorship is not compatible with both of these forms of consistency.

Perhaps a somewhat more general result on the dictatorship of social choice function was independently proven by Gibbard (1973) and Satterthwaite (1975) (see also Gärdenfors

1977). It states that any resolute social choice function with at least three possible values (choices) is either manipulable or dictatorial. To appreciate the coverage of this theorem, we need to specify what is meant by resoluteness: a social choice function is resolute if its range consists of singleton sets of alternatives only. In other words, the social choice set must consist of no more than one alternative. Obviously the theorem does not apply to the simple majority rule, the Borda count, approval voting or the maximin method as any of these rules can result in a tie. In general, it can be seen that none of these procedures is dictatorial because under each of them the social choice remains invariant under the permutation of voters, i.e., the procedures are anonymous, thereby excluding the possibility of a dictator.

Consistency

One of the "obvious" properties required of a social decision process is consistency, at least insofar as inconsistency is usually deemed an unacceptable feature of both individual and collective decisions. However, it is only after having been confronted with various specifications of consistency that one is likely to appreciate the complexity of the issue. Let us take as our point of departure the ordinary language specification of consistency in which it is stated that no one can consistently argue that p and non-p is the case where p stands for a proposition. Translated into the context of collective decisions, this requirement would obviously prohibit choosing a_1 and non-a_1 at the

Reprinted from "On the Properties of Voting Systems" by Hannu Nurmi, *Scandinavian Political Studies* 4 (1981), by permission of Norwegian University Press, Oslo.

same time. But what does it mean? Surely, any social choice function satisfies trivially (by definition) the requirement of being non-contradictory when applied in a given decision situation. But if we interpret consistency to mean stability in the sense that the individual preferences and the set of alternatives being fixed, the procedure always chooses the same set of alternatives, then we can observe that the simple majority rule with a pairwise comparison of alternatives is not consistent. In other words, the well-known parliamentary voting procedure is not consistent unless restrictions are set upon the agenda building. This observation is of course just another way of stating the Condorcet paradox, but more generally when the core of the voting game is empty and the voter preferences satisfy some fairly mild conditions and, moreover, the set of alternatives can be represented as a multidimensional real space, then any alternative can be rendered a majority winner, as McKelvey (1976; 1979) has shown.

So, under the above conditions, anyone controlling the agenda completely also determines the social choice. It must be observed, though, that the control required is, indeed, complete in the sense of allowing the agenda-controller to add any number of alternatives to the agenda in addition to dictating the voting sequence.

The Borda count, approval voting, and the maximin method are all consistent in this sense. That is, if in any given decision situation where the alternative set is fixed the social choice set differs from what it has been in another situation with the same alternative set, the difference must be due to a change in the individual preference relations.

But consistency can also be understood as referring to situations in which either the alternative set or the voter set varies. In the context of the axiomatization of the Borda count and the approval voting, the consistency axiom has the latter interpretation, i.e., it requires that

two groups when choosing from a fixed set of alternatives should fulfill a certain criterion in order to be consistent. The Borda count and approval voting thus satisfy the consistency condition in this sense. It can be noticed immediately that the simple majority rule with a fixed alternative set is also consistent if the agenda remains fixed. The maximin method, on the other hand, is not consistent (see Nurmi 1980).

Another type of consistency property is path independence. It is a requirement that regardless of the way in which we partition our alternative set into two subsets, the social choice set should be the same when we make a choice from a set consisting of the social choice set of one of the subsets and the other subset, and when the choice is made from the original alternative set. In symbols:

$$C(A, R_1, \ldots, R_n) = (C(CA_1, R_1, \ldots, R_n) \cup A_2, R_1, \ldots, R_n) \text{ for all } A_1, A_2 \subset A \text{ such that } A = A_1 \cup A_2 \text{ with } A_1 \cap A_2 = \emptyset.$$

Of course, controlling the agenda is tantamount to controlling the "path" in the relevant sense. Therefore, whenever the agenda control amounts to the control of the social choice, we are dealing with a path dependent procedure. Clearly, the simple majority rule is not a path independent procedure. It is well-known that the Borda count violates the condition of the independence of irrelevant alternatives. In particular, the number of alternatives considered affects the social choice under the Borda count. Consequently, by a suitable partitioning of the set A, one can affect the social choice from a subset of A and, thereafter, the 'overall' Borda winning set. Hence, the Borda count obviously is not a path independent procedure.

That the approval voting is path independent is obvious. The individual ballots remaining the same, any partitioning of the alternative sets leaves the set of voters voting for each subset of alternatives unaffected. When the set of winners of the subset is considered together with the complement of the subset, the number of votes ("approvals") given to each of the considered alternatives is no more or less than are given when the entire alternative set is considered simultaneously—provided, of course, that the preferences of the voters do not change and that the voting is sincere. Another way of looking at this feature of approval voting is to observe that the procedure satisfies the independence of irrelevant alternatives condition. Consequently, the removal of some of the irrelevant—i.e., socially not approved—alternatives does not affect the social choice between the rest of the alternatives.

The maximin method, on the other hand, does not have this consistency property. This can be seen upon noticing that it is not independent of irrelevant alternatives (Nurmi 1980). The winners in each subset are determined on inspecting their toughest competitors. Hence, the winners of some of the subset contests do not necessarily include all the winners of the overall contest.

Path independence thus differentiates the voting procedures discussed here. It is, however, worth pointing out that although a seemingly "nice" property, path independence is incompatible with some other intuitively plausible properties. For instance, path independence, sincere voting, Pareto optimality and non-oligarchy have been shown to be incompatible (Plott 1976, 575). So at least one notion of group rationality seems somewhat difficult to combine with one particular interpretation of consistency.

There is one further concept that could be thought of as referring to an aspect of the intuitive notion of consistency, viz. WARP. Stated informally, WARP says the following. Suppose that when a collective choice is made, it turns out that the alternative set A included some unrealistic or otherwise unrealizable alternatives and that a new choice is made among the realizable ones A'. A procedure satisfying WARP now has the property that if the preferences remain the same and an alternative belonging to A' is in the choice set when the set A is considered, then the choice set of A includes all the alternatives chosen from A' (and perhaps some others not in A') (Plott 1976, 549).

Now if we interpret the simple majority rule as the parliamentary voting procedure in a multi-candidate contest, we can observe that WARP is not satisfied even if agenda manipulation is excluded. Suppose that A_1 is the choice set from A' and A_2 is the choice set from A. Suppose moreover that $A_1 \cap A_2 \neq \phi$. The question now is whether $A_1 \subseteq A_2$ or not. Obviously some of the candidates in A_1 may be defeated in pairwise comparisons with some of the candidates in A_2 while some may survive. Hence, it is not necessary that $A_1 \subseteq A_2$. Sen's (1970, 17) well-known example of a game championship is a case in point: WARP requires that if some Pakistani is a world champion, then all champions of Pakistan must be champions of the world. Obviously, if championships are determined on the basis of the pairwise comparisons of alternatives, WARP is not necessarily satisfied.

That the Borda count does not satisfy WARP is perhaps most easily seen by noticing that in order to have the WARP property, the procedure must be such that an overall winning alternative is also the winner in every subset to which it belongs. The Borda count does not have this property (see, e.g., Riker and Ordeshook 1973, 88 for a counterexample).

Assuming that the individual preferences remain the same when the choice is made from A and when it is made from A', it is clear that the approval voting satisfies WARP. Indeed, this is a logical consequence of "approving" of candidates by giving them votes and "disapproving" of them by not giving them votes. As for the maximin method, it also satisfies WARP as has been shown elsewhere (Nurmi 1980).

Having now discussed several consistency properties of the voting procedures, let us turn to another related property, viz. rationality. While consistency is usually deemed to be a necessary condition of individual rationality, we shall now deal with a system level notion, group rationality.

Pareto Optimality

One of the most extensively discussed theoretical properties in welfare economics and social choice is Pareto optimality. Even though it is doubtful whether considerations pertaining to the justice of social institutions or arrangements are reflected in the criterion of Pareto optimality, it is difficult to deny that a failure to satisfy it—when other perhaps more "important" criteria are fulfilled—would be collectively irrational.

Stated in the context of voting procedures Pareto optimality criterion says that if everyone in a decision-making body prefers x to y, then y is not to be chosen (Plott 1976, 528). Prima facie, this principle does not appear too stringent, but it is worth noticing that we are now trying to determine whether our procedures necessarily exclude Pareto suboptimal choices.

It has been shown by McKelvey (1976; 1979) that there is nothing in the nature of the simple majority rule to exclude the possibility of Pareto suboptimal choices. Indeed, provided that the core is empty and that the voters have preferences representable by continuous utility functions, any outcome can be rendered the majority winner if the policy space is the Re^n- space ($n = 2, 3, \ldots$).

The Borda count, on the other hand, clearly fulfills the above stated condition of Pareto optimality. This is due to the fact that if x is preferred to y by everyone, then it obviously gets a higher total score than y. Consequently, y cannot be chosen.

The assessment of the approval voting is less straightforward. It is obvious that if everyone approves x (i.e., gives x a vote) and disapproves y (i.e., gives no vote to y), then y cannot be chosen. More generally, if the preferences are dichotomous, the Pareto optimality of the outcome is guaranteed. But the dichotomous nature is not necessary for this result to hold. It also holds in cases where each voter has more than two equivalence classes of alternatives provided that at least one voter puts x in a class of approved alternatives and y in a class of disapproved ones. So, we conclude that if the preference between x and y is interpreted in the relevant sense, the approval voting is Pareto optimal.

That also the maximin method satisfies the Pareto principle can be seen from the following. Suppose that x is preferred to y by everyone. Then obviously the minimum number of votes for y in all pairwise comparisons is 0. An alternative with this property cannot be chosen by the maximin method unless all the other alternatives have the same property. This, in turn, means that there is a unanimity cycle in the collective preference through every alternative. Should this be the case, the Pareto optimal set would clearly be empty. Thus, the maximin method satisfies Pareto optimality.

The above properties deal with procedures from the rationality point of view with the implicit assumption that the inputs of the procedures—i.e., the individual votes or preferences—are given in a fashion that is unproblematic for the assessment of the procedures. But there are reasons to argue that the voting procedures cannot satisfactorily be evaluated without an explicit consideration of the strategic aspects of the voting situations.

Manipulation and Implementation

It is well-known from the collective goods problematique that the sincere revelation of

preferences may not always be beneficial for the individuals participating in collective decision-making. From the viewpoint of the voting procedures this possibility has to be taken into account because the possibility of strategic manipulation—when present—is what makes the procedures unstable. Let us make a distinction between the following properties:
(i) the dominant strategy property, and
(ii) sincerity of the procedure.
Procedures having the former property allow each voter one dominant strategy. When the procedure satisfies the property (ii), in turn, it assigns to each player one dominant strategy which consists of behaving according to his (her) true preferences. Clearly, (ii) is a special case of (i). The dominant strategy property has to do with the stability of the procedure or mechanism. The problem of implementation of the social choice mechanism is customarily phrased in the following way: does a given mechanism support—i.e., choose—outcomes that are equilibria of the underlying game forms (Dasgupta, et al., 1979; Ferejohn, et al., 1980). The types of equilibria usually discussed are dominant strategy equilibria or Nash equilibria (see, however, Ferejohn, et al., 1980). We shall focus on the former type of implementability here. In other words, we restrict ourselves to discussing whether the above voting procedures have the property that for all individual preference configurations there exists for each voter a dominant strategy such that the choice of their dominant strategies by all players yields an outcome that belongs to the choice set of the voting procedure.

Clearly, the simple majority rule is non-manipulable in the case where two alternatives only are considered. The parliamentary voting procedure, on the other hand, is amenable to the strategic misrepresentation of preferences. That it has in fact been manipulated by real-world political actors is well-known (see e.g.,

Bjurulf & Niemi 1978). We can easily observe that not only does the procedure lack the sincerity property but it does not even possess the dominant strategy property. In other words, it is an unstable procedure.

Also the Borda count is obviously manipulable because given that the preferences of other voters are fixed, an individual may in some cases affect the social choice by, say, giving the largest number of points to his (her) second best alternative so as to guarantee its choice when his (her) first preference does not have any chance of being chosen. Consequently, the Borda count is not sincere. Nor is it stable as can be readily observed.

The results of Brams and Fishburn (1978) show that the approval voting procedure is less manipulable than other similar voting methods (see also Fishburn 1978a). Specifically, if the number of equivalence (or indifference) classes of alternatives for each individual is 2, then the approval voting is non-manipulable, but when the number of equivalence classes is at least 3, no single ballot non-ranked voting system is non-manipulable.

Also the maximin method is subject to strategic manipulation. This can be seen from the following example (Nurmi 1980). Consider the following table in which the results of sincere voting are tabulated when the number of alternatives is 4 and the number of voters is 4:

	x_1	x_2	x_3	x_4	row minima
x_1	-	3	2	3	2
x_2	1	-	4	4	1
x_3	2	0	-	0	0
x_4	1	0	1	-	0

Here the entry on the i'th row and the j'th column (i,j=1,2,3,4) gives the number [of] votes that x_i gets in a pairwise comparison with x_j. Suppose now that one of the voters has a strict preference order over the alternatives according to which x_4 is the best, x_2 next best, x_1 the third, and x_3 the worst of the alternatives. This voter can by misrepresenting his preferences between x_1 and x_3 bring about the following matrix:

	x_1	x_2	x_3	x_4	row minima
x_1	-	3	1	3	1
x_2	1	-	4	4	1
x_3	3	0	-	3	0
x_4	1	0	1	-	0

In the sincere voting situation the choice set consists of x_1 only while in the [latter] case it consists of x_1 and x_2. Thus, the voter has by misrepresenting his preferences brought about an outcome that is better from his viewpoint than the previous one.

CONCLUSION

In the preceding we have discussed several voting procedures in the light of various criteria of goodness. The following table (Table 1) summarizes the main observations. Obviously the check list of the properties is partial and subject to criticism on various grounds. The picture that emerges from it is favorable to the approval voting. It becomes even more so when due attention is paid to the fact that when there is an "obvious" winner, viz. the Condorcet winning alternative, the approval voting procedure always elects it if the voters vote according to their true preferences (Fishburn and Brams 1981). This feature also characterizes the maximin method (Nurmi 1980) and quite obviously the parliamentary voting procedure. In contrast, the Borda count does not necessarily choose the Condorcet winner.

One last caveat is in order: the voting methods discussed above are but a small subset of all possible methods. Similarly the criteria discussed could be augmented with many others. For an earlier account along similar lines the reader is referred to Straffin's study (1979).

Table 1 Comparison of the Voting Procedures with Respect to Various Criteria of Goodness

Rule Property	Simple majority	Borda count	Approval voting	Maximin method
Dictatorship	No	No	No	No
Consistency	No	Yes	Yes	No
Path-independence	No	No	Yes	No
WARP	No	No	Yes	Yes
Pareto optimality	No	Yes	Yes	Yes
Manipulability	Yes	Yes	Yes	Yes

References

BJURULF, B., and R. NIEMI. 1978. "Strategic Voting in Scandinavian Parliaments." *Scandinavian Political Studies* 1: 5-22.

BRAMS, S.J., and P.C. FISHBURN. 1978. "Approval Voting." *American Political Science Review* 72: 831-847.

COLMAN, A., and I. POUNTNEY. 1978. "Borda's Voting Paradox: Theoretical Likelihood and Electoral Occurrences." *Behavioral Science* 23: 15-20.

DASGUPTA, P., P. HAMMOND, and E. MASKIN. 1979. "The Implementation of Social Choice Rules." *Review of Economic Studies* 46: 185-125.

FEREJOHN, J., D. GRETHER, and R. MCKELVEY. 1980. *Implementation of Democratic Social Choice Functions.* California Institute of Technology, Social Science Working Paper 300.

FISHBURN, P.C. 1978. "Axioms for Approval Voting: Direct Proof." *Journal of Economic Theory* 19: 180-185.

FISHBURN, P.C. 1978a. "A Strategic Analysis of Nonranked Voting Systems." *SIAM Journal of Applied Mathematics* 35: 488-95.

FISHBURN, P.C. 1979. "Symmetric and Consistent Aggregation with Dichotomous Voting." In J.-J. Laffont, ed. *Aggregation and Revelation of Preferences.* Amsterdam: North-Holland.

FISHBURN, P.C., and S.J. BRAMS. 1981. "Approval Voting, Condorcet's Principle, and Runoff Elections." *Public Choice* 36: 89-114.

GIBBARD, A. 1973. "Manipulation of Voting Schemes: a General Result." *Econometrica* 41: 587-601.

GRANGER, G.-G. 1956. *La Mathématique Sociale du Marquis de Condorcet.* Paris: Presses Universitaires de France.

DE GRAZIA, A. 1953. "Mathematical Derivation of an Election System." *Isis* 44: 42-51.

GÄRDENFORS, P. 1977. "A Concise Proof of Theorem on Manipulation of Social Choice Functions." *Public Choice* 32: 137-142.

HANSSON, B., and H. SAHLQUIST. 1976. "A Proof Technique for Social Choice with Variable Electorate." *Journal of Economic Theory* 13: 193-200.

KRAMER, G.H. 1977. "A Dynamical Model of Political Equilibrium." *Journal of Economic Theory* 16: 310-334.

MAY, K.O. 1952. "A Set of Independent, Necessary and Sufficient Conditions for Simple Majority Decision." *Econometrica* 20: 680-684.

MCKELVEY, R.D. 1976. "Intransitivities in Multidimensional Voting Models and Some Implications for Agenda Control." *Journal of Economic Theory* 12: 472-482.

MCKELVEY, R.D. 1979." General Conditions for Global Intransitivities in Formal Voting Models." *Econometrica* 47: 1085-1112.

NIEMI, R.G., and W.H. RIKER. 1976. "The Choice of Voting Systems." *Scientific American* 234: 21-27.

NURMI, H. 1980. (Revised October 1980.) "Problems of and Alternatives to the Parliamentary Voting Procedure." Florence: European Public Choice Meeting.

PLOTT, C.R. 1976. "Axiomatic Social Choice Theory: an Overview and Interpretation." *American Journal of Political Science* 20: 511-596.

RIKER, W.H., and P.C. ORDESHOOK. 1973. *An Introduction to Positive Political Theory.* Englewood Cliffs: Prentice-Hall.

SATTERTHWAITE, M. 1975. "Strategy-Proofness and Arrow's Conditions." *Journal of Economic Theory* 10: 187-217.

SEN, A.K. 1970. *Collective Choice and Social Welfare.* London: Oliver & Boyd.

SIMPSON, P.B. 1969. "On Defining Areas of Voter Choice." *The Quarterly Journal of Economics* LXXXIII: 478-490.

SMITH, J.H. 1973. "Aggregation of Preferences and Variable Electorate." *Econometrica* 41: 1027-1041.

STRAFFIN, P.D., Jr. 1979. *Introduction to Social Choice Theory for Environmental Decision Making.* American Society of Civil Engineers, Urban Water Resources Research Program, Technical Memorandum No. 36.

YOUNG, H.P. 1974. "An Axiomatization of Borda's Rule." *Journal of Economic Theory* 9: 43-52.

YOUNG, H.P. 1975. "Social Choice Scoring Functions." *SIAM Journal of Applied Mathematics* 28: 824-838.

32. PARADOXES OF PREFERENTIAL VOTING

Peter C. Fishburn and Steven J. Brams

WHAT CAN GO WRONG WITH SOPHISTICATED VOTING SYSTEMS DESIGNED TO REMEDY PROBLEMS OF SIMPLER SYSTEMS

Preferential voting, developed by Thomas Hare [12] in the 1860's, is still used for major elections in Australia, Ireland and South Africa, as well as for local elections in many countries. From its inception, it has been touted as a way to promote full expression of electors' preferences and to ensure maximum and equitable consideration of each elector's vote. When used to fill several seats in a legislature, preferential voting provides representation for viable minorities and tends to distribute seats in proportion to the numbers of voters who favour the different parties.

It seeks to do all this on the basis of a single preferential (ranked) ballot by transferring votes, in part or in whole, from the most and least popular candidates to candidates with intermediate support. The most popular, elected first, don't need their "surpluses," and the least popular can never overcome their "deficits," so the transfers of both surpluses and deficits to the intermediate candidates determine which of these win. When there are n

voters and c seats to be filled, transfers are made sequentially until c candidates attain the vote quota needed for election. The quota is usually defined as

$$q = \left[\frac{n}{c+1} \right] + 1,$$

where brackets signify the integer part of the argument. We shall use this concept later.

Despite its tendencies to promote individual interests and fair representation, preferential voting has several surprising and potentially damning defects. We shall begin by illustrating four of these through an apocryphal story of an election among three contenders for mayor of a small town. In this deliberately simple case, a candidate ranked first on more than 50 percent of the ballots is elected; if there is no such candidate, the one with the fewest first-place votes is scratched, then the one of the remaining two who ranks higher on more ballots is elected. Since this procedure is tantamount to plurality (vote-for-one) voting followed by a two-candidate runoff election, the defects or paradoxes developed in our story apply also to the common plurality-runoff scheme.

The story's four paradoxes are summarized here for reference and for readers who may wish to test them on their own.

NO-SHOW PARADOX: *The addition of identical ballots with candidate x ranked last may change the winner from another candidate to x.*

Peter C. Fishburn and Steven J. Brams, "Paradoxes of Preferential Voting," *Mathematics Magazine* 56: 4 (September 1983): 207-214. Reprinted with permission of the publisher.

THWARTED-MAJORITIES PARADOX: *A candidate who can defeat every other candidate in direct-comparison majority votes may lose the election.*

MULTIPLE-DISTRICTS PARADOX: *A candidate can win in each district separately, yet lose the general election in the combined districts.*

MORE-IS-LESS PARADOX: *If the winner were ranked higher by some voters, all else unchanged, then another candidate might have won.*

Following the story, we shall discuss general problems confronting voting schemes and mention interesting mathematical work on the subject. We then return to preferential voting to illustrate two other paradoxes that arise only in more complex situations. We conclude with a note on paradox probabilities.

A Funny Thing Happened on the Way to the Polls

Mr. and Mrs. Smith's car broke down on the way to the polls just before closing time. The Smiths were intensely interested in a tight race for mayor of their town among Mrs. Bitt, Mr. Huff and Dr. Wogg.

The ballot for mayor asked each voter to rank the three candidates from first choice to third choice. The townspeople knew that the election would be decided by the simple preferential voting method, which had been instituted by local referendum some years earlier. Everyone in town was pleased that they used such a sensible procedure for electing the head of their local government.

The Smiths were of one mind about the candidates. They favoured Bitt to Huff to Wogg, and therefore both would have voted BHW. Although they liked Mrs. Bitt best, they were almost as fond of Mr. Huff but

disliked and mistrusted Dr. Wogg. Much to their regret, the Smith's car problem prevented from from making it to the polls before closing time.

Many of their fellow townspeople did. When Mrs. Smith opened her newspaper the next morning, her eye was caught by a headline proclaiming "Huff Elected as 1608 Go to Polls." She and her husband were delighted that Dr. Wogg had not won. They did feel a twinge of regret that their friend, Mrs. Bitt, was beaten. Perhaps their votes would have made a difference.

As Mrs. Smith read on, she noted that no candidate had gotten enough first-place votes to win outright. Mrs. Bitt had been scratched because she had the fewest first-place votes, and Mr. Huff went on to beat Dr. Wogg by a plurality of 917 to 691.

Toward the end of the article, on an inside page, Mrs. Smith read the tabulation of how the 1608 voters cast their ballots shown in Figure 1.

Figure 1

Totals	Rankings	H over W	W over H
417	BHW	417	0
82	BWH	0	82
143	HBW	143	0
357	HWB	357	0
285	WBH	0	285
324	WHB	0	324
1608		917	691

It made her feel good that she and her husband would have voted with the largest of the six groups. As the article had noted earlier, Mrs. Bitt barely lost out on the initial count since Bitt, Huff and Wogg had first-place tallies of 499 (417 + 82), 500 (143 + 357), and 609 (285 + 324) respectively.

Mrs. Smith realized when she read this that Mr. Huff rather than Mrs. Bitt would have been scratched if she and her husband had voted. At least their friend, Mrs. Bitt, would have made the "runoff" if their car had not broken down.

Before leaving for her job as an actuary with an insurance company headquartered in the next town, Mrs. Smith decided to see what would have happened if she and her husband had voted. Her tabulation is shown in Figure 2.

Figure 2

Totals	Rankings	B over W	W over B
419	BHW	419	0
82	BWH	82	0
143	HBW	143	0
357	HWB	0	357
285	WBH	0	285
324	WHB	0	324
1610		644	966

To her chagrin, she saw that their votes would have made Dr. Wogg the winner even though he was ranked last on their ballots! This so shocked her that she checked her figures three times. When they refused to change, it hit her: *the whole thing depended on who was scratched after the initial count.* With Bitt out, Huff wins; with Huff out, Wogg wins. Even if 300 more people had voted BHW, Dr. Wogg would still have won.

Mrs. Smith was beginning to wonder if the town's procedure for electing a mayor was that sensible after all.

That evening, while reviewing her figures again, Mrs. Smith became aware of another curious fact. She realized that the winner, Mr. Huff, would have beaten either Mrs. Bitt (824 to 784) or Dr. Wogg (917 to 691) in a direct

vote between the two. The "majority candidate"—that is, the candidate who could have beaten each of the others in direct pairwise votes—had indeed won. However, if the Smiths had voted, then not only would their last choice have won but the winner, Dr. Wogg, would not have been the candidate favoured in separate pairwise contests to each of the other candidates.

At this point, Mrs. Smith suspected that their election procedure might be more than a little flawed and wondered if further probing might uncover other unusual possibilities. She vowed to make time for this over the weekend.

The Smith's town had two voting districts, called East and West. When the weekend came round, Mrs. Smith decided to compare the outcome with what might have happened in the separate districts. She suspected that the winner, Mr. Huff, might have lost in one if not both districts. The paper had reported that 588 people voted in the East and 1020 had voted in the West. Moreover, it gave the East-West splits shown in Figure 3.

Figure 3

Totals	Rankings	East	West
417	BHW	160	257
82	BWH	0	82
143	HBW	143	0
357	HWB	0	357
285	WBH	0	285
324	WHB	285	39
1608		588	1020

Applying precisely the same election rule used for the general election to the East and the West separately, Mrs. Smith found that Mrs. Bitt would have won in both districts! She felt this was truly amazing since both Huff and Wogg had sizable majorities over Bitt in the overall electorate, so there was no way that Mrs. Bitt could have won in the combined districts.

Moreover, as Mrs. Smith noted, a multiple-district winner like Mrs. Bitt could be a "minority candidate" in the sense that this candidate would be defeated by every other candidate in direct-comparison votes. She also realized that this anomaly could arise only when different candidates were scratched on the first rounds in the several "district elections." In fact, Huff was scratched in the East, whereas Wogg was scratched in the West.

Mrs. Smith was now convinced that she had a very strong case against the supposedly sensible system used to elect the mayor of their town. At her request, the chairman of the local Election Board called a special meeting of the board to review her findings.

On the night before the board meeting, as she was going over her figures, Mrs. Smith discovered another irregularity. While pondering what would have occurred if she and her husband had voted (see Figure 2), she realized that if two or more of the 82 voters with ranking BWH had moved Wogg into first place (WBH), then Bitt rather than Huff would have been scratched and Huff rather than Wogg would have won. In other words, an increase in support for Dr. Wogg would have changed him from a winner to a loser! Extraordinary, thought Mrs. Smith, as she prepared her flip charts for her presentation to the Election Board.

The next day Mrs. Smith so impressed the board that they decided to appoint a select panel—chaired by Mrs. Smith, of course—to recommend a better election procedure. In particular, the board charged the panel with devising a system that would avoid all the paradoxes uncovered by Mrs. Smith.

At the panel's first meeting, one member suggested that they retain ranked voting but simply use the ballots to determine which of

the several candidates was the majority candidate. He explained that this would directly resolve the Thwarted-Majorities Paradox and, moreover, would also take care of Mrs. Smith's other three paradoxes.

Mrs. Smith responded that this was a very good idea up to a point, but that it would not solve all their problems. She had been reading up on the subject and proceeded to tell the panel about the most famous paradox of them all, variously known as "Condorcet's phenomenon" [4], the "paradox of voting," and the "paradox of cyclical majorities."

Condorcet's phenomenon occurs when every candidate is beaten by some other candidate under direct-comparison voting. Mrs. Smith pointed out that this was not the case in their election, but it was certainly possible. For example, if 1600 total ballots had been cast, with

400	for	BHW
500	for	WBH
700	for	HWB,

then Bitt beats Huff 900 to 700, Huff beats Wogg 1100 to 500, and Wogg beats Bitt 1200 to 400.

At this point, another panel member suggested that perhaps their problems would vanish if they used the method that his lodge used to choose its president. This method awards 2 points to a first-place vote, 1 point to a second-place vote, and 0 points to a third-place vote. The winner is the candidate with the most points. He noted that it could be extended in a straightforward way when there are more than three candidates.

The panel determined that this point-scoring system—sometimes referred to as Borda's "method of marks" [2], [5]—would resolve all of Mrs. Smith's paradoxes, with the possible exception of the Thwarted-Majorities Paradox. A quick review of the election data showed that the majority candidate, Mr. Huff, would have won under the point-scoring system. However, the panel also noticed that if 50 or so BHW voters had preferred Wogg to Huff and voted BWH, then despite the fact that Mr. Huff would remain the majority candidate, Dr. Wogg would win under the point-scoring system (see Figure 4).

Figure 4

Totals	Rankings	*B* Points	*H* Points	*W* Points
367	BHW	734	367	0
132	BWH	264	0	132
143	HBW	143	286	0
357	HWB	0	714	357
285	WBH	285	0	570
324	WHB	0	324	648
1608		1426	1691	1707

Confused and tired, the panel agreed that they had done enough for one meeting. Their next meeting was set for the following Wednesday.

Problems of Voting Systems

We end our story at this point because, in a sense, it has no end. The panel could meet forever without being able to fulfill its charge from the Election Board to avoid all four paradoxes. This is because there is a metaparadox lurking in the background which, in simplified form, says that *no* election procedure can simultaneously resolve Mrs. Smith's second and third paradoxes.

Let us elaborate. We assume, as before, that voters rank the candidates from most preferred to least preferred. With a fixed number of candidates, but any potential number of voters, Young [21] (see also [22]) showed in one of the most mathematically elegant papers on the subject that in order to avoid the Multi-

ple-Districts Paradox as well as to satisfy fundamental equity conditions for voters and candidates, one must use a type of point-scoring system. In an attempt to avoid the Thwarted-Majorities Paradox, it is necessary to assign more points to a first-place vote than to a second-place vote, and so forth, which of course takes care of the No-Show and More-Is-Less Paradoxes.

However, given any set of decreasing point values for the various places, it is always possible to construct an example with a majority candidate who is not elected by the point-scoring system. In fact, nearly two hundred years ago Condorcet recognized that it is possible to construct examples with a majority candidate who is not elected by *any* point-scoring system with decreasing point values [4], [9]. For example, if there are seven voters such that

3	have	BHW
2	have	HWB
1	has	HWB
1	has	WBH,

then B has a 4-to-3 majority over each of H and W, but H beats B under *every* point-scoring system that assigns more points to a second-place vote than to a third-place vote.

Many other problems and paradoxes that plague preferential voting and other election systems seem to have surfaced only recently. The More-Is-Less Paradox, better known in the literature as the monotonicity paradox, was shown by Smith [20] to affect virtually all successive-elimination procedures based on point scoring. Further results on the monotonicity paradox appear in [10]. Within the specific context of preferential voting, the More-Is-Less Paradox and the Multiple-Districts Paradox are discussed in [6], [7].

As far as we know, the No-Show Paradox, which is closely related to the More-Is-Less Paradox, is not discussed elsewhere.

However, another No-Show Paradox seems to have been discovered many years ago [14], [17]. This other paradox says that one of the candidates elected by preferential voting could have ended up a loser if additional people who ranked him in first place had actually voted. An example of this paradox appears in the next section.

The paradoxes discussed here and elsewhere [9], [15] reveal only the surface effects of deeper aspects of aggregation structures, such as those developed by young [21]. Recent work on these structures was stimulated in large measure by Kenneth Arrow's classic impossibility theorem [1]. This theorem shows that a few simple and appealing conditions for aggregating diverse rankings into a consensus ranking are incompatible. Numerous variants of Arrow's theorem now exist [8], [13], [19], and these have been joined by related results [11], [13], [16], [18] which show that virtually every sensible election procedure for multicandidate elections is vulnerable to strategic manipulation by voters. In other words, there will be situations in which some voters can benefit by voting contrary to their true, or sincere, preferences.

An example of the latter phenomenon occurs in our story of the Smiths. If they had voted their true preference order, BHW, then Dr. Wogg would have won under preferential voting. However, if they had voted HBW, or any other order that did not have Mrs. Bitt in first place, then Mr. Huff would have won. Hence, by voting strategically (i.e., falsely), the Smiths would have helped to elect their second choice (H) rather than their last choice (W).

More paradoxes of preferential voting

Additional flaws in preferential voting can arise only when there are more than three contenders. We shall illustrate two of these after describing a general, and widely used, procedure for preferential voting.

In the general case, voters rank the candidates from most preferred to least preferred on their ballots. To be elected, a candidate must receive a quota q of weighted votes.

Each voter begins with voting weight 1. First-place votes are tallied for each candidate; those with q or more are elected. If c' are elected on this first round and $0 < c' < c$, then the weight of each voter whose first choice was elected is decreased from 1 to a nonnegative number (0 if there is no "surplus" over quota) so that the sum of all weights becomes $n - qc'$. Elected candidates are removed from the ballots, and new rounds follow until c candidates are elected, as described below.

After removal of the elected candidates, unelected candidates move up in the ballot rankings to fill in top places, and the process is repeated with a new, weighted tally of unelected candidates now in first place. Again, q is used as the quota for election. The process continues until either all c seats have been filled, or no unelected candidate gets at least q weighted votes in the latest tally. In the latter case, the candidate with the *smallest* weighted first-place tally is scratched, ballot rankings (but not voter weights) are revised accordingly, and the process continues until c seats are filled.

Instead of our earlier story, suppose now that Bitt, Foxx, Huff and Wogg are vying for two seats on the town council, and that 100 people vote as follows:

34	BHFW
25	FBHW
26	HWBF
9	WBFH
6	WHFB

The quota is 34, so Bitt is elected first. Since exactly 34 people voted for Bitt in first place, the weights of these voters are reduced to 0, leaving

25	FHW
26	HWF
9	WFH
6	WHF

Since none of the others reaches the quota, Wogg is scratched. Then Foxx, who has 34 (25 + 9) votes to 32 (26 + 6) for Huff, wins the second seat.

Now suppose five more Foxx supporters (FBHW) had voted, giving

34	BHFW
30	FBHW
26	HWBF
9	WBFH
6	WHFB

The new quota is (105/3) + 1 = 36. Since no candidate reaches the quota, Wogg is scratched:

34	BHF
9	BFH
30	FBH
26	HBF
6	HFB

At this point Bitt passes the quota with 43 (34 + 9) votes and is elected as before. Since Bitt exceeded the quota by 7 first-place votes, each of her 43 supporters retains 7/43 of a vote, giving aggregates of

5.5	HF	
1.5	FH	from Bitt's surplus
30	FH	
26	HF	
6	HF	

Since Huff now surpasses the quota with 37.5 (26 + 6 + 5.5), he becomes the second candidate elected. Thus Foxx, a winner in the first case, becomes a loser when five more voters show up with him in first place.

Our final paradox was suggested by a statement on a recent ballot of a professional society that listed eight candidates for four

seats on the society's Nominating Committee [3]. The election was conducted by preferential voting. Society members were advised to mark candidates in order of preference until they were ignorant or indifferent concerning candidates whom they did not rank. The preferential voting system described earlier is easily modified to account for partial rankings: if a voter's marked candidates are removed or scratched before all seats are filled, that voter is then treated as if he never voted in the first place.

The ballot statement alluded to in the preceding paragraph claimed that "there is no tactical advantage to be gained by marking few candidates." Figure 2, suitably modified, shows that this is false. Suppose again that Foxx is in the race for two council seats along with Bitt, Huff, and Wogg, and that votes are precisely the same as shown in Figure 2, except that Foxx is the first choice of all 1610 voters:

Totals	Rankings
419	FBHW
82	FBWH
143	FHBW
357	FHWB
285	FWBH
324	FWHB
1610	

Then Foxx wins a seat, and matters proceed as before when he is removed from the ballots, giving Dr. Wogg the other seat.

But suppose that Mr. and Mrs. Smith had voted just F instead of FBHW, i.e., had voted only for their first choice. Then, after Foxx is removed, we revert to Figure 1, where Mr. Huff wins the other seat. By voting only for their first choice, the Smiths prevent their last choice from winning the second seat.

This example provides a second instance of how some voters might induce preferred outcomes by misrepresenting their true preferences. In the present case, misrepresentation takes the form of a deliberate truncation of one's ranking rather than a false but complete ranking.

Paradox probabilities

Although virtually all voting systems for elections with three or more candidates can produce counterintuitive and disturbing outcomes, preferential voting is especially vulnerable because of its sequential elimination and vote-transfer provisions. Nevertheless, this system is still widely used in several countries.

Defenders of preferential voting—and there have been many over the past century—might argue that the paradoxes of preferential voting are not a problem because they occur so infrequently in practice. They would, we presume, claim that a few contrived examples should not deter us from using a carefully refined system that has proved its worth in countless elections.

Although probabilities of paradoxes have been estimated in other settings [9], we know of no attempts to assess the likelihoods of the paradoxes of preferential voting discussed above, and would propose this as an interesting possibility for investigation. Is it indeed true that serious flaws in preferential voting such as the No-Shows Paradox and the More-Is-Less Paradox are sufficiently rare as to cause no practical concern?

References

[1] ARROW, K.J. 1963. *Social Choice and Individual Values* 2e. New York: Wiley.

[2] DE BORDA, JEAN-CHARLES. 1781. *Mémoire sur les élections au scrutin.* Paris: Histoire de l'Academie Royale des Sciences.

[3] BRAMS, S.J. 1982. "The AMS nominating system is vulnerable to truncation of preferences." Notices *Amer. Math. Soc.* 29: 136-138.

[4] CONDORCET, MARQUIS DE. 1785. *Essai sur l'application de l'analyse à la probabilité des décisions rendues à la pluralité des voix.* Paris.

[5] DE GRAZIA, A. 1953. "Mathematical derivation of an election system." *Isis* 44: 42-51.

[6] DORON, G. 1979. "The Hare voting system is inconsistent." *Political Studies* 27: 283-286.

[7] DORON, G., and R. KRONICK. 1977. "Single transferable vote: an example of a perverse social choice function." *American Journal of Political Science* 21: 303-311.

[8] FISHBURN, P.C. 1973. *The Theory of Social Choice.* Princeton University Press.

[9] FISHBURN, P.C. 1974. "Paradoxes of voting." *American Political Science Review* 68: 537-546.

[10] FISHBURN, P.C. 1982. "Monotonicity paradoxes in the theory of elections." *Discrete Applied Mathematics* 4: 119-134.

[11] GIBBARD, A. 1973. "Manipulation of voting schemes: a general result." *Econometrica* 41: 587-601.

[12] HARE, T. 1861. *The Election of Representatives, Parliamentary and Municipal: A Treatise.* London: Longman, Green.

[13] KELLY, J.S. 1978. *Arrow Impossibility Theorems.* New York: Academic Press.

[14] MEREDITH, J.C. 1913. *Proportional Representation in Ireland.* Dublin.

[15] NIEMI, R.G., and W.H. RIKER. 1976. "The choice of voting systems." *Scientific American* 234: 21-27.

[16] PATTANAIK, P.K. 1978. *Strategy and Group Choice.* New York: North-Holland.

[17] *Report of the Royal Commission Appointed to Enquire into Electoral Systems.* 1910. London: HMSO.

[18] SATTERTHWAITE, M.A. 1975. "Strategy-proofness and Arrow's conditions: existence and correspondence theorems for voting procedures and social welfare functions." *Journal of Economic Theory* 10: 187-217.

[19] SEN, A.K. 1970. *Collective Choice and Social Welfare.* San Francisco: Holden-Day.

[20] SMITH, J.H. 1973. "Aggregation of preferences with variable electorate." *Econometrica* 41: 1027-1041.

[21] YOUNG, H.P. 1975. "Social choice scoring functions." *SIAM Journal of Applied Mathematics* 28: 824-838.

[22] YOUNG, H.P., and A. LEVENGLICK. 1978. "A consistent extension of Condorcet's election principle." *SIAM Journal of Applied Mathematics* 35: 285-300.

33. ON THE OUTCOME OF THE 1983 CONSERVATIVE LEADERSHIP CONVENTION: How They Shot Themselves in the Other Foot

Terrence J. Levesque

INTRODUCTION

One of the most interesting and important propositions of social choice theory is that sometimes the rules which we use to make collective decisions interact with our preferences to produce perverse or nonoptimal outcomes.[1] There are profiles of voters' preferences for three or more alternatives that produce a "winner" which can be defeated by one or more other alternatives when majoritarian voting methods are used. Consider, for example, the three-voter, three-alternative case:

Voter	Preference for Alternatives		
1	A	B	C
2	B	C	A
3	C	A	B

where the alternatives A, B and C are ranked from most to least preferred (reading across from left to right). It is easy to show that if the winner is determined by pairing alternatives and putting the majority winner for a pair against the remaining alternative the outcome depends on how the agenda is structured. For example, if A is pitted against B at the first stage, A, being preferred by a majority to B, goes on to meet C which wins the contest at the second stage. But note that a majority

Terrence J. Levesque, "On the Outcome of the 1983 Conservative Leadership Convention: How They Shot Themselves in the Other Foot," *Canadian Journal of Political Science* 16 (December 1983): 779-784. Reprinted with permission of the author.

prefers B, which was not chosen, to C, which was. In this example, which is known as the "paradox of voting," there is no unambiguous victor: which alternative is chosen ultimately depends on which two are paired at the first stage. The example is special, but we may observe something of more general applicability from it, which is that rules of selection and voters' preferences may interact to yield a "winner" which is considered by a majority of voters to be inferior to another alternative.

I contend in this note that voting at the 1983 federal Conservative leadership convention probably offers an example of just such an interaction. Specifically, I conclude, under quite plausible assumptions about the convention delegates' preferences, that the Conservatives elected their second most preferred candidate from among the top three choices. Their most preferred candidate was forced off the ballot by the party's choice rule. They may very well have "shot themselves in the other foot" for want of a better choice rule because the decision they finally faced ignored the obvious compromise between two conflicting coalitions.

ANALYSIS

I begin by describing the choice rule and my assumptions about delegate preferences. Subsequently, I use these assumptions to develop an ordering of the three front-running candidates. This ordering shows that the outcome of the convention was nonoptimal from the delegates' viewpoint. I also demonstrate that this conclusion is robust with respect to a wide range of assumptions about delegate preferences.

The choice rule is majoritarian because the winner must acquire at least a simple majority of the delegates' votes. The other salient features of the rule are described in the following excerpts from a report of the party's elections committee:[2]

> 17. *Candidate Withdrawal Rules during Balloting*
>   (a) Voluntary withdrawals by candidates must be communicated in writing to the Chief Electoral Officer before the time set for the public announcement of the names of the candidates eligible for the next ballot.
>   (b) No withdrawal speeches will be permitted nor will the contents of candidate withdrawal notices be announced publicly.
> 18. Automatic elimination of candidates will occur in the following cases:
>   (a) On the first ballot:
>   i. all candidates who did not receive at least seventy-five (75) votes.
>   ii. where all candidates receive seventy-five (75) votes or more, the candidate or candidates who receive the least number of votes.
>   (b) On the second and subsequent ballots:
>   i. all candidates who did not receive at least seventy-five (75) votes.
>   ii. where all candidates receive seventy-five (75) votes or more, the candidate who receives the least number of votes.
>   iii. in the case of a tie for the least number of votes, the candidates who received an equal number of votes will be eligible for the next ballot.
> 19. Balloting shall continue until one candidate obtains an absolute majority of the votes cast in a ballot.

Table 1 presents the results of the four ballots of the 1983 Conservative leadership convention. Three candidates, namely Clark, Crosbie and Mulroney, were eligible to proceed to the third ballot. Crosbie polled the lowest total on that ballot and was forced off the fourth ballot according to the choice rule.

I require some assumptions about the delegates' second and third choices among the top three candidates in order to construct a profile. There is some information from the fourth ballot that permits a characterization of the Crosbie supporters. Barring the unlikely event that switches occurred between Clark and Mulroney supporters, the Crosbie supporters ranked the top three candidates as follows (numbers of delegates follow rankings):

Crosbie, Clark, Mulroney	286
Crosbie, Mulroney, Clark	572

These rankings are actually based on the Crosbie campaign's own estimate that their supporters would vote for Mulroney by a 2:1 margin, which proved to be quite accurate. I initially assumed that the Clark and Mulroney suppor-

Table 1   Ballots of the 1983 Conservative Leadership Convention

Candidate	First ballot	Second ballot	Third ballot	Fourth ballot
Mulroney	874	1021	1036	1584
Clark	1091	1085	1058	1325
Crosbie	639	781	858	
Crombie	116	67		
Wilson	144			
Pocklington	102			
Gamble	17			
Fraser	5			
Totals	2991	2955	2954	2928

Note: Totals include spoiled ballots. Wilson and Pocklington voluntarily withdrew after the first ballot.

ters all ranked Crosbie second. I relax this assumption later to test the tolerance of my conclusions with respect to different characterizations of delegate preferences.

It seems clear from accounts of the campaign and media coverage of the convention that Mulroney's support was based heavily on delegates who wanted a change from Clark's leadership; such delegates probably would have supported Crosbie against Clark almost unanimously. I believe that the apparent antipathy between Clark and Mulroney that appeared in their conflict over Quebec delegates would have led most Clark supporters to vote for Crosbie over Mulroney. The remainder of the delegates who voted on the third ballot are thus characterized by the following rankings:

Clark, Crosbie, Mulroney	1058
Mulroney, Crosbie, Clark	1036

If the voting method of pairwise majority (the Condorcet procedure)[3] is used on the third ballot and if the profile of delegate preferences is that summarized above, then Crosbie defeats each of Clark and Mulroney by margins of more than 800 votes. These margins suggest that there is latitude for relaxing my assumptions about delegates' preferences without affecting the conclusion that Crosbie was the convention's most preferred candidate and his election was blocked by the choice rule. Since Mulroney ultimately defeated Clark, the convention's ranking of the top three candidates seems to have been:

Crosbie, Mulroney, Clark.

Crosbie is the Condorcet choice because in pairwise contests with each of the remaining candidates he wins. Crosbie would also win if each delegate had cast one vote for each of his top two choices at the third-ballot stage, with the winner being the candidate who secured the largest number of votes; the method

known as "approval voting" would permit voting for two candidates. Finally, Crosbie would win if the delegates awarded points to each candidate in ascending order of preference—say, three points to the most preferred and one point to the least preferred with the middle candidate receiving two points. The winner is the candidate with the largest point total and is called the Borda-rule winner.

The analysis thus far might be challenged with respect to the assumption that Clark and Mulroney supporters unanimously preferred Crosbie as their second choice. In particular, there was some question about support for Crosbie from the Quebec delegates because of his unilingualism. Suppose that x of Mulroney's supporters actually preferred Clark to Crosbie and y of Clark's supporters preferred Mulroney to Crosbie. How large can x and y be before the convention's ranking described above no longer holds?

The complete delegate preference profile with the two new Mulroney and Clark delegate types is:

Crosbie, Clark, Mulroney	286
Crosbie, Mulroney, Clark	572
Clark, Mulroney, Crosbie	x
Clark, Crosbie, Mulroney	1058-x
Mulroney, Clark, Crosbie	y
Mulroney, Crosbie, Clark	1036-y

Crosbie defeats Clark in a pairwise contest if

$$858 + 1036\text{-}y > 1058 + y,$$

and Crosbie defeats Mulroney if

$$858 + 1058\text{-}x > 1036 + x.$$

Hence, as many as 440 of Clark's supporters could have preferred Mulroney to Crosbie and as many as 418 of Mulroney's supporters could have preferred Clark to Crosbie without changing the convention's ranking of the candidates.

CONCLUSIONS

The outcome of the 1983 Conservative leadership campaign depended on an interaction between the choice rule and the delegates' preferences in such a way that the convention did not pick its most preferred candidate. The choice rule was based only on the first-choice preferences of the delegates and hence, because of the lowest-vote exclusion rule, the balloting was ultimately biased against the candidate who represented a compromise between the two front runners, neither of whom was the first choice of a majority of the convention. Even though one-third of the delegates selected Clark and Mulroney as their first choice, up to a third also viewed each of them as their last choice. It is doubtful, therefore, that the final ballot between Clark and Mulroney immediately solved the Conservatives' unity problems. It seems equally apparent that had the choice rule not acted as an obstacle, Crosbie's almost certain election would have had an immediate salutary effect.

If there is a prescription in the preceding analysis, it must be that organizations that have to rely on voting to make collective decisions would do well to attend to the principles of designing choice rules articulated in social choice theory.

Notes

1. See, for example, William H. Riker, *Liberalism Against Populism* (San Francisco: W.H. Freeman, 1982).
2. Progressive Conservative Party of Canada, "1983 Leadership Convention Elections Committee Progress Report No. 1" (dated March 11, 1983; multilith), 2-3.
3. See Riker, *Liberalism Against Populism*, for description of this and other methods of election referred to in this paragraph.

34. SOCIAL CHOICE THEORY AND THE RECONSTRUCTION OF ELECTIONS: A Comment on Levesque's Analysis

Peter Woolstencroft

The import of social choice theory lies in its examination of the various choice rules available for the recording and weighing of preferences in an election and the consequences of those rules for democratic political life. A choice rule is a method for aggregating individual preferences into a collective determination. Choice rules vary in their capacities to maximize (and minimize) various values desired in a system of decision-making. They also vary in their capacities to reveal information about preferences.

Summation of preferences according to a choice rule may create a unique result; another choice rule would have produced a different result. That is, procedural accident determines the winner rather than political will. Even though individuals in the system may be rational in their political behaviour, the lack of a faithful reproduction of their preferences in the course of the aggregation for preferences may produce a perverse result. To the extent that this happens over time, democracy—which relies upon the vote as its fundamental means of taking into account preferences—is problematic.[1]

In his note, Levesque argues that the 1983 Progressive Conservative convention "probably" presents a case of nonoptimal choice inasmuch as the party's eventual winner was not the most preferred candidate, if one considers the delegates' (assumed) first, second and third rank-order preferences for the candidates who were on the third ballot.[2] On the last ballot, then, Brian Mulroney won because John Crosbie's supporters were forced to choose between Mulroney and Joe Clark and did so by a margin of approximately two to one. Yet the supporters of each of the two leading candidates—if the opportunity had been there—probably would have preferred Crosbie over the other candidate. Another set of choice rules, in which those second and third preferences were taken into account, likely would have produced victory for Crosbie.

Levesque's note is important in two respects. First, he identifies an instance of a phenomenon where few empirical cases are documented.[3] Secondly, he raises the question of the appropriateness of existing election procedures and whether suitable alternatives are available.

Without the empirical evidence at hand, one cannot contest the validity of Levesque's assumptions about the rank-order preferences of delegates. Levesque's calculations and conclusions, within the scope of his assumptions as stated, are perfectly reasonable. Indeed, for the purposes of my comments here, these assumptions will be taken as valid. It will be argued, however, that Levesque's conclusions about the likelihood of a Crosbie victory, in the event that other choice rules had been in

Peter Woolstencroft, "Social Choice Theory and the Reconstruction of Elections: A Comment on Levesque's Analysis," *Canadian Journal of Political Science* 16 (December 1983): 785-789. Reprinted with permission of the author.

place, are overstated and, moreover, that the retroactive application of various choice rules is a form of abstracted empiricism that neglects the linkages between institutional contexts and behaviour. Following that interpretation, it will be argued that decisions about which choice rules should govern collective decision-making processes are more complex than is suggested by Levesque in his claim that "the principles of designing choice rules articulated in social choice theory" should be followed.

Levesque's three-alternative choice rules depend on the delegates' rank-order preferences for the candidates. No consideration is given to the distances between these rankings; in effect, then, these distances are assumed to be equal. Such an assumption is not likely to be valid. Assume, however, that one has a cardinal utility scale from 1 to 10, low to high. Assume that each delegate is asked to assign to each candidate a number which represents the strength of the delegate's commitment to or degree of support for the candidates. A delegate undecided between two candidates, but positively inclined to both, might assign the candidates scores of eight, the others much lower. Another delegate, also undecided but less enthusiastic, might give scores of five, the others lower. And yet another, ardently committed to one candidate and hostile to all others, might assign a 10 to the highly-favoured candidate and 1's and 2's to the rest. If the choice rule is that the winner is the candidate with a plurality (or a majority) of the total cardinal utility scores, it does not take much ingenuity or mathematical dexterity to construct preference-ordering profiles for the delegates in which each of the three leading candidates would win.

The point is that the interaction between choice rules and delegates' preference could produce a number of different results. This, of course, is consistent with social choice theory. However, the fundamental question is whether

it is warrantable to impose various choice rules upon a system of behaviour such as a political convention and expect delegates' preferences to remain constant. What is being suggested, then, is that there is a very strong possibility that the delegates' rank-order preferences for and evaluations of the candidates were in good measure influenced by the convention's choice rules.

The delegates, as they went about their business of evaluating the candidates and determining whom to support, did so in light of the requirements of the choice rules (which, given their common character, can be reasonably assumed to have been widely understood). Delegates did not have to rank-order their preferences nor did they have to carry with them a cardinal utility scale. They were located in an adversarial system. This would encourage delegates to see first choices in positive terms and other candidates in negative terms. This tendency would have been exacerbated by the combative Clark/Mulroney delegate-selection contests in Quebec, and by the number of constituencies across the country in which the candidates' slates fought each other vigorously. Delegates, for the most part, would tend to believe that their first choices would be on the last ballot. Mulroney and Clark supporters certainly had plausible grounds for so believing, given each candidate's strong Quebec base. As delegates neared the time of the convention positive and negative evaluations would become accentuated for many understandable reasons, not the least of which is the system of voting which pits one candidate against another.[4]

The argument, then, is that the delegates were placed in a particular system of evaluation and contestation. This was a system of first choices, both institutionally and psychologically, which was influenced to a considerable extent by the convention's choice rules. These, then, were a condition for the delegates' behaviour. To impose the results of other choice rules upon that behaviour is to assume no interaction between an institutional context and behaviour. Other choice rules likely would have changed the process of delegate selection (more coalition-building) and how delegates went about judging the candidates (more emphasis on the relative strengths and weaknesses of the candidates, particularly second—and third—choices). To make counterfactuals explicit not only points to analytic complexity, of course, but also suggests that the lifting out of context of a pattern of behaviour, as is done when various choice rules are applied to a political convention's ballot results, is not something that is done without a price being paid by, or even violence being done to, the object under study.

The claim for the linkages between choice rules and behaviour leads to the question of appropriate choice rules for political conventions. The alleged necessity for reform is undercut by the lack of estimation by Levesque of the proportion of convention decisions in which there were arguably nonoptimal results. Does one convention warrant change? Unfortunately, moreover, Levesque is not forthcoming about which principles for designing choice rules should be followed in the event that there is a continuing problem with convention choice rules. It is noteworthy that Riker has recently succinctly pinpointed the dilemma that in fact exists within social choice theory. A system of simple majority decision between two candidates means the elimination of others through some necessarily arbitrary rule. However, "no particular decision methods for three or more alternatives can be unequivocally demonstrated to be fair or reasonable. The problem is that we cannot prove that any method truly and fairly amalgamates the judgments of citizens simply because we do not know what 'truly and fairly amalgamates' means."[5] That judgment, of course, is consistent with Arrow's theorem: any system of vot-

ing that fairly aggregates preferences has the possibility of creating a paradoxical outcome.

Canadian political conventions are relatively unstructured situations in which delegates are more or less free to do what they want. The lack of primaries and the existence of the secret ballot probably preclude the development of the structured conventions found in the United States. In a multi-candidate convention, it is reasonable to expect that, after the first ballot, a large number of delegates will have to choose between abstention and voting for candidates they did not before support (in 1983, over one-third had to do so). Others have commented on the rapidity and uncertainty with which delegates (and candidates, for that matter) have to make decisions after the first ballot's results are announced, and have proposed a number of measures to improve the probability of "delegate rationality" by increasing the amount of information and time available for delegates' decision-making.[6] The argument against these reforms is that the ability of party elites to influence delegates would be enhanced, as would the tendency of candidates to strike deals. The open character of conventions would be diminished.[7]

A similar debate is contained in the question about appropriate choice rules. Implementation of choice rules that would measure and incorporate rank-order preferences of delegates in the ballot-count would force delegates to confront directly the kinds of decisions they may be called upon to make. The role of party elites would likely be accentuated, as the organization which is able to produce the most optimal electoral result would clearly be in the strongest position. Further, as Riker has observed, any system of voting is subject to strategic voting, so that any election result is subject to doubt about its meaning.[8] Although strategic voting occurs in the present system, its incidence is "clearly the exception rather than the rule in the dynamics of Canadian convention politics."[9] Any change in choice rules must be evaluated in terms of the desirability and the likelihood of increasing the role of elites and the pattern of strategic voting in the decision-making sequences characteristic of conventions.

Notes

1. William H. Riker, *Liberalism Against Populism* (San Francisco: W.H. Freeman, 1982).

2. Terrence J. Levesque, "On the Outcome of the 1983 Conservative Leadership Convention: How They Shot Themselves in the Other Foot," *Canadian Journal of Political Science* 16 (1983): 779-784.

3. For a similar analysis, see Richard A. Joslyn, "The Impact of Decision Rules in Multi-Candidate Campaigns: The Case of the 1972 Democratic Presidential Nomination," *Public Choice* 30 (1976): 1-17.

4. Krause and LeDuc, in their analysis of the 1976 Progressive Conservative leadership convention, have argued that while some delegates "may order the preferences from the beginning.... there is little evidence that most delegates approach voting in this way" (Robert Krause and Lawrence LeDuc, "Voting Behaviour and Electoral Strategies in the Progressive Conservative Leadership Convention of 1976," *Canadian Journal of Political Science* 12 [1979]: 132). John Courtney, on the other hand, has argued that delegates, as politically active and well-informed people, are capable of rank-ordering preferences, and could do so if asked or required to (John C. Courtney, *The Selection of National Party Leaders in Canada* [Toronto: Macmillan, 1973], 208).

5. Riker, *Liberalism Against Populism*, 65-66.

6. D.V. Smiley, "The National Party Leadership Convention in Canada: A Preliminary Analysis," *Canadian Journal of Political Science* 1 (1968): 395-398.

7. Courtney, *The Selection of National Party Leaders in Canada*, 206-207.

8. Riker, *Liberalism Against Populism*, 141-168.

9. Krause and LeDuc, "Voting Behaviour and Electoral Strategies in the Progressive Conservative Leadership Convention of 1976," 102.

35. LIBERALISM, POPULISM AND THE THEORY OF SOCIAL CHOICE

William H. Riker

A. THE ADEQUACY OF VOTING

In the democratic tradition, theorists have seldom raised questions about the reliability of the voting mechanism in amalgamating individual values into a social decision. Many writers have indeed feared tyranny by the majority. But their fear has rarely, so far as I can discover, led them to question the adequacy of the way majorities are made.

Fear of majority tyranny is a fear that the values of the "majority" may be morally scarce and that enforcement of them will deprive the "minority" of its values. This fear has led some writers (from gentle Christians like T.S. Eliot to modern tyrants like Lenin or Mao) to reject democracy altogether. Others have argued that, to minimize the danger, on the more important political issues an extraordinary majority ought to be required. And still others (following the lead of Madison) have defended democracy by showing that majorities are temporary, arguing that the majority is not likely to tyrannize over people who may themselves be on top after the next election.

Given the last argument, the most frequently uttered defense of democracy against the charge of majority tyranny, one would expect traditional theorists to recognize that majorities are at best temporary artifacts and therefore to wonder whether these artifacts are well or poorly made. Unfortunately, very little such speculation has occurred, except on the part of those, from A.V. Dicey to Anthony Downs, who have recognized that all majorities are themselves coalitions of minorities. And even those theorists have not systematically inquired into how such coalitions work.

That, however, is precisely the question of social choice theory. Its main interpretation is that the process of compounding individual choices into a social choice does not inspire confidence in the quality of majorities or similar amalgamations for decision. I will now summarize the conclusions of the previous chapters, setting forth the difficulties with amalgamation.

Conclusion 1. If there are more than two alternatives on any issue—as is almost always the case for any reasonably free, open, and fair political system—then there exist a wide variety of methods by which the values of members may be incorporated into the social decision. For convenience, I have grouped these methods into three categories—majoritarian, positional, and utilitarian—although methods in the same category are often quite different. Unfortunately, the numerous methods do not necessarily lead to the same social outcome with the same set of individual values. Not only do majoritarian methods, for example, typically lead to different social choices from positional and utilitarian methods, but also the methods in any one category do not typically lead to identical outcomes.

The difference in methods would not occasion much difficulty for democratic theory if one method were clearly technically or morally superior to others. Yet this is not the case. A good argument can be made for the fairness or efficiency or both of most of the majoritarian or positional methods and even of the utilitarian methods—which is indeed why methods in each category have been invented and recommended. The difference among the methods is simply that they are fair or efficient in different ways because they embody different ethical principles. Unfortunately, there seems to be no way to show that one such ethical principle is morally superior to another. Consequently, there is no fundamental reason of prudence or morality for preferring the amalgamation produced by one method to the amalgamation produced by another.

The moral and prudential standoff among methods would not in itself occasion difficulty for democratic theory if "most of the time" most methods led to the same social choice from a given profile of individual values. But this is not the case. Between any pair of methods there may be agreement on the choice from a large proportion of possible profiles.[1] But it is not enough to consider agreement between pairs of methods. One ought instead to compare outcomes among all commonly used and frequently proposed methods. So far as I know, no one has attempted such a comparison. But it seems a safe conjecture that, if such a comparison were made, the proportion of social profiles from which all the compared methods produced identical results would indeed be tiny. How, then, can it be said that any particular method truly amalgamates individual values when different methods—all with distinguishable but nevertheless justifiable claims to fairness—amalgamate quite differently?

Different methods produce different results, and usually we are ignorant of just how different the results are. For most of the methods in wide use, not enough information on preference orders is collected to reveal how the actual outcome differs from outcomes that might have been selected by another method. This means that, *even if some method produces a reasonably justifiable amalgamation, we do not know it.* Suppose, for example, that a profile contains one kind of "reasonably justifiable outcome," namely, a Condorcet winner, and that many methods of amalgamation would produce that alternative as the actual outcome. Since we lack full detail on profiles, however, we do not know whether that alternative has actually been chosen by some given method. Furthermore, we do not even know whether the actual choice is "close" to being a Condorcet winner, or whether it is, by this standard, a very bad choice indeed.

[In Section 9.E] in my reconstruction of the election of 1860, it appears that methods other than plurality voting would have produced winners other than the actual choice. But of course we do not know if my reconstruction is right or, if wrong, how or where it is wrong. In the absence of the collection of complete preference orders from all voters—an impossible task—we will always be in doubt about whether a particular method has produced an outcome regarded as fair by some a priori standard of fairness, *even if all usable methods would in fact have produced the same winner.*

Any particular outcome from voting may be regarded as partially the outcome of a previous historical event, the selection of a constitution. Since the amalgamation often depends as much on this antecedent choice as on the individual values, today's social decisions on substance reflect in part yesterday's social decisions on procedures. It is hard to believe that a social choice that depends in some unknown degree on the constitution that happens to exist and in some equally unknown degree on voters' values is a fair amalgamation of those values.

It is not that any particular method of voting is unfair, because every method is in some sense fair. Rather it is that the very idea of truly and accurately amalgamating values by voting is unfair because one does not know the effect of different methods on (usually) incompletely known profiles. The claim that voting produces a fair and accurate outcome simply cannot be sustained when the method of counting partially determines the outcome of counting.

This is, then, the first conclusion: Outcomes of voting cannot, in general, be regarded as accurate amalgamations of voters' values. Sometimes they may be accurate, sometimes not; but since we seldom know which situation exists, we cannot, in general, expect accuracy. Hence we cannot expect fairness either.

Conclusion 2. Suppose, however, that the people in a society have decided to use a particular method of voting and to define as fair the outcomes produced by that method. Because of the revelations from Arrow's theorem, from Gibbard's and Satterthwait's theorems, and from Black and Newing's and Plott's and McKelvey's and Schofield's notions of equilibrium and related developments, there is no reason to suppose that one profile of individual values will always produce the same outcome with that method. Consequently, the alternative outcomes by a particular method on a particular profile cannot be said to be a fair or true amalgamation, even though the method itself is assumed to be fair. In that sense, we never know what an outcome means, whether it is a true expression of public opinion or not. Every reasonably fair method of voting can be manipulated in several ways. Since we cannot know whether manipulation has occurred, the truth and meaning of *all* outcomes is thereby rendered dubious.

One method of manipulation is strategic voting, wherein voters vote contrary to their true tastes in order to bring about an outcome more desirable than the outcome from voting truthfully. We know from Gibbard's theorem that all methods of voting are manipulable in this way. Since we can never be certain what "true tastes" are—all we ever know are revealed tastes—we can never be certain when voting is strategic. (Witness the difficulty [in Section 6.C] of interpreting votes on the Powell amendment.) Yet if strategic voting occurs, it is hard to say that the outcome is a fair or true amalgamation of voters' values, especially when the successful manipulators are a small minority. It is possible, even probable, that strategic voting is commonplace in the real world, as evidenced by the frequency of allegations of, for example, vote-trading. If so, then *all* voting is rendered uninterpretable and meaningless. Manipulated outcomes are meaningless because they are manipulated, and unmanipulated outcomes are meaningless because they cannot be distinguished from manipulated ones.

Another method of manipulation is by control of the agenda to change the outcome from what it would be in the absence of such control. We know from the theorems about path independence that all nonoligarchic methods of voting are susceptible to changing outcomes by rearranging the agenda. Indeed, from McKelvey's and Schofield's theorems we know that, except in the rare and fragile instances of equilibrium, simple majority voting can, when the agenda is appropriately manipulated, lead to *any* real possible outcome. Since we also know from a vast amount of conventional analysis of political institutions that much political dispute concerns control (and, presumably, manipulation) of the agenda, we can be fairly certain that this kind of manipulation is utterly commonplace. But of course we never know precisely when and how such manipulation occurs or succeeds. Since this manipulation is frequent but unidentified, again *all* outcomes of voting are rendered meaningless and uninterpretable.

A dynamic method of controlling the agenda is the introduction of new dimensions and issues in order to generate disequilibrium in which the previous kinds of manipulation are possible. Suppose that, by processes no individual person or oligarchy controls, the set of alternatives has been reduced to precisely two and that one of these always wins by a simple majority vote. This seems to be a stable equilibrium; yet it can be upset, dynamically, by the introduction of new dimensions and issues. If new issues result in situations vulnerable to strategic voting and manipulation of the agenda, then even stable equilibria are dynamically unstable. Again the meaning of outcomes is hard to interpret.

For most of the 60 years after 1800, Jeffersonian-Jacksonian agrarian expansionism with its implicit concomitants of slavery usually seemed to be a stable equilibrium. But it was upset and indeed repudiated in 1856 and 1860 over the issue of free soil. In 1860 it seems likely there was no Condorcet winner; but, if there were, it was almost certainly Douglas or Bell, not Lincoln. It is hard to say, then, that the most momentous election of American history was a fair or true amalgamation of individual values, mainly because the decision was thoroughly—and, [as I showed in Chapter 9,] deliberately—confused by the inclusion of several issues. The outcome probably was morally desirable, even though it involved a bloody civil war; but it is difficult to say that it was socially preferred. Slavery was not a false issue, as Polk believed. (Men in office always believe that new issues threatening them are "mischievous.") Rather, as a new issue it generated disequilibrium, the outcome of which could not be said to be a clear social choice. In this sense, *all* social decisions obtained by disrupting equilibria with new issues are not fair or true amalgamations of public opinion, even though the disruption may be socially and morally necessary and desirable.

This, then, is the second conclusion: Outcomes of any particular method of voting lack meaning because often they are manipulated amalgamations rather than fair and true amalgamations of voters' judgments and because we can never know for certain whether an amalgamation has in fact been manipulated.

B. THE REJECTION OF POPULISM

The social amalgamations of individual values are, for reasons just summarized, often inadequate—indeed meaningless—interpretations of public opinion. Furthermore, we seldom know whether to assign any particular social choice to the inadequate category. Hence *all* choices can be suspected of inadequacy. What does this conclusion imply for the two views of voting in democracy [set forth in Chapter 1]? Can either populism or liberalism stand up?

Clearly populism cannot survive. The essence of populism is this pair of propositions:

1. What the people, as a corporate entity, want ought to be social policy.
2. The people are free when their wishes are law.

Since social choice theory is a device to analyse moral (and descriptive) propositions, not an ethical theory to choose among them, social choice theory cannot illuminate the question, implied in proposition 1, of what *ought* to be public policy. But, if the notion of the popular will is itself unclear, then what the people want cannot be social policy simply because we do not and cannot know what the people want. An election tells us at most which alternative wins; it does not tell us that the winner would also have been chosen over another feasible alternative that might itself have a better claim to be the social choice. Hence falls proposition 1. And if we do not know the people's wishes, then we cannot make them free by enacting their wishes. Thus falls proposition 2.

Populism as a moral imperative depends on the existence of a popular will discovered by voting. But if voting does not discover or reveal a will, then the moral imperative evaporates because there is nothing to be commanded. If the people speak in meaningless tongues, they cannot utter the law that makes them free. Populism fails, therefore, not because it is morally wrong, but merely because it is empty.

In the history of political ideas, a similar rejection of a moral imperative on the ground that it was uninterpretable occurred in the sixteenth and seventeenth centuries when religious directives on politics lost their presumed clarity. So long as the spiritual authority of the pope was unquestioned, he could state the political content of moral and divine law. With the success of the Reformation, however, there were many conflicting voices speaking for God, no one of which was more clearly vested with divine quality than another. Thus, even though no one seriously questioned the existence of the Divinity or the authority of divine direction of human politics, the direction nevertheless failed simply because no one could be sure what the Divinity said. Modern secular political thought begins with that uncertainty. Similarly I believe that in the next generation populist claims will be rejected simply because it will be realized that, however desirable they might be, they are based on a flawed technique that renders populism unworkable.

Perhaps it will be said in defense of populism that, although there is always doubt about the meaning of any particular electoral outcome, a series of elections over time establishes a rough guide to policy. Yet even that defense cannot be sustained. It is possible that alternative x (say, some political platform) repeatedly beats alternative y (another platform) so that one is fairly certain that x has a good majority over y. But suppose x wins only because z was eliminated earlier or was suppressed by the Constitution or by the method of counting or by manipulation. What then is the status of x? If x is as precise as a motion, then one can still be fairly sure that x at least beats y. But if x is as vague as an ideology, it is far from certain that a clear decision is ever made.

In the history of American presidential elections, three long-enduring clusters of ideas have repeatedly been more or less endorsed by the voters. From 1800 to 1856, the agrarian expansionism of Jefferson and Jackson won most of the time; indeed it was clearly beaten only in 1840. From 1860 to 1928, the Republican program of commercial development won most of the time; it was clearly beaten (in popular vote, but not in the election itself) only in 1876. From 1932 to the present, Democratic welfare statism won most of the time; it was clearly beaten only in 1952, 1956, 1972, and 1980. Can it not be said that these repeatedly endorsed clusters of ideas have been, though rather vague, the true and revealed popular will? In a very narrow sense they have indeed been approved because x (one of these three clusters) has beaten some y (not always the same y) a number of times, frequently in two-party contests. But x has never won over *all* relevant alternatives. No party program has ever been approved *in general*.

The Jefferson-Jackson program of agrarian expansion was approved two-thirds of the time from 1800 to 1856; but it failed to obtain a majority whenever it was effectively shown that agrarian expansion entailed approval of slavery: in 1840, 1844, 1848, 1856, and 1860.

The election of 1852 and its aftermath are instructive. In 1852, Whigs, themselves in office, did not raise the slavery issue; the Free Soil party was weak; and the Democratic party, again united on its traditional economic platform, won by a clear majority. Democratic leaders, assuming they had a mandate, then produced the Kansas-Nebraska Act (1854), which, though ostensibly mere agrarian expansion and free soil at that, actually promoted the expansion and approval of slavery. Thereafter, and directly as a consequence, the Democratic party did not get a national majority for more than twenty years. Though this party with its policy of approval of slavery for the sake of expansion was apparently endorsed overwhelmingly in 1852, only a slight variation in its program resulted in savage repudiation in the next five elections. That point is clear: x (agrarian expansion and slavery) was approved against y (commercial development of Federalism and Whiggery) but lost by a huge margin to z (commercial development and free soil, ultimately the Republican combination).

In the next period, between 1860 and 1928, the Republican platform of commercial development usually triumphed against a dying agrarianism. But again, there was no general mandate for commercialism alone. Initially it succeeded (except in 1876, when, however, technically it did win) because it was associated with free soil; in its heyday it succeeded because, I believe, its commercial ideal was clearly linked to social welfare. When the welfare aspects were forgotten in an excess of commercialism (especially around the 1880s, when the old Democratic combination of agrarianism and repression of blacks was not yet fully rejected), the Republican party failed to maintain its majority: in 1876, 1880, 1884, 1888, 1892, 1912, and 1916. Notice that even the interlude of Wilson's presidency was occasioned by an internal Republican split that

presumably reflected Theodore Roosevelt's distaste for Taft's pure emphasis on commerce. Thus the mandate often thought to be overwhelming was at best conditional on an appeal to interest wider than commerce alone.

Finally, in the third period, from 1932 to the present, welfare statism appeared to receive a huge mandate under Franklin Roosevelt and thereafter as long as welfare rather than statism was emphasized. But whenever statism dominated, as in the wars undertaken by Truman and Johnson—wars involving huge statist compulsion of citizens in unpopular causes—then welfare statism lost to a combination of commerce and civil liberties as expressed in Eisenhower's mitigation of the military draft and Nixon's elimination of it. As the statist component of welfare statism becomes increasingly apparent in other ways besides military adventures, it may well be that welfare statism as a whole will be rejected. The victory of Ronald Reagan in 1980 may well be the beginning of a more general rejection of welfare statism.

In all three periods, then, a dominant program has been dominant only when it has been tested in one dimension. When more than one dimension has been salient to voters, majorities have disappeared, even when the second dimension is closely related to the first. Voters rejected agrarian expansion when its slavery component was emphasized. They rejected commercial development when mere commerce was emphasized at the expense of development, and they rejected welfare statism when the statist feature of militarism exceeded the welfare component of redistribution. Throughout all three periods, one cluster of ideas was repeatedly endorsed; but there was no clear Condorcet winner, and indeed there were probably always covert, unrevealed cycles of popular values. The inference is clear: The popular will is defined only as long as the issue dimensions are restricted. Once issue

dimensions multiply, the popular will is irreso-
lute. Slight changes in dimensions induce disequilibrium. Thus it is indeed difficult to speak
of a popular will so narrowly construed, and
that is why populism is an empty interpretation of voting and why the populist ideal is
literally unattainable.[2]

C. THE SURVIVAL OF LIBERALISM AND DEMOCRACY

Given that social choice theory reveals populism to be inconsistent and absurd, how does
the liberal interpretation of voting fare? For
democracy, this is a crucial question. Since
populism and liberalism, as I have defined
them, exhaust the possibilities and since populism must be rejected, then, if liberalism cannot survive, democracy is indefensible. Fortunately, liberalism survives, although in a
curious and convoluted way. Liberalism does
not demand much from voting, and hence the
restrictions placed on the justification of voting by social choice theory do not quite render
the liberal ideal unattainable.

The essence of the liberal interpretation of
voting is the notion that voting permits the
rejection of candidates or officials who have
offended so many voters that they cannot win
an election. This is, of course, a negative ideal.
It does *not* require that voting produce a clear,
consistent, meaningful statement of the popular will. It requires only that voting produce a
decisive result: that this official or this party is
retained in office or rejected. This very restricted expectation about voting can, I believe, easily coexist with all the defects we have
observed in the voting mechanism. If so, then
liberalism survives.

Let us investigate systematically the relation between liberalism and the discoveries of

social choice theory. To do so, I will begin by
assuming the existence of what we already
know does not exist—namely, a fair and accurate amalgamation of voters' values. That this
assumption is unrealistic does not taint the
analysis because I will use it only as an initial
standard, not as an instrument of interpretation. With this initial assumption, let us then
consider the following cases:

1. Suppose an official or candidate has not
    offended enough voters for them to reject
    him or her in a fair and true amalgamation
    of their values. If, in the actual voting
    under any particular method, the official or
    candidate is not rejected, then the method
    is working adequately in this case.

2. Suppose, however, that the actual voting
    does lead to the rejection of an unoffending
    official or candidate. Such rejection might
    occur in many ways. A Condorcet winner
    (assume him or her to be a "true winner")
    might lose in a plurality or approval or
    Borda election, or clever opponents might
    beat him or her by strategic voting or by
    manipulation of the agenda or by the intro-
    duction of additional, divisive candidates.
    If this happens, has the ideal of liberalism
    been violated? In our populistic era, even
    many liberals might say yes. Madison him-
    self would have been troubled by this case.
    But if the liberal ideal is strictly interpreted,
    it has not been violated. First and foremost
    liberalism requires the rejection of the of-
    fending, not the retention of the unoffend-
    ing. If a system admits rejection at all, then
    there is no a priori reason why it may not
    sometimes work imperfectly. One should
    expect, therefore, that some times an offi-
    cial or candidate will be rejected "wrongly."

    This means that we must modify to
    some degree our expectations from liberal-
    ism. [As originally stated in Section 1.D,]
    liberalism was said to mitigate the oppres-

sion caused by the failure of officials to act as agents of voters' participation. It is clear now, however, that the expectation of such an agency is a populist fantasy, not a tenet of liberalism (which is a wholly negative kind of control). This means that an official in a liberal regime may indeed abandon any effort to ensure voters' participation through reading the voters' will, not because the official is sophisticated enough to know that there is nothing there to read, but merely because he or she knows by experience that voters' rejection may be random. Such randomness, however, does not really matter for the liberal hope of preventing an official's abuse of office and authority. The threat of the next election retains its force. Indeed, an official who faces an electorate knowing that it sometimes works randomly and may "unfairly" reject him or her has a powerful motive to try even harder to avoid offending voters.

3. Suppose, on the other hand, that an official or candidate has—in our imaginary true and fair amalgamation—offended enough voters to be rejected. If he or she is in fact rejected, then, clearly, the voting method is working adequately.

4. But what if the offending official or candidate wins? This might happen because he or she successfully manipulates the agenda or invents additional issues or sets up spurious opponents. Has the ideal of liberalism then been violated? Again, most liberals in this populist era would say yes. I imagine that Madison would have believed this case impossible. But still, if the liberal ideal is strictly interpreted, there is no violation. Liberalism requires only that it be *possible* to reject a putatively offending official, not that the rejection actually occur. We know from social choice theory that those who should be winners in our imaginary true and fair amalgamation can

be defeated. We also know that those who should be losers can also be defeated, as, of course, they should be. Consequently, the voting system does not prevent the rejection of offenders—and that is precisely the condition liberalism requires. Of course, it may happen that an uninformed or unsophisticated or well-manipulated electorate fails to operate the voting system as its members would wish. But the fact that in particular instances people fail to make the system work well does not alter the fact that they *can* make it work. And if success is even sometimes possible, then the liberal interpretation can be sustained.[3]

It seems worthwhile to point out just how little is contained in the liberal interpretation of voting. In some sense it is very close to the cynical view that counting heads is better than breaking heads to solve the problem of succession. Let me point out some of the things that the liberal interpretation is not, simply to show how easy it is for liberalism to survive the criticisms of social choice theory. For one thing, liberalism does not require that society itself act. In the liberal interpretation, society is an anthropomorphized entity that cannot order or choose anything either consistently or inconsistently. Rather it is thought that individual people in the society choose, and what they individually choose is whether to support or oppose candidates. The social amalgamation of these choices need not be fair or just. It may even be part of a social cycle. But if it results in a decision on candidates, it is, from the liberal point of view, adequate.

Since social decisions are not, in liberal theory, required to mean anything, liberals can cheerfully acknowledge that elections do not necessarily or even usually reveal popular will. All elections do or have to do is to permit people to get rid of rulers. The people who do this do not themselves need to have a coherent will. They can be—and often are—strange bedfellows. Voters on the far right and the far left, for example, can combine to throw out a ruler in the center. The liberal purpose is then accomplished, even though one could not make a coherent ideological statement about what these voters did and even though their majority might be cyclical. The Indian rejection of Indira Gandhi in 1977 was accomplished by just such a coalition, the Janata party, which was, however, so incoherent in its combination of right and left that Mrs. Gandhi was able to win again in 1979.

The liberal interpretation of voting thus allows elections to be useful and significant even in the presence of cycles, manipulation, and other kinds of "errors" in voting. Since it is precisely cycles, manipulation, and "error" that render populism meaningless, the fact that liberalism can tolerate them demonstrates that liberalism can survive the revelations of social choice theory, while populism cannot.

The kind of democracy that thus survives is not, however, popular rule, but rather an intermittent, sometimes random, even perverse, popular veto. Social choice theory forces us to recognize that the people cannot rule as a corporate body in the way that populists suppose. Instead, officials rule, and they do not represent some indefinable popular will. Hence they can easily be tyrants, either in their own names or in the name of some putative imaginary majority. Liberal democracy is simply the veto by which it is sometimes possible to restrain official tyranny.

This may seem a minimal sort of democracy, especially in comparison with the grandiose (though intellectually absurd) claims of populism. Still, modest though liberal democracy may be, it fully satisfies the definition of democracy offered [in Chapter 1]. To begin with, it necessarily involves popular participation. Though the participation is not the abstract self-direction of a corporate people, it is the concrete self-direction of individuals who vote and organize voting to make the democratic veto work. Furthermore, since the veto does exist—even when manipulated or cyclical—it has at least the potential of preventing tyranny and rendering officials responsive.

Since officials are not responsive to some imaginary popular will, this popular participation is not the act of making policy. At best officials are responsive to a (possibly random) threat of expulsion from office. But this *may* lead them to avoid gross offense to groups of citizens who can eject them from office. Participation in this sense is then the act of placing a curb on policy, a veto at the margin. Nevertheless it is participation. Furthermore, it can engender that self-direction and self-respect that democracy is supposed to provide because candidates, trying to construct winning platforms in the face of that potential veto, also try to generate majorities, at least momentary ones.

Furthermore, the liberal veto generates freedom because of the very fact that it is a curb on tyranny. Whether one thinks of freedom as the absence of restraint ("negative liberty" in Isaiah Berlin's terms) or as the ability to direct one's own life ("positive liberty"), it is apparent that oppression by rulers eliminates either kind of freedom. Suppose freedom is simply the absence of governmental restraint on individual action. Then the chance to engage in vetoing by rejecting officials and the chance that the rejection actually occur are the very essence of this freedom, which is substantially equivalent to liberal democracy. Suppose, however, freedom is defined as the ability to use government to work one's will—the populist expectation. The agent of this (imaginary) will is government—that is, rulers who can oppress both the minority and the very majority whose will they are supposed to work. An extreme example is socialist rulers who, in order to free workers from the supposed bondage to owners, subject them to the ownership of the state and the terrorism of the police. But conventional populists turned dictator (for example, Vargas, Gandhi, and Perón) are often just as oppressive. Liberal democracy, insofar as it allows people to restrain and reject, is the main sanction against this majoritarian oppression also.

Sometimes populists argue that the true meaning of democracy is not to be found in voting, party organization, and the like, but rather in the democratic ideals of civil liberties, tolerance, and humane concern for popular rights. [As I emphasized in Chapter 1,] no one doubts that these ideals are indeed truly central in democratic thought (although I suspect that efforts to distinguish them from voting are often the first step—à la Marx—to some kind of coercive enterprise). Still, these democratic ideals depend on a vigilant citizenry. What permits a citizenry to be vigilant is the liberal method of regular elections. In that sense liberal democracy is a necessary part of what populists claim to want.

In the same way, liberal democracy promotes a kind of equality. Equal chances to restrain, to reject, and to veto inhere in the very idea of using votes to control officials. This is the notion of the equality of the right of democratic participation, which is the essence of the idea of juristic equality. Equality has many other derived meanings, including notions such as equal shares of the national treasure and equality before the law (that is, in the courtroom). But equality in these derived senses cannot occur unless juristic equality exists. In that way, juristic equality is primary, and that is what liberal democracy provides.

So the liberal interpretation of voting, however much it admits of "unfair" voting methods, manipulation, cycles, and the like, still contains the essential elements of democracy. It may, from the populist view, be a minimal kind of democracy; but this is the only kind of democracy actually attainable. It

is the kind of democracy we still have in the United States; and it is the kind of democracy so much admired by those who live in closed societies.

D. ARE LIBERAL AND POPULIST INTERPRETATIONS COMPATIBLE?

To say that the populist interpretation of voting cannot survive criticism, but the liberal interpretation can, does not necessarily imply that the two interpretations are incompatible. It may be that if voting permits the rejection of officials (the liberal goal), then from the liberal point of view it makes no difference whether people attempt, however fruitlessly, to use voting to embody the supposed popular will in law (the populist goal). Since the populist method is not valid, it will usually fail. But it may sometimes succeed. And if its failure or success are irrelevant by liberal standards, then there is no necessary incompatibility between liberalism and populism.

The case can be put thus: Let liberal rejectability or *LR* stand for "citizens are able to reject some rulers," and let populist incorporability or *PI* stand for "citizens are able to embody popular will in law." Then, if we guarantee at least *LR* and sometimes also get *PI*, we have perhaps obtained an extra benefit. This happy result can occur, however, only if *LR* and *PI* are complementary. If they are inconsistent, if, for example, *PI* is equivalent to the negative of *LR*, then populism is certainly incompatible with liberalism. It is important to discover, then, whether *LR* and *PI* can be simultaneously affirmed.

In the view of liberalism set forth by Berlin [(see Section 1.F)] populism transforms liberalism into tyranny when a coercive oligarchy claims to enforce an imaginary popular will. But that transformation assumes an oligarchy that refuses to submit to the liberal

discipline of the next election. Suppose, however, that free and regular elections are preserved. Then, even though the populist ideal may
be unattainable, populism need not destroy
freedom. So the question really is: Can liberal
institutions (that is, the ability to reject rulers)
be maintained when the populist interpretation of voting and populist institutions are
adopted?

To answer, I will first define briefly the
institutions appropriate for each interpretation
of voting.

Populist institutions. The populist ideal
requires that rulers move swiftly and surely to
embody in law the popular decision on an
electoral platform. Constitutional restraints
that retard this process are populistically intol-
erable. The appropriate institutions are those
that facilitate speedy embodiment, and the
simplest such institutions are so-called constitutional dictatorships, by which I mean dictatorial executives who submit to real elections
or plebiscites but rule by decree or through a
complaisant legislature. Latin American
governments often have this form. Mexico is
perhaps an example, though, since Mexican
presidents never stand for reelection, the one-
party plebiscites may not be real elections.

More complex populist institutions are
those that develop out of parliamentary
governments when they degenerate into a sovereign self-regenerating legislature run by a
leader (who is also the executive) of a disciplined majority party. For the legislature to be
sovereign, there cannot be external restraints
like an externally selected executive and independent courts; nor can there be internal restraints such as multiple houses with different
constituencies. For the legislature to be disciplined, members of the majority party dare
not defy the party leader. Furthermore, at
least one party must be a majority alone. With
such arrangements the party leader can then
ensure that party platforms are quickly
adopted in true populist fashion. Finally, since

the legislature is self-regenerating, this leader
can manipulate the time and conditions of
elections to facilitate his or her own continuance in office.

The closest current approximation to this
ideal is Great Britain as it has developed over
the last generation. External checks on the
House of Commons have been removed. The
House of Lords was effectively countered by
the Parliament Act of 1911, and the last attempt at even personal freedom in the Crown
was repulsed at the abdication of Edward VIII
in 1937. Strong third parties, a characteristic
feature of nineteenth century Parliaments (for
example, the Radicals, Irish, and Labour),
were eliminated with the decline of Liberalism
after the 1920s, though they may be reappear-
ing in the new Liberalism or Social Democracy. The national leaders of the two main
parties acquired control of nominations so
that the members became disciplined. And finally the national leadership of the majority
party was lodged in the prime minister, who,
once in office, could usually control all factions of his or her party and, within wide
limits, ensure his or her continuance in office.
What has so far saved the British system from
constitutional dictatorship is, I believe, a
three-century-old liberal tradition of free and
regular elections. But even that tradition now
seems threatened. The ideal of new elections
when the government loses in the House of
Commons has degenerated into the government's selection of a propitious time within the
limits of a five-year term. (And that term has
twice been doubled with the excuse of war.)
More significant evidence of the populist elimination of electoral restraint, however, is the
confiscatory and truly oppressive taxation and
inflation by which rulers have financed their
reelection, thereby acting against the society
that they are supposed to serve.

Liberal institutions. Liberalism, as here
defined, simply requires regular elections that
sometimes lead to the rejection of rulers. It is

often thought that liberalism also involves additional constitutional restraints, and it is indeed historically true that liberal regimes have always had them. This association, however, may be no more than a historical accident, owing to the fact that liberal democracy developed out of the imposition of constitutional restraints on monarchies. Perhaps, in the abstract, liberal methods do not need to be supplemented with these restraints because liberalism has only one stipulated sanction on rulers—namely, the threat of the next election. Nevertheless, in practice, liberal democracy probably does not work without the additional restraints always heretofore associated with it —multicameral legislatures, decentralized parties, and so on.

Having defined populist and liberal institutions, it is now possible to investigate the main question: Is the liberal interpretation of voting compatible with populist institutions? The answer depends on whether rulers in a populist system can be expected to maintain the electoral arrangements essential for liberal democracy.

It is difficult, I believe, for rulers of any kind to maintain free elections. The function of an election is to put at stake the rulers' jobs, even their lives. In nations where the democratic tradition is fragile or externally imposed, it is common for rulers who have won office in elections to prohibit elections they might lose. Even adherents of the democratic ideal hesitate to hold elections when they fear the electorate may do something "foolish" or "wrong." Dictators from Cromwell to Perón, who have possibly genuinely regarded themselves as caretakers until democracy can be resumed, have always been reluctant to trust an electorate that might install an alternative demagogue.

In general, therefore, the electoral system is only precariously maintained. But in populist systems both the temptation and the ability to weaken the electoral sanction are especially strong. For one thing, with a populist interpretation of voting it is easy for rulers to believe their programs are the "true" will of the people and hence more precious than the constitution and free elections. Populism reinforces the normal arrogance of rulers with a built-in justification for tyranny, the contemporary version of the divine right of rulers.

The main threat to democracy from populism is not, however, the exceptional temptation to subvert elections but the exceptional ability to do so. Populist institutions depend on the elimination of constitutional restraints, the populist interpretation of voting justifies this elimination. With the restraints removed, it is easy to change electoral arrangements, which is why populist democracies so often revert to autocracies. Perhaps the leaders of some future populism will be so thoroughly imbued with liberal ideals that they will never meddle with free elections. But since even in Britain, where liberal ideals originated, the populist elimination of constitutional limitations has begun to produce attacks on the integrity of elections, it seems that the liberal sanction can survive populist institutions. Indeed this empirical regularity suggests to me that there is a profound theoretical reason that populism induces rulers to ensconce themselves in office. At any rate, on the practical level at least, the answer is clearly negative to the main question of this section: Is liberal rejectability compatible with populist incorporability? No: because the constitutional restraints practically associated with liberalism *must* be destroyed to achieve populism.

E. THE PRESERVATION OF LIBERAL DEMOCRACY

It seems clear to me that democracy cannot be preserved simply with the liberal interpretation of voting. Suppose one had a liberal regime without the constitutional limitations typically associated with liberalism. Would the regime long remain liberal? Would it not operate for all the world as if it were populist? Would it not move certainly toward some kind of oppression by rulers? I think the answers to these questions are yes and so did Madison. Although he argued that the necessary and sufficient condition for republicanism (that is, democracy) to *exist* was simply regular, popular elections, it is still true that he did not think this condition was sufficient to *preserve* the liberal system. Instead he argued the necessity of constitutional limitations. And the constitution he was justifying in *The Federalist* contained a variety of very real restraints that together have successfully kept rulers from subverting regular, popular elections for 200 years. These restraints have the effect of preventing any single ruler or any single party from getting enough power to subvert:

1. *A multicameral legislature* (really three "houses": the President, Senate, and House of Representatives) based on different divisions of the people into constituencies. The different constituencies have typically kept the interests of rulers separate and thus forestalled the fusion of their ability to rule into a tyranny.

2. *A division between legislative and executive authority.* Though constitutional interpreters from Montesquieu on have believed this a fundamental limitation, in the American system it is no more than an extension of the differing constituencies of the multicameral legislature.

3. *A division of authority between national and local governments.* This is the famous American federalism, copied over half of the world. The constitutional restraint is not, however, the legal division of duties between central and local governments but rather the resultant localization of political

parties that renders national leadership of them impossible.

4. *An independent judiciary.* American lawyers have typically believed this to be the main limitation. Indeed, the separation of the judiciary from the rest of government does render blocking possible. But the judiciary has no independent constituency and so always loses in a crisis. Hence, this limitation is much less important than the multicameral legislature or the decentralized parties.

5. *Limited tenure and regular elections.* This is the fundamental restraint, but it is not a self-enforcing limitation. It depends rather on the force of tradition and on the other restraints previously listed.

About the only important restraint commonly found in other constitutional democracies and not included in this one is a system of more than two political parties so that no single party is ever a majority by itself. Something of that restraint, however, is provided in the American system by decentralized parties.

Madison was correct, I believe, in his assertion that constitutional limits preserve liberal democracy. Fortunately the limits he helped provide retain most of their original force. Yet in the American political tradition there has always been a strong strand of populism, usually expressed as the notion that the winners of an election ought to be able immediately to embody their platform in law and policy. This was, for example, the basis for the attack by Jacksonians on bureaucratic tenure, for the attack by populist political philosophers (such as Charles Beard and J. Allen Smith) on constitutional limitations of all sorts, for the persistent advocacy [described in Section 3.G] of a rigid system of two disciplined political parties (thus allowing a "majority" immediately to enact its program), and finally in recent decades for the idealization of "presidential leadership"—a euphemism for transcending constitutional limitations by the domination of a populistically endorsed, quasi-monarchical president.

Along with the populist notion of an unfettered agent (whether party or president) of the popular will, there is also the notion that the popular will can express itself directly, as in legislation by referenda and even by public opinion polls. The device of referendum was developed in the progressive era—an epoch of the populist spirit—to provide a "truer" expression of the popular will than statutes produced by legislatures, which were, it was argued, merely distorting intermediaries of the popular will. Since that time there has been considerable disillusionment with referenda because they have produced both inconsistent and bizarre legislation. Still, the populist belief in direct democracy dies hard, even though it can in no wise escape the defects of manipulation. So now there is considerable enthusiasm for using cable television to conduct elections on the content of statutes and even of administrative policy. Presumably citizens will listen to debate and then vote by push button, supplanting thereby the need for any kind of legislature.

Many current proposals for institutional reform are populistically intended to nullify constitutional limitations. In spite of disasters with the "imperial" presidencies of Johnson and Nixon, people continue to search for ways to enhance presidential leadership—by tightening presidential control of the bureaucracy and by elaborating presidential influence in the party. The decentralization of political parties, the fundamental restraint in federalism, is under constant attack with proposals for frequent policy-making conventions to be dominated by national leaders and proposals for centralized national financing of campaigns. While at the moment proposals to eliminate legislatures with direct law-making

over cable television or to substitute (à la Marcus Raskin, [as cited in Section 1.G]) instructions from grand juries for legislative judgment seem bizarre, I have no doubt that, as technology and opportunity combine, such populist proposals will be taken seriously.

The present situation in the United States is, therefore, that, although the fundamental constitutional limitations remain, populists persistently seek to undermine them. Since the twentieth century is a populist era worldwide, our homegrown populists may well succeed.

Populism puts democracy at risk. Democracy requires control of rulers by electoral sanctions; the spirit of populism and populist institutions allows rulers to tamper with this sanction, thereby rendering it a weak defense against the tyranny of officials. The maintenance of democracy requires therefore the minimization of the risk in populism.

How can we minimize the risk? This is the great question of political prudence forced on us by the revelations of social choice theory. I will conclude this survey with some remarks on this practical problem.

The main defense against populist excesses is the maintenance of the constitutional limitations inherited from eighteenth-century Whiggery. It would probably help also to have a citizenry aware of the emptiness of the populist interpretation of voting. And surely a wide dissemination of the discoveries of social choice theory is a desirable additional defense. But the dissemination of a rather arcane theory is a task for generations. (It took me a score of years of reflection on Black's and Arrow's discoveries to reject the populism I had initially espoused.) Consequently, the fundamental method to preserve liberty is to preserve ardently our traditional constitutional restraints—decentralized parties and multicameral government.

Almost everyone who has written about American politics has emphasized its peculiar style. Except for the one great disaster of the Civil War, the nastiest features of political scarcity have seldom flourished. One group has not persistently tried to do in another, probably because political coalitions are always shifting and constitutional restraints make it difficult to organize zero-sum situations. Consequently, there are no elaborately rationalized ideologies that carry with them a logically clear and intricately arranged set of public policies. Instead, political leaders are almost always engaged in constructing petty and pragmatic compromises for marginal adjustments in policy. Only in a few great crises have great leaders emerged, and great leaders have always disappeared as the crises have subsided.

The reason for this style is, I believe, the existence of constitutional limitations. In his famous defense in *The Federalist*, No. 51, of the notion of the separation of powers, Madison remarked:

> A dependence on the people [by which he meant democracy, or regular elections and limited tenure of office] is, no doubt, the primary control on the government; but experience has taught mankind the necessity of auxilliary precautions [by which he meant precisely the constitutional restraints here enumerated].

The experience of the subsequent two centuries has reinforced the teaching to which Madison referred. And the reason is this: Liberal democracy almost guarantees some circulation of leadership so that great power is usually fleeting and no vested interest lasts forever. The constitutional restraints have always reinforced this style. Multicameralism and federalism have enforced localism in parties, and this in turn has forced rulers to persuade rather than to control. The total effect is that policy does not change either rapidly or sharply enough to hurt anyone very badly, which is why we have usually—except in the Civil War—avoided the worst features of political scarcity. That the system has worked in this moderate way is due partly to luck; but it also is due to the happy mixture of liberal democracy and constitutional restraints that has so far preserved us from the hatreds and oppression implicit in populism.

Notes

1. See, for example, the calculation in Peter C. Fishburn, *The Theory of Social Choice* (Princeton: Princeton University Press, 1973), 172, showing similar results for the Borda and Copeland methods.

2. It probably ought to be pointed out here that the notion of a public interest, so cherished by populist propagandists, is not, technically speaking, rendered meaningless simply because the populist interpretation of voting is meaningless. A public interest is an interest attached to the collective body of the society; and as long as a society exists, it has, presumably, some purposes, which are its common or public interests. (See Brian Barry, *Political Argument* [New York: Humanities Press, 1965], passim.) By definition, however, a common or public interest is held in common, so voting is unnecessary to reveal it: Any randomly chosen member of the society can articulate public interest as well as any other, provided he or she thinks about the interest of the society rather than his or her own private interest. This fact reveals the emptiness of the populist interpretation of the public interest. No public interest can be defined in practice if people must count heads to discover it. A public interest may even

exist when people do not agree. There may really be an objectively right but not indisputably evident policy for the society-and of course every man and woman is then free to offer his or her interpretation. But when people have to vote on which interpretation is correct, then clearly the true public interest will not be revealed, without substantial unanimity. Either Ralph Nader or George Wallace might state the public interest correctly, but voting will not tell us which one has the right vision. Indeed they both may be simply opportunistic and malicious. So what is implied by the emptiness of populism is not the absence of a public interest but rather that the public interest cannot be revealed by nonunanimous voting. This means, of course, that all politicians and publicists who claim to explicate the public interest from an election are merely interpreting election results in a nonauthoritative way, although they have just as much or as

little right as anyone else to state their interpretation.

3. It may seem to some that I have applied an easier test to liberalism than to populism. I allow liberalism to survive provided it works occasionally, but I do not admit the survival of populism if it fails at all. These different standards are imposed because of the difference in the claims made in the two interpretations. Populism is supposed to reveal a substantive will, a proposition with content. Yet if voting can fail to reveal such propositions accurately and if we do not and cannot know in any particular instance whether failure has occurred, then none of the propositions supposedly revealed can be believed. Liberalism on the other hand asks only for a workable procedure—namely, that voting eliminate some offenders—and if it works sometimes, that is enough.

36. ROUSSEAU'S GENERAL WILL:
A Condorcetian Perspective

Bernard Grofman and Scott L. Feld

Rousseau's seminal contributions to democratic theory are his views on the development of the social contract and his notion of the "general will." Although the "general will" has been given various interpretations, there has been little understanding of how, in practice, political institutions might ascertain the general will for the purpose of effectuating public policy.

We illuminate the logic underlying Rousseau's notion of the general will by making use of long-neglected ideas of Rousseau's contemporary, Condorcet, especially those about the judgmental competence of individuals and groups. We also present some new results about the linkages between (individual and collective) preferences and (individual and collective) judgments about the nature of the public good. In the process, we show how some of the most obscure passages in Rousseau can be clarified by referring to results about features of majority rule first demonstrated by Condorcet some decades after *Of the Social Contract* was published. In particular, we examine the relationship between the general will and the will of all, the likelihood that the general will will err, and the subordination of individual opinions to the collective judgment. Our aim is to understand how collective decision-making processes may be appropriately used to ascertain the general will.

Almost no scholars dealing with Rousseau mention Condorcet (for important exceptions see Barry 1964, 1965, and Baker 1980), and even those who mention him customarily cite not his 1785 essay on voting but other works dealing with quite different topics (see e.g., Ellenburg 1976, 46, 84, 85). A leading interpretation of Rousseau's general will, made famous by Runciman and Sen (1965), interprets it in the context of a prisoner's dilemma game, and treats it as a problem of reconciling conflicting individual preferences rather than as a problem of developing a reliable judgment of what is in the collective interest. We view our approach, with its focus on social judgments, as complementary to that of Runciman and Sen, and providing a needed corrective to a current focus, in social choice theory, on treating all value questions in democratic theory as if they could be reduced to some aspect of the problem of aggregation of preferences.

ROUSSEAU'S GENERAL WILL

The general will can only direct the forces of the State in keeping with the end for which it was instituted, which is the common good; for if the opposition of private interests has made the establishment of societies necessary, the harmony of these same interests has made it

Bernard Grofman and Scott L. Feld, "Rousseau's General Will: A Condorcetian Perspective," *American Political Science Review* 82 (1988): 567-576. Reprinted with permission of the authors and the American Political Science Association.

possible. That which is common to these different interests forms the social bond; and if there were not some point in which all interests agree, no society could exist. Now it is only on this common interest that the society should be governed (Rousseau 1984, 66 [3.1]).

In this quote from Book 3 of *Of the Social Contract*, Rousseau recognizes that people differ in their interests but asserts that there is a common (or public) interest on which all humankind can agree in principle—even though not all would wish to pursue it: "Indeed, each individual may, as a man, have a particular will contrary to, or divergent from, the general will which he has as a citizen. His private interest may speak to him quite differently from the common interest; his absolute and naturally independent existence may make him regard what he owes to the common cause as a gratuitous contribution, the loss of which will be less harmful to others than will the payment of it be onerous to him" (53 [1.7]).

How is the general will to be ascertained? Rousseau's answer is, by voting: "The voice of the greater number always obliges all the others" (328 [4.2]). However, the vote is not to be an aggregation of self-interested preferences. Rather, "when a law is proposed in the Assembly of the People, what is asked of them is not precisely whether they approve the proposition or reject it; but whether or not it conforms to the general will which is their own: each in giving his vote states his opinion on that question, and from the counting of the voting is taken the declaration of the general will" (329 [4.2]).

This passage in Rousseau is often misunderstood. It represents an understanding of the process of voting not as a means of combining divergent interests but rather as a process that searches for "truth." Somewhere in the course of the development of capitalism, what we may think of as an essentially religious idea of voting—a search for God's mandate as revealed through man's finite cognitions (still present in some contemporary religious groups, e.g., the Bruderhof Commune [Zablocki 1971]) was replaced with a much more individual interest-based notion (Riley 1986).[1] Contemporary social welfare economics, beginning with Arrow's work (1963), has focused entirely on voting as a means of preference aggregation. The notion of voting as a process that can be thought of as a direct search for the common good—indeed, the very notion that there can be a common good that is something other than some form of summation or reconciliation of the *preferences* of individuals—has been lost.

There is another important implication of this quote about the nature of voting in the Assembly of the People, namely, that even those individuals whose vote is based on their perception of the common good may err in that perception:[2] "When the opinion contrary to mine prevails, that only proves that I was mistaken, and that what I had considered to be the general will was not" (Rousseau 1984, 329 [4.2]).

Because of the voters who seek the general will are fallible in their judgments, the collective judgment can also sometimes be wrong: "The general will is always upright and always tends towards the public utility, but it does not follow that the deliberations of the people always have the same rectitude. One wishes always his own good but does not always discern it. The people is never corrupted, though often deceived, and then only does it seem to will that which is bad" (75 [2.3]).[3]

Nonetheless, Rousseau expects the vote of the popular assembly (i.e., its "declaration of the general will") to coincide with the general will under reasonable conditions: "If, when an adequately informed people deliberate, the citizens having no communication among themselves, . . . the general will would always result" (75 [2.3]).

We should also note that Rousseau, in the passage quoted directly above, sees the "deliberative process" as one taking place within individuals rather than in terms of a process of group debate. Thus, each voter is seen as seeking to reach an individual and independent judgment about alternatives.

There are three elements of Rousseau's theory of the general will that we wish to single out:

1. There is a common good.[4]
2. Citizens are not always accurate in their judgments about what is in the common good.[5]
3. When citizens strive to identify this common good and vote in accordance with their perceptions of it, the vote of the Assembly of the People can be taken to be the most reliable means for ascertaining the common good.[6]

CONDORCET'S JURY THEOREM AS A FORMALIZATION OF ROUSSEAU'S GENERAL WILL

Rousseau has long been acknowledged as one of the great political philosophers. In contrast, Rousseau's contemporary, Condorcet, languished long in obscurity until his idea of the "paradox of cyclical majorities" was rediscovered by Black (1950, 1958) and helped lay the foundation for modern social choice theory (see, e.g., Arrow 1963; Farquharson 1969; Plott 1976; Riker 1964; Sen 1966; and a host of others). However, the idea for which Condorcet is now most famous, the paradox of cyclical majorities, was actually only an incidental by-product of the problem on which he was working, which was the problem of ascertaining how groups could best make choices that were collectively optimal (Black 1958; Grofman, Owen, and Feld 1983; Pinkham and Urken 1982; Young 1986).

Two hundred years ago Condorcet (1785) recognized that majorities of individuals are likely to be more often correct than individuals. Whether understood by the participants or not, this is one fact that makes democracy "work." Condorcet's result, however, was lost for most of the next two hundred years (Black 1958) and even today is nowhere near as well known as it deserves to be (Barry 1965; Grofman 1975; Grofman and Owen 1986a, 1986b; Miller 1986). The Condorcet jury theorem (Black 1958; Condorcet 1785; Grofman 1975) says that if each individual is somewhat more likely than not to make the "better" choice between some pair of alternatives (along some specified evaluative dimension) and each individual has the same probability of being correct in this choice, then (with each voter voting independently) the probability of the group majority being correct increases as the number of individuals increases, towards a limiting value of 1. Moreover, even if individuals have varying competence—where by *competence* we mean the individual probabilities of making the "correct" (dichotomous) choice (i.e., the choice that has the higher value along the specified evaluative dimension)—then so long as the *average* competence is greater than .5, the probability of the group majority being correct still increases to 1 as the group gets large (see Grofman, Owen, and Feld 1983).[7]

We can provide a statement of Condorcet's jury theorem in a form in which its resemblance to Rousseau's theory of the "general will" will be readily apparent. We assume that

1. There is a common good and a set of alternatives that more or less share in its virtues. Thus, alternatives can in principle be evaluated with respect to the underlying normative dimension of consonance with the public interest (general will), and this evaluative dimension permits us, in principle, to rank-order alternatives.

2. With respect to choice between any pair of alternatives, each citizen i has a probability p_i ($0 \leqslant p_i \leqslant 1$) of choosing that alternative which is more in the public interest (closer to the general will).

3. A group of size N chooses between any two alternatives by means of a majority vote in which each voter is polled about his or her independently reached choice, without any group deliberations.

Though Rousseau was not at all a formal mathematical thinker, and despite the fact that some of the basic probabilistic ideas needed to make sense of the Condorcet jury theorem were still in a very preliminary stage of development in the 1750s, we believe that the Condorcet jury theorem accurately captures the basic ideas underlying Rousseau's notion of the general will. It seems virtually certain that ideas similar to those later to be formally developed by Condorcet were "in the wind," and influenced both Rousseau and, later, Condorcet; and there certainly were various social and intellectual linkages between Rousseau and Condorcet. One connection is via the *Encyclopédie* project, in which Diderot and D'Alembert were involved. Condorcet became a close friend of the mathematician and philosopher D'Alembert, whose notion of the pursuit of the common good anticipated that of Condorcet; Rousseau, as a close friend of Diderot, may have learned of these ideas.[8]

There are five key points in understanding the relationship between the ideas of Rousseau and those of Condorcet: *First*, the Condorcet jury theorem is based on a notion of common judgment, not separate individual preferences. It thus permits us to understand better how Rousseau's distinction between the general will and the "will of all" can be implemented in a voting assembly. In Rousseau's own language, "There is often a great difference between the will of all and the general will. The latter regards only the common interest; the other regards private interests and is only the sum of particular wills."

Second, the Condorcet jury theorem permits us to understand how the majority can be a representation of the general will (when its members act in judgment of the common good and not in terms of their particularized self-interests) without the majority will being *identical* to the general will. The Condorcet jury theorem states the "limit result" that as the group size grows large, if the average citizen is more likely than not to judge correctly which of any pair of alternatives is more nearly in the public interest, the majority vote of the group will be *almost certain to be correct* in its judgment of *the public interest*.[9]

Nonetheless, the general will may err, or —in Rousseau's terminology—"the characteristics" of the general will "may not reside in the majority" (1984, 102 [4.3]). However, even for average group competence $\overline{p}$ near .5, the expected judgmental accuracy of large assemblies is considerable.[10] For example, even if $\overline{p}$ is only .51, a 399-member assembly has a competence of .66, while if $\overline{p}$ = .55, a 399-member assembly has a competence of .98. For a reasonable level of $\overline{p}$ (e.g., $\overline{p}$ = .6), even relatively small assemblies (of greater than 41) have a group competence level P_N above .9 (see Grofman 1975; Miller 1986). For $\overline{p}$ = .7, an assembly of only size 11 will have a group competence level of above .9.

Third, knowledge of the Condorcet jury theorem (and recent extensions, e.g., Miller 1986; Owen 1986) helps us better understand the logic undergirding another somewhat puzzling passage in Rousseau:

> But when factions are formed, partial associations at the expense of the whole, the will of each of these associations becomes general with regard to its members and particular with regard to the state: one is then able to say that there are no longer as many voters as there are men, but only as many as there are

associations ... and [this] yield[s] a *less general result*. Finally, when one of these associations is so large that it overcomes the rest, ... then there no longer is a general will, and the opinion which dominates is only a private opinion. (1984, 27 [2.3], emphasis ours)

We translate this remark of Rousseau in Condorcetian terms as an observation about factions reducing the *effective* size of the assembly. As the *effective* size of the assembly is reduced—because people vote as a herd (part of a faction) not as separately thinking and independently acting individuals—the Condorcet jury theorem tells us, group accuracy will be reduced. Indeed, at the extreme, if there is a majority faction, this faction is equivalent to a single voice deciding things; thus the benefits of large numbers are lost completely.[11] More generally, if individual choices are positively correlated with one another beyond the correlation to be expected from similarities in competence alone, group accuracy will be reduced (Owen 1986; Shapley and Grofman 1984).

Fourth, a focus on the judgmental basis of voting allows us to provide a mathematical foundation for Rousseau's observation that "the closer opinions approach unanimity, the more dominant is the general will" (1984, 322 [4.2]).

Using the Condorcetian probability framework, it can be shown that the more votes there are on the majority side, the more likely is the group majority to be correct.[12]

Fifth, a probabilistic approach to group judgment allows us better to understand Rousseau's views as to when supermajoritarian decision rules are called for: "The more important and serious the deliberations, the closer the prevailing opinion should approach unanimity; [on the other hand,] in decisions that must be resolved immediately, a majority of one vote should suffice" (p. 103 [4.2]).

If certain kinds of decisions are more subject to error than others (or are simply more important than others so that we wish to have a higher level of confidence that the group vote is an accurate expression of the general will), we might wish to require more than a bare majority vote, since this will reduce the error level since it can be shown that the more votes there are in favour, the more likely is the group judgment to be correct (Grofman 1978; Nitzan and Paroush 1985; cf. Buchanan and Tullock 1962; Rae 1969).[13]

Our emphasis has been on how individual judgments about what is in the public interest aggregate to indicate the general will. We believe that this approach captures the central notion of Rousseau's concept of the general will. However, Rousseau recognized that individuals were not always so nobly motivated and that they sometimes expressed their personal preferences, rather than seeking the general will (see n. 5). He also noted that the general will could sometimes emerge as the residue from the cancelling out of individual self-interest in the process of aggregation: "The [general will] looks only to the common interest. The [will of all] looks only to private interests and is only the sum of particular wills: but take away from these same wills the pluses and minuses which cancel each other out and the general will remains as the sum of the differences" (1984, 76 [2.3]).

While this language has proved incomprehensible or nonsensical to some (e.g., Plamenatz quoted in Gildin 1983, 55), Gildin (1983, 55-57) provides a simple illustration of what Rousseau almost certainly meant. In Gildin's illustration of a Common's Dilemma, each fisherman would like to fish above the limit set by long-run social advantage, since, ceteris paribus, the few fish netted will not be sufficient to drive the fish population to extinction; yet if each fisherman "cheats," all will suffer (cf. Goodin 1982). Clearly, each fisherman wishes the rule to be one where *all other* fishermen must obey the limit. If we subtract out these egocentric peculiarities, the "common" preference is for a ban on fishing above the socially optimal limit for *all* fishermen (see Gildin 1983; cf. Runciman and Sen 1965).

However, as is clear from many passages from him, Rousseau believed that the most certain route to finding the general will was one in which individuals were primarily oriented toward the general will rather than to their own narrow self-interest.

CONCLUSIONS

We hope that our reconstruction of Rousseau's theory can lead to a broader understanding of democracy as a means to collective ends, rather than as just as a means for aggregating narrow interests residing in, and confined to, individuals. While it is often assumed that democracy should be based upon individuals following their own self-interests, Rousseau's and Condorcet's contributions suggest that democracy "works" better when individuals try to see beyond their narrow self-interests to the collective good. Democracy may require a certain amount of shared collective consciousness to achieve competent collective judgments; consequently, polities that lack such consciousness may not function well as democracies.[14]

Even while many politicians and researchers recognize that voters often vote to further the collective rather than their individual interests, other researchers and theorists (especially those working in a social choice framework) tend to overlook the importance of these collective orientations. Politicians obviously recognize that appeals to "right," "good," and "fair" policies have some political appeal. Similarly, empirical research consistently shows that norms of citizen duty are one of the main determinants of whether citizens vote at all. However, theorists of democracy may fail to recognize that even relatively small amounts of collective orientation (i.e., only slightly more than none), especially in the context of negatively correlated individual interests, can aggregate to collective decisions with a high probability of serving the public good. That small differences in each individual's amount of collective orientation can make large differences in the likely ability of the electorate as a whole to make collectively beneficial judgments is one of the clear implications of the Condorcet jury theorem. Thus, it may not matter that individuals are not very "sociotropic" in their voting, as long as there are *some* elements of sociotropic voting present in a significant number of voters (cf. Miller 1986).[15]

We see Rousseau as a propounder of enlightened democracy, not dehumanized collectivism.[16] For Rousseau, as for Condorcet, the process of voting is a means whereby the common good can be identified and implemented, albeit imperfectly.[17] In voting, however, social judgments, not individual preferences, are to be the basis of voter choice.[18] Democracy as a process for making good decisions based upon the aggregation of individual judgments has only recently begun to receive the attention that it deserves (Grofman and Owen 1986a, 1986b; Miller 1986; Nitzan and Paroush 1985; Pinkham and Urken 1982; Young 1986).[19] We hope our reinterpretation of Rousseau's views may encourage others to pursue the topic of collective judgments in terms of both descriptive and normative theory of democratic behaviour.[20]

Notes

This research was begun while Grofman was a fellow at the Center for Advanced Study in the Behavioral Sciences, Stanford. We are indebted to the staff of the Word Processing Center, School of Social Sciences, UCI for typing and table preparation and to Dorothy Gormick for bibliographic assistance.

1. Riley (1986, ix) characterizes his book as "a study of the transformation of a theological idea, the general will of God to save all men, into a political one, the general will of the citizen to place common good of the city above his particular will as a private self, and thereby to 'save the polity.'"

2. Compare this idea with that of the "impartial spectator" that, according to Adam Smith in his *Theory of Moral Sentiments* (1971, 171) is contained within each of us and would be "forced" to agree on what is right. Such intuitionist notions of moral judgment are common in the seventeenth and eighteenth centuries.

3. We have omitted the continuation of this quote, which indicates what happens when the assembly is divided into factions. We will return to this problem later.

4. "If there were not some point in which all interests agree, no society could exist" (Rousseau 1984, 66 [2.1]).

5. Moreover, individuals may falter in their allegiance to the common good over self-interest: "If it is not impossible that a private will will agree at some point with the general, it is at least impossible that this agreement should be lasting and constant; for the private will naturally tends to preferences, and the general will to equality" (Rousseau 1984, 68 [2.1]).

6. Thus, from the vote of the Assembly "is taken the declaration of the general will" (Rousseau 1984, 329 [4.2]).

7. Let P_N be the majority judgmental accuracy of a group of size N ($m = (N + 1)/2$, if we assume, for convenience, N odd), i.e., let P_N be the probability that the group majority will, in a pairwise comparison, pick the alternative that is better with respect to the common interest. Let $\bar{p}$ be the average accuracy level of voters. Then, if voter choices are mutually independent,

$$P_N \approx \sum_{h=m}^{N} \binom{N}{h} (\bar{p})^h (1 - \bar{p})^{N-h}$$

and if $\bar{p} > .5$,

$$\lim_{N \to \infty} P_N \to 1.$$

If $\bar{p} < .5$,

$$\lim_{N \to \infty} P_N \to 0,$$

while if $\bar{p} = .5$, then, not so intuitively,

$$1 - e^{1/2} < \lim_{N \to \infty} P_N < e^{-1/2}$$

(Grofman, Owen, and Feld 1983).

8. In his *Encyclopédie* essays on natural rights and on the ancient Greeks, Diderot himself deals with the conflict between individual wills and the general will (see Riley 1986, 203-05). We are not, however, aware of any mention of Rousseau by Condorcet in his 1785 essay.

9. Grofman (1975) characterizes this aspect of the Condorcet jury theorem as "vox populi, vox dei," i.e., the voice of the people approaches infallibility.

10. The calculations below are based on a normal approximation to the situation in which all group members have identical accuracy levels. However, for $m > 10$ or so, distributional effects of competence are minimal, and the results given above may be used even for extreme cases (e.g., ones where some members of the group have $p_i = 0$ or 1). Grofman, Owen, and Feld (1983) and Grofman, Feld, and Owen (1982) give precise bounds.

11. See n. 10.

12. To look at the differing competences of group judgments with differing margins of votes, we make use of the formula for the ratio of the probability of the correct choice by a group majority of size $m + k$ to the probability of an

incorrect choice by a group majority of that same size, where *m* is a simple majority (= (N + 1)/2 if N odd), and $\overline{p}$ is mean group competence. We have

$$\frac{(\overline{p})^{m+k}(1-\overline{p})^{N-m-k}}{(\overline{p})^{N-m-k}(1-\overline{p})^{m+k}} = \frac{\overline{p}^{(2m+2k-N)}}{(1-\overline{p})^{N-2m-2k}}$$

It is apparent that the above expression increases with *k*.

It should be clear that no single will can ever be expected to divine the general will reliably (i.e., more formally, we would not expect any p_i to equal 1). Furthermore it is likely that any long-lasting faction, even if a majority, will turn away from a search for the common good to a concern for the private good of its own members (see n. 5; cf. *Federalist Papers*, no. 10).

13. If we insist on a supermajority, of course, then we must risk deadlock; e.g., if juries require unanimity, this opens the possibility of hung juries (see Grofman 1979, 1981; cf. Buchanan and Tullock 1962).

14. Thomas Schwartz (personal communication, March 1985) has proposed that "Rousseau and other radical democrats want to have a society without politics." In one sense, this is correct; but we prefer to stress the way in which, for Rousseau, politics in effect becomes redefined as the search for the general will.

15. Compare the view of Tocqueville: "Not only is common opinion the only guide which private judgment retains among a democratic people, but amongst such a people it possess a power infinitely beyond what it has elsewhere. At periods of equality men have no faith in one another, by reason of their common resemblance; but this very resemblance gives them almost unbounded confidence in the judgment of the public; for it would not seem probable, as they are all endowed with equal means of judging, but that the greater truth should go with the greater number" (1945, 2:11).

16. Some of the same language we have cited to show how the majority will can become the general will if citizens strive to identify the common good and vote in accordance with their perceptions of it, other authors interpret to mean that Rousseau takes the position that

individuals do not count, only society matters. For example, Peter Drucker contends that Rousseau believes that

> whatever human existence there is; whatever freedom, rights and duties the individual has; whatever meaning there is in individual life—all is determined by society according to society's objective need of survival. The individual, in other words, is not autonomous. He is determined by society. He is free only in matters that do not matter. He has rights only because society concedes them. He has a will only if he wills what society needs. His life has meaning only insofar as it relates to the social meaning and as it fulfills itself in fulfilling the objective goal of society. There is, in short, no human existence, there is only social existence. There is no individual, there is only the citizen. (1971, 51).

This seems far too extreme a reading of Rousseau. Certainly, the language in Rousseau about the "general will" is susceptible to a much more straightforward interpretation. Rousseau merely sees a public interest that is the proper concern of citizens acting in the legislative arena but does not make the extravagant claim that the legislative arena is the sole, or even the superordinate, arena (see Riley 1986, 248-250; cf. Cobban 1964).

17. The clause "albeit imperfectly" is a critical one. It is sometimes claimed that Arrow's theorem demonstrates the inherent impossibility of there being such a thing as a general will: "The theorem provides an unambiguous answer to the question 'Is there a foolproof way to derive complete and transitive social preference relations?' The answer is no. This clearly negative result casts doubts on all assertions that there is a 'general will,' a 'social contract,' a 'social good,' a 'will of the people,' a 'people's government,' a 'people's voice', a 'social benefit,' and so forth" (Feldman 1980, 191). We believe this (common) view of what Arrow's theorem allegedly demonstrates about democratic theory is simply wrong. Our position, like Rousseau's, is that the general will may exist but that the outcome of any voting process is but an imperfect reflection of it.

18. As previously noted, we believe that the Condorcetian perspective on social judgments provides a useful corrective to the standard emphasis of economists on social welfare as the aggregation of *individual preferences* (cf. Dummett 1984, 170; Grofman, Owen, and Feld 1983; Lehrer and Wagner 1981; Margolis 1982, 66-69; Nurmi 1984). We also believe that the educative role of politicians in the political process must also be acknowledged (cf. Kelly 1987; Shklar 1969, 186-187). Similarly, accounts of political actors as vote maximizers neglect the role of politicians as innovators of organizational solutions to common problems (Glazer and McMillan 1987).

19. As we have seen, Condorcet, who was concerned with the search for the public good, is remembered only for his analysis of the effects of combining individual *preferences* in such a fashion as to give rise to intransitivities (the paradox of cyclical majorities).

20. One such application might be the analysis of judicial decision making. Clearly, Supreme Court justices are not supposed to be reconciling competing personal preferences for policy when they vote; rather they are seeking to arrive at a judgment of what the Constitution —or some statute—means (in the given context). Thus, to use terminology from early U.S. (and Continental) political thought, Supreme Court justices are to exercise "judgment," not "will" (Chamberlin n.d.). Whether such distinction is meaningful and, even if meaningful, whether human beings can be expected to restrain their will and exercise only their judgment are questions relevant to the present debate over the proper role of evaluation of judicial philosophies as a factor in shaping Senate nonconfirmation of U.S. Supreme Court justices such as Robert Bork.

References

ARROW, KENNETH J. 1963. *Social Choice and Individual Values.* New York: Wiley.

BAKER, MICHAEL. 1980. *Condorcet.* Chicago: University of Chicago Press.

BARRY, BRIAN. 1964. "The Public Interest." *Proceedings of the Aristotelian Society* 38:9-14.

BARRY, BRIAN. 1965. *Political Argument.* London: Routledge & Kegan Paul.

BLACK, DUNCAN. 1950. "The Unity of Political and Economic Science." *Economic Journal* 60:506-14.

BLACK, DUNCAN. 1958. *The Theory of Committees and Elections.* Cambridge: Cambridge University Press.

BUCHANAN, JAMES M., and GORDON TULLOCK. 1962. *The Calculus of Consent.* Ann Arbor: University of Michigan Press.

CHAMBERLIN, JOHN. "Assessing the Power of the Supreme Court." N.d. Forthcoming in Bernard Grofman and Donald Wittman, eds. *The "Federalist Papers" and the New Institutionalism.* New York: Agathon.

COBBAN, ALFRED. 1964. *Rousseau and the Modern State.* 2e. London: Allen & Unwin.

CONDORCET, MARQUIS DE. 1785. *Essai sur l'application de l'analyse à la probabilité des decisions rendues à la pluralité des voix.* Paris.

DRUCKER, PETER F. 1971. *Men, Ideas, and Politics.* New York: Harper & Row.

DUMMETT, MICHAEL. 1984. *Voting Procedures.* Oxford: Oxford University Press.

ELLENBURG, STEPEH. 1976. *Rousseau's Political Philosophy.* Ithaca, NY: Cornell University Press.

FARQUHARSON, ROBIN. 1969. *Theory of Voting.* New Haven: Yale University Press.

FELDMAN, ALLAN. 1980. *Welfare Economics and Social Choice Theory.* Boston: Martinus Nijhoff.

GILDEN, HILAIL. 1983. *Rousseau's Social Contract: The Design of the Argument.* Chicago: University of Chicago Press.

GLAZER, AMIHAI, and HENRY McMILLAN. 1987. "Legislation and the Cost of Making Proposals." University of California, Irvine. Photo-offset.

GOODIN, ROBERT. 1982. *Political Theory and Public Policy*. Chicago: University of Chicago Press.

GROFMAN, BERNARD. 1975. "A Comment on Democratic Theory: A Preliminary Mathematical Model." *Public Choice* 21:99-104.

GROFMAN, BERNARD. 1978. "Judgmental Competence of Individuals and Groups in a Dichotomous Choice Situation: Is a Majority of Heads Better Than One?" *Journal of Mathematical Sociology* 6: 47-60.

GROFMAN, BERNARD. 1979. "A Preliminary Model of Jury Decision Making as a Function of Jury Size, Effective Jury Decision Rule, and Mean Juror Judgmental Competence." In Gordon Tullock, ed. *Frontiers of Economics*, Vol. 3. Blacksburg, VA: Center for Study of Public Choice.

GROFMAN, BERNARD. 1981. "Mathematical Models of Jury/Juror Decision Making." In Bruce D. Sales, ed. *Perspectives in Law and Psychology*, Vol. 2, *The Jury, Judicial, and Trial Processes*. New York: Plenum.

GROFMAN, BERNARD, SCOTT L. FELD, and GUILLERMO OWEN. 1982. "Evaluating the Competence of Experts, Pooling Individual Judgments into a Collective Choice, and Delegating Decision Responsibility to Subgroups." In Felix Geyer and Hans van der Zouwen, eds. *Dependence and Inequality*. New York: Pergamon.

GROFMAN, BERNARD, and GUILLERMO OWEN, eds. 1986a. "Condorcet Models: Avenues for Future Research." In Bernard Grofman and Guillermo Owen, eds. *Information Pooling and Group Decision Making*. Greenwich, CT:JAI.

GROFMAN, BERNARD, GUILLERMO OWEN, and SCOTT L. FELD. 1983. "Thirteen Theorems in Search of the Truth." *Theory and Decision* 15:261-278.

KELLY, CHRISTOPHER. 1987. "To Persuade without Convincing: The Language of Rousseau's Legislator." *American Journal of Political Science* 31: 321-335.

LEHRER, KEITH, and CARL WAGNER. 1981. *Rational Consensus in Science and Society*. Dordrecht: D. Reidel.

MARGOLIS, HOWARD. 1982. *Selfishness, Altruism, and Rationality: A Theory of Social Choice*. Chicago: University of Chicago Press.

MILLER, NICHOLAS. 1986. "Information, Electorates, and Democracy: Some Extensions and Interpretations of the Condorcet Jury Theorem." In Bernard Grofman and Guillermo Owen, eds. *Information Pooling and Group Decision Making*. Greenwich, CT:JAI.

NITZAN, SHMUEL, and JACOB PAROUSH. 1985. *Collective Decision Making: An Economic Approach*. New York: Cambridge University Press.

NURMI, HANNU. 1984. "Social Choice Theory and Democracy: A Comparison of Two Recent Views." *European Journal of Political Research* 12:325-333.

OWEN, GUILLERMO. 1986. "'Fair' Indirect Majority Rules." In Bernard Grofman and Guillermo Owen, eds. *Information Pooling and Group Decision Making*. Westport, CT:JAI.

PINKHAM, ROGER S., and ARNOLD B. URKEN. 1982. "Competence and the Choice of a Voting System." Stevens Institute of Technology. Typescript.

PLOTT, CHARLES R. 1976. "Axiomatic Social Choice Theory: An Overview and Interpretation." *American Journal of Political Science* 20:511-96.

RAE, DOUGLAS. 1969. "Decision Rules and Individual Values in Constitutional Choice." *American Political Science Review* 63:40-56.

RIKER, WILLIAM. 1964. "Voting and the Summation of Preferences." *American Political Science Review* 58:341-349.

RILEY, PATRICK. 1986. *The General Will before Rousseau*. Princeton: Princeton University Press.

ROUSSEAU, JEAN-JACQUES. 1984. *Of the Social Contract*. Trans. Charles M. Sherover. New York: Harper & Row.

RUNCIMAN, W.G., and AMARTYA K. SEN. 1965. "Games, Justice, and the General Will." *Mind* 74: 554-562.

SEN, AMARTYA K. 1966. "A Possibility Theorem on Majority Decisions." *Econometrica* 34:491-499.

SHAPLEY, LLOYD S., and BERNARD GROFMAN. 1984. "Optimizing Group Judgmental Accuracy in the Presence of Interdependencies." *Public Choice* 43: 329-343.

SHKLAR, JUDITH. 1969. *Men and Citizens: A Study of Rousseau's Social Theory.* Oxford: Cambridge University Press.

SMITH, ADAM. 1971. *The Theory of Moral Sentiments.* New York: Garland.

TOCQUEVILLE, ALEXIS DE. 1945. *Democracy in America.* New York: Random House Vintage.

YOUNG, H. PEYTON. 1986. "Optimal Ranking and Choice from Pairwise Comparisons." In Bernard Grofman and Guillermo Owen, eds. *Information Pooling and Group Decision Making.* Westport, CT:JAI.

ZABLOCKI, BENJAMIN. 1971. *The Joyful Community.* New York: Pelican.

DISCUSSION QUESTIONS

1. Identify those features of the social choice theory approach that are most useful in evaluating voting procedures and assessing the quality of representative institutions.

2. Discuss the properties that are absolutely essential to a collective choice procedure. Indicate why you think those specific properties are most desirable.

3. Social choice theorists are concerned with the quality of the choices made through collective decision-making processes. Debate the criteria one might profitably use in assessing that quality. Note how these criteria relate to issues regarding the quality of representation that is afforded through the use of such processes.

4. Which of the several properties of voting systems discussed by Nurmi seem to be most desirable? On what bases can one judge those properties?

5. Discuss the role that each of the various aspects of election systems described by Fishburn plays in the making of collective choices through the use of voting in elections.

6. Explain the underlying causes of the several paradoxes of preferential choice described by Fishburn and Brams. Indicate what property of the choice procedure used seems to result in each of these paradoxes.

7. Debate the positions taken by Levesque and Woolstencroft about the extent to which the selection of Brian Mulroney as the Progressive Conservative leader was produced by a biased procedure.

8. Evaluate Woolstencroft's claim that social choice theory, as employed by Levesque, neglects the impact of the institutional context on the process of making collective choices. What aspects of that context seem to be relevant to his charge?

9. Debate the merits of Riker's rejection of the "populist" conception of democracy. Indicate what aspects of the social choice theory are most pertinent to his argument and why.

10. Discuss the extent to which Riker's article places the age-old debate between the Levellers and the Whigs in a modern perspective, informed by the principles of social choice theory.

11. Discuss the implications of the Condorcetian resolution of Rousseau's problem of making collective choices based on the "general will," as set forward in the selection by Grofman and Feld.

12. Discuss the extent to which a relatively small body of representatives might be capable of making collective decisions that truly conformed to the "general will" if they adopted the procedure set out in the Grofman and Feld selection. What important implications seem to follow from this regarding the workings of representative democracy?

SELECT BIBLIOGRAPHY

Section One

Bardach, Eugene. "On Representing the Public Interest." *Ethics*91 (1981): 486-490.

Birch, Anthony H. *Representation*. London: MacMillan, 1971.

_____. *Representative and Responsible Government*. Toronto: University of Toronto Press, 1964.

de Grazia, Alfred. *Public and Republic*. New York: A.A. Knopf, 1951.

Eulau, Heinz. *Politics, Self and Society: A Theme and Variations*. Cambridge, Massachusetts: Harvard University Press, 1986.

Eulau, Heinz, and Paul Karps. "The Puzzle of Representation: Specifying Components of Responsiveness." *Legislative Studies Quarterly* 2 (1977): 233-254.

Grofman, Bernard. "Fair and Equal Representation." *Ethics* 91 (1981): 477-485.

Johnston, J. Paul. "Representation." In *Liberal Democracy in Canada and the United States*, edited by T.C. Pocklington, 92-221. Toronto: Holt Rinehart and Winston, 1985.

Kateb, George. "The Moral Distinctiveness of Representative Democracy." *Ethics* 91 (1981): 357-374.

MacCallum, Gerald. *Political Philosophy*. Chapter 10, 141-154. Englewood Cliffs, New Jersey: Prentice Hall, Inc., 1987.

Mansbridge, Jane J. "Living with Conflict: Representation in the Theory of Adversary Democracy." *Ethics* 91 (1981): 466-476.

Mayo, Henry B. *An Introduction to Democratic Theory*. New York: Oxford University Press, 1960.

Mill, J.S. *Considerations on Representative Government*. London: Parker, Son and Bourn, 1861.

Monahan, Arthur P. *Consent, Coercion, and Limit: The Medieval Origins of Parliamentary Democracy*. Kingston and Montreal: McGill-Queen's University Press, 1987.

Pennock, J.R. *Democratic Political Theory*. Princeton: Princeton University Press, 1979.

Pitkin, Hanna F. *The Concept of Representation*. Berkeley: University of California Press, 1967.

_____. *Representation*. New York: Atherton Press, 1969.

Rae, Douglas, "Two Contradictory Ideas of (Political) Equality." *Ethics* 91 (1981): 451-456.

Redner, Harry. "Representation and the Crisis of Post-Modernism." *Political Science* 20 (1987): 673-679.

Rogowski, Ronald. "Representation in Political Theory and in Law." *Ethics* 91 (1981): 395-430.

Spafford, Duff. "Mill's Majority Principle." *Canadian Journal of Political Science* 18 (1985): 599-608.

Spitz, Elaine. *Majority Rule*. Chatham, New Jersey: Chatham House Publishers, Inc., 1984.

Stewart, Robert M. *Readings in Social and Political Philosophy*. Oxford: Oxford University Press, 1986.

Still, Jonathan W. "Political Equality and Election Systems." *Ethics* 91 (1981): 375-394.

Weale, Albert P. "Representation, Individualism and Collectivism." *Ethics* 91 (1981): 457-465.

Section Two

Clarke, Harold D., Colin Campbell, F.Q. Quo, and Arthur Goddard, eds. *Parliament, Policy and Representation*. Toronto: Methuen, 1980.

Fleras, Augie. "From Social Control Towards Political Self-Determination? Maori Seats and the Politics of Separate Maori Representation in New Zealand." *Canadian Journal of Political Science* 13 (1985): 551-576.

Fox, Russell H. *State and Local Representation: An Annotated Bibliography*. New York: National Municipal League, 1980.

Franks, C.E.S. *The Parliament of Canada*. Toronto: University of Toronto Press, 1987.

Gagnon, Alain G., and A. Brian Tanguay, eds. *Canadian Parties in Transition: Discourse, Organization, and Representation*. Scarborough: Nelson Canada, 1989.

Gormley, William T., Jr. "The Representation Revolution: Reforming State Regulation Through Public Representation." *Administration and Society* 18 (1986): 179-196.

Jackson, Robert J., and Michael M. Atkinson. *The Canadian Legislative System*. 2nd ed., rev. Chapter 7, 155-173. Toronto: MacMillan Co. of Canada, 1980.

Johnson, Peter, and Graham White. "To Everything There is an Agency: Boards, Agencies and Commissions." In *The Government and Politics of Ontario*. 2nd ed. Edited by Donald C. MacDonald, 123-144. Toronto: Van Nostrand Reinhold Ltd., 1980.

Kernaghan, Kenneth, and David Siegel. *Public Administration in Canada: A Text.* 445-451 and 482-490. Toronto: Methuen, 1987.

Kornberg, Allan, William Mishler, and Harold D. Clarke. *Representative Democracy in the Canadian Provinces.* Scarborough: Prentice-Hall Canada Inc., 1982.

Legislative Studies Quarterly 12 (1987). Issue on "Representation in France: A Symposium," 169-241.

McCormick, Peter, Ernest C. Manning, and Gordon Gibson. *The Canadian Partnership: A Task Force Report.* Calgary: Canada West Foundation, 1981.

McLeay, E.M. "Political Argument about Representation: The Case of the Maori Seats." *Political Studies* 28 (1980): 43-62.

Paltiel, Khayyam Z. "The Changing Environment and Role of Special Interest Groups." *Canadian Public Administration* 25 (1982): 198-210.

Papayanopoulos, Lee, ed. *Democratic Representation and Apportionment: Quantitative Methods, Measures and Criteria.* New York: Annals of the New York Academy of Sciences, 1973.

Russell, Peter H. *The Judiciary in Canada: The Third Branch of Government,* 164-169. Toronto: McGraw-Hill Ryerson, 1987.

Ward, Norman. "The Basis of Representation in the House of Commons." *Canadian Journal of Economics and Political Science* 15 (1949): 477-494.

Section Three

Backstrom, Charles H., et al. "Issues in gerrymandering: an exploratory measure of partisan gerrymandering applied to Minnesota." *Minnesota Law Review* 62 (1978): 1121-1159.

Backstrom, Charles H. "The Practice and Effect of Redistricting." *Political Geography Quarterly* 1 (1982): 351-359.

Baker, Gordon. "Judicial determination of political gerrymandering: a 'totality of circumstances' approach." *Journal of Law and Politics* 3 (1986): 1-19.

Balinski, Michel, and H. Young. "Fair Electoral Distribution." *Policy Options* 4 (July 1983): 30-32.

————. *Fair Representation.* New Haven: Yale University Press, 1982.

————. "Parliamentary Representation and the Amalgam Method." *Canadian Journal of Political Science* 14 (1981): 797-812.

Barnes, G.P. "The Use of Computers in Redistributing Constituencies." *Electoral Studies* 6 (1987): 133-138.

Brugger, B., and Dean Jaensch. *Australian Politics: Theory and Practice.* Part IV, "Electoral System," 203-214. Sydney: George Allen and Unwin, 1985.

Butler, David, and Bruce Cain. "Reapportionment: A Study in Comparative Government." *Electoral Studies* 4 (1985): 197-213.

Cain, Bruce E. "Assessing the Partisan Effects of Redistricting." *American Political Science Review* 79 (1985): 320-333.

———. *The Reapportionment Puzzle.* Berkeley: University of California Press, 1984.

Cain, Bruce, John Ferejohn, and Morris Fiorina. *The Personal Vote: Constituency Service and Electoral Independence.* Cambridge, Massachusetts: Harvard University Press, 1987.

Cain, Bruce E., and Janet C. Campagne. "Predicting Partisan Redistricting Disputes." *Legislative Studies Quarterly* 12 (1987): 265-274.

Carty, R.K. "The Electoral Boundary Revolution in Canada." *The American Review of Canadian Studies* 15 (1985): 273-287.

Chi, N.H. "Mathematical Modeling of Politics From Electoral Representation To Superpowers' Stockpiles." Unpublished paper presented at annual meeting of Canadian Political Science Association: Winnipeg, Manitoba, June 1986.

Copeland, Gary W., and Jean G. McDonald. "Reapportionment and Partisan Competition: When Does Reapportionment Matter?" *Political Behavior* 9 (1987): 160-173.

Coulson, Michael. "Reforming Electoral Distribution." *Policy Options* 4 (January/February 1983): 25-28.

Courtney, John C. "Parliament and Representation: The Unfinished Agenda of Electoral Redistributions." *Canadian Journal of Political Science* 21 (1988): 675-690.

———. "Theories Masquerading As Principles: Canadian Electoral Boundary Commissions and the Australian Model." In *The Canadian House of Commons: Essays in Honour of Norman Ward*, edited by John C. Courtney, 135-172. Calgary: University of Calgary Press, 1985.

———. "The Size of Canada's Parliament: An Assessment of the Implications of a Larger House of Commons?" In *Institutional Reforms for Representative Government* by Peter Aucoin, 1-39. Toronto: University of Toronto Press, 1985.

Cranor, John D., Gary L. Crawley, and Raymond H. Scheele. "The Anatomy of a Gerrymander." *American Journal of Political Science* 33 (1989): 222-239.

Dawson, R. MacGregor. "The Gerrymander of 1882." *Canadian Journal of Economics and Political Science* 1 (1935): 197-221.

Dixon, Robert G. *Democratic Representation: Reapportionment in Law and Politics.* New York: Oxford University Press, 1968.

Dye, Thomas. *Understanding Public Policy.* 6th ed. Englewood Cliffs, New Jersey: Prentice Hall Inc. 1987.

Dye, Thomas, and V. Gray, eds. *The Determinants of Public Policy.* Lexington, Massachusetts: D.C. Heath and Co., 1980.

Engstrom, Richard. "District Magnitudes and the Election of Women to the Irish Dail." *Electoral Studies* 6 (1987): 123-132.

———. "Post-census representative districting: the Supreme Court, one person one vote, and the gerrymandering issue." *Southern University Law Review* 7 (1981): 173-226.

Falcone, David, and W. Mishler. "Canadian Provincial Legislatures and System Outputs: A Diachronic Analysis of the Determinants of Health Policy." Unpublished paper prepared for delivery at 46th convention of Southern Political Science Association, New Orleans, Louisiana, 1974.

Feig, Douglas. "Expenditures in the American States: The Impact of Court-Ordered Legislative Reapportionment." *American Politics Quarterly* 6 (1978): 309-324.

Fenno, Richard F. *Home Style: House Members in Their Districts.* Boston: Little Brown, 1978.

Glazer, Amihai, Bernard Grofman, and Marc Robbins. "Partisan and Incumbency Effects of the 1970s Congressional Redistricting." *American Journal of Political Science* 31 (1987): 680-707.

Greer, David. "Redistribution of Seats in the B.C. Legislature, 1952-1978." *B.C. Studies* 38 (1978): 24-46.

Grofman, Bernard. "Criteria for redistricting: a social science perspective." *UCLA Law Review* 33 (1985): 77-184.

Grofman, Bernard, and H. Scarrow. *Current Issues in Reapportionment.* Irvine, California: School of Social Sciences, 1981.

———. "The Riddle of Apportionment: Equality of What?" *National Civic Review* 70 (1981): 242-254.

———. "Current Issues in Reapportionment." *Law and Policy Quarterly* 4 (1982): 435-474.

Grofman, Bernard, et al. *Representation and Redistricting Issues.* Lexington: D.C. Heath and Co., 1982.

Grofman, Bernard, et al. "The Totality of Circumstances Test in the Voting Rights Act." *Law and Policy Quarterly* 7 (1985): 199-223.

Hardy, Leroy, et al., eds. *Reapportionment Politics: The History of Redistricting in the 50 States.* Beverly Hills: Sage, 1981.

Hibbing, John R., and Samuel C. Patterson. "Representing a Territory: Constituency Boundaries for the British House of Commons of the 1980s." *The Journal of Politics* 48 (1986): 992-1005.

Hofferbert, Richard. "State and Community Policy Studies: A Review of Comparative-Output Analysis." In *Political Science Annual*, edited by James A. Robinson. Indianapolis: Bobbs-Merrill 3 (1972): 3-72.

Hogan, James B. "Social Structure and Public Policy." *Comparative Politics* 4 (1972): 477-509.

Hughes, Colin. "Fair and Equal Electoral Districts—The Problem At The State Level." Unpublished paper on Australia, 1983.

Irvine, William P. "Does the Candidate Make a Difference? The Macro-Politics and Micro-Politics of Getting Elected." *Canadian Journal of Political Science* 15 (1982): 755-782.

Johnston, Ronald J. "Political Geography of Contemporary Events II: A Reapportionment Revolution that Failed." *Political Geography Quarterly* 2 (1983): 309-317.

Johnston, Ronald J., S. Openshaw, D.W. Rhind, and D.J. Rossiter. "Spatial Scientists and Representational Democracy: The Role of Information—Processing Technology in the Design of Parliamentary and other Constituencies." *Environment and Planning: C* 2 (1984): 57-66.

Levinson, Sanford. "Gerrymandering and the Brooding Omnipresence of Proportional Representation: Why Won't It Go Away?" *UCLA Law Review* 33 (1985): 257-281.

Lijphart, Arend. "Comparative Perspectives on Fair Representation, The Plurality–Majority Rule, Geographical Districting and Alternate Electoral Arrangements." *Policy Studies Journal* 9 (1980-81): 899-915.

Lowenstein, Daniel, and Jonathan Steinberg. "The Quest for Legislative Districting in the Public Interest: Elusive or Illusory?" *UCLA Law Review* 33 (1985): 1-75.

Lyons, William E. *One Man—One Vote*. Toronto: McGraw-Hill Ryerson, 1970.

Markowitz, J. "Constitutional Challenges to Gerrymandering." *University of Chicago Law Review* 45 (1978): 845-881.

McCrone, Donald J., and Walter J. Stone. "The Structure of Constituency Representation: On Theory and Method." *The Journal of Politics* 48 (1986): 956-975.

McCubbins, Matthew D., and Thomas Schwartz. "Congress, the Courts, and Public Policy: Consequences of the One Man, One Vote Rule." *American Journal of Political Science* 32 (1988): 388-415.

McKay, D.H., and Samuel Patterson. "Population Equality and the Distribution of Seats in the British House of Commons." *Comparative Politics* 4 (1971): 59-76.

McWhinney, Edward. *Supreme Courts and Judicial Law-Making: Constitutional Tribunals and Constitutional Law.* Chapter 9, 187-210. Dordrecht: Martinus Nijhoff Publishers, 1986.

Morrill, Richard L. "Redistricting, region and representation." *Political Geography Quarterly* 6 (1987): 241-260.

———. "Redistricting Standards and Strategies After 20 years." *Political Geography Quarterly* 1 (1982): 361-369.

———. *Political Redistricting and Geographic Theory.* Washington: Association of American Geographers, 1981.

Musgrove, Philipp. *The General Theory of Gerrymandering.* Beverly Hills: Sage Publications, 1977.

Niemi, Richard, and J. Deegan. "A Theory of Political Districting." *American Political Science Review* 72 (1978): 1304-1323.

Norcliffe, G.B. "Discretionary Aspects of Scientific Districting." *Area* 9 (1977): 240-246.

Owen, Guillermo, and Bernard Grofman. "Optimal Partisan Gerrymandering." *Political Geography Quarterly* 7 (1988): 5-22.

Pasis, Harvey. "The Courts and Redistribution." *Canadian Parliamentary Review* 10 (1987): 8-9.

———. "Achieving Population Equality Among Constituencies of the Canadian House, 1903-1976. *Legislative Studies Quarterly* 8 (1983): 111-115.

———. "The Inequality of Distribution in the Canadian Provincial Assemblies." *Canadian Journal of Political Science* 5 (1972): 433-436.

Petit, J.L., and E. Terouanne. "Proportional Methods, Extremal Values and Manipulability." *European Journal of Political Research* 16 (1988): 339-356.

Poel, Dale. "The Diffusion of Legislation among the Canadian Provinces: A Statistical Analysis." *Canadian Journal of Political Science* 9 (1976): 605-626.

Political Geography Quarterly 1 (1982). Special Issue on The Theory and Practice of Redistricting.

Qualter, Terence. "Representation by Population: A Comparative Study." *Canadian Journal of Economics and Political Science* 33 (1967): 246-268.

Representation in the Federal Parliament. Ottawa: Elections Canada, Minister of Supply and Services, 1986.

Robertson, Andrew. "American Redistricting in the 1980s: The Effect on the Mid-term Elections." *Electoral Studies* 2 (1983): 113-129.

Ruff, Norman J., and William M. Ross. "Towards a More Equitable Distribution of Seats in British Columbia." *Canadian Parliamentary Review* 12 (1989): 21-23.

Shapiro, Martin. "Gerrymandering, Unfairness, and the Supreme Court." *UCLA Law Review* 33 (1985): 227-256.

Waller, Robert. "The 1983 Boundary Commission: Policies and Effects." *Electoral Studies* 2 (1983): 195-206.

Ward, Norman. "A Century of Constituencies." *Canadian Public Administration* 10 (1967): 105-122.

_____. "The Redistribution of 1952." *Canadian Journal of Economics and Political Science* 19 (1953): 341-360.

_____. *The Canadian House of Commons: Representation.* Toronto: University of Toronto Press, 1950.

Weaver, James B. *Fair and Equal Districts: A How-To-Do-It Manual on Computer Use.* New York: National Municipal League, 1970.

Weinstein, H. "Partisan Gerrymandering: The Next Hurdle in the Political Thicket?" *Journal of Law and Politics* 1 (1984): 357-380.

Weissberg, Robert. "Collective vs. Dyadic Representation in Congress." *American Political Science Review* 72 (1978): 535-547.

Young, H.P. "Measuring the Compactness of Legislative Districts." *Legislative Studies Quarterly* 13 (1988): 105-115.

Section Four

Archer, J. Clark, F.M. Shelley, and E.R. White. *American Electoral Mosaics.* Washington: Association of American Geographers, 1986.

Balinski, and Michel L., and H.P. Young. "Stability, Coalitions and Schisms in Proportional Representation Systems." *American Political Science Review* 72 (1978): 848-858.

Basehart, Harry. "The Seats/Votes Relationship and the Identification of Partisan Gerrymandering in State Legislatures." *American Politics Quarterly* 15 (1987): 484-498.

Blais, Andre. "The Classification of Electoral Systems." *European Journal of Political Research* 16 (1988): 99-110.

Blais, Andre, and R.K. Carty. "The Impact of Electoral Formulae on the Creation of Majority Government." *Electoral Studies* 6 (1987): 209-218.

Bogdanor, Vernon. "Electoral Reform and British Politics." *Electoral Studies* 6 (1987): 115-121.

———. *Representation of the People? Parliamentarians and Constituents in Western Democracies.* Aldershot: Gower, 1985.

Boston, Jonathan. "Electoral Reform in New Zealand: The Report of the Royal Commission." *Electoral Studies* 6 (1987): 105-114.

———. *What is Proportional Representation?* Oxford: Martin Robertson and Co., 1984.

Boyer, J. Patrick. *Election Law in Canada: The Law and Procedure of Federal, Provincial and Territorial Elections.* 2 vols. Toronto and Vancouver: Butterworths, 1987.

Brookes, R.H. "Electoral Distortion in New Zealand." *Australian Journal of Politics and History* 5-6 (1959-60): 218-223.

———. "The Analysis of Distorted Representation in Two-Party Single-Member Elections." *Political Science* (New Zealand) 12 (1960): 158-167.

———. "Seats and Votes in New Zealand." *Political Science* (New Zealand) 5 (1953): 37-44.

Butler, David E. *The Electoral System in Britain Since 1918.* Oxford: Oxford University Press, 1963, 196-202.

Cairns, Alan C. "The Electoral System and the Party System in Canada, 1921-1965." *Canadian Journal of Political Science* 1 (1968): 55-80.

Carter, Cyril. "Some Properties of Divisor Methods for Legislative Apportionment and Proportional Representation." *American Political Science Review* 76 (1982): 575-584.

Carty, R.K. "Politicians and Electoral Laws: An Anthropology of Party Competition in Ireland." *Political Studies* 28 (1980): 550-566.

Casstevens, T.W., and W.D. Morris. "The Cube Law and the Decomposed System." *Canadian Journal of Political Science* 5 (1972): 521-531.

Chandler, J.A. "The Plurality Vote: A Reappraisal." *Political Studies* 30 (1982): 87-94.

Courtney, John C. "Reflections on Reforming the Canadian Electoral System." *Canadian Public Administration* 23 (1980): 427-457.

Curtise J., and M. Steed. "Proportionality and Exaggeration in the British Electoral System." *Electoral Studies* 5 (1986): 209-228.

Davidson, Chandler, and George Korbel. "At-large Elections and Minority Group Representation: A Re-examination of Historical and Contemporary Evidence." *Journal of Politics* 43 (1981): 982-1005.

Dobell, W.M. "Updating Duverger's Law." *Canadian Journal of Political Science* 19 (1986): 585-595.

Duverger, Maurice. *Political Parties.* New York: Wiley, 1954. "Effective Representation." In *Policy Options*, introduced by George Cooper. Halifax: The Institute for Research on Public Policy, n.d.

Elkins, David. "Electoral Reform and Political Culture in Australia and Canada." Unpublished paper presented at annual conference of Canadian Political Science Association. Hamilton: McMaster University, June 1987.

European Journal of Political Research 13 (1985). Issue on electoral systems.

Fielding, Geoff, and Hans Liebeck. "Voting Structures and the Square Root Law." *British Journal of Political Science* 5 (1975): 249-256.

Gallagher, Michael. "The Political Consequences of the Electoral System in the Republic of Ireland." *Electoral Studies* 5 (1986): 253-276.

Goot, Murray. "Electoral Systems." In *Surveys of Australian Political Science*, edited by Don Aitken. Sydney: George Allen and Unwin, 1985.

Grofman, Bernard, and Arend Lijphart. *Electoral Laws and their Consequences.* New York: Agathon Press, 1986.

Gudgin, Graham, and P.J. Taylor. *The Spatial Organization of Elections.* London: Pion 1978.

Irvine, William P. "Measuring the Effects of Electoral Systems on Regionalism." *Electoral Studies* 7 (1988): 15-26.

———. "A Review and Evaluation of Electoral System Reform Proposals." In *Institutional Reforms for Representative Government*, by Peter Aucoin, 71-109. Toronto: University of Toronto Press, 1985.

Jackman, Robert W. "Political Institutions and Voter Turnout in the Industrial Democracies." *American Political Science Review* 81 (1987): 405-423.

Johnston, Richard, and J. Ballantyne. "Geography and the Electoral System." *Canadian Journal of Political Science* 10 (1977): 857-866.

Johnston, Ronald J. "Review Essay: Can we leave electoral reform to politicians?" *Political Geography Quarterly* 6 (1987): 279-282.

———. *Political Electoral and Spatial Systems.* Oxford: Oxford University Press, 1979.

Kendall, M.G., and A. Stuart. "The Law of the Cubic Proportion in Election Results." *British Journal of Sociology* 1 (1950): 183-196.

King, Gary, and Robert X. Browning. "Democratic Representation and Partisan Bias in Congressional Elections." *American Political Science Review* 81 (1987): 1251-1273.

Lijphart, Arend. "The Demise of the Last Westminster System? Comments on the Report of New Zealand's Royal Commission on the Electoral System." *Electoral Studies* 6 (1987): 97-103.

———. "The Field of Electoral Systems Research: A Critical Survey." *Electoral Studies* 4 (1985): 3-14.

———. *Democracies.* New Haven: Yale University Press, 1984.

Lijphart, Arend, and Bernard Grofman. *Choosing an Electoral System: Issues and Alternatives.* New York: Praeger, 1984.

Lijphart, Arend, and Robert Gibberd. "Thresholds and Payoffs in List Systems of Proportional Representation." *European Journal of Political Research* 5 (1977): 219-244.

Lovink, J.A.A. "On Analysing the Impact of the Electoral System on the Party System in Canada." *Canadian Journal of Political Science* 3 (1970): 497-516.

Mackenzie, W.J.M. *Free Elections.* London: George Allen and Unwin, 1958.

Mamadouh, V.D., and H.H. van der Wusten. "The Influence of the Change of Electoral System on Political Representation: The Case of France in 1985." *Political Geography Quarterly* 8 (1989): 145-159.

March, James G. "Party Legislative Representation as a Function of Election Results." *Public Opinion Quarterly* 21 (1957): 521-542.

Marsh, Michael. "The Voters Decide?: Preferential Voting in European List Systems." *European Journal of Political Research* 13 (1985): 365-378.

Merrill, Samuel III. "A Comparison of Efficiency of Multicandidate Electoral Systems." *American Journal of Political Science* 28 (1984): 23-48.

Niemi, Richard. "The Relationship Between Votes and Seats: The Ultimate Question in Political Gerrymandering." *UCLA Law Review* 33 (1986): 185-212.

O'Loughlin, J. "District Size and Party Electoral Strength: A Comparison of Sixteen Democracies." *Environment and Planning A* 12 (1980): 247-262.

Parliamentary Government 1 (1980): Issue on Canada's Electoral System: Assessments and Alternatives.

Pinard, Maurice. "Third Parties in Canada Revisted: A Rejoinder and Elaboration of the Theory of One-party Dominance." *Canadian Journal of Political Science* 6 (1973): 439-460.

———. "One-party Dominance and Third Parties." *Canadian Journal of Economics and Political Science* 33 (1967): 358-373.

Qualter, Terrence H. *The Electoral Process in Canada.* Toronto: McGraw-Hill, 1970.

———. "Seats and Votes: An Application of the Cube Law to the Canadian Electoral System." *Canadian Journal of Political Science* 1 (1968): 336-344.

Rae, Douglas. *The Political Consequences of Electoral Laws.* New Haven: Yale University Press, 1971.

Report of the Royal Commission on the Electoral System: Towards a Better Democracy. Wellington, New Zealand: Government Printer, 1986.

Reynolds, David R., and Fred M. Shelley. "Application of Procedural Justice to Electoral Systems." *European Journal of Political Research* 13 (1985): 401-408.

Riker, William. "The Two-party System and Duverger's Law: An Essay on the History of Political Science." *American Political Science Review* 76 (1982): 753-766.

Rydon, Joan. "The Relation of Votes to Seats in Elections for the Australian House of Representatives, 1949-54." *Political Science* (New Zealand) 9 (1957): 49-61.

Schindeler, Fred. "One Man One Vote: One Vote One Value." *Journal of Canadian Studies* 3 (1968): 13-20.

Shugart, Matthew F. "The Two Effects of District Magnitude: Venezuela as a Crucial Experiment." *European Journal of Political Research* 13 (1985): 353-364.

Soper, C.S. "Distorted Representation: A Note." *Political Science* (New Zealand) 16 (1964): 81-82.

Soper, C.S., and J. Rydon. "Under-representation and Electoral Prediction." *Australian Journal of Politics and History* 3-4 (1957-58): 94-106.

Spafford, Duff. "Electoral Systems and Voters' Behavior: Comment and a Further Test." *Comparative Politics* 5 (1972): 129-134.

_____. "The Electoral System of Canada." *American Political Science Review* 64 (1970): 168-176.

Taagepera, Rein. "Reformulating The Cube Law For Proportional Representation Elections." *American Political Science Review* 80 (1986): 489-504.

Taagepera, Rein and Bernard Grofman. "Rethinking Duverger's Law: Predicting the Effective Number of Parties in Plurality and PR Systems—Parties Minus Issues Equals One." *European Journal of Political Research* 13 (1985): 341-352.

Taagepera, Rein and Matthew S. Shugart. "Designing Electoral Systems." *Electoral Studies* 8 (1989): 49-58.

Taylor, Peter J., and Arend Lijphart. "Proportional Tenure vs Proportional Representation: Introducing a New Debate." *European Journal of Political Research* 13 (1985): 387-399.

Taylor, Peter J., and R.J. Johnston. *Georgraphy of Elections*. London: Penguin, 1979.

Tufte, Edward. "The Relationship between Seats and Votes in Two-Party Systems." *American Political Science Review* 67 (1973): 540-554.

Section Five

Arrow, Kenneth. *Social Choice and Individual Values*. New York: Wiley, 1941.

Barbut, Marc. "Does the Majority Ever Rule?" *Portfolio and Art News Annual* 4 (1961): 79-83 and 161-168.

Barton, David. "Constitutional Choice and Simple Majority Rule: Comment." *Journal of Political Economy* 81 (1973): 471-479 and Tullock's reply: 480-484.

Black, Duncan. *Theory of Committees and Elections.* Cambridge: Cambridge University Press, 1958.

———. "The Theory of Elections in Single-Member Constituencies." *Canadian Journal of Economics and Political Science* 15 (1949): 158-175.

———. "Some Theoretical Schemes of Proportional Representation." *Canadian Journal of Economics and Political Science* 15 (1949): 334-343.

Buchanan, James, and G. Tullock. *The Calculus of Consent.* Ann Arbor: University of Michigan Press, 1962.

Cox, G. "Electoral Equilibrium under Alternative Voting Institutions." *American Journal of Political Science* 31 (1987): 82-108.

de Grazia, Alfred. "Mathematical Derivation of an Election System." *ISIS* 44 (1953): 42-51.

deMeur, Gisele, and X. Hubaut. "Fair Models of Political Fairness." *European Journal of Political Research* 14 (1986): 237-252.

Denzau, Arthur, William Riker, and Kenneth Shepsle. "Farquharson and Fenno: Sophisticated Voting and Home Style." *American Political Science Review* 79 (1985): 1117-1134.

Doron, Gideon, and Richard Kronick. "Single Transferrable Vote: An Example of a Perverse Social Choice Function." *American Journal of Political Science* 21 (1977): 303-311.

Feld, Scott, and Bernard Grofman. "Necessary and Sufficient Conditions for a Majority Winner in n-Dimensional Spatial Voting Games: An Intuitive Geometric Approach." *American Journal of Political Science* 31 (1987): 709-728.

———. "On the Possibility of Faithfully Representing Committees." *American Political Science Review* 80 (1986): 863-879.

Ferejohn, J., M. Fiorina, and R. McKelney. "Sophisticated Voting and Agenda Independence in the Distributive Politics Setting." *American Journal of Political Science* 31 (1987): 169-193.

Fishburn, Peter C. "Dimensions of Election Procedures: Analyses and Comparisons." *Theory and Decision* 15 (1983): 371-397.

Fishburn, Peter C., and S. Brams. "Paradoxes of Preferential Voting." *Mathematics Magazine* 56 (1983): 207-214.

Gardner, Martin, written by L.A. Steen. "Mathematical Games (From Counting Votes to Making Votes Count: The Mathematics of Elections)." *Scientific American* 243 (1980): 16-26B.

Gibbard, Allan. "Manipulation of Voting Systems: A General Result." *Econometrica* 41 (1973): 587-601.

Grofman, Bernard, and Scott L. Feld. "Rousseau's General Will: A Condorcetian Perspective." *American Political Science Review* 82 (1988): 567-576.

Holler, Manfred J., ed. *The Logic of Multiparty Systems.* Dordrecht: Kluwer Academic Publishers, 1987.

Huntington, E.V. "A Paradox in the Scoring of Competing Teams." *Science* 88 (1938): 287-288.

Laver, Michael. "Coalition Bargaining, Interest Representation and Government Responsiveness." *Political Studies* 31 (1983): 650-655.

Laver, Michael, and John Underhill. "The Bargaining Advantages of Combining with Others." *British Journal of Political Science* 12 (1982): 27-42.

Levesque, Terrence J. "On the Outcome of the 1983 Conservative Leadership Convention: How They Shot Themselves in the Other Foot." *Canadian Journal of Political Science* 16 (1983): 779-784.

May, Kenneth O. "A Set of Independent Necessary and Sufficient Conditions for Simple Majority Decisions." *Econometrica* 20 (1952): 680-684.

McLean, Iain. *Public Choice: An Introduction.* Oxford: Basil Blackwell Ltd., 1987.

Merrill, Samuel III. *Making Multicandidate Elections More Democratic.* Princeton, New Jersey: Princeton University Press, 1988.

Merrill, Samuel III, and Jack Nagel. "The Effect of Approval Ballotting On Strategic Voting Under Alternative Decision Rules." *American Political Science Review* 81 (1987): 509-524.

Murakami, Y. *Logic and Social Choice.* London: Routledge and Kegan Paul Ltd., 1968.

Niemi, Richard, and W.H. Riker. "The Choice of Voting Systems." *Scientific American* 234 (1976): 21-27.

Niemi, Richard, and H. Weisberg. *Probability Models of Collective Decision Making.* Columbus: Charles E. Merrill, 1972.

Nurmi, Hannu. "Mathematical Models of Elections and their Relevance for Institutional Design." *Electoral Studies* 5 (1986): 167-181.

———. "On the Properties of Voting Systems." *Scandinavian Political Studies* 4 (1981): 19-32.

Ordeshook, Peter C. *Game Theory and Political Theory: An Introduction.* Cambridge: Cambridge University Press, 1986.

Perlin, George. "Did the Best Candidate Win? A Comment on Levesque's Analysis." *Canadian Journal of Political Science* 16 (1983): 791-794.

Rae, Douglas. "Decision Rules and Individual Values in Constitutional Choice." *American Political Science Review* 63 (1969): 40-56.

Riker, William. *Liberalism Against Populism.* San Francisco: W.H. Freeman and Co., 1982.

Riker, William, and P. Ordeshook. "The Paradox of Voting and Majority Rule." In *An Introduction to Positive Political Theory*, by Wm. Riker and P. Ordeshook, 78-115. Englewood Cliffs, New Jersey: Prentice Hall Inc., 1973.

Schwartz, Thomas. *The Logic of Collective Action*. New York: Columbia University Press, 1986.

Sen, A.K. "A Possibility Theorem on Majority Decision." *Econometrica* 34 (1966): 491-499.

Sugden, Robert. "Free Association and the Theory of proportional Representation." *American Political Science Review* 78 (1984): 31-43.

Woolstencroft, Peter. "Social Choice Theory and the Reconstruction of Elections: A Comment on Levesque's Analysis." *Canadian Journal of Political Science* 16 (1983): 785-789.

Young, H.P. "Condorcet's Theory of Voting." *American Political Science Review* 82 (1988): 1231-1244.

INDEX